Contents

Kaleidoscope

Introduction

The American Multicultural Experience

WHEN EUROPEANS first arrived on the shores of the land that was to become the United States, they were greeted by a native population that was already multicultural. In the South and Southwest, these Native Americans inhabited permanent villages and lived by farming. There they created stable cultures and in some cases—the Acoma pueblo in New Mexico, for example—they had lived in the same communities for as long as a thousand years when, in the sixteenth century, the first Spaniards arrived in search of the fabled Seven Cities of Cibola, whose walls would be shining with gold. On the East Coast, there were more or less stable communities that subsisted by fishing and growing corn. In the forests of the Northeast, people pursued game throughout large tribal territories and covered astonishing distances by means of birchbark canoes. In the prairies of the Midwest and West, some tribes were wanderers, with the buffalo central to their existence, while others found particularly favorable locations for their towns and farms. In the Northwest, in spawning season, they fished the streams for salmon. In the mountains they picked berries and dug for roots.

There were hundreds of tribes, hundreds of languages, hundreds of cultures. Some, such as the Mound Builders of the Midwest, had already passed out of existence long before the coming of the Europeans. Others did not survive the radical changes that accompanied European exploration and settlement. Because they lacked written languages, their stories were first told in print by others, by the explorers who met them, the soldiers who made war upon them, the traders, priests, and captives who lived among them. Their oral traditions survived, however, becoming the basis for later stories told by their descendants directly in writing or else as recorded by folklorists, anthropologists, and ethnologists. In time, oral traditions became merged with or gave way to eyewitness histories, autobiographies, and fictions. Much of the best of the early literature was written by white men, but later came fine contributions from men and women of Native American heritage, who have been especially impressive as writers in our own time.

Today the literature of the Native American experience shines with particular luster among the ever-changing patterns of the American kaleidoscope.

The Native Americans—Indians, as we came to know them—were here first. But so was the land. And so was the promise. When Shakespeare put into Miranda's mouth in *The Tempest* the words "O brave new world, that has such people in it," he voiced the part of the promise that suggests that in this new world on the other side of the Atlantic Ocean, the wrongs of the Old World can be put right, perhaps by magic, perhaps by the love of a generation young enough to be unhampered by the bitter experience of the past. The goal of becoming American has remained for many a goal of youth, a goal for parents to pass on to their children. Three hundred years after the Italians of Shakespeare's *Tempest* were discovering the promise of the Caribbean in their children, Jerre Mangione was being told by his Sicilian father in Rochester, New York, "Your children will be *Americani*. But you, my son, are half-and-half." The land was there, the promise was there, but to become American was not always as easy as magic. It took time.

Not all the early explorers had the same sense of what the land was. Columbus never overcame the belief that he had discovered India. Not all had the same sense of what the promise consisted of. For some there was the promise of gold, for others the promise of empire, for still others the promise of glories to be won by converting the natives to the one true faith. The idea that the land itself was the prize, that emigration could lead to a new life, that a brave new world might arise on those foreign shores was slow to develop, but its foundations were well established by the time of *The Tempest*, written four years after the settlement of Jamestown, Virginia.

Meanwhile, before there were any permanent English settlements in the territory that became the United States, there had been almost a century of cross-cultural exchange between Europeans and Native Americans. A Florentine, Giovanni da Verrazzano, explored the East Coast, meeting the Indians at several points and staying with them briefly in Rhode Island. Alvar Núñez Cabeza de Vaca, with two fellow Spaniards and a Moroccan slave, lived eight years among the Indians of the South and Southwest. Coronado and his men ranged through the Southwest and as far north as Kansas. The Englishman Sir Francis Drake sailed up the West Coast as far as Washington and accepted the area around Point Reyes, California, from the natives, naming it Nova Albion. The French explorer Samuel de Champlain helped establish a settlement on the Bay of Fundy and examined the coast of New England as far south as Martha's Vineyard before establishing a trading post at Quebec in 1608. And there were many others, some simply traders or fishermen. By the time of the settlement at Jamestown, the Spanish town of St. Augustine, Florida, was forty-two years old. When Squanto met the Pilgrims at Plymouth Colony, he had already been to England, perhaps twice.

Whatever else the early settlers knew, whatever dreams or ambitions they carried with them, they knew, as all newcomers after them have known, that their lives in the New World would be different from the lives they left behind. Opportunity and difference—these two strong senses of the American experience—are themes running through the reports of immigrants from the first to the most recent. Because they expected much from both, and because they saw that there would be no opportunities if there were not differences, from the first they were impelled to write down their observations, to tell their stories.

Their new worlds in the seventeenth century were often small and isolated, but they were not always culturally cohesive. There were the planters of Virginia, mostly Anglican, with African slaves; the Pilgrims of Plymouth, Separatists; the Puritans of Massachusetts Bay, non-Separatist; the mingled Catholics and Protestants in Maryland; the Dutch of New Netherlands; the haven of religious toleration established by Roger Williams in Rhode Island; the Quaker bastion founded by William Penn in Pennsylvania; and the mingled English, Barbadian, French Huguenot, and Scottish settlers, who together with their black slaves made up the population of the Carolinas. Further south, in Florida and Mexico, were the Spaniards; to the north, in Canada, the French. Even in the most strictly ordered of these communities, cultural cohesiveness was never whole and entire. Years later Nathaniel Hawthorne delighted in portraying the diverse races, classes, and beliefs that tried the patience of community leaders in his ancestral Massachusetts. Arrests, imprisonments, banishments, and even the death penalty failed to maintain for long a society of complete cultural homogeneity.

After 1664, when the Dutch colony of New Netherlands fell to the British and became New York, the American colonies from the Carolinas north to New England were politically British, but they retained their cultural differences, which by the eighteenth century were substantial. In addition to the racial, religious, ethnic, and class differences existing within and among colonies, there were increasing regional differences that distinguished North from South, seaboard from interior, town from country, prosperous farming community from pioneer village. Moving from one to another of the colonies, as Benjamin Franklin did when he left Boston for Philadelphia in 1723, could become a severe test of cultural adaptability.

Much of the literature of the British colonies in America is utilitarian or religious: descriptions of the land, advertisements of the benefits of emigration, testimonies of faith, evangelical or polemical religious tracts, sermons, political documents, histories, diaries. A significant product of the impetus to provide useful information or moral instruction, however, was the literature that focused on the ways of the varied people of the New World. Relations with the Indians bulk large in this early record; among some of the more interesting accounts are John Smith's and William Bradford's reports from Jamestown and Plymouth and the captivity narratives of Mary Rowlandson and James Smith. Among cultural conflicts between white communities, the Puritan dispute with the Anglican settlement at Merrymount is famous. Narrated first by participants, including William Bradford in *The History of Plymouth Plantation* (written 1630–1646) and Thomas Morton in his *New English Canaan* (1637), it formed the basis for many later tellings, including Hawthorne's "The Maypole of Merry Mount." In the South, William Byrd recorded in his books and diaries a Virginia gentleman's observations on life in the backwoods and in the "Lubberland" of North Carolina. Writing later in England as a free man, Olaudah Equiano included passages on his American slave experiences in his *Interesting Narrative of the Life of Olaudah Equiano* (1789). Summing up his life in his *Autobiography* (written 1771–1788), Benjamin Franklin touched frequently on the numerous religious, ethnic, and racial strains that made up the population of Pennsylvania.

In his *Letters from an American Farmer* (1782), written as the new nation was about to be born, a Frenchman, St. Jean de Crèvecoeur, considered the question "What is an American?" Emphasizing the diversity of national origins, he wrote:

> I could point out to you a family whose grandfather was an Englishman, whose wife was Dutch, whose son married a French woman, and whose present four sons have now four wives of different nations. *He* is an American, who, leaving behind him all his ancient prejudices and manners, receives new ones from the new mode of life he has embraced, the new government he obeys, and the new rank he holds. He becomes an American by being received in the broad lap of our great *Alma Mater*. Here individuals of all nations are melted into a new race of men, whose labours and posterity will one day cause great changes in the world.

If taken too literally, however, Crèvecoeur's vision of the country as a great melting pot, with its implications of an homogenous stew, seems to deny the heterogeneity that had characterized the country from the beginning and continued during and after the Revolutionary War. James Fenimore Cooper was closer to the mark in *The Pioneers* (1823) when he portrayed the settlers of upstate New York just after the war as a conglomerate gathered from the far reaches of Europe and America, each carrying ineradicable marks of birth or alien experience. A reader is not likely to mistake the Pennsylvania Quaker for the Massachusetts Yankee or the Vermont woodsman, or for the Welsh, Irish, Cornish, German, French, African, and Mohegan inhabitants of Cooper's fictional Templeton, a community modeled closely on the Cooperstown of the author's youth.

The nineteenth century brought vast changes that dramatically extended the range of American multiculturalism.

Expansion westward brought a rise of sectionalism. Although a stubborn tenet of faith, particularly in the first half of the century, held that all freeborn citizens were equal, observation suggested that at least in manners and culture they were not. Huge cultural differences between East Coast and frontier were highlighted in 1829 when Andrew Jackson arrived at the White House and his followers trampled the floors and furniture with their muddy boots, forcing the new President to escape through the window. The humorists of the old Southwest, writers like Augustus Baldwin Longstreet, T. B. Thorpe, George Washington Harris, and Johnson Jones Hooper, portrayed a region inhabited by braggarts, scalawags, and sharpers: "It is good to be shifty in a new country," said Hooper's Simon Suggs. Particularly in this early period, tours of the new country by English citizens curious to see what had become of their old colony became fashionable; widely read and widely objected to by Americans were Frances Trollope's *Domestic Manners of the Americans* (1832) and Charles Dickens's *American Notes* (1842).

Later, the westward push through the prairies, the gold rush of 1849, the great impetus to western settlement and commerce symbolized by the golden spike driven in 1869 in Promontory, Utah, all created new regions replete with cultural differences. Early accounts such as Caroline Kirkland's *A New Home—Who'll Follow?* (1839), on pioneer life in Michigan, were themselves followed by numerous journalistic, autobiographical, and fictional works on the many new homelands—or potential homelands—of America, each with its distinctive cultural identity. Among its other qualities, Richard Henry Dana Jr.'s *Two Years Before the Mast* (1840) remains a classic portrayal of Spanish California before the gold rush. In *The Oregon Trail* (1849), Francis Parkman depicted the Sioux a generation before they became the hated enemies of the white man. The California of the mining camps was memorialized by Bret Harte in *The Luck of Roaring Camp* (1868) and other fictions, while Mark Twain's adventures in the Far West produced "The Notorious Jumping Frog of Calaveras County" and *Roughing It* (1872). In the area once roamed by the Sioux, Hamlin Garland set many of his stories of pioneer life, beginning with *Main-Travelled Roads* (1891) and later including accounts of the Indians as their hereditary ways of life were disappearing.

Accompanying westward expansion was an increased attention to literature concerning the Indians. James Fenimore Cooper's Leatherstocking series (1823–1841) gained most lasting fame and made Chingachgook one of the enduring creations of American literature, but there were many other works, both fiction and nonfiction. In the South, William Gilmore Simms, who had visited the Creeks, Choctaws, and Cherokees as a young man, wrote with particular sensitivity in works that included the novel *The Yemassee* (1835) and the stories collected in *The Wigwam and the Cabin* (1845–1846). Longfellow's verse narrative *The Song of Hiawatha* (1855) provided generations with vivid but not always completely accurate pictures of Ojibway life. Later, Helen Hunt Jackson reached an enormous audience with her novel *Ramona* (1884), a mixed-blood romance of California. Meanwhile, the captivity narrative continued as an American genre, with works like *A Narrative Attending the Capture, Detention, and Ransom of Charles Johnston of Virginia* (1827) and *Narrative of the Captivity and Adventures of John Tanner during 30 Years' Residence among the Indians* (1830). By the nineteenth century, moreover, Native Americans were beginning to tell their own stories. Autobiographies include William Apes's *A Son of the Forest* (1829); *Black Hawk's Autobiography* (1833; narrated by Black Hawk, translated and edited by others); George Copway's *The Life, History, and Travels of Kah-ge-ga-gah-bowh* (1847); and Sarah Winnemucca Hopkins's *Life among the Piutes* (1883). Novels by Indians mostly came later, but include in mid-nineteenth century John Rollin Ridge's *The Life and Adventures of Joaquin Murieta* (1854), about a mixed-blood California bandit.

The events culminating in the Civil War did much to emphasize cultural differences as Americans became, even more than they had been before, northerners or southerners. Fictions like John Pendleton Kennedy's *Swallow Barn* (1832) helped create the stereotype of the old plantation South, and in the years before the war no European visitor could feel that a tour of the country was complete without at least a glimpse at the institution of slavery, which they wrote about in letters, journal articles, and books. Northerners, too, went to look, treating the South almost as a foreign land: An example is Frederick Law Olmsted's *A Journey in the Seaboard Slave States, with Remarks on Their Economy* (1856). Meanwhile, important contributions to the abolition movement were being made by escaped slaves, notably Frederick Douglass in *Narrative of the Life of Frederick Douglass* (1845) and Harriet Jacobs in *Incidents in the Life of a Slave Girl* (1861). The best seller of the period, of course, was Harriet Beecher Stowe's novel *Uncle Tom's Cabin* (1852), which spawned anti-Tom novels intent on showing what the South insisted were the true conditions of slave and slave owner. A year after *Uncle Tom*, William Wells Brown's *Clotel, or the President's Daughter* appeared in London; this novel, perhaps the first by an American black, professed to tell of a daughter of Jefferson by one of his slaves. When the war came, it was not only a military and political but also a cultural conflict, Johnny Reb defending a feudal way of life against the Yankee march of nineteenth-century progress. The literature of the war is vast, much of it centered on accounts by participants, as in the *Memoirs* of General William T. Sherman (1875) and General Ulysses S. Grant (1885–1886). Especially interesting for the light shed on the cultural changes and conflicts forced on the wartime South are Mary Boykin Chesnut's *A Diary from Dixie* (1905) and Sarah Morgan's *A Confederate Girl's Diary* (1915).

After the war came Reconstruction, and with it still more literature displaying the South's cultural differences from the rest of the nation. In *Uncle Remus: His Songs and His Sayings* (1880) and other works Joel Chandler Harris drew on black folklore and portrayed a mostly benign relationship between master and slave. Thomas Nelson Page, too, presented an essentially nostalgic picture in *In Ole Virginia* (1887) and other books. Less romantic were the portraits of the South that emerged from the pen of George Washington Cable, whose stories of New Orleans, beginning with *Old Creole Days* (1879), centered on racial confusion and accommodation in a city with a rich multicultural heritage. Outside the heart of the old South, but connected to New Orleans by the Mississippi River, was Mark Twain's Missouri, scene of some of the finest multicultural writings of the period. There is much to ponder concerning interracial relations not only in *Huckleberry Finn* (1884), Twain's masterpiece, but in *Pudd'nhead Wilson* (1894) as well. By the end of the century, Charles W. Chesnutt, the son of free blacks from North Carolina, had begun his brief career as a chronicler of racial matters in both North and South in books like *The Conjure Woman* (1899) and *The Wife of His Youth and Other Stories of the Color Line* (1899).

Additional strong cultural differences within the United States resulted when freedom of belief in the new nation combined with nineteenth-century intellectual and economic forces to produce a vast expansion of religious choices. The divisions evident within Protestantism from the earliest settlements were enlarged and multiplied under the onslaught of newer religious and intellectual trends, including Deism, Unitarianism, and Transcendentalism. Methodism increased its membership as the circuit rider and the camp meeting became distinguishing features of the American cultural landscape—admired by many, parodied by writers like Johnson Jones Hooper and Mark Twain. Quakerism prospered. Roman Catholicism increased its numbers and influence as immigrants flocked to America, first from Ireland and then from other largely Catholic countries. From eastern Europe, particularly at the end of the century, came many Jews to add immense weight to an earlier quite small community of belief. The influence of Orientalism burgeoned with the China trade and increased with immigration. Meanwhile, there emerged a number of strong and distinctively American religions: the Shaking Quakers of England emigrated and became the Shakers of the United States, from Joseph Smith's revelations came Mormonism, from Mary Baker Eddy the teachings of Christian Science.

Religious belief often combined with social promise as the nineteenth became in the United States the century of social utopias. The Shakers had their communities—celibate—the Mormons theirs—polygamous. From Germany came the Rappites to Harmony, Pennsylvania, and New Harmony, Indiana; the latter they sold to the Scottish Robert Owen for his short-lived model community. Transcendentalists were prominent in the establishment of Brook Farm, the model for Hawthorne's *The Blithedale Romance*. Albert Drisbane promulgated Fourierism in America, leading to the establishment of more than forty phalanxes, intricately organized communities of independent individuals. In Iowa, German "Inspirationists" founded the successful Amana communities. Oneida, New York, was the scene of John Humphrey Noyes's experiment in communal living and "complex marriage." Much of the literature that arose from these experiments was polemic, for or against, but William Dean Howells, for example, wrote interesting fiction about the Shakers.

This was also the century of the rise of the rich. Vast fortunes lifted the privileged classes far above the masses in material possessions, while the growth of industrial cities created at the other end of the social scale the grinding poverty of the slum as a new feature of American life. For many writers wealth—the lack of it, the attainment of it, the loss of it—became a dominant American theme. Money, after all, was the visible embodiment of the American dream, the proof that the opportunity existed, the promise could be fulfilled. Early in the century novelists complained that the country lacked the settled social climate that provided the background for much of the best European fiction, but as the century wore on they made of America's very fluidity the stuff of which they wove their tales of American cultural interchange. Although the Horatio Alger story of rags to riches provided the dominant myth, in the hands of more serious writers the problems of life were not so simple as they turned out to be for Ragged Dick.

Fittingly, one of the master chroniclers of the rich was the grandson of a poor immigrant from Ireland who had become one of this country's first millionaires. Henry James possessed an unmatched sensitivity to questions of money and class, especially as they concerned women. He wrote much of his best fiction about Americans in Europe, but also explored cross-cultural confrontations in novels set in the United States, including *The Europeans* (1878), *Washington Square* (1881), and *The Bostonians* (1886). His friend Howells, who had himself risen from a poor country background to intellectual eminence in Boston, wrote one of America's most memorable novels of class confrontation in *The Rise of Silas Lapham* (1885). And Howells's friend Twain, writing with Charles Dudley Warner, produced the novel on financial aspiration that in its title suggested an emblematic summary of the period: *The Gilded Age* (1873). At the end of the century, focusing the money problem more closely on the poor, came Stephen Crane's *Maggie: A Girl of the Streets* (1893), Frank Norris's *McTeague* (1899), and Theodore Dreiser's *Sister Carrie* (1900).

With the political and economic success of the United States in the nineteenth century came a renewed impetus to immigration, founded as before on the opportunities afforded in the New World but accompanied by a greatly enhanced vision of the different lives awaiting in a country as yet unspoiled by history—a vision of freedom and equality under a new form of government. Political and social upheavals in Europe, together with displacements brought about by wars, famines, and the industrial revolution, combined with the rapid growth in the power and prestige of the United States to produce wave after wave of immigration. Until mid-century, most of the newcomers were from northern Europe, the majority Irish or German. They came at an increasingly rapid rate—fewer than two hundred thousand in the 1820s, a half million in the 1830s, a million and a half in the 1840s. They kept coming up to and during the Civil War, and then in the first ten years of peace came three and a quarter million more. As the century wore on, the places of origin began to change: Of the nearly three and three-quarter million who arrived in the last decade of the nineteenth century, over 50 percent were from southern and eastern Europe; of the nearly nine million who came in the first decade of the twentieth century, 70 percent were from the same region. Meanwhile, immigration from China, which had begun as a trickle as early as the 1830s, had peaked at over a hundred and twenty thousand during the railroad building days of the 1870s, only to fall dramatically in the next few decades. By 1900, substantial numbers of immigrants had arrived also from Norway, Sweden, Denmark, Switzerland, Poland, Austria, Hungary, Russia, Finland, Rumania, Turkey, Greece, Italy, Spain, Portugal, Mexico, and the West Indies.

The stories of the newer immigrant groups were told initially by writers from more settled generations who comprised the mainstream of literary activity in the nineteenth century. As part of the changing constituency of American life, they appear as pioneers in Cooper's forests, as sailors on Herman Melville's ships. They inhabit the West of Bret Harte, the Midwest of Hamlin Garland. They appear in Henry David Thoreau's *Walden* (1854) and in his posthumously printed *Journals*. They form a significant part of the life of New York City in Howells's *A Hazard of New Fortunes* (1890) and contribute in major ways to the intellectual and social climate of upstate New York in Harold Frederic's *The Damnation of Theron Ware* (1896). Stories of the experience of nineteenth-century immigrants written by the immigrants themselves, however, mostly came later. At first they typically kept diaries or wrote letters home in the language of the old country. Somewhat afterward, they turned to autobiographies and stories of personal observation. Only still later, for the most part, did they turn their experiences into fiction.

By the 1890s, the literature of the newer immigrants had begun. Within a generation a number of significant works appeared. In 1890 Jacob Riis, from Denmark, called attention to the plight of New York City slum dwellers in *How the Other Half Lives*; later he told his own story in *The Making of an American* (1901). Abraham Cahan, a Russian Jew, wrote of New York's Lower East Side in *The Imported Bridegroom and Other Stories of the New York Ghetto* (1898) and the novel *The Rise of David Levinsky* (1917). Mary Antin, also a Jew from Russia, turned her early *From Plotzk to Boston* (1899) into the hugely popular autobiography *The Promised Land* (1912). Anzia Yezierska, from Russian Poland, depicted New York Jewish life in the stories of *Hungry Hearts* (1920) and in the novel *Bread Givers* (1925). Ludwig Lewisohn, a German Jew whose parents had converted to Christianity, wrote of his experiences in the American academic world in his autobiographical *Up Stream* (1922). These were set mostly in the urban East; another kind of life was depicted in Ole Rölvaag's masterful novel of Norwegians in North Dakota, *Giants in the Earth: A Saga of the Prairies* (1924–1925; in English, 1927). Less noticed were the first stories of Asian life in America as told by Asian Americans in books such as Yung Wing's *My Life in China and America* (1909) and Edith Eaton's *Mrs. Spring Fragrance* (1912).

In the same period, from the 1890s into the 1920s, the American kaleidoscope took another turn as American blacks, many now born in freedom, found stronger and more numerous voices than those that had presented their experience in the past. After Chesnutt broke the ground for distinguished black fiction, winning the praise of the powerful critic William Dean Howells, many writers of both fiction and nonfiction followed, including Booker T. Washington, with *Up from Slavery* (1900), an autobiography; W. E. B. DuBois, with *The Souls of Black Folk* (1903), essays, and sketches; and James Weldon Johnson, with *The Autobiography of an Ex-Colored Man* (1912), a novel. Then came the 1920s and the Harlem Renaissance, a period when black culture suddenly became fashionable, and works by blacks began to appear in unprecedented numbers. An influential experimental work, combining verse and prose, was Jean Toomer's *Cane* (1923). Among many novels were Walter White's *The Fire in the Flint* (1924), about a lynching; Jessie Redmon Fauset's several novels of black middle-class life; Claude McKay's *Home to Harlem* (1928), about a black soldier's return after World War I; Wallace Thurman's *The Blacker the Berry* (1929), about black prejudice stemming from variations in skin color; and Nella Larsen's *Passing* (1929), about blacks living as whites.

From 1930 until 1945, black publication was slowed somewhat, as was publication generally, under the influence of economic depression and war, but nevertheless the period was marked by the appearance of some especially strong writers and books. These included, in fiction, Langston Hughes's *Not without Laughter* (1930) and *The Ways of White Folks* (1934), Zora Neale Hurston's *Their Eyes Were Watching God* (1937), Richard Wright's *Native Son* (1940), and Chester Himes's *If He Hollers Let Him Go* (1945). Autobiography was important as well, as blacks attempted under the newer circumstances of American life to examine their cultural identity in works like Hughes's *The Big Sea* (1940), Hurston's *Dust Tracks on a Road* (1942), and Wright's *Black Boy* (1945).

Meanwhile, for Jewish writing in America, the years from 1930 to 1945 proved a time of consolidation and extension, with much of the best work produced by second- and third-generation writers, some of whom paid little attention to ethnicity. Questions of Jewish identity and of cross-cultural interchange with other Americans continued to bulk large, however, in novels such as Michael Gold's *Jews without Money* (1930), Henry Roth's *Call It Sleep* (1934), Meyer Levin's *The Old Bunch* (1937), Jerome Weidman's *I Can Get It for You Wholesale* (1937), and Budd Schulberg's *What Makes Sammy Run?* (1941).

The oldest Americans also found more voices in print from the 1890s into the middle of the twentieth century, though their literature was hampered by the special conditions of their relationship to the rest of America that limited most Indians to minimal education in government-sponsored schools. In 1891 there appeared what is probably the first novel by an Indian woman, Sophia Alice Callahan's *Wynema, a Child of the Forest*. A Canadian Mohawk, Emily Pauline Johnson had some success as a platform performer, publishing books of verse and *Moccasin Maker* (1913), stories. Later came several novels, including Mourning Dove's *Cogewea, the Half Blood* (1927), John Joseph Mathews's *Sundown* (1934), John Oskinson's *Brothers Three* (1935), and D'Arcy McNickle's *The Surrounded* (1936), all focused at least in part on the problems of mixed blood. Autobiographies in this period included Charles Eastman's *Indian Boyhood* (1902) and *From the Deep Woods to Civilization* (1916) and, much later, Mathews's *Talking to the Moon* (1945). Mathews's *Wah 'Kon-Tah: The Osage and the White Man's Road* (1932) approaches history through the life of an idealistic Indian agent.

By the 1930s and 1940s, other voices were also being heard, mostly in lesser numbers than those chronicled above. Although the Irish had arrived in great numbers a century earlier, no one had portrayed the lives of Irish Americans in such copious and faithful detail as James T. Farrell lavished on the Irish of Chicago in *Young Lonigan* (1932) and the many novels that followed it. Born in California, the popular and prolific writer William Saroyan wrote often of his Armenian heritage, for example, in the autobiographical stories collected in *My Name Is Aram* (1940). Significant literature emphasizing the lives of Italian Americans appeared in Pietro Di Donato's *Christ in Concrete* (1939) and in Jerre Mangione's *Mount Allegro* (1943). To the few stories of the Asian American experience from earlier years there now were added such books as Younghill Kang's *The Grass Roof* (1931) and *East Goes West* (1937), by a Korean American; Jade Snow Wong's *Fifth Chinese Daughter* (1945), an autobiography; Carlos Bulosan's *America Is in the Heart* (1946), an autobiographical novel by a Filipino immigrant; and Lin Yutang's novel *A Chinatown Family* (1948).

The four decades that began with the 1950s witnessed an enormous increase in multicultural literature by Americans. In part this increase was a reflection of general increases in population, in the level of American education, and in the annual production of books. Much of it was also attributable, however, to a renewed awareness of the kaleidoscopic nature of the American experience, emphasized in social and political phenomena such as the Beat Generation; protests against the war in Vietnam; Woodstock; the Civil Rights movement; Affirmative Action; Women's Liberation; and consciousness-raising movements for American Indians, Chicanos, and Asian Americans. In a country increasingly heterogenous in its experience, but still heavily under the influence of the myth of the melting pot, many ethnic groups found themselves enmeshed in issues of cultural identity versus assimilation.

For Jews the problem was enormously magnified by the memory of the millions who died in the Holocaust of World War II; as a result, Jewish writers after the war had to deal with the immense burden of deciding the extent of their obligation to remain identifiably Jewish in their writing or of their willingness to risk charges of contributing to the death of their culture. The immigrant Isaac Bashevis Singer responded to his own mostly internal pressures by writing in Yiddish, and mostly of his native Poland, although a few stories and one novel, *Enemies: A Love Story* (1972), are set in the United States. Saul Bellow won early fame with a kind of Jewish *Adventures of Huckleberry Finn*, paying tribute to the earlier novel in his title *The Adventures of Augie March* (1953), then went on to a distinguished career as a chronicler of twentieth-century urban anxieties, rooted in Jewishness. Bernard Malamud wrote magical fictions, mostly centered on the lives of New York Jews; among them is *The Tenants* (1971), an allegorical confrontation between a black and a Jew caught in the threatening matrix of a disintegrating New York City. Philip Roth offended some Jews with pictures they considered unflattering in the stories of his first book, *Goodbye, Columbus* (1959), continued to find both detractors and champions in later books, then turned the anguish of a writer's life into a series of novels that in some ways parallel his own life; *The Ghost Writer* (1979) was first and remains one of the best. Such are the riches of literature by Jews within this period, however, that this small catalog touches on only a few of those whose cultural portraits are most memorable.

In the work of American blacks, too, in recent decades, tensions between cultural identity and assimilation have often been clearly marked. For some, after three centuries of coexistence with whites on this continent, after a history of racial mixture that left many with at least as much "white" as "black" blood, after a century or more in which for many the solution to integration was "passing" for white, it has seemed a reasonable ambition to write as Americans rather than as African Americans, leaving others to deal with questions of black culture, black history, or cultural conflict. Thus, Frank Yerby, for example, wrote a succession of historical romances, beginning with *The Foxes of Harrow* (1946), that sold over fifty million copies but did not materially address racial issues. James Baldwin, among the most critically acclaimed writers of his time and hailed as a spokesman for his race, took time to write one novel, *Giovanni's Room* (1946), in which human sexuality, not race, is the issue. Most of the stronger works of the recent period, however, have centered on black culture or on cross-cultural conflict or interchange. A brief list of some of the best, restricted to novels only, includes Baldwin's *Go Tell It on the Mountain* (1953) and *Another Country* (1962), Ralph Ellison's *Invisible Man* (1962), Toni Morrison's *Song of Solomon* (1977) and *Beloved* (1987), Alice Walker's *The Color Purple* (1982), and Charles Johnson's *Middle Passage* (1990).

For American Indians, questions of identity and of cultural heritage have also seemed especially important recently. Because the history of mixed blood and of mixed cultures goes back four centuries, to the Spanish presence in the Southwest in the sixteenth century, and because many individuals with Indian ancestors have long ceased to call themselves Indians (though many more than in the past made that claim in the 1990 census), tribal affiliation is often the measure by which an Indian identity is affirmed. For writers, the practical result is that Indians appear most clearly to be Indians when they write of the Native American heritage or of the interchange with white culture. At the same time, cultural pride has sometimes claimed for Native American literature earlier writers who in their time scarcely seemed to draw on their Indian heritage at all: Will Rogers, the popular cowboy humorist, for example, and Lynn Riggs, author of the folk drama *Green Grow the Lilacs* (1931), the basis for the musical comedy *Oklahoma!* (1943). Counting only the strongest novels of recent decades that have an Indian focus, however, the list remains impressive. It includes N. Scott Momaday's *The House Made of Dawn* (1968), Leslie Marmon Silko's *Ceremony* (1977), Darcy McNickle's *Wind from an Enemy Sky* (1978), James Welch's *Fool's Crow* (1986), and Louise Erdrich's *Love Medicine* (1984), *Beet Queen* (1986), and *Tracks* (1988).

The recent rise in attention to ethnic origins in the United States has been accompanied by a heightened consciousness of Hispanic heritage, from

Spain, from the West Indies, from the early Spanish settlements in the Southwest, and from Mexico. Apart from the early narratives of explorations, with rare exceptions prior to World War II the Hispanic presence had been chronicled by non-Hispanics. In 1945, however, Josephina Niggli's *Mexican Village* found a wide readership with its linked stories of Mexican-Anglo love, illegitimacy, and rejection. That and the success of José Antonio Villarreal's *Pocho* (1959), a family saga, gave great impetus to much that followed, some in English, some in Spanish. Among the most memorable are Tomás Rivera's *And the Earth Did Not Part* (1971), sketches of farm workers; Rodolfo Anaya's *Bless Me, Ultima* (1972), a novel of changes in New Mexico after the atomic explosion at White Sands in 1945; Rolando Hinoja-Smith's *Sketches of the Valley* (1972); and Sandra Cisneros's *Woman Hollering Creek and Other Stories* (1991), feminist in its rendering of human relations.

By the 1950s, most of America's ethnic groups were well settled, had established at least the beginnings of literary traditions in the United States, and continued to see their numbers swollen by newer arrivals. With respect to Asians, however, a major change occurred after 1965 when a new Immigration and Naturalization Act ended many years of severe restriction. Asian immigration soon changed from a trickle to a flood, with many of the newcomers refugees from Southeast Asia. Although the full impact of these newcomers on literature is yet to be felt, already the literature of Asian Americans has increased enormously in both bulk and quality. Among the most interesting books thus far by Americans of Japanese descent are John Okada's *No-No Boy* (1957), telling of the consequences of a nisei's refusal of the draft; Jeanne Wakatsuki Houston's *Farewell to Manzanar* (1973), a memoir, written with her husband, of her family's removal to a World War II internment camp; and Hisaye Yamamoto's *Seventeen Syllables* (1988), including stories of internment camps. Chinese Americans have contributed fine fiction that includes Maxine Hong Kingston's *The Woman Warrior* (1976), *China Men* (1980), and *Tripmaster Monkey: His Fake Book* (1989); Amy Tan's *The Joy Luck Club* (1989) and *The Kitchen God's Wife* (1991); and Frank Chin's *Donald Duk* (1991). Among the writings of Americans from India, Ved Mehta's memoirs, especially *Sound-Shadows of the New World* (1985) and *The Stolen Light* (1989), portray the difficult adjustments for an immigrant who was, when he came, an Indian, an unaccompanied child, and blind. Bharati Mukherjee, another Indian American, fictionalizes the problems of immigrants to Canada and the United States in books that include *The Middleman* (1988), stories, and *Jasmine* (1989), a novel.

Recent abandonment of restrictive policies has led also to greatly increased immigration from the Middle East, Central and South America, and the West Indies. New cultural communities have been created in America's cities, and new cross-cultural relationships established. Many stories are yet to be told, some by the members of the first generation, others by their descendants, born in the United States, as the American kaleidoscope continues to reflect its changing patterns.

Notes toward Understanding

From the beginning, stories of American multiculturalism have sprung from the common storytelling impulses: to record, interpret, and enlighten. The writers of the stories have been concerned with creating lasting accounts of their experiences in the world, with organizing their observations to make the incoherencies and accidentals of life coherently understandable, and with presenting their knowledge and insights to others.

Like all stories, the stories of American multiculturalism are fundamentally narrative: They are accounts of events happening in time. Although storytellers may temporarily suspend the narrative movement, introducing passages of description, analysis, or moralization, the element that characterizes their productions as stories is the return to the pull of the basic narrative question, What happens next? After that basic pull has been exhausted, the question that next engages the reader—making it worthwhile and perhaps necessary to reread—is, What does it mean? Fact or fiction, realistic or fantastic, complete or incomplete, stories are narratives pointed toward meaning.

A problem for the reader of stories is that there are many kinds of meanings, many clues toward interpretations that may not be consistent with one another. One story may be presented as fact, an autobiographical account of a personal experience, but memory is not always accurate, and distortions may arise from hidden motives or prejudices. Another story may be presented as realistic fiction: In this case the obvious inventions of detail point toward general truths, but the truths that appeared clear to the writer may prove controversial in a discussion among readers. We look sometimes to sober history to tell us where truth resides, forgetting that historians, too, are human and subject to error, prey to subtle distortions arising from birth and upbringing.

Narrative Perspective

Clues to meaning are often most fruitfully pursued through considerations of narrative perspective: Who narrates the story? when? where? The slave's story is not the same as the master's, the husband's not the same as the wife's, the rebel's not the same as the patriot's, the story told by an objective observer not the same as one told by a passionate participant. Moreover, when and where are frequently as important as who, since stories sometimes change with changing circumstances.

In some instances, the narrator of an individual story becomes the narrator of history, as is especially the case with the first stories of European contact with Native Americans. Europeans, possessing writing and printing presses, produced their narratives for three hundred years, from the sixteenth to the nineteenth century, before Native Americans began to write their own versions. Obviously a careful reader of the early narratives of exploration and captivity will proceed with some sense of the limitations imposed by the perspectives, both as they bear upon the individual tales and upon the collective account we call history. Similarly, a consideration of narrative perspective will shed light on the displacements of other historical narratives, serving as a reminder of how often the slave's story has not been told by the slave or the woman's told by a woman. An interesting development within our own times is the strong push to reject stories written by outsiders, to reconstruct history as seen from perspectives once considered marginal. In Frank Chin's novel *Donald Duk* (1991), for example, the issue is expressed as a challenge. Dismayed to find the history of the Chinese who built the railroads in the American West largely missing from the books he reads, Donald is confronted with the view of his father:

> "They don't want our names in their history books. So what? You're surprised. If we don't write our history, why should they, huh?"
> "It's not fair."
> "Fair? What's fair? History is war, not sport! * * * You gotta keep the history yourself or lose it forever, boy. That's the mandate of heaven."

If keeping the history yourself is an important reason for writing stories, an important reason for reading them is discovering the history of others. But the reader should always become an interpreter, considering the source.

Ethos

Just as stories are colored by the personality of the narrator, they are also colored by the time and place of their telling—and of their happening. The social ethos, the spirit underlying the characteristic beliefs and practices of a community, affects the narrative even in instances in which the teller's response to the ethos is to rebel against it. Huckleberry Finn struggles to escape the lessons of school and church in Missouri in the 1840s, and Mark Twain, his creator, had at the time of his writing largely escaped them, but neither could tell the story effectively in the abstract, removed from the pressures imposed by the ethos of time and place, happening before the Civil War, written afterward. Similarly, a persistent theme of the literature of American immigration is the conflict engendered between an ethos transported from the old country and a quite different ethos encountered in the new.

The Narrator and the Experiencer

In many stories it is important to distinguish between the person who tells the story and the person who experienced it. The point seems obvious when the two people are different, since it is easy to see that the narrator's different character and different placement in time and space may produce judgments about the story that are different from those of the person involved in it. Indeed, writers often signal the importance of this difference by placing the narrator within a context of education, social class, and sophistication that is dramatically different from the position occupied by the subject of the narration. Less obvious is the importance of the distinctions that frequently need to be made even for stories in which the narrator and the experiencer are in the simplest sense one and the same; for these a reader needs to ask whether there are signs that in the interval between happening and telling the narrator has grown in judgment, has become in effect a different person. Autobiographies, like Franklin's, sometimes gain much of their power from the play of youth against age, the innocent "I" that experienced the events against the wiser "I" who tells of them. Works of fiction, too, frequently mimic this lesson from life: Experience comes first, then understanding.

Voice

Consequently, considerations of the narrative voice may provide strong clues to meaning. Putting aside the tale itself, the reader asks whether in the manner of telling the narrator betrays personal characteristics, particularly of attitude: Is the narrative voice dispassionate concerning the events narrated or emotionally involved in them? Is it biased, for example, by race, religion, gender, or politics? Is it the voice of an individual only or of an individual who desires to be understood as speaking for a group?

Focus

Sometimes the narrative voice is not easy to characterize, at least in its governing attitudes. It betrays few personal characteristics or none at all. If it is ruled by bias, or programmed toward particular moral or philosophic conclusions, it displays no overt signs of its position with respect to other possible voices. Sometimes it becomes almost self-effacing, appearing with such restraint that the story appears as a collection of voices and actions, presented in dramatic fashion directly to the mind of the reader, with little of the mediating effect normally associated with a narrator. In these instances there is always the question of focus.

Narrators display their interests in their focus, the elements of the story that they most insistently call to a reader's attention. What characters get most attention? Through whose eyes within the story are the events most consistently seen? Is the reader given the thoughts of one character only (or a few characters), but not others, thereby forcing attention to a limited viewpoint on what has happened? Why are some scenes developed at length, others scarcely detailed at all, and still others—scenes within the wider story that we can imagine—omitted entirely?

The Author

In fiction, author and narrator may be very different, like Mark Twain and Huckleberry Finn, or they may share so many characteristics that the distinction becomes blurred, as it does also in autobiography, biography, and history. Nevertheless, it is generally worthwhile to maintain the distinction between author and narrator, remembering that the author has a life outside the room in which the words are committed to paper. In that outside life the author may hold opinions quite different from those the book seems to suggest, or in a long life may generally have subscribed to a personal philosophy that seems at odds with the philosophy that for a few weeks or months seems to have dominated the mind that placed the words on paper. The narrator, on the other hand, is present only in the story and has no life outside that suggested by the unchanging words that are printed on the pages of the story. Although the interpretations of the story that the narrator points toward may be clear enough, it is safest to ascribe them strictly to the narrator. Whether the author also holds them is another question.

Irony

Situations in which author and narrator hold drastically different opinions, as do Mark Twain and Huckleberry Finn, for example, about the morality of slavery, can produce powerful ironies: The narrator presents views the author does not share. Ironic effects, however, are not restricted to fiction and are not necessarily the product of an imagined narrator played off against a real author. Something like the ironies between author and narrator occurs in autobiography, for example, where an ironic tension may arise between the vision of the younger person who experiences the events and the older one who narrates. Consideration of these kinds of ironies leads to the conclusion that the meanings of narratives may be layered. In brief, the experiences and characters that provide the subject for a narration may on their own level suggest one kind of interpretation, the narrator may suggest quite a different one, and the author may suggest yet a third. The key to full comprehension lies often in the reader's ability to perceive one or more levels of irony.

The Reader's Response

In the end it is impossible to discount the response of the reader. Not all readers pick up the same clues from a narrative or respond to them in the same way. Complete understanding of the meaning of a story, therefore, sometimes requires attention to the personal values and interpretative strategies of other people. Moreover, since reading climates change with changing times and with the changing cultural conditions in which stories are read, a narrative that seemed generally to convey a particular message in, say, the last decade of the nineteenth century may convey a substantially different message in the last decade of the twentieth. For this reason, complete understanding frequently requires an attempt to comprehend what the story meant within the community that produced it and within the subsequent reading communities of its literary history.

Textual Notes

We have tried to reproduce accurately the best reading text for each author. The specific source of each piece, unless it is obvious, is identified in the author introduction or notes. Omissions from the original text are marked by three asterisks. Important dates are given either in the author introduction or in the footnotes. Where portions of longer pieces are used, the bracketed word [From] is employed. Except when printed between brackets, titles are those of the original text. Some early texts have been newly edited for this book, as indicated in headnotes or footnotes, and where it seems appropriate some have been modernized in spelling and punctuation. The diction has not been changed. Archaic usages are explained in footnotes.

Giovanni da Verrazzano
(c. 1485–1528)

The first description of the East Coast of the territory that was to become
the United States, together with an account of its inhabitants, was written
by a Florentine explorer in the service of a French king. Like Columbus, he
was seeking a route to Cathay. Unlike Columbus, he recognized that the
land that lay before him was a new continent, though he believed that the
Pacific Ocean was not far beyond the Atlantic coast.

Giovanni da Verrazzano was an inhabitant of Lyons, France, when he
secured the support of bankers and merchants there and in Florence for his
trip, which was made under the French flag. In 1524, after an aborted start
in four ships, he left with fifty men in La Dauphine, sailing west from the
Madeira Islands and reaching fifty days later "a new country, which had
never before been seen by any one, either in ancient or modern times." This
was either Cape Fear, North Carolina, or nearby. From there he explored
northward as far as Newfoundland, touching probably on the shore of Virgina and discovering New York Harbor and Narragansett Bay. At the site
of the present Newport, Rhode Island, he encountered and described the
Wampanoag Indians, almost a hundred years before they befriended the
Pilgrims at Plymouth Colony.

Verrazzano's later career took him to the Caribbean, where he was
apparently killed by natives of Guadaloupe in 1528. Meanwhile he had
written the story of his North American explorations in a letter to King
Francis I of France. It was first translated into English by Richard Hakluyt
for his Divers Voyages Touching on the Discovery of America (1582), a
work that helped to pave the way for British exploration and colonization.

The text reproduced here is from "Verrazzano's Voyage: 1524," Old South Leaflets,
Gen. Series, No. 17; the translation, by J. G. Cogswell, was first printed in 1841.
L. C. Wroth edited The Voyages of Giovanni da Verrazzano, 1524–1528, trans. S.
Tarrow, 1970. See also S. E. Morison, The European Discovery of America: The
Northern Voyages, A.D. 500–1600, 1971.

[From] Verrazzano's Voyage: 1524

CAPTAIN JOHN DE VERRAZZANO TO HIS MOST SERENE MAJESTY, THE KING OF FRANCE, WRITES: Since the tempests which we encountered on the northern coasts, I have not written to your most Serene and Christian Majesty concerning the four ships sent out by your orders on the ocean to discover new lands, because I thought you must have been before apprized of all that had happened to us—that we had been compelled by the impetuous violence of the winds to put into Britany in distress with only the two ships Normandy and Dolphin; and that after having repaired these ships, we made a cruise in them, well armed, along the coast of Spain, as your Majesty must have heard, and also of our new plan of continuing our begun voyage with the Dolphin alone; from this voyage being now returned, I proceed to give your Majesty an account of our discoveries.

On the 17th of last January we set sail from a desolate rock near the island of Madeira, belonging to his most Serene Majesty, the King of Portugal, with fifty men, having provisions sufficient for eight months, arms and other warlike munition and naval stores. Sailing westward with a light and pleasant easterly breeze, in twenty-five days we ran eight hundred leagues. On the 24th of February we encountered as violent a hurricane as any ship ever weathered, from which we escaped unhurt by the divine assistance and goodness, to the praise of the glorious and fortunate name of our good ship, that had been able to support the violent tossing of the waves. Pursuing our voyage towards the West, a little northwardly, in twenty-four days more, having run four hundred leagues, we reached a new country, which had never before been seen by any one, either in ancient or modern times. At first it appeared to be very low, but on approaching it to within a quarter of a league from the shore we perceived, by the great fires near the coast, that it was inhabited. We perceived that it stretched to the south, and coasted along in that direction in search of some port, in which we might come to anchor, and examine into the nature of the country, but for fifty leagues we could find none in which we could lie securely. Seeing the coast still stretch to the south, we resolved to change our course and stand to the northward, and as we still had the same difficulty, we drew in with the land and sent a boat on shore. Many people who were seen coming to the sea-side fled at our approach, but occasionally stopping, they looked back upon us with astonishment, and some were at length induced, by various friendly signs, to come to us. These showed the greatest delight on beholding us, wondering at our dress, countenances and complexion. They then showed us by signs where we could more conveniently secure our boat, and offered us some of their provisions. That your Majesty may know all that we learned, while on shore, of their manners and customs of life, I will relate what we saw as briefly as possible. They go entirely naked, except that about the loins they wear skins of small animals like martens fastened by a girdle of plaited grass, to which they tie, all round the body, the tails of other animals hanging down to the knees; all other parts of the body and the head are naked. Some wear garlands similar to birds' feathers.

The complexion of these people is black, not much different from that of the Ethiopians; their hair is black and thick, and not very long, it is worn tied back upon the head in the form of a little tail. In person they are of good proportions, of middle stature, a little above our own, broad across the breast, strong in the arms, and well formed in the legs and other parts of the body; the only exception to their good looks is that they have broad faces, but not all, however, as we saw many that had sharp ones, with large black eyes and a fixed expression. They are not very strong in body, but acute in mind, active and swift of foot, as far as we could judge by observation. In these last two particulars they resemble the people of the east, especially those the most remote. We could not learn a great many particulars of their usages on account of our short stay among them, and the distance of our ship from the shore.

We found not far from this people another whose mode of life we judged to be similar. The whole shore is covered with fine sand, about fifteen feet thick, rising in the form of little hills about fifty paces broad. Ascending farther, we found several arms of the sea which make in through inlets, washing the shores on both sides as the coast runs. An outstretched country appears at a little distance rising somewhat above the sandy shore in beautiful fields and broad plains, covered with immense forests of trees, more or less dense, too various in colours, and too delightful and charming in appearance to be described. I do not believe that they are like the Hercynian forest[1] or the rough wilds of Scythia,[2] and the northern regions full of vines and common trees, but adorned with palms, laurels, cypresses, and other varieties unknown in Europe, that send forth the sweetest fragrance to a great distance, but which we could not examine more closely for the reasons before given, and not on account of any difficulty in traversing the woods, which, on the contrary, are easily penetrated.

As the "East" stretches around this country, I think it cannot be devoid of the same medicinal and aromatic drugs, and various riches of gold and the like, as is denoted by the colour of the ground. It abounds also in animals, as deer, stags, hares, and many other similar, and with a great variety of birds for every kind of pleasant and delightful sport. It is plentifully supplied with lakes and ponds of running water, and being in the latitude of 34,[3] the air is salubrious, pure and temperate, and free from the extremes of both heat and cold. There are no violent winds in these regions, the most prevalent are the north-west and west. In summer, the season in which we were there, the sky is clear, with but little rain: if fogs and mists are at any time driven in by the south wind, they are instantaneously dissipated, and at once it becomes

---

1. In Germany.

2. In Southeast Europe and Asia.

3. Immediately north of Cape Fear, North Carolina.

serene and bright again. The sea is calm, not boisterous, and its waves are gentle. Although the whole coast is low and without harbours, it is not dangerous for navigation, being free from rocks and bold, so that within four or five fathoms from the shore there is twenty-four feet of water at all times of tide, and this depth constantly increases in a uniform proportion. The holding ground is so good that no ship can part her cable, however violent the wind, as we proved by experience; for while riding at anchor on the coast, we were overtaken by a gale in the beginning of March, when the winds are high, as is usual in all countries, we found our anchor broken before it started from its hold or moved at all.

We set sail from this place, continuing to coast along the shore, which we found stretching out to the west (east?); the inhabitants being numerous, we saw everywhere a multitude of fires. While at anchor on this coast, there being no harbour to enter, we sent the boat on shore with twenty-five men to obtain water, but it was not possible to land without endangering the boat, on account of the immense high surf thrown up by the sea, as it was an open roadstead. Many of the natives came to the beach, indicating by various friendly signs that we might trust ourselves on shore. One of their noble deeds of friendship deserves to be made known to your Majesty. A young sailor was attempting to swim ashore through the surf to carry them some knick-knacks, as little bells, looking-glasses, and other like trifles; when he came near three or four of them he tossed the things to them, and turned about to get back to the boat, but he was thrown over by the waves, and so dashed by them that he lay as it were dead upon the beach. When these people saw him in this situation, they ran and took him up by the head, legs and arms, and carried him to a distance from the surf; the young man, finding himself borne off in this way, uttered very loud shrieks in fear and dismay, while they answered as they could in their language, showing him that he had no cause for fear. Afterwards they laid him down at the foot of a little hill, when they took off his shirt and trowsers, and examined him, expressing the greatest astonishment at the whiteness of his skin. Our sailors in the boat seeing a great fire made up, and their companion placed very near it, full of fear, as is usual in all cases of novelty, imagined that the natives were about to roast him for food. But as soon as he had recovered his strength after a short stay with them, showing by signs that he wished to return aboard, they hugged him with great affection, and accompanied him to the shore, then leaving him, that he might feel more secure, they withdrew to a little hill, from which they watched him until he was safe in the boat. This young man remarked that these people were black like the others, that they had shining skins, middle stature, and sharper faces, and very delicate bodies and limbs, and that they were inferior in strength, but quick in their minds; this is all that he observed of them.

Departing hence, and always following the shore, which stretched to the north, we came, in the space of fifty leagues, to another land, which appeared very beautiful and full of the largest forests. We approached it, and going ashore with twenty men, we went back from the coast about two leagues, and found that the people had fled and hid themselves in the woods for fear. By searching around we discovered in the grass a very old woman and a young girl of about eighteen or twenty, who had concealed themselves for the same reason; the old woman carried two infants on her shoulders, and behind her neck a little boy eight years of age; when we came up to them they began to shriek and make signs to the men who had fled to the woods. We gave them a part of our provisions, which they accepted with delight, but the girl would not touch any; every thing we offered to her being thrown down in great anger. We took the little boy from the old woman to carry with us to France, and would have taken the girl also, who was very beautiful and very tall, but it was impossible because of the loud shrieks she uttered as we attempted to lead her away; having to pass some woods, and being far from the ship, we determined to leave her and take the boy only. We found them fairer than the others, and wearing a covering made of certain plants, which hung down from the branches of the trees, trying them together with threads of wild hemp; their heads are without covering and of the same shape as the others. Their food is a kind of pulse[4] which there abounds, different in colour and size from ours, and of a very delicious flavour. Besides they take birds and fish for food, using snares and bows made of hard wood, with reeds for arrows, in the ends of which they put the bones of fish and other animals. The animals in these regions are wilder than in Europe from being continually molested by the hunters. We saw many of their boats made of one tree twenty feet long and four feet broad, without the aid of stone or iron or other kind of metal. In the whole country for the space of two hundred leagues, which we visited, we saw no stone of any sort. To hollow out their boats they burn out as much of a log as is requisite, and also from the prow and stern to make them float well on the sea. The land, in situation, fertility and beauty, is like the other, abounding also in forests filled with various kinds of trees, but not of such fragrance, as it is more northern and colder.

We saw in this country many vines growing naturally, which entwine about the trees, and run up upon them as they do in the plains of Lombardy. These vines would doubtless produce excellent wine if they were properly cultivated and attended to, as we have often seen the grapes which they produce very sweet and pleasant, and not unlike our own. They must be held in estimation by them, as they carefully remove the shrubbery from around them, wherever they grow, to allow the fruit to ripen better. We found also wild roses, violets, lilies, and many sorts of plants and fragrant flowers different from our own. We cannot describe their habitations, as they are in the interior of the country, but from various indications we conclude they must be formed of trees and shrubs. We saw also many grounds for conjecturing that they often sleep in the open air, without any covering but the sky. Of their other usages we know nothing; we believe, however, that all the people we were among live in the same way.

---

4. Peas or beans.

After having remained here three days, riding at anchor on the coast, as we could find no harbour we determined to depart, and coast along the shore to the north-east, keeping sail on the vessel only by day, and coming to anchor by night. After proceeding one hundred leagues, we found a very pleasant situation[5] among some steep hills, through which a very large river, deep at its mouth, forced its way to the sea; from the sea to the estuary of the river, any ship heavily laden might pass, with the help of the tide, which rises eight feet. But as we were riding at anchor in a good berth, we would not venture up in our vessel, without a knowledge of the mouth; therefore we took the boat, and entering the river, we found the country on its banks well peopled, the inhabitants not differing much from the others, being dressed out with the feathers of birds of various colours. They came towards us with evident delight, raising loud shouts of admiration, and showing us where we could most securely land with our boat. We passed up this river, about half a league, when we found it formed a most beautiful lake three leagues in circuit, upon which they were rowing thirty or more of their small boats, from one shore to the other, filled with multitudes who came to see us. All of a sudden, as is wont to happen to navigators, a violent contrary wind blew in from the sea, and forced us to return to our ship, greatly regretting to leave this region which seemed so commodious and delightful, and which we supposed must also contain great riches, as the hills showed many indications of minerals. Weighing anchor, we sailed fifty leagues toward the east, as the coast stretched in that direction, and always in sight of it; at length we discovered an island[6] of a triangular form, about ten leagues from the mainland, in size about equal to the island of Rhodes, having many hills covered with trees, and well peopled, judging from the great number of fires which we saw all around its shores; we gave it the name of your Majesty's illustrious mother.

We did not land there, as the weather was unfavourable, but proceeded to another place, fifteen leagues distant from the island, where we found a very excellent harbour.[7] Before entering it, we saw about twenty small boats full of people, who came about our ship, uttering many cries of astonishment, but they would not approach nearer than within fifty paces; stopping, they looked at the structure of our ship, our persons and dress, afterwards they all raised a loud shout together, signifying that they were pleased. By imitating their signs, we inspired them in some measure with confidence, so that they came near enough for us to toss to them some little bells and glasses, and many toys, which they took and looked at, laughing, and then came on board without fear. Among them were two kings more beautiful in form and stature than can possibly be described; one was about forty years old, the other about twenty-four, and they were dressed in the following manner: The oldest had a deer's skin around his body, artificially wrought in

---

5. New York Harbor.

6. Perhaps Block Island, off Rhode Island.

7. Narragansett Bay. The Indians met there were Narragansetts and Wampanoags.

damask figures, his head was without covering, his hair was tied back in various knots; around his neck he wore a large chain ornamented with many stones of different colours. The young man was similar in his general appearance. This is the finest looking tribe, and the handsomest in their costumes, that we have found in our voyage. They exceed us in size, and they are of a very fair complexion (?); some of them incline more to a white (bronze?), and others to a tawny colour; their faces are sharp, their hair long and black, upon the adorning of which they bestow great pains; their eyes are black and sharp, their expression mild and pleasant, greatly resembling the antique. I say nothing to your Majesty of the other parts of the body, which are all in good proportion, and such as belong to well-formed men. Their women are of the same form and beauty, very graceful, of fine countenances and pleasing appearance in manners and modesty; they wear no clothing except a deer skin, ornamented like those worn by the men; some wear very rich lynx skins upon their arms, and various ornaments upon their heads, composed of braids of hair, which also hang down upon their breasts on each side. Others wear different ornaments, such as the women of Egypt and Syria use. The older and the married people, both men and women, wear many ornaments in their ears, hanging down in the oriental manner. We saw upon them several pieces of wrought copper, which is more esteemed by them than gold, as this is not valued on account of its colour, but is considered by them as the most ordinary of the metals—yellow being the colour especially disliked by them; azure and red are those in highest estimation with them. Of those things which we gave them, they prized most highly the bells, azure crystals, and other toys to hang in their ears and about their necks; they do not value or care to have silk or gold stuffs, or other kinds of cloth, nor implements of steel or iron. When we showed them our arms, they expressed no admiration, and only asked how they were made; the same was the case of the looking-glasses, which they returned to us, smiling, as soon as they had looked at them. They are very generous, giving away whatever they have. We formed a great friendship with them, and one day we entered into the port with our ship, having before rode at the distance of a league from the shore, as the weather was adverse. They came off to the ship with a number of their little boats, with their faces painted in divers colours, showing us real signs of joy, bringing us of their provisions, and signifying to us where we could best ride in safety with our ship, and keeping with us until we had cast anchor. We remained among them fifteen days, to provide ourselves with many things of which we were in want, during which time they came every day to see our ship, bringing with them their wives, of whom they were very careful; for, although they came on board themselves, and remained a long while, they made their wives stay in the boats, nor could we ever get them on board by any entreaties or any presents we could make them. One of the two kings often came with his queen and many attendants, to see us for his amusement; but he always stopped at the distance of about two hundred paces, and sent a boat to inform us of his intended visit, saying they would come and see our ship—this was done for safety, and as soon as they had an answer from us they came off, and remained awhile to look around; but on hearing the annoying cries of the sailors, the king sent the queen, with her attendants, in a very light boat, to wait, near an island a quarter of a league distant from us, while he remained a long time on board, talking with us by signs, and expressing his fanciful notions about every thing in the ship, and asking the use of all. After imitating our modes of salutation, and tasting our food, he courteously took leave of us. Sometimes, when our men stayed two or three days on a small island, near the ship, for their various necessities, as sailors are wont to do, he came with seven or eight of his attendants, to inquire about our movements, often asking us if we intended to remain there long, and offering us everything at his command, and then he would shoot with his bow, and run up and down with his people, making great sport for us. We often went five or six leagues into the interior, and found the country as pleasant as is possible to conceive, adapted to cultivation of every kind, whether of corn, wine or oil; there are open plains twenty-five or thirty leagues in extent, entirely free from trees or other hindrances, and of so great fertility, that whatever is sown there will yield an excellent crop. On entering the woods, we observed that they might all be traversed by an army ever so numerous; the trees of which they were composed, were oaks, cypresses, and others, unknown in Europe. We found, also, apples, plumbs, filberts, and many other fruits, but all of a different kind from ours. The animals, which are in great numbers, as stags, deer, lynxes, and many other species, are taken by snares, and by bows, the latter being their chief implement; their arrows are wrought with great beauty, and for the heads of them, they use emery, jasper, hard marble, and other sharp stones, in the place of iron. They also use the same kind of sharp stones in cutting down trees, and with them they construct their boats of single logs, hollowed out with admirable skill, and sufficiently commodious to contain ten or twelve persons; their oars are short, and broad at the end, and are managed in rowing by force of the arms alone, with perfect security, and as nimbly as they choose. We saw their dwellings, which are of a circular form, of about ten or twelve paces in circumference, made of logs split in halves, without any regularity of architecture, and covered with roofs of straw, nicely put on, which protect them from wind and rain. There is no doubt that they would build stately edifices if they had workmen as skilful as ours, for the whole sea-coast abounds in shining stones, crystals, and alabaster, and for the same reason it has ports and retreats for animals. They change their habitations from place to place as circumstances of situation and season may require; this is easily done, as they have only to take with them their mats, and they have other houses prepared at once. The father and the whole family dwell together in one house in great numbers; in some we saw twenty-five or thirty persons. Their food is pulse, as with the other tribes, which is here better than elsewhere, and more carefully cultivated; in the time of sowing they are governed by the moon, the sprouting of grain, and many other ancient usages. They live by hunting and fishing, and they are long-lived. If they fall sick, they cure themselves without medicine, by the heat of the fire, and their death at last comes from extreme old age. We judge them to be very affectionate and charitable towards their relatives—making loud lamentations in their adversity, and in their misery calling to mind all their good fortune. At their departure out of life, their relations mutually join in weeping, mingled with singing, for a long while. This is all that we could learn of them. This region is situated in the parallel of Rome, being 41° 40' of north latitude, but much colder from accidental circumstances, and not by nature, as I shall hereafter explain to your Majesty, and confine myself at present to the description of its local situation. It looks towards the south, on which side the harbour is half a league broad; afterwards, upon entering it, the extent between the coast and north is twelve leagues, and then enlarging itself it forms a very large bay, twenty leagues in circumference, in which are five small islands, of great fertility and beauty, covered with large and lofty trees. Among these islands any fleet, however large, might ride safely, without fear of tempests or other dangers. Turning towards the south, at the entrance of the harbour, on both sides, there are very pleasant hills, and many streams of clear water, which flow down to the sea. In the midst of the entrance, there is a rock of free-stone, formed by nature, and suitable for the construction of any kind of machine or bulwark for the defence of the harbour.[8]

Having supplied ourselves with every thing necessary, on the fifth of May we departed from the port, and sailed one hundred and fifty leagues, keeping so close to the coast as never to lose it from our sight; the nature of the country appeared much the same as before, but the mountains were a little higher, and all in appearance rich in minerals. We did not stop to land as the weather was very favorable for pursuing our voyage, and the country presented no variety. The shore stretched to the east, and fifty leagues beyond more to the north, where we found a more elevated country,[9] full of very thick woods of fir trees, cypresses and the like, indicative of a cold climate. The people were entirely different from the others we had seen, whom we had found kind and gentle, but these were so rude and barbarous that we were unable by any signs we could make, to hold communication with them. They clothe themselves in the skins of bears, lynxes, seals and other animals. Their food, as far as we could judge by several visits to their dwellings, is obtained by hunting and fishing, and certain fruits, which are a sort of root of spontaneous growth. They have no pulse, and we saw no signs of cultivation; the land appears sterile and unfit for growing of fruit or grain of any kind. If we wished at any time to traffick with them, they came to the sea shore and stood upon the rocks, from which they lowered down by a cord to our boats beneath whatever they had to barter, continually crying out to us, not to come nearer, and instantly demanding from us that which was to be given in exchange; they took from us only knives, fish hooks and sharpened

8. At Newport.
9. The coast of Maine.

steel. No regard was paid to our courtesies; when we had nothing left to exchange with them, the men at our departure made the most brutal signs of disdain and contempt possible. Against their will we penetrated two or three leagues into the interior[1] with twenty-five men; when we came to the shore, they shot at us with their arrows, raising the most horrible cries and afterwards fleeing to the woods. In this region we found nothing extraordinary except vast forests and some metalliferous hills, as we infer from seeing that many of the people wore copper ear-rings. Departing from thence, we kept along the coast, steering north-east, and found the country more pleasant and open, free from woods, and distant in the interior we saw lofty mountains, but none which extended to the shore. Within fifty leagues we discovered thirty-two islands, all near the main land, small and of pleasant appearance, but high and so disposed as to afford excellent harbours and channels, as we see in the Adriatic gulph, near Illyria and Dalmatia. We had no intercourse with the people, but we judge that they were similar in nature and usages to those we were last among. After sailing between east and north the distance of one hundred and fifty leagues more,[2] and finding our provisions and naval stores nearly exhausted, we took in wood and water and determined to return to France, having discovered 502, that is 700 (sic) leagues of unknown lands.

As to the religious faith of all these tribes, not understanding their language, we could not discover either by sign or gestures any thing certain. It seemed to us that they had no religion nor laws, nor any knowledge of a First Cause or Mover, that they worshipped neither the heavens, stars, sun, moon nor other planets; nor could we learn if they were given to any kind of idolatry, or offered any sacrifices or supplications, or if they have temples or houses of prayer in their villages;—our conclusion was, that they have no religious belief whatever, but live in this respect entirely free. All which proceeds from ignorance, as they are very easy to be persuaded, and imitated us with earnestness and fervour in all which they saw us do as Christians in our acts of worship.

*   *   *

On board the ship Dolphin, in the port of Dieppe in Normandy, the 8th of July, 1524.

> *Your humble servitor,*
> John de Verrazzano.

---

1. Perhaps near Portland, Maine.
2. That is, approximately to Cape Breton, Nova Scotia.

Alvar Núñez Cabeza de Vaca
(c. 1490–c. 1557)

Almost a century before the English settled Jamestown and Plymouth Colony, three Spaniards and a Moroccan slave lived eight years among Native American tribes of the Southwest. Their story is the first account of extended contact on the soil that was to become the United States between Old World people and the inhabitants of the New World that they called Indians.

Alvar Núñez Cabeza de Vaca was a native of Cadiz, in southern Spain. In June 1527 he left Spain with the expedition of Pánfilo de Narváez, whose intent was to conquer and colonize Florida. By April 1528, when the expedition arrived at Tampa Bay, the six hundred colonists and soldiers who sailed from Spain had been severely reduced in numbers by shipwreck and disease. Among the approximately three hundred who set out on foot and by ship to explore the region westward, only four survived: Cabeza de Vaca, Alonzo del Castillo, Andrés Dorantes, and Dorantes's black slave Estévan. Although their routes remain uncertain, they seem to have come ashore after a shipwreck on what is now Galveston Island, off the coast of Texas. From there they wandered as captives and slaves, but they were also venerated for shamanistic healing powers, visiting West Texas, New Mexico, Arizona, and perhaps California before reaching a Spanish outpost in Mexico in 1536. They were probably the first non-Indians to see buffalo, and the stories they brought back of richer Indians (Pueblos) to the north contributed to legends of the Seven Cities of Cibola and El Dorado, inspiring Coronado's expedition of 1540. Cabeza de Vaca wrote his account almost immediately on his return, and it was first published six years later, in 1542. Later he went to Brazil and published an account of his South American experiences in Commentarios *(1555).*

The Narrative of Cabeza de Vaca *was translated into English by Thomas Buckingham Smith in 1851 and reprinted by Frederick W. Hodge in* Spanish Explorers in the Southern United States, 1528–1543 *(1907), the source of the present text. Studies include Morris Bishop,* The Odyssey of Cabeza de Vaca *(1933) and Haniel Long,* The Marvelous Adventures of Cabeza de Vaca *(1973).*

[From] The Narrative of Cabeza de Vaca

CHAPTER 11. OF WHAT BEFELL LOPE DE OVIEDO WITH THE INDIANS[1]

AFTER THE PEOPLE had eaten, I ordered Lope de Oviedo, who had more strength and was stouter than any of the rest, to go to some trees that were near by, and climbing into one of them to look about and try to gain knowledge of the country. He did as I bade, and made out that we were on an island. He saw that the land was pawed up in the manner that ground is wont to be where cattle range, whence it appeared to him that this should be a country of Christians; and thus he reported to us. I ordered him to return and examine much more particularly, and see if there were any roads that were worn, but without going far, because there might be danger.

He went, and coming to a path, took it for the distance of half a league, and found some huts, without tenants, they having gone into the field. He took from these an earthen pot, a little dog, some few mullets, and returned. As it appeared to us he was gone a long time, we sent two men that they should look to see what might have happened. They met him near by, and saw that three Indians with bows and arrows followed and were calling to him, while he, in the same way, was beckoning them on. Thus he arrived where we were, the natives remaining a little way back, seated on the shore. Half an hour after, they were supported by one hundred other Indian bowmen, who if they were not large, our fears made giants of them. They stopped near us with the first three. It were idle to think that any among us could make defence, for it would have been difficult to find six that could rise from the ground. The assessor[2] and I went out and called to them, and they came to us. We endeavored the best we could to encourage them and secure their favor. We gave them beads and hawk-bells, and each of them gave me an arrow, which is a pledge of friendship. They told us by signs that

---

1. The members of the expedition had arrived in Florida at St. Clement's Point, near Tampa Bay, on April 14, 1528. After traveling overland to Appalachee Bay, their numbers reduced by hardship, illness, and conflicts with the Indians, they constructed a forge, built five boats, and sailed west along the Gulf coast, past the Mississippi Delta. Separated by storms from the other boats, Cabeza de Vaca and his men found themselves on the morning of November 6, 1528 shipwrecked and cast ashore off the coast of Texas, probably on Galveston Island.

2. Alonzo de Solis.

they would return in the morning and bring us something to eat, as at that time they had nothing.

CHAPTER 12. THE INDIANS BRING US FOOD

At sunrise the next day, the time the Indians appointed, they came according to their promise, and brought us a large quantity of fish with certain roots, some a little larger than walnuts, others a trifle smaller, the greater part got from under the water and with much labor. In the evening they returned and brought us more fish and roots. They sent their women and children to look at us, who went back rich with the hawk-bells and beads given them, and they came afterwards on other days, returning as before. Finding that we had provision, fish, roots, water, and other things we asked for, we determined to embark again and pursue our course. Having dug out our boat from the sand in which it was buried, it became necessary that we should strip, and go through great exertion to launch her, we being in such a state that things very much lighter sufficed to make us great labor.

Thus embarked, at the distance of two crossbow shots in the sea we shipped a wave that entirely wet us. As we were naked, and the cold was very great, the oars loosened in our hands, and the next blow the sea struck us, capsized the boat. The assessor and two others held fast to her for preservation, but it happened to be far otherwise; the boat carried them over and they were drowned under her. As the surf near the shore was very high, a single roll of the sea threw the rest into the waves and half drowned upon the shore of the island, without our losing any more than those the boat took down. The survivors escaped naked as they were born, with the loss of all they had; and although the whole was of little value, at that time it was worth much, as we were then in November, the cold was severe, and our bodies were so emaciated the bones might be counted with little difficulty, having become the perfect figures of death. For myself I can say that from the month of May passed, I had eaten no other thing than maize, and sometimes I found myself obliged to eat it unparched; for although the beasts were slaughtered while the boats were building, I could never eat their flesh, and I did not eat fish ten times. I state this to avoid giving excuses, and that every one may judge in what condition we were. Besides all these misfortunes, came a north wind upon us, from which we were nearer to death than life. Thanks be to our Lord that, looking among the brands we had used there, we found sparks from which we made great fires. And thus were we asking mercy of Him and pardon for our transgressions, shedding many tears, and each regretting not his own fate alone, but that of his comrades about him.

At sunset, the Indians thinking that we had not gone, came to seek us and bring us food; but when they saw us thus, in a plight so different from what it was before, and so extraordinary, they were alarmed and turned back. I went toward them and called, when they returned much frightened. I gave them to understand by signs that our boat had sunk and three of our number had been drowned. There, before them, they saw two of the departed, and we who remained were near joining them. The Indians, at sight of what had befallen us, and our state of suffering and melancholy destitution, sat down among us, and from the sorrow and pity they felt, they all began to lament so earnestly that they might have been heard at a distance, and continued so doing more than half an hour. It was strange to see these men, wild and untaught, howling like brutes over our misfortunes. It caused in me as in others, an increase of feeling and a livelier sense of our calamity.

The cries having ceased, I talked with the Christians, and said that if it appeared well to them, I would beg these Indians to take us to their houses. Some, who had been in New Spain, replied that we ought not to think of it; for if they should do so, they would sacrifice us to their idols. But seeing no better course, and that any other led to a nearer and more certain death, I disregarded what was said, and besought the Indians to take us to their dwellings. They signified that it would give them delight, and that we should tarry a little, that they might do what we asked. Presently thirty men loaded themselves with wood and started for their houses, which were far off, and we remained with the others until near night, when, holding us up, they carried us with all haste. Because of the extreme coldness of the weather, lest any one should die or fail by the way, they caused four or five very large fires to be placed at intervals, and at each they warmed us; and when they saw that we had regained some heat and strength, they took us to the next so swiftly that they hardly let us touch our feet to the ground. In this manner we went as far as their habitations, where we found that they had made a house for us with many fires in it. An hour after our arrival, they began to dance and hold great rejoicing, which lasted all night, although for us there was no joy, festivity nor sleep, awaiting the hour they should make us victims. In the morning they again gave us fish and roots, showing us such hospitality that we were reassured, and lost somewhat the fear of sacrifice.

CHAPTER 13. WE HEAR OF OTHER CHRISTIANS

This day I saw a native with an article of traffic I knew was not one we had bestowed; and asking whence it came, I was told by signs that it had been given by men like ourselves who were behind. Hearing this I sent two Indians, and with them two Christians to be shown those persons. They met near by,[3] as the men were coming to look after us; for the Indians of the place where they were, gave them information concerning us. They were Captains Andrés Dorantes and Alonzo del Castillo, with all the persons of their boat. Having come up they were surprised at seeing us in the condition we were, and very much pained at having nothing to give us, as they had brought no other clothes than what they had on.

Thus together again, they related that on the fifth day of that month,[4] their boat had capsized a league and a half[5] from there, and they escaped without losing any thing. We all agreed to refit their [our] boat, that those of us might go in her who had vigor sufficient and disposition to do so, and the rest should remain until they became well enough to go, as they best might, along the coast until God our Lord should be pleased to conduct us alike to a land of Christians. Directly as we arranged this, we set ourselves to work. Before we threw the boat out into the water, Tavera, a gentleman of our company, died; and the boat, which we thought to use, came to its end, sinking from unfitness to float.

As we were in the condition I have mentioned, the greater number of us naked, and the weather boisterous for travel, and to cross rivers and bays by swimming, and we being entirely without provisions or the means of carrying any, we yielded obedience to what necessity required, to pass the winter in the place where we were. We also agreed that four men of the most robust should go on to Panunco,[6] which we believed to be near, and if, by Divine favor, they should reach there, they could give information of our remaining on that island, and of our sorrows and destitution.

*   *   *

CHAPTER 14. THE DEPARTURE OF FOUR CHRISTIANS

The four Christians being gone, after a few days such cold and tempestuous weather succeeded that the Indians could not pull up roots, the cane weirs in which they took fish no longer yielded any thing, and the houses being very open, our people began to die. Five Christians, of a mess [quartered] on the

---

3. This would seem to indicate that Dorantes's boat was cast ashore on the same island. [Hodge's note]

4. November 1528. Dorantes' boat was therefore cast ashore the day before the landing of Cabeza de Vaca's party. [Hodge's note]

5. About four miles. [Hodge's note]

6. Pánuco, a Spanish province in Mexico.

coast, came to such extremity that they ate their dead; the body of the last one only was found unconsumed. Their names were Sierra, Diego Lopez, Corral, Palacios and Gonçalo Ruiz. This produced great commotion among the Indians giving rise to so much censure that had they known it in season to have done so, doubtless they would have destroyed any survivor, and we should have found ourselves in the utmost perplexity. Finally, of eighty men who arrived in the two instances, fifteen only remained alive.

After this, the natives were visited by a disease of the bowels, of which half their number died. They conceived that we had destroyed them,[7] and believing it firmly, they concerted among themselves to dispatch those of us who survived. When they were about to execute their purpose, an Indian who had charge of me, told them not to believe we were the cause of those deaths, since if we had such power we should also have averted the fatality from so many of our people, whom they had seen die without our being able to minister relief, already very few of us remaining, and none doing hurt or wrong, and that it would be better to leave us unharmed. God our Lord willed that the others should heed this opinion and counsel, and be hindered in their design.

To this island we gave the name Malhado.[8] The people[9] we found there are large and well formed; they have no other arms than bows and arrows, in the use of which they are very dexterous. The men have one of their nipples bored from side to side, and some have both, wearing a cane in each, the length of two palms and a half, and the thickness of two fingers. They have the under lip also bored, and wear in it a piece of cane the breadth of half a finger. Their women are accustomed to great toil. The stay they make on the island is from October to the end of February. Their subsistence then is the root I have spoken of, got from under the water in November and December. They have weirs of cane and take fish only in this season; afterwards they live on the roots. At the end of February, they go into other parts to seek food; for then the root is beginning to grow and is not food.

Those people love their offspring the most of any in the world, and treat them with the greatest mildness. When it occurs that a son dies, the parents and kindred weep as does everybody; the wailing continuing for him a whole year. They begin before dawn every day, the parents first and after them the whole town. They do the same at noon and at sunset. After a year of mourning has passed, the rites of the dead are performed; then they wash and purify themselves from the stain of smoke. They lament all the deceased in this manner, except the aged, for whom they show no regret, as they say that their season has passed, they having no enjoyment, and that living they would occupy the earth and take aliment from the young. Their custom is to bury the dead, unless it be those among them who have been physicians. These they burn. While the fire kindles they are all dancing and making

---

7. That is, the Indians believed the Christians to be sorcerers. [Hodge's note]

8. "Misfortune," "ill-fate." [Hodge's note]

9. The Capoques, or Cahoques, and the Hans. [Hodge's note]

high festivity, until the bones become powder. After the lapse of a year the funeral honors are celebrated, every one taking part in them, when that dust is presented in water for the relatives to drink.

* * *

CHAPTER 16. THE CHRISTIANS LEAVE THE ISLAND OF MALHADO

After Dorantes and Castillo returned to the island, they brought together the Christians, who were somewhat separated, and found them in all to be fourteen. As I have said, I was opposite on the main, where my Indians had taken me, and where so great sickness had come upon me, that if anything before had given me hopes of life, this were enough to have entirely bereft me of them.

When the Christians heard of my condition, they gave an Indian the cloak of marten skins we had taken from the cacique, as before related, to pass them over to where I was that they might visit me. Twelve of them crossed; for two were so feeble that their comrades could not venture to bring them. The names of those who came were Alonzo del Castillo, Andrés Dorantes, Diego Dorantes, Valdevieso, Estrada, Tostado, Chaves, Gutierrez, Asturiano a clergyman, Diego de Huelva, Estevanico the black, and Benitez; and when they reached the main land, they found another, who was one of our company, named Francisco de Leon. The thirteen together followed along the coast. So soon as they had come over, my Indians informed me of it, and that Hieronymo de Alvaniz and Lope de Oviedo remained on the island. But sickness prevented me from going with my companions or even seeing them.

I was obliged to remain with the people belonging to the island more than a year, and because of the hard work they put upon me and the harsh treatment, I resolved to flee from them and go to those of Charruco, who inhabit the forests and country of the main, the life I led being insupportable. Besides much other labor, I had to get out roots from below the water, and from among the cane where they grew in the ground. From this employment I had my fingers so worn that did a straw but touch them they would bleed. Many of the canes are broken, so they often tore my flesh, and I had to go in the midst of them with only the clothing on I have mentioned.

Accordingly, I put myself to contriving how I might get over to the other Indians, among whom matters turned somewhat more favorably for me. I set to trafficking, and strove to make my employment profitable in the ways I could best contrive, and by that means I got food and good treatment.

The Indians would beg me to go from one quarter to another for things of which they have need; for in consequence of incessant hostilities, they cannot traverse the country, nor make many exchanges. With my merchandise and trade I went into the interior as far as I pleased, and travelled along the coast forty or fifty leagues. The principal wares were cones and other pieces of sea-snail, conchs used for cutting, and fruit like a bean of the highest value among them, which they use as a medicine and employ in their dances and festivities. Among other matters were sea-beads. Such were what I carried into the interior; and in barter I got and brought back skins, ochre with which they rub and color the face, hard canes of which to make arrows, sinews, cement and flint for the heads, and tassels of the hair of deer that by dyeing they make red. This occupation suited me well; for the travel allowed me liberty to go where I wished, I was not obliged to work, and was not a slave. Wherever I went I received fair treatment, and the Indians gave me to eat out of regard to my commodities. My leading object, while journeying in this business, was to find out the way by which I should go forward, and I became well known. The inhabitants were pleased when they saw me, and I had brought them what they wanted; and those who did not know me sought and desired the acquaintance, for my reputation. The hardships that I underwent in this were long to tell, as well of peril and privation as of storms and cold. Oftentimes they overtook me alone and in the wilderness; but I came forth from them all by the great mercy of God our Lord. Because of them I avoided pursuing the business in winter, a season in which the natives themselves retire to their huts and ranches, torpid and incapable of exertion.

I was in this country nearly six years, alone among the Indians, and naked like them. The reason why I remained so long, was that I might take with me the Christian, Lope de Oviedo, from the island; Alaniz, his companion, who had been left with him by Alonzo del Castillo, and by Andrés Dorantes, and the rest, died soon after their departure; and to get the survivor out from there, I went over to the island every year, and entreated him that we should go, in the best way we could contrive, in quest of Christians. He put me off every year, saying in the next coming we would start. At last I got him off, crossing him over the bay, and over four rivers in the coast, as he could not swim. In this way we went on with some Indians, until coming to a bay a league in width, and everywhere deep. From the appearance we supposed it to be that which is called Espiritu Sancto. We met some Indians on the other side of it, coming to visit ours, who told us that beyond them were three men like us, and gave their names. We asked for the others, and were told that they were all dead of cold and hunger; that the Indians farther on, of whom they were, for their diversion had killed Diego Dorantes, Valdevieso, and Diego de Huelva, because they left one house for another; and that other Indians, their neighbors with whom Captain Dorantes now was, had in consequence of a dream, killed Esquivel and Mendez. We asked how the living were situated, and they answered that they were very ill used, the boys and some of the Indian men being very idle, out of cruelty gave them many kicks, cuffs, and blows with sticks; that such was the life they led.

We desired to be informed of the country ahead, and of the subsistence:

they said there was nothing to eat, and that it was thin of people, who suffered of cold, having no skins or other things to cover them. They told us also if we wished to see those three Christians, two days from that time the Indians who had them would come to eat walnuts a league from there on the margin of that river; and that we might know what they told us of the ill usage to be true, they slapped my companion and beat him with a stick, and I was not left without my portion. Many times they threw lumps of mud at us, and every day they put their arrows to our hearts, saying that they were inclined to kill us in the way that they had destroyed our friends. Lope Oviedo, my comrade, in fear said that he wished to go back with the women of those who had crossed the bay with us, the men having remained some distance behind. I contended strongly against his returning, and urged my objections; but in no way could I keep him. So he went back, and I remained alone with those savages. They are called Quevenes, and those with whom he returned, Deaguanes.

Chapter 17. The Coming of Indians with Andrés Dorantes, Castillo, and Estevanico

Two days after Lope de Oviedo left, the Indians who had Alonzo del Castillo and Andrés Dorantes, came to the place of which we had been told, to eat walnuts. These are ground with a kind of small grain, and this is the subsistence of the people two months in the year without any other thing; but even the nuts they do not have every season, as the tree produces in alternate years. The fruit is the size of that in Galicia; the trees are very large and numerous.

An Indian told me of the arrival of the Christians, and that if I wished to see them I must steal away and flee to the point of a wood to which he directed me, and that as he and others, kindred of his, should pass by there to visit those Indians, they would take me with them to the spot where the Christians were. I determined to attempt this and trust to them, as they spoke a language distinct from that of the others. I did so, and the next day they left, and found me in the place that had been pointed out, and accordingly took me with them.

When I arrived near their abode, Andrés Dorantes came out to see who it could be, for the Indians had told him that a Christian was coming. His astonishment was great when he saw me, as they had for many a day considered me dead, and the natives had said that I was. We gave many thanks at seeing ourselves together, and this was a day to us of the greatest pleasure we had enjoyed in life. Having come to where Castillo was, they inquired of me where I was going. I told them my purpose was to reach the land of Christians, I being then in search and pursuit of it. Andrés Dorantes said that for a long time he had entreated Castillo and Estevanico to go forward; but that they dared not venture, because they knew not how to swim, and greatly dreaded the rivers and bays they should have to cross, there being many in that country. Thus the Almighty had been pleased to preserve me through many trials and diseases, conducting me in the end to the fellowship of those who had abandoned me, that I might lead them over the bays and rivers that obstructed our progress. They advised me on no account to let the natives know or have a suspicion of my desire to go on, else they would destroy me; and that for success it would be necessary for me to remain quiet until the end of six months, when comes the season in which these Indians go to another part of the country to eat prickly pears. People would arrive from parts farther on, bringing bows to barter and for exchange, with whom, after making our escape, we should be able to go on their return. Having consented to this course, I remained. The prickly pear is the size of a hen's egg, vermillion and black in color, and of agreeable flavor. The natives live on it three months in the year, having nothing beside.

I was given as a slave to an Indian, with whom was Dorantes. He was blind of one eye, as were also his wife and sons, and likewise another who was with him; so that of a fashion they were all blind. These are called Marians; Castillo was with another neighboring people, called Yguases.

While here the Christians related to me how they had left the island of Malhado, and found the boat in which the comptroller and the friars had sailed, bottom up on the seashore; and that going along crossing the rivers, which are four, very large and of rapid current, their boats were swept away and carried to sea, where four of their number were drowned; that thus they proceeded until they crossed the bay, getting over it with great difficulty, and fifteen leagues thence they came to another. By the time they reached this, they had lost two companions in the sixty leagues they travelled, and those remaining were nearly dead, in all the while having eaten nothing but crabs and rockweed. Arrived at this bay, they found Indians eating mulberries, who, when they saw them, went to a cape opposite. While contriving and seeking for some means to cross the bay, there came over to them an Indian, and a Christian whom they recognized to be Figueroa, one of the four we had sent forward from the island of Malhado. He there recounted how he and his companions had got as far as that place, when two of them and an Indian died of cold and hunger, being exposed in the most inclement of seasons. He and Mendez were taken by the Indians, and while with them his associate fled, going as well as he could in the direction of Pánuco, and the natives pursuing, put him to death.

While living with these Indians, Figueroa learned from them that there was a Christian among the Mariames, who had come over from the opposite side, and he found him among the Quevenes. This was Hernando de Esquivel, a native of Badajoz, who had come in company with the commissary. From him Figueroa learned the end to which the Governor, the comptroller, and the others had come. Esquivel told him that the comptroller and the friars had upset their boat at the confluence of the rivers,[1] and that the boat of the Governor, moving along the coast, came with its people to land. Narváez went in the boat until arriving at that great bay, where he took in the people, and, crossing them to the opposite point, returned for the comptroller, the friars, and the rest. And he related that being disembarked, the Governor had recalled the commission the comptroller held as his lieutenant, assigning the duties to a captain with him named Pantoja: that Narváez stayed the night in his boat, not wishing to come on shore, having a cockswain with him and a page who was unwell, there being no water nor anything to eat on board; that at midnight, the boat having only a stone for anchor, the north wind blowing strongly took her unobserved to sea, and they never knew more of their commander.

The others then went along the coast, and as they were arrested by a wide extent of water, they made rafts with much labor, on which they crossed to the opposite shore. Going on, they arrived at a point of woods on the banks of the water where were Indians, who, as they saw them coming, put their houses into their canoes and went over to the opposite side. The Christians, in consideration of the season, for it was now the month of November, stopped at this wood, where they found water and fuel, some crabs and shellfish. They began, one by one, to die of cold and hunger; and, more than this, Pantoja, who was Lieutenant-Governor, used them severely, which Soto-Mayor (the brother of Vasco Porcallo, of the island of Cuba), who had come with the armament as camp-master, not being able to bear, had a struggle with him, and, giving him a blow with a club, Pantoja was instantly killed.

Thus did the number go on diminishing. The living dried the flesh of them that died; and the last that died was Soto-Mayor, when Esquivel preserved his flesh, and, feeding on it, sustained existence until the first of March, when an Indian of those that had fled, coming to see if they were alive, took Esquivel with him. While he was in the possession of the native, Figueroa saw him, and learned all that had been related.

* * *

CHAPTER 19. OUR SEPARATION BY THE INDIANS

When the six months were over, I had to spend with the Christians to put in execution the plan we had concerted, the Indians went after prickly pears,

---

1. The Mississippi Delta. [Hodge's note]

the place at which they grew being thirty leagues off; and when we approached the point of flight, those among whom we were, quarrelled about a woman. After striking with fists, beating with sticks and bruising heads in great anger, each took his lodge and went his way, whence it became necessary that the Christians should also separate, and in no way could we come together until another year.

In this time I passed a hard life, caused as much by hunger as ill usage. Three times I was obliged to run from my masters, and each time they went in pursuit and endeavored to slay me; but God our Lord in his mercy chose to protect and preserve me; and when the season of prickly pears returned, we again came together in the same place. After we had arranged our escape, and appointed a time, that very day the Indians separated and all went back. I told my comrades I would wait for them among the prickly-pear plants until the moon should be full. This day was the first of September,[2] and the first of the moon; and I said that if in this time they did not come as we had agreed, I would leave and go alone. So we parted, each going with his Indians. I remained with mine until the thirteenth day of the moon, having determined to flee to others when it should be full.

At this time Andrés Dorantes arrived with Estevanico and informed me that they had left Castillo with other Indians near by, called Lanegados; that they had encountered great obstacles and wandered about lost; that the next day the Indians, among whom we were, would move to where Castillo was, and were going to unite with those who held him and become friends, having been at war until then, and that in this way we should recover Castillo.

We had thirst all the time we ate the pears, which we quenched with their juice. We caught it in a hole made in the earth, and when it was full we drank until satisfied. It is sweet, and the color of must. In this manner they collect it for lack of vessels. There are many kinds of prickly pears, among them some very good, although they all appeared to me to be so, hunger never having given me leisure to choose, nor to reflect upon which were the best.

Nearly all these people drink rain-water, which lies about in spots. Although there are rivers, as the Indians never have fixed habitations, there are no familiar or known places for getting water. Throughout the country are extensive and beautiful plains with good pasturage; and I think it would be a very fruitful region were it worked and inhabited by civilized men. We nowhere saw mountains.

These Indians told us that there was another people next in advance of us, called Camones, living towards the coast, and that they had killed the people who came in the boat of Peñalosa and Tellez, who arrived so feeble that even while being slain they could offer no resistance, and were all destroyed. We were shown their clothes and arms, and were told that the

---

2. 1534. Cabeza de Vaca had evidently lost his reckoning (perhaps during his illness), as the date of the new moon in this year was September 8. [Hodge's note]

boat lay there stranded. This, the fifth boat, had remained till then unaccounted for. We have already stated how the boat of the Governor had been carried out to sea, and that of the comptroller and the friars had been cast away on the coast, of which Esquivel narrated the fate of the men. We have once told how the two boats in which Castillo, I, and Dorantes came, foundered near the Island of Malhado.

Chapter 20. Of Our Escape

The second day after we had moved, we commended ourselves to God and set forth with speed, trusting, for all the lateness of the season and that the prickly pears were about ending, with the mast which remained in the woods [field], we might still be enabled to travel over a large territory. Hurrying on that day in great dread lest the Indians should overtake us, we saw some smokes, and going in the direction of them we arrived there after vespers, and found an Indian. He ran as he discovered us coming, not being willing to wait for us. We sent the negro[3] after him, when he stopped, seeing him alone. The negro told him we were seeking the people who made those fires. He answered that their houses were near by, and he would guide us to them. So we followed him. He ran to make known our approach, and at sunset we saw the houses. Before our arrival, at the distance of two cross-bow shots from them, we found four Indians, who waited for us and received us well. We said in the language of the Mariames, that we were coming to look for them. They were evidently pleased with our company, and took us to their dwellings. Dorantes and the negro were lodged in the house of a physician,[4] Castillo and myself in that of another.

These people speak a different language, and are called Avavares. They are the same that carried bows to those with whom we formerly lived, going to traffic with them, and although they are of a different nation and tongue, they understand the other language. They arrived that day with their lodges, at the place where we found them. The community directly brought us a great many prickly pears, having heard of us before, of our cures, and of the wonders our Lord worked by us, which, although there had been no others, were adequate to open ways for us through a country poor like this, to afford us people where oftentimes there are none, and to lead us through immediate dangers, not permitting us to be killed, sustaining us under great want, and putting into those nations the heart of kindness, as we shall relate hereafter.

---

3. Estévanico [Hodge's note]

4. A shaman, or "medicine-man" [Hodge's note]

CHAPTER 21. OUR CURE OF SOME OF THE AFFLICTED

That same night of our arrival, some Indians came to Castillo and told him that they had great pain in the head, begging him to cure them. After he made over them the sign of the cross, and commended them to God, they instantly said that all the pain had left, and went to their houses bringing us prickly pears, with a piece of venison, a thing to us little known. As the report of Castillo's performances spread, many came to us that night sick, that we should heal them, each bringing a piece of venison, until the quantity became so great we knew not where to dispose of it. We gave many thanks to God, for every day went on increasing his compassion and his gifts. After the sick were attended to, they began to dance and sing, making themselves festive, until sunrise; and because of our arrival, the rejoicing was continued for three days.

When these were ended, we asked the Indians about the country farther on, the people we should find in it, and of the subsistence there. They answered us, that throughout all the region prickly-pear plants abounded; but the fruit was now gathered and all the people had gone back to their houses. They said the country was very cold, and there were few skins. Reflecting on this, and that it was already winter, we resolved to pass the season with these Indians.

Five days after our arrival, all the Indians went off, taking us with them to gather more prickly pears, where there were other peoples speaking different tongues. After walking five days in great hunger, since on the way was no manner of fruit, we came to a river[5] and put up our houses. We then went to seek the product of certain trees, which is like peas. As there are no paths in the country, I was detained some time. The others returned, and coming to look for them in the dark I got lost. Thank God I found a burning tree, and in the warmth of it I passed the cold of that night. In the morning, loading myself with sticks, and taking two brands with me, I returned to seek them. In this manner I wandered five days, ever with my fire and load; for if the wood had failed me where none could be found, as many parts are without any, though I might have sought sticks elsewhere, there would have been no fire to kindle them. This was all the protection I had against cold, while walking naked as I was born. Going to the low woods near the rivers, I prepared myself for the night, stopping in them before sunset. I made a hole in the ground and threw in fuel which the trees abundantly afforded, collected in good quantity from those that were fallen and dry. About the whole I made four fires, in the form of a cross, which I watched and made up from time to time. I also gathered some bundles of the coarse straw that

---

5. This may have been the San Antonio or the San Marcos-Guadalupe. [Hodge's note]

there abounds, with which I covered myself in the hole. In this way I was sheltered at night from cold. On one occasion while I slept, the fire fell upon the straw, when it began to blaze so rapidly that notwithstanding the haste I made to get out of it, I carried some marks on my hair of the danger to which I was exposed. All this while I tasted not a mouthful, nor did I find anything I could eat. My feet were bare and bled a good deal. Through the mercy of God, the wind did not blow from the north in all this time, otherwise I should have died.

At the end of the fifth day I arrived on the margin of a river,[6] where I found the Indians, who with the Christians, had considered me dead, supposing that I had been stung by a viper. All were rejoiced to see me, and most so were my companions. They said that up to that time they had struggled with great hunger, which was the cause of their not having sought me. At night, all gave me of their prickly pears, and the next morning we set out for a place where they were in large quantity, with which we satisfied our great craving, the Christians rendering thanks to our Lord that He had ever given us His aid.

Chapter 22. The Coming of Other Sick to Us the Next Day

The next day morning, many Indians came, and brought five persons who had cramps and were very unwell. They came that Castillo might cure them. Each offered his bow and arrows, which Castillo received. At sunset he blessed them, commending them to God our Lord, and we all prayed to Him the best we could to send health; for that He knew there was no other means, than through Him, by which this people would aid us, so we could come forth from this unhappy existence. He bestowed it so mercifully, that, the morning having come, all got up well and sound, and were as strong as though they never had a disorder. It caused great admiration, and inclined us to render many thanks to God our Lord, whose goodness we now clearly beheld, giving us firm hopes that He would liberate and bring us to where we might serve Him. For myself I can say that I ever had trust in His providence that He would lead me out from that captivity, and thus I always spoke of it to my companions.

The Indians having gone and taken their friends with them in health, we departed for a place at which others were eating prickly pears. These people are called Cuthalchuches and Malicones, who speak different tongues. Adjoining them were others called Coayos and Susolas, who were on the

---

6. Presumably the river last mentioned, where they had erected their shelters. [Hodge's note]

opposite side, others called Atayos, who were at war with the Susolas, exchanging arrow shots daily. As through all the country they talked only of the wonders which God our Lord worked through us, persons came from many parts to seek us that we might cure them. At the end of the second day after our arrival, some of the Susolas came to us and besought Castillo that he would go to cure one wounded and others sick, and they said that among them was one very near his end. Castillo was a timid practitioner, most so in serious and dangerous cases, believing that his sins would weigh, and some day hinder him in performing cures. The Indians told me to go and heal them, as they liked me; they remembered that I had ministered to them in the walnut grove when they gave us nuts and skins, which occurred when I first joined the Christians. So I had to go with them, and Dorantes accompanied me with Estevanico. Coming near their huts, I perceived that the sick man we went to heal was dead. Many persons were around him weeping, and his house was prostrate, a sign that the one who dwelt in it is no more. When I arrived I found his eyes rolled up, and the pulse gone, he having all the appearances of death, as they seemed to me and as Dorantes said. I removed a mat with which he was covered, and supplicated our Lord as fervently as I could, that He would be pleased to give health to him, and to the rest that might have need of it. After he had been blessed and breathed upon many times, they brought me his bow, and gave me a basket of pounded prickly pears.

The natives took me to cure many others who were sick of a stupor, and presented me two more baskets of prickly pears, which I gave to the Indians who accompanied us. We then went back to our lodgings. Those to whom we gave the fruit tarried, and returned at night to their houses, reporting that he who had been dead and for whom I wrought before them, had got up whole and walked, had eaten and spoken with them and that all to whom I had ministered were well and much pleased. This caused great wonder and fear, and throughout the land the people talked of nothing else. All to whom the fame of it reached, came to seek us that we should cure them and bless their children.

When the Cuthalchuches, who were in company with our Indians, were about to return to their own country, they left us all the prickly pears they had, without keeping one: they gave us flints of very high value there, a palm and a half in length, with which they cut. They begged that we would remember them and pray to God that they might always be well, and we promised to do so. They left, the most satisfied beings in the world, having given us the best of all they had.

We remained with the Avavares eight months, reckoned by the number of moons. In all this time people came to seek us from many parts, and they said that most truly we were children of the sun. Dorantes and the negro to this time had not attempted to practise; but because of the great solicitation made by those coming from different parts to find us, we all became physicians, although in being venturous and bold to attempt the performance of any cure, I was the most remarkable. No one whom we treated, but told us he was left well; and so great was the confidence that they would become healed if we administered to them, they even believed that whilst we remained none of them could die.

* * *

CHAPTER 33. WE SEE TRACES OF CHRISTIANS

When we saw sure signs of Christians, and heard how near we were to them, we gave thanks to God our Lord for having chosen to bring us out of a captivity so melancholy and wretched. The delight we felt let each one conjecture, when he shall remember the length of time we were in that country, the suffering and perils we underwent. That night I entreated my companions that one of them should go back three day's journey after the Christians who were moving about over the country, where we had given assurance of protection. Neither of them received this proposal well, excusing themselves because of weariness and exhaustion; and although either might have done better than I, being more youthful and athletic, yet seeing their unwillingness, the next morning I took the negro with eleven Indians, and, following the Christians by their trail, I travelled ten leagues, passing three villages, at which they had slept.

The day after I overtook four of them on horseback, who were astonished at the sight of me, so strangely habited as I was, and in company with Indians. They stood staring at me a length of time, so confounded that they neither hailed me nor drew near to make an inquiry. I bade them take me to their chief: accordingly we went together half a league to the place where was Diego de Alcaraz, their captain.

After we had conversed, he stated to me that he was completely undone; he had not been able in a long time to take any Indians; he knew not which way to turn, and his men had well begun to experience hunger and fatigue. I told him of Castillo and Dorantes, who were behind, ten leagues off, with a multitude that conducted us. He thereupon sent three cavalry to them, with fifty of the Indians who accompanied him. The negro returned to guide them, while I remained. I asked the Christians to give me a certificate of the year, month, and day I arrived there, and of the manner of my coming, which they accordingly did. From this river[7] to the town of the Christians, named San Miguel,[8] within the government of the province called New Galicia, are thirty leagues.

---

7. Evidently the Rio Sinaloa. [Hodge's note]

8. San Miguel Culiacan. [Hodge's note]

Samuel de Champlain
(c. 1567–1635)

Born in Brouage, France, on the Bay of Biscay, Samuel de Champlain served in France under King Henry IV (Henry of Navarre), then for three years commanded a Spanish fleet in the New World, visiting the West Indies, Mexico, and Panama. In 1603, he accompanied a fur-trading expedition to New France, reporting on the experience in Des Sauvages *(1604). For most of the remaining three decades of his life, he lived in North America, though he returned briefly to France on several occasions and was for four years a prisoner in England after the fall of Quebec in 1629. In 1604, he helped to establish a colony on the Bay of Fundy and in the next few years explored the coast from Nova Scotia south to Martha's Vineyard, compiling the first detailed charts of the region. After the abandonment of that early colony, in 1608 he settled Quebec. In 1609, with a war party of Huron Indians he became the European discoverer of Lake Champlain and defeated the Iroquois near the later Fort Ticonderoga, a battle largely responsible for the longstanding Iroquois enmity toward the French. He explored as far west as Georgian Bay, visited Lake Ontario, and accompanied another Huron war party on an attack on an Iroquois fort near Oneida Lake in New York. His was largely the initiative that set the pattern for the French explorers and voyageurs who soon pushed west to the Rocky Mountains and down the Mississippi River to St. Louis and New Orleans.*

The source of the present text is W. L. Grant, ed., *Voyages of Samuel de Champlain, 1604–1618,* 1907, which reproduces the translations of Charles Pomery Otis, first printed in Edmund F. Slafter's *Voyages of Samuel de Champlain,* 3 vols., 1878–1882. Studies include Francis Parkman, *Pioneers of France in the New World,* 1865; Morris Bishop, *Champlain: The Life of Fortitude,* 1948; and Samuel Eliot Morison, *Samuel de Champlain: Father of New France,* 1972.

[From] *Voyages of Samuel de Champlain,* 1604–1618

[An Attack on an Iroquois Fort; Life among the Hurons]

*   *   *

WE CONTINUED OUR COURSE by land for about twenty-five or thirty leagues. In the space of four days we crossed many brooks, and a river which proceeds from a lake that discharges into that of the Entouhonorons.[1] This lake is twenty-five or thirty leagues in circuit, contains some fine islands, and is the place where our enemies, the Iroquois, catch their fish, in which it abounds.

On the 9th of the month of October, our savages going out to reconnoitre met eleven savages, whom they took prisoners. They consisted of four women, three boys, one girl, and three men, who were going fishing and were distant some four leagues from the fort of the enemy. Now it is to be noted that one of the chiefs, on seeing the prisoners, cut off the finger of one of these poor women as a beginning of their usual punishment; upon which I interposed and reprimanded the chief, Iroquet, representing to him that it was not the act of a warrior, as he declared himself to be, to conduct himself with cruelty towards women, who have no defence but their tears, and that one should treat them with humanity on account of their helplessness and weakness; and I told him that on the contrary this act would be deemed to proceed from a base and brutal courage, and that if he committed any more of these cruelties he would not give me heart to assist them or favor them in the war. To which the only answer he gave me was that their enemies treated them in the same manner, but that, since this was displeasing to me, he would not do anything more to the women, although he would to the men.

The next day, at three o'clock in the afternoon, we arrived before the fort[2] of their enemies, where the savages made some skirmishes with each other, although our design was not to disclose ourselves until the next day, which however the impatience of our savages would not permit, both on account of their desire to see fire opened upon their enemies, and also that they might rescue some of their own men who had become too closely engaged, and were hotly pressed. Then I approached the enemy, and although I had only a few men, yet we showed them what they had never seen nor heard before; for, as soon as they saw us and heard the arquebus shots and the balls whizzing in their ears, they withdrew speedily to their fort, carrying the dead and wounded in this charge. We also withdrew to our main body, with five or six wounded, one of whom died.

---

1. The Oneida River, flowing from Oneida Lake into Lake Ontario. [Grant's note]
2. Situated south of Oneida Lake, perhaps in the present town of Fenner, not far from Cazenovia, New York.

This done, we withdrew to the distance of cannon range, out of sight of the enemy, but contrary to my advice and to what they had promised me. This moved me to address them very rough and angry words in order to incite them to do their duty, foreseeing that if everything should go according to their whim and the guidance of their council, their utter ruin would be the result. Nevertheless I did not fail to send to them and propose means which they should use in order to get possession of their enemies.

These were, to make with certain kinds of wood a *cavalier*[3] which should be higher than the palisades. Upon this were to be placed four or five of our arquebusiers, who should keep up a constant fire over their palisades and galleries, which were well provided with stones, and by this means dislodge the enemy who might attack us from their galleries. Meanwhile orders were to be given to procure boards for making a sort of mantelet[4] to protect our men from the arrows and stones of which the savages generally make use. These instruments, namely the cavalier and mantelets, were capable of being carried by a large number of men. One mantelet was so constructed that the water could not extinguish the fire, which might be set to the fort, under cover of the arquebusiers who were doing their duty on the cavalier. In this manner, I told them, we might be able to defend ourselves so that the enemy could not approach to extinguish the fire which we should set to their ramparts.

This proposition they thought good and very seasonable, and immediately proceeded to carry it out as I directed. In fact the next day they set to work, some to cut wood, others to gather it, for building and equipping the cavalier and mantelets. The work was promptly executed and in less than four hours, although the amount of wood they had collected for burning against the ramparts, in order to set fire to them, was very small. Their expectation was that the five hundred men who had promised to come would do so on this day, but doubt was felt about them, since they had not appeared at the rendezvous, as they had been charged to do, and as they had promised. This greatly troubled our savages; but seeing that they were sufficiently numerous to take the fort without other assistance, and thinking for my part that delay, if not in all things at least in many, is prejudicial, I urged them to attack it, representing to them that the enemy, having become aware of their force and our arms, which pierced whatever was proof against arrows, had begun to barricade themselves and cover themselves with strong pieces of wood, with which they were well provided and their village filled. I told them that the least delay was the best, since the enemy had already strengthened themselves very much; for their village was enclosed by four good palisades, which were made of great pieces of wood, interlaced with each other, with an opening of not more than half a foot between two, and which were thirty feet high, with galleries after the manner of a parapet, which they had

3. An elevated wooden platform, walled, as depicted in Champlain's drawing included in the first edition of his *Voyages*.
4. Shield.

furnished with double pieces of wood that were proof against our arquebus shots. Moreover it was near a pond where the water was abundant, and was well supplied with gutters, placed between each pair of palisades, to throw out water, which they had also under cover inside, in order to extinguish fire. Now this is the character of their fortifications and defences, which are much stronger than the villages of the Attigouautan and others.

We approached to attack the village, our cavalier being carried by two hundred of the strongest men, who put it down before the village at a pike's length off. I ordered three arquebusiers to mount upon it, who were well protected from the arrows and stones that could be shot or hurled at them. Meanwhile the enemy did not fail to send a large number of arrows which did not miss, and a great many stones, which they hurled from their palisades. Nevertheless a hot fire of arquebusiers forced them to dislodge and abandon their galleries, in consequence of the cavalier which uncovered them, they not venturing to show themselves, but fighting under shelter. Now when the cavalier was carried forward, instead of bringing up the mantelets according to order, including that one under cover of which we were to set the fire, they abandoned them and began to scream at their enemies, shooting arrows into the fort, which in my opinion did little harm to the enemy.

But we must excuse them, for they are not warriors, and besides will have no discipline nor correction, and will do only what they please. Accordingly one of them set fire inconsiderately to the wood placed against the fort of the enemy, quite the wrong way and in the face of the wind, so that it produced no effect.

This fire being out, the greater part of the savages began to carry wood against the palisades, but in so small quantity that the fire could have no great effect. There also arose such disorder among them that one could not understand another, which greatly troubled me. In vain did I shout in their ears and remonstrate to my utmost with them as to the danger to which they exposed themselves by their bad behavior, but on account of the great noise they made they heard nothing. Seeing that shouting would only burst my head, and that my remonstrances were useless for putting a stop to the disorder, I did nothing more, but determined together with my men to do what we could, and fire upon such as we could see.

Meanwhile the enemy profited by our disorder to get water and pour it so abundantly that you would have said brooks were flowing through their spouts, the result of which was that the fire was instantly extinguished, while they did not cease shooting their arrows, which fell upon us like hail. But the men on the cavalier killed and maimed many. We were engaged in this combat about three hours, in which two of our chiefs and leading warriors were wounded, namely, one called Ochateguain and another Orani, together with some fifteen common warriors. The others, seeing their men and some of the chiefs wounded, now began to talk of a retreat without farther fighting, in expectation of the five hundred men, whose arrival could not be much delayed. Thus they retreated, a disorderly rabble.

Moreover the chiefs have in fact no absolute control over their men, who are governed by their own will and follow their own fancy, which is the cause of their disorder and the ruin of all their undertakings; for, having determined upon anything with their leaders, it needs only the whim of a villain, or nothing at all, to lead them to break it off and form a new plan. Thus there is no concert of action among them, as can be seen by this expedition.

Now we withdrew into our fort, I having received two arrow wounds, one in the leg, the other in the knee, which caused me great inconvenience, aside from the severe pain. When they were all assembled, I addressed them some words of remonstrance on the disorder that had occurred. But all I said availed nothing, and had no effect upon them. They replied that many of their men had been wounded, like myself, so that it would cause the others much trouble and inconvenience to carry them as they retreated, and that it was not possible to return again against their enemies, as I told them it was their duty to do. They agreed, however, to wait four days longer for the five hundred men who were to come; and, if they came, to make a second effort against their enemies, and execute better what I might tell them than they had done in the past. With this I had to content myself, to my great regret.

Herewith is indicated the manner in which they fortify their towns, from which representation it may be inferred that those of their friends and enemies are fortified in like manner.

The next day there was a violent wind, which lasted two days, and was very favorable for setting fire anew to the fort of the enemy, which, although I urged them strongly, they were unwilling to do, as if they were afraid of getting the worst of it, and besides they pleaded their wounded as an excuse.

We remained in camp until the 16th of the month,[5] during which time there were some skirmishes between the enemy and our men, who were very often surrounded by the former, rather through their imprudence than from lack of courage; for I assure you that every time we went to the charge it was necessary for us to go and disengage them from the crowd, since they could only retreat under cover of our arquebusiers, whom the enemy greatly dreaded and feared; for as soon as they perceived any one of the arquebusiers they withdrew speedily, saying in a persuasive manner that we should not interfere in their combats, and that their enemies had very little courage to require us to assist them, with many other words of like tenor, in order to prevail upon us.

I have represented by figure E the manner in which they arm themselves in going to war.

After some days, seeing that the five hundred men did not come, they determined to depart, and enter upon their retreat as soon as possible. They proceeded to make a kind of basket for carrying the wounded, who are put into it crowded up in a heap, being bound and pinioned in such a manner

---

5. October. [Grant's note]

Champlain's plan of the fort of the Iroquois. From a copy of the first edition of the *Voyages of 1619*. Courtesy of the Rare Books and Manuscripts Division, The New York Public Library; Astor, Lenox, and Tilden Foundation.

that it is as impossible for them to move as for an infant in its swaddling clothes; but this is not without causing the wounded much extreme pain. This I can say with truth from my own experience, having been carried some days, since I could not stand up, particularly on account of an arrow-wound which I had received in the knee. I never found myself in such a *gehenna* as during this time, for the pain which I suffered in consequence of the wound in my knee was nothing in comparison with that which I endured while I was carried bound and pinioned on the back of one of our savages; so that I lost my patience, and as soon as I could sustain myself, got out of this prison, or rather *gehenna*.

The enemy followed us about half a league, though at a distance, with the view of trying to take some of those composing the rear guard; but their efforts were vain, and they retired.

Now the only good point that I have seen in their mode of warfare is that they make their retreat very securely, placing all the wounded and aged in their centre, being well armed on the wings and in the rear, and continuing this order without interruption until they reach a place of security.

Their retreat was very long, being from twenty-five to thirty leagues, which caused the wounded much fatigue, as also those who carried them, although the latter relieved each other from time to time.

On the 18th day of the month there fell much snow and hail, accompanied by a strong wind, which greatly incommoded us. Nevertheless we succeeded in arriving at the shore of the lake of the Entouhonorons, at the place where our canoes were concealed, which we found all intact, for we had been afraid lest the enemy might have broken them up.

When they were all assembled, and I saw that they were ready to depart to their village, I begged them to take me to our settlement, which, though unwilling at first, they finally concluded to do, and sought four men to conduct me. Four men were found, who offered themselves of their own accord; for, as I have before said, the chiefs have no control over their men, in consequence of which they are often unable to do as they would like. Now the men having been found, it was necessary also to find a canoe, which was not to be had, each one needing his own, and there being no more than they required. This was far from being pleasant to me, but on the contrary greatly annoyed me, since it led me to suspect some evil purpose, inasmuch as they had promised to conduct me to our settlement after their war. Moreover I was poorly prepared for spending the winter with them, or else should not have been concerned about the matter. But not being able to do anything, I was obliged to resign myself in patience. Now after some days I perceived that their plan was to keep me and my companions, not only as a security for themselves, for they feared their enemies, but also that I might listen to what took place in their councils and assemblies, and determine what they should do in the future against their enemies for their security and preservation.

The next day, the 28th of the month, they began to make preparations; some to go deer-hunting, others to hunt bears and beavers, others to go fishing, others to return to their villages. An abode and lodging were furnished me by one of the principal chiefs, called D'Arontal, with whom I already had some acquaintance. Having offered me his cabin, provisions, and accommodations, he set out also for the deer-hunt, which is esteemed by them the greatest and most noble one. After crossing, from the island, the end of the lake, we entered a river[6] some twelve leagues in extent. They then carried their canoes by land some half a league, when we entered a lake[7] which was some ten or twelve leagues in circuit, where there was a large amount of game, as swans, white cranes, *outardes*,[8] ducks, teal, song-thrush, larks, snipe, geese, and several other kinds of fowl too numerous to mention. Of these I killed a great number, which stood us in good stead while waiting for the capture of a deer. From there we proceeded to a certain place some ten leagues distant, where our savages thought there were deer in abundance.

6. Probably Cataraqui Creek, in the province of Ontario. [Grant's note]

7. Probably Loughborough Lake. [Grant's note]

8. Bustards.

Assembled there were some twenty-five savages, who set to building two or three cabins out of pieces of wood fitted to each other, the chinks of which they stopped up by means of moss to prevent the entrance of the air, covering them with the bark of trees.

When they had done this they went into the woods to a small forest of firs, where they made an enclosure in the form of a triangle, closed up on two sides and open on one. This enclosure was made of great stakes of wood closely pressed together, from eight to nine feet high, each of the sides being fifteen hundred paces long. At the extremity of this triangle there was a little enclosure, constantly diminishing in size, covered in part with boughs and with only an opening of five feet, about the width of a medium-sized door, into which the deer were to enter. They were so expeditious in their work, that in less than ten days they had their enclosure in readiness. Meanwhile other savages had gone fishing, catching trout and pike of prodigious size, and enough to meet all our wants.

All preparations being made, they set out half an hour before day to go into the wood, some half a league from the before-mentioned enclosure, separated from each other some eighty paces. Each had two sticks, which they struck together, and they marched in this order at a slow pace until they arrived at their enclosure. The deer hearing this noise flee before them until they reach the enclosure, into which the savages force them to go. Then they gradually unite on approaching the bay and opening of their triangle, the deer skirting the sides until they reach the end, to which the savages hotly pursue them, with bow and arrow in hand ready to let fly. On reaching the end of the triangle they begin to shout and imitate wolves, which are numerous, and which devour the deer. The deer, hearing this frightful noise, are constrained to enter the retreat by the little opening, whither they are very hotly pursued by arrow shots. Having entered this retreat, which is so well closed and fastened that they can by no possibility get out, they are easily captured. I assure you that there is a singular pleasure in this chase, which took place every two days, and was so successful that, in the thirty-eight days during which we were there, they captured one hundred and twenty deer, which they make good use of, reserving the fat for winter, which they use as we do butter, and taking away to their homes some of the flesh for their festivities.

They have other contrivances for capturing the deer; as snares, with which they kill many. You see depicted opposite the manner of their chase, enclosure, and snare. Out of the skins they make garments. Thus you see how we spent the time while waiting for the frost, that we might return the more easily, since the country is very marshy.

When they first went out hunting, I lost my way in the woods, having followed a certain bird that seemed to me peculiar. It had a beak like that of a parrot, and was of the size of a hen. It was entirely yellow, except the head which was red, and the wings which were blue, and it flew by intervals like a partridge. The desire to kill it led me to pursue it from tree to tree for a very long time, until it flew away in good earnest. Thus losing all hope, I desired to retrace my steps, but found none of our hunters, who had been constantly getting ahead, and had reached the enclosure. While trying to overtake them, and going, as it seemed to me, straight to where the enclosure was, I found myself lost in the woods, going now on this side now on that, without being able to recognize my position. The night coming on, I was obliged to spend it at the foot of a great tree, and in the morning set out and walked until three o'clock in the afternoon, when I came to a little pond of still water. Here I noticed some game, which I pursued, killing three or four birds, which were very acceptable, since I had had nothing to eat. Unfortunately for me there had been no sunshine for three days, nothing but rain and cloudy weather, which increased my trouble. Tired and exhausted I prepared to rest myself and cook the birds in order to alleviate the hunger which I began painfully to feel, and which by God's favor was appeased.

When I had made my repast I began to consider what I should do, and to pray God to give me the will and courage to sustain patiently my misfortune if I should be obliged to remain abandoned in this forest without counsel or consolation except the Divine goodness and mercy, and at the same time to exert myself to return to our hunters. Thus committing all to His mercy I gathered up renewed courage, going here and there all day, without perceiving any foot-print or path, except those of wild beasts, of which I generally saw a good number. I was obliged to pass here this night also. Unfortunately I had forgotten to bring with me a small compass which would have put me on the right road, or nearly so. At the dawn of day, after a brief repast, I set out in order to find, if possible, some brook and follow it, thinking that it must of necessity flow into the river on the border of which our hunters were encamped. Having resolved upon this plan, I carried it out so well that at noon I found myself on the border of a little lake, about a league and a half in extent, where I killed some game, which was very timely for my wants; I had likewise remaining some eight or ten charges of powder, which was a great satisfaction.

I proceeded along the border of this lake to see where it discharged, and found a large brook, which I followed until five o'clock in the evening, when I heard a great noise, but on carefully listening failed to perceive clearly what it was. On hearing the noise, however, more distinctly, I concluded that it was a fall of water in the river which I was searching for. I proceeded nearer, and saw an opening, approaching which I found myself in a great and far-reaching meadow, where there was a large number of wild beasts, and looking to my right I perceived the river, broad and long. I looked to see if I could not recognize the place, and walking along on the meadow I noticed a little path where the savages carried their canoes. Finally, after careful observation, I recognized it as the same river, and that I had gone that way before.

I passed the night in better spirits than the previous ones, supping on the little I had. In the morning I re-examined the place where I was, and concluded from certain mountains on the border of the river that I had not been deceived, and that our hunters must be lower down by four or five good leagues. This distance I walked at my leisure along the border of the river, until I perceived the smoke of our hunters, where I arrived to the great pleasure not only of myself but of them, who were still searching for me, but had about given up all hopes of seeing me again. They begged me not to stray off from them any more, or never to forget to carry with me my compass, and they added: If you had not come, and we had not succeeded in finding you, we should never have gone again to the French, for fear of their accusing us of having killed you. After this he was very careful of me when I went hunting, always giving me a savage as companion, who knew how to find again the place from which he started so well that it was something very remarkable.

* * *

John Smith
(1580–1631)

John Smith, the author of the first book written in English on the North American continent, was a champion of colonization. The Italian and Spanish accounts emphasized exploration for fabulous riches as well as dangers and hardships. Smith drew maps that made the country look familiar and inhabitable to his fellow Englishmen; his descriptions of the climate, the agricultural possibilities, and the rewards of colonization were designed to attract not only the adventurous and ambitious but those eager for a fresh start.

Smith was born in Willoughby, Lincolnshire. With only a grammar school education, he was apprenticed to business at fifteen and, after his father's death, enlisted for military service at sixteen, serving in France and the Netherlands. During the next decade he traveled over the European continent, was captured and held as a slave in Turkey, escaped to Morocco, and returned to England.

An investor in the New London Company, he joined the expedition to Virginia led by Captain Christopher Newport in 1606. Arriving in April, he was, with difficulty, named to the seven-member governing council and set out to explore the surrounding countryside. He established trade relations with the Indians of Algonquian linguistic stock led by Chief Powhatan, despite some near escapes from death. In addition to the famous anecdote of his rescue by the chief's twelve-year-old daughter, Pocahontas, Smith recounts several examples of alternating warfare and friendly relations between the settlers and the native inhabitants. His first report, A True Relation of Such Occurrences and Accidents of Note as Hath Happened in Virginia since the First Planting of That Colony, *was printed in London in 1608.*

Only 38 of the original 105 colonists survived by the spring of 1608. Smith was elected president of the small group in September. He led them through the starvation and suffering of the winter until, wounded by the explosion of his gunpowder bag, he returned to England in August 1609. A Map of Virginia, with a Description of the Country, the Commodities, People, Government and Religion *appeared in 1612.*

Smith spent the spring and summer of 1614 exploring the New England coast from Maine to Cape Cod. He saw New England as an alternative to the harsh conditions of Virginia and presented his vision of a settlement of farmers, fisherman, craftsmen, and free landowners in A Description of New England *(1616).*

In his most important book, The General History of Virginia, New England, and the Summer Isles *(1624), Smith revised and expanded his earlier work; the story of Pocahontas, for instance, appears first in this volume. In this and his final work,* Advertisements for the Unexperienced Planters of New England, or Any Where *(1631), he laid out for English readers the vision of a great future in the New World. Though he expressed his preference to live in New England, he died in England just as the settlement of Massachusetts Bay was getting under way.*

The following text, with spelling and punctuation modernized, is taken from John Smith, *Works*, edited by Edward Arber (1884). Other editions are *The Complete Works of Captain John Smith*, 3 vols., edited by Philip L. Barbour (1986); and *Captain John Smith: A Select Edition of His Writings*, edited by Karen Ordahl Kupperman (1988). Biographical studies include Bradford Smith, *Captain John Smith, His Life and Legend* (1953); and A. T. Vaughan, *American Genesis: Captain John Smith and the Founding of Virginia* (1975). Philip L. Barbour wrote *The Three Worlds of Captain John Smith* (1964) and *Pocahontas and Her World* (1970).

[From] *The General History of Virginia, New England, and the Summer Isles*

* * *

BUT OUR COMEDIES never endured long without a tragedy, some idle exceptions being muttered against Captain Smith[1] for not discovering the head of Chickahominy river, and [being] taxed by the Council, to be too slow in so worthy an attempt. The next voyage he proceeded so far that with much labor by cutting of trees asunder he made his passage, but when his barge could pass no farther, he left her in a broad bay out of danger of shot, com-

---

1. Smith commonly refers to himself in the third person in his writings.

manding none should go ashore till his return. Himself with two English and two savages went up higher in a canoe; but he was not long absent but his men went ashore, whose want of government gave both occasion and opportunity to the savages to surprise one George Cassen, whom they slew, and much failed not to have cut off the boat and all the rest.

Smith little dreaming of that accident, being got to the marshes at the river's head, twenty miles in the desert, had his two men slain (as is supposed) sleeping by the canoe, while himself by fowling sought them victual: who finding he was beset with 200 savages, two of them he slew, still defending himself with the aid of a savage his guide, whom he bound to his arm with his garters, and used him as a buckler. Yet he was shot in his thigh a little, and had many arrows that stuck in his clothes but no great hurt, till at last they took him prisoner.

When this news came to Jamestown, much was their sorrow for his loss, few expecting what ensued.

Six or seven weeks[2] those barbarians kept him prisoner. Many strange triumphs and conjurations they made of him, yet he so demeaned himself among them, as he not only diverted them from surprising the fort, but procured his own liberty, and got himself and his company such estimation among them, that those savages admired him more than their own *Qutyoughkasoucks*.[3]

The manner how they used and delivered him is as follows.

The savages having drawn from George Cassen whether Captain Smith was gone, prosecuting that opportunity they followed him with 300 bowmen, conducted by the King of Pamaunkee[4] who in divisions searching the turnings of the river found Robinson and Emry by the fireside. Those they shot full of arrows and slew. Then finding the captain, as is said, that used the savage that was his guide as his shield (three of them being slain and divers others so galled) all the rest would not come near him. Thinking thus to have returned to his boat, regarding them, as he marched, more then his way, [he] slipped up to the middle in an oozy creek and his savage with him, yet durst they not come to him till being near dead with cold he threw away his arms. Then according to their composition[5] they drew him forth and led him to the fire where his men were slain. Diligently they chafed his benumbed limbs.

He demanding for their captain, they showed him Opechankanough, King of Pamaunkee, to whom he gave a round ivory double compass dial. Much they marvelled at the playing of the fly[6] and needle, which they could

---

2. The actual time Smith was held (December 16, 1607 to January 8, 1608) is a little over three weeks.

3. Priests.

4. Opechankanough was the brother of Chief Powhatan.

5. Agreement.

6. A circular card suspended on a pivot so that it can move freely. Magnets are attached to its underside and the face is divided into the points of the compass.

see so plainly, and yet not touch it, because of the glass that covered them. But when he demonstrated by that globe-like jewel, the roundness of the earth, and skies, the sphere of the sun, moon, and stars, and how the sun did chase the night round about the world continually; the greatness of the land and sea, the diversity of nations, variety of complexions, and how we were to them antipodes, and many other such like matters, they all stood as amazed with admiration.

Notwithstanding, within an hour after they tied him to a tree, and as many as could stand about him prepared to shoot him, but the King holding up the compass in his hand, they all laid down their bows and arrows, and in a triumphant manner led him to Orapaks, where he was after their manner kindly feasted and well used.

Their order in conducting him was thus: Drawing themselves all in file, the King in the midst had all their pieces and swords borne before him. Captain Smith was led after him by three great savages, holding him fast by each arm, and on each side six went in file with their arrows nocked. But arriving at the town (which was but only thirty or forty hunting houses made of mats, which they remove as they please, as we our tents) all the women and children staring to behold him, the soldiers first all in file performed the form of a bissone[7] so well as could be; and on each flank, officers as sergeants to see them keep their orders. A good time they continued this exercise, and then cast themselves in a ring, dancing in such several postures, and singing and yelling out such hellish notes and screeches, being strangely painted, every one his quiver of arrows, and at his back a club, on his arm a fox or an otter's skin, or some such matter for his vambrace;[8] their heads and shoulders painted red, with oil and pocones[9] mingled together, which scarlet-like color made an exceeding handsome show; his bow in his hand, and the skin of a bird with her wings abroad dried, tied on his head, a piece of copper, a white shell, a long feather, with a small rattle growing at the tails of their snakes tied to it, or some such like toy. All this while Smith and the King stood in the midst guarded, as before is said, and after three dances they all departed. Smith they conducted to a long house, where thirty or forty tall fellows did guard him, and ere long more bread and venison was brought him than would have served twenty men. I think his stomach at that time was not very good, what he left they put in baskets and tied over his head. About midnight they set the meat again before him. All this time not one of them would eat a bit with him, till the next morning they brought him as much more, and then did they eat all the old, and reserved the new as they had done the other, which made him think they would fat him to eat him. Yet in this desperate estate to defend him from the cold, one Maocassater brought him his gown, in requital of some beads and toys Smith had given him at his first arrival in Virginia.

Two days after, a man would have slain him (but that the guard pre-

---

7. Military formation.

8. In plate armor terms, a piece to protect the forearm.

9. Bloodroot.

vented it) for the death of his son, to whom they conducted him to recover the poor man then breathing his last. Smith told them that at Jamestown he had a water[1] would do it, if they would let him fetch it, but they would not permit that; but made all the preparations they could to assault Jamestown, craving his advice, and for recompense he should have life, liberty, land, and women. In part of a table book[2] he writ his mind to them at the fort, what was intended, how they should follow that direction to affright the messengers, and without fail send him such things as he writ for. And an inventory with them. The difficulty and danger he told the savages of the mines, great guns, and other engines exceedingly affrighted them, yet according to his request they went to Jamestown, in as bitter weather as could be of frost and snow, and within three days returned with an answer.

But when they came to Jamestown, seeing men sally out as he had told them they would, they fled; yet in the night they came again to the same place where he had told them they should receive an answer, and such things as he had promised them, which they found accordingly, and with which they returned with no small expedition, to the wonder of them all that heard it, that he could either divine, or the paper could speak.

Then they led him to the Youthtanunds, the Mattapanients, the Payankatanks, the Nantaughtacunds, and Onawmanients upon the rivers of Rappahannock and Potomac; over all those rivers, and back again by divers other several nations, to the King's habitation at Pamaunkee, where they entertained him with most strange and fearful conjurations:

> As if near led to hell,
> Amongst the devils to dwell.[3]

Not long after, early in a morning a great fire was made in a long house, and a mat spread on the one side, as on the other, on the one they caused him to sit, and all the guard went out of the house, and presently came skipping in a great grim fellow, all painted over with coal, mingled with oil, and many snakes' and weasels' skins stuffed with moss, and all their tails tied together, so as they met on the crown of his head in a tassel; and round about the tassel was as a coronet of feathers, the skins hanging round about his head, back, and shoulders, and in a manner covered his face, with a hellish voice, and a rattle in his hand. With most strange gestures and passions he began his invocation, and environed the fire with a circle of meal; which done, three more such like devils came rushing in with the like antique tricks, painted half black, half red, but all their eyes were painted white, and some red strokes like mutchatos,[4] along their cheeks Round about him those fiends danced a pretty while, and then came in three more as ugly as the rest, with red eyes, and white strokes over their black faces. At last

---

1. Medicine.

2. Notebook.

3. A quote from a contemporary translation (Bishop Martin Fotherby) of the Roman philosopher Seneca (4 B.C.–A.D. 65).

4. Mustaches.

they all sat down right against him, three of them on the one hand of the chief priest, and three on the other. Then all with their rattles began a song, which ended, the chief priest laid down five wheat corns. Then straining his arms and hands with such violence that he sweat, and his veins swelled, he began a short oration. At the conclusion they all gave a short groan and then laid down three grains more. After that, began their song again, and then another oration, ever laying down so many corns as before, till they had twice encircled the fire. That done, they took a bunch of little sticks prepared for that purpose, continuing still their devotion, and at the end of every song and oration, they laid down a stick betwixt the divisions of corn. Till night, neither he nor they did either eat or drink, and then they feasted merrily, with the best provisions they could make. Three days they used this ceremony, the meaning whereof they told him was to know if he intended them well or no. The circle of meal signified their country, the circles of corn the bounds of the sea, and the sticks his country. They imagined the world to be flat and round, like a trencher,[5] and they in the midst.

After this they brought him a bag of gunpowder, which they carefully preserved till the next spring, to plant as they did their corn, because they would be acquainted with the nature of that seed

Opitchapam, the King's brother, invited him to his house, where, with as many platters of bread, fowl, and wild beasts as did environ him, he bid him welcome; but not any of them would eat a bit with him, but put up all the remainder in baskets.

At his return to Opechancanoughs, all the King's women and their children flocked about him for their parts, as a due by custom, to be merry with such fragments.

> But his waking mind in hideous dreams did oft see wondrous shapes,
> Of bodies strange, and huge in growth, and of stupendous makes.[6]

At last they brought him to Meronocomoco[7] where was Powhatan their Emperor. Here more than two hundred of those grim countiers stood wondering at him, as he had been a monster, till Powhatan and his train had put themselves in their greatest braveries. Before a fire upon a seat like a bedstead, he sat covered with a great robe, made of rarowcun[8] skins, and all the tails hanging by. On either hand did sit a young wench of 16 or 18 years, and along on each side the house, two rows of men, and behind them as many women, with all their heads and shoulders painted red, many of their heads bedecked with the white down of birds, but every one with something, and a great chain of white beads about their necks.

At his entrance before the King, all the people gave a great shout. The Queen of Appamatuck was appointed to bring him water to wash his hands, and another brought him a bunch of feathers, instead of a towel to dry them.

---

5. Platter.

6. From Lucretius (c. 98–55 B.C.), the Roman Poet, as translated by Fotherby.

7. A town on the James River. They arrived there January 5.

8. Raccoon.

Having feasted him after their best barbarous manner they could, a long consultation was held, but the conclusion was, two great stones were brought before Powhatan; then as many as could laid hands on him, dragged him to them, and thereon laid his head, and being ready with their clubs to beat out his brains, Pocahontas, the King's dearest daughter, when no entreaty could prevail, got his head in her arms, and laid her own upon his to save him from death, whereat the Emperor was contented he should live to make him hatchets, and her bells, beads, and copper, for they thought him as well[9] of all occupations as themselves. For the King himself will make his own robes, shoes, bows, arrows, pots; plant, hunt, or do any thing so well as the rest.

> They say he bore a pleasant show,
> But sure his heart was sad.
> For who can pleasant be, and rest,
> That lives in fear and dread:
> And having life suspected, doth
> It still suspected lead.[1]

Two days after, Powhatan having disguised himself in the most fearfulest manner he could, caused Captain Smith to be brought forth to a great house in the woods, and there upon a mat by the fire to be left alone. Not long after from behind a mat that divided the house, was made the most dolefulest noise he ever heard. Then Powhatan more like a devil than a man, with some two hundred more as black as himself, came unto him and told him now they were friends, and presently he should go to Jamestown, to send him two great guns, and a grindstone, for which he would give him the country of Capahowosick, and forever esteem him as his son Nantaquoud.

So to Jamestown with 12 guides Powhatan sent him. That night they quartered in the woods, he still expecting (as he had done all this long time of his imprisonment) every hour to be put to one death or other, for all their feasting. But almighty God (by his divine providence) had mollified the hearts of those stern barbarians with compassion. The next morning betimes they came to the fort, where Smith, having used the savages with what kindness he could, he showed Rawhunt, Powhattan's trusty servant, two demiculverins[2] and a millstone to carry Powhatan. They found them somewhat too heavy, but when they did see him discharge them, being loaded with stones, among the boughs of a great tree loaded with icicles, the ice and branches came so tumbling down, that the poor savages ran away half dead with fear. But at last we regained some conference with them, and gave them such toys; and sent to Powhatan, his women, and children such presents, as gave them in general full content.

*   *   *

---

9. Capable.

1. A Fotherby translation of lines from the Greek dramatist Euripides (c. 480–405 B.C.).

2. Cannons capable of firing 10-pound shots.

The Fourth Book. The Proceedings of the English after the Alteration of the Government of Virginia

John Smith's Relation to Queen Anne of Pocahontas (1616)

To the most high and virtuous Princess, Queen Anne of Great Britain

Most admired Queen, The love I bear my God, my King and Country, hath so oft emboldened me in the worst of extreme dangers, that now honesty doth constrain me [to] presume thus far beyond myself, to present your Majesty this short discourse. If ingratitude be a deadly poison to all honest virtues, I must be guilty of that crime if I should omit any means to be thankful. So it is,

That some ten years ago [i.e., Jan 1608] being in Virginia, and taken prisoner by the power of Powhatan their chief King, I received from this great savage exceeding great courtesy, especially from his son Nantaquaus, the most manliest, comeliest, boldest spirit I ever saw in a savage, and his sister Pocahontas, the King's most dear and well-beloved daughter, being but a child of twelve or thirteen years of age, whose compassionate pitiful heart, of my desperate estate, gave me much cause to respect her, I being the first Christian this proud King and his grim attendants ever saw, and thus enthralled in their barbarous power, I cannot say I felt the least occasion of want that was in the power of those my mortal foes to prevent, notwithstanding all their threats. After some six weeks [rather, about three weeks] fatting amongst those savage courtiers, at the minute of my execution, she hazarded the beating out of her own brains to save mine; and not only that, but so prevailed with her father, that I was safely conducted to Jamestown, where I found about eight and thirty miserable poor and sick creatures, to keep possession of all those large territories of Virginia. Such was the weakness of this poor commonwealth, as had the savages not fed us, we directly had starved. And this relief, most gracious Queen, was commonly brought us by this Lady Pocahontas.

Notwithstanding all these passages, when inconstant fortune turned our peace to war, this tender virgin would still not spare to dare to visit us, and by her our jars[3] have been oft appeased, and our wants still supplied. Were it the policy of her father thus to employ her, or the ordinance of God thus to make her his instrument, or her extraordinary affection to our nation, I know not; but of this I am sure when her father with the utmost of his policy and power, sought to surprise me [at Werowocomoco, about 15 Jan. 1609], having but eighteen with me, the dark night could not affright her from coming through the irksome woods, and with watered eyes gave me

---

3. Conflicts.

intelligence, with her best advice to escape his fury, which had he known, he had surely slain her.

Jamestown with her wild train she as freely frequented as her father's habitation; and during the time of two or three years [1608-9], she next under God, was still the instrument to preserve this colony from death, famine and utter confusion; which if in those times, [it] had once been dissolved, Virginia might have lain as it was at our first arrival to this day.

Since then, this business having been turned and varied by many accidents from that I left it at, it is most certain, after a long and troublesome war after my departure, betwixt her father and our colony, all which time she was not heard of.

About two years after [April 1613] she herself was taken prisoner, being so detained near two years longer, the colony by that means was relieved, peace concluded; and at last rejecting her barbarous condition, [she] was married [1 April 1614] to an English gentleman,[4] with whom at this present she is in England, the first Christian ever of that nation, the first Virginian ever spake English, or had a child in marriage by an Englishman: a matter surely, if my meaning be truly considered and well understood, worthy a Prince's understanding.

Thus, most gracious Lady, I have related to your Majesty, what at your best leisure our approved histories will account you at large, and done in the time of your Majesty's life; and however this might be presented you from a more worthy pen, it cannot from a more honest heart, as yet I never begged anything of the state, or any: and it is my want of ability and her exceeding desert; your birth, means and authority; her birth, virtue, want and simplicity, doth make me thus bold, humbly to beseech your Majesty to take this knowledge of her, though it be from one so unworthy to be the reporter, as myself, her husband's estate not being able to make her fit to attend your Majesty. The most and least I can do is to tell you this, because none so oft hath tried it as myself, and the rather being of so great a spirit, however her stature. If she should not be well received, seeing this kingdom may rightly have a kingdom by her means, her present love to us and Christianity might turn to such scorn and fury as to divert all this good to the worst of evil: where[as] finding so great a Queen should do her some honor more than she can imagine, for being so kind to your servants and subjects, would so ravish her with content, as endear her dearest blood to effect that your Majesty and all the King's honest subjects most earnestly desire.

And so I humbly kiss your gracious hands.

* * *

---

4. John Rolfe.

William Bradford
(1590–1657)

William Bradford defined many of the ideal traits of the American charac-
ter through the anecdotes he chose to tell in Of Plymouth Plantation. *His*
description of the hazardous voyage of the Mayflower *emphasized strength*
in the face of adversity; details of the negotiations leading to the
Mayflower Compact communicated the determination to govern by
mutual consent; the story of the First Thanksgiving demonstrated gratitude
to God and to the friendly Wampanoags whose help was so crucial to the
Pilgrims' survival. Less desirable traits, such as religious intolerance, are
also depicted in what became, without publication, a seminal text of Ameri-
can history and legend.

Bradford's account, describing persecution in England, exile in Holland,
the journey to the New World, and the early history of the colony, was uti-
lized by other colonial historians from the time of its composition, before
1646, but the manuscript disappeared from the Old South Church in
Boston during the Revolution. It was found in a British library in 1855 and
was first published in 1856, more than two hundred years after the last sec-
tions were written. By the time the manuscript was returned to Mas-
sachusetts in 1897, the Pilgrim story it recounted was already a familiar
part of the national myth through the work of other historians and writers
such as Nathaniel Hawthorne and Henry Wadsworth Longfellow.

Bradford, an orphan by age seven, had almost no formal education, but
he was self-educated and was able to read both English and Dutch well, as
well as a smattering of French, Greek, Latin, and Hebrew. When he arrived
in the New World, his baggage included a collection of books. He began
attending meetings of the outlawed Separatists when he was twelve. At six-
teen, he joined the Scrooby group and fled to Holland with them in 1608 to
avoid persecution. A decade later they decided to sail for the New World,
along with secular representatives of the sponsoring Virginia Company of
London. Bradford was a leader of the sect's organizing committee.

After a stormy two-month voyage, an exploratory group went ashore
on Cape Cod on November 11, 1620. While they were anchored in Cape
Cod Bay, Bradford's first wife was lost overboard. She was one of the fifty
people, nearly half the group, who did not survive the first year. When John

Carver, the first elected governor of the colony, fell victim, Bradford was elected to succeed him. Probably Bradford had already begun to write an account of the journey by this time. It is believed that his journal and that of Edward Winslow were combined by George Morton, the English agent for the Pilgrims, in the first published account of the colony, A Relation or Journall of the Beginnings and Proceedings of the Plantation Settled at Plimoth, *commonly known as* Mourt's Relation, *which appeared in London in 1622.*

Before disembarking at Plymouth, the Pilgrims drew up and signed the Mayflower Compact, pledging themselves to work "together into a Civil Body Politic" to preserve and govern the group. From 1621 until his death, Bradford was the most powerful person in the colony; most of the time he held the title of governor and was re-elected to that honor thirty times. He persuaded the Pilgrims to share their rights with the secular settlers and helped raise the money to liquidate the colony's debt to the British investors who had financed the voyage. Though the second book of his history is less optimistic than the first, because of the internal problems and economic depression the colonists experienced, Bradford remained convinced that the Pilgrim's success was evidence of God's providence. At his death he was owner of a small house and some orchards in Plymouth as well as a library of about 400 books.

The following text is taken from *Of Plymouth Plantation, 1620–1647*, edited by Samuel Eliot Morison (1952). The standard edition is *History of Plymouth Plantation, 1620–1647*, 2 vols., edited, with notes, by W. C. Ford (1912).

Mourt's Relation, first published as *A Relation or Journall of the Beginning and Proceedings of the Plantation Settled at Plimouth* (1622), is available in editions edited by Theodore Besterman (1939) and Dwight B. Heath (1963).

Good biographical studies are to be found in the Introduction to the Morison edition and in Bradford Smith's *Bradford of Plymouth* (1951).

[From] Of *Plymouth Plantation*, Book I

Chapter X. Showing How They Sought Out a Place of Habitation; and What Befell Them Thereabout

BEING THUS ARRIVED at Cape Cod the 11th of November,[1] and necessity calling them to look out a place for habitation (as well as the master's and mariners' importunity); they having brought a large shallop with them out of England, stowed in quarters in the ship, they now got her out and set their carpenters to work to trim her up; but being much bruised and shattered in the ship with foul weather, they saw she would be long in mending. Whereupon a few of them tendered themselves to go by land and discover those nearest places, whilst the shallop was in mending; and the rather because as they went into that harbor there seemed to be an opening some two or three leagues off, which the master judged to be a river. It was conceived there might be some danger in the attempt, yet seeing them resolute, they were permitted to go, being sixteen of them well armed under the conduct of Captain Standish,[2] having such instructions given them as was thought meet.

They set forth the 15th of November,[3] and when they had marched about the space of a mile by the seaside, they espied five or six persons with a dog coming towards them, who were savages; but they fled from them and ran up into the woods, and the English followed them, partly to see if they could speak with them, and partly to discover if there might not be more of them lying in ambush. But the Indians seeing themselves thus followed, they again forsook the woods and ran away on the sands as hard as they could, so as they could not come near them but followed them by the track of their feet sundry miles and saw that they had come the same way. So, night coming on, they made their rendezvous and set out their sentinels, and rested in quiet that night; and the next morning followed their track till they had headed a great creek and so left the sands, and turned another way

---

1. Bradford used the "Old Style," or Julian, calendar. Under the modern (Gregorian) calendar, dates are ten days later. Thus Bradford's November 11 is November 21 by our reckoning.

2. Standish (c. 1584–1656) was not a Puritan; he had been hired as their military leader. The anecdote of his sending John Alden to court Priscilla Mullens was popularized in Longfellow's *The Courtship of Miles Standish*.

3. That is, November 25.

into the woods. But they still followed them by guess, hoping to find their dwellings; but they soon lost both them and themselves, falling into such thickets as were ready to tear their clothes and armor in pieces; but were most distressed for want of drink. But at length they found water and refreshed themselves, being the first New England water they drunk of, and was now in great thirst as pleasant unto them as wine or beer had been in foretimes.

Afterwards they directed their course to come to the other shore, for they knew it was a neck of land they were to cross over, and so at length got to the seaside and marched to this supposed river, and by the way found a pond of clear, fresh water, and shortly after a good quantity of clear ground where the Indians had formerly set corn, and some of their graves. And proceeding further they saw new stubble where corn had been set the same year; also they found where lately a house had been, where some planks and a great kettle was remaining, and heaps of sand newly paddled with their hands. Which, they digging up, found in them divers fair Indian baskets filled with corn, and some in ears, fair and good, of divers colours, which seemed to them a very goodly sight (having never seen any such before). This was near the place of that supposed river they came to seek, unto which they went and found it to open itself into two arms with a high cliff of sand in the entrance[4] but more like to be creeks of salt water than any fresh, for aught they saw; and that there was good harborage for their shallop, leaving it further to be discovered by their shallop, when she was ready. So, their time limited them being expired, they returned to the ship lest they should be in fear of their safety; and took with them part of the corn and buried up the rest. And so, like the men from Eshcol, carried with them of the fruits of the land and showed their brethren,[5] of which, and their return, they were marvelously glad and their hearts encouraged.

After this, the shallop being got ready, they set out again for the better discovery of this place, and the master of the ship desired to go himself.[6] So there went some thirty men but found it to be no harbor for ships but only for boats. There was also found two of their houses covered with mats, and sundry of their implements in them, but the people were run away and could not be seen. Also there was found more of their corn and of their beans of various colours; the corn and beans they brought away, purposing to give them full satisfaction when they should meet with any of them as, about some six months afterward they did, to their good content.

And here is to be noted a special providence of God, and a great mercy to this poor people, that here they got seed to plant them corn the next year, or else they might have starved, for they had none nor any likelihood to get any

---

4. According to S. E. Morison, the river described is the Pamet River, a salt creek in the present-day Truro, where there are sections called Pond Village and Corn Hill.

5. In the Old Testament (Numbers xiii:23–26) Moses sent out scouts who brought back fruit from the valley of Eshcol in Canaan.

6. The second expedition of the Truro area took place from November 28 to 30.

till the season had been past, as the sequel did manifest. Neither is it likely they had had this, if the first voyage had not been made, for the ground was now all covered with snow and hard frozen; but the Lord is never wanting unto His in their greatest needs; let His holy name have all the praise.

The month of November being spent in these affairs, and much foul weather falling in, the 6th [16th] of December they sent out their shallop again with ten of their principal men and some seamen, upon further discovery, intending to circulate that deep bay of Cape Cod. The weather was very cold and it froze so hard as the spray of the sea lighting on their coats, they were as if they had been glazed. Yet that night betimes they got down into the bottom of the bay, and as they drew near the shore they saw some ten or twelve Indians very busy about something. They landed about a league or two from them,[7] and had much ado to put ashore anywhere—it lay so full of flats. Being landed, it grew late and they made themselves a barricado with logs and boughs as well as they could in the time, and set out their sentinel and betook them to rest, and saw the smoke of the fire the savages made that night. When morning was come they divided their company, some to coast along the shore in the boat, and the rest marched through the woods to see the land, if any fit place might be for their dwelling. They came also to the place where they saw the Indians the night before, and found they had been cutting up a great fish like a grampus,[8] being some two inches thick of fat like a hog, some pieces whereof they had left by the way. And the shallop found two more of these fishes dead on the sands, a thing usual after storms in that place, by reason of the great flats of sand that lie off.

So they ranged up and down all that day, but found no people, nor any place they liked. When the sun grew low, they hasted out of the woods to meet with their shallop, to whom they made signs to come to them into a creek hard by,[9] the which they did at high water, of which they were very glad, for they had not seen each other all that day since the morning. So they made them a barricado as usually they did every night, with logs, stakes and thick pine boughs, the height of a man, leaving it open to leeward, partly to shelter them from the cold and wind (making their fire in the middle and lying round about it) and partly to defend them from any sudden assaults of the savages, if they should surround them; so being very weary, they betook them to rest. But about midnight they heard a hideous and great cry, and their sentinel called "Arm! arm!" So they bestirred them and stood to their arms and shot off a couple of muskets, and then the noise ceased. They concluded it was a company of wolves or such like wild beasts, for one of the seamen told them he had often heard such a noise in Newfoundland.

So they rested till about five of the clock in the morning; for the tide, and

---

7. In the present-day town of Eastham, perhaps in the area of Kingsbury Beach. The Native Americans of Cape Cod were members of the Nauset tribe. Their descendants still live on the Cape, especially in Mashpee.

8. Probably a pilot whale. There are still periodic beachings of pilot whales along this coast of Cape Cod Bay.

9. The Herring River, Eastham.

their purpose to go from thence, made them be stirring betimes. So after prayer they prepared for breakfast, and it being day dawning it was thought best to be carrying things down to the boat. But some said it was not best to carry the arms down, others said they would be the readier, for they had lapped them up in their coats from the dew; but some three or four would not carry theirs till they went themselves. Yet as it fell out, the water being not high enough, they laid them down on the bank side and came up to breakfast.

But presently, all on the sudden, they heard a great and strange cry, which they knew to be the same voices they heard in the night, though they varied their notes; and one of their company being abroad came running in and cried, "Men, Indians! Indians!" And withal, their arrows came flying amongst them. Their men ran with all speed to recover their arms, as by the good providence of God they did. In the meantime, of those that were there ready, two muskets were discharged at them, and two more stood ready in the entrance of their rendezvous but were commanded not to shoot till they could take full aim at them. And the other two charged again with all speed, for there were only four had arms there, and defended the barricado, which was first assaulted. The cry of the Indians was dreadful, especially when they saw their men run out of the rendezvous toward the shallop to recover their arms, the Indians wheeling about upon them. But some running out with coats of mail on, and cutlasses in their hands, they soon got their arms and let fly amongst them and quickly stopped their violence. Yet there was a lusty man, and no less valiant, stood behind a tree within half a musket shot, and let his arrows fly at them; he was seen [to] shoot three arrows, which were all avoided. He stood three shots of a musket, till one taking full aim at him and made the bark or splinters of the tree fly about his ears, after which he gave an extraordinary shriek and away they went, all of them. They left some to keep the shallop and followed them about a quarter of a mile and shouted once or twice, and shot off two or three pieces, and so returned. This they did that they might conceive that they were not afraid of them or any way discouraged.

Thus it pleased God to vanquish their enemies and give them deliverance; and by His special providence so to dispose that not any one of them were either hurt or hit, though their arrows came close by them and on every side [of] them; and sundry of their coats, which hung up in the barricado, were shot through and through. Afterwards they gave God solemn thanks and praise for their deliverance, and gathered up a bundle of their arrows and sent them into England afterward by the master of the ship, and called that place the First Encounter.[1]

From hence they departed and coasted all along but discerned no place likely for harbor, and therefore hasted to a place that their pilot (one Mr. Coppin who had been in the country before) did assure them was a good harbor, which he had been in and they might fetch it before night; of which they were glad for it began to be foul weather.

---

1. Now First Encounter Beach, in Eastham.

After some hours' sailing it began to snow and rain, and about the middle of the afternoon the wind increased and the sea became very rough, and they broke their rudder, and it was as much as two men could do to steer her with a couple of oars. But their pilot bade them be of good cheer for he saw the harbor; but the storm increasing, and night drawing on, they bore what sail they could to get in, while they could see. But herewith they broke their mast in three pieces and their sail fell overboard in a very grown sea, so as they had like to have been cast away. Yet by God's mercy they recovered themselves, and having the flood[2] with them, struck into the harbor. But when it came to, the pilot was deceived in the place, and said the Lord be merciful unto them for his eyes never saw that place before; and he and the master's mate would have run her ashore in a cove full of breakers before the wind. But a lusty seaman which steered bade those which rowed, if they were men, about with her or else they were all cast away; the which they did with speed. So he bid them to be of good cheer and row lustily, for there was a fair sound before them, and he doubted not but they should find one place or other where they might ride in safety. And though it was very dark and rained sore, yet in the end they got under the lee of a small island and remained there all that night in safety.[3] But they knew not this to be an island till morning, but were divided in their minds; some would keep the boat for fear they might be amongst the Indians, others were so wet and cold they could not endure but got ashore, and with much ado got fire (all things being so wet); and the rest were glad to come to them, for after midnight the wind shifted to the northwest and it froze hard.

But though this had been a day and night of much trouble and danger unto them, yet God gave them a morning of comfort and refreshing (as usually He doth to His children) for the next day was a fair, sunshining day, and they found themselves to be on an island secure from the Indians, where they might dry their stuff, fix their pieces and rest themselves, and gave God thanks for His mercies in their manifold deliverances. And this being the last day of the week, they prepared there to keep the Sabbath.

On Monday they sounded the harbor and found it fit for shipping, and marched into the land and found divers cornfields and little running brooks, a place (as they supposed) fit for the situation.[4] At least it was the best they could find, and the season and their present necessity made them glad to accept of it. So they returned to their ship again with this news to the rest of the people, which did much comfort their hearts.

On the 15th of December they weighed anchor to go to the place they had discovered, and came within two leagues of it, but were fain to bear up

---

2. "The mean rise and fall of tide there is about 9 ft. Plymouth Bay * * * is a bad place to enter in thick weather with a sea running and night coming on." [Morison's note]

3. Morison identifies the anchorage as the lee of Naguish Head, and the island there as Clarks Island, where they spent Saturday and Sunday, December 9/19–10/20.

4. "Here is the only contemporary authority for the 'Landing of the Pilgrims on Plymouth Rock' on Monday, 11/21 Dec. 1620. * * * The landing took place from the shallop, not the *Mayflower*. * * * Nor is it clear that they landed on * * * Plymouth Rock, [although] it would have been very convenient for that purpose at half tide." [Morison's note]

again; but the 16th day, the wind came fair, and they arrived safe in this harbor. And afterwards took better view of the place, and resolved where to pitch their dwelling; and the 25th day began to erect the first house for common use to receive them and their goods.[5]

[Compact with the Indians (1621)]

All this while[6] the Indians came skulking about them, and would sometimes show themselves aloof off, but when any approached near them, they would run away; and once they stole away their tools where they had been at work and were gone to dinner. But about the 16th of March, a certain Indian[7] came boldly amongst them and spoke to them in broken English, which they could well understand but marveled at it. At length they understood by discourse with him, that he was not of these parts, but belonged to the eastern parts where some English ships came to fish, with whom he was acquainted and could name sundry of them by their names, amongst whom he had got his language. He became profitable to them in acquainting them with many things concerning the state of the country in the east parts where he lived, which was afterwards profitable unto them; as also of the people here, of their names, number and strength, of their situation and distance from this place, and who was chief amongst them. His name was Samoset. He told them also of another Indian whose name was Squanto,[8] a native of this place, who had been in England and could speak better English than himself.

Being, after some time of entertainment and gifts dismissed, a while after he came again, and five more with him, and they brought again all the tools that were stolen away before, and made way for the coming of their great Sachem, called Massasoit. Who, about four or five days after, came with the chief of his friends and other attendance, with the aforesaid Squanto. With whom, after friendly entertainment and some gifts given him, they made a peace with him (which hath now continued this 24 years)[9] in these terms:

1. That neither he nor any of his should injure or do hurt to any of their people.
2. That if any of his hurt to any of theirs, he should send the offender, that they might punish him.

---

5. The *Mayflower* reached Plymouth Harbor on December 16/26. Building of shelters began nine days later, after exploration for the best sites.

6. January, February, and early March of 1621, a period of starvation and great suffering. The settlers built a large common house and several cottages. They lived on scant game and fish; many died of disease. Only twenty-one of the men survived.

7. Samoset was from Maine and returned there shortly after this meeting.

8. Squanto or Tisquantum (d. 1622) was a member of the Pawtuxet tribe. He lived in England from 1615 to 1619. He helped negotiate the treaty with the Wampanoag tribe led by Chief Massasoit. On an expedition to Cape Cod with William Bradford the following year, he fell ill with smallpox and died.

9. This first American treaty was faithfully kept for fifty-four years, until 1675 when Massasoit's son, Metacomet, or King Philip, began the attacks known as King Philip's War.

3. That if anything were taken away from any of theirs, he should cause it to be restored; and they should do the like to his.

4. If any did unjustly war against him, they would aid him; if any did war against them, he should aid them

5. He should send to his neighbours confederates to certify them of this, that they might not wrong them, but might be likewise comprised in the conditions of peace.

6. That when their men came to them, they should leave their bows and arrows behind them.

After these things he returned to his place called Sowams,[1] some 40 miles from this place, but Squanto continued with them and was their interpreter and was a special instrument sent of God for their good beyond their expectation. He directed them how to set their corn, where to take fish, and to procure other commodities, and was also their pilot to bring them to unknown places for their profit, and never left them till he died. He was a native of this place, and scarce any left alive besides himself. He was carried away with divers others by one Hunt, a master of a ship, who thought to sell them for slaves in Spain. But he got away for England and was entertained by a merchant in London, and employed to Newfoundland and other parts, and lastly brought hither into these parts by one Mr. Dermer, a gentleman employed by Sir Ferdinando Gorges and others for discovery and other designs in these parts.

[First Thanksgiving (1621)]

They began now to gather in the small harvest they had, and to fit up their houses and dwellings against winter, being all well recovered in health and strength and had all things in good plenty. For as some were thus employed in affairs abroad, others were exercised in fishing, about cod and bass and other fish, of which they took good store, of which every family had their portion. All the summer there was no want; and now began to come in store of fowl, as winter approached, of which this place did abound when they came first (but afterward decreased by degrees). And besides waterfowl there was great store of wild turkeys, of which they took many, besides venison, etc. Besides they had about a peck a meal a week to a person, or now since harvest, Indian corn to that proportion. Which made many afterwards write so largely of their plenty here to their friends in England, which were not feigned but true reports.[2]

---

1. Now Barrington, Rhode Island.

2. The actual date of the "First Thanksgiving" is not recorded, but it was in the autumn of 1621, since Winslow's letter describing it, printed in *Mourt's Relation*, is dated December 11, 1621. He relates that their store of wild meat and produce was such that they were able to entertain Massasoit and "some 90 men" for three days with feasting and competitive games.

Mary Rowlandson
(1636?–1711?)

In the early years of English settlement at Plymouth and Massachusetts Bay, relationships with the Native Americans were remarkably good. There were bloody conflicts, including the Pequot War of 1637, but the treaty of 1621 signed between the Pilgrims and Massasoit, Chief of the Wampanoags, was honored on both sides until his death in 1661. By that time Roger Williams had also found a friendly welcome for his settlement in Rhode Island. Indeed, generally good relations between Wampanoags and whites had begun as early as 1524, when Verrazzano and his men "formed a great friendship with them" during their brief stay in Narragansett Bay. Not the least of the tragedies of King Philip's War (1675–1676) was that it brought to an end a period of a century and a half when, at least in this portion of New England, peaceful coexistence seemed possible.

Many circumstances contributed to the war. The English were arriving in large numbers and pushing farther and farther into Native American territory. Some Indians, such as the Praying Indians of Natick, were adopting the ways of the whites. Others were attempting to maintain their cultural traditions and seeking to control their own destinies, but finding themselves more and more dependent on trade with the English, more and more subject to English law. In these circumstances, Massasoit's son, Metacomet (King Philip), continued for some years his father's policy of peace, but war broke out after three Indians were accused of murder, tried, and executed in Plymouth. The conflict lasted barely a year. By the end, over 1,000 homes had been burned, 600 whites and 3,000 Indians had been killed, tribal life had essentially come to an end in New England, and a pattern of westward expansion and frontier warfare had been clearly established.

Mary Rowlandson was probably born in England, the daughter of John White, and came with her parents to Salem, Massachusetts, in 1638. Later the family settled in Lancaster, thirty-five miles west of Boston, and in 1656 she married the Reverend Joseph Rowlandson. Taken in the attack on Lancaster in the winter of 1676, she spent nearly three months in captivity, then lived briefly in Boston before settling in in Wethersfield, Connecticut. Her book, first published in 1682, displays a continual concern with the role of God in her experience, an emphasis also apparent in its full title: The Soveraignty and Goodness of GOD, Together with the Faithfulness of His Promises Displayed; Being a Narrative of the Captivity and Restauration of Mrs. Mary Rowlandson. *Hugely popular in America and in England in the seventeenth and eighteenth centuries, it was the most famous of the many captivity narratives that for a long while formed a distinct genre in American literature.*

The present text is a modernized version of that printed in *Narratives of the Indian Wars, 1675–1679*, edited by Charles H. Lincoln (1913). A study is Richard Van Der Beets, *The Indian Captivity Narrative: An American Genre* (1984).

A Narrative of the Captivity and Restoration of Mrs. Mary Rowlandson

ON THE TENTH OF FEBRUARY 1675[1] came the Indians with great numbers upon Lancaster: Their first coming was about sun-rising; hearing the noise of some guns, we looked out; several houses were burning, and the smoke ascending to heaven. There were five persons taken in one house, the father, and the mother and a sucking child, they knocked on the head; the other two they took and carried away alive. There were two others, who being out of their garrison upon some occasion were set upon; one was knocked on the head, the other escaped: Another there was who running along was shot and wounded, and fell down; he begged of them his life, promising them money (as they told me) but they would not hearken to him but knocked him in head, and stripped him naked, and split open his bowels. Another seeing many of the Indians about his barn, ventured and went out, but was quickly shot down. There were three others belonging to the same garrison who were killed; the Indians getting up upon the roof of the barn, had advantage to shoot down upon them over their fortification. Thus these murderous wretches went on, burning, and destroying before them.

At length they came and beset our own house, and quickly it was the dolefullest day that ever mine eyes saw. The house stood upon the edge of a

---

1. By the present Gregorian calendar, the date was February 20, 1676. The calendar at use in Mary Rowlandson's time is now called Old Style.

hill; some of the Indians got behind the hill, others into the barn, and others behind any thing that could shelter them; from all which places they shot against the house, so that the bullets seemed to fly like hail; and quickly they wounded one man among us, then another, and then a third, About two hours (according to my observation, in that amazing time) they had been about the house before they prevailed to fire it (which they did with flax and hemp, which they brought out of the barn, and there being no defense about the house, only two flankers[2] at two opposite corners and one of them not finished) they fired it once and one ventured out and quenched it, but they quickly fired it again, and that took. Now is the dreadful hour come, that I have often heard of (in time of war, as it was the case of others) but now mine eyes see it. Some in our house were fighting for their lives, others wallowing in their blood, the house on fire over our heads, and the bloody heathen ready to knock us on the head, if we stirred out. Now might we hear mothers and children crying out for themselves, and one another, Lord, what shall we do? Then I took my children (and one of my sisters, hers) to go forth and leave the house: but as soon as we came to the door and appeared, the Indians shot so thick that the bullets rattled against the house, as if one had taken an handful of stones and threw them, so that we were fain to give back. We had six stout dogs belonging to our garrison, but none of them would stir, though another time, if any Indian had come to the door, they were ready to fly upon him and tear him down. The Lord hereby would make us the more to acknowledge his hand, and to see that our help is always in him. But out we must go, the fire increasing, and coming along behind us, roaring, and the Indians gaping before us with their guns, spears and hatchets to devour us. No sooner were we out of the house, but my brother-in-law (being before wounded, in defending the house, in or near the throat) fell down dead, whereat the Indians scornfully shouted, and hallowed, and were presently upon him, stripping off his clothes, the bullets flying thick, one went through my side, and the same (as would seem) through the bowels and hand of my dear child in my arms. One of my elder sister's children, named William, had then his leg broken, which the Indians perceiving, they knocked him on head. Thus were we butchered by those merciless heathen, standing amazed, with the blood running down to our heels. My eldest sister being yet in the house, and seeing those woeful sights, the infidels hauling mothers one way, and children another, and some wallowing in their blood: and her elder son telling her that her son William was dead, and my self was wounded, she said, And, Lord, let me die with them; which was no sooner said, but she was struck with a bullet, and fell down dead over the threshold. I hope she is reaping the fruit of her good labors, being faithful to the service of God in her place. In her younger years she lay under much trouble upon spiritual accounts, till it pleased God to make that precious scripture take hold of her heart, 2 Cor. 12. 9. *And he said unto me, my Grace is sufficient for thee.* More then twenty years after I

---

2. Fortified projections.

have heard her tell how sweet and comfortable that place was to her. But to return: The Indians laid hold of us, pulling me one way, and the children another, and said, Come go along with us; I told them they would kill me: they answered, If I were willing to go along with them, they would not hurt me.

Oh the doleful sight that now was to behold at this house! *Come, behold the works of the Lord, what dissolations he has made in the Earth.*[3] Of thirty-seven persons who were in this one house, none escaped either present death, or a bitter captivity, save only one, who might say as he, Job 1. 15, *And I only am escaped alone to tell the News.* There were twelve killed, some shot, some stabbed with their spears, some knocked down with their hatchets. When we are in prosperity, oh the little that we think of such dreadful sights, and to see our dear friends, and relations lie bleeding out their heart-blood upon the ground. There was one who was chopped into the head with a hatchet, and stripped naked, and yet was crawling up and down. It is a solemn sight to see so many Christians lying in their blood, some here, and some there, like a company of sheep torn by wolves, all of them stripped naked by a company of hell-hounds, roaring, singing, ranting and insulting, as if they would have torn our very hearts out; yet the Lord by his Almighty power preserved a number of us from death, for there were twenty-four of us taken alive and carried captive.

I had often before this said, that if the Indians should come, I should choose rather to be killed by them then taken alive but when it came to the trial my mind changed; their glittering weapons so daunted my spirit, that I chose rather to go along with those (as I may say) ravenous beasts, then that moment to end my days; and that I may the better declare what happened to me during that grievous captivity, I shall particularly speak of the several removes we had up and down the wilderness.

THE FIRST REMOVE

Now away we must go with those barbarous creatures, with our bodies wounded and bleeding, and our hearts no less than our bodies. About a mile we went that night, up upon a hill within sight of the town, where they intended to lodge. There was hard by a vacant house (deserted by the English before, for fear of the Indians). I asked them whether I might not lodge in the house that night to which they answered, what will you love English men still? This was the dolefullest night that ever my eyes saw. Oh the roaring, and singing and dancing, and yelling of those black creatures in the night, which made the place a lively resemblance of hell. And as miser-

---

3. Psalm xlvi:8.

able was the waste that was there made, of horses, cattle, sheep, swine, calves, lambs, roasting pigs, and fowl (which they had plundered in the town) some roasting, some lying and burning, and some boiling to feed our merciless enemies; who were joyful enough though we were disconsolate. To add to the dolefulness of the former day, and the dismalness of the present night: my thoughts ran upon my losses and sad bereaved condition. All was gone, my husband gone (at least separated from me, he being in the Bay;[4] and to add to my grief, the Indians told me they would kill him as he came homeward) my children gone, my relations and friends gone, our house and home and all our comforts within door, and without, all was gone, (except my life) and I knew not but the next moment that might go too. There remained nothing to me but one poor wounded babe, and it seemed at present worse than death that it was in such a pitiful condition, bespeaking compassion, and I had no refreshing for it, not suitable things to revive it. Little do many think what is the savageness and brutishness of this barbarous enemy, aye, even those that seem to profess more than others among them, when the English have fallen into their hands.

Those seven that were killed at Lancaster the summer before upon a Sabbath day, and the one that was afterward killed upon a week day, were slain and mangled in a barbarous manner, by one-eyed John, and Marlborough's Praying Indians, which Capt. Mosely brought to Boston,[5] as the Indians told me.

THE SECOND REMOVE[6]

But now, the next morning, I must turn my back upon the town, and travel with them into the vast and desolate wilderness, I knew not whither. It is not my tongue, or pen can express the sorrows of my heart, and bitterness of my spirit, that I had at this departure: but God was with me, in a wonderful manner, carrying me along, and bearing up my spirit, that it did not quite fail. One of the Indians carried my poor wounded babe upon a horse; it went moaning all along, I shall die, I shall die. I went on foot after it, with sorrow that cannot be expressed. At length I took it off the horse, and carried it in my arms till my strength failed, and I fell down with it: Then they set me upon a horse with my wounded child in my lap, and there being no furniture upon the horse's back, as we were going down a steep hill, we both fell

---

4. That is, at Massachetts Bay, in or near Boston.

5. On August 22, 1765 seven people had been killed at Lancaster. On August 30, Captain Samuel Mosely brought to Boston fifteen Praying Indians (Christianized) from Marlborough, Massachusetts, who were thought to be involved in the attack.

6. To Princeton, Massachusetts, about ten miles west of Lancaster.

over the horse's head, at which they like inhumane creatures laughed, and
rejoiced to see it, though I thought we should there have ended our days, as
overcome with so many difficulties. But the Lord renewed my strength still,
and carried me along, that I might see more of his Power; yea, so much that
I could never have thought of, had I not experienced it.

After this it quickly began to snow, and when night came on, they
stopped: and now down I must sit in the snow by a little fire, and a few
boughs behind me, with my sick child in my lap; and calling much for water,
being now (through the wound) fallen into a violent fever. My own wound
also growing so stiff, that I could scarce sit down or rise up; yet so it must be,
that I must sit all this cold winter night upon the cold snowy ground, with
my sick child in my arms, looking that every hour would be the last of its
life; and having no Christian friend near me, either to comfort or help me.
Oh, I may see the wonderful power of God, that my spirit did not utterly
sink under my affliction: still the Lord upheld me with his gracious and
merciful, spirit and we were both alive to see the light of the next morning.

THE THIRD REMOVE[7]

The morning being come, they prepared to go on their way. One of the
Indians got up upon a horse, and they set me up behind him, with my poor
sick babe in my lap. A very wearisome and tedious day I had of it, what
with my own wound, and my child's being so exceeding sick, and in a
lamentable condition with her wound. It may be easily judged what a poor
feeble condition we were in, there being not the least crumb of refreshing
that came within either of our mouths, from Wednesday night to Saturday
night, except only a little cold water. This day in the afternoon, about an
hour by sun, we came to the place where they intended, *viz.* an Indian
Town, called Wenimesset, north of Quabaug.[8] When we were come, Oh the
number of pagans (now merciless enemies) that there came about me, that I
may say as David, Psal. 27. 13, *I had fainted, unless I had believed,* etc. The
next day was the sabbath: I then remembered how careless I had been of
God's holy time, how many sabbaths I had lost and mispent, and how evilly
I had walked in God's sight; which lay so close unto my spirit, that it was
easy for me to see how righteous it was with God to cut off the thread of
my life, and cast me out of his presence for ever. Yet the Lord still showed
mercy to me, and upheld me; and as he wounded me with one hand, so he
healed me with the other. This day there came to me one Robbert Pepper (a

---

7. February 12–27, to an Indian Village on the Ware River, near New Braintree, fifteen miles
southwest of Princeton.
8. Now Brookfield.

man belonging to Roxbury) who was taken in Captain Beers his fight,[9] and had been now a considerable time with the Indians; and up with them almost as far as Albany,[1] to see King Philip, as he told me, and was now very lately come into these parts. Hearing, I say, that I was in this Indian town, he obtained leave to come and see me. He told me, he himself was wounded in the leg at Captain Beers his fight; and was not able some time to go, but as they carried him, and as he took oak leaves and laid to his wound, and through the blessing of God he was able to travel again. Then I took oak leaves and laid to my side, and with the blessing of God it cured me also; yet before the cure was wrought, I may say, as it is in Psal. 38. 5, 6. *My wounds stink and are corrupt, I am troubled, I am bowed down greatly, I go mourning all the day long.* I sat much alone with a poor wounded child in my lap, which moaned night and day, having nothing to revive the body, or cheer the spirits of her, but instead of that, sometimes one Indian would come and tell me one hour, that your master will knock your child in the head, and then a second, and then a third, your master will quickly knock your child in the head.

This was the comfort I had from them, miserable comforters are ye all, as he said.[2] Thus nine days I sat upon my knees, with my babe in my lap, till my flesh was raw again; my child being even ready to depart this sorrowful world, they bade me carry it out to another wigwam (I suppose because they would not be troubled with such spectacles) whither I went with a very heavy heart, and down I sat with the picture of death in my lap. About two hours in the night, my sweet babe like a lamb departed this life, on Feb. 18, 1675. It being about six years, and five months old. It was nine days from the first wounding, in this miserable condition, without any refreshing of one nature or other, except a little cold water. I cannot, but take notice, how at another time I could not bear to be in the room where any dead person was, but now the case is changed; I must and could lie down by my dead babe, side by side all the night after. I have thought since of the wonderful goodness of God to me, in preserving me in the use of my reason and senses, in that distressed time, that I did not use wicked and violent means to end my own miserable life. In the morning, when they understood that my child was dead they sent for me home to my master's wigwam: (by my master in this writing, must be understood Quanopin, who was a sagamore, and married King Philip's wive's sister; not that he first took me, but I was sold to him by another Narragansett Indian,[3] who took me when first I came out of the garrison). I went to take up my dead child in my arms to carry it with me, but they bid me let it alone: there was no resisting, but go I must and leave it. When I had been at my master's wigwam, I took the first opportu-

---

9. On September 4, 1675 Beers and most of his men had been killed in a fight at Northfield.

1. Albany, New York. King Philip spent the winter of 1675–1676 somewhat east of there.

2. See Job xvi:2.

3. Other tribes, including the Narragansetts and Nipmucks, had joined with the Wampanoags under the leadership of King Philip. A sagamore was a lesser chief.

nity I could get, to go look after my dead child: when I came I asked them
what they had done with it? Then they told me it was upon the hill: then
they went and showed me where it was, where I saw the ground was newly
digged, and there they told me they had buried it. There I left that child in
the wilderness, and must commit it, and myself also in this wilderness-con-
dition, to him who is above all. God having taken away this dear child, I
went to see my daughter Mary, who was at this same Indian town, at a wigwam not very far off, though we had little liberty or opportunity to see one
another. She was about ten years old, and taken from the door at first by a
Praying Indian and afterward sold for a gun. When I came in sight, she
would fall a-weeping; at which they were provoked, and would not let me
come near her, but bade me be gone, which was a heart-cutting word to me. I
had one child dead, another in the wilderness, I knew not where, the third
they would not let me come near to: *Me* (as he said) *have ye bereaved of my
Children, Joseph is not, and Simeon is not, and ye will take Benjamin also,
all these things are against me.*[4] I could not sit still in this condition, but
kept walking from one place to another. And as I was going along, my heart
was even overwhelmed with the thoughts of my condition, and that I should
have children, and a nation which I knew not ruled over them. Whereupon I
earnestly entreated the Lord, that he would consider my low estate, and
show me a token for good, and if it were his blessed will, some sign and hope
of some relief. And indeed quickly the Lord answered, in some measure, my
poor prayers: for as I was going up and down mourning and lamenting my
condition, my son came to me, and asked me how I did; I had not seen him
before, since the destruction of the town, and I knew not where he was, till I
was informed by himself, that he was amongst a smaller parcel of Indians,
whose place was about six miles off. With tears in his eyes, he asked me
whether his sister Sarah was dead; and told me he had seen his sister Mary;
and prayed me, that I would not be troubled in reference to himself. The
occasion of his coming to see me at this time, was this: There was, as I said,
about six miles from us, a smal plantation of Indians, where it seems he had
been during his captivity: and at this time, there were some forces of the
Indians gathered out of our company, and some also from them (among
whom was my son's master) to go to assault and burn Medfield: In this time
of the absence of his master, his dame brought him to see me. I took this to
be some gracious answer to my earnest and unfeigned desire. The next day,
viz. to this, the Indians returned from Medfield, all the company, for those
that belonged to the other small company, came thorough the town that
now we were at. But before they came to us, Oh! the outragious roaring and
whooping that there was: They began their din about a mile before they
came to us. By their noise and whooping they signified how many they had
destroyed (which was at that time twenty-three.) Those that were with us at
home, were gathered together as soon as they heard the whooping, and
every time that the others went over their number, these at home gave a

---

4. Jacob's lament in Genesis xlii:36.

shout, that the very earth rung again: And thus they continued till those that had been upon the expedition were come up to the sagamore's wigwam; and then, Oh, the hideous insulting and triumphing that there was over some Englishmen's scalps that they had taken (as their manner is) and brought with them. I cannot but take notice of the wonderful mercy of God to me in those afflictions, in sending me a Bible. One of the Indians that came from Medfield fight, had brought some plunder, came to me, and asked me, if I would have a Bible, he had got one in his basket. I was glad of it, and asked him, whether he thought the Indians would let me read? he answered, yes: So I took the Bible, and in that melancholy time, it came into my mind to read first the 28. Chap. of Deut., which I did, and when I had read it, my dark heart wrought on this manner, That there was no mercy for me, that the blessings were gone, and the curses come in their room, and that I had lost my opportunity. But the Lord helped me still to go on reading till I came to Chap. 30 the seven first verses, where I found, there was mercy promised again, if we would return to him by repentance; and though we were scattered from one end of the earth to the other, yet the Lord would gather us together, and turn all those curses upon our enemies. I do not desire to live to forget this scripture, and what comfort it was to me.

Now the Indians began to talk of removing from this place, some one way, and some another. There were now besides myself nine English captives in this place (all of them children, except one woman). I got an opportunity to go and take my leave of them; they being to go one way, and I another, I asked them whether they were earnest with God for deliverance; they told me, they did as they were able, and it was some comfort to me, that the Lord stirred up children to look to him. The woman, *viz.* Goodwife Joslin, told me, she should never see me again, and that she could find in her heart to run away; I wished her not to run away by any means, for we were near thirty miles from any English town, and she very big with child, and had but one week to reckon; and another child in her arms, two years old, and bad rivers there were to go over, and we were feeble, with our poor and course entertainment. I had my Bible with me, I pulled it out, and asked her whether she would read; we opened the Bible and lighted on Psal. 27, in which Psalm we especially took notice of that, *ver. ult., Wait on the Lord, Be of good courage, and he shall strengthen thine Heart, wait I say on the Lord.*

THE FOURTH REMOVE[5]

And now I must part with that little company I had. Here I parted from my daughter Mary, (whom I never saw again till I saw her in Dorchester,

---

5. February 28–March 3, to the present Petersham, east of the Quabbin Reservoir.

returned from captivity), and from four little cousins and neighbours, some of which I never saw afterward: the Lord only knows the end of them. Amongst them also was that poor woman before mentioned, who came to a sad end, as some of the company told me in my travel: She having much grief upon her spirit, about her miserable condition, being so near her time, she would be often asking the Indians to let her go home; they not being willing to that, and yet vexed with her importunity, gathered a great company together about her, and stripped her naked, and set her in the midst of them; and when they had sung and danced about her (in their hellish manner) as long as they pleased, they knocked her on head, and the child in her arms with her: when they had done that, they made a fire and put them both into it, and told the other children that were with them, that if they attempted to go home, they would serve them in like manner: The children said, she did not shed one tear, but prayed all the while. But to return to my own journey; we travelled about half a day or little more, and came to a desolate place in the wilderness, where there were no wigwams or inhabitants before; we came about the middle of the afternoon to this place, cold and wet, and snowy, and hungry, and weary, and no refreshing, for man, but the cold ground to sit on, and our poor Indian cheer.

Heart-aching thoughts here I had about my poor children, who were scattered up and down among the wild beasts of the forest: My head was light and dizzy (either through hunger or hard lodging, or trouble or altogether) my knees feeble, my body raw by sitting double night and day, that I cannot express to man the affliction that lay upon my spirit, but the Lord helped me at that time to express it to himself. I opened my Bible to read, and the Lord brought that precious scripture to me, Jer. 31. 16. *Thus saith the Lord, refrain thy voice from weeping, and thine eyes from tears, for thy work shall be rewarded, and they shall come again from the land of the Enemy.* This was a sweet cordial to me, when I was ready to faint, many and many a time have I sat down, and wept sweetly over this scripture. At this place we continued about four days.

THE FIFTH REMOVE[6]

The occasion (as I thought) of their moving at this time, was, the English army, it being near and following them: For they went, as if they had gone for their lives, for some considerable way, and then they made a stop, and chose some of their stoutest men, and sent them back to hold the English army in play whilst the rest escaped: And then, like Jehu,[7] they marched on

---

6. To the Bacquag River (Miller's River) at Orange.

7. King of Israel noted as a furious charioteer: II Kings:9.

furiously, with their old, and with their young: some carried their old decrepit mothers, some carried one, and some another. Four of them carried a great Indian upon a bier; but going through a thick wood with him, they were hindered, and could make no haste; whereupon they took him upon their backs, and carried him, one at a time, till they came to Bacquaug River. Upon a Friday, a little after noon we came to this river. When all the company was come up, and were gathered together, I thought to count the number of them, but they were so many, and being somewhat in motion, it was beyond my skill. In this travel, because of my wound, I was somewhat favored in my load; I carried only my knitting work and two quarts of parched[8] meal: Being very faint I asked my mistress[9] to give me one spoonful of the meal, but she would not give me a taste. They quickly fell to cutting dry trees, to make rafts to carry them over the river: and soon my turn came to go over: By the advantage of some brush which they had laid upon the raft to sit upon, I did not wet my foot (which many of themselves at the other end were mid-leg deep) which cannot but be acknowledged as a favor of God to my weakened body, it being a very cold time. I was not before acquainted with such kind of doings or dangers. *When thou passeth through the waters I will be with thee, and through the Rivers they shall not overflow thee*, Isai. 43. 2. A certain number of us got over the river that night, but it was the night after the sabbath before all the company was got over. On the Saturday they boiled an old horse's leg which they had got, and so we drank of the broth, as soon as they thought it was ready, and when it was almost all gone, they filled it up again.

The first week of my being among them, I hardly ate any thing; the second week, I found my stomach grow very faint for want of something; and yet it was very hard to get down their filthy trash: but the third week, though I could think how formerly my stomach would turn against this or that, and I could starve and die before I could eat such things, yet they were sweet and savory to my taste. I was at this time knitting a pair of white cotton stockings for my mistress; and had not yet wrought upon a sabbath day; when the sabbath came they bade me go to work; I told them it was the sabbath-day, and desired them to let me rest, and told them I would do as much more to morrow; to which they answered me, they would break my face. And here I cannot but take notice of the strange providence of God in preserving the heathen: They were many hundreds, old and young, some sick, and some lame, many had papooses at their backs, the greatest number at this time with us, were squaws, and they travelled with all they had, bag and baggage, and yet they got over this river aforesaid; and on Monday they set their wigwams on fire, and away they went: On that very day came the English army after them to this river, and saw the smoke of their wigwams, and yet this river put a stop to them. God did not give them courage or activity to go over after us; we were not ready for so great a mercy as victory

---

8. Dried.

9. Weetamo, one of Quanopin's wives, to whom Mary Rowlandson had been given as a servant.

and deliverance; if we had been, God would have found out a way for the English to have passed this river, as well as for the Indians with their squaws and children, and all their luggage. *Oh that my People had hearkened to me, and Israel had walked in my ways, I should soon have subdued their Enemies, and turned my hand against their Adversaries,* Psal. 81: 13. 14.

THE EIGHTH REMOVE[1]

* * *

But to return, We travelled on till night; and in the morning, we must go over the river to Philip's crew. When I was in the canoe, I could not but be amazed at the numerous crew of pagans that were on the bank on the other side. When I came ashore, they gathered all about me, I sitting alone in the midst: I observed they asked one another questions, and laughed, and rejoiced over their gains and victories. Then my heart began to fail: and I fell a-weeping, which was the first time to my remembrance, that I wept before them. Although I had met with so much affliction, and my heart was many times ready to break, yet could I not shed one tear in their sight: but rather had been all this while in a maze, and like one astonished: but now I may say as, Psal. 137. 1. *By the Rivers of Babylon, there we sate down: yea, we wept when we remembered Zion.* There one of them asked me, why I wept; I could hardly tell what to say: yet I answered, they would kill me: No, said he, none will hurt you. Then came one of them and gave me two spoonfuls of meal to comfort me, and another gave me half a pint of peas; which was more worth than many bushels at another time. Then I went to see King Philip. He bade me come in and sit down, and asked me whether I would smoke it (a usual compliment nowadays amongst saints and sinners) but this no way suited me. For though I had formerly used tobacco, yet I had left it ever since I was first taken. It seems to be a bait, the devil lays to make men loose their precious time: I remember with shame, how formerly, when I had taken two or three pipes, I was presently ready for another, such a bewitching thing it is: But I thank God, he has now given me power over it; surely there are many who may be better imployed than to lie sucking a stinking tobacco-pipe.

Now the Indians gather their forces to go against Northhampton:[2] overnight one went about yelling and hooting to give notice of the design. Whereupon they fell to boiling of ground-nuts, and parching of corn (as many as had it) for their Provision: and in the morning away they went. During my abode in this place, Philip spoke to me to make a shirt for his boy, which I did, for which he gave me a shilling: I offered the mony to my

---

1. To modern South Vernon, Vermont.

2. The attack on Northampton, Massachusetts, on March 14, was repulsed, but six of the inhabitants were killed.

master, but he bade me keep it: and with it I bought a piece of horse flesh. Afterwards he asked me to make a cap for his boy, for which he invited me to dinner. I went, and he gave me a pancake, about as big as two fingers; it was made of parched wheat, beaten, and fried in bear's grease, but I thought I never tasted pleasanter meat in my life. There was a squaw who spoke to me to make a shirt for her *sannup*,[3] for which she gave me a piece of bear. Another asked me to knit a pair of stockings, for which she gave me a quart of peas: I boiled my peas and bear together, and invited my master and mistress to dinner, but the proud gossip,[4] because I served them both in one dish, would eat nothing, except one bit that he gave her upon the point of his knife. Hearing that my son was come to this place, I went to see him, and found him lying flat upon the ground: I asked him how he could sleep so? he answered me, that he was not asleep, but at prayer; and lay so, that they might not observe what he was doing. I pray God he may remember these things now he is returned in safety. At this place (the sun now getting higher) what with the beams and heat of the sun, and the smoke of the wigwams, I thought I should have been blind. I could scarce discern one wigwam from another. There was here one Mary Thurston of Medfield, who seeing how it was with me, lent me a hat to wear: but as soon as I was gone, the squaw (who owned that Mary Thurston) came running after me, and got it away again. Here was the squaw that gave me one spoonful of meal. I put it in my pocket to keep it safe: yet notwithstanding somebody stole it, but put five Indian corns in the room of it: which corns were the greatest provisions I had in my travel for one day.

The Twentieth Remove[5]

* * *

But to return again to my going home, where we may see a remarkable change of Providence: At first they were all against it, except my husband would come for me; but afterwards they assented to it, and seemed much to rejoice in it; some asked me to send them some bread, others some tobacco, others shaking me by the hand, offering me a hood and scarf to ride in; not one moving hand or tongue against it. Thus hath the Lord answered my poor desire, and the many earnest requests of others put up unto God for me. In my travels an Indian came to me, and told me, if I were willing, he and his squaw would run away, and go home along with me: I told him No: I was not willing to run away, but desired to wait God's time, that I might go home quietly, and without fear. And now God hath granted me my desire. O the wonderful power of God that I have seen, and the experience that I have

---

3. Husband.

4. Wife, or friend.

5. April 28–May 2, to the south end of Wachusett Lake, Princeton.

had: I have been in the midst of those roaring lions, and savage bears, that feared neither God, nor man, nor the Devil, by night and day, alone and in company: sleeping all sorts together, and yet not one of them ever offered me the least abuse of unchastity to me, in word or action. Though some are ready to say, I speak it for my own credit; But I speak it in the presence of God, and to his glory. God's power is as great now, and as sufficient to save, as when he preserved Daniel in the lion's den; or the three children in the fiery furnace.[6] I may well say as his Psal. 107. 12, *Oh give thanks unto the Lord for he is good, for his mercy endureth for ever.* Let the redeemed of the Lord say so, whom he hath redeemed from the hand of the enemy, especially that I should come away in the midst of so many hundreds of enemies quietly and peacably, and not a dog moving his tongue. So I took my leave of them, and in coming along my heart melted into tears, more then all the while I was with them, and I was almost swallowed up with the thoughts that ever I should go home again. About the sun going down, Mr. Hoar,[7] and myself, and the two Indians came to Lancaster, and a solemn sight it was to me. There had I lived many comfortable years amongst my relations and neighbors, and now not one Christian to be seen, nor one house left standing. We went on to a farm house[8] that was yet standing, where we lay all night: and a comfortable lodging we had, though nothing but straw to lie on. The Lord preserved us in safety that night, and raised us up again in the morning, and carried us along, that before noon, we came to Concord. Now was I full of joy, and yet not without sorrow: joy to see such a lovely sight, so many Christians together, and some of them my neighbors: There I met with my brother, and my brother-in-law, who asked me, if I knew where his wife was? Poor heart! he had helped to bury her, and knew it not; she being shot down by the house was partly burnt: so that those who were at Boston at the desolation of the town, and came back afterward, and buried the dead, did not know her. Yet I was not without sorrow, to think how many were looking and longing, and my own children amongst the rest, to enjoy that deliverance that I had now received, and I did not know whether ever I should see them again. Being recruited[9] with food and raiment we went to Boston that day, where I met with my dear husband, but the thoughts of our dear children, one being dead, and the others we could not tell where, abated our comfort each to other.

* * *

We were hurried up and down in our thoughts, sometimes we should hear a report that they were gone this way, and sometimes that; and that they were come in, in this place or that: We kept enquiring and listening to hear con-

---

6. Daniel iii:13–30.

7. John Hoar, who had negotiated the ransom.

8. On the road to Marlborough.

9. Replenished.

cerning them, but no certain news as yet. About this time the council had ordered a day of public. Thanksgiving:[1] though I thought I had still cause of mourning, and being unsettled in our minds, we thought we would ride toward the eastward, to see if we could hear any thing concerning our children. And as we were riding along (God is the wise disposer of all things) between Ipswich and Rowley we met with Mr. William Hubbard, who told us that our son Joseph was come in to Major Waldren's, and another with him, which was my sister's son. I asked him how he knew it? He said, the Major himself told him so. So along we went till we came to Newbury; and their minister being absent, they desired my husband to preach the Thanksgiving for them; but he was not willing to stay there that night, but would go over to Salisbury, to hear further, and come again in the morning; which he did, and preached there that day. At night, when he had done, one came and told him that his daughter was come in at Providence. Here was mercy on both hands: Now hath God fulfiled that precious scripture which was such a comfort to me in my distressed condition. When my heart was ready to sink into the earth (my children being gone I could not tell whither) and my knees trembled under me, and I was walking through the valley of the shadow of Death: Then the Lord brought, and now has fulfilled that reviving word unto me: *Thus saith the Lord, Refrain thy voice from weeping, and thine eyes from tears, for thy Work shall be rewarded, saith the Lord, and they shall come again from the Land of the Enemy.*[2]

* * *

I can remember the time, when I used to sleep quietly without workings in my thoughts, whole nights together, but now it is other ways with me. When all are fast about me, and no eye open, but his whoever waketh, my thoughts are upon things past, upon the awful dispensation of the Lord towards us; upon his wonderful power and might, in carrying of us through so many difficulties, in returning us in safety, and suffering none to hurt us. I remember in the night season, how the other day I was in the midst of thousands of enemies, and nothing but death before me: It is then hard work to persuade myself, that ever I should be satisfied with bread again. But now we are fed with the finest of the wheat, and, as I may say, with honey out of the rock.[3] In stead of the husk, we have the fatted calf[4]: The thoughts of these things in the particulars of them, and of the love and goodness of God towards us, make it true of me, what David said of himself, Psal. 6.6 *I watered my Couch with my tears.* Oh! the wonderful power of God that mine eyes have seen, affording matter enough for my thoughts to run in, that when others are sleeping mine eyes are weeping.

---

1. June 9, 1676.
2. Jeremiah xxi:16.
3. Psalm lxxxi:16.
4. Luke xv:23.

I have seen the extreme vanity of this world: One hour I have been in health, and wealth, wanting nothing: But the next hour in sickness and wounds, and death, having nothing but sorrow and affliction.

Before I knew what affliction meant, I was ready sometimes to wish for it. When I lived in prosperity, having the comforts of the world about me, my relations by me, my heart cheerful, and taking little care for anything; and yet seeing many, whom I preferred before my self, under many trials and afflictions, in sickness, weakness, poverty, losses, crosses, and cares of the world, I should be sometimes jealous least I should have my portion in this life, and that scripture would come to my mind, Heb. 12.6. *For whom the Lord loveth he chasteneth, and scourgeth every Son whom he receiveth.* But now I see the Lord had his time to scourge and chasten me. The portion of some is to have their afflictions by drops, now one drop and then another; but the dregs of the cup, the wine of astonishment, like a sweeping rain that leaveth no food, did the Lord prepare to be my portion. Affliction I wanted, and affliction I had, full measure (I thought) pressed down and running over; yet I see, when God calls a person to anything, and though never so many difficulties, yet he is fully able to carry them through and make them see, and say they have been gainers thereby: And I hope I can say in some measure, As David did, *It is good for me that I have been afflicted.*[5] The Lord hath showed me the vanity of these outward things. That they are the vanity of vanities, and vexation of spirit; that they are but a shadow, a blast, a bubble, and things of no continuance. That we must rely on God himself, and our whole dependence must be upon him. If trouble from smaller matters begins to arise in me, I have something at hand to check myself with, and say, why am I troubled? It was but the other day that if I had had the world, I would have given it for my freedom, or to have been a servant to a Christian. I have learned to look beyond present and smaller troubles, and to be quieted under them, as Moses said, Exod. 14. 13. *Stand still and see the salvation of the Lord.*

Finis.

---

5. Psalm cxix:71.

James Smith
(1737–1812)

James Smith was born on the frontier in Franklin County, Pennsylvania. At eighteen he joined a crew cutting a road across the Alleghenies for the use of General Edward Braddock's troops in their planned assault on Fort Duquesne. Captured shortly before Braddock's defeat, he spent four years living with the Indians, finally escaping in 1759 and making his way back to his family in 1760. Later he married, had seven children, and after his wife's death married again, a widow with five children. He was at times an Indian fighter, both in the service of the English and as a leader of an irregular group of rangers who defied British law in their attempts to assert the rights of the western pioneers. He served in the Revolutionary War, attaining the rank of colonel in 1778, and in 1788 settled in Kentucky. In later years he was a missionary to the Indians of Tennessee.

Smith kept a journal during his captivity and revised it shortly after his return, but waited almost forty years to publish his account, believing, he said, that "at that time the Americans were so little acquainted with Indian affairs I apprehended a great part of it would be viewed as fable or romance." An Account of the Remarkable Occurrences in the Life and Travels of Col. James Smith (1799) tells the story of his captivity and adds material on his later life and campaigns.

The source of the present text is the Ohio Valley Historical Series reprinting of Smith's *Account* (1870), with an appendix by W. M. Darlington. Spelling has been normalized. Smith also wrote two pamphlets attacking the Shakers (*Remarkable Occurrences* and *Shakerism Detected*, both 1810) and *A Treatise on the Mode and Manner of Indian War* (1812).

[From] an Account of the Remarkable Occurrences in the Life and Travels of Col. James Smith

IN MAY 1755, the province of Pennsylvania agreed to send out three hundred men in order to cut a wagon road from Fort Loudon,[1] to join Braddock's road,[2] near the Turkey Foot; or three forks of Yohogania.[3] My brother-in-law, William Smith esq. of Conococheague, was appointed commissioner, to have the oversight of these road-cutters.

Though I was at that time only eighteen years of age, I had fallen violently in love with a young lady, whom I apprehended was possessed of a large share of both beauty and virtue; but being born between Venus and Mars, I concluded I must also leave my dear fair one, and go out with this company of road-cutters, to see the event of this campaign; but still expecting that some time in the course of this summer I should again return to the arms of my beloved.

We went on with the road, without interruption, until near the Allegheny Mountain; when I was sent back, in order to hurry up some provision wagons that were on the way after us; I proceeded down the road as far as the crossings of Juniata, where, finding the wagons were coming on as fast as possible, I returned up the road again towards the Allegheny Mountain, in company with one Arnold Vigoras. About four or five miles above Bedford, three Indians had made a blind of bushes, stuck in the ground, as though they grew naturally, where they concealed themselves, about fifteen yards from the road. When we came opposite to them, they fired upon us, at this short distance, and killed my fellow traveller, yet their bullets did not touch me; but my horse making a violent start, threw me, and the Indians immediately ran up, and took me prisoner. The one that laid hold on me was a Canasatauga, the other two were Delawares. One of them could speak English, and asked me if there were any more white men coming after? I told them not any near, that I knew of. Two of these Indians stood by me, whilst the other scalped my comrade: they then set off and ran at a smart rate, through the woods, for about fifteen miles, and that night we slept on the Allegheny Mountain, without fire.

The next morning they divided the last of their provision which they had brought from Fort DuQuesne, and gave me an equal share, which was about two or three ounces of mouldy biscuit—this and a young groundhog,

---

1. Near Chambersburg, Pennsylvania.

2. Extending westward from Cumberland, Maryland, over the route that was to become the National Road.

3. The Youghiogheny River.

about as large as a rabbit, roasted, and also equally divided, was all the provision we had until we came to the Loyal-Hannan, which was about fifty miles; and a great part of the way we came through exceeding rocky laurel-thickets, without any path. When we came to the west side of Laurel Hill, they gave the scalp halloo, as usual, which is a long yell or halloo, for every scalp or prisoner they have in possession; the last of these scalp halloos was followed with quick and sudden, shrill shouts of joy and triumph. On their performing this, we were answered by the firing of a number of guns on the Loyal-Hannan, one after another, quicker than one could count, by another party of Indians, who were encamped near where Ligoneer[4] now stands. As we advanced near this party, they increased with repeated shouts of joy and triumph; but I did not share with them in their excessive mirth. When we came to this camp, we found they had plenty of turkeys and other meat, there; and though I never before eat venison without bread or salt, yet as I was hungry, it relished very well. There we lay that night, and the next morning the whole of us marched on our way for Fort DuQuesne. The night after we joined another camp of Indians, with nearly the same ceremony, attended with great noise, and apparent joy, among all, except one. The next morning we continued our march, and in the afternoon we came in full view of the fort, which stood on the point, near where Fort Pitt now stands. We then made a halt on the bank of the Allegheny, and repeated the scalp halloo, which was answered by the firing of all the firelocks in the hands of both Indians and French who were in and about the fort, in the aforesaid manner, and also the great guns, which were followed by the continued shouts and yells of the different savage tribes who were then collected there.

As I was at this time unacquainted with this mode of firing and yelling of the savages, I concluded that there were thousands of Indians there, ready to receive General Braddock; but what added to my surprise, I saw numbers running towards me, stripped naked, excepting breech-clouts, and painted in the most hideous manner, of various colors, though the principal color was vermillion, or a bright red; yet there was annexed to this, black, brown, blue, &c. As they approached, they formed themselves into two long ranks, about two or three rods apart. I was told by an Indian that could speak English, that I must run betwixt these ranks, and that they would flog me all the way, as I ran, and if I ran quick, it would be so much the better, as they would quit when I got to the end of the ranks. There appeared to be a general rejoicing around me, yet I could find nothing like joy in my breast; but I started to the race with all the resolution and vigor I was capable of exerting, and found that it was as I had been told, for I was flogged the whole way. When I had got near the end of the lines, I was struck with something that appeared to me to be a stick, or the handle of a tomahawk, which caused me to fall to the ground. On my recovering my senses, I endeavored to renew my race; but as I arose, some one cast sand in my eyes, which blinded me so, that I could not see where to run. They continued beating me most intolera-

---

4. Ligonier, Pennsylvania, on the Loyalhanna creek, twenty miles west of Johnstown.

bly, until I was at length insensible; but before I lost my senses, I remember my wishing them to strike the fatal blow, for I thought they intended killing me, but apprehended they were too long about it.

The first thing I remember was my being in the fort, amidst the French and Indians, and a French doctor standing by me, who had opened a vein in my left arm: after which the interpreter asked me how I did, I told him I felt much pain; the doctor then washed my wounds, and the bruised places of my body, with French brandy. As I felt faint, and the brandy smelt well, I asked for some inwardly, but the doctor told me, by the interpreter, that it did not suit my case.

When they found I could speak, a number of Indians came around me, and examined me with threats of cruel death, if I did not tell the truth. The first question they asked me, was, how many men were there in the party that were coming from Pennsylvania, to join Braddock? I told them the truth, that there were three hundred. The next question was, were they well armed? I told them they were all well armed, (meaning the arm of flesh) for they had only about thirty guns among the whole of them; which, if the Indians had known, they would certainly have gone and cut them all off; therefore I could not in conscience let them know the defenseless situation of these road-cutters. I was then sent to the hospital, and carefully attended by the doctors, and recovered quicker than what I expected.

Some time after I was there, I was visited by the Delaware Indian already mentioned, who was at the taking of me, and could speak some English. Though he spoke but bad English, yet I found him to be a man of considerable understanding. I asked him if I had done any thing that had offended the Indians, which caused them to treat me so unmercifully? He said no, it was only an old custom the Indians had, and it was like how do you do; after that he said I would be well used. I asked him if I should be admitted to remain with the French? He said no—and told me that as soon as I recovered, I must not only go with the Indians, but must be made an Indian myself. I asked him what news from Braddock's army? He said the Indians spied them every day, and he showed me by making marks on the ground with a stick, that Braddock's army was advancing in very close order, and that the Indians would surround them, take trees, and (as he expressed it) *Shoot um down all one pigeon.*

Shortly after this, on the 9th day of July 1755, in the morning I heard a great stir in the fort. As I could then walk with a staff in my hand, I went out of the door which was just by the wall of the fort, and stood upon the wall and viewed the Indians in a huddle before the gate, where were barrels of powder, bullets, flints &c., and every one taking what suited; I saw the Indians also march off in rank entire—likewise the French Canadians, and some regulars. After viewing the Indians and French in different positions, I computed them to be about four hundred, and wondered that they attempted to go out against Braddock with so small a party. I was then in high hopes that I would soon see them flying before the British troops, and that General Braddock would take the fort and rescue me.

I remained anxious to know the event of this day; and in the afternoon I again observed a great noise and commotion in the fort, and though at that time I could not understand French, yet I found it was the voice of joy and triumph, and feared that they had received what I called bad news.

I had observed some of the old country soldiers speak Dutch, as I spoke Dutch I went to one of them and asked him what was the news? he told me that a runner had just arrived, who said that Braddock would certainly be defeated; that the Indians and French had surrounded him, and were concealed behind trees and in gullies, and kept a constant fire upon the English, and that they saw the English falling in heaps, and if they did not take the river which was the only gap, and make their escape, there would not be one man left alive before sundown. Some time after this I heard a number of scalp halloo's and saw a company of Indians and French coming in. I observed they had a great many bloody scalps, grenadiers' caps, British canteens, bayonets &c. with them. They brought the news that Braddock was defeated. After that another company came in which appeared to be about one hundred, and chiefly Indians, and it seemed to me that almost every one of this company was carrying scalps; after this came another company with a number of wagon-horses, and also a great many scalps. Those that were coming in, and those that had arrived, kept a constant firing of small arms, and also the great guns in the fort, which were accompanied with the most hideous shouts and yells from all quarters; so that it appeared to me as if the infernal regions had broke loose.

About sundown I beheld a small party coming in with about a dozen prisoners, stripped naked, with their hands tied behind their backs, and their faces, and part of their bodies blacked—these prisoners they burned to death on the bank of Allegheny River opposite to the fort. I stood on the fort wall until I beheld them begin to burn one of these men, they had him tied to a stake and kept touching him with fire-brands, red-hot irons &c. and he screaming in a most doleful manner,—the Indians in the meantime yelling like infernal spirits. As this scene appeared too shocking for me to behold, I retired to my lodging both sore and sorry.

When I came into my lodgings I saw Russel's *Seven Sermons*, which they had brought from the field of battle, which a Frenchman made a present of to me. From the best information I could receive there were only seven Indians and four French killed in this battle, and five hundred British lay dead in the field; besides what were killed in the river on their retreat.

The morning after the battle I saw Braddock's artillery brought into the fort, the same day I also saw several Indians in British officers' dress with sash, half-moon, laced hats &c. which the British then wore.

A few days after this the Indians demanded me and I was obliged to go with them. I was not yet well able to march, but they took me in a canoe, up the Allegheny River to an Indian town[5] that was on the north side of the river, about forty miles above Fort DuQuesne. Here I remained about three

---

5. Now Kittanning, Pennsylvania.

weeks, and was then taken to an Indian town on the west branch of Musk-ingum, about twenty miles above the forks, which was called Tullihas,[6] inhabited by Delawares, Caughnewagas and Mohicans.—On our route betwixt the aforesaid towns, the country was chiefly black-oak and white-oak land, which appeared generally to be good wheat land, chiefly second and third rate, intermixed with some rich bottoms.

The day after my arrival at the aforesaid town, a number of Indians col-lected about me, and one of them began to pull the hair out of my head. He had some ashes on a piece of bark, in which he frequently dipped his fingers in order to take the firmer hold, and so he went on, as if he had been pluck-ing a turkey, until he had all the hair clean out of my head, except a small spot about three or four inches square on my crown; this they cut off with a pair of scissors, excepting three locks, which they dressed up in their own mode. Two of these they wrapped round with a narrow beaded garter made by themselves for that purpose, and the other they platted at full length, and then stuck it full of silver brooches. After this they bored my nose and ears, and fixed me off with ear rings and nose jewels, then they ordered me to strip off my clothes and put on a breechclout, which I did; then they painted my head, face and body in various colors. They put a large belt of wampum on my neck, and silver bands on my hands and right arm; and so an old chief led me out in the street and gave the alarm halloo, *coo-wigh,* several times repeated quick, and on this all that were in the town came running and stood round the old chief, who held me by the hand in the midst. As I at that time knew nothing of their mode of adoption, and had seen them put to death all they had taken, and as I never could find that they saved a man alive at Braddock's defeat, I made no doubt but they were about putting me to death in some cruel manner. The old chief holding me by the hand made a long speech very loud, and when he had done he handed me to three young squaws, who led me by the hand down the bank into the river until the water was up to our middle. The squaws then made signs to me to plunge myself into the water, but I did not understand them; I thought that the result of the council was that I should be drowned, and that these young ladies were to be the executioners. They all three laid violent hold of me, and I for some time opposed them with all my might; which occasioned loud laughter by the multitude that were on the bank of the river. At length one of the squaws made out to speak a little English (for I believe they began to be afraid of me) and said, *no hurt you;* on this I gave myself up to their ladyships, who were as good as their word; for though they plunged me under water, and washed and rubbed me severely, yet I could not say they hurt me much.

These young women then led me up to the council house, where some of the tribe were ready with new clothes for me. They gave me a new ruffled shirt, which I put on, also a pair of leggings done off with ribbons and beads, likewise a pair of moccasins, and garters dressed with beads, porcupine-

---

6. Near Coshocton, Ohio.

quills, and red hair—also a tinsel laced cap. They again painted my head and face with various colors, and tied a bunch of red feathers to one of these locks they had left on the crown of my head, which stood up five or six inches. They seated me on a bear skin, and gave me a pipe, tomahawk, and polecat skin pouch, which had been skinned pocket fashion, and contained tobacco, killegenico, or dry sumach leaves, which they mix with their tobacco,—also spunk, flint and steel. When I was thus seated, the Indians came in dressed and painted in their grandest manner. As they came in they took their seats and for a considerable time there was a profound silence, every one was smoking,—but not a word was spoken among them.—At length one of the chiefs made a speech which was delivered to me by an interpreter,—and was as followeth:—"My son, you are now flesh of our flesh, and bone of our bone. By the ceremony which was performed this day, every drop of white blood was washed out of your veins; you are taken into the Caughnewago nation, and initiated into a warlike tribe; you are adopted into a great family, and now received with great seriousness and solemnity in the room and place of a great man; after what has passed this day, you are now one of us by an old strong law and custom—My son, you have now nothing to fear, we are now under the same obligations to love, support and defend you, that we are to love and defend one another, therefore you are to consider yourself as one of our people."—At this time I did not believe this fine speech, especially that of the white blood being washed out of me; but since that time I have found that there was much sincerity in said speech,— for from that day I never knew them to make any distinction between me and themselves in any respect whatever until I left them.—If they had plenty of clothing I had plenty, if we were scarce we all shared one fate.

* * *

Though the Indians had given me a gun, I had not yet been admitted to go out from the camp to hunt. At this place[7] Mohawk Solomon[8] asked me to go out with him to hunt, which I readily agreed to. After some time we came upon some fresh buffalo tracks. I had observed before this that the Indians were upon their guard, and afraid of an enemy; for, until now they and the southern nations had been at war. As we were following the buffalo tracks, Solomon seemed to be upon his guard, went very slow, and would frequently stand and listen, and appeared to be in suspense. We came to where the tracks were very plain in the sand, and I said it is surely buffalo tracks; he said *hush, you know nothing, may be buffalo tracks, may be Catawba.* He went very cautious until we found some fresh buffalo dung: he then smiled and said *Catawba can not make so.* He then stopped and told me an odd story about the Catawbas. He said that formerly the Catawbas came near one of their hunting camps, and at some distance from the camp lay in ambush, and in order to decoy them out, sent two or three Catawbas

---

7. Near Newark, Ohio.

8. Identified earlier by Smith as a chief whose Indian name was Afallecoa.

in the night, past their camp, with buffalo hoofs fixed on their feet, so as to make artificial tracks. In the morning those in the camp followed after these tracks, thinking they were buffalo, until they were fired on by the Catawbas, and several of them killed; the others fled, collected a party and pursued the Catawbas; but they in their subtlety brought with them rattlesnake poison, which they had collected from the bladder that lieth at the root of the snakes' teeth; this they had corked up in a short piece of cane-stalk; they had also brought with them small cane or reed, about the size of a rye straw, which they made sharp at the end like a pen, and dipped them in this poison, and stuck them in the ground among the grass, along their own tracks, in such a position that they might stick into the legs of the pursuers, which answered the design; and as the Catawbas had runners behind to watch the motions of the pursuers, when they found that a number of them were lame, being artifically snake bit, and that they were all turning back, the Catawbas turned upon the pursuers, and defeated them, and killed and scalped all those that were lame.—When Solomon had finished this story, and found that I understood him, [he] concluded by saying, *you don't know, Catawba velly bad Indian, Catawba all one Devil Catawba.*

Some time after this, I was told to take the dogs with me and go down the creek, perhaps I might kill a turkey; it being in the afternoon, I was also told not to go far from the creek, and to come up the creek again to the camp, and to take care not to get lost. When I had gone some distance down the creek I came upon fresh buffalo tracks, and as I had a number of dogs with me to stop the buffalo, I concluded I would follow after and kill one; and as the grass and weeds were rank, I could readily follow the track. A little before sundown, I despaired of coming up with them: I was then thinking how I might get to camp before night; I concluded as the buffalo had made several turns, if I took the track back to the creek, it would be dark before I could get to camp; therefore I thought I would take a near way through the hills, and strike the creek a little below the camp; but as it was cloudy weather, and I a very young woodsman, I could find neither creek or camp. When night came on I fired my gun several times, and hallooed, but could have no answer. The next morning early, the Indians were out after me, and as I had with me ten or a dozen dogs, and the grass and weeds rank, they could readily follow my track. When they came up with me, they appeared to be in a very good humor. I asked Solomon if he thought I was running away, he said *no no, you go too much clooked.* On my return to camp they took my gun from me, and for this rash step I was reduced to a bow and arrows, for near two years.

* * *

After the departure of these warriors[9] we had hard times, and tho we were not altogether out of provisions we were brought to short allowance.

---

9. In the winter, with game scarce, the warriors decided on a raid in search of horses, to help with the hunting.

At length Tontileaugo[1] had considerable success; and we had meat brought into camp sufficient to last ten days. Tontileaugo then took me with him in order to encamp some distance from this winter cabin,[2] to try his luck there. We carried no provision with us, he said we would leave what was there for the squaws and children, and that we could shift for ourselves. We steered about a south course up the waters of this creek, and encamped about ten or twelve miles from the winter cabin. As it was still cold weather and a crust upon the snow, which made a noise as we walked and alarmed the deer, we could kill nothing, and consequently went to sleep without supper. The only chance we had under these circumstances, was to hunt bear holes; as the bears about Christmas search out a winter lodging place, where they lie about three or four months without eating or drinking. This may appear to some incredible; but it is now well known to be the case, by those who live in the remote western parts of North America.

The next morning early we proceeded on, and when we found a tree scratched by the bears climbing up, and the hole in the tree sufficiently large for the reception of the bear; we then fell a sapling or small tree against or near the hole; and it was my business to climb up and drive out the bear, while Tontileaugo stood ready with his gun and bow. We went on in this manner until evening, without success; at length we found a large elm scratched, and a hole in it about forty feet up; but no tree nigh suitable to lodge against the hole. Tontileaugo got a long pole and some dry rotten wood which he tied in bunches, with bark, and as there was a tree that grew near the elm, and extended up near the hole; but leaned the wrong way; so that we could not lodge it to advantage; but to remedy this inconvenience, he climbed up this tree and carried with him his rotten wood, fire and pole. The rotten wood he tied to his belt, and to one end of the pole he tied a hook, and a piece of rotten wood which he set fire to, as it would retain fire almost like spunk; and reached this hook from limb to limb as he went up; when he got up, with this pole he put dry wood on fire into the hole, after he put in the fire he heard the bear snuff and he came speedily down, took his gun in his hand and waited until the bear would come out; but it was some time before it appeared, and when it did appear he attempted taking sight with his rifle, but it being then too dark to see the sights, he set it down by a tree, and instantly bent his bow, took hold of an arrow, and shot the bear a little behind the shoulder; I was preparing also to shoot an arrow, but he called to me to stop, there was no occasion; and with that the bear fell to the ground.

Being very hungry we kindled a fire, opened the bear, took out the liver, and wrapped some of the caul fat round and put it on a wooden spit which we stuck in the ground by the fire to roast, we then skinned the bear, got on our kettle, and had both roast and boiled, and also sauce to our meat, which appeared to me to be delicate fare. After I was fully satisfied I went to sleep,

---

1. Smith's adopted brother.
2. They had camped for the winter in or near the present Hinckley or Royalton, Ohio.

Tontileaugo awoke me, saying, come eat hearty, we have got meat plenty now.

The next morning we cut down a lynn tree, peeled bark and made a snug little shelter, facing the southeast, with a large log betwixt us and the north west; we made a good fire before us, and scaffolded up our meat at one side.—When we had finished our camp we went out to hunt, searched two trees for bears, but to no purpose. As the snow thawed a little in the afternoon, Tontileaugo killed a deer, which we carried with us to camp.

The next day we turned out to hunt, and near the camp we found a tree well scratched; but the hole was above forty feet high, and no tree that we could lodge against the hole; but finding that it was very hollow, we concluded that we would cut down the tree with our tomahawks, which kept us working a considerable part of the day. When the tree fell we ran up, Tontileaugo with his gun and bow, and I with my bow ready bent. Tontileaugo shot the bear through with his rifle, a little behind the shoulders, I also shot, but too far back; and not being then much accustomed to the business, my arrow penetrated only a few inches through the skin. Having killed an old she bear and three cubs, we hauled her on the snow to the camp, and only had time afterwards, to get wood, make a fire, cook &c. before dark.

Early the next morning we went to business, searched several trees, but found no bears. On our way home we took three racoons out of a hollow elm, not far from the ground.

We remained here about two weeks, and in this time killed four bears, three deer, several turkeys, and a number of racoons. We packed up as much meat as we could carry, and returned to our winter cabin. On our arrival, there was great joy, as they were all in a starving condition,—the three hunters that we had left having killed but very little.—All that could carry a pack repaired to our camp to bring in meat.

Some time in February the four warriors returned, who had taken two scalps, and six horses from the frontiers of Pennsylvania. The hunters could then scatter out a considerable distance from the winter cabin, and encamp, kill meat and pack it in upon horses; so that we commonly after this had plenty of provision.

* * *

When we were ready to embark, Tontileaugo would not go to town, but go up the river and take a hunt. He asked me if I choosed to go with him? I told him I did. We then got some sugar, bears oil bottled up in a bear's gut, and some dry venison, which we packed up, and went up Canesadooharie,[3] about thirty miles, and encamped. At this time I did not know either the day of the week or the month; but I supposed it to be about the first of April. We had considerable success in our business. We also found some stray horses, or a horse, mare, and a young colt; and though they had run in the woods all winter, they were in exceeding good order. There is plenty of grass here all

---

3. The Black River, Lorain County, Ohio.

winter, under the snow, and horses accustomed to the woods can work it out.—These horses had run in the woods until they were very wild.

Tontileaugo one night concluded that we must run them down. I told him I thought we could not accomplish it. He said he had run down bears, buffaloes and elks: and in the great plains, with only a small snow on the ground, he had run down a deer; and he thought that in one whole day, he could tire, or run down any four footed animal except a wolf. I told him that though a deer was the swiftest animal to run a short distance, yet it would tire sooner than a horse. He said he would at all events try the experiment. He had heard the Wiandots say, that I could run well, and now he would see whether I could or not. I told him that I never had run all day, and of course was not accustomed to that way of running. I never had run with the Wiandots more than seven or eight miles at one time. He said that was nothing, we must either catch these horses or run all day.

In the morning early we left camp, and about sunrise we started after them, stripped naked excepting breechclouts and moccasins. About ten o'clock I lost sight of both Tontileaugo and the horses, and did not see them again until about three o'clock in the afternoon. As the horses run all day, in about three or four miles square, at length they passed where I was, and I fell in close after them. As I then had a long rest, I endeavored to keep ahead of Tontileaugo, and after some time I could hear him after me calling *chakoh, chakoanaugh*, which signifies, pull away or do your best. We pursued on, and after some time Tontileaugo passed me, and about an hour before sundown, we despaired of catching these horses and returned to camp where we had left our clothes.

I reminded Tontileaugo of what I had told him; he replied he did not know what horses could do. They are wonderful strong to run; but withal we made them very tired. Tontileaugo then concluded, he would do as the Indians did with wild horses, when out at war: which is to shoot them through the neck under the name, and above the bone, which will cause them to fall and lie until they can halter them, and then they recover again. This he attempted to do; but as the mare was very wild, he could not get sufficiently nigh to shoot her in the proper place; however he shot, the ball passed too low, and killed her. As the horse and colt stayed at this place, we caught the horse, and took him and the colt with us to camp.

* * *

I went out with Tecaughretanego,[4] and some others a beaver hunting: but we did not succeed, and on our return we saw where several racoons had passed, while the snow was soft; tho' there was now a crust upon it, we all made a halt looking at the racoon tracks. As they saw a tree with a hole in it they told me to go and see if they had gone in thereat; and if they had to halloo, and they would come and take them out. When I went to that tree I

---

4. At this point, Smith has left Tontileaugo and gone on a hunt with an elderly adopted brother, Tecaughretanego.

found they had gone past; but I saw another the way they had went, and proceeded to examine that, and found they had gone up it. I then began to halloo, but could have no answer.

As it began to snow and blow most violently, I returned and proceeded after my company, and for some time could see their tracks; but the old snow being only about three inches deep, and a crust upon it, the present driving snow soon filled up the tracks. As I had only a bow, arrows, and tomahawk, with me, and no way to strike fire, I appeared to be in a dismal situation—and as the air was dark with snow, I had little more prospect of steering my course, than I would in the night. At length I came to a hollow tree, with a hole at one side that I could go in at. I went in, and found that it was a dry place, and the hollow about three feet diameter, and high enough for me to stand in. I found that there was also a considerable quantity of soft, dry rotten wood, around this hollow: I therefore concluded that I would lodge here; and that I would go to work, and stop up the door of my house. I stripped off my blanket, (which was all the clothes that I had, excepting a breech-clout, leggings, and moccasins) and with my tomahawk fell to chopping at the top of a fallen tree that lay near and carried wood and set it up on end against the door, until I had it three or four feet thick, all round, excepting a hole I had left to creep in at. I had a block prepared that I could haul after me, to stop this hole: and before I went in I put in a number of small sticks, that I might more effectually stop it on the inside. When I went in, I took my tomahawk and cut down all the dry, rotten wood I could get, and beat it small. With it I made a bed like a goose-nest or hog-bed, and with the small sticks stopped every hole, until my house was almost dark. I stripped off my moccasins, and danced in the center of my bed for about half an hour, in order to warm myself. In this time my feet and whole body were agreeably warmed. The snow, in the mean while, had stopped all the holes, so that my house was as dark as a dungeon; though I knew it could not yet be dark out of doors. I then coiled myself up in my blanket, lay down in my little round bed, and had a tolerable nights lodging. When I awoke, all was dark— not the least glimmering of light was to be seen. Immediately I recollected that I was not to expect light in this new habitation, as there was neither door nor window in it. As I could hear the storm raging, and did not suffer much cold, as I was then situated, I concluded I would stay in my nest until I was certain it was day. When I had reason to conclude that it surely was day, I arose and put on my moccasins, which I had laid under my head to keep from freezing. I then endeavored to find the door, and had to do all by the sense of feeling, which took me some time. At length I found the block, but it being heavy, and a large quantity of snow having fallen on it, at the first attempt I did not move it. I then felt terrified—among all the hardships I had sustained, I never knew before, what it was to be thus deprived of light. This, with the other circumstances attending it, appeared grievous. I went straightway to bed again, wrapped my blanket round me, and lay and mused awhile, and then prayed to Almighty God to direct and protect me, as he had done heretofore. I once again attempted to move away the block, which proved successful: it moved about nine inches. With this a considerable quantity of snow fell in from above, and I immediately received light; so that I found a very great snow had fallen, above what I had ever seen in one night. I then knew why I could not easily move the block, and I was so rejoiced at obtaining the light, that all my other difficulties seemed to vanish. I then turned into my cell, and returned God thanks for having once more received the light of Heaven. At length I belted my blanket about me, got my tomahawk, bow and arrows, and went out of my den.

I was now in tolerable high spirits, tho' the snow had fallen above three feet deep, in addition to what was on the ground before; and the only imperfect guide I had, in order to steer my course to camp, was the trees; as the moss generally grows on the north-west side of them, if they are straight. I proceeded on, wading through the snow, and about twelve o'clock (as it appeared afterwards, from that time to night, for it was yet cloudy) I came upon the creek that our camp was on, about half a mile below the camp; and when I came in sight of the camp, I found that there was great joy, by the shouts and yelling of the boys, &c.

When I arrived, they all came round me, and received me gladly; but at this time no questions were asked, and I was taken into a tent, where they gave me plenty of fat beaver meat, and then asked me to smoke. When I had done, Tecaughretanego desired me to walk out to a fire they had made. I went out, and they all collected round me, both men, women, and boys. Tecaughretanego asked me to give them a particular account of what had happened from the time they left me yesterday, until now. I told them the whole of the story, and they never interrupted me; but when I made a stop, the intervals were filled with loud acclamations of joy. As I could not, at this time, talk Ottawa or Jibewa well, (which is nearly the same) I delivered my story in Caughnewaga. As my sister Molly's husband was a Jibewa and could understand Caughnewaga, he acted as interpreter, and delivered my story to the Jibewas and Ottawas, which they received with pleasure. When all this was done, Tecaughretanego made a speech to me in the following manner:

"Brother,

"You see we have prepared snow shoes to go after you, and were almost ready to go, when you appeared; yet, as you had not been accustomed to hardships in your country, to the east, we never expected to see you alive. Now, we are glad to see you, in various respects; we are glad to see you on your own account; and we are glad to see the prospect of your filling the place of a great man, in whose room you were adopted. We do not blame you for what has happened, we blame ourselves; because, we did not think of this driving snow filling up the tracks, until after we came to camp.

"Brother,

"Your conduct on this occasion hath pleased us much: You have given us an evidence of your fortitude, skill and resolution: and we hope you will always go on to do great actions, as it is only great actions that can make a great man."

I told my brother Tecaughretanego, that I thanked them for their care of me, and for the kindness I always received. I told him that I always wished to do great actions, and hoped I never would do any thing to dishonor any of those with whom I was connected. I likewise told my Jibewa brother-in-law to tell his people that I also thanked them for their care and kindness.

*   *   *

Tecaughretanego who had been a first rate warrior, statesman and hunter; and though he was now near sixty years of age, he was yet equal to the common run of hunters, but subject to the rheumatism, which deprived him of the use of his legs.

Shortly after Tontileaugo left us, Tecaughretanego became lame, and could scarcely walk out of our hut for two months. I had considerable success in hunting and trapping. Though Tecaughretanego endured much pain and misery, yet he bore it all with wonderful patience, and would often endeavor to entertain me with chearful conversation. Sometimes he would applaud me for my diligence, skill and activity—and at other times he would take great care in giving me instructions concerning the hunting and trapping business. He would also tell me that if I failed of success, we would suffer very much, as we were about forty miles from any one living, that we knew of; yet he would not intimate that he apprehended we were in any danger, but still supposed that I was fully adequate to the task.

Tontileaugo left us a little before Christmas, and from that until some time in February, we had always plenty of bear meat, venison, &c. During this time I killed much more than we could use, but having no horses to carry in what I killed, I left part of it in the woods. In February there came a snow, with a crust, which made a great noise when walking on it, and frightened away the deer; and as bear and beaver were scarce here, we got entirely out of provision. After I had hunted two days without eating any thing, and had very short allowance for some days before, I returned late in the evening faint and weary. When I came into out hut, Tecaughretanego asked what success? I told him not any. He asked me if I was not very hungry? I replied that the keen appetite seemed to be in some measure removed, but I was both faint and weary. He commanded Nunganey his little son, to bring me something to eat, and he brought me a kettle with some bones and broth—after eating a few mouthfuls my appetite violently returned, and I thought the victuals had a most agreeable realish, though it was only fox and wildcat bones, which lay about the camp, which the ravens and turkey-buzzards had picked—these Nunganey had collected and boiled, until the sinews that remained on the bones would strip off. I speedily finished my allowance, such as it was, and when I had ended my *sweet* repast, Tecaughretanego asked me how I felt? I told him that I was much refreshed. He then handed me his pipe and pouch, and told me to take a smoke. I did so. He then said he had something of importance to tell me, if I was now composed and ready to hear it. I told him that I was ready to hear him. He said the reason why he deferred his speech till now, was because few men are in a right humor to hear good talk, when they are extremely hungry, as they are then generally fretful and discomposed; but as you appear now to enjoy calmness and serenity of mind, I will now communicate to you the thoughts of my heart, and those things that I know to be true.

"*Brother,*

"As you have lived with the white people, you have not had the same advantage of knowing that the great being above feeds his people, and gives them their meat in due season, as we Indians have, who are frequently out of provisions, and yet are wonderfully supplied, and that so frequently that it is evidently the hand of the great Owaneeyo[5] that doth this: whereas the white people have commonly large stocks of tame cattle, that they can kill when they please, and also their barns and cribs filled with grain, and therefore have not the same opportunity of seeing and knowing that they are supported by the ruler of Heaven and Earth.

"*Brother,*

"I know that you are now afraid that we will all perish with hunger, but you have no just reason to fear this.

"*Brother,*

"I have been young, but am now old—I have been frequently under the like circumstance that we now are, and that some time or other in almost every year of my life; yet, I have hitherto been supported, and my wants supplied in time of need.

"*Brother,*

"Owaneeyo some times suffers us to be in want, in order to teach us our dependance upon him, and to let us know that we are to love and serve him: and likewise to know the worth of the favors that we receive, and to make us more thankful.

"*Brother,*

"Be assured that you will be supplied with food, and that just in the right time; but you must continue diligent in the use of means—go to sleep, and rise early in the morning and go a hunting—be strong and exert yourself like a man, and the great spirit will direct your way."

The next morning I went out, and steered about an east course. I proceeded on slowly for about five miles, and saw deer frequently, but as the crust on the snow made a great noise, they were always running before I spied them, so that I could not get a shoot. A violent appetite returned, and I became intolerably hungry;—it was now that I concluded I would run off to Pennsylvania, my native country. As the snow was on the ground, and Indian hunters almost the whole of the way before me, I had but a poor prospect of making my escape; but my case appeared desperate. If I staid here I thought I would perish with hunger, and if I met with Indians, they could but kill me.

I then proceeded on as fast as I could walk, and when I got about ten or

---

5. This is the name of God, in their tongue, and signifies the owner and ruler of all things. [Smith's note]

twelve miles from our hut, I came upon fresh buffalo tracks,—I pursued after, and in a short time came in sight of them, as they were passing through a small glade—I ran with all my might, and headed them, where I lay in ambush, and killed a very large cow. I immediately kindled a fire and began to roast meat, but could not wait till it was done—I ate it almost raw. When hunger was abated I began to be tenderly concerned for my old Indian brother, and the little boy I had left in a perishing condition. I made haste and packed up what meat I could carry, secured what I left from the wolves, and returned homewards.

I scarcely thought on the old man's speech while I was almost distracted with hunger, but on my return was much affected with it, reflected on myself for my hard-heartedness and ingratitude, in attempting to run off and leave the venerable old man and little boy to perish with hunger. I also considered how remarkably the old man's speech had been verified in our providentially obtaining a supply. I thought also of that part of his speech which treated of the fractious dispositions of hungry people, which was the only excuse I had for my base inhumanity, in attempting to leave them in the most deplorable situation.

As it was moon-light, I got home to our hut, and found the old man in his usual good humor. He thanked me for my exertion, and bid me sit down, as I must certainly be fatigued, and he commanded Nunganey to make haste and cook. I told him I would cook for him, and let the boy lay some meat on the coals, for himself—which he did, but ate it almost raw, as I had done. I immediately hung on the kettle with some water, and cut the beef in thin slices, and put them in:—when it had boiled awhile, I proposed taking it off the fire, but the old man replied, "let it be done enough." This he said in as patient and unconcerned a manner, as if he had not wanted one single meal. He commanded Nunganey to eat no more beef at that time, lest he might hurt himself; but told him to sit down, and after some time he might sup some broth—this command he reluctantly obeyed.

When we were all refreshed, Tecaughretanego delivered a speech upon the necessity and pleasure of receiving the necessary supports of life with thankfulness, knowing that Owaneeyo is the great giver. Such speeches from an Indian, may be tho't by those who are unacquainted with them, altogether incredible; but when we reflect on the Indian war, we may readily conclude that they are not an ignorant or stupid sort of people, or they would not have been such fatal enemies. When they came into our country they outwitted us—and when we sent armies into their country, they out-generalled, and beat us with inferior force. Let us also take into consideration that Tecaughretanego was no common person, but was among the Indians, as Socrates in the ancient Heathen world; and it may be, equal to him—if not in wisdom and learning, yet, perhaps in patience and fortitude. Notwithstanding Tecaughretanego's uncommon natural abilities, yet in the sequel of this history you will see the deficiency of the light of nature, unaided by revelation, in this truly great man.

The next morning Tecaughretanego desired me to go back and bring another load of buffalo beef: As I proceeded to do so, about five miles from our hut I found a bear tree. As a sapling, grew near the tree, and reached near the hole that the bear went in at, I got dry dozed or rotten wood, that would catch and hold fire almost as well as spunk. This wood I tied up in bunches, fixed them on my back, and then climbed up the sapling, and with a pole, I put them touched with fire, into the hole, and then came down and took my gun in my hand. After some time the bear came out, and I killed and skinned it, packed up a load of the meat, (after securing the remainder from the wolves) and returned home before night. On my return my old brother and his son were much rejoiced at my success. After this we had plenty of provision.

We remained here until some time in April 1758. At this time Tecaughretanego had recovered so, that he could walk about. We made a bark canoe, embarked, and went down Ollentangy some distance, but the water being low, we were in danger of splitting our canoe upon the rocks: therefore Tecaughretanego concluded we would encamp on shore, and pray for rain.

* * *

Early in the year 1760, I came home to Conococheague, and found that my people could never ascertain whether I was killed or taken, until my return. They received me with great joy, but were surprised to see me so much like an Indian, both in my gait and gesture.

Upon enquiry, I found that my sweetheart was married a few days before I arrived. My feelings I must leave on this occasion, for those of my readers to judge, who have felt the pangs of disappointed love, as it is impossible now for me to describe the emotion of soul I felt at that time.

Olaudah Equiano
(1745?–1797?)

Equiano's autobiography, The Interesting Narrative of the Life of Olaudah Equiano, or Gustavus Vassa the African, *written by himself, was first published in London in 1789. It sold well and went through a number of English and American editions. Equiano's travels as an antislavery speaker in England undoubtedly added to the book's popularity.*

Equiano was born in what is now Nigeria, and his language was Ibo. He and his sister were captured by local slave raiders when Equiano was ten or eleven years old. After a journey down a large river, probably the Niger, he was sold to slavers bound for the West Indies. He was given several names by various masters; Captain Pascal, with whom he traveled in military campaigns, called him Gustavus Vassa, the name he used for the rest of his life. In the service of his last master, the Quaker Robert King of Philadelphia, he traveled back and forth between America and the West Indies.

With the help of several friends and owners, Equiano learned reading, writing, calculation, and rudimentary navigation. Given the privilege of investing in his master's cargoes, he was able to save enough money to purchase his own freedom for forty pounds by the time he was twenty-one years old. As a free man he was converted to Calvinism, toured the Mediterranean, traveled to the Arctic and the coast of South America, and took part in planning for the first expedition of freed slaves to settle in Sierra Leone in 1787. His book, written in a plain, direct style, was favorably reviewed by the leading magazines of the day.

The following text is taken from *Equiano's Travels*, edited by Paul Edwards (1967). In addition to the first London edition of 1789, Equiano's narrative is included in several collections, including *The Classic Slave Narratives*, edited by Henry Louis Gates, Jr. (1987).

––––––

[From] The Interesting Narrative of the Life of Olaudah Equiano

THE SLAVE SHIP

THE FIRST OBJECT which saluted my eyes when I arrived on the coast was the sea, and a slave ship which was then riding at anchor and waiting for its cargo. These filled me with astonishment, which was soon converted into terror when I was carried on board. I was immediately handled and tossed up to see if I were sound by some of the crew, and I was now persuaded that I had gotten into a world of bad spirits and that they were going to kill me. Their complexions too differing so much from ours, their long hair and the language they spoke (which was very different from any I had ever heard) united to confirm me in this belief. Indeed such were the horrors of my views and fears at the moment that, if ten thousand worlds had been my own, I would have freely parted with them all to have exchanged my condition with that of the meanest slave in my own country. When I looked round the ship too and saw a large furnace or copper boiling and a multitude of black people of every description chained together, every one of their countenances expressing dejection and sorrow, I no longer doubted of my fate; and quite overpowered with horror and anguish, I fell motionless on the deck and fainted. When I recovered a little I found some black people about me, who I believed were some of those who had brought me on board and had been receiving their pay; they talked to me in order to cheer me, but all in vain. I asked them if we were not to be eaten by those white men with horrible looks, red faces, and loose hair. They told me I was not, and one of the crew brought me a small portion of spirituous liquor in a wine glass, but being afraid of him I would not take it out of his hand. One of the blacks therefore took it from him and gave it to me, and I took a little down my palate, which instead of reviving me, as they thought it would, threw me into the greatest consternation at the strange feeling it produced, having never tasted such any liquor before. Soon after this the blacks who brought me on board went off, and left me abandoned to despair.[1]

I now saw myself deprived of all chance of returning to my native country or even the least glimpse of hope of gaining the shore, which I now considered as friendly; and I even wished for my former slavery in preference to my present situation, which was filled with horrors of every kind, still heightened by my ignorance of what I was to undergo. I was not long suffered to indulge my grief; I was soon put down under the decks, and there I received such a salutation in my nostrils as I had never experienced in my life: so that with the loathsomeness of the stench and crying together, I became so sick and low that I was not able to eat, nor had I the least desire to taste anything. I now wished for the last friend, death, to relieve me; but soon, to my grief, two of the white men offered me eatables, and on my refusing to eat, one of them held me fast by the hands and laid me across I think the windlass,[2] and tied my feet while the other flogged me severely. I had never experienced anything of this kind before, and although, not being used to the water, I naturally feared that element the first time I saw it, yet nevertheless could I have got over the nettings I would have jumped over the side, but I could not; and besides, the crew used to watch us very closely who were not chained down to the decks, lest we should leap into the water: and I have seen some of these poor African prisoners most severely cut for attempting to do so, and hourly whipped for not eating. This indeed was often the case with myself. In a little time after, amongst the poor chained

---

1. He had been separated from his sister shortly after they were taken from their home. His arrival at the slave ship took place six or seven months after his capture.

2. A winch used for lifting the anchor.

men I found some of my own nation, which in a small degree gave ease to my mind. I inquired of these what was to be done with us; they gave me to understand we were to be carried to these white people's country to work for them. I then was a little revived, and thought if it were no worse than working, my situation was not so desperate: but still I feared I should be put to death, the white people looked and acted, as I thought, in so savage a manner; for I had never seen among my people such instances of brutal cruelty, and this not only shewn towards us blacks but also to some of the whites themselves. One white man in particular I saw, when we were permitted to be on deck, flogged so unmercifully with a large rope near the foremast that he died in consequence of it; and they tossed him over the side as they would have done a brute. This made me fear these people the more, and I expected nothing less than to be treated in the same manner. I could not help expressing my fears and apprehensions to some of my countrymen: I asked them if these people had no country but lived in this hollow place (the ship): they told me they did not, but came from a distant one. 'Then,' said I, 'how comes it in all our country we never heard of them?' They told me because they lived so very far off. I then asked where were their women? had they any like themselves? I was told they had: 'and why,' said I, 'do we not see them?' They answered, because they were left behind. I asked how the vessel could go? They told me they could not tell, but that there were cloths put upon the masts by the help of the ropes I saw, and then the vessel went on; and the white men had some spell or magic they put in the water when they liked in order to stop the vessel. I was exceedingly amazed at this account and really thought they were spirits. I therefore wished much to be from amongst them for I expected they would sacrifice me: but my wishes were vain, for we were so quartered that it was impossible for any of us to make our escape. While we stayed on the coast I was mostly on deck, and one day, to my great astonishment, I saw one of these vessels coming in with the sails up. As soon as the whites saw it they gave a great shout, at which we were amazed; and the more so as the vessel appeared larger by approaching nearer. At last she came to an anchor in my sight, and when the anchor was let go I and my countrymen who saw it were lost in astonishment to observe the vessel stop, and were now convinced it was done by magic. Soon after this the other ship got her boats out, and they came on board of us, and the people of both ships seemed very glad to see each other. Several of the strangers also shook hands with us black people, and made motions with their hands, signifying I suppose we were to go to their country; but we did not understand them. At last, when the ship we were in had got in all her cargo, they made ready with many fearful noises, and we were all put under deck so that we could not see how they managed the vessel. But this disappointment was the last of my sorrow. The stench of the hold while we were on the coast was so intolerably loathsome that it was dangerous to remain there for any time, and some of us had been permitted to stay on the deck for the fresh air; but now that the whole ship's cargo were confined together it became absolutely pestilential.

The closeness of the place and the heat of the climate, added to the number in the ship, which was so crowded that each had scarcely room to turn himself, almost suffocated us. This produced copious perspirations, so that the air soon became unfit for respiration from a variety of loathsome smells, and brought on a sickness among the slaves, of which many died, thus falling victims to the improvident avarice, as I may call it, of their purchasers. This wretched situation was again aggravated by the galling of the chains, now become insupportable, and the filth of the necessary tubs, into which the children often fell and were almost suffocated. The shrieks of the women and the groans of the dying rendered the whole a scene of horror almost inconceivable. Happily perhaps for myself I was soon reduced so low here that it was thought necessary to keep me almost always on deck, and from my extreme youth I was not put in fetters. In this situation I expected every hour to share the fate of my companions, some of whom were almost daily brought upon deck at the point of death, which I began to hope would soon put an end to my miseries. Often did I think many of the inhabitants of the deep much more happy than myself. I envied them the freedom they enjoyed, and as often wished I could change my condition for theirs. Every circumstance I met with served only to render my state more painful, and heighten my apprehensions and my opinion of the cruelty of the whites. One day they had taken a number of fishes, and when they had killed and satisfied themselves with as many as they thought fit, to our astonishment who were on the deck, rather than give any of them to us to eat as we expected, they tossed the remaining fish into the sea again, although we begged and prayed for some as well as we could, but in vain; and some of my countrymen, being pressed by hunger, took an opportunity when they thought no one saw them of trying to get a little privately; but they were discovered, and the attempt procured them some very severe floggings. One day, when we had a smooth sea and moderate wind, two of my wearied country-men who were chained together (I was near them at the time), preferring death to such a life of misery, somehow made through the nettings and jumped into the sea: immediately another quite dejected fellow, who on account of his illness was suffered to be out of irons, also followed their example; and I believe many more would very soon have done the same if they had not been prevented by the ship's crew, who were instantly alarmed. Those of us that were the most active were in a moment put down under the deck, and there was such a noise and confusion amongst the people of the ship as I never heard before, to stop her and get the boat out to go after the slaves. However two of the wretches were drowned, but they got the other and afterwards flogged him unmercifully for thus attempting to prefer death to slavery. In this manner we continued to undergo more hardships than I can now relate, hardships which are inseparable from this accursed trade. Many a time we were near suffocation from the want of fresh air, which we were often without for whole days together. This and the stench of the necessary tubs carried off many. During our passage I first saw flying fishes, which surprised me very much: they used frequently to fly across the ship and many of them fell on the deck. I also now first saw the use of the quadrant,[3] I had often with astonishment seen the mariners make observations with it, and I could not think what it meant. They at last took notice of my surprise, and one of them, willing to increase it as well as to gratify my curiosity, made me one day look through it. The clouds appeared to me to be land, which disappeared as they passed along. This heightened my wonder, and I was now more persuaded than ever that I was in another world and that everything about me was magic. At last we came in sight of the island of Barbados, at which the whites on board gave a great shout and made many signs of joy to us. We did not know what to think of this, but as the vessel drew nearer we plainly saw the harbour and other ships of different kinds and sizes, and we soon anchored amongst them off Bridgetown. Many merchants and planters now came on board, though it was in the evening. They put us in separate parcels[4] and examined us attentively. They also made us jump[5] and pointed to the land, signifying we were to go there. We thought by this we should be eaten by these ugly men, as they appeared to us; and when soon after we were all put down under the deck again, there was much dread and trembling among us, and nothing but bitter cries to be heard all the night from these apprehensions, insomuch that at last the white people got some old slaves from the land to pacify us. They told us we were not to be eaten but to work, and were soon to go on land where we should see many of our country people. This report eased us much; and sure enough soon after we were landed there came to us Africans of all languages. We were conducted immediately to the merchant's yard, where we were all pent up together like so many sheep in a fold without regard to sex or age. As every object was new to me everything I saw filled me with surprise. What struck me first was that the houses were built with storeys, and in every other respect different from those in Africa: but I was still more astonished on seeing people on horseback. I did not know what this could mean, and indeed I thought these people were full of nothing but magical arts. While I was in this astonishment one of my fellow prisoners spoke to a countryman of his about the horses, who said they were the same kind they had in their country. I understood them though they were from a distant part of Africa, and I thought it odd I had not seen any horses there; but afterwards when I came to converse with different Africans I found they had many horses amongst them, and much larger than those I then saw. We were not many days in the merchant's custody before we were sold after their usual manner, which is this: On a signal given, (as the beat of a drum) the buyers rush at once into the yard where the slaves are confined, and make choice of that parcel they like best. The noise and clamour with which this is attended and the eagerness visible in the countenances of the buyers

---

3. An instrument for measuring the angle of the sun. It consists of a graduated arc of 90° with a movable index and a sight.

4. Sale groupings.

5. To ascertain the state of their health.

serve not a little to increase the apprehensions of the terrified Africans, who may well be supposed to consider them as the ministers of that destruction to which they think themselves devoted. In this manner, without scruple, are relations and friends separated, most of them never to see each other again. I remember in the vessel in which I was brought over, in the men's apartment there were several brothers who, in the sale, were sold in different lots; and it was very moving on this occasion to see and hear their cries at parting. O, ye nominal Christians! might not an African ask you, Learned you this from your God who says unto you, Do unto all men as you would men should do unto you? Is it not enough that we are torn from our country and friends to toil for your luxury and lust of gain? Must every tender feeling be likewise sacrificed to your avarice? Are the dearest friends and relations, now rendered more dear by their separation from their kindred, still to be parted from each other and thus prevented from cheering the gloom of slavery with the small comfort of being together and mingling their sufferings and sorrows? Why are parents to lose their children, brothers their sisters, or husbands their wives? Surely this is a new refinement in cruelty which, while it has no advantage to atone for it, thus aggravates distress and adds fresh horrors even to the wretchedness of slavery.

Voyage to England

I now totally lost the small remains of comfort I had enjoyed in conversing with my countrymen; the women too who used to wash and take care of me were all gone different ways, and I never saw one of them afterwards.

I stayed in this island for a few days, I believe it could not be above a fortnight, when I and some few more slaves that were not saleable amongst the rest, from very much fretting, were shipped off in a sloop for North America. On the passage we were better treated than when we were coming from Africa and we had plenty of rice and fat pork. We were landed up a river a good way from the sea, about Virgina county, where we saw few or none of our native Africans and not one soul who could talk to me. I was a few weeks weeding grass and gathering stones in a plantation, and at last all my companions were distributed different ways and only myself was left. I was now exceedingly miserable and thought myself worse off than any of the rest of my companions, for they could talk to each other, but I had no person to speak to that I could understand. In this state I was constantly grieving and pining and wishing for death rather than anything else. While I was in this plantation the gentleman to whom I suppose the estate belonged being unwell, I was one day sent for to his dwelling house to fan him; when I came into the room where he was I was very much affrighted at some things I saw, and the more so as I had seen a black woman slave as I came through the house who was cooking the dinner, and the poor creature was cruelly loaded with various kinds of iron machines; she had one particularly on her head which locked her mouth so fast that she could scarcely speak, and could not eat nor drink. I was much astonished and shocked at this contrivance, which I afterwards learned was called the iron muzzle. Soon after I had a fan put into my hand to fan the gentleman while he slept, and so I did indeed with great fear. While he was fast asleep I indulged myself a great deal in looking about the room, which to me appeared very fine and curious. The first object that engaged my attention was a watch which hung on the chimney and was going. I was quite surprised at the noise it made and was afraid it would tell the gentleman anything I might do amiss: and when I immediately after observed a picture hanging in the room which appeared constantly to look at me, I was still more affrighted, having never seen such things as these before. At one time I thought it was something relative to magic, and not seeing it move I thought it might be some way the whites had to keep their great men when they died and offer them libation as we used to do to our friendly spirits. In this state of anxiety I remained till my master awoke, when I was dismissed out of the room to my no small satisfaction and relief, for I though that these people were all made up of wonders. In this place I was called Jacob, but on board the *African* snow[6] I was called Michael. I had been some time in this miserable, forlorn, and much dejected state without having anyone to talk to, which made my life a burden, when the kind and unknown hand of the Creator (who in very deed leads the blind in a way they know not) now began to appear, to my comfort; for one day the captain of a merchant ship called the *Industrious Bee* came on some business to my master's house. This gentleman, whose name was Michael Henry Pascal, was a lieutenant in the Royal Navy, but now commanded this trading ship which was somewhere in the confines of the county many miles off. While he was at my master's house it happened that he saw me and liked me so well that he made a purchase of me. I think I have often heard him say he gave thirty or forty pounds sterling[7] for me, but I do not now remember which. However, he meant me for a present to some of his friends in England, and I was sent accordingly from the house of my then master, one Mr Campbell, to the place where the ship lay; I was conducted on horseback by an elderly black man, (a mode of travelling which appeared very odd to me). When I arrived I was carried on board a fine large ship, loaded with tobacco, etc. and just ready to sail for England. I now thought my condition much mended; I had sails to lie on and plenty of good victuals to eat, and everybody on board used me very kindly, quite contrary to what I had seen of any white people before; I therefore began to think that they were not all of the same disposition. A few days after I was on board we sailed for England. I was still at a loss to conjecture my destiny. By this time however I could smatter a little imperfect English, and I wanted

---

6. Small sailing vessel used in the slave trade.

7. A fairly high price to pay for a child

to know as well as I could where we were going. Some of the people of the ship used to tell me they were going to carry me back to my own country and this made me very happy. I was quite rejoiced at the sound of going back, and thought if I should get home what wonders I should have to tell. But I was reserved for another fate and was soon undeceived when we came within sight of the English coast. While I was on board this ship, my captain and master named me *Gustavus Vasa*.[8] I at that time began to understand him a little, and refused to be called so, and told him as well as I could that I would be called Jacob; but he said I should not, and still called me Gustavus; and when I refused to answer to my new name, which at first I did, it gained me many a cuff; so at length I submitted and was obliged to bear the present name, by which I have been known ever since. The ship had a very long passage,[9] and on that account we had very short allowance of provisions. Towards the last we had only one pound and a half of bread per week, and about the same quantity of meat, and one quart of water a day. We spoke with only one vessel the whole time we were at sea, and but once we caught a few fishes. In our extremities the captain and people told me in jest they would kill and eat me, but I thought them in earnest and was depressed beyond measure, expecting every moment to be my last. While I was in this situation, one evening they caught, with a good deal of trouble, a large shark, and got it on board. This gladdened my poor heart exceedingly, as I thought it would serve the people to eat instead of their eating me; but very soon, to my astonishment, they cut off a small part of the tail and tossed the rest over the side. This renewed my consternation, and I did not know what to think of these white people, though I very much feared they would kill and eat me. There was on board the ship a young lad who had never been at sea before, about four or five years older than myself; his name was Richard Baker. He was a native of America,[1] had received an excellent education, and was of a most amiable temper. Soon after I went on board he showed me a great deal of partiality and attention and in return I grew extremely fond of him. We at length became inseparable, and for the space of two years he was of very great use to me and was my constant companion and instructor. Although this dear youth had many slaves of his own, yet he and I have gone through many sufferings together on shipboard, and we have many nights lain in each other's bosoms when we were in great distress. Thus such a friendship was cemented between us as we cherished till his death, which to my very great sorrow happened in the year 1759, when he was up the Archipelago on board his Majesty's ship the *Preston*, an event which I have never ceased to regret as I lost at once a kind interpreter, an agreeable companion, and a faithful friend; who, at the age of fifteen, discovered a mind

---

8. The original Gustavas Vasa was a King of Sweden (1496–1560). Equiano sometimes spelled the name *Vassa*.

9. Thirteen weeks.

1. Since this voyage took place twenty years before the Declaration of Independence, Baker would have been a British subject though born in North America.

superior to prejudice, and who was not ashamed to notice, to associate with, and to be the friend and instructor of one who was ignorant, a stranger, of a different complexion, and a slave!

* * *

FREE MAN

Every day now brought me nearer to my freedom, and I was impatient till we proceeded again to sea, that I might have an opportunity of getting a sum large enough to purchase it. I was not long ungratified, for in the beginning of 1766 my master bought another sloop, named the *Nancy*, the largest I had ever seen. She was partly laden, and was to proceed to Philadelphia. Our captain had his choice of three, and I was well pleased he chose this, which was the largest, for from his having a large vessel I had more room and could carry a larger quantity of goods with me. Accordingly, when we had delivered our old vessel, the *Prudence*, and completed the lading of the *Nancy*, having made near 300 per cent by four barrels of pork I brought from Charleston, I laid in as large a cargo as I could, trusting to God's providence to prosper my undertaking. With these views I sailed for Philadelphia.

We arrived safe and in good time at Philadelphia, and I sold my goods there chiefly to the Quakers. They always appeared to be a very honest discreet sort of people, and never attempted to impose on me; I therefore liked them, and ever after chose to deal with them in preference to any others. One Sunday morning while I was here, as I was going to church, I chanced to pass a meeting-house. The doors being open, and the house full of people, it excited my curiosity to go in. When I entered the house, to my great surprise, I saw a very tall woman standing in the midst of them, speaking in an audible voice something which I could not understand. Having never seen anything of this kind before, I stood and stared about me for some time, wondering at this odd scene. As soon as it was over I took an opportunity to make inquiry about the place and people, when I was informed they were called Quakers. I particularly asked what that woman I saw in the midst of them had said, but none of them were pleased to satisfy me; so I quitted them, and soon after, as I was returning, I came to a church crowded with people: the churchyard was full likewise, and a number of people were even mounted on ladders, looking in at the windows. I thought this a strange sight, as I had never seen churches, either in England or the East Indies, crowded in this manner before. I therefore made bold to ask some people the meaning of all this, and they told me the Rev. Mr George Whitfield[2] was

---

2. A follower of John Wesley who attracted great crowds.

preaching. I had often heard of this gentleman, and had wished to see and hear him; but I had never before had an opportunity. I now therefore resolved to gratify myself with the sight and pressed in amidst the multitude. When I got into the church I saw this pious man exhorting the people with the greatest fervour and earnestness, and sweating as much as I ever did while in slavery on Montserrat beach. I was very much struck and impressed with this; I thought it strange I had never seen divines exert themselves in this manner before, and I was no longer at a loss to account for the thin congregations they preached to.

When we had discharged our cargo here and were loaded again, we left this fruitful land once more and set sail for Montserrat. My traffic had hitherto succeeded so well with me that I thought, by selling my goods when we arrived at Montserrat,[3] I should have enough to purchase my freedom.

*   *   *

When we had unladen the vessel and I had sold my venture, finding myself master of about forty-seven pounds I consulted my true friend, the captain, how I should proceed in offering my master the money for my freedom. He told me to come on a certain morning, when he and my master would be at breakfast together. Accordingly, on that morning I went and met the captain there as he had appointed. When I went in I made my obeisance to my master, and with money in my hand and many fears in my heart I prayed him to be as good as his offer to me, when he was pleased to promise me my freedom as soon as I could purchase it. This speech seemed to confound him; he began to recoil: and my heart that instant sunk within me. 'What,' said he, 'give you your freedom? Why, where did you get the money? Have you got forty pounds sterling?[4] 'Yes, sir,' I answered. 'How did you get it?' replied he. I told him very honestly. The captain then said he knew I got the money very honestly and with much industry, and that I was particularly careful. On which my master replied I got money much faster than he did, and said he would not have made me the promise he did if he had thought I should have got money so soon. 'Come, come,' said my worthy captain, clapping my master on the back, 'Come, Robert, (which was his name) I think you must let him have his freedom; you have laid your money out very well; you have received good interest for it all this time, and here is now the principal at last. I know Gustavus has earned you more than an hundred a year, and he will still save you money, as he will not leave you. Come, Robert, take the money.' My master then said he would not be worse than his promise, and taking the money, told me to go to the Secretary at the Register Office and get my manumission drawn up. These words of my master were like a voice from Heaven to me. In an instant all my trepidation was turned into unutterable bliss, and I most reverently bowed myself with gratitude, unable to express my feelings but by the overflowing of my eyes,

---

3. A British island of the Leeward group.

4. Equiano's certificate of manumission actually shows that King was paid seventy pounds.

while my true and worthy friend, the captain, congratulated us both with a peculiar degree of heartfelt pleasure. As soon as the first transports of my joy were over, and that I had expressed my thanks to these my worthy friends in the best manner I was able, I rose with a heart full of affection and reverence and left the room, in order to obey my master's joyful mandate of going to the Register Office. As I was leaving the house I called to mind the words of the Psalmist, in the 126th Psalm, and like him, 'I glorified God in my heart, in whom I trusted.' These words had been impressed on my mind from the very day I was forced from Deptford to the present hour, and I now saw them, as I thought, fulfilled and verified. My imagination was all rapture as I flew to the Register Office, and in this respect, like the apostle Peter, (whose deliverance from prison was so sudden and extraordinary, that he thought he was in a vision)[5] I could scarcely believe I was awake. Heavens! who could do justice to my feelings at this moment! Not conquering heroes themselves in the midst of a triumph—Not the tender mother who has just regained her long-lost infant, and presses it to her heart—Not the weary, hungry mariner at the sight of the desired friendly port—Not the lover, when he once more embraces his beloved mistress after she had been ravished from his arms!—All within my breast was tumult, wildness, and delirium! My feet scarcely touched the ground, for they were winged with joy, and like Elijah, as he rose to Heaven, they 'were with lightning sped as I went on.' Everyone I met I told of my happiness and blazed about the virtue of my amiable master and captain.

When I got to the office and acquainted the Register with my errand he congratulated me on the occasion and told me he would draw up my manumission for half price, which was a guinea. I thanked him for his kindness, and having received it and paid him I hastened to my master to get him to sign it, that I might be fully released. Accordingly he signed the manumission that day, so that before night, I who had been a slave in the morning, trembling at the will of another, was become my own master and completely free. I thought this was the happiest day I had ever experienced; and my joy was still heightened by the blessings and prayers of the sable race, particularly the aged, to whom my heart had ever been attached with reverence.

---

5. See Acts xii:9.

Charles Johnston
(1769–1833)

In March 1790, while traveling with five other passengers in a flatboat down the Ohio River heading for western Kentucky, Charles Johnston, an attorney from Virginia, was captured by a mixed band of fifty-four Shawnee, Delaware, Wyandot, and Cherokee. By the terms of the treaty of Fort Stanwix in 1768, the Native Americans had withdrawn from western Pennsylvania and Virginia and were confined north of the Ohio River; the north bank of that river was thus known as "the Indian side," and the travelers had been warned away from it. The swell of settlers westward at the close of the Revolutionary War and the opening up of the Northwest Territory had angered the Indians, and continual warfare was in progress throughout this period. Johnston and his companion, Mr. May, were making their second trip to Kentucky and, knowing the dangers, were resolved not to land. But near the mouth of the Scioto River and the site of present-day Portsmouth, Ohio, they were lured close to shore by a ruse of two white men pretending to have escaped the Indians. John May and one woman were killed in the fighting, and another man was wounded. Along with two children captured in Kentucky, Johnston and a group led by the Shawnee Chickatommo set off for the Indian towns on the Upper Sandusky River.

Johnston was put under the protection of Messhawa, whom he described as "tall, straight and muscular" with a face of "mildness and humanity" and qualities "which would have done honour to human nature in a state of the most refined civilization." Messhawa and another friendly Indian named Tom Lewis kept him from harsh treatment and death at the hands of Chickatommo and others for five weeks until, on his twenty-first birthday, Johnston was ransomed for 600 silver brooches by a Canadian trader. Returning by way of Detroit, the Great Lakes, and New York City, he was interviewed by President George Washington and made a deposition to Secretary of War Henry Knox about his captivity and conditions in the Northwest Territories.

In later years Johnston repaid his rescuer, Francis Duchouquet, and learned from him the fate of some of his captors: Chickatommo died in a fight against the army of General Anthony Wayne near Fort Defiance in

1795; Messhawa became a follower of the great Shawnee chief Tecumseh and his brother Tenskwatawa the Prophet, and may have fallen in one of the battles waged by the confederation; Tom Lewis, who became a chief of the Shawnee and fought on the American side in the War of 1812, was still alive in 1826. Johnston became a successful lawyer and owned an estate in Roanoke County, Virginia, where Duchouquet visited him in 1826. The next year he published his memoir of captivity, A Narrative of the Incidents Attending the Capture, Detention and Ransom of Charles Johnston.

The source of the present text is a 1905 printing, with introduction and notes by Edwin Erle Sparks.

A Narrative of the Incidents Attending the Capture, Detention, and Ransom of Charles Johnston of Virginia

CHAPTER VI

✳ ✳ ✳

WE HAD NOW PENETRATED a great distance into the interior of a wild and uninhabited country; and I was compelled to abandon every thing like an effort or a hope to escape from my captors.[1] Even though I had succeeded in eluding their incessant vigilance, so far as to get out of their power, I should have been unable to procure sustenance of any kind, or to explore my way through woods and deserts, for I knew not how many miles; and must have perished with hunger, or fallen into the hands of other Indians, parties of whom were wandering about in every direction. I was therefore reconciled to a continuance with them until we should arrive at their towns, where I flattered myself I might be purchased or ransomed by some benevolent trader.

---

1. The time is early April, about two weeks after capture. The band of Indians holding his wounded companion, Mr. Skyles, have left and have headed for the villages on the Miami River. Johnston's group travels toward the Sandusky.

During the whole march, we subsisted on bear's meat, venison, turkeys, and racoons, with which we were abundantly supplied, as the ground over which we passed afforded every species of game in profusion, diminishing, however, as we approached their villages. But we were destitute of bread and salt, necessaries of life to a white man, while they are considered mere superfluities by the Indian warrior or hunter, when he is occupied in war or the chase. A mode of living perfectly new to me; the fatigues of the journey; my exposure to all the inclemencies of the season and climate; and the uneasiness of mind under which I constantly laboured, wasted my strength and depressed my spirits.

* * *

The gloom, which reflection on such subjects had spread over my mind, was in some degree dispelled by an incident, which, under ordinary circumstances would have been disregarded. We found a negro in the woods, under cover of a tent, which contained a quantity of whiskey and peltry belonging to his master, an Indian of the Wyandot tribe, then at peace with the United States. This negro was a runaway from the state of Kentucky,[2] and had fled across the Ohio to the country of the savages; among whom it was a law, as I was informed, that the first who should lay hands on such runaway had a right to hold him as his property. The negro had been thus acquired by the Wyandot, who was, when we fell in with the negro, engaged in hunting, and had, on a trading expedition, recently visited the Muskingum, where he had obtained the whiskey now in the possession and care of his negro man.

I now felt myself quite at home; and the poor negro, whom under other circumstances, I should have kept at a distance, became my companion and friend. He treated me with great kindness and hospitality, offering me such refreshments as he had, the most acceptable of which were bread and salt. I had not tasted either since we left the Ohio river. My captors, as soon as they ascertained that the negro had whiskey for sale, began to barter for it a part of the booty which they had acquired on the Ohio. A pair of new boots, which they had taken from my saddlebags, and for which I had paid eight dollars at Petersburg, was given for a pint of whiskey; and other articles were exchanged at a similar rate. The scenes which had passed on the Ohio were now to be acted over again. A disgusting revelry commenced, which lasted for three days. As usual, a sufficient number remained sober to guard the prisoners, consisting, at this time only of the two children and myself.

On the first night, about the time when we were composing ourselves for rest, we were removed to some distance from the spot occupied by those who were in a state of intoxication, that we might not, while asleep, be disturbed by them. The two children had never been tied; but I was confined by cords, and Indians laid themselves on each side of me as before. In this situation I slept, until about midnight, when I was awaked by the falling of rain.

---

2. This incident of a fugitive slave is not unique. There were many among the Seminoles in Florida as well as some among northern tribes.

Soon after, the negro, who had observed the direction in which we had gone when removed from the place where the drunken Indians were, arrived at our camp, and kindly proposed to me, that I should go with him to his tent, and sleep under it, protected from the rain. I pointed out the impossibility of accepting his invitation, without the consent of my guard, lying on each side of me, upon the rope with which I was confined. These men, hearing a conversation between the negro and myself which they did not understand, conceived a suspicion that he was concerting with me measures for my escape. They immediately sprung up, and seizing the negro, set up a tremendous yell, which was answered by the drunken party, and presently most of them came running towards us with their tomahawks in their hands. The negro, who could speak their language, was taken off a short distance and interrogated as to the object of his visit to me; after which I was separately questioned on the same point by one of those who spoke English. As there was an entire correspondence in our answers, the Indians did not doubt their truth; and I was permitted to accept the invitation of my new friend. I soon reached his tent, accompanied by nearly all the Indians, who appeared to have been much sobered by the incident which had just occurred. I then laid myself down within the tent, near its entrance, in front of which there was a fire. Sheltered from the rain, and no longer encumbered by ropes, I soon fell into a profound sleep, which I should probably have enjoyed till the morning, had not my slumbers been interrupted by a sensation like that called the night-mare; but which was, in fact, produced by the weight of a large Indian sitting composedly on my breast, before the fire, and smoking his pipe. I turned over and dropped him on the ground, where he continued to sit, indulging, as if nothing had occurred, in his favourite amusement of smoking, until I again sunk into sleep.

Chapter VII

In the morning, a frightful scene presented itself: they were preparing for the war dance. A pole had been cut from the woods; after taking the bark from it, it was painted black, with streaks of red, winding like snakes around it: the lower end was sharpened, and at the top the scalps of my late companions,[3] with others which they had obtained during their excursion, were suspended. Each Indian had dressed himself for the occasion. Some had painted their faces black, with red round the eyes; others, reversing it, had painted their faces red, with black round the eyes: all with feathers stuck in their heads, and all with the aspect of so many demons. When they had finished adorning themselves in this manner, the pole was stuck fast into the ground. They formed themselves into a circle around it: and then the dance began. It

---

3. John May and Dolly Fleming, killed in the attack on the flatboat.

commenced with the fell war-whoop, which had not ceased to ring in my ears since the fatal morning of our capture. They danced around the pole, writhing their bodies and distorting their faces in a most hideous manner. It is their practice, on such occasions, to repeat the injuries which have been inflicted on them by their enemies the whites; their lands taken from them—their villages burnt—their cornfields laid waste—their fathers and brothers killed—their women and children carried into captivity. In this instance, by these repetitions of their wrongs and sufferings, they had wrought themselves up to a pitch of the greatest fury.

The dance lasted for about half an hour. The scene being new to me, I had seated myself on a log to witness it. When it ended, Chickatommo, with eyes flashing fire, advanced towards me, and when in reach struck me a violent blow on the head. I immediately quitted my seat, seized him over the arms, and demanded why he struck me? He replied, by saying, "Sit down!—sit down!" I accordingly loosened my grasp, and resumed my seat on the log. At that moment, perceiving the two prisoner children near, who, like myself, had been attentive spectators of the dance, he snatched up a tomahawk that was at hand, and advanced towards them with a quick step and determined look. Alarmed at his menacing approach they fled:—he pursued. My humane friend Messhawa, seeing the imminent danger to which they were exposed, bounded like a deer to their relief. The boy being older and stronger than his sister, she was the first to be overtaken by Chickatommo, and would have been the first to fall a victim to his rage; but at the moment when the fatal instrument was raised to strike her dead, Messhawa had reached the spot. Coming up behind Chickatommo, he seized him around the arms, and with violence slung him back. He then darted towards the affrighted child, whom he reached in an instant, snatched her up in his arms, and pursued the boy. Misconstruing the good intentions of Messhawa, he redoubled his exertions to escape, and they had run a considerable distance before he was overtaken. When his deliverer came up with him, he thought all was over, and gave a bitter shriek, which was answered by one still more bitter from his sister, then in the arms of Messhawa and who had not yet understood his object. They were both, however, soon undeceived. Although he spoke to them in an unknown tongue, his language, from the manner of it, could not be misunderstood. They found that they had been mistaken, and that they had been pursued by a friend instead of an enemy. When this was ascertained, their little palpitating hearts were soon calmed into repose, and presently they arrived at our camp, walking by the side of Messhawa, who held each by the hand, and soothed them as they advanced with his caresses. The wood being an open one, I had viewed the scene with intense gaze; and nothing could exceed the delight I felt at finding my poor little companions thus relieved from the dangers of so perilous a situation.

On the next day two Mingo Indians[4] arrived, and immediately partici-

---

4. Name used by the Delawares to denote people from the Six Nations of the Iroquois. Whites applied the word to a band of Iroquois speakers residing around the headwaters of the Ohio River. They were allies of the Shawnee.

pated in the drunken debauchery of our camp. One of these men had killed
in the course of the preceding summer, an Indian of the Wyandot tribe, who
was a husband, and the father of several children. Among all the savage
nations of America, the usage prevails, of adopting prisoners taken in war
for the purpose of supplying any loss incurred by those, who have had their
friends slain in battle, or otherwise. If one takes the life of another belonging
to his own or a different tribe, he is bound to make reparation to the family
of the dead man, either by the payment of a certain value in property, or by
furnishing a substitute for the deceased, who occupies precisely the same
station, and fills all the relations of such deceased in the community to
which he belonged; becomes the husband of his widow, should he have left
one, the father of his children, and is required to perform all the duties
appertaining to these connexions. If reparation is not made for the death of a
man by one of the modes which have been mentioned, within a period limited by their usages, the murderer becomes liable to be killed with impunity
by the relatives of him who has fallen, or by any other of his tribe. In this
instance, the Mingo stated to my captors his wretched situation. He declared
himself so poor, that he was not able to render the requisite value for the
Wyandot whom he had slain; and therefore that his own life must be for-
feited, unless the alternative condition was fulfilled by him. While their
hearts were warmed more by the operation of the spirituous liquor they had
drank, than by any genuine emotions of liberality, they did not hesitate to
yield to his solicitations; and I was delivered over to this new master, to be
substituted for the Wyandot whom he had murdered.

When I had ascertained, that those with whom I had travelled from the
Ohio River, were preparing to resume their journey, and to leave me in the
hands of my new possessor, I was utterly astonished and incapable of con-
ceiving the cause of so unexpected a determination. For the purpose of
relieving my mind from the anxiety and alarm necessarily produced by my
transfer to the Mingo, I requested the negro to explain its object. He was
equally ignorant with myself of the negotiations between my present and
former proprietors, and applied to both parties for explanation. The intelligence, unreservedly communicated to him by each, was perfectly concur-
rent, and the perturbation of my feelings was in a great degree diminished,
when I learnt, that I was destined shortly to become a husband and a father.
The prospect, indeed, was not very rapturous, of leading to the altar of
Hymen and Indian squaw, already the mother of several children. But there
was something extremely consoling in the hope, I might say in the persuasion, that such an event would bring within my reach those chances of
escape from the savages, and for restoration to my country and friends,
which I had thus far vainly exerted myself to obtain.

The Indians, whose captive I had heretofore been, took up their packs
immediately after surrendering me to the Mingo, and continued their
march. But before they set out, every individual made it a point to take leave
of me, and to shake me by the hand. Several of them, by their countenances
and manner, evinced feelings of kindness, and even of regret, at parting. My

excellent friend Messhawa, who had certainly formed an attachment to me, seemed to partake more of this feeling than any of them.

After they left us, I had leisure to reflect on my new condition, and believed I had reason to congratulate myself on a change so auspicious. The matrimonial connexion, which had been designed for me, without my consent, occupied my mind, and I entertained an earnest curiosity with respect to the female, the place of whose husband I was to supply, and with whom I was to be allied by the ties of marriage. Whether she was old or young, ugly or handsome, deformed or beautiful, were the questions not without their interest to me. I therefore inquired on those subjects from the Mingo, by the aid of my interpreter, the negro. But he had never seen her, and could give me no information, except that she was the mother of three or four children. But whatever might be her personal appearance, or the qualities of her heart; whether she was destitute of charms, or distinguished for them; the plan to be pursued by me was clear, and my resolution was not to deviate from it. I was not to be consulted in relation to the marriage intended for me by those who claimed the disposal of my person: whether it was to be productive of happiness or misery to me, was no concern of theirs. The only benefit which could result on my side would be, that I should be free, and no longer continue the object of suspicion and vigilance; and might seize on the first favourable opportunity which presented itself, of returning to the comforts, the security, and the enjoyments of civilized life. For the more certain attainment of my purpose, it was my intention, after assuming the charge of the family which I was about to enter by compulsion, thoroughly to devote myself to it, to reconcile myself as far as was in my power to the necessity by which I was overwhelmed; but by no means to delay my escape, when the moment should arrive at which there was a possibility of its being accomplished. It may well be conceived, that with such hopes and views, I became impatient for our arrival at the place of residence of my intended bride.

These reveries, which I continued hourly to indulge, were not of long duration. After the lapse of two or three days, the Mingo, who now considered me as his property, began to move on with me towards the town at which I was to be delivered, and where the bridal ceremony was to be performed at the proper period subsequent to my arrival. Before he fell in with the party from the Ohio, we had struck the war-path leading from the country on that river, to the Indian towns on the Sandusky and Miami. Upon this war-path my late proprietors had proceeded, when they took leave of the Mingo and myself; and as he conducted me along the same route in their rear, it would happen, that if delayed a few days, we should overtake them. The fact was, that my former possessors, after the generous feeling excited by the whiskey, which they were quaffing when the Mingo joined them, had subsided, began to repent of their liberality, and determined to reclaim me. They accordingly halted until we came up with them. We were received with smiles, and every indication of civility. They all shook us by the hand, and there was nothing which induced the slightest apprehension of ill humour. But this temper did not long display itself. A bitter altercation commenced, which soon proceeded to a high quarrel; in the course of which I was not exempt from uneasiness when I observed, by their frequent pointing to me, that I was the subject of controversy. The danger was, that one party might despatch me with the tomahawk or rifle, rather than yield me to the claim of the other. The dispute was terminated by the act of Messhawa, who caught two of the horses that were browsing in the immediate neighbourhood and in view of our position, mounted one of them, required me to get on the other, and conducted me, with his rifle on his shoulder, to the Indian town at upper Sandusky.[5] This was done by instruction from Chickatommo.

We reached that place after riding about five miles. Those of our party, who had been left in the rear by Messhawa and myself, did not long delay to follow us; and, when they arrived at the town, encamped about the centre of it. Mr. Francis Duchouquet, a Canadian trader,[6] who had resided for some years among the Indians at this place, had met us at the point where the party had waited for the Mingo and me, and had then, on my earnest solicitation, assured me, that overtures for my redemption should be made on our arrival at Upper Sandusky. He visited us in a short time after we had encamped in that village. At the first moment when I saw this gentleman, I was animated with the hope, that I might prevail on him to treat with the Indians for my ransom, and that he might succeed in rescuing me from the pains and horrors of a captivity which I had then suffered for many weeks. I instantly renewed my application to him on this subject, and he did not hesitate to exert his good offices in my favour. But his propositions were decisively rejected; and the Indians expressed a determination not to let me go from their hands. The failure of this negotiation, when disclosed to me, produced an agonizing effect, which perhaps may be conceived, but cannot be expressed. All the terrors of a cruel death, inflicted by merciless savages, ingenious in the invention and practice of torture, recurred to my imagination, and filled me with despair.

Chapter VIII

I had forgotten my copy of the Debates of the Virginia Convention,[7] at the place from which I had been hurried by order of Chickatommo, on the day

---

5. This town of the Wyandot or Huron Indians was located near the present town of Upper Sandusky, Ohio. A note in the original edition describes bark houses constructed on a timber frame, with a smoke hole in the center.

6. French traders had been common in this region for fifty years. They collected furs and transported them to Detroit, where they were taken by boat to Quebec.

7. Johnston was keeping a journal of his captivity in the margins of this book. He lost it again, however, and wrote his account many years later from memory.

that we reached Upper Sandusky. Next morning the Mingo Indian, to whom I had been for a short time transferred, and from whom I had been reclaimed by my captors, appeared at our encampment. Recollection of the contest which he had lately maintained, for possession of my person, induced a suspicion, that his views were not propitious to my safety; and I was disposed to avoid him. My fears, however, were entirely dispelled, when, on his approach towards me, he drew from his bosom the book in which I had kept my journal, and presented it to me with a smiling face.

Soon afterwards, the party who held me a prisoner, was gladdened by the arrival of several Wyandots from Muskingum, with a quantity of whiskey in kegs, each of which contained about ten gallons, brought on horses, and lashed across their backs with hickory wythes. Immediately they began to barter with their guests for the article, which of all others, is most valuable in their eyes. The Wyandots turned their whiskey to good account. Five gallons were enough for the purchase of a horse worth two hundred dollars; a finely formed, handsome animal, now reduced in his plight by the journey from the Ohio river. Others of inferior value, were exchanged at a price proportioned to the first; and drunkenness soon spread itself over our encampment. But their customary precaution was not neglected; and a small number refusing to drink, remained sober, for the purpose of guarding me.

I had observed the liberality of their disposition while under the influence of drink, when they gratuitously yielded me to the Mingo; and therefore, pressed Mr. Duchouquet to renew his efforts for my ransom, at a moment which seemed favorable to my hopes. Again his propositions were rejected. I then begged him to ascertain, by inquiry from the Indians, to what point it was their intention to convey me; and what was the fate to which I was destined. To the first question they answered, by telling him that they intended to take me to their towns on the Miami river: to the second their reply was, that they did not know what final destination they should make of me. I had before this distinctly understood, that captives conveyed to the Miami towns, were certain of meeting the most dreadful fate; and that it is the invariable practice of the savages, to conceal their purposes from the prisoners whom they meant to sacrifice. When Mr. Duchouquet, therefore, reported to me the result of the inquiries which he had made at my request, my alarm and despondency were greater, if possible, than I had yet experienced; and every thing like hope was banished from my bosom.

The spirit of drunken debauchery prevailed, until the funds for purchasing whiskey, and the article itself, were about the same time exhausted. Four or five days of unbounded riot and intoxication had been passed, when the Indians to whom I belonged, finding themselves suddenly reduced from affluence to their usual poverty: ashamed of their wasteful expenditures, after having boasted of their exploits and their acquisitions on the Ohio; unwilling to return to their homes and their countrymen with nothing in their hands, of the wealth which they had recently possessed; adopted a resolution to go back to the river on which they had succeeded so well, and to make farther captures of white men and their property. They communicated their intention to Mr. Duchouquet, and informed him, that as the scalp of their captive might be transported with greater facility and safety than his person, they had determined to put me to death: but if he was in a temper to treat for my ransom, this was his time. A negotiation was then commenced, and concluded happily for me, without my knowledge or intervention. It was agreed, that he should pay one hundred dollars[8] worth of goods as the price of my liberation; and that I should be forthwith surrendered to him. The price was paid down in six hundred silver broaches; which answers all the purposes of a circulating medium with them.

This event, to me the most important of my life, by a singular coincidence occurred on the 28th of April, in the year 1790;[9] the day on which I attained the age of twenty-one years. It might be truly and literally denominated my second birth; since, within the preceding twenty-four hours, I might have been considered as dead to any prospect which my condition presented, except the most miserable, and sunk to the lowest depth of despair. The extravagance of my joy was such, that I know not any terms in our language adequate to its expression. Subsequent circumstances, presently to be noticed, threw me again into uneasiness and alarm.

After the Indians had disposed of me, they separated themselves into two parties. A small number of the Shawanese, the Mingo, the women, and the two captive children, set out for the Miami towns. Chickatommo, with the other Shawanese, commenced their route back to the Ohio river. Their departure seemed to ensure my safety, and therefore my mind was perfectly quieted. But there was a white man among the Wyandots at Upper Sandusky, who had been carried into captivity by those Indians when very young, and had been reared and naturalized with their tribe. He spoke the English language sufficiently to enable me to understand him; and we entered into conversation; in the course of which he intimated, that my emancipation was not yet reduced to certainty; and that he suspected it was the intention of Chickatommo and his party, to regain possession of my person. This suggestion, from a man who knew the savages well; their characteristic treachery; and the fact, that they had already once reclaimed me after having consigned me to the Mingo, induced an apprehension, that what I had heard was not to be disregarded. This apprehension was greatly strengthened, when on the succeeding day, the Shawanese chief with his followers, actually presented themselves again at Upper Sandusky.

Once more terror and despondency seized on me. I reflected on the events which had passed; the miseries which I had endured; and the dreadful fate which was inevitable, should I now, for the third time, fall into the hands of my captors. I deliberately and solemnly resolved, to resist their whole force by exertion of all my powers, and to perish on the spot before they should ever again become my masters. I provided myself with a tomahawk, and calmly sat down on a log, fixed in my purpose should they

---

8. One half the price of a good horse.

9. Johnston traveled about 200 miles in his five-week captivity.

approach, but chopping the log with an air of indifference. They made no attempt upon me, and retired to an encampment which they formed on the river near the town, yet out of our view. Mr. Duchouquet concurred with me in the opinion, that all the circumstances of their conduct were such, as ought to excite strong suspicion that they meditated my recapture. They had disappeared on the preceding day, after receiving the price for which I had been sold; had declared a design of returning to the Ohio; had suddenly returned, without any apparent reason or business; had encamped at a place different from that which they had before occupied, more remote from view, and better suited for a plan of surprise from it on us by night. We determined to prepare for the attack, and remain, with the utmost vigilance, on our guard. Mr. Duchouquet, and a labourer then in his service, continued to watch with me throughout the night. We locked and barred our door. We were in possession of an axe, several guns, and tomahawks. But there was no necessity for their use. The Indians permitted us to remain undisturbed; and on the next day quitted their camp. Their whole party, with their packs on their backs, came out of their course through the town; shook hands with Mr. Duchouquet and myself, declaring an intention to visit the British post at Detroit, and departed. I could not yet banish from my mind all disquiet, and continued under some apprehension that they might lurk in the neighbourhood, for a favourable opportunity to return and bear me off. But after several days of anxiety, we were informed by a party of strolling Indians from Lower Sandusky, that they had met Chickatommo and his followers, at a considerable distance from our village, pursuing their journey steadily towards Detroit. My fears and dangers were now at an end: my spirits became buoyant, and I indulged none but the most joyous feelings.

Frances Trollope
(1780–1863)

In the expansionist years of the early nineteenth century, the United States became a popular visiting place for Europeans who, not necessarily desiring to live here, wanted at least to discover for themselves what were the conditions of life in this upstart nation, what were its promises for the future. Most substantial of the books that resulted was Alexis de Tocqueville's Democracy in America *(1835, 1840), a classic of political analysis aimed at instructing European nations in the successes and failures of the American experiment. Other books of the same period generally aimed more simply*

at reporting travels and observations; those by English observers alone included Harriet Martineau's Society in America *(1837), Frederick Marryat's* A Diary in America *(1839) and* Second Series of a Diary in America *(1840), and Charles Dickens's* American Notes *(1842). Not finished with the subject, in* Martin Chuzzlewit *(1843–1844) Dickens turned into fiction some of the scenes and characters that had offended Americans in his travel book. Somewhat earlier on the scene was Frances Trollope, who began a prolific career as a writer with* Domestic Manners of the Americans *(1832).*

Born in England, Mrs. Trollope sailed to the United States in 1827 with three of her children in hopes of finding the fortune that had eluded her family in England, where her husband had failed as a lawyer and a farmer. She spent nearly four years in America, over half of it in the frontier town of Cincinnati, where she failed in an attempt to found a department store. Later she traveled in the eastern part of the country, but the fortune she sought in America came only on her return to England, with the appearance of her book, the first of over forty published during her lifetime. Widely read, the book outraged Americans, who thought its depictions scurrilous. "Yet," wrote Mark Twain later, "she was merely telling the truth, and this indignant nation knew it." For all her posturings, her account remains interesting as the record of a seeker tinged with disillusion, frequently mocking, as she observes American institutions and social relations, including landowners, servants and slaves, a revival meeting, a camp meeting, and the treatment of the Native Americans.

Four editions of *Domestic Manners of the Americans* were printed in 1832 and a fifth in 1839. Donald Smalley's 1949 edition includes an introduction and notes. The text that follows is from the edition of 1901, with an introduction by Harry Thurston Peck.

———

[From] Domestic Manners of the Americans

CHAPTER XXII. SMALL LANDED PROPRIETORS—SLAVERY

I NOW, for the first time since I crossed the mountains, found myself sufficiently at leisure to look deliberately round, and mark the different aspects of men and things in a region which, though bearing the same name, and calling itself the same land, was, in many respects, as different from the one I had left, as Amsterdam from St. Petersburg. There every man was straining, and struggling, and striving for himself (heaven knows!) Here every white man was waited upon, more or less, by a slave. There, the newly-cleared lands, rich with the vegetable manure accumulated for ages, demanded the slightest labour to return the richest produce; where the plough entered, crops the most abundant followed; but where it came not, no spot of native verdure, no native fruits, no native flowers cheered the eye; all was close, dark, stifling forest. Here the soil had long ago yielded its first fruits; much that had been cleared and cultivated for tobacco (the most exhausting of crops) by the English, required careful and laborious husbandry to produce any return; and much was left as sheep-walks. It was in these spots that the natural bounty of the soil and climate was displayed by the innumerable wild fruits and flowers which made every dingle and bushy dell seem a garden.

On entering the cottages I found also a great difference in the manner of living. Here, indeed, there were few cottages without a slave, but there were fewer still that had their beef-steak and onions for breakfast, dinner, and supper. The herrings of the bountiful Potomac supply their place. These are excellent "relish," as they call it, when salted, and, if I mistake not, are sold at a dollar and a half per thousand. Whiskey, however, flows every where at the same fatally cheap rate of twenty cents (about one shilling) the gallon, and its hideous effects are visible on the countenance of every man you meet.

The class of people the most completely unlike any existing in England, are those who, farming their own freehold estates, and often possessing several slaves, yet live with as few of the refinements, and I think I may say, with as few of the comforts of life, as the very poorest English peasant. When in Maryland, I went into the houses of several of these small proprietors, and remained long enough, and looked and listened sufficiently, to obtain a tolerably correct idea of their manner of living.

One of these families consisted of a young man, his wife, two children, a female slave, and two young lads, slaves also. The farm belonged to the wife, and, I was told, consisted of about three hundred acres of indifferent land, but all cleared. The house was built of wood, and looked as if the three slaves might have overturned it, had they pushed hard against the gable end. It contained one room, of about twelve feet square, and another adjoining it, hardly larger than the closet; this second chamber was the lodging-room of the white part of the family. Above these rooms was a loft, without windows, where I was told the "staying company" who visited them, were lodged. Near this mansion was a "shanty," a black hole, without any window, which served as a kitchen and all other offices, and also as the lodging of the blacks.

We were invited to take tea with this family, and readily consented to do so. The furniture of the room was one heavy huge table, and about six wooden chairs. When we arrived the lady was in rather a dusky dishabille, but she vehemently urged us to be seated, and then retired into the closet-chamber above mentioned, whence she continued to address to us from behind the door all kinds of "genteel country visiting talk," and at length emerged upon us in a smart new dress.

Her female slave set out the great table, and placed upon it cups of the very coarsest blue ware, a little brown sugar in one and a tiny drop of milk in another, no butter, though the lady assured us she had a "*deary*" and two cows. Instead of butter, she "hoped we would fix a little relish with our crackers," in ancient English, eat salt meat and dry biscuits. Such was the fare, and for guests that certainly were intended to be honoured. I could not help recalling the delicious repasts which I remembered to have enjoyed at little dairy farms in England, not *possessed*, but rented, and at high rents too; where the clean, fresh-coloured, bustling mistress herself skimmed the delicious cream, herself spread the yellow butter on the delightful brown loaf, and placed her curds, and her junket, and all the delicate treasures of her dairy before us, and then, with hospitable pride, placed herself at her board, and added the more delicate "relish" of good tea and good cream. I remembered all this, and did not think the difference atoned for, by the dignity of having my cup handed to me by a slave. The lady I now visited, however, greatly surpassed my quondam friends in the refinement of her conversation. She ambled through the whole time the visit lasted, in a sort of elegantly mincing familiar style of gossip, which, I think, she was imitating from some novel, for I was told she was a great novel reader, and left all household occupations to be performed by her slaves. To say she addressed us in a tone of equality, will give no adequate idea of her manner; I am persuaded that no misgiving on the subject ever entered her head. She told us that their estate was her divi-*dend* of her father's property. She had married a first cousin, who was as fine a gentleman as she was a lady, and as idle, preferring hunting (as they call shooting) to any other occupation. The consequence was that but a very small portion of the divi-*dend* was cultivated, and their poverty was extreme. The slaves, particularly the lads, were considerably more than half naked, but the air of dignity with which, in the midst of all this misery, the lanky lady said to one of the young negroes, "Attend to your young master, Lycurgus," must have been heard to be conceived in the full extent of its mock heroic.

Another dwelling of one of these landed proprietors was a hovel as wretched as the one above described, but there was more industry within it. The gentleman, indeed, was himself one of the numerous tribe of regular whiskey drinkers, and was rarely capable of any work; but he had a family of twelve children, who, with their skeleton mother, worked much harder than I ever saw negroes do. They were, accordingly, much less elegant and much less poor than the heiress; yet they lived with no appearance of comfort, and with, I believe, nothing beyond the necessaries of life. One proof of this was, that the worthless father would not suffer them to raise, even by their own labour, any garden vegetables, and they lived upon their fat pork, salt fish, and corn bread, summer and winter, without variation. This I found was frequently the case among the farmers. The luxury of whiskey is more appreciated by the men than all the green delicacies from the garden, and if all the ready money goes for that and their darling chewing tobacco, none can be spent by the wife for garden seeds; and as far as my observation extended, I never saw any American *ménage* where the toast and no toast question would have been decided in favour of the lady.

There are some small farmers who hold their lands as tenants, but these are by no means numerous; they do not pay their rent in money, but by making over a third of the produce to the owner; a mode of paying rent considerably more advantageous to the tenant than the landlord; but the difficulty of obtaining *money* in payment, excepting for mere retail articles, is very great in all American transactions. "I can pay in pro-*duce*," is the offer which I was assured is constantly made on all occasions, and if rejected, "Then I guess we can't deal," is the usual rejoinder. This statement does not, of course, include the great merchants of great cities, but refers to the mass of the people scattered over the country; it has, indeed, been my object, in speaking of the customs of the people, to give an idea of what they are *generally*.

The effect produced upon English people by the sight of slavery in every direction is very new, and not very agreeable, and it is not the less painfully felt from hearing upon every breeze the mocking words, "All men are born free and equal." One must be in the heart of American slavery, fully to appreciate that wonderfully fine passage in Moore's Epistle to Lord Viscount Forbes,[1] which describes perhaps more faithfully, as well as more powerfully, the political state of America, than any thing that has ever been written upon it.

> Oh! Freedom, Freedom, how I hate thy cant!
> Not eastern bombast, nor the savage rant
> Of purpled madmen, were they numbered all

---

1. Thomas Moore (1779–1852), Irish poet. The poem was a result of his visit to America in 1804.

From Roman Nero, down to Russian Paul,
Could grate upon my ear so mean, so base,
As the rank jargon of that factious race,
Who, poor of heart, and prodigal of words,
Born to be slaves, and struggling to be lords,
But pant for licence, while they spurn controul,
And shout for rights, with rapine in their soul!
Who can, with patience, for a moment see
The medley mass of pride and misery,
Of whips and charters, manacles and rights,
Of slaving blacks, and democratic whites,
Of all the pyebald polity that reigns
In free confusion o'er Columbia's plains?
To think that man, thou just and gentle God!
Should stand before thee with a tyrant's rod,
O'er creatures like himself, with soul from thee,
Yet dare to boast of perfect liberty;
Away, away, I'd rather hold my neck
By doubtful tenure from a Sultan's beck,
In climes where liberty has scarce been named,
Nor any right, but that of ruling claimed,
Than thus to live, where bastard freedom waves
Her fustian flag in mockery o'er slaves;
Where (motley laws admitting no degree
Betwixt the vilely slaved, and madly free)
Alike the bondage and the licence suit,
The brute made ruler, and the man made brute!

The condition of domestic slaves, however, does not generally appear to be bad; but the ugly feature is, that should it be so, they have no power to change it. I have seen much kind attention bestowed upon the health of slaves; but it is on these occasions impossible to forget, that did this attention fail, a valuable piece of property would be endangered. Unhappily the slaves, too, know this; and the consequence is, that real kindly feeling very rarely can exist between the parties. It is said that slaves born in a family are attached to the children of it, who have grown up with them. This may be the case where the petty acts of infant tyranny have not been sufficient to conquer the kindly feeling naturally produced by long and early association; and this sort of attachment may last as long as the slave can be kept in that state of profound ignorance which precludes reflection. The law of Virginia has taken care of this. The State legislators may truly be said to be "wiser in their generation than the children of light," and they ensure their safety by forbidding light to enter among them. By the law of Virginia it is penal to teach any slave to read, and it is penal to be aiding and abetting in the act of instructing them. This law speaks volumes. Domestic slaves are, generally speaking, tolerably well fed, and decently clothed; and the mode in which they are lodged seems a matter of great indifference to them. They are rarely exposed to the lash, and they are carefully nursed in sickness. These are the favourable features of their situation. The sad one is, that they *may* be sent to *the south* and sold. This is the dread of all the slaves north of Louisiana. The sugar plantations, and more than all, the rice grounds of Georgia and the Carolinas, are the terror of American negroes; and well they may be, for they open an early grave to thousands; and to *avoid loss*, it is needful to make their previous labour pay their value.

There is something in the system of breeding and rearing negroes in the Northern States, for the express purpose of sending them to be sold in the South, that strikes painfully against every feeling of justice, mercy, or common humanity. During my residence in America I became perfectly persuaded that the state of a domestic slave in a gentleman's family was preferable to that of a hired American "help," both because they are more cared for and valued, and because their condition being born with them, their spirits do not struggle against it with that pining discontent which seems the lot of all free servants in America. But the case is widely different with such as, in their own persons, or those of their children, "loved in vain," are exposed to the dreadful traffic above mentioned. In what is their condition better than that of the kidnapped negroes on the coast of Africa? Of the horror in which this enforced migration is held I had a strong proof during our stay in Virginia. The father of a young slave, who belonged to the lady with whom we boarded, was destined to this fate, and within an hour after it was made known to him, he sharpened the hatchet with which he had been felling timber, and with his right hand severed his left from the wrist.

But this is a subject on which I do not mean to dilate; it has been lately treated most judiciously by a far abler hand.[2] Its effects on the moral feelings and external manners of the people are all I wish to observe upon, and these are unquestionably most injurious. The same man who beards his wealthier and more educated neighbour with the bullying boast, "I'm as good as you," turns to his slave, and knocks him down, if the furrow he has ploughed, or the log he has felled, please not this sticker for equality. There is a glaring falsehood on the very surface of such a man's principles that is revolting. It is not among the higher classes that the possession of slaves produces the worst effects. Among the poorer class of landholders, who are often as profoundly ignorant as the negroes they own, the effect of this plenary power over males and females is most demoralising; and the kind of coarse, not to say brutal, authority which is exercised, furnishes the most disgusting moral spectacle I ever witnessed. In all ranks, however, it appeared to me that the greatest and best feelings of the human heart were paralyzed by the relative positions of slave and owner. The characters, the hearts of children, are irretrievably injured by it. In Virginia we boarded for some time in a family consisting of a widow and her four daughters, and I there witnessed a scene strongly indicative of the effect I have mentioned. A young female slave, about eight years of age, had found on the shelf of a

---

2. See Captain Hall's Travels in America. [Trollope note] Basil Hall's *Travels in North America* appeared in 1829. Mrs, Trollope discusses its reception in the United States in her Chapter XXXI.

cupboard a biscuit, temptingly buttered, of which she had eaten a considerable portion before she was observed. The butter had been copiously sprinkled with arsenic for the destruction of rats, and had been thus most
incautiously placed by one of the young ladies of the family. As soon as the
circumstance was known, the lady of the house came to consult me as to
what had best be done for the poor child; I immediately mixed a large cup of
mustard and water (the most rapid of all emetics) and got the little girl to
swallow it. The desired effect was instantly produced, but the poor child,
partly from nausea, and partly from the terror of hearing her death proclaimed by half a dozen voices round her, trembled so violently that I
thought she would fall. I sat down in the court where we were standing, and,
as a matter of course, took the little sufferer in my lap. I observed a general
titter among the white members of the family, while the black stood aloof,
and looked stupefied. The youngest of the family, a little girl about the age
of the young slave, after gazing at me for a few moments in utter astonishment, exclaimed, "My! if Mrs. Trollope has not taken her in her lap, and
wiped her nasty mouth! Why I would not have touched her mouth for two
hundred dollars!"

The little slave was laid on a bed, and I returned to my own apartments;
some time afterwards I sent to enquire for her, and learnt that she was in
great pain. I immediately went myself to inquire farther, when another
young lady of the family, the one by whose imprudence the accident had
occurred, met my anxious enquiries with ill-suppressed mirth—told me
they had sent for the doctor—and then burst into uncontrollable laughter.
The idea of really sympathising in the sufferings of a slave appeared to them
as absurd as weeping over a calf that had been slaughtered by the butcher.
The daughters of my hostess were as lovely as features and complexion
could make them; but the neutralizing effect of this total want of feeling
upon youth and beauty, must be witnessed, to be conceived.

There seems in general a strong feeling throughout America, that none
of the negro race can be trusted; and as fear, according to their notions, is the
only principle by which a slave can be actuated, it is not wonderful if the
imputation be just. But I am persuaded that were a different mode of moral
treatment pursued, most important and beneficial consequences would
result from it. Negroes are very sensible to kindness, and might, I think, be
rendered more profitably obedient by the practice of it towards them, than
by any other mode of discipline whatever. To emancipate them entirely
throughout the Union cannot, I conceive, be thought of, consistently with
the safety of the country; but were the possibility of amelioration taken into
the consideration of the legislature, with all the wisdom, justice, and mercy,
that could be brought to bear upon it, the negro population of the Union
might cease to be a terror, and their situation no longer be a subject either of
indignation or of pity.

I observed every where, throughout the slave states, that all articles
which can be taken and consumed are constantly locked up, and in large
families, where the extent of the establishment multiplies the number of

keys, these are deposited in a basket, and consigned to the care of a little negress, who is constantly seen following her mistress's steps with this basket on her arm, and this, not only that the keys may be always at hand, but because, should they be out of sight one moment, that moment would infallibly be employed for purposes of plunder. It seemed to me in this instance, as in many others, that the close personal attendance of these sable shadows, must be very annoying; but whenever I mentioned it, I was assured that no such feeling existed, and that use rendered them almost unconscious of their presence.

I had, indeed, frequent opportunities of observing this habitual indifference to the presence of their slaves. They talk of them, of their condition, of their faculties, of their conduct, exactly as if they were incapable of hearing. I once saw a young lady, who, when seated at table between a male and a female, was induced by her modesty to intrude on the chair of her female neighbour to avoid the indelicacy of touching the elbow of *a man*. I once saw this very young lady lacing her stays with the most perfect composure before a negro footman. A Virginian gentleman told me that ever since he had married, he had been accustomed to have a negro girl sleep in the same chamber with himself and his wife. I asked for what purpose this nocturnal attendance was necessary? "Good heaven!" was the reply, "if I wanted a glass of water during the night, what would become of me?"

Washington Irving
(1783–1859)

Washington Irving was the first American to win international acclaim as a writer. Although a few books by earlier writers had found interested readers in Europe, his were the first to gain a solid reputation that placed their author on a par with the major writers of the Old World. The Sketch Book (1820) was classic, a model of English prose style and a pioneering work in the development of the short story as a literary form. Irving was America's first successful familiar essayist, its first accomplished humorist, one of the first American writers to turn history and biography into entertaining reading. Not incidentally, he was also his country's first professional recorder of the multiculturalism that was to form so large a part of its heritage.

Born in New York City, the youngest of eleven children of a prosperous merchant, Irving began reading for the law at sixteen and passed the bar at twenty-three. Meanwhile, he had written newspaper satires under the name Jonathan Oldstyle and had spent two years in Europe in leisurely study and travel. In 1807, with his brother William and James Kirke Paulding, he published Salmagundi, satires on New York society. Two years later came A History of New York, a burlesque account of early Dutch settlers written under the pseudonym Dietrich Knickerbocker. No new work followed immediately, however, as Irving turned to other interests. When The Sketch Book appeared, he had been several years in England, and he was to remain abroad another dozen years before returning to the United States. In Europe he wrote such works as Bracebridge Hall (1822), Tales of a Traveller (1824), and several works with Spanish backgrounds, including A History of the Life and Voyages of Christopher Columbus (1828), A Chronicle of the Conquest of Granada (1829), and the stories and sketches collected in The Alhambra (1832). After his return, he published books on western America—A Tour on the Prairies (1835), Astoria (1836), and The Adventures of Captain Bonneville (1837)—and solid biographies of Oliver Goldsmith (1840) and George Washington (1855–1859).

"Rip Van Winkle," from The Sketch Book, is an exemplary tale of cultures in transition, Dutch and Yankee, colony and new nation.

The Works of Washington Irving (21 vols., 1860–1861), long standard, is the source of the present text. A Complete Works of Washington Irving is being published by Twayne. Stanley T. Williams wrote The Life of Washington Irving (2 vols., 1935).

———

Rip Van Winkle

A Posthumous Writing of Diedrich Knickerbocker

By Woden, God of Saxons,
From whence comes Wensday, that is Wodensday.
Truth is a thing that ever I will keep
Unto thylke day in which I creep into
My sepulchre—

—Cartwright[1]

———

1. William Cartwright (1611–1643), English poet and playwright.

THE FOLLOWING TALE was found among the papers of the late Diedrich Knickerbocker, an old gentleman of New York, who was very curious in the Dutch history of the province, and the manners of the descendants from its primitive settlers. His historical researches, however, did not lie so much among books as among men; for the former are lamentably scanty on his favorite topics; whereas he found the old burghers, and still more their wives, rich in that legendary lore, so invaluable to true history. Whenever, therefore, he happened upon a genuine Dutch family, snugly shut up in its low-roofed farmhouse, under a spreading sycamore, he looked upon it as a little clasped volume of black-letter, and studied it with the zeal of a bookworm.

The result of all these researches was a history of the province during the reign of the Dutch governors, which he published some years since. There have been various opinions as to the literary character of his work, and, to tell the truth, it is not a whit better than it should be. Its chief merit is its scrupulous accuracy, which indeed was a little questioned on its first appearance, but has since been completely established; and it is now admitted into all historical collections, as a book of unquestionable authority.

The old gentleman died shortly after the publication of his work, and now that he is dead and gone, it cannot do much harm to his memory to say that his time might have been much better employed in weightier labors. He, however, was apt to ride his hobby his own way; and though it did now and then kick up the dust a little in the eyes of his neighbors, and grieve the spirit of some friends, for whom he felt the truest deference and affection; yet his errors and follies are remembered "more in sorrow than in anger,"[2] and it begins to be suspected, that he never intended to injure or offend. But however his memory may be appreciated by critics, it is still held dear by many folk, whose good opinion is well worth having; particularly by certain biscuit-bakers, who have gone so far as to imprint his likeness on their new-year cakes; and have thus given him a chance for immortality, almost equal to the being stamped on a Waterloo Medal,[3] or a Queen Anne's Farthing.[4]

Whoever has made a voyage up the Hudson must remember the Kaatskill mountains. They are a dismembered branch of the great Appalachian family, and are seen away to the west of the river, swelling up to a noble height, and lording it over the surrounding country. Every change of season, every change of weather, indeed, every hour of the day, produces some change in the magical hues and shapes of these mountains, and they are regarded by all the good wives, far and near, as perfect barometers. When the weather is fair and settled, they are clothed in blue and purple, and print their bold outlines on the clear evening sky; but, sometimes, when the rest of the landscape is cloudless, they will gather a hood of gray vapors about

---

2. Shakespeare's *Hamlet* I, ii, 232.

3. A medal given by England to participants of the Battle of Waterloo.

4. A coin worth a quarter of a penny, bearing the likeness of Queen Anne and minted during her reign (1702–1714).

their summits, which, in the last rays of the setting sun, will glow and light up like a crown of glory.

At the foot of these fairy mountains, the voyager may have descried the light smoke curling up from a village, whose shingle-roofs gleam among the trees, just where the blue tints of the upland melt away into the fresh green of the nearer landscape. It is a little village, of great antiquity, having been founded by some of the Dutch colonists, in the early times of the province, just about the beginning of the government of the good Peter Stuyvesant, (may he rest in peace!) and there were some of the houses of the original settlers standing within a few years, built of small yellow bricks brought from Holland, having latticed windows and gable fronts, surmounted with weathercocks.

In that same village, and in one of these very houses (which, to tell the precise truth, was sadly time-worn and weather-beaten), there lived many years since, while the country was yet a province of Great Britain, a simple good-natured fellow, of the name of Rip Van Winkle. He was a descendant of the Van Winkles who figured so gallantly in the chivalrous days of Peter Stuyvesant, and accompanied him to the siege of Fort Christina.[5] He inherited, however, but little of the martial character of his ancestors. I have observed that he was a simple good-natured man; he was, moreover, a kind neighbor, and an obedient hen-pecked husband. Indeed, to the latter circumstance might be owing that meekness of spirit which gained him such universal popularity; for those men are most apt to be obsequious and conciliating abroad, who are under the discipline of shrews at home. Their tempers, doubtless, are rendered pliant and malleable in the fiery furnace of domestic tribulation; and a curtain lecture is worth all the sermons in the world for teaching the virtues of patience and long-suffering. A termagant wife may, therefore, in some respects, be considered a tolerable blessing; and if so, Rip Van Winkle was thrice blessed.

Certain it is, that he was a great favorite among all the good wives of the village, who, as usual, with the amiable sex, took his part in all family squabbles; and never failed, whenever they talked those matters over in their evening gossipings, to lay all the blame on Dame Van Winkle. The children of the village, too, would shout with joy whenever he approached. He assisted at their sports, made their playthings, taught them to fly kites and shoot marbles, and told them long stories of ghosts, witches, and Indians. Whenever he went dodging about the village, he was surrounded by a troop of them, hanging on his skirts, clambering on his back, and playing a thousand tricks on him with impunity; and not a dog would bark at him throughout the neighborhood.

The great error in Rip's composition was an insuperable aversion to all kinds of profitable labor. It could not be from the want of assiduity or perseverance; for he would sit on a wet rock, with a rod as long and heavy as a Tartar's lance, and fish all day without a murmur, even though he should

---

5. An event treated in Irving's *History of New York*.

not be encouraged by a single nibble. He would carry a fowling-piece on his shoulder for hours together, trudging through woods and swamps, and up hill and down dale, to shoot a few squirrels or wild pigeons. He would never refuse to assist a neighbor even in the roughest toil, and was a foremost man at all country frolics for husking Indian corn, or building stone-fences; the women of the village, too, used to employ him to run their errands, and to do such little old jobs as their less obliging husbands would not do for them. In a word Rip was ready to attend to anybody's business but his own; but as to doing family duty, and keeping his farm in order, he found it impossible.

In fact, he declared it was of no use to work on his farm; it was the most pestilent little piece of ground in the whole country; every thing about it went wrong, and would go wrong, in spite of him. His fences were continually falling to pieces; his cow would either go astray, or get among the cabbages; weeds were sure to grow quicker in his fields than anywhere else; the rain always made a point of setting in just as he had some outdoor work to do; so that though his patrimonial estate had dwindled away under his management, acre by acre, until there was little more left than a mere patch of Indian corn and potatoes, yet it was the worst conditioned farm in the neighborhood.

His children, too, were as ragged and wild as if they belonged to nobody. His son Rip, an urchin begotten in his own likeness, promised to inherit the habits, with the old clothes of his father. He was generally seen trooping like a colt at his mother's heels, equipped in a pair of his father's cast-off galligaskins,[6] which he had much ado to hold up with one hand, as a fine lady does her train in bad weather.

Rip Van Winkle, however, was one of those happy mortals, of foolish, well-oiled dispositions, who take the world easy, eat white bread or brown, whichever can be got with least thought or trouble, and would rather starve on a penny than work for a pound. If left to himself, he would have whistled life away in perfect contentment; but his wife kept continually dinning in his ears about his idleness, his carelessness, and the ruin he was bringing on his family. Morning, noon, and night, her tongue was incessantly going, and every thing he said or did was sure to produce a torrent of household eloquence. Rip had but one way of replying to all lectures of the kind, and that, by frequent use, had grown into a habit. He shrugged his shoulders, shook his head, cast up his eyes, but said nothing. This, however, always provoked a fresh volley from his wife; so that he was fain to draw off his forces, and take to the outside of the house—the only side which, in truth, belongs to a hen-pecked husband.

Rip's sole domestic adherent was his dog Wolf, who was as much hen-pecked as his master; for Dame Van Winkle regarded them as companions in idleness, and even looked upon Wolf with an evil eye, as the cause of his master's going so often astray. True it is, in all points of spirit befitting an honorable dog, he was as courageous an animal as ever scoured the woods—

---

6. Knee breeches.

but what courage can withstand the ever-during and all-besetting terrors of a woman's tongue? The moment Wolf entered the house his crest fell, his tail drooped to the ground, or curled between his legs, he sneaked about with a gallows air, casting many a side-long glance at Dame Van Winkle, and at the least flourish of a broomstick or ladle, he would fly to the door with yelping precipitation.

Times grew worse and worse with Rip Van Winkle as years of matrimony rolled on; a tart temper never mellows with age, and a sharp tongue is the only edged tool that grows keener with constant use. For a long while he used to console himself, when driven from home, by frequenting a kind of perpetual club of the sages, philosophers, and other idle personages of the village; which held its sessions on a bench before a small inn, designated by a rubicund portrait of His Majesty George the Third. Here they used to sit in the shade through a long lazy summer's day, talking listlessly over village gossip, or telling endless sleepy stories about nothing. But it would have been worth any statesman's money to have heard the profound discussions that sometimes took place, when by chance an old newspaper fell into their hands from some passing traveller. How solemnly they would listen to the contents, as drawled out by Derrick Van Bummel, the schoolmaster, a dapper learned little man, who was not to be daunted by the most gigantic word in the dictionary; and how sagely they would deliberate upon public events some months after they had taken place.

The opinions of this junto were completely controlled by Nicholas Vedder, a patriarch of the village, and landlord of the inn, at the door of which he took his seat from morning till night, just moving sufficiently to avoid the sun and keep in the shade of a large tree; so that the neighbors could tell the hour by his movements as accurately as by a sun-dial. It is true he was rarely heard to speak, but smoked his pipe incessantly. His adherents, however (for every great man has his adherents), perfectly understood him, and knew how to gather his opinions. When any thing that was read or related displeased him, he was observed to smoke his pipe vehemently, and to send forth short, frequent and angry puffs; but when pleased, he would inhale the smoke slowly and tranquilly, and emit it in light and placid clouds; and sometimes, taking the pipe from his mouth, and letting the fragrant vapor curl about his nose, would gravely nod his head in token of perfect approbation.

From even this stronghold the unlucky Rip was at length routed by his termagant wife, who would suddenly break in upon the tranquillity of the assemblage and call the members all to naught; nor was that august personage, Nicholas Vedder himself, sacred from the daring tongue of this terrible virago, who charged him outright with encouraging her husband in habits of idleness.

Poor Rip was at last reduced almost to despair; and his only alternative, to escape from the labor of the farm and clamor of his wife, was to take gun in hand and stroll away into the woods. Here he would sometimes seat himself at the foot of a tree, and share the contents of his wallet with Wolf, with whom he sympathized as a fellow-sufferer in persecution. "Poor Wolf," he would say, "thy mistress leads thee a dog's life of it; but never mind, my lad, whilst I live thou shalt never want a friend to stand by thee!" Wolf would wag his tail, look wistfully in his master's face, and if dogs can feel pity I verily believe he reciprocated the sentiment with all his heart.

In a long ramble of the kind on a fine autumnal day, Rip had unconsciously scrambled to one of the highest parts of the Kaatskill mountains. He was after his favorite sport of squirrel shooting, and the still solitudes had echoed and re-echoed with the reports of his gun. Panting and fatigued, he threw himself, late in the afternoon, on a green knoll, covered with mountain herbage, that crowned the brow of a precipice. From an opening between the trees he could overlook all the lower country for many a mile of rich woodland. He saw at a distance the lordly Hudson, far, far below him, moving on its silent but majestic course, with the reflection of a purple cloud, or the sail of a lagging bark, here and there sleeping on its glassy bosom, and at last losing itself in the blue highlands.

On the other side he looked down into a deep mountain glen, wild, lonely, and shagged, the bottom filled with fragments from the impending cliffs, and scarcely lighted by the reflected rays of the setting sun. For some time Rip lay musing on this scene; evening was gradually advancing; the mountains began to throw their long blue shadows over the valleys; he saw that it would be dark long before he could reach the village, and he heaved a heavy sigh when he thought of encountering the terrors of Dame Van Winkle.

As he was about to descend, he heard a voice from a distance, hallooing, "Rip Van Winkle! Rip Van Winkle!" He looked round, but could see nothing but a crow winging its solitary flight across the mountain. He thought his fancy must have deceived him, and turned again to descend, when he heard the same cry through the still evening air; "Rip Van Winkle! Rip Van Winkle!"—at the same time Wolf bristled up his back, and giving a low growl, skulked to his master's side, looking fearfully down into the glen. Rip now felt a vague apprehension stealing over him; he looked anxiously in the same direction, and perceived a strange figure slowly toiling up the rocks, and bending under the weight of something he carried on his back. He was surprised to see any human being in this lonely and unfrequented place, but supposing it to be some one of the neighborhood in need of his assistance, he hastened down to yield it.

On nearer approach he was still more surprised at the singularity of the stranger's appearance. He was a short square-built old fellow, with thick bushy hair, and a grizzled beard. His dress was of the antique Dutch fashion—a cloth jerkin strapped round the waist—several pair of breeches, the outer one of ample volume, decorated with rows of buttons down the sides, and bunches at the knees. He bore on his shoulder a stout keg, that seemed full of liquor, and made signs for Rip to approach and assist him with the load. Though rather shy and distrustful of this new acquaintance, Rip complied with his usual alacrity; and mutually relieving one another, they clambered up a narrow gully, apparently the dry bed of a mountain torrent. As they ascended, Rip every now and then heard long rolling peals, like distant thunder, that seemed to issue out of a deep ravine, or rather cleft, between lofty rocks, toward which their rugged path conducted. He paused for an instant, but supposing it to be the muttering of one of those transient thunder-showers which often take place in mountain heights, he proceeded. Passing through the ravine, they came to a hollow, like a small amphitheatre, surrounded by perpendicular precipices, over the brinks of which impending trees shot their branches, so that you only caught glimpses of the azure sky and the bright evening cloud. During the whole time Rip and his companion had labored on in silence; for though the former marvelled greatly what could be the object of carrying a keg of liquor up this wild mountain, yet there was something strange and incomprehensible about the unknown, that inspired awe and checked familiarity.

On entering the amphitheatre, new objects of wonder presented themselves. On a level spot in the centre was a company of odd-looking personages playing at nine-pins. They were dressed in a quaint outlandish fashion; some wore short doublets, others jerkins, with long knives in their belts, and most of them had enormous breeches, of similar style with that of the guide's. Their visages, too, were peculiar: one had a large head, broad face, and small piggish eyes: the face of another seemed to consist entirely of nose, and was surmounted by a white sugar-loaf hat, set off with a little red cock's tail. They all had beards, of various shapes and colors. There was one who seemed to be the commander. He was a stout old gentleman, with a weather-beaten countenance; he wore a laced doublet, broad belt and hanger[7] high crowned hat and feather, red stockings, and high-heeled shoes, with roses[8] in them. The whole group reminded Rip of the figures in an old Flemish painting, in the parlor of Dominie Van Shaick, the village parson, and which had been brought over from Holland at the time of the settlement.

What seemed particularly odd to Rip was, that though these folks were evidently amusing themselves, yet they maintained the gravest faces, the most mysterious silence, and were, withal, the most melancholy party of pleasure he had ever witnessed. Nothing interrupted the stillness of the scene but the noise of the balls, which, whenever they were rolled, echoed along the mountains like rumbling peals of thunder.

As Rip and his companion approached them, they suddenly desisted from their play, and stared at him with such fixed statue-like gaze, and such strange, uncouth, lack-lustre countenances, that his heart turned within him, and his knees smote together. His companion now emptied the contents of the keg into large flagons, and made signs to him to wait upon the company. He obeyed with fear and trembling; they quaffed the liquor in profound silence, and then returned to their game.

By degrees Rip's awe and apprehension subsided. He even ventured, when no eye was fixed upon him, to taste the beverage, which he found had

---

7. A light saber.
8. Rosettes.

much of the flavor of excellent Hollands.[9] He was naturally a thirsty soul, and was soon tempted to repeat the draught. One taste provoked another; and he reiterated his visits to the flagon so often that at length his senses were overpowered, his eyes swam in his head, his head gradually declined, and he fell into a deep sleep.

On waking, he found himself on the green knoll whence he had first seen the old man of the glen. He rubbed his eyes—it was a bright sunny morning. The birds were hopping and twittering among the bushes, and the eagle was wheeling aloft, and breasting the pure mountain breeze. "Surely," thought Rip, "I have not slept here all night." He recalled the occurrences before he fell asleep. The strange man with a keg of liquor—the mountain ravine—the wild retreat among the rocks—the wobegone party at nine-pins—the flagon—"Oh! that flagon! that wicked flagon!" thought Rip—"what excuse shall I make to Dame Van Winkle!"

He looked round for his gun, but in place of the clean well-oiled fowling-piece, he found an old firelock lying by him, the barrel incrusted with rust, the lock falling off, and the stock worm-eaten. He now suspected that the grave roysters of the mountain had put a trick upon him, and, having dosed him with liquor, had robbed him of his gun. Wolf, too, had disappeared, but he might have strayed away after a squirrel or partridge. He whistled after him and shouted his name, but all in vain; the echoes repeated his whistle and shout, but no dog was to be seen.

He determined to revisit the scene of the last evening's gambol, and if he met with any of the party, to demand his dog and gun. As he rose to walk, he found himself stiff in the joints, and wanting in his usual activity. "These mountain beds do not agree with me," thought Rip, "and if this frolic should lay me up with a fit of the rheumatism, I shall have a blessed time with Dame Van Winkle." With some difficulty he got down into the glen: he found the gully up which he and his companion had ascended the preceding evening; but to his astonishment a mountain stream was now foaming down it, leaping from rock to rock, and filling the glen with babbling murmurs. He, however, made shift to scramble up its sides, working his toilsome way through thickets of birch, sassafras, and witch-hazel, and sometimes tripped up or entangled by the wild grapevines that twisted their coils or tendrils from tree to tree, and spread a kind of network in his path.

At length he reached to where the ravine had opened through the cliffs to the amphitheatre; but no traces of such opening remained. The rocks presented a high impenetrable wall over which the torrent came tumbling in a sheet of feathery foam, and fell into a broad deep basin, black from the shadows of the surrounding forest. Here, then, poor Rip was brought to a stand. He again called and whistled after his dog; he was only answered by the cawing of a flock of idle crows, sporting high in air about a dry tree that overhung a sunny precipice; and who, secure in their elevation, seemed to look down and scoff at the poor man's perplexities. What was to be done? the morning was passing away, and Rip felt famished for want of his break-

---

9. A Dutch gin.

fast. He grieved to give up his dog and gun; he dreaded to meet his wife; but it would not do to starve among the mountains. He shook his head, shouldered the rusty firelock, and, with a heart full of trouble and anxiety, turned his steps homeward.

As he approached the village he met a number of people, but none whom he knew, which somewhat surprised him, for he had thought himself acquainted with every one in the country round. Their dress, too, was of a different fashion from that to which he was accustomed. They all stared at him with equal marks of surprise, and whenever they cast their eyes upon him, invariably stroked their chins. The constant recurrence of this gesture induced Rip, involuntarily, to do the same, when, to his astonishment, he found his beard had grown a foot long!

He had now entered the skirts of the village. A troop of strange children ran at his heels, hooting after him, and pointing at his gray beard. The dogs, too, not one of which he recognized for an old acquaintance, barked at him as he passed. The very village was altered; it was larger and more populous. There were rows of houses which he had never seen before, and those which had been his familiar haunts had disappeared. Strange names were over the doors—strange faces at the windows—every thing was strange. His mind now misgave him; he began to doubt whether both he and the world around him were not bewitched. Surely this was his native village, which he had left but the day before. There stood the Kaatskill mountains—there ran the silver Hudson at a distance—there was every hill and dale precisely as it had always been—Rip was sorely perplexed—"That flagon last night," thought he, "has addled my poor head sadly!"

It was with some difficulty that he found the way to his own house, which he approached with silent awe, expecting every moment to hear the shrill voice of Dame Van Winkle. He found the house gone to decay—the roof fallen in, the windows shattered, and the doors off the hinges. A half-starved dog that looked like Wolf was skulking about it. Rip called him by name, but the cur snarled, showed his teeth, and passed on. This was an unkind cut indeed—"My very dog," sighed poor Rip, "has forgotten me!"

He entered the house, which, to tell the truth, Dame Van Winkle had always kept in neat order. It was empty, forlorn, and apparently abandoned. This desolateness overcame all his connubial fears—he called loudly for his wife and children—the lonely chambers rang for a moment with his voice, and then all again was silence.

He now hurried forth, and hastened to his old resort, the village inn—but it too was gone. A large rickety wooden building stood in its place, with great gaping windows, some of them broken and mended with old hats and petticoats, and over the door was painted, "the Union Hotel, by Jonathan Doolittle." Instead of the great tree that used to shelter the quiet little Dutch inn of yore, there now was reared a tall naked pole, with something on the top that looked like a red night-cap,[1] and from it was fluttering a flag, on which was a singular assemblage of stars and stripes—all this was strange

---

1. The "liberty cap," a symbol of the French Revolution often displayed in the United States.

and incomprehensible. He recognized on the sign, however, the ruby face of King George, under which he had smoked so many a peaceful pipe; but even this was singularly metamorphosed. The red coat was changed for one of blue and buff, a sword was held in the hand instead of a sceptre, the head was decorated with a cocked hat, and underneath was painted in large characters, GENERAL WASHINGTON.

There was, as usual, a crowd of folk about the door, but none that Rip recollected. The very character of the people seemed changed. There was a busy, bustling, disputatious tone about it, instead of the accustomed phlegm and drowsy tranquillity. He looked in vain for the sage Nicholas Vedder, with his broad face, double chin, and fair long pipe, uttering clouds of tobacco-smoke instead of idle speeches; or Van Bummel, the schoolmaster, doling forth the contents of an ancient newspaper. In place of these, a lean, bilious-looking fellow, with his pockets full of handbills, was haranguing vehemently about rights of citizens—elections—members of congress—liberty—Bunker's Hill—heroes of seventy-six—and other words, which were a perfect Babylonish jargon to the bewildered Van Winkle.

The appearance of Rip, with his long grizzled beard, his rusty fowling-piece, his uncouth dress, and an army of women and children at his heels, soon attracted the attention of the tavern politicians. They crowded round him, eyeing him from head to foot with great curiosity. The orator bustled up to him, and, drawing him partly aside, inquired "on which side he voted?" Rip stared in vacant stupidity. Another short but busy little fellow pulled him by the arm, and, rising on tiptoe, inquired in his ear, "Whether he was Federal or Democrat?"[2] Rip was equally at a loss to comprehend the question; when a knowing, self-important old gentleman, in a sharp cocked hat, made his way through the crowd, putting them to the right and left with his elbows as he passed, and planting himself before Van Winkle, with one arm akimbo, the other resting on his cane, his keen eyes and sharp hat penetrating, as it were, into his very soul, demanded in an austere tone, "what brought him to the election with a gun on his shoulder, and a mob at his heels, and whether he meant to breed a riot in the village?"—"Alas! gentlemen," cried Rip, somewhat dismayed, "I am a poor quiet man, a native of the place, and a loyal subject of the king, God bless him!"

Here a general shout burst from the by-standers—"A tory! a tory! a spy! a refugee! hustle him! away with him!" It was with great difficulty that the self-important man in the cocked hat restored order; and, having assumed a tenfold austerity of brow, demanded again of the unknown culprit, what he came there for, and whom he was seeking? The poor man humbly assured him that he meant no harm, but merely came there in search of some of his neighbors, who used to keep about the tavern.

"Well—who are they?—name them."

Rip bethought himself a moment, and inquired, "Where's Nicholas Vedder?"

There was a silence for a little while, when an old man replied, in a thin

---

2. The Federalists were followers of Hamilton, the Democratic Republicans, of Jefferson.

piping voice, "Nicholas Vedder! why, he is dead and gone these eighteen years! There was a wooden tombstone in the churchyard that used to tell all about him, but that's rotten and gone too."

"Where's Brom Dutcher?"

"Oh, he went off to the army in the beginning of the war; some say he was killed at the storming of Stony Point[3]—others say he was drowned in a squall at the foot of Antony's Nose.[4] I don't know—he never came back again."

"Where's Van Bummel, the schoolmaster?"

"He went off to the wars too, was a great militia general, and is now in congress."

Rip's heart died away at hearing of these sad changes in his home and friends, and finding himself thus alone in the world. Every answer puzzled him too, by treating of such enormous lapses of time, and of matters which he could not understand: war—congress—Stony Point;—he had no courage to ask after any more friends, but cried out in despair, "Does nobody here know Rip Van Winkle?"

"Oh, Rip Van Winkle!" exclaimed two or three, "Oh, to be sure! that's Rip Van Winkle yonder, leaning against the tree."

Rip looked, and beheld a precise counterpart of himself, as he went up the mountain: apparently as lazy, and certainly as ragged. The poor fellow was now completely confounded. He doubted his own identity, and whether he was himself or another man. In the midst of his bewilderment, the man in the cocked hat demanded who he was, and what was his name?

"God knows," exclaimed he, at his wit's end; "I'm not myself—I'm somebody else—that's me yonder—no—that's somebody else got into my shoes—I was myself last night, but I fell asleep on the mountain, and they've changed my gun, and every thing's changed, and I'm changed, and I can't tell what's my name, or who I am!"

The by-standers began now to look at each other, nod, wink significantly, and tap their fingers against their foreheads. There was a whisper, also, about securing the gun, and keeping the old fellow from doing mischief, at the very suggestion of which the self-important man in the cocked hat retired with some precipitation. At this critical moment a fresh comely woman passed through the throng to get a peep at the gray-bearded man. She had a chubby child in her arms, which, frightened at his looks, began to cry. "Hush, Rip," cried she, "hush, you little fool; the old man won't hurt you." The name of the child, the air of the mother, the tone of her voice, all awakened a train of recollections in his mind. "What is your name, my good woman?" asked he.

"Judith Gardenier."

"And your father's name?"

"Ah, poor man, Rip Van Winkle was his name, but it's twenty years since he went away from home with his gun, and never has been heard of

---

3. A headland on the Hudson below West Point, captured in 1779 by Mad Anthony Wayne.

4. Another promontory on the Hudson.

since—his dog came home without him; but whether he shot himself, or was carried away by the Indians, nobody can tell. I was then but a little girl."

Rip had but one question more to ask; but he put it with a faltering voice:

"Where's your mother?"

"Oh, she too had died but a short time since; she broke a blood-vessel in a fit of passion at a New-England peddler."

There was a drop of comfort, at least, in this intelligence. The honest man could contain himself no longer. He caught his daughter and her child in his arms. "I am your father!" cried he—"Young Rip Van Winkle once— old Rip Van Winkle now!—Does nobody know poor Rip Van Winkle?"

All stood amazed, until an old woman, tottering out from among the crowd, put her hand to her brow, and peering under it in his face for a moment, exclaimed, "Sure enough! it is Rip Van Winkle—it is himself! Welcome home again, old neighbor—Why, where have you been these twenty long years?"

Rip's story was soon told, for the whole twenty years had been to him but as one night. The neighbors stared when they heard it; some were seen to wink at each other, and put their tongues in their cheeks: and the self-important man in the cocked hat, who, when the alarm was over, had returned to the field, screwed down the corners of his mouth, and shook his head—upon which there was a general shaking of the head throughout the assemblage.

It was determined, however, to take the opinion of old Peter Vander-donk, who was seen slowly advancing up the road. He was a descendant of the historian[5] of that name, who wrote one of the earliest accounts of the province. Peter was the most ancient inhabitant of the village, and well versed in all the wonderful events and traditions of the neighborhood. He recollected Rip at once, and corroborated his story in the most satisfactory manner. He assured the company that it was a fact, handed down from his ancestor the historian, that the Kaatskill mountains had always been haunted by strange beings. That it was affirmed that the great Hendrick Hudson, the first discover of the river and country, kept a kind of vigil there every twenty years, with his crew of the Halfmoon; being permitted in this way to revisit the scenes of his enterprise, and keep a guardian eye upon the river, and the great city called by his name.[6] That his father had once seen them in their old Dutch dresses playing at nine-pins in a hollow of the mountain; and that he himself had heard, one summer afternoon, the sound of their balls, like distant peals of thunder.

To make a long story short, the company broke up, and returned to the more important concerns of the election. Rip's daughter took him home to live with her; she had a snug, well-furnished house, and a stout cheery farmer for a husband, whom Rip recollected for one of the urchins that used to climb upon his back. As to Rip's son and heir, who was the ditto of him-

---

5. Adriaen Van der Donck (c. 1620–1655).

6. Hudson, on the Hudson River.

self, seen leaning against the tree, he was employed to work on the farm; but evinced an hereditary disposition to attend to any thing else but his business.

Rip now resumed his old walks and habits; he soon found many of his former cronies, though all rather the worse for the wear and tear of time; and preferred making friends among the rising generation, with whom he soon grew into great favor.

Having nothing to do at home, and being arrived at that happy age when a man can be idle with impunity, he took his place once more on the bench at the inn door, and was reverenced as one of the patriarchs of the village, and a chronicle of the old times "before the war." It was some time before he could get into the regular track of gossip, or could be made to comprehend the strange events that had taken place during his torpor. How that there had been a revolutionary war—that the country had thrown off the yoke of old England—and that, instead of being a subject of His Majesty George the Third, he was now a free citizen of the United States. Rip, in fact, was no politician; the changes of states and empires made but little impression on him; but there was one species of despotism under which he had long groaned, and that was—petticoat government. Happily that was at an end; he had got his neck out of the yoke of matrimony, and could go in and out whenever he pleased, without dreading the tyranny of Dame Van Winkle. Whenever her name was mentioned, however, he shook his head, shrugged his shoulders, and cast up his eyes; which might pass either for an expression of resignation to his fate, or joy at his deliverance.

He used to tell his story to every stranger that arrived at Mr. Doolittle's Hotel. He was observed, at first, to vary on some points every time he told it, which was, doubtless, owing to his having so recently awaked. It at last settled down precisely to the tale I have related, and not a man, woman, or child in the neighborhood, but knew it by heart. Some always pretended to doubt the reality of it, and insisted that Rip had been out of his head, and that this was one point on which he always remained flighty. The old Dutch inhabitants, however, almost universally gave it full credit. Even to this day they never hear a thunderstorm of a summer afternoon about the Kaatskill, but they say Hendrick Hudson and his crew are at their game of nine-pins; and it is a common wish of all hen-pecked husbands in the neighborhood, when life hangs heavy on their hands, that they might have a quieting draught out of Rip Van Winkle's flagon.

Note.—The foregoing tale, one would suspect, had been suggested to Mr. Knickerbocker by a little German superstition about the Emperor Frederick *der Rothbart*[7] and the Kypphauser mountain; the subjoined note, however, which he had appended to the tale, shows that it is an absolute fact, narrated with his usual fidelity.

"The story of Rip Van Winkle may seem incredible to many, but nevertheless I give it my full belief, for I know the vicinity of our old Dutch settlements to have been very

---

7. According to legend, Frederick I, Holy Roman Emperor (1152–1190), called "Rothbart" or "Barbarossa" for his red beard, slept in a cave in the mountain.

subject to marvelous events and appearances. Indeed, I have heard many stranger stories than this, in the villages along the Hudson, all of which were too well authenticated to admit of a doubt. I have even talked with Rip Van Winkle myself, who, when last I saw him, was a very venerable old man, and so perfectly rational and consistent on every other point that I think no conscientious person could refuse to take this into the bargain; nay, I have seen a certificate on the subject taken before a country justice, and signed with a cross, in the justice's own handwriting. The story, therefore, is beyond the possibility of doubt."

John James Audubon
(1785–1851)

Born in Les Cayes, Santo Domingo, in the area that is now Haiti, John James Audubon was the son of a French naval officer and a Creole woman. Educated in France, he came at eighteen to his family's estate near Philadelphia. He was married in 1808 and lived for the next dozen years mostly in Kentucky and then in the 1820s mostly in Louisiana. Much of the time, however, he lived apart from his family, wandering through the forests and along the streams with his dog, his gun, and his sketchbook, obsessed with picturing the birds of the American wilderness. His collection complete, he went to England to find a publisher for The Birds of North America, *first published in four volumes as a double elephant folio (1827–1838), then in seven volumes in royal octavo form (1840–1844). To accompany the plates of that work, he published his* Ornithological Biography *(5 vols., 1831–1839), a compilation of descriptive ornithological notes interspersed with sketches of his travels, including the encounter reprinted here. Turning then to animals, he traveled into the Yellowstone area, gathering the material for* The Viviparous Quadrupeds of North America *(plates, 1842–1845; text, 1846–1854). Famous and wealthy, he settled with his family on an estate on the Hudson River, on the northern end of Manhattan Island, but did not live to see the final text of his* Viviparous Quadrupeds *in print.*

Posthumous editions of Audubon's writings include *Delineations of American Scenery and Character*, edited by Francis Hobart Herrick (1926), which reprints most of the sketches from *Ornithological Biography; Journal of John James Audubon, Made During a Trip to New Orleans in 1820–21*, edited by Howard Corning (1929); and *Letters*, edited by Howard Corning (1930).

The Prairie[1]

ON MY RETURN from the Upper Mississippi, I found myself obliged to cross one of the wide Prairies, which, in that portion of the United States vary the appearance of the country. The weather was fine, all around me was as fresh and blooming as if it had just issued from the bosom of nature. My knapsack, my gun, and my dog, were all I had for baggage and company. But, although well moccasined, I moved slowly along, attracted by the brilliancy of the flowers, and the gambols of the fawns around their dams, to all appearance as thoughtless of danger as I felt myself.

My march was of long duration; I saw the sun sinking beneath the horizon long before I could perceive any appearance of woodland, and nothing in the shape of man had I met with that day. The track which I followed was only an old Indian trace, and as darkness overshadowed the prairie, I felt some desire to reach at least a copse, in which I might lie down to rest. The Night-hawks were skimming over and around me, attracted by the buzzing wings of the beetles which form their food, and the distant howling of wolves gave me some hope that I should soon arrive at the skirts of some woodland.

I did so, and almost at the same instant a fire-light attracting my eye, I moved towards it, full of confidence that it proceeded from the camp of some wandering Indians. I was mistaken:—I discovered by its glare that it was from the hearth of a small log cabin, and that a tall figure passed and repassed between it and me, as if busily engaged in household arrangements.

I reached the spot, and presenting myself at the door, asked the tall figure, which proved to be a woman, if I might take shelter under her roof for the night. Her voice was gruff, and her attire negligently thrown about her. She answered in the affirmative. I walked in, took a wooden stool, and quitely seated myself by the fire. The next object that attracted my notice was a finely formed young Indian, resting his head between his hands, with his elbows on his knees. A long bow rested against the log wall near him, while a quantity of arrows and two or three raccoon skins lay at his feet. He moved not; he apparently breathed not. Accustomed to the habits of the Indians, and knowing that they pay little attention to the approach of civilized strangers (a circumstance which in some countries is considered as evincing the apathy of their character), I addressed him in French, a language not unfrequently partially known to the people in that neighborhood. He raised his head, pointed to one of his eyes with his finger, and gave me a significant glance with the other. His face was covered with blood. The fact was, that an hour before this, as he was in the act of discharging an arrow at a raccoon in the top of a tree, the arrow had split upon the cord, and sprung back with such violence into his right eye as to destroy it for ever.

---

1. First published in *Ornithological Biography*, reprinted in *Delineations of American Scenery and Character*.

Feeling hungry, I inquired what sort of fare I might expect. Such a thing as a bed was not to be seen, but many large untanned bear and buffalo hides lay piled in a corner. I drew a fine time-piece from my breast, and told the woman that it was late, and that I was fatigued. She had espyed my watch, the richness of which seemed to operate upon her feelings with electric quickness. She told me that there was plenty of venison and jerked buffalo meat, and that on removing the ashes I should find a cake. But my watch had struck her fancy, and her curiosity had to be gratified by an immediate sight of it. I took off the gold chain that secured it from around my neck, and presented it to her. She was all ecstasy, spoke of its beauty, asked me its value, and put the chain round her brawny neck, saying how happy the possession of such a watch should make her. Thoughtless, and, as I fancied myself, in so retired a spot, secure, I paid little attention to her talk or her movements. I helped my dog to a good supper of venison, and was not long in satisfying the demands of my own appetite.

The Indian rose from his seat, as if in extreme suffering. He passed and repassed me several times, and once pinched me on the side so violently, that the pain nearly brought forth an exclamation of anger. I looked at him. His eye met mine; but his look was so forbidding, that it struck a chill into the more nervous part of my system. He again seated himself, drew his butcher-knife from its greasy scabbard, examined its edge, as I would do that of a razor suspected dull, replaced it, and again taking his tomahawk from his back, filled the pipe of it with tobacco, and sent me expressive glances whenever our hostess chanced to have her back towards us.

Never until that moment had my senses been awakened to the danger which I now suspected to be about me. I returned glance for glance to my companion, and rested well assured that, whatever enemies I might have, he was not of their number.

I asked the woman for my watch, wound it up, and under pretence of wishing to see how the weather might probably be on the morrow, took up my gun, and walked out of the cabin. I slipped a ball into each barrel, scraped the edges of my flints, renewed the primings, and returning to the hut, gave a favourable account of my observations. I took a few bearskins, made a pallet of them, and calling my faithful dog to my side, lay down, with my gun close to my body, and in a few minutes was, to all appearance, fast asleep.

A short time had elapsed, when some voices were heard, and from the corner of my eyes I saw two athletic youths making their entrance, bearing a dead stag on a pole. They disposed of their burden, and asking for whisky, helped themselves freely to it. Observing me and the wounded Indian, they asked who I was, and why the devil that rascal (meaning the Indian, who, they knew, understood not a word of English) was in the house. The mother—for so she proved to be, bade them speak less loudly, made mention of my watch, and took them to a corner, where a conversation took place, the purport of which it required little shrewdness in me to guess. I tapped my dog gently. He moved his tail, and with indescribable pleasure I saw his fine eyes alternately fixed on me and raised towards the trio in the corner. I felt that he perceived danger in my situation. The Indian exchanged a last glance with me.

The lads had eaten and drunk themselves into such condition, that I already looked upon them as *hors de combat;* and the frequent visits of the whisky bottle to the ugly mouth of their dam I hoped would soon reduce her to a like state. Judge of my astonishment, reader, when I saw this incarnate fiend take a large carving-knife, and go to the grindstone to whet its edge. I saw her pour the water on the turning machine, and watched her working away with the dangerous instrument, until the sweat covered every part of my body, in despite of my determination to defend myself to the last. Her task finished, she walked to her reeling sons, and said. "There, that'll soon settle him! Boys, kill yon———, and then for the watch."

I turned, cocked my gun-locks silently, touched my faithful companion, and lay ready to start up and shoot the first who might attempt my life. The moment was fast approaching, and that night might have been my last in this world, had not Providence made preparations for my rescue. All was ready. The infernal hag was advancing slowly, probably contemplating the best way of despatching me, whilst her sons should be engaged with the Indian. I was several times on the eve of rising and shooting her on the spot:—but she was not to be punished thus. The door was suddenly opened, and there entered two stout travellers, each with a long rifle on his shoulder. I bounced up on my feet, and making them most heartily welcome, told them how well it was for me that they should have arrived at that moment. The tale was told in a minute. The drunken sons were secured, and the woman, in spite of her defence and vociferations, shared the same fate. The Indian fairly danced with joy, and gave us to understand that, as he could not sleep for pain, he would watch over us. You may suppose we slept much less than we talked. The two strangers gave me an account of their once having been themselves in a somewhat similar situation. Day came, fair and rosy, and with it the punishment of our captives.

They were now quite sobered. Their feet were unbound, but their arms were still securely tied. We marched them into the woods off the road, and having used them as Regulators[2] were wont to use such delinquents, we set

---

2. In his sketch "The Regulators" Audubon clarifies the term as follows:

> In those remote parts, no sooner is it discovered that an individual has conducted himself in a notoriously vicious manner, or has committed some outrage upon society, than a conclave of the honest citizens takes place, for the purpose of investigating the case with a rigour without which no good result could be expected. These honest citizens, selected from among the most respectable persons in the district, and vested with powers suited to the necessity of preserving order on the frontiers, are named *Regulators.* The accused person is arrested, his conduct laid open, and if he is found guilty of a first crime, he is warned to leave the country, and go farther from society, within an appointed time. Should the individual prove so callous as to disregard the sentence, and remain in the same neighbourhood, to commit new crimes, then woe be to him; for the Regulators, after proving him guilty a second time, pass and execute a sentence, which, if not enough to make him perish under the infliction, is at least forever impressed upon his memory. The punishment inflicted is generally a severe castigation, and the destruction, by fire, of his cabin. Sometimes, in cases of reiterated theft or murder, death is considered necessary; and, in some instances, delinquents of the worst species have been shot, after which their heads have been stuck on poles, to deter others from following their example.

fire to the cabin, gave all the skins and implements to the young Indian warrior, and proceeded, well pleased, towards the settlements.

During upwards of twenty-five years, when my wanderings extended to all parts of our country, this was the only time at which my life was in danger from my fellow creatures. Indeed, so little risk do travellers run in the United States, that no one born there ever dreams of any to be encountered on the road; and I can only account for this occurrence by supposing that the inhabitants of the cabin were not Americans.

Will you believe, reader, that not many miles from the place where this adventure happened, and where fifteen years ago, no habitation belonging to civilized man was expected, and very few ever seen, large roads are now laid out, cultivation has converted the woods into fertile fields, taverns have been erected, and much of what we Americans call comfort is to be met with. So fast does improvement proceed in our abundant and free country.

William Apes
(1798–?)

In A Son of the Forest *(1829), William Apes contributed to American literature the first Native American autobiography, inaugurating a genre that was to include such later nineteenth-century works as George Copway's* The Life, History, and Travels of Kah-ge-ga-gah-bowh *(1847) and Sarah Winnemucca Hopkins's* Life among the Piutes *(1883). Americans with their roots in Europe had already a considerable interest in the Indians, but their knowledge, when it had not come from direct personal contact, had hitherto come almost exclusively through the filter of white sensibilities. From the reports of the early Spanish explorers through the captivity narratives of the seventeenth and eighteenth centuries, the view had been that of outsiders, even though some of the captives had been adopted by their tribal hosts, had lived long with them, and had accepted Indian ways: James Smith, for example, spent four years with tribes of Pennsylvania and Ohio, and John Tanner, the "white Indian," lived nearly thirty years with Ottawas and Ojibways around the Great Lakes.*

By the 1820s the Indians had become a major subject in American literature, most recently and most famously in the Leatherstocking *series of James Fenimore Cooper, three of which—*The Pioneers *(1823),* The Last of the Mohicans *(1826), and* The Prairie *(1827)—had appeared before* A Son of the Forest. *To the view of the Indian then current, Apes's autobiography* *was in one sense no corrective since it dealt not at all with the Indian in a tribal setting in the wilderness. Apes's story was of an Indian among whites, and as such a reminder of how intertwined the differing cultures had become in New England in the two centuries subsequent to the landing of the Pilgrims. Descended from King Philip—the chief whose name is commemorated in King Philip's War and whose followers kidnapped Mary Rowlandson—Apes was also a descendant of a white man married to a granddaughter of King Philip. Taken as a child from his Indian home, he was raised by whites, fought in the War of 1812, and became a Methodist preacher.*

A *Son of the Forest* (1829) was reprinted in a second, revised edition in 1831, the source of the present text. Apes's other works include *The Experience of Five Christian Indians of the Pequod Tribe* (1833) and *Eulogy on King Philip* (1836). *On Our Ground: The Complete Writings of William Apes, a Pequot* (1992) was edited by Barry O'Connell.

———

[From] A Son of the Forest

CHAPTER I. [EARLY YEARS]

WILLIAM APES, the author of the following narrative, was born in the town of Colereign,[1] Massachusetts, on the thirty-first of January, in the year of our Lord seventeen hundred and ninety-eight. My grandfather was a white man, and married a female attached to the royal family of Philip,[2] king of the Pequod[3] tribe of Indians, so well known in that part of American history, which relates to the wars between the whites and the natives. My grandmother was, if I am not misinformed, the king's granddaughter, and a fair

---

1. Or Colrain.

2. King Philip, or Metacomet (?–1676), son of Massasoit, who had befriended the Pilgrims. King Philip's War (1675–1676) ended years of relatively peaceful relations between whites and Indians in New England.

3. Usually Pequot.

and beautiful woman. This statement is given not with a view of appearing great, in the estimation of others—what I would ask, is *royal* blood—the blood of a king is no better than that of the subject—we are in fact but one family; we are all the descendants of one great progenitor—Adam. I would not boast of my extraction, as I consider myself nothing more than a worm of the earth.

I have given the above account of my origin, with the simple view of narrating the truth as I have received it; and under the settled conviction that I must render an account at the last day, to the sovereign Judge of all men, for every word contained in this little book.

As the story of King Philip, is perhaps generally known, and consequently the history of the Pequod tribe, over whom he reigned; it will suffice to say, that he was overcome by treachery, and the goodly heritage occupied by this once happy, powerful, yet peaceful people, was possessed in the process of time, by their avowed enemies the whites, who had been welcomed to their land in that spirit of kindness, so peculiar to the red-men of the woods. But the violation of their inherent rights, by those to whom they had extended the hand of friendship, was not the only act of injustice which this oppressed and afflicted nation, was called to suffer at the hands of their white neighbours—alas! they were subject to a more intense and heart-corroding affliction, that of having their daughters claimed by the conquerers, and however much subsequent efforts were made to sooth their sorrows, in this particular, they considered the glory of their nation as having departed.

From what I have already stated, it will appear that my father was of mixed blood; his father being a white man, and his mother a native, or in other words, a red woman.—On attaining a sufficient age to act for himself, he joined the Pequod tribe, to which he was maternally connected. He was well received, and in a short time afterwards, married a female of the tribe, in whose veins a single drop of the white man's blood never flowed. Not long after his marriage, he removed to what was then called the back settlements, directing his course first to the west, and afterwards to the northeast, where he pitched his tent in the woods of a town called Colreign, near the Connecticut river, in the state of Massachusetts. In this, the place of my birth, he continued some time, and afterwards removed to Colchester, New London county, Connecticut. At the latter place, our little family lived for nearly three years in comparative comfort.

Circumstances however changed with us, as with many other people, in consequence of which, I was taken together with my two brothers and sisters into my grandfather's family.—One of my uncles dwelt in the same hut. Now my grand parents, were not the best people in the world—like all others, who are wedded to the beastly vice of intemperance, they would drink to excess whenever they could procure rum, and as usual in such cases, when under the influence of liquor, they would not only quarrel and fight with each other, but would at times, turn upon their unoffending grand children, and beat them in a most cruel manner. It makes me shudder even at this this time, to think how frequent, and how great have been our sufferings in consequence of the introduction of this "cursed stuff" into our family—and I could wish, in the sincerity of my soul, that it were banished from our land.

Our fare was of the poorest kind, and even of this we had not enough—our clothing also was of the worst description: literally speaking, we were clothed with rags, so far only as rags would suffice to cover our nakedness. We were always contented and happy to get a cold potato for our dinner—of this at times we were denied, and many a night have we gone supperless to rest, if stretching our limbs on a bundle of straw, without any covering against the weather, may be called rest. Truly we were in a most deplorable condition. Too young to obtain subsistence for ourselves, by the labour of our hands, and our wants almost totally disregarded by those who should have made every exertion to supply them. Some of our white neighbours however took pity on us, and measurably administered to our wants, by bringing us frozen milk, with which we were glad to satisfy the calls of hunger. We lived in this way for some time, suffering both from cold and hunger. Once in particular, I remember that when it rained very hard, my grandmother put us all down cellar, and when we complained of cold and hunger, she unfeelingly bid us dance and thereby warm ourselves—but we had no food of any kind; and one of my sisters, almost died of hunger.—Poor dear girl she was quite overcome.—Young as I was, my very heart bled for her. I merely relate this circumstance, without any embellishment or exaggeration, to show the reader how we were treated. The intensity of our sufferings I cannot tell. Happily we did not continue in this very deplorable condition for a great length of time. Providence smiled on us, but in a particular manner.

Our parents quarrelled, parted and went off to a great distance, leaving their helpless children to the care of their grandparents. We lived at this time in an old house, divided into two apartments—one of which was occupied by my uncle. Shortly after my father left us, my grandmother, who had been out among the whites, returned in a state of intoxication, and without any provocation whatever on my part, began to belabour me most unmercifully with a club; she asked me if I hated her, and I very innocently answered in the affirmative as I did not then know what the word meant, and thought all the while that I was answering aright; and so she continued asking me the same question, and I as often answered her in the same way, whereupon she continued beating me, by which means one of my arms was broken in three different places. I was then only four years of age, and consequently could not take care of, or defend myself—and I was equally unable to seek safety in flight. But my uncle who lived in the other part of the house, being alarmed for my safety, came down to take me away, when my grandfather made towards him with a fire-brand, but very fortunately he succeeded in rescuing me, and thus saved my life, for had he not come at the time he did, I would most certainly have been killed. My grandparents who acted in this unfeeling and cruel manner, were by my mother's side—those by my father's side, were Christians, lived and died happy in the love of God; and if

I continue faithful in improving that measure of grace, with which God hath blessed me, I expect to meet them in a world of unmingled and ceaseless joys. But to return:—

The next morning when it was discovered that I had been most dangerously injured, my uncle determined to make the whites acquainted with my condition. He accordingly went to a Mr. Furman, the person who had occasionally furnished us with milk, and the good man came immediately to see me. He found me dreadfully beaten, and the other children in a state of absolute suffering; and as he was extremely anxious that something should be done for our relief, he applied to the selectmen of the town in our behalf, who after duly considering the application, adjudged that we should be severally taken and bound out. Being entirely disabled in consequence of the wounds I had received, I was supported at the expense of the town for about twelve months.

When the selectmen were called in, they ordered me to be carried to Mr. Furman's—where I received the attention of two surgeons. Some considerable time elapsed before my arm was set, which was consequently very sore, and during this painful operation I scarcely murmured. Now this dear man and family were sad on my account. Mrs. Furman was a kind, benevolent and tender hearted lady—from her I received the best possible care: had it been otherwise I believe that I could not have lived. It pleased God however to support me. The great patience that I manifested I attribute mainly to my improved situation. Before, I was almost always naked, or cold, or hungry— now, I was comfortable with the exception of my wounds.

In view of this treatment, I presume that the reader will exclaim, "what savages your grandparents were to treat unoffending helpless children in this cruel manner." But this cruel and unnatural conduct was the effect of some cause. I attribute it in a great measure to the whites, inasmuch as they introduced among my countrymen, that bane of comfort and happiness, ardent spirits—seduced them into a love of it, and when under its unhappy influence, wronged them out of their lawful possessions—that land, where reposed the ashes of their sires; and not only so, but they committed violence of the most revolting kind upon the persons of the female portion of the tribe, who previous to the introduction among them of the arts, and vices, and debaucheries of the whites, were as unoffending and happy as they roamed over their goodly possessions, as any people on whom the sun of heaven ever shown. The consequence was, that they were scattered abroad. Now many of them were seen reeling about intoxicated with liquor, neglecting to provide for themselves and families, who before were assiduously engaged in supplying the necessities of those depending on them for support. I do not make this statement in order to justify those who had treated me so unkindly, but simply to show, that inasmuch as I was thus treated only when they were under the influence of spirituous liquor, that the whites were justly chargeable with at least some portion of my sufferings.

After I had been nursed for about twelve months, I had so far recovered that it was deemed expedient to bind me out, until I should attain the age of twenty-one years. Mr. Furman the person with whom the selectmen had placed me was a poor man, a cooper by trade, and obtained his living by the labour of his hands. As I was only five years old, he at first thought that his circumstances would not justify him in keeping me, as it would be some considerable time before I could render him much service. But such was the attachment of the family towards me, that he came to the conclusion to keep me until I was of age, and he further agreed to give me so much instruction as would enable me to read and write. Accordingly, when I attained my sixth year, I was sent to school, and continued for six successive winters—during this time I learned to read and write, though not so well as I could have wished. This was all the instruction of the kind I ever received—Small and imperfect as was the amount of the knowledge I obtained, yet in view of the advantages I have thus derived, I bless God for it.

CHAPTER II. [FEAR OF INDIANS]

* * *

After a while I became very fond of attending on the word of God—then again I would meet the enemy of my soul, who would strive to lead me away, and in many instances he was but too successful, and to this day I remember that nothing scarcely grieved me so much, when my mind had been thus petted, than to be called by a nickname. If I was spoken to in the spirit of kindness, I would be instantly disarmed of my stubborness, and ready to perform anything required of me. I know of nothing so trying to a child as to be repeatedly called by an improper name. I thought it disgraceful to be called an Indian; it was considered as a slur upon an oppressed and scattered nation, and I have often been led to inquire where the whites received this word, which they so often threw as an opprobrious epithet at the sons of the forest. I could not find it in the Bible, and therefore concluded, that it was a word imported for the special purpose of degrading us. At other times I thought it was derived from the term in-gen-uity. But the proper term which ought to be applied to our nation, to distinguish it from the rest of the human family, is that of *"Natives"*—and I humbly conceive that the natives of this country are the only people under heaven who have a just title to the name, inasmuch as we are the only people who retain the original complexion of our father Adam. Notwithstanding my thoughts on this matter, so completely was I weaned from the interests and affections of my brethren, that a mere threat of being sent away among the Indians into the dreary woods, had a much better effect in making me obedient to the commands of my superiors, than any corporeal punishment that they ever inflicted. I had received a lesson in the unnatural treatment of my own relations, which could not be effaced; and I thought that if those who should have loved and protected me, treated me with such unkindness, surely I had no reason to expect mercy or favour at the hands of those who knew me in no other relation than that of a cast-off member of the tribe. A threat, of the kind alluded to, invariably produced obedience on my part, so far as I understood the nature of the command.

I cannot perhaps give a better idea of the dread which prevaded my mind on seeing any of my brethren of the forest, than by relating the following occurrence. One day several of the family went into the woods to gather berries, taking me with them. We had not been out long before we fell in with a company of white females, on the same errand—their complexion was, to say the least, as *dark* as that of the natives. This circumstance filled my mind with terror, and I broke from the party with my utmost speed, and I could not muster courage enough to look behind until I had reached home. By this time my imagination had pictured out a tale of blood, and as soon as I regained breath sufficient to answer the questions which my master asked, I informed him that we had met a body of the natives in the woods, but what had become of the party I could not tell. Notwithstanding the manifest incredibility of my tale of terror, Mr. Furman was agitated; my very appearance was sufficient to convince him that I had been terrified by something, and summoning the remainder of the family, he sallied out in quest of the absent party, whom he found searching for me among the bushes. The whole mystery was soon unravelled. It may be proper for me here to remark, that the great fear I entertained of my brethren, was occasioned by the many stories I had heard of their cruelty towards the whites—how they were in the habit of killing and scalping men, women and children. But the whites did not tell me that they were in a great majority of instances the aggressors—that they had imbrued their hands in the life blood of my brethren, driven them from their once peaceful and happy homes—that they introduced among them the fatal and exterminating diseases of civilized life. If the whites had told me how cruel they had been to the "poor Indian," I should have apprehended as much harm from them.

* * *

Chapter III. [New Masters]

* * *

Nothing very extraordinary occurred until I had attained my eleventh year. At this time it was fashionable for boys to run away, and the wicked one put it into the head of the oldest boy on the farm to persuade me to follow the fashion. He told me that I could take care of myself, and get my own living. I thought it was a very pretty notion to be a man—to *do business for myself and become rich*. Like a fool I concluded to make the experiment, and accordingly began to pack up my clothes as deliberately as could be, and in which my adviser assisted. I had been once or twice at New London, where I saw, as I thought, every thing wonderful: thither I determined to bend my course, as I expected, that on reaching the town I should be metamorphosed into a person of consequence; I had the world and every thing my little heart could desire in a string, when behold, my companion who had persuaded me to act thus, informed my master that I was going to run off. At first he would not believe the boy, but my clothing already packed up was ample evidence of my intention. On being questioned I acknowledged the fact. I did not wish to leave them—told Mr Furman so; he believed me, but thought best that for a while I should have another master. He accordingly agreed to transfer my indentures to Judge Hillhouse for the sum of twenty dollars. Of course after the bargain was made, my consent was to be obtained, but I was as unwilling to go now, as I had been anxious to run away before. After some persuasion, I agreed to try it for a fortnight, on condition that I should take my dog with me, and my request being granted, I was soon under the old man's roof, as he only lived about six miles off. Here every thing was done to make me contented, because they thought to promote their own interests by securing my services. They fed me with nicknacks, and soon after I went among them, I had a jack knife presented to me, which was the first one I had ever seen. Like other boys, I spent my time either in whittling or playing with my dog, and was withal very happy. But I was home sick at heart, and as soon as my fortnight had expired, I went home without cere-mony. Mr. Furman's family were surprised to see me, but that surprise was mutual satisfaction in which my faithful dog appeared to participate.

The joy I felt on returning home as I hoped, was turned to sorrow on being informed that I had been *sold* to the judge, and must instantly return. This I was compelled to do. And reader, all this sorrow was in consequence of being led away by a bad boy: if I had not listened to him I should not have lost my home. Such treatment I conceive to be the best means to accomplish the ruin of a child, as the reader will see in the sequel. I was sold to the judge at a time when age had rendered him totally unfit to manage an unruly lad. If he undertook to correct me, which he did at times, I did not regard it as I knew that I could run off from him if he was too severe, and besides I could do what I pleased in defiance of his authority. Now the old gentleman was a member of the Presbyterian church, and withal a very strict one. He never neglected family prayer, and he always insisted on my being present. I did not believe, or rather had no faith in his prayer, because it was the same thing from day to day, and I had heard it repeated so often, that I knew it as well as he. Although I was so young, I did not think that Christians ought to learn their prayers, and knowing that he repeated the same thing from day to day, is I have no doubt, the very reason why his petitions did me no good. I could fix no value on his prayers.

After a little while the conduct of my new guardians was changed towards me. Once secured I was no longer the favourite. The few clothes I had were not taken care of, by which I mean, no pains were taken to keep them clean and whole, and the consequence was that in a little time they were all "tattered and torn," and I was not fit to be seen in decent company. I had not the opportunity of attending meeting as before. Yet as the divine and reclaiming impression had not been entirely defaced, I would frequently retire behind the barn, and attempt to pray in my weak manner. I now became quite anxious to attend evening meetings a few miles off: I asked the judge if I should go and take one of the horses, to which he consented. This promise greatly delighted me—but when it was time for me to go, all my hopes were dashed at once, as the judge had changed his mind. I was not to be foiled so easily; I watched the first opportunity and slipped off with one of the horses, reached the meeting, and returned in safety. Here I was to blame; if he acted wrong, it did not justify me in doing so; but being success- ful in one grand net of disobedience, I was encouraged to make another simi- lar attempt, whenever my unsanctified dispositions prompted; for the very next time I wished to go to meeting, I thought I would take the horse again, and in the same manner too, without the knowledge of my master. As he was by some means apprised of my intention, he prevented my doing so, and had the horses locked up in the stable. He then commanded me to give him the bridle; I was obstinate for a time, then threw it at the old gentleman, and run off. I did not return until the next day, when I received a flogging for my bad conduct, which determined me to run away. Now the judge was partly to blame for all this. He had in the first place treated me with the utmost kindness until he had made sure of me. Then the whole course of his conduct changed, and I believed he fulfilled only one item of the transferred indentures, and that was work. Of this there was no lack. To be sure I had enough to eat, such as it was, but he did not send me to school as he had promised.

A few days found me on my was to New London, where I staid awhile. I then pushed on to Waterford, and as my father lived about twenty miles off, I concluded to go and see him. I got there safely, and told him I had come on a visit, and that I should stay one week. At the expiration of the week he bid me go home, and I obeyed him. On my return I was treated rather coolly, and this not suiting my disposition, I run off again, but returned in a few days. Now, as the judge found he could not control me, he got heartily tired of me, and wished to hand me over to some one else, so he obtained a place for me in New London. I knew nothing of it, and I was greatly mortified to think that I was sold in this way. If my consent had been solicited as a matter of form, I should not have felt so bad. But to be sold to, and treated unkindly, by those who had got our father's lands for nothing, was too much to bear. When all things were ready, the judge told me that he wanted me to go to New London with a neighbour, to purchase salt. I was delighted, and went with the man, expecting to return that night. When I reached the place I found my mistake. The name of the person to whom I was transferred this time, was Gen. William Williams, and as my treatment at the Judge's was none of the best, I went home with him contentedly. Indeed I felt glad that I had changed masters, and more especially that I was to reside in the city. The finery and show caught my eye, and captivated my heart. I can truly say that my situation was better now than it had been previously to my residence in New London. In a little time I was furnished with good new clothes. I had enough to eat, both as it respects quality and quantity, and my work was light. The whole family treated me kindly, and the only difficulty of moment was that they all wished to be masters. But I would not obey all of them. There was a French boy in the family, who one day told Mr. Williams a wilful lie about me, which he believed, and gave me a horse-whipping, without asking me a single question about it. Now I do not suppose that he whipped so much on account of what the boy told him, as he did from the influence of the Judge's directions. He used the falsehood as a pretext for flogging me as from what he said he was determined to make a good boy of me at once—as if stripes were calculated to effect that which love, kindness and instruction can only successfully accomplish. He told me that if I ever run away from him he would follow me to the uttermost parts of the earth. I knew from this observation that the Judge had told him that I was a runaway. However cruel this treatment appeared, for the accusation was false, yet it did me much good, as I was ready to obey the general and his lady at all times. But I could not and would not obey any but my superiors. In short, I got on very smoothly for a season.

* * *

Chapter IV. [A Runaway and Soldier]

The calm and sunshine did not however continue uninterrupted for any length of time; my peace of mind, which flowed as a river, was disturbed. While the adversary tempted me, the fire of persecution was rekindled. It was considered by some members of the family, that I was too young to be religiously inclined, and consequently that I was under a strong delusion. After a time, Mr. Williams came to the conclusion, that it was advisable for me to absent myself entirely from the Methodist meetings.

This restriction was the more galling, as I had joined the class, and was extremely fond of this means of grace. I generally attended once in each week, so when the time came round, I went off to the meeting, without permission. When I returned, Mrs. Williams prepared to correct me for acting contrary to my orders; in the first place, however, she asked me where I had been, I frankly told her that I had been to meeting to worship God. This reply completely disarmed her, and saved me a flogging for the time. But this was not the end of my persecution or my troubles.

The chamber-maid was in truth a treacherous woman; her heart appeared to me to be filled with deceit and guile, and she persecuted me with as much bitterness as Paul did the disciples of old. She had a great dislike towards me, and would not hesitate to tell a falsehood in order to have me whipped. But my mind was stayed upon God, and I had much comfort in reading the holy Scriptures. One day after she had procured me a flogging, and no very mild one either, she pushed me down a long flight of stairs. In the fall I was greatly injured, especially my head: in consequence of this I was disabled, and laid up for a long time. When I told Mr. Williams that the maid had pushed me down stairs, she denied it, but I succeeded in making them believe it. In all this trouble the Lord was with me of a truth. I was happy in the enjoyment of his love. The abuse heaped on me was in consequence of my being a Methodist.

Sometimes I would get permission to attend meetings in the evening, and once or twice on the Sabbath. And oh, how thankful I felt for these opportunities for hearing the word of God. But the waves of persecution, and affliction, and sorrow, rolled on, and gathered strength in their progress, and for a season overwhelmed my dispirited soul. I was flogged several times very unjustly for what the maid said respecting me. My treatment in this respect was so bad that I could not brook it, and in an evil hour I listened to the suggestions of the devil, who was not slow in prompting me to pursue a course directly at variance with the Gospel. He put it into my head to abscond from my master, and I made arrangements with a boy of my acquaintance to accompany me. So one day Mr. Williams had gone to Stonington, I left his house, notwithstanding he had previously threatened if I did so, to follow me to the ends of the earth. While my companion was getting ready I hid my clothes in a barn, and went to buy some bread and cheese, and while at the store, although I had about four dollars in my pocket, I so far forgot myself, as to buy a pair of shoes on my master's account. Then it was that I began to lose sight of religion and of God. We now set out; it being a rainy night, we bought a bottle of rum, of which poisonous stuff I drank heartily. Now the shadows of spiritual death began to gather around my soul. It was half past nine o'clock at night when we started, and to keep up our courage we took another drink of the liquor. As soon as we left the city, that is, as we descended the hill, it became very dark, and my companion, who was always fierce enough by daylight, began to hang back. I saw that his courage was failing, and endeavoured to cheer him up. Sometimes I would take a drink of rum to drown my sorrows—but in vain, it appears to me now as if my sorrows neutralized the effects of the liquor.

This night we travelled about seven miles, and being weary and wet with the rain, we crept into a barn by the wayside, and for fear of being detected in the morning, if we should happen to sleep too long, we burrowed into the hay a considerable depth. We were aroused in the morning by the people feeding their cattle; we laid still and they did not discover us. After they had left the barn we crawled out, made our breakfast on rum, bread, and cheese, and set off for Colchester, about fourteen miles distant, which we reached that night. Here we ventured to put up at a tavern. The next morning we started for my father's, about four miles off. I told him that we had come to stay only one week, and when that week had expired he wished me to redeem my promise and return home. So I had seemingly to comply, and when we had packed up our clothes, he said he would accompany us part of the way; and when we parted I thought he had some suspicions of my intention to take another direction, as he begged me to go straight home. He then sat down on the wayside and looked after us as long as we were to be seen. At last we descended a hill, and as soon as we lost sight of him, we struck into the woods. I did not see my father again for eight years. At this time, I felt very much disturbed. I was just going to step out on the broad theatre of the world, as it were, without father, mother, or friends.

After travelling some distance in the woods, we shaped our course towards Hartford. We were fearful of being taken up, and my companion coined a story, which he thought would answer very well. It was to represent ourselves, whenever questioned, as having belonged to a privateer, which was captured by the British, who kindly sent us on shore near New London; that our parents lived in the city of New York, and that we were travelling thither to see them.

Now John was a great liar. He was brought up by dissipated parents, and accustomed in the way of the world to all kinds of company. He had a good memory, and having been where he heard war songs and tales of blood and carnage, he treasured them up. He therefore agreed to be spokesman, and I assure my dear reader that I was perfectly willing, for abandoned as I was I could not lie without feeling my conscience smite me. This part of the business being arranged, it was agreed that I should sell part of my clothing to defray our expenses. Our heads were full of schemes, and we journeyed on until night overtook us. We then went into a farmhouse to test our plan. The people soon began to ask us questions, and John as readily answered them. He gave them a great account of our having been captured by the enemy, and so straight, that they believed the whole of it. After supper we went to bed, and in the morning they gave us a good breakfast, and some bread and cheese, and we went on our way, satisfied with our exploits. John now studied to make his story appear as correct as possible. The people pitied us, and sometimes we had a few shillings put into our hands. We did not suffer for the want of food. At Hartford we stayed some time, and we here agreed to work our passage down to New York on board of a brig—but learning that the British fleet was on the coast, the captain declined going.

We then set out to reach New York by land. We thought it a good way to walk. We went by way of New Haven, expecting to reach the city from that place by water. Again we were disappointed. We fell in company with some sailors who had been exchanged,[4] and we listened to their story—it was an affecting one, and John concluded to incorporate a part of it with his own. So shortly afterwards he told some people that while we were prisoners, we had to eat bread mixed with pounded glass. The people were foolish enough to believe us. At Kingsbridge an old lady gave us several articles of clothing. Here we agreed with the captain of a vessel to work our way to New York. When we got under weigh, John undertook to relate our sufferings to the crew. They appeared to believe it all, until he came to the incredible story of the "glass bread." This convinced the captain that all he said was false. He told us that he knew that we were runaways, and pressed us to tell him, but we declined. At length he told us that we were very near to Hellgate,[5] (Hurlgate,)—that when we reached it the devil would come on board in a stone canoe, with an iron paddle, and make a terrible noise, and that he intended to give us to him. I thought all he said was so. I therefore confessed that we were runaways—where, and with whom we had lived. He said he would take me back to New London, as my master was rich and would pay him a good price. Here the devil prompted me to tell a lie, and I replied that the General had advertised me one cent reward. He then said that he would do nothing with me further than to keep my clothes until we paid him. When the vessel reached the dock, John slipped off, and I was not slow to follow. In a few days we got money to redeem our clothing; we took board in Cherrystreet, at two dollars per week; we soon obtained work and received sixty-two and a half cents per day. While this continued, we had no difficulty in paying our board. My mind now became tolerably calm, but in the midst of this I was greatly alarmed; as I was informed that my master had offered fifteen dollars reward for me, and that the captain of one of the packets was looking for me. I dared not go back, and therefore determined to go to Philadelphia; to this John objected, and advised me to go to sea, but I could find no vessel. He entered on board a privateer, and I was thus left entirely alone in a strange city. Wandering about, I fell in company with a sergeant and a file of men who were enlisting soldiers for the United States army. They thought I would answer their purpose, but how to get me was the thing. Now they began to talk to me, then treated me to some spirits and when that began to operate they told me all about the war, and what a fine thing it was to be a soldier. I was pleased with the idea of being a soldier, took some more liquor and some money, had a cockade fastened on my hat, and was off in high spirits for my uniform. Now my enlistment was against the law, but I did not know it; I could not think why I should risk my life

---

4. As prisoners during the War of 1812.
5. A narrow channel in the East River, between Manhattan and Queens.

and limbs in fighting for the white man, who had cheated my forefathers out of their land. By this time I had acquired many bad practices. I was sent over to Governor's Island, opposite the city, and here I remained some time. Too much liquor was dealt out to the soldiers, who got drunk very often. Indeed the island was like a hell upon earth, in consequence of the wickedness of the soldiers. I have known sober men to enlist, who afterwards became confirmed drunkards, and appear like fools upon the earth. So it was among the soldiers, and what should a child do, who was entangled in their net. Now, although I made no profession of religion, yet I could not bear to hear sacred things spoken of lightly, or the sacred name of God blasphemed; and I often spoke to the soldiers about it, and in general they listened attentively to what I had to say. I did not tell them that I had ever made a profession of religion. In a little time I became almost as bad as any of them; could drink rum, play cards, and act as wickedly as any. I was at times tormented with the thoughts of death, but God had mercy on me, and spared my life, and for this I feel thankful to the present day. Some people are of opinion that if a person is once born of the Spirit of God he can never fall away entirely, and because I acted thus, they may pretend to say that I had not been converted to the faith. I believe firmly, that if ever Paul was born again, I was; if not, from whence did I derive all the light and happiness I had heretofore experienced? To be sure it was not to be compared to Paul's—but the change I felt in my very soul.

I felt anxious to obtain forgiveness from every person I had injured in any manner whatever. Sometimes I thought I would write to my old friends and request forgiveness—then I thought I had done right. I could not bear to hear any order of Christians ridiculed, especially the Methodists—it grieved me to the heart.

Nathaniel Hawthorne
(1804–1864)

Born in Salem, Massachusetts, Nathaniel Hawthorne sprang from a family that had inhabited New England for five generations. His father was a sea captain who died of yellow fever and was buried in Dutch Guiana when Hawthorne was four. A grandfather had commanded a privateer during the Revolutionary War. An earlier ancestor had served as a judge in the Salem witchcraft trials. Raised in Salem and in Raymond in the territory that

became Maine in 1820, he graduated from Bowdoin College, having met there Henry Wadsworth Longfellow and Franklin Pierce. Solitary and bookish from his childhood, he was influenced by his reading—especially, perhaps, Sir Walter Scott—to try his hand at writing.

For a dozen years after his graduation from college, he lived mostly in the family home in Salem, turning out stories and sketches of New England. Fanshawe *(1828), a gothic romance, was published at his own expense, but later he burned every copy he could find. In 1830 his work began appearing in gift annuals like* The Token, *and in 1837 he gathered some of his best, including "The Maypole of Merry Mount," in* Twice-Told Tales. *Married in 1842, he moved with his new wife into the Old Manse in Concord and a few years later published* Mosses from an Old Manse *(1846), another collection of tales. From 1846 to 1849 he was surveyor of customs in Salem; partly from that experience came his greatest novel,* The Scarlet Letter *(1850), which was soon followed by* The House of the Seven Gables *(1851) and* The Blithedale Romance *(1852). Now famous, and invigorated by his friendship with the younger Herman Melville, Hawthorne was publishing rapidly but still earning little money when he took the opportunity to strengthen his finances by accepting an appointment from President Pierce, his old college friend, as United States Consul at Liverpool, England. After four years in England and a shorter time in Italy, he wrote one more novel,* The Marble Faun *(1860), and a collection of English sketches,* Our Old Home *(1863). He died while on a trip to New Hampshire with Franklin Pierce.*

Few Americans have written as well or influenced as many later readers and writers as Hawthorne. Brooding on American history, he made the particularities of the American condition his great subject, and with his gift for allegory he raised considerations of Puritan sin and atonement to universal examinations of the human condition. "The Maypole of Merry Mount," solidly rooted in an historical encounter between radically differing cultures, magically thrusts down the ages its reverberations of questions raised about a time when "Jollity and gloom were contending for an empire."

Hawthorne's *Complete Works* (12 vols. 1883), ed. by George P. Lathrop, long standard, is the source of the present text. A modern scholarly edition, in progress, is Ohio State's *Centenary Edition of the Works of Nathaniel Hawthorne.* A recent and authoritative biography is Arlin Turner's *Nathaniel Hawthorne* (1980).

The Maypole of Merry Mount[1]

There is an admirable foundation for a philosophic romance in the curious history of the early settlement of Mount Wollaston, or Merry Mount. In the slight sketch here attempted, the facts, recorded on the grave pages of our New England annalists, have wrought themselves, almost spontaneously, into a sort of allegory. The masques, mummeries, and festive customs, described in the text, are in accordance with the manners of the age. Authority on these points may be found in Strutt's Book of English Sports and Pastimes.[2]

BRIGHT WERE THE DAYS at Merry Mount,[3] when the Maypole was the banner staff of that gay colony! They who reared it, should their banner be triumphant, were to pour sunshine over New England's rugged hills, and scatter flower seeds throughout the soil. Jollity and gloom were contending for an empire. Midsummer eve had come, bringing deep verdure to the forest, and roses in her lap, of a more vivid hue than the tender buds of Spring. But May, or her mirthful spirit, dwelt all the year round at Merry Mount, sporting with the Summer months, and revelling with Autumn, and basking in the glow of Winter's fireside. Through a world of toil and care she flitted with a dreamlike smile, and came hither to find a home among the lightsome hearts of Merry Mount.

Never had the Maypole been so gayly decked as at sunset on midsummer eve. This venerated emblem was a pine-tree, which had preserved the slender grace of youth, while it equalled the loftiest height of the old wood monarchs. From its top streamed a silken banner, colored like the rainbow. Down nearly to the ground the pole was dressed with birchen boughs, and others of the liveliest green, and some with silvery leaves, fastened by ribbons that fluttered in fantastic knots of twenty different colors, but no sad ones. Garden flowers, and blossoms of the wilderness, laughed gladly forth amid the verdure, so fresh and dewy that they must have grown by magic on that happy pine-tree. Where this green and flowery splendor terminated, the shaft of the Maypole was stained with the seven brilliant hues of the banner at its top. On the lowest green bough hung an abundant wreath of roses, some that had been gathered in the sunniest spots of the forest, and others, of still richer blush, which the colonists had reared from English seed. O, people of the Golden Age, the chief of your husbandry was to raise flowers!

But what was the wild throng that stood hand in hand about the Maypole? It could not be that the fauns and nymphs, when driven from their classic groves and homes of ancient fable, had sought refuge, as all the perse-

---

1. "The Maypole of Merry Mount" was first published in *The Token* for 1836, and was collected in *Twice-Told Tales* (1837).

2. Joseph Strutt, *The Sports and Pastimes of the People of England* (1801).

3. Now the Wollaston area of Quincy, Massachusetts.

cuted did, in the fresh woods of the West. These were Gothic monsters, though perhaps of Grecian ancestry. On the shoulders of a comely youth uprose the head and branching antlers of a stag; a second, human in all other points, had the grim visage of a wolf; a third, still with the trunk and limbs of a mortal man, showed the beard and horns of a venerable he-goat. There was the likeness of a bear erect, brute in all but his hind legs, which were adorned with pink silk stockings. And here again, almost as wondrous, stood a real bear of the dark forest, lending each of his fore paws to the grasp of a human hand, and as ready for the dance as any in that circle. His inferior nature rose half way, to meet his companions as they stooped. Other faces wore the similitude of man or woman, but distorted or extravagant, with red noses pendulous before their mouths, which seemed of awful depth, and stretched from ear to ear in an eternal fit of laughter. Here might be seen the Salvage Man,[4] well known in heraldry, hairy as a baboon, and girdled with green leaves. By his side, a noble figure, but still a counterfeit, appeared an Indian hunter, with feathery crest and wampum belt. Many of this strange company wore foolscaps, and had little bells appended to their garments, tinkling with a silvery sound, responsive to the inaudible music of their gleesome spirits. Some youths and maidens were of soberer garb, yet well maintained their places in the irregular throng by the expression of wild revelry upon their features. Such were the colonists of Merry Mount, as they stood in the broad smile of sunset round their venerated Maypole.

Had a wanderer, bewildered in the melancholy forest, heard their mirth, and stolen a half-affrighted glance, he might have fancied them the crew of Comus,[5] some already transformed to brutes, some midway between man and beast, and the others rioting in the flow of tipsy jollity that foreran the change. But a band of Puritans, who watched the scene, invisible themselves, compared the masques to those devils and ruined souls with whom their superstition peopled the black wilderness.

Within the ring of monsters appeared the two airiest forms that had ever trodden on any more solid footing than a purple and golden cloud. One was a youth in glistening apparel, with a scarf of the rainbow pattern crosswise on his breast. His right hand held a gilded staff, the ensign of high dignity among the revellers, and his left grasped the slender fingers of a fair maiden, not less gayly decorated than himself. Bright roses glowed in contrast with the dark and glossy curls of each, and were scattered round their feet, or had sprung up spontaneously there. Behind this lightsome couple, so close to the Maypole that its boughs shaded his jovial face, stood the figure of an English priest, canonically dressed, yet decked with flowers, in heathen fashion, and wearing a chaplet of the native vine leaves. By the riot of his rolling eye, and the pagan decorations of his holy garb, he seemed the wildest monster there, and the very Comus of the crew.

---

4. That is, Savage Man—one of the green men of folklore, alluded to three paragraphs below.

5. Classical god of revelry, who, in Milton's *Comus* (1634), has the power to change human beings to animals.

"Votaries of the Maypole," cried the flower-decked priest, "merrily, all day long, have the woods echoed to your mirth. But be this your merriest hour, my hearts! Lo, here stand the Lord and Lady of the May, whom I, a clerk of Oxford, and high priest of Merry Mount, am presently to join in holy matrimony. Up with your nimble spirits, ye morris-dancers, green men, and glee maidens, bears and wolves, and horned gentlemen! Come; a chorus now, rich with the old mirth of Merry England, and the wilder glee of this fresh forest; and then a dance, to show the youthful pair what life is made of, and how airily they should go through it! All ye that love the Maypole, lend your voices to the nuptial song of the Lord and Lady of the May!"

This wedlock was more serious than most affairs of Merry Mount, where jest and delusion, trick and fantasy, kept up a continual carnival. The Lord and Lady of the May, though their titles must be laid down at sunset, were really and truly to be partners for the dance of life, beginning the measure that same bright eve. The wreath of roses, that hung from the lowest green bough of the Maypole, had been twined for them, and would be thrown over both their heads, in symbol of their flowery union. When the priest had spoken, therefore, a riotous uproar burst from the rout of monstrous figures.

"Begin you the stave, reverend Sir," cried they all; "and never did the woods ring to such a merry peal as we of the Maypole shall send up!"

Immediately a prelude of pipe, cithern, and viol, touched with practised minstresly, began to play from a neighboring thicket, in such a mirthful cadence that the boughs of the Maypole quivered to the sound. But the May Lord, he of the gilded staff, chancing to look into his Lady's eyes, was wonder struck at the almost pensive glance that met his own.

"Edith, sweet Lady of the May," whispered he reproachfully, "is yon wreath of roses a garland to hang above our graves, that you look so sad? O, Edith, this is our golden time! Tarnish it not by any pensive shadow of the mind; for it may be that nothing of futurity will be brighter than the mere remembrance of what is now passing."

"That was the very thought that saddened me! How came it in your mind too?" said Edith, in a still lower tone than he, for it was high treason to be sad at Merry Mount. "Therefore do I sigh amid this festive music. And besides, dear Edgar, I struggle as with a dream, and fancy that these shapes of our jovial friends are visionary, and their mirth unreal, and that we are no true Lord and Lady of the May. What is the mystery in my heart?"

Just then, as if a spell had loosened them, down came a little shower of withering rose leaves from the Maypole. Alas, for the young lovers! No sooner had their hearts glowed with real passion than they were sensible of something vague and unsubstantial in their former pleasures, and felt a dreary presentiment of inevitable change. From the moment that they truly loved, they had subjected themselves to earth's doom of care and sorrow, and troubled joy, and had no more a home at Merry Mount. That was Edith's mystery. Now leave we the priest to marry them, and the masquers to sport round the Maypole, till the last sunbeam be withdrawn from its summit, and the shadows of the forest mingle gloomily in the dance. Meanwhile, we may discover who these gay people were.

Two hundred years ago, and more, the old world and its inhabitants became mutually weary of each other. Men voyaged by thousands to the West: some to barter glass beads, and such like jewels, for the furs of the Indian hunter; some to conquer virgin empires; and one stern band to pray. But none of these motives had much weight with the colonists of Merry Mount. Their leaders were men who had sported so long with life, that when Thought and Wisdom came, even these unwelcome guests were led astray by the crowd of vanities which they should have put to flight. Erring Thought and perverted Wisdom were made to put on masques, and play the fool. The men of whom we speak, after losing the heart's fresh gayety, imagined a wild philosophy of pleasure, and came hither to act out their latest day-dream. They gathered followers from all that giddy tribe whose whole life is like the festal days of soberer men. In their train were minstrels, not unknown in London streets; wandering players, whose theatres had been the halls of noblemen; mummers, rope-dancers, and mountebanks, who would long be missed at wakes, church ales, and fairs; in a word, mirth makers of every sort, such as abounded in that age, but now began to be discountenanced by the rapid growth of Puritanism. Light had their footsteps been on land, and as lightly they came across the sea. Many had been maddened by their previous troubles into a gay despair; others were as madly gay in the flush of youth, like the May Lord and his Lady; but whatever might be the quality of their mirth, old and young were gay at Merry Mount. The young deemed themselves happy. The elder spirits, if they knew that mirth was but the counterfeit of happiness, yet followed the false shadow wilfully, because at least her garments glittered brightest. Sworn triflers of a lifetime, they would not venture among the sober truths of life not even to be truly blest.

All the hereditary pastimes of Old England were transplanted hither. The King of Christmas was duly crowned, and the Lord of Misrule bore potent sway. On the Eve of St. John,[6] they felled whole acres of the forest to make bonfires, and danced by the blaze all night, crowned with garlands, and throwing flowers into the flame. At harvest time, though their crop was of the smallest, they made an image with the sheaves of Indian corn, and wreathed it with autumnal garlands, and bore it home triumphantly. But what chiefly characterized the colonists of Merry Mount was their veneration for the Maypole. It has made their true history a poet's tale. Spring decked the hallowed emblem with young blossoms and fresh green boughs; Summer brought roses of the deepest blush, and the perfected foliage of the forest; Autumn enriched it with that red and yellow gorgeousness which converts each wildwood leaf into a painted flower; and Winter silvered it with sleet, and hung it round with icicles, till it flashed in the cold sunshine,

---

6. Midsummer eve.

itself a frozen sunbeam. Thus each alternate season did homage to the Maypole, and paid it a tribute of its own richest splendor. Its votaries danced round it, once, at least, in every month; sometimes they called it their religion, or their altar; but always, it was the banner staff of Merry Mount.

Unfortunately, there were men in the new world of a sterner faith than these Maypole worshippers. Not far from Merry Mount was a settlement of Puritans, most dismal wretches, who said their prayers before daylight, and then wrought in the forest or the cornfield till evening made it prayer time again. Their weapons were always at hand to shoot down the straggling savage. When they met in conclave, it was never to keep up the old English mirth, but to hear sermons three hours long, or to proclaim bounties on the heads of wolves and the scalps of Indians. Their festivals were fast days, and their chief pastime the singing of psalms. Woe to the youth or maiden who did but dream of a dance! The selectman nodded to the constable; and there sat the light-heeled reprobate in the stocks; or if he danced, it was round the whipping-post, which might be termed the Puritan Maypole.

A party of these grim Puritans, toiling through the difficult woods, each with a horseload of iron armor to burden his footsteps, would sometimes draw near the sunny precincts of Merry Mount. There were the silken colonists, sporting round their Maypole; perhaps teaching a bear to dance, or striving to communicate their mirth to the grave Indian; or masquerading in the skins of deer and wolves, which they had hunted for that especial purpose. Often, the whole colony were playing at blindman's buff, magistrates and all, with their eyes bandaged, except a single scapegoat, whom the blinded sinners pursued by the tinkling of the bells at his garments. Once, it is said, they were seen following a flower-decked corpse, with merriment and festive music, to his grave. But did the dead man laugh? In their quietest times, they sang ballads and told tales, for the edification of their pious visitors; or perplexed them with juggling tricks; or grinned at them through horse collars; and when sport itself grew wearisome, they made game of their own stupidity, and began a yawning match. At the very least of these enormities, the men of iron shook their heads and frowned so darkly that the revellers looked up, imagining that a momentary cloud had overcast the sunshine, which was to be perpetual there. On the other hand, the Puritans affirmed that, when a psalm was pealing from their place of worship, the echo which the forest sent them back seemed often like the chorus of a jolly catch, closing with a roar of laughter. Who but the fiend, and his bond slaves, the crew of Merry Mount, had thus disturbed them? In due time, a feud arose, stern and bitter on one side, and as serious on the other as anything could be among such light spirits as had sworn allegiance to the Maypole. The future complexion of New England was involved in this important quarrel. Should the grizzly saints establish their jurisdiction over the gay sinners, then would their spirits darken all the clime, and make it a land of clouded visages, of hard toil, of sermon and psalm forever. But should the banner staff of Merry Mount be fortunate, sunshine would break upon the hills, and flowers would beautify the forest, and late posterity do homage to the Maypole.

After these authentic passages from history, we return to the nuptials of the Lord and Lady of the May. Alas! we have delayed too long, and must darken our tale too suddenly. As we glance again at the Maypole, a solitary sunbeam is fading from the summit, and leaves only a faint, golden tinge blended with the hues of the rainbow banner. Even that dim light is now withdrawn, relinquishing the whole domain of Merry Mount to the evening gloom, which has rushed so instantaneously from the black surrounding woods. But some of these black shadows have rushed forth in human shape.

Yes, with the setting sun, the last day of mirth had passed from Merry Mount. The ring of gay masquers was disordered and broken; the stag lowered his antlers in dismay; the wolf grew weaker than a lamb; the bells of the morris-dancers tinkled with tremulous affright. The Puritans had played a characteristic part in the Maypole mummeries. Their darksome figures were intermixed with the wild shapes of their foes, and made the scene a picture of the moment, when waking thoughts start up amid the scattered fantasies of a dream. The leader of the hostile party stood in the centre of the circle, while the route of monsters cowered around him, like evil spirits in the presence of a dread magician. No fantastic foolery could look him in the face. So stern was the energy of his aspect, that the whole man, visage, frame, and soul, seemed wrought of iron, gifted with life and thought, yet all of one substance with his headpiece and breastplate. It was the Puritan of Puritans; it was Endicott[7] himself!

"Stand off, priest of Baal!" said he, with a grim frown, and laying no reverent hand upon the surplice. "I know thee, Blackstone![8] Thou art the man who couldst not abide the rule even of thine own corrupted church, and hast come hither to preach iniquity, and to give example of it in thy life. But now shall it be seen that the Lord hath sanctified this wilderness for his peculiar people. Woe unto them that would defile it! And first, for this flower-decked abomination, the altar of thy worship!"

And with his keen sword Endicott assaulted the hallowed Maypole. Nor long did it resist his arm. It groaned with a dismal sound; it showered leaves and rosebuds upon the remorseless enthusiast; and finally, with all its green boughs and ribbons and flowers, symbolic of departed pleasures, down fell the banner staff of Merry Mount. As it sank, tradition says, the evening sky grew darker, and the woods threw forth a more sombre shadow.

"There," cried Endicott, looking triumphantly on his work, "there lies the only Maypole in New England! The thought is strong within me that, by its fall, is shadowed forth the fate of light and idle mirth makers, amongst us and our posterity. Amen, saith John Endicott."

"Amen!" echoed his followers.

---

7. John Endicott (c. 1589–1665), several times governor of Massachusetts Bay.

8. "Did Governor Endicott speak less positively, we should suspect a mistake here. The Rev. Mr. Blackstone, though an eccentric, is not known to have been an immoral man. We rather doubt his identity with the priest of Merry Mount." [Hawthorne's note] William Blackstone (died 1675), nonconformist Anglican clergyman, moved to Rhode Island in 1631 following disputes with the Massachusetts Bay settlers. The story of the slaying of the priests of Baal is told in I Kings xviii.

But the votaries of the Maypole gave one groan for their idol. At the sound, the Puritan leader glanced at the crew of Comus, each a figure of broad mirth, yet, at this moment, strangely expressive of sorrow and dismay.

"Valiant captain," quoth Peter Palfrey, the Ancient[9] of the band, "what order shall be taken with the prisoners?"

"I thought not to repent me of cutting down a Maypole," replied Endicott, "yet now I could find in my heart to plant it again, and give each of these bestial pagans one other dance round their idol. It would have served rarely for a whipping-post!"

"But there are pine-trees enow," suggested the lieutenant.

"True, good Ancient," said the leader. "Wherefore, bind the heathen crew, and bestow on them a small matter of stripes apiece, as earnest of our future justice. Set some of the rogues in the stocks to rest themselves, so soon as Providence shall bring us to one of our own well-ordered settlements, where such accommodations may be found. Further penalties, such as branding and cropping of ears, shall be thought of hereafter."

"How many stripes for the priest?" inquired Ancient Palfrey.

"None as yet," answered Endicott, bending his iron frown upon the culprit. "It must be for the Great and General Court to determine, whether stripes and long imprisonment, and other grievous penalty, may atone for his transgressions. Let him look to himself! For such as violate our civil order, it may be permitted us to show mercy. But woe to the wretch that troubleth our religion!"

"And this dancing bear," resumed the officer. "Must he share the stripes of his fellows?"

"Shoot him through the head!" said the energetic Puritan. "I suspect witchcraft in the beast."

"Here be a couple of shining ones," continued Peter Palfrey, pointing his weapon at the Lord and Lady of the May. "They seem to be of high station among these misdoers. Methinks their dignity will not be fitted with less than a double share of stripes."

Endicott rested on his sword, and closely surveyed the dress and aspect of the hapless pair. There they stood, pale, downcast, and apprehensive. Yet there was an air of mutual support, and of pure affection, seeking aid and giving it, that showed them to be man and wife, with the sanction of a priest upon their love. The youth, in the peril of the moment, had dropped his gilded staff, and thrown his arm about the Lady of the May, who leaned against his breast, too lightly to burden him, but with weight enough to express that their destinies were linked together, for good or evil. They looked first at each other, and then into the grim captain's face. There they stood, in the first hour of wedlock, while the idle pleasures, of which their companions were the emblems, had given place to the sternest cares of life, personified by the dark Puritans. But never had their youthful beauty seemed so pure and high as when its glow was chastened by adversity.

---

9. Standard-bearer or lieutenant. *Cf.* ensign.

"Youth," said Endicott, "ye stand in an evil case thou and thy maiden wife. Make ready presently, for I am minded that ye shall both have a token to remember your wedding day!"

"Stern man," cried the May Lord, "how can I move thee? Were the means at hand, I would resist to the death. Being powerless, I entreat! Do with me as thou wilt, but let Edith go untouched!"

"Not so," replied the immitigable zealot. "We are not wont to show an idle courtesy to that sex, which requireth the stricter discipline. What sayest thou, maid? Shall thy silken bridegroom suffer thy share of the penalty, besides his own?"

"Be it death," said Edith, "and lay it all on me!"

Truly, as Endicott had said, the poor lovers stood in a woful case. Their foes were triumphant, their friends captive and abased, their home desolate, the benighted wilderness around them, and a rigorous destiny, in the shape of the Puritan leader, their only guide. Yet the deepening twilight could not altogether conceal that the iron man was softened; he smiled at the fair spectacle of early love; he almost sighed for the inevitable blight of early hopes.

"The troubles of life have come hastily on this young couple," observed Endicott. "We will see how they comport themselves under their present trials ere we burden them with greater. If, among the spoil, there be any garments of a more decent fashion, let them be put upon this May Lord and his Lady, instead of their glistening vanities. Look to it, some of you."

"And shall not the youth's hair be cut?"[1] asked Peter Palfrey, looking with abhorrence at the lovelock and long glossy curls of the young man.

"Crop it forthwith, and that in the true pumpkin-shell fashion," answered the captain. "Then bring them along with us, but more gently than their fellows. There be qualities in the youth, which may make him valiant to fight, and sober to toil, and pious to pray; and in the maiden, that may fit her to become a mother in our Israel, bringing up babes in better nurture than her own hath been. Nor think ye, young ones, that they are the happiest, even in our lifetime of a moment, who misspend it in dancing round a Maypole!"

And Endicott, the severest Puritan of all who laid the rock foundation of New England, lifted the wreath of roses from the ruin of the Maypole, and threw it, with his own gauntleted hand, over the heads of the Lord and Lady of the May. It was a deed of prophecy. As the moral gloom of the world overpowers all systematic gayety, even so was their home of wild mirth made desolate amid the sad forest. They returned to it no more. But as their flowery garland was wreathed of the brightest roses that had grown there, so, in the tie that united them, were intertwined all the purest and best of their early joys. They went heavenward, supporting each other along the difficult path which it was their lot to tread, and never wasted one regretful thought on the vanities of Merry Mount.

---

1. The Puritans, or "roundheads," wore their hair short, in contrast to the long hair of the English "Cavaliers."

William Gilmore Simms
(1806–1870)

Born in Charleston, South Carolina, William Gilmore Simms was reared in poverty by a grandmother after his mother died when he was an infant and his father, an Irish immigrant, moved West. Apprenticed to a druggist, he left Charleston at eighteen to stay briefly with his father on a Mississippi farm. While in the West he visited the Indians of the Creek, Choctaw, and Cherokee nations, writing poetry and prose accounts of them. Returning to Charleston, he published his first book of verse at nineteen, practiced law, and wrote for newspapers. Before long, he had become one of America's leading writers, in the course of a long career publishing over thirty volumes of fiction and another thirty books of verse and nonfiction prose. Increasingly a spokesperson for the South, he urged secession for South Carolina, and later saw his plantation house and fine library burned by stragglers from the Union army.

Heavily influenced by Sir Walter Scott and James Fenimore Cooper, Simms was at his best in historical novels that focus on cultures in conflict or play upon the conflict inherent in situations in which a dying culture is being supplanted by a growing and vigorous one. In The Yemassee (1835), the most admired of his novels, Simms tells of a 1715 conflict between Carolina settlers and Indians, portraying the Indians with sympathy and a high degree of accuracy. Novels of the Revolutionary War focus on action in the Carolinas and include The Partisan (1835), Mellichampe (1836), Katherine Walton (1851), and The Sword and the Distaff (1853; revised as Woodcraft, 1856). Among other novels are the Border Romances, including Guy Rivers (1834), set in Georgia; Richard Hurdis (1838), Alabama; Border Beagles (1840), Mississippi; and Beauchampe: or, The Kentucky Tragedy (1842), based on a famous case of seduction, murder, and suicide. Stories, including sympathetic portrayals of Native Americans, are collected in The Wigwam and the Cabin (1845).

Simms's Works appeared in twenty volumes (1853–1866). J. C. Guilds and J. B. Meriwether edited The Centennial Edition of the Writings of William Gilmore Simms (1969–). Studies are by William B. Trent (1892) and Joseph V. Ridgely (1962).

The Two Camps

A Legend of the Old North State[1]

CHAPTER I

IT IS FREQUENTLY THE CASE, in the experience of the professional novelist or tale-writer, that his neighbour comes in to his assistance when he least seeks, and, perhaps, least desires any succour. The worthy person, man or woman, however,—probably some excellent octogenarian whose claims to be heard are based chiefly upon the fact that he himself no longer possesses the faculty of hearing,—has some famous incident, some wonderful fact, of which he has been the eye-witness, or of which he has heard from his great-grandmother, which he fancies is the very thing to be woven into song or story. Such is the strong possession which the matter takes of his brain, that, if the novelist whom he seeks to benefit does not live within trumpet-distance, he gives him the narrative by means of post, some three sheets of stiff foolscap, for which the hapless tale-writer, whose works are selling in cheap editions at twelve or twenty cents, pays a sum of one dollar sixty-two postage. Now, it so happens, to increase the evil, that, in ninety-nine cases in the hundred, the fact thus laboriously stated is not worth a straw—consisting of some simple deed of violence, some mere murder, a downright blow with gunbutt or cudgel over the skull, or a hidden thrust, three inches deep, with dirk or bowie knife, into the abdomen, or at random among the lower ribs. The man dies and the murderer gets off to Texas, or is prematurely caught and stops by the way—and still stops by the way! The thing is fact, no doubt. The narrator saw it himself, or his brother saw it, or—more solemn, if not more certain testimony still—his grandmother saw it, long before he had eyes to see at all. The circumstance is attested by a cloud of witnesses—a truth solemnly sworn to—and yet, for the purposes of the tale-writer, of no manner of value. This assertion may somewhat conflict with the received opinions of many, who, accustomed to find deeds of violence recorded in almost every work of fiction, from the time of Homer to the present day, have rushed to the conclusion that this is all, and overlook that labour of the artist, by which an ordinary event is made to assume the character of novelty; in other words, to become an extraordinary event. The least difficult thing in the world, on the part of the writer of fiction, is to find the assassin and the bludgeon; the art is to make them appear in the right place, strike at

---

1. First published in *The Gift*, an annual, in 1844, "The Two Camps" was collected in *The Wigwam and the Cabin* (1845).

the right time, and so adapt one fact to another, as to create mystery, awaken curiosity, inspire doubt as to the result, and bring about the catastrophe, by processes which shall be equally natural and unexpected. All that class of sagacious persons, therefore, who fancy they have found a mare's nest, when, in fact, they are only gazing at a goose's, are respectfully counselled that no fact—no tradition—is of any importance to the artist, unless it embodies certain peculiar characteristics of its own, or unless it illustrates some history about which curiosity has already been awakened. A mere brutality, in which John beats and bruises Ben, and Ben in turn shoots John, putting eleven slugs, or thereabouts, between his collar-bone and vertebrae—or, maybe, stabs him under his left pap, or any where you please, is just as easily conceived by the novelist, without the help of history. Nay, for that matter, he would perhaps rather not have any precise facts in his way, in such cases, as then he will be able to regard the picturesque in the choice of his weapon, and to put the wounds in such parts of the body, as will better bear the examination of all persons. I deem it right to throw out this hint, just at this moment, as well for the benefit of my order as for my own protection. The times are hard, and the post-office requires all its dues in hard money. Literary men are not proverbially prepared at all seasons for any unnecessary outlay—and to be required to make advances for commodities of which they have on hand, at all times, the greatest abundance, is an injustice which, it is to be hoped, that this little intimation will somewhat lessen. We take for granted, therefore, that our professional brethren will concur with us in saying to the public, that we are all sufficiently provided with "disastrous chances" for some time to come—that our "moving accidents by flood and field" are particularly numerous, and of "hair-breadth 'scapes" we have enough to last a century. Murders, and such matters, as they are among the most ordinary events of the day, are decidedly vulgar; and, for mere cudgelling and bruises, the taste of the belles-lettres reader, rendered delicate by the monthly magazines, has voted them equally gross and unnatural.

But, if the character of the materials usually tendered to the novelist by the incident-mongers, is thus ordinarily worthless as we describe it, we sometimes are fortunate in finding an individual, here and there, in the deep forests,—a sort of recluse, hale and lusty, but white-headed,—who unfolds from his own budget of experience a rare chronicle, on which we delight to linger. Such an one breathes life into his deeds. We see them as we listen to his words. In lieu of the dead body of the fact, we have its living spirit—subtle, active, breathing and burning, and fresh in all the provocations and associations of life. Of this sort was the admirable characteristic narrative of Horse-Shoe Robinson, which we owe to Kennedy,[2] and for which he was indebted to the venerable hero of the story. When we say that the subject of the sketch which follows was drawn from not dissimilar sources, we must

---

2. John Pendleton Kennedy (1795–1870) wrote a romance called *Horse-Shoe Robinson* (1835) based on the experiences of an informant of that name, according to the author.

beg our readers not to understand us as inviting any reference to that able and national story—with which it is by no means our policy or wish to invite or provoke comparison.

CHAPTER II

There are probably some old persons still living upon the upper dividing line between North and South Carolina, who still remember the form and features of the venerable Daniel Nelson. The old man was still living so late as 1817. At that period he removed to Mississippi, where, we believe, he died in less than three months after his change of residence. An old tree does not bear transplanting easily, and does not long survive it. Daniel Nelson came from Virginia when a youth. He was one of the first who settled on the southern borders of North Carolina, or, at least in that neighbourhood where he afterwards passed the greatest portion of his days.

At that time the country was not only a forest, but one thickly settled with Indians. It constituted the favourite hunting-grounds for several of their tribes. But this circumstance did not discourage young Nelson. He was then a stalwart youth, broad-chested, tall, with a fiery eye, and an almost equally fiery soul—certainly with a very fearless one. His companions, who were few in number, were like himself. The spirit of old Daniel Boone was a more common one than is supposed. Adventure gladdened and excited their hearts,—danger only seemed to provoke their determination,—and mere hardship was something which their frames appeared to covet. It was as refreshing to them as drink. Having seen the country, and struck down some of its game,—tasted of its bear-meat and buffalo, its deer and turkey,—all, at that time, in the greatest abundance,—they returned for the one thing most needful to a brave forester in a new country,—a good, brisk, fearless wife, who, like the damsel in Scripture, would go whithersoever went the husband to whom her affections were surrendered. They had no fear, these bold young hunters, to make a home and rear an infant family in regions so remote from the secure walks of civilization. They had met and made an acquaintance and a sort of friendship with the Indians, and, in the superior vigour of their own frames, their greater courage, and better weapons, they perhaps had come to form a too contemptuous estimate of the savage. But they were not beguiled by him into too much confidence. Their log houses were so constructed as to be fortresses upon occasion, and they lived not so far removed from one another, but that the leaguer of one would be sure, in twenty-four hours, to bring the others to his assistance. Besides, with a stock of bear-meat and vension always on hand, sufficient for a winter, either of these fortresses might, upon common calculations, be maintained for several weeks against any single band of the Indians, in the small numbers in which they were wont to range together in those neighbourhoods. In this way these bold pioneers took possession of the soil, and paved the way for still mightier generations. Though wandering, and somewhat averse to the tedious labours of the farm, they were still not wholly unmindful of its duties; and their open lands grew larger every season, and increasing comforts annually spoke for the increasing civilization of the settlers. Corn was in plenty in proportion to the bear-meat, and the squatters almost grew indifferent to those first apprehensions, which had made them watch the approaches of the most friendly Indian as if he had been an enemy. At the end of five years, in which they had suffered no hurt and but little annoyance of any sort from their wild neighbours, it would seem as if this confidence in the security of their situation was not without sufficient justification.

But, just then, circumstances seemed to threaten an interruption of this goodly state of things. The Indians were becoming discontented. Other tribes, more frequently in contact with the larger settlements of the whites,—wronged by them in trade, or demoralized by drink,—complained of their sufferings and injuries, or, as is more probable, were greedy to obtain their treasures, in bulk, which they were permitted to see, but denied to enjoy, or only in limited quantity. Their appetites and complaints were transmitted, by inevitable sympathies, to their brethren of the interior, and our worthy settlers upon the Haw,[3] were rendered anxious at signs which warned them of a change in the peaceful relations which had hitherto existed in all the intercourse between the differing races. We need not dwell upon or describe these signs, with which, from frequent narratives of like character, our people are already sufficiently familiar. They were easily understood by our little colony, and by none more quickly than Daniel Nelson. They rendered him anxious, it is true, but not apprehensive; and, like a good husband, while he strove not to frighten his wife by what he said, he deemed it necessary to prepare her mind for the worst that might occur. This task over, he felt somewhat relieved, though, when he took his little girl, now five years old, upon his knee that evening, and looked upon his infant boy in the lap of his mother, he felt his anxieties very much increase; and that very night he resumed a practice which he had latterly abandoned, but which had been adopted as a measure of strict precaution, from the very first establishment of their little settlement. As soon as supper was over, he resumed his rifle, thrust his *couteau de chasse*[4] into his belt, and, taking his horn about his neck, and calling up his trusty dog, Clinch, he proceeded to scour the woods immediately around his habitation. This task, performed with the stealthy caution of the hunter, occupied some time, and, as the night was clear, a bright starlight, the weather moderate, and his own mood restless, he determined to strike through the forest to the settlement of Jacob

---

3. A river in north-central North Carolina, east of Greensboro.

4. Hunting knife.

Ransom, about four miles off, in order to prompt him, and, through him, others of the neighbourhood, to the continued exercise of a caution which he now thought necessary. The rest of this night's adventure we propose to let him tell in his own words, as he has been heard to relate it a thousand times in his old age, at a period of life when, with one foot in his grave, to suppose him guilty of falsehood, or of telling that which he did not himself fervently believe, would be, among all those who knew him, to suppose the most impossible and extravagant thing in the world.

Chapter III

"Well, my friends," said the veteran, then seventy, drawing his figure up to its fullest height, and extending his right arm, while his left still grasped the muzzle of his ancient rifle, which he swayed from side to side, the butt resting on the floor—"Well, my friends, seeing that the night was cl'ar, and there was no wind, and feeling as how I didn't want for sleep, I called to Clinch and took the path for Jake Ransom's. I knew that Jake was a sleepy sort of chap, and if the redskins caught any body napping, he'd, most likely, be the man. But I confess, 'twarn't so much for his sake, as for the sake of all,—of my own as well as the rest;—for, when I thought how soon, if we warn't all together in the business, I might see, without being able to put in, the long yellow hair of Betsy and the babies twirling on the thumbs of some painted devil of the tribe,—I can't tell you how I felt, but it warn't like a human, though I shivered mightily like one,—'twas wolfish, as if the hair was turned in and rubbing agin the very heart within me. I said my prayers, where I stood, looking up at the stars, and thinking that, after all, all was in the hands and the mercy of God. This sort o' thinking quieted me, and I went ahead pretty free, for I knew the track jest as well by night as by day, though I didn't go so quick, for I was all the time on the look-out for the enemy. Now, after we reached a place in the woods where there was a gully and a mighty bad crossing, there were two roads to get to Jake's—one by the hollows, and one jest across the hills. I don't know why, but I didn't give myself time to think, and struck right across the hill, though that was rather the longest way.

"Howsomedever, on I went, and Clinch pretty close behind me. The dog was a good dog, with a mighty keen nose to hunt, but jest then he didn't seem to have the notion for it. The hill was a sizeable one, a good stretch to foot, and I began to remember, after awhile, that I had been in the woods from blessed dawn; and that made me see how it was with poor Clinch, and why he didn't go for'ad; but I was more than half way, and wasn't guine to turn back till I had said my say to Jake. Well, when I got to the top of the hill, I stopped, and rubbed my eyes. I had cause to rub 'em, for what should I see at a distance but a great fire. At first I was afeard lest it was Jake's house, but I considered, the next moment, that he lived to the left, and this fire was cl'ar to the right, and it did seem to me as if 'twas more near to my own. Here was something to scare a body. But I couldn't stay there looking, and it warn't now a time to go to Jake's; so I turned off, and, though Clinch was mighty onwilling, I bolted on the road to the fire. I say road, but there was no road; but the trees warn't over-thick, and the land was too poor for undergrowth; so we got on pretty well, considering. But, what with the tire I had had, and the scare I felt, it seemed as if I didn't get for'ad a bit. There was the fire still burning as bright and almost as far off as ever. When I saw this I stopt and looked at Clinch, and he stopped and looked at me, but neither of us had any thing to say. Well, after a moment's thinking, it seemed as if I shouldn't be much of a man to give up when I had got so far, so I pushed on. We crossed more than one little hill, then down and through the hollow, and then up the hill again. At last we got upon a small mountain the Indians called Nolleehatchie, and then it seemed as if the fire had come to a stop, for it was now burning bright, on a little hill below me, and not two hundred yards in front. It was a regular camp fire, pretty big, and there was more than a dozen Indians sitting round it. 'Well,' says I to myself, 'it's come upon us mighty sudden, and what's to be done? Not a soul in the settlement knows it but myself, and nobody's on the watch. They'll be sculped, every human of them, in their very beds, or, moutbe, waken up in the blaze, to be shot with arrows as they run.' I was in a cold sweat to think of it. I didn't know what to think and what to do. I looked round to Clinch, and the strangest thing of all was to see him sitting quiet on his haunches, looking at me, and at the stars, and not at the fire jest before him. Now, Clinch was a famous fine hunting dog, and jest as good on an Indian trail as any other. He know'd my ways, and what I wanted, and would give tongue, or keep it still, jest as I axed him. It was sensible enough, jest then, that he shouldn't bark, but, dang it!—he didn't even seem to see. Now, there warn't a dog in all the settlement so quick and keen to show sense as Clinch, even when he didn't say a word;—and to see him looking as if he didn't know and didn't care what was a-going on, with his eyes sot in his head and glazed over with sleep, was, as I may say, very onnatural, jest at that time, in a dog of any onderstanding. So I looked at him, half angry, and when he saw me looking at him, he jest stretched himself off, put his nose on his legs, and went to sleep in 'arnest. I had half a mind to lay my knife-handle over his head, but I considered better of it, and though it did seem the strangest thing in the world that he shouldn't even try to get to the fire, for warm sake, yet I recollected that dog natur', like human natur', can't stand every thing, and he hadn't such good reason as I had, to know that the Indians were no longer friendly to us. Well, there I stood, a pretty considerable chance, looking, and wondering, and onbeknowing what to do. I was mighty beflustered. But at last I felt ashamed to be so oncertain, and then again it was a needcessity that we should know the worst one time or another, so I determined to push for'ad. I was no slouch of a hunter, as you may suppose; so, as I was nearing the camp, I begun sneaking; and, taking it sometimes on hands and knees, and sometimes flat to the ground, where there was neither tree nor bush to cover me, I went ahead, Clinch keeping close behind me, and not showing any notion of what I was after. It was a slow business, because it was a ticklish business; but I was a leetle too anxious to be altogether so careful as a good sneak ought to be, and I went on rather faster than I would advise any young man to go in a time of war, when the inimy is in the neighbourhood. Well, as I went, there was the fire, getting larger and larger every minute, and there were the Indians round it, getting plainer and plainer. There was so much smoke that there was no making out, at any distance, any but their figures, and these, every now and then, would be so wrapt in the smoke that not more than half of them could be seen at the same moment. At last I stopped, jest at a place where I thought I could make out all that I wanted. There was a sizeable rock before me, and I leaned my elbows on it to look. I reckon I warn't more than thirty yards from the fire. There were some bushes betwixt us, and what with the bushes and the smoke, it was several minutes before I could separate man from man, and see what they were all adoing, and when I did, it was only for a moment at a time, when a puff of smoke would wrap them all, and make it as difficult as ever. But when I did contrive to see clearly, the sight was one to worry me to the core, for, in the midst of the redskins, I could see a white one, and that white one a woman. There was no mistake. There were the Indians, some with their backs, and some with their faces to me; and there, a little a-one side, but still among them, was a woman. When the smoke blowed off, I could see her white face, bright like any star, shining out of the clouds, and looking so pale and ghastly that my blood cruddled in my veins to think lest she might be dead from fright. But it couldn't be so, for she was sitting up and looking about her. But the Indians were motionless. They jest sat or lay as when I first saw them—doing nothing—saying nothing, but jest as motionless as the stone under my elbow. I couldn't stand looking where I was, so I began creeping again, getting nigher and nigher, until it seemed to me as if I ought to be able to read every face. But what with the paint and smoke, I couldn't make out a single Indian. Their figures seemed plain enough in their buffalo-skins and blankets, but their faces seemed always in the dark. But it wasn't so with the woman. I could make her out clearly. She was very young; I reckon not more than fifteen, and it seemed to me as if I knew her looks very well. She was very handsome, and her hair was loosed upon her back. My heart felt strange to see her. I was weak as any child. It seemed as if I could die for the gal, and yet I hadn't strength enough to raise my rifle to my shoulder. The weakness kept on me the more I looked; for every moment seemed to make the poor child more and more dear to me. But the strangest thing of all was to see how motionless was every Indian in the camp. Not a word was spoken—not a limb or finger stirred. There they sat, or lay, round about the fire, like so many effigies, looking at the gal, and she looking at them. I never was in such a fix of fear and weakness in my life. What was I to do? I had got so nigh that I could have stuck my knife, with a jerk, into the heart of any one of the party, yet I hadn't the soul to lift it; and before I knew where I was, I cried like a child. But my crying didn't make 'em look about 'em. It only brought my poor dog Clinch leaping upon me, and whining, as if he wanted to give me consolation. Hardly knowing what I did, I tried to set him upon the camp, but the poor fellow didn't seem to understand me; and in my desperation, for it was a sort of madness growing out of my scare, I jumped headlong for 'ad, jest where I saw the party sitting, willing to lose my life rather than suffer from such a strange sort of misery.

CHAPTER IV

"Will you believe me! there were no Indians, no young woman, no fire! I stood up in the very place where I had seen the blaze and the smoke, and there was nothing! I looked for'ad and about me—there was no sign of fire any where. Where I stood was covered with dry leaves, the same as the rest of the forest. I was stupefied. I was like a man roused out of sleep by a strange dream, and seeing nothing. All was dark and silent. The stars were overhead, but that was all the light I had. I was more scared than ever, and, as it's a good rule when a man feels that he can do nothing himself, to look to the great God who can do every thing, I kneeled down and said my prayers—the second time that night that I had done the same thing, and the second time, I reckon, that I had ever done so in the woods. After that I felt stronger. I felt sure that this sign hadn't been shown to me for nothing; and while I was turning about, looking and thinking to turn on the back track for home, Clinch began to prick up his ears and waken up. I clapped him on his back, and got my knife ready. It might be a *painter* that stirred him, for he could scent that beast a great distance. But, as he showed no fright, only a sort of quickening, I knew there was nothing to fear. In a moment he started off, and went boldly ahead. I followed him, but hadn't gone twenty steps down the hill and into the hollow, when I heard something like a groan. This quickened me, and keeping up with the dog, he led me to the foot of the hollow, where was a sort of pond. Clinch ran right for it, and another groan set me in the same direction. When I got up to the dog, he was on the butt-end of an old tree that had fallen, I reckon, before my time, and was half buried in the water. I jumped on it, and walked a few steps for'ad, when, what should I see but a human, half across the log, with his legs hanging in the water, and his head down. I called Clinch back out of my way, and went to the spot. The groans were pretty constant. I stopped down and laid my hands upon the person, and, as I felt the hair, I knew it was an Indian. The head was clammy with blood, so that my fingers stuck, and when I attempted to turn it, to look at the face, the groan was deeper than ever; but 'twarn't a time to suck one's fingers. I took him up, clapped my shoulders to it, and, fixing my feet firmly on the old tree, which was rather slippery, I brought the poor fellow out without much trouble. Though tall, he was not heavy, and was only a boy of fourteen or fifteen. The wonder was how a lad like that should get into such a fix. Well, I brought him out and laid him on the dry leaves. His groans stopped, and I thought he was dead, but I felt his heart, and it was still warm, and I thought, though I couldn't be sure, there was a beat under my fingers. What to do was the next question. It was now pretty late in the night. I had been all day a-foot, and, though still willing to go, yet the thought of such a weight on my shoulders made me stagger. But 'twouldn't do to leave him where he was to perish. I thought, if so be I had a son in such a fix, what would I think of the stranger who should go home and wait till daylight to give him help! No, darn my splinters, said I,— though I had just done my prayers,—if I leave the lad—and, tightening my girth, I give my whole soul to it, and hoisted him on my shoulders. My cabin, I reckoned, was good three miles off. You can guess what trouble I had, and what a tire under my load, before I got home and laid the poor fellow down by the fire. I then called up Betsy, and we both set to work to see if we could stir up the life that was in him. She cut away his hair, and I washed the blood from his head, which was chopped to the bone, either with a knife or hatchet. It was a God's blessing it hadn't gone into his brain, for it was fairly enough aimed for it, jest above the ear. When we come to open his clothes, we found another wound in his side. This was done with a knife, and, I suppose, was pretty deep. He had lost blood enough, for all his clothes were stiff with it. We knew nothing much of doctoring, but we had some rum in the cabin, and after washing his wounds clean with it, and pouring some down his throat, he began to groan more freely, and by that we knew he was coming to a nateral feeling. We rubbed his body down with warm cloths, and after a little while, seeing that he made some signs, I give him water as much as he could drink. This seemed to do him good, and having done every thing that we thought could help him, we wrapped him up warmly before the fire, and I stretched myself off beside him. 'Twould be a long story to tell, step by step, how he got on. It's enough to say that he didn't die that bout. We got him on his legs in a short time, doing little or nothing for him more than we did at first. The lad was a good lad, though, at first, when he first came to his senses, he was mighty shy, wouldn't look steadily in our faces, and, I do believe, if he could have got out of the cabin, would have done so as soon as he could stagger. But he was too weak to try that, and, meanwhile, when he saw our kindness, he was softened. By little and little, he got to play with my little Lucy, who was not quite six years old; and, after a while, he seemed to be never better pleased than when they played together. The child, too, after her first fright, leaned to the lad, and was jest as willing to play with him as if he had been a cl'ar white like herself. He could say a few words of English from the beginning, and learnt quickly; but, though he talked tolerable free for an Indian, yet I could never get him to tell me how he was wounded, or by whom. His brow blackened when I spoke of it, and his lips would be shut together, as if he was ready to

fight sooner than to speak. Well, I didn't push him to know, for I was pretty
sure the head of the truth will be sure to come some time or other, if you
once have it by the tail, provided you don't jerk it off by straining too hard
upon it.

Chapter V

"I suppose the lad had been with us a matter of six weeks, getting better
every day, but so slowly that he had not, at the end of that time, been able to
leave the picket. Meanwhile, our troubles with the Indians were increasing.
As yet, there had been no bloodshed in our quarter, but we heard of murders
and sculpings on every side, and we took for granted that we must have our
turn. We made our preparations, repaired the pickets, laid in ammunition,
and took turns for scouting nightly. At length, the signs of Indians got to be
thick in our parts, though we could see none. Jake Ransom had come upon
one of their camps after they had left it; and we had reason to apprehend
every thing, inasmuch as the outlyers didn't show themselves, as they used
to do, but prowled about the cabins and went from place to place, only by
night, or by close skulking in the thickets. One evening after this, I went out
as usual to go the rounds, taking Clinch with me, but I hadn't got far from
the gate, when the dog stopped and gave a low bark;—then I knew there was
mischief, so I turned round quietly, without making any show of scare, and
got back safely, though not a minute too soon. They trailed me to the gate
the moment after I had got it fastened, and were pretty mad, I reckon, when
they found their plan had failed for surprising me. But for the keen nose of
poor Clinch, with all my skill in scouting,—and it was not small even in that
early day,—they'd 'a had me, and all that was mine, before the sun could
open his eyes to see what they were after. Finding they had failed in their
ambush, they made the woods ring with the war-whoop, which was a sign
that they were guine to give us a regular siege. At the sound of the whoop,
we could see the eyes of the Indian boy brighten, and his ears prick up, jest
like a hound's when he first gets scent of the deer, or hears the horn of the
hunter. I looked closely at the lad, and was dub'ous what to do. He moutbe
only an enemy in the camp, and while I was fighting in front, he might be
cutting the throats of my wife and children within. I did not tell you that I
had picked up his bow and arrows near the little lake where I had found him,
and his hunting-knife was sticking in his belt when I brought him home.
Whether to take these away from him, was the question. Suppose I did, a
billet of wood would answer pretty near as well. I thought the matter over
while I watched him. Thought runs mighty quick in time of danger! Well,
after turning it over on every side, I concluded 'twas better to trust him jest
as if he had been a sure friend. I couldn't think, after all we had done for

him, that he'd be false, so I said to him—'Lenatewá!'—'twas so he called himself—'those are your people!' 'Yes!' he answered slowly, and lifting himself up as if he had been a lord—he was a stately-looking lad, and carried himself like the son of a Micco,[5] as he was—'Yes, they are the people of Lenatewá—must he go to them?' and he made the motion of going out. But I stopped him. I was not willing to lose the security which I had from his being a sort of prisoner. 'No,' said I; 'no, Lenatewá, not to-night. To-morrow will do. To-morrow you can tell them I am a friend, not an enemy, and they should not come to burn my wigwam.' 'Brother—friend!' said the lad, advancing with a sort of freedom and taking my hand. He then went to my wife, and did the same thing,—not regarding she was a woman,— 'Brother—friend!' I watched him closely, watched his eye and his motions, and I said to Betsy, 'The lad is true; don't be afeard!' But we passed a weary night. Every now and then we could hear the whoop of the Indians. From the loop-holes we could see the light of three fires on different sides, by which we knew that they were prepared to cut off any help that might come to us from the rest of the settlement. But I didn't give in or despair. I worked at one thing or another all night, and though Lenatewá gave me no help, yet he sat quietly, or laid himself down before the fire, as if he had nothing in the world to do in the business. Next morning by daylight, I found him already dressed in the same bloody clothes which he had on when I found him. He had thrown aside all that I gave him, and though the hunting-shirt and leggins which he now wore, were very much stained with blood and dirt, he had fixed them about him with a good deal of care and neatness, as if preparing to see company. I must tell you that an Indian of good family always has a nateral sort of grace and dignity which I never saw in a white man. He was busily engaged looking through one of the loop-holes, and though I could distinguish nothing, yet it was cl'ar that he saw something to interest him mightily. I soon found out that, in spite of all my watchfulness, he had contrived to have some sort of correspondence and communication with those outside. This was a wonder to me then, for I did not recollect his bow and arrows. It seems that he had shot an arrow through one of the loop-holes, to the end of which he had fastened a tuft of his own hair. The effect of this was considerable, and to this it was owing that, for a few hours after-wards, we saw not an Indian. The arrow was shot at the very peep of day. What they were about, in the meantime, I can only guess, and the guess was only easy, after I had known all that was to happen. That they were in coun-cil what to do was cl'ar enough. I was not to know that the council was like to end in cutting some of their own throats instead of ours. But when we did see the enemy fairly, they came out of the woods in two parties, not actually separated, but not moving together. It seemed as if there was some strife among them. Their whole number could not be less than forty, and some eight or ten of these walked apart under the lead of a chief, a stout, dark-looking fellow, one-half of whose face was painted black as midnight, with a

---

5. A chief.

red circle round both his eyes. The other party was headed by an old white-headed chief, who couldn't ha' been less than sixty years—a pretty fellow, you may be sure, at his time of life, to be looking after sculps of women and children. While I was kneeling at my loop-hole looking at them, Lenatewá came to me, and touching me on the arm, pointed to the old chief, saying—'Micco Lenatewá Glucco,' by which I guessed he was the father or grandfather of the lad. 'Well,' I said, seeing that the best plan was to get their confidence and friendship if possible,—'Well, lad, go to your father and tell him what Daniel Nelson has done for you, and let's have peace. We can fight, boy, as you see; we have plenty of arms and provisions; and with this rifle, though you may not believe it, I could pick off your father, the king, and that other chief, who has so devilled himself up with paint.' 'Shoot!' said the lad quickly, pointing to the chief of whom I had last spoken. 'Ah! he is your enemy then?' The lad nodded his head, and pointed to the wound on his temple, and that in his side. I now began to see the true state of the case. 'No,' said I; 'no, Lenatewá, I will shoot none. I am for peace. I would do good to the Indians, and be their friend. Go to your father and tell him so. Go, and make him be my friend.' The youth caught my hand, placed it on the top of his head, and exclaimed, 'Good!' I then attended him down to the gate, but, before he left the cabin, he stopped and put his hand on the head of little Lucy,—and I felt glad, for it seemed to say, 'you shan't be hurt—not a hair of your head!' I let him out, fastened up, and then hastened to the loop-hole.

Chapter VI

"And now came a sight to tarrify. As soon as the Indians saw the young prince, they set up a general cry. I couldn't tell whether it was of joy, or what. He went for'ad boldly, though he was still quite weak, and the king at the head of his party advanced to meet him. The other and smaller party, headed by the black chief, whom young Lenatewá had told me to shoot, came forward also, but very slowly, and it seemed as if they were doubtful whether to come or go. Their leader looked pretty much beflustered. But they hadn't time for much study, for, after the young prince had met his father, and a few words had passed between them, I saw the finger of Lenatewá point to the black chief. At this, he lifted up his clenched fists, and worked his body as if he was talking angrily. Then, sudden, the war-whoop sounded from the king's party, and the other troop of Indians began to run, the black chief at their head; but he had not got twenty steps when a dozen arrows went into him, and he tumbled for'a'ds, and grappled with the earth. It was all over with him. His party was scattered on all sides, but were not pursued. It seemed that all the arrows had been aimed at the one person, and when he sprawled, there was an end to it: the whole affair was over in five minutes.

Chapter VII

"It was a fortunate affair for us. Lenatewá soon brought the old Micco to terms of peace. For that matter, he had only consented to take up the red stick because it was reported by the black chief—who was the uncle of the young Micco, and had good reasons for getting him out of the way—that he had been murdered by the whites. This driv' the old man to desperation, and brought him down upon us. When he knew the whole truth, and saw what friends we had been to his son, there was no end to his thanks and promises. He swore to be my friend while the sun shone, while the waters run, and while the mountains stood, and I believe, if the good old man had been spared so long, he would have been true to his oath. But, while he lived, he kept it, and so did his son when he succeeded him as Micco Glucco. Year after year went by, and though there was frequent war between the Indians and the whites, yet Lenatewá kept it from our doors. He himself was at war several times with our people, but never with our settlement. He put his *totem* on our trees, and the Indians knew that they were sacred. But, after a space of eleven years, there was a change. The young prince seemed to have forgotten our friendship. We now never saw him among us, and, unfortunately, some of your young men—the young men of our own settlement—murdered three young warriors of the Ripparee tribe, who were found on horses stolen from us. I was very sorry when I heard it, and began to fear the consequences; and they came upon us when we least looked for it. I had every reason to think that Lenatewá would still keep the warfare from my little family, but I did not remember that he was the prince of a tribe only, and not of the nation. This was a national warfare, in which the whole Cherokee people were in arms. Many persons, living still, remember that terrible war, and how the Carolinians humbled them at last; but there's no telling how much blood was shed in that war, how many sculps taken, how much misery suffered by young and old, men, women, and children. Our settlement had become so large and scattered that we had to build a sizeable blockhouse, which we stored, and to which we could retreat whenever it was necessary. We took possession of it on hearing from our scouts that Indian trails had been seen, and there we put the women and children, under a strong guard. By day we tended our farms, and only went to our families at night. We had kept them in this fix for five weeks or thereabouts, and there was no attack. The Indian signs disappeared, and we all thought the storm had blown over, and began to hope and to believe that the old friendship of

Lenatewá had saved us. With this thinking, we began to be less watchful. The men would stay all night at the farms, and sometimes, in the day, would carry with them the women, and sometimes some even the children. I cautioned them agin this, but they mocked me, and said I was gitting old and scary. I told them, 'Wait and see who'll scare first.' But, I confess, not seeing any Indians in all my scouting, I began to feel and think like the rest, and to grow careless. I let Betsy go now and then with me to the farm, though she kept it from me that she had gone there more than once with Lucy, without any man protector. Still, as it was only a short mile and a half from the block, and we could hear of no Indians, it did not seem so venturesome a thing. One day we heard of some very large b'ars among the thickets—a famous range for them, about four miles from the settlement; and a party of us, Simon Lorris, Hugh Darling, Jake Ransom, William Harkless, and myself, taking our dogs, set off on the hunt. We started the b'ar with a rush, and I got the first shot at a mighty big she b'ar, the largest I had ever seen— lamed the critter slightly, and dashed into the thickets after her! The others pushed, in another direction, after the rest, leaving me to finish my work as I could.

"I had two dogs with me, Clap and Claw, but they were young things, and couldn't be trusted much in a close brush with a b'ar. Old Clinch was dead, or he'd ha' made other guess-work with the varmint. But, hot after the b'ar, I didn't think of the quality of the dogs till I found myself in a fair wrestle with the brute. I don't brag, my friends, but that *was* a fight. I tell you my breath was clean gone, for the b'ar had me about the thin of my body, and I thought I was doubled up enough to be laid down without more handling. But my heart was strong when I thought of Betsy and the children, and I got my knife, with hard *jugging*—though I couldn't use my arm above my elbow—through the old critter's hide, and in among her ribs. That only seemed to make her hug closer, and I reckon I was clean gone, if it hadn't been that she blowed out before me. I had worked a pretty deep window in her waist, and then life run out plentiful. Her nose dropped agin my breast, and then her paws; and when the strain was gone, I fell down like a sick child, and she fell on top of me. But she warn't in a humour to do more mischief. She roughed me once or twice more with her paws, but that was only because she was at her last kick. There I lay a matter of half an hour, with the dead b'ar alongside o' me. I was almost as little able to move as she, and I vomited as if I had taken physic. When I come to myself and got up, there was no sound of the hunters. There I was with the two dogs and the b'ar, all alone, and the sun already long past the turn. My horse, which I had fastened outside of the thicket, had slipped his bridle, and, I reckoned, had either strayed off grazing, or had pushed back directly for the block. These things didn't make make me feel much better. But, though my stomach didn't feel altogether right, and my ribs were as sore as if I had been sweating under a coating of hickory, I felt that there was no use and no time to stand there grunting. But I made out to skin and to cut up the b'ar, and a noble mountain of fat she made. I took the skin with me, and, covering the flesh with bark, I whistled off the dogs, after they had eat to fill, and pushed after my horse. I followed his track for some time, till I grew fairly tired. He had gone off in a scare and at a full gallop, and, instead of going home, had dashed down the lower side of the thicket, then gone aside, to round some of the hills, and thrown himself out of the track, it moutbe seven miles or more. When I found this, I saw there was no use to hunt him that day and afoot, and I had no more to do but turn about, and push as fast as I could for the block. But this was work enough. By this time the sun was pretty low, and there was now a good seven miles, work it how I could, before me. But I was getting over my b'ar-sickness, and though my legs felt weary enough, my stomach was better, and my heart braver; and, as I was in no hurry, having the whole night before me, and knowing the way by night as well as by light, I began to feel cheerful enough, all things considering. I pushed on slowly, stopping every now and then for rest, and recovering my strength this way. I had some parched meal and sugar in my pouch which I ate, and it helped me mightily. It was my only dinner that day. The evening got to be very still. I wondered I had seen and heard nothing of Jake Ransom and the rest, but I didn't feel at all oneasy about them, thinking that, like all other hunters, they would naterally follow the game to any distance. But, jest when I was thinking about them, I heard a gun, then another, and after that all got to be as quiet as ever. I looked to my own rifle and felt for my knife, and put forward a little more briskly. I suppose I had walked an hour after this, when it came on close dark, and I was still four good miles from the block. The night was cloudy, there were no stars, and the feeling in the air was damp and oncomfortable. I began to wish I was safe home, and felt queerish, almost as bad as I did when the b'ar was 'bracing me; but it warn't so much the body-sickness as the heart-sickness. I felt as if something was going wrong. Jest as this feeling was most worrisome, I stumbled over a human. My blood cruddled, when, feeling about, I put my hand on his head, and found the sculp was gone. Then I knew there was mischief. I couldn't make out who 'twas that was under me, but I reckoned 'twas one of the hunters. There was nothing to be done but to push for'ad. I didn't feel any more tire. I felt ready for fight, and when I thought of our wives and children in the block, and what might become of them, I got wolfish, though the Lord only knows what I was minded to do. I can't say I had any raal sensible thoughts of what was to be done in the business. I didn't trust myself to think whether the Indians had been to the block yet or no; though ugly notions came across me when I remembered how we let the women and children go about to the farms. I was in a complete fever and agy. I scorched one time and shivered another, but I pushed on, for there was now no more feeling of tire in my limbs than if they were made of steel. By this time I had reached that long range of hills where I first saw that strange campfire, now eleven years gone, that turned out to be a deception, and it was nateral enough that the thing should come fresh into my mind, jest at that moment. While I was thinking over the wonder, and asking myself, as I had done over and often before, what it possibly could mean, I reached the top of one of the hills, from which I could see, in daylight, the whole country for a matter of ten miles or more on every side. What was my surprise, do you reckon, when there, jest on the very same hill opposite where I had seen that apparition of a camp, I saw another, and this time it was a raal one. There was a rousing blaze, and though the woods and undergrowth were thicker on this than on the other side, from which I had seen it before, yet I could make out that there were several figures, and them Indians. It sort o' made me easier to see the enemy before, and then I could better tell what I had to do. I was to spy out the camp, see what the red-devils were thinking to do, and what they had already done. I was a little better scout and hunter this time than when I made the same sort o' search before, and I reckoned that I could get nigh enough to see all that was going on, without stirring up any dust among 'em. But I had to keep the dogs back. I couldn't tie 'em up, for they'd howl; so I stripped my hunting-shirt and put it down for one to guard, and I gave my cap and horn to another. I knew they'd never leave 'em, for I had l'arned 'em all that sort of business—to watch as well as to fetch and carry. I then said a sort of short running prayer, and took the trail. I had to work for'ad slowly. If I had gone on this time as I did in that first camp transaction, I'd ha' lost my sculp to a sartainty. Well, to shorten a long business, I tell you that I got nigh enough, without scare or surprise, to see all that I cared to see, and a great deal more than I wished to see; and now, for the first time, I saw the meaning of that sight which I had, eleven years before, of the camp that come to nothing. I saw that first sight over again, the Indians round the fire, a young woman in the middle, and that young woman my own daughter, my child, my poor, dear Lucy!

Chapter VIII

"That was a sight for a father. I can't tell you—and I won't try—how I felt. But I lay there, resting upon my hands and knees, jest as if I had been turned into stone with looking. I lay so for a good half hour, I reckon, without stirring a limb; and you could only tell that life was in me, by seeing the big drops that squeezed out of my eyes now and then, and by a sort of shivering that shook me as you sometimes see the canebrake shaking with the gust of the pond inside. I tried to pray to God for help, but I couldn't pray, and as for thinking, that was jest as impossible. But I could do nothing by looking, and, for that matter, it was pretty cla'r to me, as I stood, with no help—by myself—one rifle only and knife—I couldn't do much by moving. I could have lifted the gun, and in a twinkle, tumbled the best fellow in the gang, but what good was that guine to do me? I was never fond of blood-spilling, and if I could have been made sure of my daughter, I'd ha' been willing that the red devils should have had leave to live for ever. What was I to do? Go to the block? Who know'd if it warn't taken, with every soul in it? And where else was I to look for help? Nowhere, nowhere but to God! I groaned—I groaned so loud that I was dreadful 'feared that they'd hear me; but they were too busy among themselves, eating supper, and poor Lucy in the midst, not eating, but so pale, and looking so miserable—jest as I had seen her, when she was only a child—in the same fix, though 'twas only an appearance—eleven years ago! Well, at last, I turned off. As I couldn't say what to do, I was too miserable to look, and I went down to the bottom of the hill and rolled about on the ground, pulling the hair out of my head and groaning, as if that was to do me any good. Before I knew where I was, there was a hand on my shoulder. I jumped up to my feet, and flung my rifle over my head, meaning to bring the butt down upon the stranger—but his voice stopped me.

"'Brother,' said he, 'me Lenatewá!'

"The way he talked, his soft tones, made me know that the young prince meant to be friendly, and I gave him my hand; but the tears gushed out as I did so, and I cried out like a man struck in the very heart, while I pointed to the hill—'My child, my child!'

"'Be man!' said he, 'come!' pulling me away.

"'But, will you save her, Lenatewá?'

"He did not answer instantly, but led me to the little lake, and pointed to the old tree over which I had borne his lifeless body so many years ago. By that I knew he meant to tell me, he had not forgotten what I had done for him; and would do for me all he could. But this did not satisfy me. I must know how and when it was to be done, and what was his hope; for I could see from his caution, and leading me away from the camp, that he did not command the party, and had no power over them. He then asked me, if I had not seen the paint of the warriors in the camp. But I had seen nothing but the fix of my child. He then described the paint to me, which was his way of showing me that the party on the hill were his deadly enemies. The paint about their eyes was that of the great chief, his uncle, who had tried to murder him years ago, and who had been shot, in my sight, by the party of his father. The young chief, now in command of the band on the hill was the son of his uncle, and sworn to revenge the death of his father upon him, Lenatewá. This he made me onderstand in a few minutes. And he gave me farther to onderstand, that there was no way of getting my child from them onless by cunning. He had but two followers with him, and they were even then busy in making preparations. But of these preparations he either would not or could not give me any account; and I had to wait on him with all the patience I could muster; and no easy trial it was, for an Indian is the most cool and slow-moving creature in the world, unless he's actually fighting, and then he's about the quickest. After awhile, Lenatewá led me round the hill. We fetched a pretty smart reach, and before I knew where I was, he led me into a hollow that I had never seen before. Here, to my surprise, there

were no less than twelve or fourteen horses fastened, that these red devils
had stolen from the settlement that very day, and mine was among them. I
did not know it till the young prince told me.

"'Him soon move,' said he, pointing to one on the outside, which a close
examination showed me to be my own—'Him soon move,'—and these
words gave me a notion of his plan. But he did not allow me to have any
hand in it—not jest then, at least. Bidding me keep a watch on the fire
above, for the hollow in which we stood was at the foot of the very hill the
Indians had made their camp on—though the stretch was a long one
between—he pushed for'ad like a shadow, and so slily, so silently, that,
though I thought myself a good deal of a scout before, I saw then that I
warn't fit to hold a splinter to him. In a little time he had unhitched my
horse, and quietly led him farther down the hollow, half round the hill, and
then up the opposite hill. There was very little noise, the wind was from the
camp, and, though they didn't show any alarm, I was never more scary in
my life. I followed Lenatewá, and found where he had fastened my nag. He
had placed him several hundred yards from the Indians, on his way to the
block; and, where we now stood, owing to the bend of the hollow, the camp
of the Indians was between us and where they had hitched the stolen horses.
When I saw this, I began to guess something of his plan. Meantime, one
after the other, his two followers came up, and made a long report to him in
their own language. This done, he told me that three of my hunting companions had been sculped, the other, who was Hugh Darling, had got off
cl'ar, though fired upon twice, and had alarmed the block, and that my
daughter had been made prisoner at the farm to which she had gone without
any company. This made me a little easier, and Lenatewá then told me what
he meant to do. In course, I had to do something myself towards it. Off he
went, with his two men, leaving me to myself. When I thought they had got
pretty fairly round the hill, I started back for the camp, trying my best, you
may be sure, to move as slily as Lenatewá. I got within twenty-five yards, I
reckon, when I thought it better to lie by quietly and wait. I could see every
head in the huddle, and my poor child among them, looking whiter than a
sheet, beside their ugly painted skins. Well, I hadn't long to wait, when there
was such an uproar among the stolen horses in the hollow on the opposite
side of the hill—such a trampling, such a whinnying and whickering, you
never heard the like. Now, you must know, that a stolen horse, to an Indian,
is jest as precious as a sweetheart to a white man; and when the rumpus
reached the camp, there was a rush of every man among them, for his critter. Every redskin, but one, went over the hill after the horses, and he
jumped up with the rest, but didn't move off. He stood over poor Lucy with
his tomahawk, shaking it above her head, as if guine to strike every minute.
She, poor child—I could see her as plain as the fire-light, for she sat jest on
one side of it—her hands were clasped together. She was praying, for she
must have looked every minute to be knocked on the head. You may depend,
I found it very hard to keep in. I was a'most biling over, the more when I
saw the red devil making his flourishes, every now and then, close to the

child's ears, with his bloody we'pon. But it was a needcessity to keep in till the sounds died off pretty much, so as not to give them any scare this side, till they had dashed ahead pretty far 'pon the other. I don't know that I waited quite as long as I ought to, but I waited as long as my feelings would let me, and then I dropped the sight of my rifle as close as I could fix it on the breast of the Indian that had the keeping of my child. I took aim, but I felt I was a little tremorsome, and I stopped. I know'd I had but one shoot, and if I didn't onbutton him in that one, it would be a bad shoot for poor Lucy. I didn't fear to hit *her*, and I was pretty sure I'd hit him. But it must be a dead shot to do good, for I know'd if I only hurt him, that he'd sink the tomahawk in her head with what strength he had left him. I brought myself to it again, and this time I felt strong. I could jest hear a little of the hubbub of men and horses afar off. I knew it was the time, and, resting the side of the muzzle against a tree, I give him the whole blessing of the bullet. I didn't stop to ask what luck, but run in, with a sort o' cry, to do the finishing with the knife. But the thing was done a'ready. The beast was on his back, and I only had to use the knife in cutting the vines that fastened the child to the sapling behind her. The brave gal didn't scream or faint. She could only say, 'Oh, my father!' and I could only say, 'Oh! my child!' And what a precious hug followed; but it was only for a minute. We had no time to waste in hugging. We pushed at once for the place where I had left the critter, and if the good old nag ever used his four shanks to any purpose, he did that night. I reckon it was a joyful surprise to poor Betsy when we broke into the block. She had given it out for sartin that she'd never see me or the child again, with a nateral sculp on our heads.

CHAPTER IX

"There's no need to tell you the whole story of this war between our people and the redskins. It's enough that I tell you of what happened to us, and our share in it. Of the great affair, and all the fights and burnings, you'll find enough in the printed books and newspapers. What I tell you, though you can't find it in any books, is jest as true, for all that. Of our share in it, the worst has already been told you. The young chief, Oloschottee—for that was his name—the cousin and the enemy of Lenatewá, had command of the Indians that were to surprise our settlements; and though he didn't altogether do what he expected and intended, he worked us quite enough of mischief as it was. He soon put fire to all our farms to draw us out of the block, but finding that wouldn't do, he left us; for an Indian gets pretty soon tired of a long siege where there is neither rum nor blood to git drunk on. His force was too small to trouble us in the block, and so he drawed off his warriors, and we saw no more of him until the peace. That followed pretty soon after General Middleton gave the nation that licking at Echotee,—a licking, I reckon, that they'll remember long after my day. At that affair Lenatewá got an ugly bullet in his throat, and if it hadn't been for one of his men, he'd ha' got a bag'net in his breast. They made a narrow run with him, head foremost down the hill, with a whole swad of the mounted men from the low country at their heels. It was some time after the peace before he got better of his hurt, though the Indians are naterally more skilful in cures than white men. By this time we had all gone home to our farms, and had planted and rebuilt, and begun to forget our troubles, when who should pop into our cabin one day, but Lenatewá. He had got quite well of his hurts. He was a monstrous fine-looking fellow, tall and handsome, and he was dressed in his very best. He wore pantaloons, like one of us, and his hunting shirt was a raally fine blue, with a white fringe. He wore no paint, and was quite nice and neat with his person. We all received him as an old friend, and he stayed with us three days. Then he went, and was gone for a matter of two weeks, when he came back and stayed with us another three days. And so, off and on, he came to visit us, until Betsy said to me one day, 'Daniel, that Indian, Lenatewá, comes here after Lucy. Leave a woman to guess these things.' After she told me, I recollected that the young prince was quite watchful of Lucy, and would follow her out into the garden, and leave us, to walk with her. But then, again, I thought—'What if he is favorable to my daughter? The fellow's a good fellow; and a raal, noble-hearted Indian, that's sober, is jest as good, to my thinking, as any white man in the land.' But Betsy wouldn't hear to it. 'Her daughter never should marry a savage, and a heathen, and a redskin, while her head was hot':—and while her head was so hot, what was I to do? All I could say was this only, 'Don't kick, Betsy, till you're spurred. 'Twill be time enough to give the young Chief his answer when he asks the question; and it won't do for us to treat him rudely, when we consider how much we owe him.' But she was of the mind that the boot was on the other leg,—that it was he and not us that owed the debt; and all that I could do couldn't keep her from showing the lad a sour face of it whenever he came. But he didn't seem much to mind this, since I was civil and kind to him. Lucy too, though her mother warned her against him, always treated him civilly as I told her; though she naterally would do so, for she couldn't so easily forget that dreadful night when she was a prisoner in the camp of the enemy, not knowing what to expect, with an Indian toma-hawk over her head, and saved, in great part, by the cunning and courage of this same Lenatewá. The girl treated him kindly, and I was not sorry she did so. She walked and talked with him jest as if they had been brother and sis-ter, and he was jest as polite to her as if he had been a born Frenchman.

"You may be sure, it was no pleasant sight to my wife to see them two go out to walk. 'Daniel Nelson,' said she, 'do you see and keep an eye on those people. There's no knowing what may happen. I do believe that Lucy has a liking for that redskin, and should they run!'—'Psho!' said I,—but that wouldn't do for her, and so she made me watch the young people sure enough. 'Twarn't a business that I was overfond of, you may reckon, but I was a rough man and didn't know much of woman natur'. I left the judgment of such things to my wife, and did pretty much what she told me. Whenever they went out to walk, I followed them, rifle in hand; but it was only to please Betsy, for if I had seen the lad running off with the girl, I'm pretty sure, I'd never ha' been the man to draw trigger upon him. As I said before, Lenatewá was jest as good a husband as she could have had. But, poor fellow, the affair was never to come to that. One day, after he had been with us almost a week, he spoke softly to Lucy, and she got up, got her bonnet and went out with him. I didn't see them when they started, for I happened to be in the upper story,—a place where we didn't so much live, but where we used to go for shelter and defence whenever any Indians came about us. 'Daniel,' said my wife, and I knew by the quickness and sharpness of her voice what 'twas she had to tell me. But jest then I was busy, and moreover, I didn't altogether like the sort of business upon which she wanted me to go. The sneaking after an enimy, in raal warfare, is an onpleasant sort of thing enough; but this sneaking after one that you think your friend is worse than running in a fair fight, and always gave me a sheepish feeling after it. Besides, I didn't fear Lenatewá, and I didn't fear my daughter. It's true, the girl treated him kindly and sweetly, but that was owing to the nateral sweetness of her temper, and because she felt how much sarvice he had been to her and all of us. So, instead of going out after them, I thought I'd give them a look through one of the loop-holes. Well, there they went, walking among the trees, not far from the picket, and no time out of sight. As I looked at them, I thought to myself, 'Would n't they make a handsome couple!' Both of them were tall and well made. As for Lucy, there wasn't, for figure, a finer set girl in all the settlement, and her face was a match for her figure. And then she was so easy in her motion, so graceful, and walked, or sate, or danced,—jest, for all the world, as if she was born only to do the particular thing she was doing. As for Lenatewá, he was a lad among a thousand. Now, a young Indian warrior, when he don't drink, is about the noblest-looking creature, as he carries himself in the woods, that God ever did make. So straight, so proud, so stately, always as if he was doing a great action—as if he knew the whole world was looking at him. Lenatewá was pretty much the handsomest and noblest Indian I had ever seen; and then, I know'd him to be raally so noble. As they walked together, their heads a little bent downwards, and Lucy's pretty low, the thought flashed across me that, jest then, he was telling her all about his feelings; and perhaps, said I to myself, the girl thinks about it pretty much as I do. Moutbe now, she likes him better than any body she has ever seen, and what more nateral? Then I thought, if there is any picture in this life more sweet and beautiful than two young people jest beginning to feel love for one another, and walking together in the innocence of their hearts, under the shady trees,—I've never seen it! I laid the rifle on my lap, and sat down on the floor and watched 'em through the loop until I felt the water in my eyes. They walked backwards and for'ads, not a hundred yards off, and I could see all their motions, though I couldn't hear their words. An Indian don't use his hands much generally, but I could see that Lenatewá was using his,—not a great deal, but as if he felt every word he was saying. Then I began to think, what was I to do, if so be he was raally offering to marry Lucy, and she willing! How was I to do? what was I to say?—how could I refuse him when I was willing? how could I say 'yes,' when Betsy said 'no!'

"Well, in the midst of this thinking, what should I hear but a loud cry from the child, then a loud yell,—a regular war-whoop,—sounded right in front, as if it came from Lenatewá himself. I looked up quickly, for, in thinking, I had lost sight of them, and was only looking at my rifle; I looked out, and there, in the twinkle of an eye, there was another sight. I saw my daughter flat upon the ground, lying like one dead, and Lenatewá staggering back as if he was mortally hurt; while, pressing fast upon him, was an Indian warrior, with his tomahawk uplifted, and striking—once, twice, three times—hard and heavy, right upon the face and forehead of the young prince. From the black paint on his face, and the red ring about his eyes, and from his figure and the eagle feathers in his head, I soon guessed it was Oloschottee and I then knew it was the old revenge for the killing of his father; for an Indian never forgets that sort of obligation. Of course, I didn't stand quiet to see an old friend, like Lenatewá, tumbled in that way, without warning, like a bullock; and there was my own daughter lying flat, and I wasn't to know that he hadn't struck her too. It was only one motion for me to draw sight upon the savage, and another to pull trigger; and I reckon he dropped jest as soon as the young Chief. I gave one whoop for all the world as if I was an Indian myself, and run out to the spot; but Lenatewá had got his discharge from further service. He warn't exactly dead, but his sense was swimming. He couldn't say much, and that warn't at all to the purpose. I could hear him, now and then, making a sort of singing noise, but that was soon swallowed up in a gurgle and a gasp, and it was all over. My bullet was quicker in its working than Oloschottee's hatchet; he was stone dead before I got to him. As for poor Lucy, she was not hurt, either by bullet or hatchet; but she had a hurt in the heart, whether from the scare she had, or because she had more feeling for the young prince than we reckoned, there's no telling. She warn't much given to smiling after that. But, whether she loved Lenatewá, we couldn't know, and I never was the man to ask her. It's sartain she never married, and she had about as many chances, and good ones, too, as any girl in our settlement. You've seen her—some among you—and warn't she a beauty—though I say it myself—the very flower of the forest!"

Harriet Jacobs
(C.1813–1897)

Harriet Jacobs was born a slave in Edenton, North Carolina. Her parents, owned by two different families, soon died, and she became the property of Margaret Horniblow, who taught her to read and to sew. At her mistress's death, Jacobs was bequeathed to the three-year-old Mary Matilda Norcom, whose father, called Dr. Flint in Incidents in the Life of a Slave Girl, *harassed Jacobs throughout her life as a slave. The Norcom family home was only a block away from that of Jacobs's maternal grandmother, Molly Horniblow, called Aunt Martha in the book, who was a free woman.*

To thwart the continual sexual threats of Dr. Norcom, Jacobs became the mistress of Samuel Tredwell Sawyer (called Mr. Sands) and gave birth to a son (Joseph, born 1829, book name Benjamin) and a daughter (Louisa Matilda, born 1833, called Ellen). When Norcom, punishing Jacobs for rejecting his sexual demands, threatened to enslave her children and sent her to do field work at his plantation several miles out of town, her family hid her—first in a swamp and then under the roof of a storage shed attached to her grandmother's house. Mr. Sawyer bought the children, promising to free them at a later time, and allowing them to live in the home of their freed great-grandmother.

During the seven years (1835–1842) Jacobs remained hidden in the attic, her lover was elected to Congress and married a northern woman, her brother John escaped from slavery, her aunt Betty died a slave to the Norcoms, and her daughter was sent to live with the Congressman's family in the North.

On her arrival in Philadelphia, Jacobs was aided by the Vigilant Committee, visited her daughter in Brooklyn, and took employment as a nurse-maid in New York and as a seamstress in Boston. Even after Dr. Norcom's death in 1850, she was constantly harassed by the Norcom family's attempts to re-enslave her. In 1853 she decided to write her own story, using the pen name Linda Brent. The manuscript was completed in 1858, but the failure of two Boston publishers delayed the publication until 1861. An English version appeared the following year under the title The Deeper Wrong. *After the war, Jacobs and her daughter allied themselves with the relief work of the Freedmen's Bureau and made visits to several places in the South, including Edenton.*

The following text is taken from the Schomburg Library reprinting of the 1861 edition (New York: Oxford University Press, 1988).

———

[From] *Incidents in the Life of a Slave Girl*

XXI. THE LOOPHOLE OF RETREAT[1]

A SMALL SHED had been added to my grandmother's house years ago. Some boards were laid across the joists at the top, and between these boards and the roof was a very small garret, never occupied by any thing but rats and mice. It was a pent roof, covered with nothing but shingles, according to the southern custom for such buildings. The garret was only nine feet long and seven wide. The highest part was three feet high, and sloped down abruptly to the loose board floor. There was no admission for either light or air. My uncle Philip, who was a carpenter, had very skilfully made a concealed trapdoor, which communicated with the storeroom. He had been doing this while I was waiting in the swamp. The storeroom opened upon a piazza. To this hole I was conveyed as soon as I entered the house. The air was stifling; the darkness total. A bed had been spread on the floor. I could sleep quite comfortably on one side; but the slope was so sudden that I could not turn on the other without hitting the roof. The rats and mice ran over my bed; but I was weary, and I slept such sleep as the wretched may, when a tempest has passed over them. Morning came. I knew it only by the noises I heard; for in my small den day and night were all the same. I suffered for air even more than for light. But I was not comfortless. I heard the voices of my children. There was joy and there was sadness in the sound. It made my tears flow. How I longed to speak to them! I was eager to look on their faces; but

---

1. An ironic use of a phrase from William Cowper's "The Task" (IV, 88–90), in which he describes as "pleasant" peeping at the world from a removed location. The lines were also used as an epigraph for an 1838 column, "The Curtain," in *Freedom's Journal,* published in New York.

there was no hole, no crack, through which I could peep. This continued darkness was oppressive. It seemed horrible to sit or lie in a cramped position day after day, without one gleam of light. Yet I would have chosen this, rather than my lot as a slave, though white people considered it an easy one; and it was so compared with the fate of others. I was never cruelly overworked; I was never lacerated with the whip from head to foot; I was never so beaten and bruised that I could not turn from one side to the other; I never had my heel-strings cut to prevent my running away; I was never chained to a log and forced to drag it about, while I toiled in the fields from morning till night; I was never branded with hot iron, or torn by bloodhounds. On the contrary, I had always been kindly treated, and tenderly cared for, until I came into the hands of Dr. Flint. I had never wished for freedom till then. But though my life in slavery was comparatively devoid of hardships, God pity the woman who is compelled to lead such a life!

My food was passed up to me through the trap-door my uncle had contrived; and my grandmother, my uncle Phillip,[2] and aunt Nancy[2] would seize such opportunities as they could, to mount up there and chat with me at the opening. But of course this was not safe in the daytime. It must all be done in darkness. It was impossible for me to move in an erect position, but I crawled about my den for exercise. One day I hit my head against something, and found it was a gimlet. My uncle had left it sticking there when he made the trap-door. I was as rejoiced as Robinson Crusoe could have been at finding such a treasure. It put a lucky thought into my head. I said to myself, "Now I will have some light. Now I will see my children." I did not dare to begin my work during the daytime, for fear of attracting attention. But I groped round; and having found the side next the street, where I could frequently see my children, I stuck the gimlet in and waited for evening. I bored three rows of holes, one above another; then I bored out the interstices between. I thus succeeded in making one hole about an inch long and an inch broad. I sat by it till late into the night, to enjoy the little whiff of air that floated in. In the morning I watched for my children. The first person I saw in the street was Dr. Flint. I had a shuddering, superstitious feeling that it was a bad omen. Several familiar faces passed by. At last I heard the merry laugh of children, and presently two sweet little faces were looking up at me, as though they knew I was there, and were conscious of the joy they imparted. How I longed to *tell* them I was there!

My condition was now a little improved. But for weeks I was tormented by hundreds of little red insects, fine as a needle's point, that pierced through my skin, and produced an intolerable burning. The good grandmother gave me herb teas and cooling medicines, and finally I got rid of them. The heat of my den was intense, for nothing but thin shingles protected me from the scorching summer's sun. But I had my consolations. Through my peeping-hole I could watch the children, and when they were

---

2. Characters based on Jacob's real-life uncle, Mark Ramsey, and her Aunt Betty, a slave in the Norcom household.

near enough, I could hear their talk. Aunt Nancy brought me all the news she could hear at Dr. Flint's. From her I learned that the doctor had written to New York to a colored woman, who had been born and raised in our neighborhood, and had breathed his contaminating atmosphere. He offered her a reward if she could find out any thing about me. I know not what was the nature of her reply; but he soon after started for New York in haste, saying to his family that he had business of importance to transact. I peeped at him as he passed on his way to the steamboat. It was a satisfaction to have miles of land and water between us, even for a little while; and it was a still greater satisfaction to know that he believed me to be in the Free States. My little den seemed less dreary than it had done. He returned, as he did from his former journey to New York, without obtaining any satisfactory information. When he passed our house next morning, Benny[3] was standing at the gate. He had heard them say that he had gone to find me, and he called out, "Dr. Flint, did you bring my mother home? I want to see her." The doctor stamped his foot at him in a rage, and exclaimed, "Get out of the way, you little damned rascal! If you don't, I'll cut off your head."

Benny ran terrified into the house, saying, "You can't put me in jail again. I don't belong to you now." It was well that the wind carried the words away from the doctor's ear. I told my grandmother of it, when we had our next conference at the trap-door; and begged of her not to allow the children to be impertinent to the irascible old man.

Autumn came, with a pleasant abatement of heat. My eyes had become accustomed to the dim light, and by holding my book or work in a certain position near the aperture I contrived to read and sew. That was a great relief to the tedious monotony of my life. But when winter came, the cold penetrated through the thin shingle roof, and I was dreadfully chilled. The winters there are not so long, or so severe, as in northern latitudes; but the houses are not built to shelter from cold, and my little den was peculiarly comfortless. The kind grandmother brought me bed-clothes and warm drinks. Often I was obliged to lie in bed all day to keep comfortable; but with all my precautions, my shoulders and feet were frostbitten. O, those long, gloomy days, with no object for my eye to rest upon, and no thoughts to occupy my mind, except the dreary past and the uncertain future! I was thankful when there came a day sufficiently mild for me to wrap myself up and sit at the loophole to watch the passers by. Southerners have the habit of stopping and talking in the streets, and I heard many conversations not intended to meet my ears. I heard slave-hunters planning how to catch some poor fugitive. Several times I heard allusions to Dr. Flint, myself, and the history of my children, who, perhaps, were playing near the gate. One would say, "I wouldn't move my little finger to catch her, as old Flint's property." Another would say, "I'll catch *any* nigger for the reward. A man ought to have what belongs to him, if he *is* a damned brute." The opinion was often expressed that I was in the Free States. Very rarely did any one suggest that I might be in the vicinity. Had the least suspicion rested on my

---

3. Jacobs's six-year-old son.

grandmother's house, it would have been burned to the ground. But it was the last place they thought of. Yet there was no place, where slavery existed, that could have afforded me so good a place of concealment.

Dr. Flint and his family repeatedly tried to coax and bribe my children to tell something they had heard said about me. One day the doctor took them into a shop, and offered them some bright little silver pieces and gay handkerchiefs if they would tell where their mother was. Ellen shrank away from him, and would not speak; but Benny spoke up, and said, "Dr. Flint, I don't know where my mother is. I guess she's in New York; and when you go there again, I wish you'd ask her to come home, for I want to see her; but if you put her in jail, or tell her you'll cut her head off, I'll tell her to go right back."

XXII. Christmas Festivities

Christmas was approaching. Grandmother brought me materials, and I busied myself making some new garments and little playthings for my children. Were it not that hiring day is near at hand,[4] and many families are fearfully looking forward to the probability of separation in a few days, Christmas might be a happy season for the poor slaves. Even slave mothers try to gladden the hearts of their little ones on that occasion. Benny and Ellen had their Christmas stockings filled. Their imprisoned mother could not have the privilege of witnessing their surprise and joy. But I had the pleasure of peeping at them as they went into the street with their new suits on. I heard Benny ask a little playmate whether Santa Claus brought him any thing. "Yes," replied the boy; "but Santa Claus ain't a real man. It's the children's mothers that put things into the stockings." "No, that can't be," replied Benny, "for Santa Claus brought Ellen and me these new clothes, and my mother has been gone this long time."

How I longed to tell him that his mother made those garments, and that many a tear fell on them while she worked!

Every child rises early on Christmas morning to see the Johnkannaus.[5] Without them, Christmas would be shorn of its greatest attraction. They consist of companies of slaves from the plantations, generally of the lower class. Two athletic men, in calico wrappers, have a net thrown over them, covered with all manner of bright-colored stripes.[6] Cows' tails are fastened to their backs, and their heads are decorated with horns. A box, covered with

---

4. At the New Year, slaves were hired out to different masters.

5. Also written John Koonah, John Konnu, or John Canoe; a masquerade tradition incorporating African and English forms. Compare to Hawthorne's description of mumming in "The Maypole of Merry Mount" and Sir Walter Scott's in Chapter XIV of *The Abbot*.

6. Similar striped and animal costumes are used in celebrations along the coast of West Africa.

sheepskin, is called the gumbo box. A dozen beat on this, while others strike triangles and jawbones, to which bands of dancers keep time. For a month previous they are composing songs, which are sung on this occasion. These companies, of a hundred each, turn out early in the morning, and are allowed to go round till twelve o'clock, begging for contributions. Not a door is left unvisited where there is the least chance of obtaining a penny or a glass of rum. They do not drink while they are out, but carry the rum home in jugs, to have a carousal. These Christmas donations frequently amount to twenty or thirty dollars. It is seldom that any white man or child refuses to give them a trifle. If he does, they regale his ears with the following song:—

> Poor massa, so dey say;
> Down in de heel, so dey say;
> Got no money, so dey say;
> Not one shillin, so dey say;
> God A'mighty bress you, so dey say.

Christmas is a day of feasting, both with white and colored people. Slaves, who are lucky enough to have a few shillings, are sure to spend them for good eating; and many a turkey and pig is captured, without saying, "By your leave, sir." Those who cannot obtain these, cook a 'possum, or a raccoon, from which savory dishes can be made. My grandmother raised poultry and pigs for sale; and it was her established custom to have both a turkey and a pig roasted for Christmas dinner.

On this occasion, I was warned to keep extremely quiet, because two guests had been invited. One was the town constable, and the other was a free colored man, who tried to pass himself off for white, and who was always ready to do any mean work for the sake of currying favor with white people. My grandmother had a motive for inviting them. She managed to take them all over the house. All the rooms on the lower floor were thrown open for them to pass in and out; and after dinner, they were invited up stairs to look at a fine mocking bird my uncle had just brought home. There, too, the rooms were all thrown open, that they might look in. When I heard them talking on the piazza, my heart almost stood still. I knew this colored man had spent many nights hunting for me. Every body knew he had the blood of a slave father in his veins; but for the sake of passing himself off for white, he was ready to kiss the slaveholders' feet. How I despised him! As for the constable, he wore no false colors. The duties of his office were despicable, but he was superior to his companion, inasmuch as he did not pretend to be what he was not. Any white man, who could raise money enough to buy a slave, would have considered himself degraded by being a constable; but the office enabled its possessor to exercise authority. If he found any slave out after nine o'clock, he could whip him as much as he liked; and that was a privilege to be coveted. When the guests were ready to depart, my grandmother gave each of them some of her nice pudding, as a present for their wives. Through my peep-hole I saw them go out of the gate, and I was glad when it closed after them. So passed the first Christmas in my den.

XXIII. STILL IN PRISON

When spring returned, and I took in the little patch of green the aperture commanded, I asked myself how many more summers and winters I must be condemned to spend thus. I longed to draw in a plentiful draught of fresh air, to stretch my cramped limbs, to have room to stand erect, to feel the earth under my feet again. My relatives were constantly on the lookout for a chance of escape; but none offered that seemed practicable, and even tolerably safe. The hot summer came again, and made the turpentine drop from the thin roof over my head.

During the long nights I was restless for want of air, and I had no room to toss and turn. There was but one compensation; the atmosphere was so stifled that even mosquitos would not condescend to buzz in it. With all my detestation of Dr. Flint, I could hardly wish him a worse punishment, either in this world or that which is to come, than to suffer what I suffered in one single summer. Yet the laws allowed *him* to be out in the free air, while I, guiltless of crime, was pent up here, as the only means of avoiding the cruelties the laws allowed him to inflict upon me! I don't know what kept life within me. Again and again, I thought I should die before long; but I saw the leaves of another autumn whirl through the air, and felt the touch of another winter. In summer the most terrible thunder storms were acceptable, for the rain came through the roof, and I rolled up my bed that it might cool the hot boards under it. Later in the season, storms sometimes wet my clothes through and through, and that was not comfortable when the air grew chilly. Moderate storms I could keep out by filling the chinks with oakum.

But uncomfortable as my situation was, I had glimpses of things out of doors, which made me thankful for my wretched hiding-place. One day I saw a slave pass our gate, muttering, "It's his own, and he can kill it if he will." My grandmother told me that woman's history. Her mistress had that day seen her baby for the first time, and in the lineaments of its fair face she saw a likeness to her husband. She turned the bondwoman and her child out of doors, and forbade her ever to return. The slave went to her master, and told him what had happened. He promised to talk with her mistress, and make it all right. The next day she and her baby were sold to a Georgia trader.

Another time I saw a woman rush wildly by, pursued by two men. She was a slave, the wet nurse of her mistress's children. For some trifling offence her mistress ordered her to be stripped and whipped. To escape the degradation and the torture, she rushed to the river, jumped in, and ended her wrongs in death.

Senator Brown,[7] of Mississippi, could not be ignorant of many such facts as these, for they are of frequent occurrence in every Southern State.

---

7. Albert Gallatin Brown (1813–1880), in a debate on the Kansas-Nebraska Bill (Feb. 24, 1854), described slavery as of divine origin and used the phrase cited here.

Yet he stood up in the Congress of the United States, and declared that slavery was "a great moral, social, and political blessing; a blessing to the master, and a blessing to the slave!"

I suffered much more during the second winter than I did during the first. My limbs were benumbed by inaction, and the cold filled them with cramp. I had a very painful sensation of coldness in my head; even my face and tongue stiffened, and I lost the power of speech. Of course it was impossible, under the circumstances, to summon any physician. My brother William[8] came and did all he could for me. Uncle Phillip also watched tenderly over me; and poor grandmother crept up and down to inquire whether there were any signs of returning life. I was restored to consciousness by the dashing of cold water in my face, and found myself leaning against my brother's arm, while he bent over me with streaming eyes. He afterwards told me he thought I was dying, for I had been in an unconscious state sixteen hours. I next became delirious, and was in great danger of betraying myself and my friends. To prevent this, they stupefied me with drugs. I remained in bed six weeks, weary in body and sick at heart. How to get medical advice was the question. William finally went to a Thompsonian[9] doctor, and described himself as having all my pains and aches. He returned with herbs, roots, and ointment. He was especially charged to rub on the ointment by a fire; but how could a fire be made in my little den? Charcoal in a furnace was tried, but there was no outlet for the gas, and it nearly cost me my life. Afterwards coals, already kindled, were brought up in an iron pan, and placed on bricks. I was so weak, and it was so long since I had enjoyed the warmth of a fire, that those few coals actually made me weep. I think the medicines did me some good; but my recovery was very slow. Dark thoughts passed through my mind as I lay there day after day. I tried to be thankful for my little cell, dismal as it was, and even to love it, as part of the price I had paid for the redemption of my children. Sometimes I thought God was a compassionate Father, who would forgive my sins for the sake of my sufferings. At other times, it seemed to me there was no justice or mercy in the divine government. I asked why the curse of slavery was permitted to exist, and why I had been so persecuted and wronged from youth upward. These things took the shape of mystery, which is to this day not so clear to my soul as I trust it will be hereafter.

In the midst of my illness, grandmother broke down under the weight of anxiety and toil. The idea of losing her, who had always been my best friend and a mother to my children, was the sorest trial I had yet had. O, how earnestly I prayed that she might recover! How hard it seemed, that I could not tend upon her, who had so long and so tenderly watched over me!

One day the screams of a child nerved me with strength to crawl to my peeping-hole, and I saw my son covered with blood. A fierce dog, usually kept chained, had seized and bitten him. A doctor was sent for, and I heard

---

8. A character based on her real brother John S. Jacobs.

9. A medical system based on raising body temperature devised by Samuel Thomson (1763–1843).

the groans and screams of my child while the wounds were being sewed up. O, what torture to a mother's heart, to listen to this and be unable to go to him!

But childhood is like a day in spring, alternately shower and sunshine. Before night Benny was bright and lively, threatening the destruction of the dog; and great was his delight when the doctor told him the next day that the dog had bitten another boy and been shot. Benny recovered from his wounds; but it was long before he could walk.

When my grandmother's illness became known, many ladies, who were her customers, called to bring her some little comforts, and to inquire whether she had every thing she wanted. Aunt Nancy one night asked permission to watch with her sick mother, and Mrs. Flint replied, "I don't see any need of your going. I can't spare you." But when she found other ladies in the neighborhood were so attentive, not wishing to be outdone in Christian charity, she also sallied forth, in magnificent condescension, and stood by the bedside of her who had loved her in her infancy, and who had been repaid by such grievous wrongs. She seemed surprised to find her so ill, and scolded uncle Phillip for not sending for Dr. Flint. She herself sent for him immediately, and he came. Secure as I was in my retreat, I should have been terrified if I had known he was so near me. He pronounced my grandmother in a very critical situation, and said if her attending physician wished it, he would visit her. Nobody wished to have him coming to the house at all hours, and we were not disposed to give him a chance to make out a long bill.

As Mrs. Flint went out, Sally told her the reason Benny was lame was, that a dog had bitten him. "I'm glad of it," replied she. "I wish he had killed him. It would be good news to send to his mother. *Her* day will come. The dogs will grab *her* yet." With these Christian words she and her husband departed, and, to my great satisfaction, returned no more.

I heard from uncle Phillip, with feelings of unspeakable joy and gratitude, that the crisis was passed and grandmother would live. I could now say from my heart, "God is merciful. He has spared me the anguish of feeling that I caused her death."

* * *

XXIX. PREPARATIONS FOR ESCAPE

I hardly expect that the reader will credit me, when I affirm that I lived in that little dismal hole, almost deprived of light and air, and with no space to move my limbs, for nearly seven years. But it is a fact; and to me a sad one, even now; for my body still suffers from the effects of that long imprisonment, to say nothing of my soul. Members of my family, now living in New York and Boston, can testify to the truth of what I say.

Countless were the nights that I sat late at the little loophole scarcely large enough to give me a glimpse of one twinkling star. There, I heard the patrols and slave-hunters conferring together about the capture of runaways, well knowing how rejoiced they would be to catch me.

Season after season, year after year, I peeped at my children's faces, and heard their sweet voices, with a heart yearning all the while to say, "Your mother is here." Sometimes it appeared to me as if ages had rolled away since I entered upon that gloomy, monotonous existence. At times, I was stupefied and listless; at other times I became very impatient to know when these dark years would end, and I should again be allowed to feel the sunshine, and breathe the pure air.

After Ellen left us,[1] this feeling increased. Mr. Sands had agreed that Benny might go to the north whenever his uncle Phillip could go with him; and I was anxious to be there also, to watch over my children, and protect them so far as I was able. Moreover, I was likely to be drowned out of my den, if I remained much longer; for the slight roof was getting badly out of repair, and uncle Phillip was afraid to remove the shingles, lest some one should get a glimpse of me. When storms occurred in the night, they spread mats and bits of carpet, which in the morning appeared to have been laid out to dry; but to cover the roof in the daytime might have attracted attention. Consequently, my clothes and bedding were often drenched; a process by which the pains and aches in my cramped and stiffened limbs were greatly increased. I revolved various plans of escape in my mind, which I sometimes imparted to my grandmother, when she came to whisper with me at the trap-door. The kind-hearted old woman had an intense sympathy for runaways. She had known too much of the cruelties inflicted on those who were captured. Her memory always flew back at once to the sufferings of her bright and handsome son, Benjamin[2] the youngest and dearest of her flock. So, whenever I alluded to the subject, she would groan out, "O, don't think of it, child. You'll break my heart." I had no good old aunt Nancy now to encourage me; but my brother William and my children were continually beckoning me to the north.

And now I must go back a few months in my story. I have stated that the first of January was the time for selling slaves, or leasing them out to new masters. If time were counted by heart-throbs, the poor slaves might reckon years of suffering during that festival so joyous to the free. On the New Year's day preceding my aunt's death, one of my friends, named Fanny,

---

1. Louisa Matilda was sent to live with the Brooklyn family of her father's first cousin, James Iredell Tredwell.

2. Joseph, son of Molly Horniblow, fought with his master, and faced with a public whipping, escaped. When his ship was forced ashore during a storm, Joseph was recaptured, imprisoned, and shipped South and escaped a second time. Seen once by his brother Mark in New York, Joseph was never heard of again by his family.

was to be sold at auction, to pay her master's debts. My thoughts were with her during all the day, and at night I anxiously inquired what had been her fate. I was told that she had been sold to one master, and her four little girls to another master, far distant; that she had escaped from her purchaser, and was not to be found. Her mother was the old Aggie I have spoken of. She lived in a small tenement belonging to my grandmother, and built on the same lot with her own house. Her dwelling was searched and watched, and that brought the patrols so near me that I was obliged to keep very close in my den. The hunters were somehow eluded; and not long afterwards Benny accidentally caught sight of Fanny in her mother's hut. He told his grandmother, who charged him never to speak of it, explaining to him the frightful consequences; and he never betrayed the trust. Aggie little dreamed that my grandmother knew where her daughter was concealed, and that the stooping form of her old neighbor was bending under a similar burden of anxiety and fear; but these dangerous secrets deepened the sympathy between the two old persecuted mothers.

My friend Fanny and I remained many weeks hidden within call of each other; but she was unconscious of the fact. I longed to have her share my den, which seemed a more secure retreat than her own; but I had brought so much trouble on my grandmother, that is seemed wrong to ask her to incur greater risks. My restlessness increased. I had lived too long in bodily pain and anguish of spirit. Always I was in dread that by some accident, or some contrivance, slavery would succeed in snatching my children from me. This thought drove me nearly frantic, and I determined to steer for the North Star at all hazards. At this crisis, Providence opened an unexpected way for me to escape. My friend Peter[3] came one evening, and asked to speak with me. "Your day has come, Linda," said he. "I have found a chance for you to go to the Free States. You have a fortnight to decide." The news seemed too good to be true; but Peter explained his arrangements, and told me all that was necessary was for me to say I would go. I was going to answer him with a joyful yes, when the thought of Benny came to my mind. I told him the temptation was exceedingly strong, but I was terribly afraid of Dr. Flint's alleged power over my child, and that I could not go and leave him behind. Peter remonstrated earnestly. He said such a good chance might never occur again; that Benny was free, and could be sent to me; and that for the sake of my children's welfare I ought not to hesitate a moment. I told him I would consult with uncle Phillip. My uncle rejoiced in the plan, and bade me go by all means. He promised, if his life was spared, that he would either bring or send my son to me as soon as I reached a place of safety. I resolved to go, but thought nothing had better be said to my grandmother till very near the time of departure. But my uncle thought she would feel it more keenly if I left her so suddenly. "I will reason with her," said he, "and convince her how necessary it is, not only for your sake, but for hers also. You cannot be blind to the fact that she is sinking under her burdens." I was not blind to it. I

---

3. A slave who had been apprenticed to Jacobs's carpenter father. Peter had helped her before.

knew that my concealment was an ever-present source of anxiety, and that the older she grew the more nervously fearful she was of discovery. My uncle talked with her, and finally succeeded in persuading her that it was absolutely necessary for me to seize the chance so unexpectedly offered.

*   *   *

I was to escape in a vessel; but I forbear to mention any further particulars. I was in readiness, but the vessel was unexpectedly detained several days. Meantime, news came to town of a most horrible murder committed on a fugitive slave, named James. Charity, the mother of this unfortunate young man, had been an old acquaintance of ours. I have told the shocking particulars of his death, in my description of some of the neighboring slaveholders. My grandmother, always nervously sensitive about runaways, was terribly frightened. She felt sure that a similar fate awaited me, if I did not desist from my enterprise. She sobbed, and groaned, and entreated me not to go. Her excessive fear was somewhat contagious, and my heart was not proof against her extreme-agony. I was grievously disappointed, but I promised to relinquish my project.

When my friend Peter was apprised of this, he was both disappointed and vexed. He said, that judging from our past experience, it would be a long time before I had such another chance to throw away. I told him it need not be thrown away; that I had a friend concealed near by, who would be glad enough to take the place that had been provided for me. I told him about poor Fanny, and the kind-hearted, noble fellow, who never turned his back upon any body in distress, white or black, expressed his readiness to help her. Aggie was much surprised when she found that we knew her secret. She was rejoiced to hear of such a chance for Fanny, and arrangements were made for her to go on board the vessel the next night. They both supposed that I had long been at the north, therefore my name was not mentioned in the transaction. Fanny was carried on board at the appointed time, and stowed away in a very small cabin. This accommodation had been purchased at a price that would pay for a voyage to England. But when one proposes to go to fine old England, they stop to calculate whether they can afford the cost of the pleasure; while in making a bargain to escape from slavery, the trembling victim is ready to say, "Take all I have, only don't betray me!"

The next morning I peeped through my loophole, and saw that it was dark and cloudy. At night I received news that the wind was ahead, and the vessel had not sailed. I was exceedingly anxious about Fanny, and Peter too, who was running a tremendous risk at my instigation. Next day the wind and weather remained the same. Poor Fanny had been half dead with fright when they carried her on board, and I could readily imagine how she must be suffering now. Grandmother came often to my den, to say how thankful she was I did not go. On the third morning she rapped for me to come down to the storeroom. The poor old sufferer was breaking down under her weight of trouble. She was easily flurried now. I found her in a nervous, excited state, but I was not aware that she had forgotten to lock the door behind her, as usual. She was exceedingly worried about the detention of the vessel. She was afraid all would be discovered, and then Fanny, and Peter, and I, would all be tortured to death, and Phillip would be utterly ruined, and her house would be torn down. Poor Peter! If he should die such a horrible death as the poor slave James had lately done, and all for his kindness in trying to help me, how dreadful it would be for us all! Alas, the thought was familiar to me, and had sent many a sharp pang through my heart. I tried to suppress my own anxiety, and speak soothingly to her. She brought in some allusion to aunt Nancy, the dear daughter she had recently buried, and then she lost all control of herself. As she stood there, trembling and sobbing, a voice from the piazza called out, "Whar is you, aunt Marthy?" Grandmother was startled, and in her agitation opened the door, without thinking of me. In stepped Jenny,[4] the mischievous housemaid, who had tried to enter my room, when I was concealed in the house of my white benefactress. "I's bin huntin ebery whar for you, aunt Marthy," said she. "My missis wants you to send her some crackers." I had slunk down behind a barrel, which entirely screened me, but I imagined that Jenny was looking directly at the spot, and my heart beat violently. My grand mother immediately thought what she had done, and went out quickly with Jenny to count the crackers locking the door after her. She returned to me, in a few minutes, the perfect picture of despair. "Poor child!" she exclaimed, "my carelessness has ruined you. The boat ain't gone yet. Get ready immediately, and go with Fanny. I ain't got another word to say against it now; for there's no telling what may happen this day."

Uncle Phillip was sent for, and he agreed with his mother in thinking that Jenny would inform Dr. Flint in less than twenty-four hours. He advised getting me on board the boat, if possible; if not, I had better keep very still in my den, where they could not find me without tearing the house down. He said it would not do for him to move in the matter, because suspicion would be immediately excited; but he promised to communicate with Peter. I felt reluctant to apply to him again, having implicated him too much already; but there seemed to be no alternative. Vexed as Peter had been by my indecision, he was true to his generous nature, and said at once that he would do his best to help me, trusting I should show myself a stronger woman this time.

He immediately proceeded to the wharf, and found that the wind had shifted, and the vessel was slowly beating down stream. On some pretext of urgent necessity, he offered two boatmen a dollar apiece to catch up with her. He was of lighter complexion than the boatmen he hired, and when the captain saw them coming so rapidly, he thought officers were pursuing his vessel in search of the runaway slave he had on board. They hoisted sails, but the boat gained upon them, and the indefatigable Peter sprang on board.

---

4. A slave in the home of a friendly white woman who had allowed Jacobs to hide in her home on a prior occasion.

The captain at once recognized him. Peter asked him to go below, to speak about a bad bill he had given him. When he told his errand, the captain replied, "Why, the woman's here already; and I've put her where you or the devil would have a tough job to find her."

"But it is another woman I want to bring," said Peter. "*She* is in great distress, too, and you shall be paid any thing within reason, if you'll stop and take her."

"What's her name?" inquired the captain.

"Linda," he replied.

"That's the name of the woman already here," rejoined the captain. "By George! I believe you mean to betray me."

"O!" exclaimed Peter, "God knows I wouldn't harm a hair of your head. I am too grateful to you. But there really *is* another woman in great danger. Do have the humanity to stop and take her!"

After a while they came to an understanding. Fanny, not dreaming I was any where about in that region, had assumed my name, though she called herself Johnson. "Linda is a common name," said Peter, "and the woman I want to bring is Linda Brent."

The captain agreed to wait at a certain place till evening, being handsomely paid for his detention.

Of course, the day was an anxious one for us all. But we concluded that if Jenny had seen me, she would be too wise to let her mistress know of it; and that she probably would not get a chance to see Dr. Flint's family till evening, for I knew very well what were the rules in that household. I afterwards believed that she did not see me; for nothing ever came of it, and she was one of those base characters that would have jumped to betray a suffering fellow being for the sake of thirty pieces of silver.

I made all my arrangements to go on board as soon as it was dusk. The intervening time I resolved to spend with my son. I had not spoken to him for seven years, though I had been under the same roof, and seen him every day, when I was well enough to sit at the loophole. I did not dare to venture beyond the storeroom; so they brought him there, and locked us up together, in a place concealed from the piazza door. It was an agitating interview for both of us. After we had talked and wept together for a little while, he said, "Mother, I'm glad you're going away. I wish I could go with you. I knew you was here; and I have been *so* afraid they would come and catch you!"

I was greatly surprised, and asked him how he had found it out.

He replied, "I was standing under the eaves, one day, before Ellen went away, and I heard somebody cough up over the wood shed. I don't know what made me think it was you, but I did think so. I missed Ellen, the night before she went away; and grandmother brought her back into the room in the night; and I thought maybe she'd been to see *you*, before she went, for I heard grandmother whisper to her, 'Now go to sleep; and remember never to tell.'"

I asked him if he ever mentioned his suspicions to his sister. He said he never did; but after he heard the cough, if he saw her playing with other children on that side of the house, he always tried to coax her round to the other side, for fear they would hear me cough, too. He said he had kept a close lookout for Dr. Flint, and if he saw him speak to a constable, or a patrol, he always told grandmother. I now recollected that I had seen him manifest uneasiness, when people were on that side of the house, and I had at the time been puzzled to conjecture a motive for his actions. Such prudence may seem extraordinary in a boy of twelve years, but slaves, being surrounded by mysteries, deceptions, and dangers, early learn to be suspicious and watchful, and prematurely cautious and cunning. He had never asked a question of grandmother, or uncle Phillip, and I had often heard him chime in with other children, when they spoke of my being at the north.

I told him I was now really going to the Free States, and if he was a good, honest boy, and a loving child to his dear old grandmother, the Lord would bless him, and bring him to me, and we and Ellen would live together. He began to tell me that grandmother had not eaten any thing all day. While he was speaking, the door was unlocked, and she came in with a small bag of money, which she wanted me to take. I begged her to keep a part of it, at least, to pay for Benny's being sent to the north; but she insisted, while her tears were falling fast, that I should take the whole. "You may be sick among strangers," she said, "and they would send you to the poorhouse to die." Ah, that good grandmother!

For the last time I went up to my nook. Its desolate appearance no longer chilled me, for the light of hope had risen in my soul. Yet, even with the blessed prospect of freedom before me, I felt very sad at leaving forever that old homestead, where I had been sheltered so long by the dear old grandmother; where I had dreamed my first young dream of love; and where, after that had faded away, my children came to twine themselves so closely round my desolate heart. As the hour approached for me to leave, I again descended to the storeroom. My grandmother and Benny were there. She took me by the hand, and said, "Linda, let us pray." We knelt down together, with my child pressed to my heart, and my other arm round the faithful, loving old friend I was about to leave forever. On no other occasion has it ever been my lot to listen to so fervent a supplication for mercy and protection. It thrilled through my heart, and inspired me with trust in God.

Peter was waiting for me in the street. I was soon by his side, faint in body, but strong of purpose. I did not look back upon the old place, though I felt that I should never see it again.

XXX. Northward Bound

I never could tell how we reached the wharf. My brain was all of a whirl, and my limbs tottered under me. At an appointed place we met my uncle Phillip, who had started before us on a different route, that he might reach the wharf first, and give us timely warning if there was any danger. A row-boat was in readiness. As I was about to step in, I felt something pull me gently, and turning round I saw Benny, looking pale and anxious. He whispered in my ear, "I've been peeping into the doctor's window, and he's at home. Good by, mother. Don't cry; I'll come." He hastened away. I clasped the hand of my good uncle, to whom I owed so much, and of Peter, the brave, generous friend who had volunteered to run such terrible risks to secure my safety. To this day I remember how his bright face beamed with joy, when he told me he had discovered a safe method for me to escape. Yet that intelligent, enterprising, noble-hearted man was a chattel! liable, by the laws of a country that calls itself civilized, to be sold with horses and pigs! We parted in silence. Our hearts were all too full for words!

Swiftly the boat glided over the water. After a while, one of the sailors said, "Don't be down-hearted, madam. We will take you safely to your husband, in⸺." At first I could not imagine what he meant; but I had presence of mind to think that it probably referred to something the captain had told him; so I thanked him, and said I hoped we should have pleasant weather.

When I entered the vessel the captain came forward to meet me. He was an elderly man, with a pleasant countenance. He showed me to a little box of a cabin, where sat my friend Fanny. She started as if she had seen a spectre. She gazed on me in utter astonishment, and exclaimed, "Linda, can this be *you?* or is it your ghost?" When we were locked in each other's arms, my overwrought feelings could no longer be restrained. My sobs reached the ears of the captain, who came and very kindly reminded us, that for his safety, as well as our own, it would be prudent for us not to attract any attention. He said that when there was a sail in sight he wished us to keep below; but at other times, he had no objection to our being on deck. He assured us that he would keep a good lookout, and if we acted prudently, he thought we should be in no danger. He had represented us as women going to meet our husbands in⸺. We thanked him, and promised to observe carefully all the directions he gave us.

Fanny and I now talked by ourselves, low and quietly, in our little cabin. She told me of the sufferings she had gone through in making her escape, and of her terrors while she was concealed in her mother's house. Above all, she dwelt on the agony of separation from all her children on that dreadful auction day. She could scarcely credit me, when I told her of the place where I had passed nearly seven years. "We have the same sorrows," said I. "No," replied she, "you are going to see your children soon, and there is no hope that I shall ever even hear from mine."

The vessel was soon under way, but we made slow progress. The wind was against us. I should not have cared for this, if we had been out of sight of the town; but until there were miles of water between us and our enemies, we were filled with constant apprehensions that the constables would come on board. Neither could I feel quite at ease with the captain and his men. I was an entire stranger to that class of people, and I had heard that sailors were rough, and sometimes cruel. We were so completely in their power, that if they were bad men, our situation would be dreadful. Now that the captain was paid for our passage, might he not be tempted to make more money by giving us up to those who claimed us as property? I was naturally of a confiding disposition, but slavery had made me suspicious of every body. Fanny did not share my distrust of the captain or his men. She said she was afraid at first, but she had been on board three days while the vessel lay in the dock, and nobody had betrayed her, or treated her otherwise than kindly.

The captain soon came to advise us to go on deck for fresh air. His friendly and respectful manner, combined with Fanny's testimony, reassured me, and we went with him. He placed us in a comfortable seat, and occasionally entered into conversation. He told us he was a Southerner by birth, and had spent the greater part of his life in the Slave States, and that he had recently lost a brother who traded in slaves. "But," said he, "it is a pitiable and degrading business, and I always felt ashamed to acknowledge my brother in connection with it." As we passed Snaky Swamp, he pointed to it, and said, "There is a slave territory that defies all the laws." I thought of the terrible days I had spent there, and though it was not called Dismal Swamp, it made me feel very dismal as I looked at it.

I shall never forget that night. The balmy air of spring was so refreshing! And how shall I describe my sensations when we were fairly sailing on Chesapeake Bay? O, the beautiful sunshine! the exhilarating breeze! and I could enjoy them without fear or restraint. I had never realized what grand things air and sunlight are till I had been deprived of them.

Ten days after we left land we were approaching Philadelphia. The captain said we should arrive there in the night, but he thought we had better wait till morning, and go on shore in broad daylight, as the best way to avoid suspicion.

I replied, "You know best. But will you stay on board and protect us?"

He saw that I was suspicious, and he said he was sorry, now that he had brought us to the end of our voyage, to find I had so little confidence in him. Ah, if he had ever been a slave he would have known how difficult it was to trust a white man. He assured us that we might sleep through the night without fear; that he would take care we were not left unprotected. Be it said to the honor of this captain, Southerner as he was, that if Fanny and I had been white ladies, and our passage lawfully engaged, he could not have treated us more respectfully. My intelligent friend, Peter, had rightly estimated the character of the man to whose honor he had intrusted us.

The next morning I was on deck as soon as the day dawned. I called Fanny to see the sun rise, for the first time in our lives, on free soil; for such I *then* believed it to be. We watched the reddening sky, and saw the great orb come up slowly out of the water, as it seemed. Soon the waves began to sparkle, and every thing caught the beautiful glow. Before us lay the city of strangers. We looked at each other, and the eyes of both were moistened with tears. We had escaped from slavery, and we supposed ourselves to be safe from the hunters. But we were alone in the world, and we had left dear ties behind us; ties cruelly sundered by the demon Slavery.

Frederick Douglass
(c. 1818–1895)

Born on the Maryland shore near Easton, Frederick Douglass was the son of a slave woman, Harriet Bailey, and an unknown white father. After his escape from slavery in 1838, he added the surname Douglass from the character in Sir Walter Scott's The Lady of the Lake. *His 1841 speech to the Nantucket Anti-Slavery Society was such a success he was drafted by the national group to speak against slavery throughout the country.*

In response to criticism that such an impressive speaker could never have been enslaved, he wrote his autobiography, Narrative of the Life of Frederick Douglass, *in 1845. Because so many previous slave narratives had been dictated or ghostwritten, Douglass appended to his text the subtitle "Written by Himself." The book became an international best seller, with nine English editions and translations into Dutch and French. Out of fear that the notice his book had generated would make him a tempting target for slave catchers, Douglass spent two years in England and Ireland, returning in 1847 after English friends had purchased his freedom.*

He established the abolitionist newspaper North Star *in Rochester, New York, and edited it for seventeen years, later changing its name to* Frederick Douglass' Paper. *Douglass's novel* The Heroic Slave, *published in the paper in March 1853, can lay claim, by a margin of a few months, to being the first work of fiction published by an African American. Later the same year, Julia Griffiths published it in her* Autographs for Freedom, *the source of the text below. The work is based on a historical figure and events well known in abolitionist circles; Douglass had often made reference to the story in his antislavery speeches.*

In November 1841, Madison Washington was part of a cargo of 134 slaves on the ship Creole *sailing out of Hampton, Virginia, heading for New Orleans. He led a mutiny and, having secured control of the vessel, changed its destination to Nassau, the Bahamas, where the slaves were given asylum and freed. The takeover was so orderly and restrained that in testimony before a Senate committee, one passenger credited Washington with saving the lives of the captain and passengers. Douglass praised Washington as a hero who balanced a love for freedom with mercy and, in the Introduction to the novel, equated him with heroes of the American*

Revolution. Acknowledging the lack of documentary evidence relating to Washington's life, Douglass merged fictional devices such as invented conversations with the bare outline of the story.

During the Civil War, Douglass helped to organize groups of African American volunteers for the northern Army, including the famous 54th Massachusetts Regiment commanded by Robert Gould Shaw (1837–1863). After the war, he continued to speak out on behalf of civil rights, held offices in the District of Columbia and served as minister to Haiti from 1889 to 1891.

A solid critical biography is William S. McFeely's *Frederick Douglass* (1991).

[From] The Heroic Slave

PART I

> *Oh! child of grief, why weepest thou?*
> *Why droops thy sad and mournful brow?*
> *Why is thy look so like despair?*
> *What deep, sad sorrow lingers there?*

THE STATE OF VIRGINIA is famous in American annals for the multitudinous array of her statesmen and heroes. She has been dignified by some the mother of statesmen. History has not been sparing in recording their names, or in blazoning their deeds. Her high position in this respect, has given her an enviable distinction among her sister States. With Virginia for his birthplace, even a man of ordinary parts, on account of the general partiality for her sons, easily rises to eminent stations. Men, not great enough to attract special attention in their native States, have, like a certain distinguished citizen in the State of New York, sighed and repined that they were not born in Virginia. Yet not all the great ones of the Old Dominion have, by the fact of their birth-place, escaped undeserved obscurity. By some strange neglect, *one* of the truest, manliest, and bravest of her children,—one who, in after years, will, I think, command the pen of genius to set his merits forth, holds now no higher place in the records of that grand old Commonwealth than is held by a horse or an ox. Let those account for it who can, but there stands the fact, that a man who loved liberty as well as did Patrick Henry,—who deserved it as much as Thomas Jefferson,—and who fought for it with a valor as high, an arm as strong, and against odds as great, as he who led all the armies of the American colonies through the great war for freedom and independence, lives now only in the chattel records of his native State.

Glimpses of this great character are all that can now be presented. He is brought to view only by a few transient incidents, and these afford but partial satisfaction. Like a guiding star on a stormy night, he is seen through the parted clouds and the howling tempests; or, like the gray peak of a menacing rock on a perilous coast, he is seen by the quivering flash of angry lightning, and he again disappears covered with mystery.

Curiously, earnestly, anxiously we peer into the dark, and wish even for the blinding flash, or the light of northern skies to reveal him. But alas! he is still enveloped in darkness, and we return from the pursuit like a wearied and disheartened mother, (after a tedious and unsuccessful search for a lost child,) who returns weighed down with disappointment and sorrow. Speaking of marks, traces, possibles, and probabilities, we come before our readers.

In the spring of 1835, on a Sabbath morning, within hearing of the solemn peals of the church bells at a distant village, a Northern traveller through the State of Virginia drew up his horse to drink at a sparkling brook near the edge of a dark pine forest. While his weary and thirsty steed drew in the grateful water, the rider caught the sound of a human voice, apparently engaged in earnest conversation.

Following the direction of the sound, he descried, among the tall pines, the man whose voice had arrested his attention. "To whom can he be speaking?" thought the traveller. "He seems to be alone." The circumstance interested him much, and he became intensely curious to know what thoughts and feelings, or, it might be, high aspirations, guided those rich and mellow accents. Tieing his horse at a short distance from the brook, he stealthily drew near the solitary speaker; and, concealing himself by the side of a huge fallen tree, he distinctly heard the following soliloquy:—

"What, then, is life to me? it is aimless and worthless, and worse than worthless. Those birds, perched on yon swinging boughs, in friendly conclave, sounding forth their merry notes in seeming worship of the rising sun, though liable to the sportsman's fowling-piece, are still my superiors. They *live free*, though they may die slaves. They fly where they list by day, and retire in freedom at night. But what is freedom to me, or I to it? I am a *slave*,—born a slave, an abject slave,—even before I made part of this breathing world, the scourge was platted for my back; the fetters were forged for my limbs. How mean a thing am I. That accursed and crawling snake, that miserable reptile, that has just glided into its slimy home, is freer and better off than I. He escaped my blow, and is safe. But here am I, a man,—yes, *a man!*—with thoughts and wishes, with powers and faculties as far as angel's flight above that hated reptile,—yet he is my superior, and scorns to own me as his master, or to stop to take my blows. When he saw my uplifted arm, he darted beyond my reach, and turned to give me battle. I dare not do as much as that. I neither run nor fight, but do meanly stand, answering each heavy blow of a cruel master with doleful wails and piteous cries. I am galled with irons; but even these are more tolerable than the consciousness, the *galling* consciousness of cowardice and indecision. Can it be that I *dare* not run away? *Perish the thought,* I *dare* do any thing which may be done by another. When that young man struggled with the waves *for life,* and others stood back appalled in helpless horror, did I not plunge in, forgetful of life, to save his? The raging bull from whom all others fled, pale with fright, did I not keep at bay with a single pitchfork? Could a coward do that? *No,—no,—*I wrong myself,—I am no coward. *Liberty* I will have, or die in the attempt to gain it. This working that others may live in idleness! This cringing submission to insolence and curses! This living under the constant dread and apprehension of being sold and transferred, like a mere brute, is *too* much for me. I will stand it no longer. What others have done, I will do. These trusty legs, or these sinewy arms shall place me among the free. Tom escaped; so can I. The North Star will not be less kind to me than to him. I will follow it. I will at least make the trial. I have nothing to lose. If I am caught, I shall only be a slave. If I am shot, I shall only lose a life which is a burden and a curse. If I get clear, (as something tells me I shall,) liberty, the inalienable birth-right of every man, precious and priceless, will be mine. My resolution is fixed. *I shall be free.*"

At these words the traveller raised his head cautiously and noiselessly, and caught, from his hiding-place, a full view of the unsuspecting speaker. Madison (for that was the name of our hero) was standing erect, a smile of satisfaction rippled upon his expressive countenance, like that which plays upon the face of one who has but just solved a difficult problem, or vanquished a malignant foe; for at that moment he was free, at least in spirit. The future gleamed brightly before him, and his fetters lay broken at his feet. His air was triumphant.

Madison was of manly form. Tall, symmetrical, round, and strong. In his movements he seemed to combine, with the strength of the lion, a lion's elasticity. His torn sleeves disclosed arms like polished iron. His face was "black, but comely." His eye, lit with emotion, kept guard under a brow as dark and as glossy as the raven's wing. His whole appearance betokened Herculean strength; yet there was nothing savage or forbidding in his aspect. A child might play in his arms, or dance on his shoulders. A giant's strength, but not a giant's heart was in him. His broad mouth and nose spoke only of good nature and kindness. But his voice, that unfailing index of the soul, though full and melodious, had that in it which could terrify as well as charm. He was just the man you would choose when hardships were to be endured, or danger to be encountered,—intelligent and brave. He had the head to conceive, and the hand to execute. In a word, he was one to be sought as a friend, but to be dreaded as an enemy.

As our traveller gazed upon him, he almost trembled at the thought of his dangerous intrusion. Still he could not quit the place. He had long desired to sound the mysterious depths of the thoughts and feelings of a slave. He was not, therefore, disposed to allow so providential an opportunity to pass unimproved. He resolved to hear more; so he listened again for those mellow and mournful accents which, he says, made such an impression upon him as can never be erased. He did not have to wait long. There came another gush from the same full fountain; now bitter, and now sweet. Scathing denunciations of the cruelty and injustice of slavery; heart-touching narrations of his own personal suffering, intermingled with prayers to the God of the oppressed for help and deliverance, were followed by presentations of the dangers and difficulties of escape, and formed the burden of his eloquent utterances; but his high resolution clung to him,—for he ended each speech by an emphatic declaration of his purpose to be free. It seemed that the very repetition of this, imparted a glow to his countenance. The hope of freedom seemed to sweeten, for a reason, the bitter cup of slavery, and to make it, for a time, tolerable; for when in the very whirlwind of anguish,—when his heart's cord seemed screwed up to snapping tension, hope sprung up and soothed his troubled spirit. Fitfully he would exclaim. "How can I leave her? Poor thing! what can she do when I am gone? Oh! oh! 't is impossible that I can leave poor Susan!"

A brief pause intervened. Our traveller raised his head, and saw again the sorrow-smitten slave. His eye was fixed upon the ground. The strong man staggered under a heavy load. Recovering himself, he argued thus aloud: "All is uncertain here. To-morrow's sun may not rise before I am sold, and separated from her I love. What, then, could I do for her? I should be in more hopeless slavery, and she no nearer to liberty,—whereas if I were free,—my arms my own,—I might devise the means to rescue her."

This said, Madison cast around a searching glance, as if the thought of being overheard had flashed across his mind. He said no more, but, with measured steps walked away, and was lost to the eye of our traveller amidst the wildering woods.

Long after Madison had left the ground, Mr. Listwell (our traveller) remained in motionless silence, meditating on the extraordinary revelations to which he had listened. He seemed fastened to the spot, and stood half hoping, half fearing the return of the sable preacher to his solitary temple. The speech of Madison rung through the chambers of his soul, and vibrated through his entire frame. "Here is indeed a man," though he, "of rare endowments,—a child of God,—guilty of no crime but the color of his skin,—hiding away from the face of humanity, and pouring out his thoughts and feelings, his hopes and resolutions to the lonely woods; to him those distant church bells have no grateful music. He shuns the church, the altar, and the great congregation of christian worshippers, and wanders away to the gloomy forest, to utter in the vacant air complaints and griefs, which the religion of his times and his country can neither console nor relieve. Goaded almost to madness by the sense of the injustice done him, he resorts hither to give vent to his pent up feelings, and to debate with himself the feasibility of plans, plans of his own invention, for his own deliverance. From this hour I am an abolitionist. I have seen enough and heard enough, and I shall go to my home in Ohio resolved to atone for my past indifference to this ill-starred race, by making such exertions as I shall be able to do, for the speedy emancipation of every slave in the land.

PART II

The gaudy, blabbling and remorseful day
Is crept into the bosom of the sea;
And now loud-howling wolves arouse the jades
That drag the tragic melancholy night;
Who with their drowsy, slow, and flagging wings
Clip dead men's graves, and from their misty jaws
Breathe foul contagions, darkness in the air.

SHAKSPEARE

Five years after the foregoing singular occurrence, in the winter of 1840, Mr. and Mrs. Listwell sat together by the fireside of their own happy home, in the State of Ohio. The children were all gone to bed. A single lamp burnt brightly on the centre-table. All was still and comfortable within; but the night was cold and dark; a heavy wind sighed and moaned sorrowfully around the house and barn, occasionally bringing against the clattering windows a stray leaf from the large oak trees that embowered their dwelling. It was a night for strange noises and for strange fancies. A whole wilderness of thought might pass through one's mind during such an evening. The smouldering embers, partaking of the spirit of the restless night, became fruitful of varied and fantastic pictures, and revived many bygone scenes and old impressions. The happy pair seemed to sit in silent fascination, gazing on the fire. Suddenly this *reverie* was interrupted by a heavy growl. Ordinarily such an occurrence would have scarcely provoked a single word, or excited the least apprehension. But there are certain seasons when the slightest sound sends a jar through all the subtle chambers of the mind; and such a season was this. The happy pair started up, as if some sudden danger had come upon them. The growl was from their trusty watch-dog.

"What can it mean? certainly no one can be out on such a night as this," said Mrs. Listwell.

"The wind has deceived the dog, my dear; he has mistaken the noise of falling branches, brought down by the wind, for that of the footsteps of persons coming to the house. I have several times to-night thought that I heard the sound of footsteps. I am sure, however, that it was but the wind. Friends would not be likely to come out at such an hour, or such a night; and thieves are too lazy and self-indulgent to expose themselves to this biting frost; but should there be any one about, our brave old Monte, who is on the lookout, will not be slow in sounding the alarm."

Saying this they quietly left the window, whither they had gone to learn the cause of the menacing growl, and re-seated themselves by the fire, as if reluctant to leave the slowly expiring embers, although the hour was late. A few minutes only intervened after resuming their seats, when again their sober meditations were disturbed. Their faithful dog now growled and barked furiously, as if assailed by an advancing foe. Simultaneously the good couple arose, and stood in mute expectation. The contest without seemed fierce and violent. It was, however, soon over,—the barking ceased, for, with true canine instinct, Monte quickly discovered that a friend, not an enemy of the family, was coming to the house, and instead of rushing to repel the supposed intruder, he was now at the door, whimpering and dancing for the admission of himself and his newly made friend.

Mr. Listwell knew by this movement that all was well; he advanced and opened the door, and saw by the light that streamed out into the darkness, a tall man advancing slowly towards the house, with a stick in one hand, and a small bundle in the other. "It is a traveller," thought he, "who has missed his way, and is coming to inquire the road. I am glad we did not go to bed earlier,—I have felt all the evening as if somebody would be here to-night."

The man had now halted a short distance from the door, and looked prepared alike for flight or battle. "Come in, sir, don't be alarmed, you have probably lost your way."

Slightly hesitating, the traveller walked in; not, however, without regarding his host with a scrutinizing glance. "No, sir," said he "I have come to ask you a greater favor."

Instantly Mr. Listwell exclaimed, (as the recollection of the Virginia forest scene flashed upon him,) "Oh, sir, I know not your name, but I have seen your face, and heard your voice before. I am glad to see you. *I know all.* You are flying for your liberty,—be seated,—be seated,—banish all fear. You are safe under my roof."

This recognition, so unexpected, rather disconcerted and disquieted the noble fugitive. The timidity and suspicion of persons escaping from slavery are easily awakened, and often what it intended to dispel the one, and to allay the other, has precisely the opposite effect. It was so in this case. Quickly observing the unhappy impression made by his words and action, Mr. Listwell assumed a more quiet and inquiring aspect, and finally succeeded in removing the apprehensions which his very natural and generous salutation had aroused.

Thus assured, the stranger said, "Sir, you have rightly guessed, I am, indeed, a fugitive from slavery. My name is Madison,—Madison Washington my mother used to call me. I am on my way to Canada, where I learn that persons of my color are protected in all the rights of men; and my object in calling upon you was, to beg the privilege of resting my weary limbs for the night in your barn. It was my purpose to have continued my journey till morning; but the piercing cold, and the frowning darkness compelled me to seek shelter; and, seeing a light through the lattice of your window, I was encouraged to come here to beg the privilege named. You will do me a great favor by affording me shelter for the night."

"A resting-place, indeed, sir, you shall have; not, however, in my barn, but in the best room of my house. Consider yourself, if you please, under the roof of a friend; for such I am to you, and to all your deeply injured race."

While this introductory conversation was going on, the kind lady had revived the fire, and was diligently preparing supper; for she, not less than her husband, felt for the sorrows of the oppressed and hunted ones of earth, and was always glad of an opportunity to do them a service. A bountiful repast was quickly prepared, and the hungry and toil-worn bondman was cordially invited to partake thereof. Gratefully he acknowledged the favor of his benevolent benefactress; but appeared scarcely to understand what such hospitality could mean. It was the first time in his life that he had met so humane and friendly a greeting at the hands of persons whose color was unlike his own; yet it was impossible for him to doubt the charitableness of his new friends, or the genuineness of the welcome so freely given; and he therefore, with many thanks, took his seat at the table with Mr. and Mrs. Listwell, who, desirous to make him feel at home, took a cup of tea themselves, while urging upon Madison the best that the house could afford.

Supper over, all doubts and apprehensions banished, the three drew around the blazing fire, and a conversation commenced which lasted till long after midnight.

"Now," said Madison to Mr. Listwell, "I was a little surprised and alarmed when I came in, by what you said; do tell me, sir, *why* you thought you had seen my face before, and by what you knew me to be a fugitive from slavery; for I am sure that I never was before in this neighborhood, and I certainly sought to conceal what I supposed to be the manner of a fugitive slave."

Mr. Listwell at once frankly disclosed the secret; describing the place where he first saw him; rehearsing the language which he (Madison) had used; referring to the effect which his manner and speech had made upon him; declaring the resolution he there formed to be an abolitionist; telling how often he had spoken of the circumstance, and the deep concern he had ever since felt to know what had become of him; and whether he had carried out the purpose to make his escape, as in the woods he declared he would do.

"Ever since that morning," said Mr. Listwell, "you have seldom been absent from my mind, and though now I did not dare to hope that I should ever see you again, I have often wished that such might be my fortune; for, from that hour, your face seemed to be daguerreotyped on my memory."

Madison looked quite astonished, and felt amazed at the narration to which he had listened. After recovering himself he said, "I well remember that morning, and the bitter anguish that wrung my heart; I will state the occasion of it. I had, on the previous Saturday, suffered a cruel lashing; had been tied up to the limb of a tree, with my feet chained together, and a heavy iron bar placed between my ankles. Thus suspended, I received on my naked back forty stripes, and was kept in this distressing position three or four hours, and was then let down, only to have my torture increased; for my bleeding back, gashed by the cow-skin, was washed by the overseer with old brine, partly to augment my suffering, and partly, as he said, to prevent inflammation. My crime was that I had stayed longer at the mill, the day previous, than it was thought I ought to have done, which, I assured my master and the overseer, was no fault of mine; but no excuses were allowed. 'Hold your tongue, you impudent rascal,' met my every explanation. Slaveholders are so imperious when their passions are excited, as to construe every word of the slave into insolence. I could do nothing but submit to the agonizing infliction. Smarting still from the wounds, as well as from the consciousness of being whipt for no cause, I took advantage of the absence of my master, who had gone to church, to spend the time in the woods, and brood over my wretched lot. Oh, sir, I remember it well,—and can never forget it."

"But this was five years ago; where have you been since?"

"I will try to tell you," said Madison. "Just four weeks after that Sabbath morning, I gathered up the few rags of clothing I had, and started, as I supposed, for the North and for freedom. I must not stop to describe my feelings on taking this step. It seemed like taking a leap into the dark. The thought of leaving my poor wife and two little children caused me indescribable anguish; but consoling myself with the reflection that once free, I could, possibly, devise ways and means to gain their freedom also, I nerved myself up to make the attempt. I started, but ill-luck attended me; for after being out a whole week, strange to say, I still found myself on my master's grounds; the third night after being out, a season of clouds and rain set in, wholly preventing me from seeing the North Star, which I had trusted as my guide, not dreaming that clouds might intervene between us.

"This circumstance was fatal to my project, for in losing my star, I lost my way; so when I supposed I was far towards the North, and had almost gained my freedom, I discovered myself at the very point from which I had started. It was a severe trial, for I arrived at home in great destitution; my feet were sore, and in travelling in the dark, I had dashed my foot against a stump, and started a nail, and lamed myself. I was wet and cold; one week had exhausted all my stores; and when I landed on my master's plantation, with all my work to do over again,—hungry, tired, lame, and bewildered,—I almost cursed the day that I was born. In this extremity I approached the quarters. I did so stealthily, although in my desperation I hardly cared whether I was discovered or not. Peeping through the rents of the quarters, I saw my fellow-slaves seated by a warm fire, merrily passing away the time, as though their hearts knew no sorrow. Although I envied their seeming contentment, all wretched as I was, I despised the cowardly acquiescence in their own degradation which it implied, and felt a kind of pride and glory in my own desperate lot. I dared not enter the quarters,—for where there is seeming contentment with slavery, there is certain treachery to freedom. I proceeded towards the great house, in the hope of catching a glimpse of my poor wife, whom I knew might be trusted with my secrets even on the scaffold. Just as I reached the fence which divided the field from the garden, I saw a woman in the yard, who in the darkness I took to be my wife; but a nearer approach told me it was not she. I was about to speak; had I done so, I would not have been here this night; for an alarm would have been sounded, and the hunters been put on my track. Here were hunger, cold, thirst, disappointment, and chagrin, confronted only by the dim hope of liberty. I tremble to think of that dreadful hour. To face the deadly cannon's mouth in warm blood unterrified, is, I think, a small achievement, compared with a conflict like this with gaunt starvation. The gnawings of hunger conquers by degrees, till all that a man has he would give in exchange for a single crust of bread. Thank God, I was not quite reduced to this extremity.

"Happily for me, before the fatal moment of utter despair, my good wife made her appearance in the yard. It was she; I knew her step. All was well now. I was, however, afraid to speak, lest I should frighten her. Yet speak I did; and, to my great joy, my voice was known. Our meeting can be more easily imagined than described. For a time hunger, thirst, weariness, and lameness were forgotten. But it was soon necessary for her to return to the house. She being a house-servant, her absence from the kitchen, if discovered, might have excited suspicion. Our parting was like tearing the flesh from my bones; yet it was the part of wisdom for her to go. She left me with the purpose of meeting me at midnight in the very forest where you last saw me. She knew the place well, as one of my melancholy resorts, and could easily find it, though the night was dark.

"I hastened away, therefore, and concealed myself, to await the arrival of my good angel. As I lay there among the leaves, I was strongly tempted to return again to the house of my master and give myself up; but remembering my solemn pledge on that memorable Sunday morning, I was able to linger out the two long hours between ten and midnight. I may well call them long hours. I have endured much hardship; I have encountered many perils; but the anxiety of those two hours, was the bitterest I ever experienced. True to her word, my wife came laden with provisions, and we sat down on the side of a log, at that dark and lonesome hour of the night. I cannot say we talked; our feelings were too great for that; yet we came to an understanding that I should make the woods my home, for if I gave myself up, I should be whipped and sold away; and if I started for the North, I should leave a wife doubly dear to me. We mutually determined, therefore, that I should remain in the vicinity. In the dismal swamps I lived, sir, five long years,—a cave for my home during the day. I wandered about at night with the wolf and the bear,—sustained by the promise that my good Susan would meet me in the pine woods at least once a week. This promise was redeemed, I assure you, to the letter, greatly to my relief. I had partly become contented with my mode of life, and had made up my mind to spend my days there; but the wilderness that sheltered me thus long took fire, and refused longer to be my hiding-place.

"I will not harrow up your feeling by portraying the terrific scene of this awful conflagration. There is nothing to which I can liken it. It was horribly and indescribably grand. The whole world seemed on fire, and it appeared to me that the day of judgment had come; that the burning bowels of the earth had burst forth, and that the end of all things was at hand. Bears and wolves, scorched from their mysterious hiding-places in the earth, and all the wild inhabitants of the untrodden forest, filled with a common dismay, ran forth, yelling, howling, bewildered amidst the smoke and flame. The very heavens seemed to rain down fire through the towering trees; it was by the merest chance that I escaped the devouring element. Running before it, and stopping occasionally to take breath, I looked back to behold its frightful ravages, and to drink in its savage magnificence. It was awful, thrilling, solemn, beyond compare. When aided by the fitful wind, the merciless tempest of fire swept on, sparkling, creaking, cracking, curling, roaring, out-doing in its dreadful splendor a thousand thunderstorms at once. From tree to tree it leaped, swallowing them up in its lurid, baleful glare; and leaving them leafless, limbless, charred, and lifeless behind. The scene was overwhelming, stunning,—nothing was spared,—cattle, tame and wild, herds of swine and of deer, wild beasts of every name and kind,—huge night-birds, bats, and owls, that had retired to their homes in lofty tree-tops to rest, perished in that fiery storm. The long-winged buzzard and croaking raven mingled their dismal cries with those of the countless myriads of small birds that rose up to the skies, and were lost to the sight in clouds of smoke and flame. Oh, I shudder when I think of it! Many a poor wandering fugitive, who, like myself, had sought among wild beasts the mercy denied by our fellow men, saw, in helpless consternation, his dwelling-place and city of refuge reduced to ashes forever. It was this grand conflagration that drove me hither; I ran alike from fire and from slavery."

After a slight pause, (for both speaker and hearers were deeply moved by the above recital,) Mr. Listwell, addressing Madison, said, "If it does not weary you too much, do tell us something of your journeyings since this disastrous burning,—we are deeply interested in everything which can throw light on the hardships of persons escaping from slavery; we could hear you talk all night; are there no incidents that you could relate of your travels hither? or are they such that you do not like to mention them."

"For the most part, sir, my course has been uninterrupted; and, considering the circumstances, at times even pleasant. I have suffered little for want of food; but I need not tell you how I got it. Your moral code may differ from mine, as your customs and usages are different. The fact is, sir, during my flight, I felt myself robbed by society of all my just rights; that I was in an enemy's land, who sought both my life and my liberty. They had transformed me into a brute; made merchandise of my body, and, for all the purposes of my flight, turned day into night,—and guided by my own necessities, and in contempt of their conventionalities, I did not scruple to take bread where I could get it."

"And just there you were right," said Mr. Listwell; "I once had doubts on this point myself, but a conversation with Gerrit Smith, (a man, by the way, that I wish you could see, for he is a devoted friend of your race, and I know he would receive you gladly,) put an end to all my doubts on this point. But do not let me interrupt you."

"I had but one narrow escape during my whole journey," said Madison.

"Do let us hear of it," said Mr. Listwell.

"Two weeks ago," continued Madison, "after travelling all night, I was overtaken by daybreak, in what seemed to me an almost interminable wood. I deemed it unsafe to go farther, and, as usual, I looked around for a suitable tree in which to spend the day. I liked one with a bushy top, and found one just to my mind. Up I climbed, and hiding myself as well as I could, I, with this strap, (pulling one out of his old coat-pocket,) lashed myself to a bough, and flattered myself that I should get a *good night's* sleep that day; but in this I was soon disappointed. I had scarcely got fastened to my natural hammock, when I heard the voices of a number of persons, apparently approaching the part of the woods where I was. Upon my word, sir, I dreaded more these human voices than I should have done those of wild beasts. I was at a loss to know what to do. If I descended, I should probably be discovered by the men; and if they had dogs I should, doubtless, be 'treed.' It was an anxious moment, but hardships and dangers have been the accompaniments of my life; and have, perhaps, imparted to me a certain hardness of character, which, to some extent, adapts me to them. In my present predicament, I decided to hold my place in the tree-top, and abide the consequences. But here I must disappoint you; for the men, who were all colored, halted at least a hundred yards from me, and began with their axes, in right good earnest, to attack the trees. The sound of their laughing axes was like the report of as many well-charged pistols. By and by there came down at least a dozen trees with a terrible crash. They leaped upon the fallen trees with an air of victory. I could see no dog with them, and felt myself comparatively safe, though I could not forget the possibility that some freak or fancy might bring the axe a little nearer my dwelling than comported with my safety.

"There was no sleep for me that day, and I wished for night. You may imagine that the thought of having the tree attacked under me was far from agreeable, and that it very easily kept me on the look-out. The day was not without diversion. The men at work seemed to be a gay set; and they would often make the woods resound with that uncontrolled laughter for which we, as a race, are remarkable. I held my place in the tree till sunset,—saw the men put on their jackets to be off. I observed that all left the ground except one, whom I saw sitting on the side of a stump, with his head bowed, and his eyes apparently fixed on the ground. I became interested in him. After sitting in the position to which I have alluded ten or fifteen minutes, he left the stump, walked directly towards the tree in which I was secreted, and halted almost under the same. He stood for a moment and looked around, deliberately and reverently took off his hat, by which I saw that he was a man in the evening of life, slightly bald and quite gray. After laying down his hat carefully, he knelt and prayed aloud, and such a prayer, the most fervent, earnest, and solemn, to which I think I ever listened. After reverently addressing the Almighty, as the all-wise, all-good, and the common Father of all mankind, he besought God for grace, for strength, to bear up under, and to endure, as a good soldier, all the hardships and trials which beset the journey of life, and to enable him to live in a manner which accorded with the gospel of Christ. His soul now broke out in humble supplication for deliverance from bondage. 'O thou,' said he, 'that hearest the raven's cry, take pity on poor me! O deliver me! O deliver me! in mercy, O God, deliver me from the chains and manifold hardships of slavery! With thee, O Father, all things are possible. Thou canst stand and measure the earth. Thou hast beheld and drove asunder the nations,—all power is in thy hand,—thou didst say of old, "I have seen the affliction of my people, and am come to deliver them,"—Oh look down upon our afflictions, and have mercy upon us.' But I cannot repeat his prayer, nor can I give you an idea of its deep pathos. I had given but little attention to religion, and had but little faith in it; yet, as the old man prayed, I felt almost like coming down and kneel by his side, and mingle my broken complaint with his.

"He had already gained my confidence; as how could it be otherwise? I knew enough of religion to know that the man who prays in secret is far more likely to be sincere than he who loves to pray standing in the street, or in the great congregation. When he arose from his knees, like another Zacheus, I came down from the tree. He seemed a little alarmed at first, but I told him my story, and the good man embraced me in his arms, and assured me of his sympathy.

"I was now about out of provisions, and thought I might safely ask him to help me replenish my store. He said he had no money; but if he had, he would freely give it me. I told him I had *one dollar*; it was all the money I had in the world. I gave it to him, and asked him to purchase some crackers and cheese, and to kindly bring me the balance; that I would remain in or near that place, and would come to him on his return, if he would whistle. He was gone only about an hour. Meanwhile, from some cause or other, I know not what, (but as you shall see very wisely,) I changed my place. On his return I started to meet him; but it seemed as if the shadow of approaching danger fell upon my spirit, and checked my progress. In a very few minutes, closely on the heels of the old man, I distinctly saw *fourteen men*, with something like guns in their hands."

"Oh! the old wretch!" exclaimed Mrs. Listwell "he had betrayed you, had he?"

"I think not," said Madison, "I cannot believe that the old man was to blame. He probably went into a store, asked for the articles for which I sent, and presented the bill I gave him; and it is so unusual for slaves in the country to have money, that fact, doubtless, excited suspicion, and gave rise to inquiry. I can easily believe that the truthfulness of the old man's character compelled him to disclose the facts; and thus were these blood-thirsty men put on my track. Of course I did not present myself; but hugged my hiding-place securely. If discovered and attacked, I resolved to sell my life as dearly as possible.

"After searching about the woods silently for a time, the whole company gathered around the old man; one charged him with lying, and called him an old villain; said he was a thief; charged him with stealing money; said if he did not instantly tell where he got it, they would take the shirt from his old back, and give him thirty-nine lashes.

"'I did *not* steal the money,' said the old man it was given me, as I told you at the store; and if the man who gave it me is not here, it is not my fault.'

"'Hush! you lying old rascal; we'll make you smart for it. You shall not leave this spot until you have told where you got that money.'

"They now took hold of him, and began to strip him; while others went to get sticks with which to beat him. I felt, at the moment, like rushing out in the midst of them; but considering that the old man would be whipped the more for having aided a fugitive slave, and that, perhaps, in the *melée* he might be killed outright, I disobeyed this impulse. They tied him to a tree, and began to whip him. My own flesh crept at every blow, and I seem to hear the old man's piteous cries even now. They laid thirty-nine lashes on his bare back, and were going to repeat that number, when one of the company besought his comrades to desist. 'You'll kill the d—d old scoundrel! You've already whipt a dollar's worth out of him, even if he stole it!' 'O yes,' said another, 'let him down. He'll never tell us another lie, I'll warrant ye!' With this, one of the company untied the old man, and bid him go about his business.

The old man left, but the company remained as much as an hour, scouring the woods. Round and round they went, turning up the underbrush, and peering about like so many bloodhounds. Two or three times they came within six feet of where I lay. I tell you I held my stick with a firmer grasp than I did in coming up to your house tonight. I expected to level one of them at least. Fortunately, however, I eluded their pursuit, and they left me alone in the woods.

"My last dollar was now gone, and you may well suppose I felt the loss of it; but the thought of being once again free to pursue my journey, prevented that depression which a sense of destitution causes; so swinging my little bundle on my back, I caught a glimpse of the *Great Bear* (which ever points the way to my beloved star,) and I started again on my journey. What I lost in money I made up at a hen-roost that same night, upon which I fortunately came."

"But you didn't eat your food raw? How did you cook it?" said Mrs. Listwell.

"O no, Madam," said Madison, turning to his little bundle,—"I had the means of cooking." Here he took out of his bundle an old-fashioned tinder-box, and taking up a piece of a file, which he brought with him, he struck it with a heavy flint, and brought out at least a dozen sparks at once. "I have had this old box," said he, "more than five years. It is the *only* property saved from the fire in the dismal swamp. It has done me good service. It has given me the means of broiling many a chicken!"

It seemed quite a relief to Mrs. Listwell to know that Madison had, at least, lived upon cooked food. Women have a perfect horror of eating uncooked food.

By this time thoughts of what was best to be done about getting Madison to Canada, began to trouble Mr. Listwell; for the laws of Ohio were very stringent against any one who should aid, or who were found aiding a slave to escape through that State. A citizen, for the simple act of taking a fugitive slave in his carriage, had just been stripped of all his property, and thrown penniless upon the world. Notwithstanding this, Mr. Listwell was determined to see Madison safely on his way to Canada. "Give yourself no uneasiness, said he to Madison, for if it cost my farm, I shall see you safely out of the States, and on your way to a land of liberty. Thank God that there Is such a land so near us! You will spend to-morrow with us, and to-morrow night I will take you in my carriage to the Lake. Once upon that, and you are safe."

"Thank you! thank you," said the fugitive; "I will commit myself to your care."

For the *first* time during *five* years, Madison enjoyed the luxury of resting his limbs on a comfortable bed, and inside a human habitation. Looking at the white sheets, he said to Mr. Listwell, "What, sir! you don't mean that I shall sleep in that bed?"

"Oh yes, oh yes."

After Mr. Listwell left the room, Madison said he really hesitated whether or not he should lie on the floor; for that was *far* more comfortable and inviting than any bed to which he had been used.

We pass over the thoughts and feelings, the hopes and fears, the plans and purposes, that revolved in the mind of Madison during the day that he was secreted at the house of Mr. Listwell. The reader will be content to know that nothing occurred to endanger his liberty, or to excite alarm. Many were the little attentions bestowed upon him in his quiet retreat and hiding-place. In the evening, Mr. Listwell, after treating Madison to a new suit of winter clothes, and replenishing his exhausted purse with five dollars, all in silver, brought out his two-horse wagon, well provided with buffaloes,[1] and silently started off with him to Cleveland. They arrived there without interruption, a few minutes before sunrise the next morning. Fortunately the steamer Admiral lay at the wharf, and was to start for Canada at nine o'clock. Here the last anticipated danger was surmounted. It was feared that just at this point the hunters of men might be on the look-out, and, possibly, pounce upon their victim. Mr. Listwell saw the captain of the boat; cautiously

---

1. Fur carriage robes.

sounded him on the matter of carrying liberty-loving passengers, before he introduced his precious charge. This done, Madison was conducted on board. With usual generosity this true subject of the emancipating queen[2] welcomed Madison, and assured him that he should be safely landed in Canada, free of charge. Madison now felt himself no more a piece of merchandise, but a passenger, and, like any other passenger, going about his business, carrying with him what belonged to him, and nothing which rightfully belonged to anybody else.

Wrapped in his new winter suit, snug and comfortable, a pocket full of silver, safe from his pursuers, embarked for a free country, Madison gave every sign of sincere gratitude, and bade his kind benefactor farewell, with such a grip of the hand as bespoke a heart full of honest manliness, and a soul that knew how to appreciate kindness. It need scarcely be said that Mr. Listwell was deeply moved by the gratitude and friendship he had excited in a nature so noble as that of the fugitive. He went to his home that day with a joy and gratification which knew no bounds. He had done something "to deliver the spoiled out of the hands of the spoiler," he had given bread to the hungry, and clothes to the naked; he had befriended a man to whom the laws of his country forbade all friendship,—and in proportion to the odds against his righteous deed, was the delightful satisfaction that gladdened his heart. On reaching home, he exclaimed, "*He is safe,—he is safe,—he is safe,*"— and the cup of his joy was shared by his excellent lady. The following letter was received from Madison a few days after.

Windsor, Canada West, Dec. 16, 1840.

My dear Friend,—for such you truly are:—Madison is out of the woods at last; I nestle in the mane of the British lion, protected by his mighty paw from the talons and the beak of the American eagle. I am free, and breathe an atmosphere too pure for *slaves,* slave-hunters, or slave-holders. My heart is full. As many thanks to you, sir, and to your kind lady, as there are pebbles on the shores of Lake Erie; and may the blessing of God rest upon you both. You will never be forgotten by your profoundly grateful friend.

Madison Washington.

✳ ✳ ✳

---

2. The Abolition Act in Great Britain was actually passed four years before Victoria's ascension to the throne in 1837, but emancipation was gradual in all lands under British control.

Francis Parkman
(1823–1893)

Born into wealth and social position in Boston, the son a Unitarian minister, Francis Parkman early developed a case of "Injuns on the brain" that led to his great work. Educated at Harvard, he spent vacations in the wilderness areas of New Hampshire and New York. As an undergraduate he had already developed ambitions to write a history of the French and Indian War, an idea later expanded, as he said, "to include the whole course of the American conflict between France and England; or in other words, the history of the American forest." Never robust, Parkman traveled frequently, partly for his health, but partly also to visit the historical sites that he would describe so vividly in his writings. From a journey West in 1846, when he visited the Great Plains, lived among the Sioux, and hunted buffalo, came his most popular book, The California and Oregon Trail *(1849, later reprinted as* The Oregon Trail*), which he dictated to a friend. Two years later he published the first of his great histories,* The Conspiracy of Pontiac *(1851). Nearly blind when he began* The Conspiracy, *he completed as few as six lines a day, writing with a crayon, guiding his hand with wires stretched across a frame over the paper. For years he worked in his rose garden and published little except an autobiographical novel,* Vassall Morton *(1856), but he returned to history in 1865 with* Pioneers in France and the New World. *His "History of France and England in North America" continued, with volumes appearing regularly for the next quarter century, culminating with* A Half Century of Conflict *(1892).*

In La Salle and the Discovery of the Great West *(1869), Parkman recounts a story nearly two hundred years old at the time of his telling. The English settlements were strung out along the Atlantic coast, with the Appalachian Mountains still a barrier to be crossed in the future. In New England, King Philip's War (1675–1676) had effectively ended tribal resistance in New England, but had also shown that westward expansion would not necessarily come easily. By a bold stroke, with major consequences for the inhabitants of North America of all races, La Salle led a band of French and Indians down the Mississippi to Louisiana, in 1682 laying claim to territory they had explored "In the name of the most high, mighty, invincible, and victorious * * * King of France."*

The Works of Francis Parkman, Frontenac edition, appeared in 20 volumes (1901–1907). Studies include Otis A. Pease, *Parkman's History: The Historian as Literary Artist* (1953); Howard Doughty, *Francis Parkman* (1962); and Robert L. Gale, *Francis Parkman* (1973).

———

[From] La Salle and the Discovery of the Great West[1]

CHAPTER XIX. 1681. LA SALLE BEGINS ANEW

His Constancy; His Plans; His Savage Allies; He Becomes Snow-Blind. —Negotiations.—Grand Council.—La Salle's Oratory.— Meeting with Tonty.—Preparation.—Departure.

IN TRACING THE ADVENTURES of Tonty and the rovings of Hennepin,[2] we have lost sight of La Salle, the pivot of the enterprise. Returning from the desolation and horror in the valley of the Illinois, he had spent the winter at Fort Miami, on the St. Joseph, by the borders of Lake Michigan. Here he might have brooded on the redoubled ruin that had befallen him,—the desponding friends, the exulting foes; the wasted energies, the crushing load of debt, the stormy past, the black and lowering future. But his mind was of a different temper. He had no thought but to grapple with adversity, and out of the fragments of his ruin to build up the fabric of success.

He would not recoil; but he modified his plans to meet the new contingency. His white enemies had found, or rather perhaps had made, a savage ally in the Iroquois. Their incursions must be stopped, or his enterprise would come to nought; and he thought he saw the means by which this new danger

———

1. The source of the present text is the Centenary Edition (1922). A number of Parkman's notes are here omitted.

2. Henri de Tonty, an Italian officer, and Father Louis Hennepin, a Franciscan friar, had joined with La Salle about two years earlier.

could be converted into a source of strength. The tribes of the West, threatened by the common enemy, might be taught to forget their mutual animosities and join in a defensive league, with La Salle at its head. They might be colonized around his fort in the valley of the Illinois, where in the shadow of the French flag, and with the aid of French allies, they could hold the Iroquois in check, and acquire in some measure the arts of a settled life. The Franciscan friars could teach them the Faith; and La Salle and his associates could supply them with goods, in exchange for the vast harvest of furs which their hunters could gather in these boundless wilds. Meanwhile, he would seek out the mouth of the Mississippi; and the furs gathered at his colony in the Illinois would then find a ready passage to the markets of the world. Thus might this ancient slaughter-field of warring savages be redeemed to civilization and Christianity; and a stable settlement, half-feudal, half-commercial, grow up in the heart of the western wilderness. This plan was but a part of the original scheme of his enterprise, adapted to new and unexpected circumstances; and he now set himself to its execution with his usual vigor, joined to an address which, when dealing with Indians, never failed him.

There were allies close at hand. Near Fort Miami were the huts of twenty-five or thirty savages, exiles from their homes, and strangers in this western world. Several of the English colonies, from Virginia to Maine, had of late years been harassed by Indian wars; and the Puritans of New England, above all, had been scourged by the deadly outbreak of King Philip's war.[3] Those engaged in it had paid a bitter price for their brief triumphs. A band of refugees, chiefly Abenakis and Mohegans, driven from their native seats, had roamed into these distant wilds, and were wintering in the friendly neighborhood of the French. La Salle soon won them over to his interests. One of their number was the Mohegan hunter, who for two years had faithfully followed his fortunes, and who had been four years in the West. He is described as a prudent and discreet young man, in whom La Salle had great confidence, and who could make himself understood in several western languages, belonging, like his own, to the great Algonquin tongue. This devoted henchman proved an efficient mediator with his countrymen. The New-England Indians, with one voice, promised to follow La Salle, asking no recompense but to call him their chief, and yield to him the love and admiration which he rarely failed to command from this hero-worshipping race.

New allies soon appeared. A Shawanoe chief from the valley of the Ohio, whose following embraced a hundred and fifty warriors, came to ask the protection of the French against the all-destroying Iroquois. "The Shawanoes are too distant," was La Salle's reply; "but let them come to me at the Illinois, and they shall be safe." The chief promised to join him in the autumn, at Fort Miami, with all his band. But, more important than all, the consent and co-operation of the Illinois must be gained; and the Miamis, their neighbors and of late their enemies, must be taught the folly of their

---

3. 1675–1676.

league with the Iroquois, and the necessity of joining in the new confederation. Of late, they had been made to see the perfidy of their dangerous allies.
A band of the Iroquois, returning from the slaughter of the Tamaroa Illinois,
had met and murdered a band of Miamis on the Ohio, and had not only
refused satisfaction, but had intrenched themselves in three rude forts of
trees and brushwood in the heart of the Miami country. The moment was
favorable for negotiating; but, first, La Salle wished to open a communication with the Illinois, some of whom had begun to return to the country
they had abandoned. With this view, and also, it seems, to procure provisions, he set out on the first of March, with his lieutenant La Forest, and fifteen men.

The country was sheeted in snow, and the party journeyed on snow-
shoes; but when they reached the open prairies, the white expanse glared in
the sun with so dazzling a brightness that La Salle and several of the men
became snow-blind. They stopped and encamped under the edge of a forest;
and here La Salle remained in darkness for three days, suffering extreme
pain. Meanwhile, he sent forward La Forest and most of the men, keeping
with him his old attendant Hunaut. Going out in quest of pine-leaves,—a
decoction of which was supposed to be useful in cases of snow-blindness,—
this man discovered the fresh tracks of Indians, followed them, and found a
camp of Outagamies, or Foxes, from the neighborhood of Green Bay. From
them he heard welcome news. They told him that Tonty was safe among the
Pottawattamies, and that Hennepin had passed through their country on his
return from among the Sioux.

A thaw took place; the snow melted rapidly; the rivers were opened; the
blind men began to recover; and launching the canoes which they had
dragged after them, the party pursued their way by water. They soon met a
band of Illinois. La Salle gave them presents, condoled with them on their
losses, and urged them to make peace and alliance with the Miamis. Thus, he
said, they could set the Iroquois at defiance; for he himself, with his Frenchmen and his Indian friends, would make his abode among them, supply
them with goods, and aid them to defend themselves. They listened, well
pleased, promised to carry his message to their countrymen, and furnished
him with a large supply of corn. Meanwhile he had rejoined La Forest,
whom he now sent to Michilimackinac to await Tonty, and tell him to
remain there till he, La Salle, should arrive.

Having thus accomplished the objects of his journey, he returned to Fort
Miami, whence he soon after ascended the St. Joseph to the village of the
Miami Indians, on the portage, at the head of the Kankakee. Here he found
unwelcome guests. These were three Iroquois warriors, who had been for
some time in the place, and who, as he was told, had demeaned themselves
with the insolence of conquerors, and spoken of the French with the utmost
contempt. He hastened to confront them, rebuked and menaced them, and
told them that now, when he was present, they dared not repeat the calum-
nies which they has uttered in his absence. They stood abashed and confounded, and during the following night secretly left the town and fled. The

effect was prodigious on the minds of the Miamis, when they saw that La Salle, backed by ten Frenchmen, could command from their arrogant visitors a respect which they, with their hundreds of warriors, had wholly failed to inspire. Here, at the outset, was an augury full of promise for the approaching negotiations.

There were other strangers in the town,—a band of eastern Indians, more numerous than those who had wintered at the fort. The greater number were from Rhode Island, including, probably, some of King Philip's warriors; others were from New York, and others again from Virginia. La Salle called them to a council, promised them a new home in the West under the protection of the Great King, with rich lands, an abundance of game, and French traders to supply them with the goods which they had once received from the English. Let them but help him to make peace between the Miamis and the Illinois, and he would insure for them a future of prosperity and safety. They listened with open ears, and promised their aid in the work of peace.

On the next morning, the Miamis were called to a grand council. It was held in the lodge of their chief, from which the mats were removed, that the crowd without might hear what was said. La Salle rose and harangued the concourse. Few men were so skilled in the arts of forest rhetoric and diplomacy. After the Indian mode, he was, to follow his chroniclers, "the greatest orator in North America."[4] He began with a gift of tobacco, to clear the brains of his auditory; next, for he had brought a canoe-load of presents to support his eloquence, he gave them cloth to cover their dead, coats to dress them, hatchets to build a grand scaffold in their honor, and beads, bells, and trinkets of all sorts, to decorate their relatives at a grand funeral feast. All this was mere metaphor. The living, while appropriating the gifts to their own use, were pleased at the compliment offered to their dead; and their delight redoubled as the orator proceeded. One of their great chiefs had lately been killed; and La Salle, after a eulogy of the departed, declared that he would now raise him to life again; that is, that he would assume his name and give support to his squaws and children. This flattering announcement drew forth an outburst of applause; and when, to confirm his words, his attendants placed before them a huge pile of coats, shirts, and hunting-knives, the whole assembly exploded in yelps of admiration.

Now came the climax of the harangue, introduced by a further present of six guns:—

"He who is my master, and the master of all this country, is a mighty chief, feared by the whole world; but he loves peace, and the words of his lips are for good alone. He is called the King of France, and he is the mightiest among the chiefs beyond the great water. His goodness reaches even to your dead, and his subjects come among you to raise them up to life. But it is his will to preserve the life he has given; it is his will that you should obey his laws, and make no war without the leave of Onontio, who commands in his name at Quebec, and who loves all the nations alike, because such is the

---

4. "En ce genre, il étoit le plus grand orateur de l'Amérique Septentrionale."—*Relation des Découvertes.* [Parkman's note]

will of the Great King. You ought, then, to live at peace with your neighbors, and above all with the Illinois. You have had causes of quarrel with them; but their defeat has avenged you. Though they are still strong, they wish to make peace with you. Be content with the glory of having obliged them to ask for it. You have an interest in preserving them; since, if the Iroquois destroy them, they will next destroy you. Let us all obey the Great King, and live together in peace, under his protection. Be of my mind, and use these guns that I have given you, not to make war, but only to hunt and to defend yourselves."[5]

So saying, he gave two belts of wampum to confirm his words; and the assembly dissolved. On the following day, the chiefs again convoked it, and made their reply in form. It was all that La Salle could have wished. "The Illinois is our brother, because he is the son of our Father, the Great King." "We make you the master of our beaver and our lands, of our minds and our bodies." "We cannot wonder that our brothers from the East wish to live with you. We should have wished so too, if we had known what a blessing it is to be the children of the Great King." The rest of this auspicious day was passed in feasts and dances, in which La Salle and his Frenchmen all bore part. His new scheme was hopefully begun. It remained to achieve the enterprise, twice defeated, of the discovery of the mouth of the Mississippi,—that vital condition of his triumph, without which all other success was meaningless and vain.

To this end he must return to Canada, appease his creditors, and collect his scattered resources. Towards the end of May he set out in canoes from Fort Miami, and reached Michilimackinac after a prosperous voyage. Here, to his great joy, he found Tonty and Zenobe Membré,[6] who had lately arrived from Green Bay. The meeting was one at which even his stoic nature must have melted. Each had for the other a tale of disaster; but when La Salle recounted the long succession of his reverses, it was with the tranquil tone and cheerful look of one who relates the incidents of an ordinary journey. Membré looked on him with admiration. "Any one else," he says, "would have thrown up his hand and abandoned the enterprise; but, far from this, with a firmness and constancy that never had its equal, I saw him more resolved than ever to continue his work and push forward his discovery."[7]

Without loss of time they embarked together for Fort Frontenac, paddled their canoes a thousand miles, and safely reached their destination. Here, in this third beginning of his enterprise, La Salle found himself beset with embarrassments. Not only was he burdened with the fruitless costs of his two former efforts, but the heavy debts which he had incurred in building and maintaining Fort Frontenac had not been wholly paid. The fort and

---

5. Translated from the *Relation*, where these councils are reported at great length. [Parkman's note]

6. A Franciscan friar.

7. Membré in Le Clerc, ii. 208. Tonty, in his memoir of 1693, speaks of the joy of La Salle at the meeting. The *Relation*, usually very accurate, says, erroneously, that Tonty had gone to Fort Frontenac. La Forest had gone thither, not long before La Salle's arrival. [Parkman's note]

the seigniory were already deeply mortgaged; yet through the influence of Count Frontenac, the assistance of his secretary Barrois, a consummate man of business, and the support of a wealthy relative, he found means to appease his creditors and even to gain fresh advances. To this end, however, he was forced to part with a portion of his monopolies. Having first made his will at Montreal, in favor of a cousin who had befriended him, he mustered his men, and once more set forth, resolved to trust no more to agents, but to lead on his followers, in a united body, under his own personal command.

At the beginning of autumn he was at Toronto, where the long and difficult portage to Lake Simcoe detained him a fortnight. He spent a part of it in writing an account of what had lately occurred to a correspondent in France, and he closes his letter thus: "This is all I can tell you this year. I have a hundred things to write, but you could not believe how hard it is to do it among Indians. The canoes and their lading must be got over the portage, and I must speak to them continually and bear all their importunity, or else they will do nothing I want, I hope to write more at leisure next year, and tell you the end of this business, which I hope will turn out well: for I have M. de Tonty, who is full of zeal; thirty Frenchmen, all good men, without reckoning such as I cannot trust; and more than a hundred Indians, some of them Shawanoes, and others from New England, all of whom know how to use guns."

It was October before he reached Lake Huron. Day after day and week after week the heavy-laden canoes crept on along the lonely wilderness shores, by the monotonous ranks of bristling moss-bearded firs; lake and forest, forest and lake; a dreary scene haunted with yet more dreary memories—disasters, sorrows, and deferred hopes; time, strength, and wealth spent in vain; a ruinous past and a doubtful future; slander, obloquy, and hate. With unmoved heart, the patient voyager held his course, and drew up his canoes at last on the beach at Fort Miami.

CHAPTER XX. 1681–1682. SUCCESS OF LA SALLE

His Followers—The Chicago Portage.—Descent of the Mississippi.—The Lost Hunter.—The Arkansas.—The Taensas.—The Natchez.—Hostility.—The Mouth of the Mississippi.—Louis XIV Proclaimed Sovereign of the Great West.

THE season was far advanced. On the bare limbs of the forest hung a few withered remnants of its gay autumnal livery; and the smoke crept upward through the sullen November air from the squalid wigwams of La Salle's Abenaki and Mohegan allies. These, his new friends, were savages whose midnight yells had startled the border hamlets of New England; who had danced around Puritan scalps, and whom Puritan imaginations painted as incarnate fiends. La Salle chose eighteen of them, whom he added to the twenty-three Frenchmen who remained with him, some of the rest having deserted and others lagged behind. The Indians insisted on taking their squaws with them. These were ten in number, besides three children; and thus the expedition included fifty-four persons, of whom some were useless, and others a burden.

On the 21st of December, Tonty and Membré set out from Fort Miami with some of the party in six canoes, and crossed to the little river Chicago. La Salle, with the rest of the men, joined them a few days later. It was the dead of winter, and the streams were frozen. They made sledges, placed on them the canoes, the baggage, and a disabled Frenchman; crossed from the Chicago to the northern branch of the Illinois, and filed in a long procession down its frozen course. They reached the site of the great Illinois village, found it tenantless, and continued their journey, still dragging their canoes, till at length they reached open water below Lake Peoria.

La Salle had abandoned for a time his original plan of building a vessel for the navigation of the Mississippi. Bitter experience had taught him the difficulty of the attempt, and he resolved to trust to his canoes alone. They embarked again, floating prosperously down between the leafless forests that flanked the tranquil river; till, on the sixth of February, they issued upon the majestic bosom of the Mississippi. Here, for the time, their progress was stopped; for the river was full of floating ice. La Salle's Indians, too, had lagged behind; but within a week all had arrived, the navigation was once more free, and they resumed their course. Towards evening they saw on their right the mouth of a great river; and the clear current was invaded by the headlong torrent of the Missouri, opaque with mud. They built their campfires in the neighboring forest; and at daylight, embarking anew on the dark and mighty stream, drifted swiftly down towards unknown destinies. They passed a deserted town of the Tamaroas; saw, three days after, the mouth of the Ohio; and, gliding by the wastes of bordering swamp, landed on the twenty-fourth of February near the Third Chickasaw Bluffs. They encamped, and the hunters went out for game. All returned, excepting Pierre Prudhomme; and as the others had seen fresh tracks of Indians, La Salle feared that he was killed. While some of his followers built a small stockade fort on a high bluff by the river, others ranged the woods in pursuit of the missing hunter. After six days of ceaseless and fruitless search, they met two Chickasaw Indians in the forest; and through them La Salle sent presents and peace-messages to that warlike people, whose villages were a few days' journey distant. Several days later Prudhomme was found, and brought into the camp, half-dead. He had lost his way while hunting; and to console him for his woes La Salle christened the newly built fort with his name, and left him, with a few others, in charge of it.

Again they embarked; and with every stage of their adventurous progress the mystery of this vast New World was more and more unveiled. More and more they entered the realms of spring. The hazy sunlight, the warm and drowsy air, the tender foliage, the opening flowers, betokened the reviving life of Nature. For several days more they followed the writhings of the great river on its tortuous course through wastes of swamp and cane-brake, till on the thirteenth of March they found themselves wrapped in a thick fog. Neither shore was visible; but they heard on the right the boom-ing of an Indian drum and the shrill outcries of the war-dance. La Salle at once crossed to the opposite side, where, in less than an hour, his men threw up a rude fort of felled trees. Meanwhile the fog cleared; and from the far-ther bank the astonished Indians saw the strange visitors at their work. Some of the French advanced to the edge of the water, and beckoned them to come over. Several of them approached, in a wooden canoe, to within the distance of a gun-shot. La Salle displayed the calumet, and sent a Frenchman to meet them. He was well received; and the friendly mood of the Indians being now apparent, the whole party crossed the river.

On landing, they found themselves at a town of the Kappa band of the Arkansas, a people dwelling near the mouth of the river which bears their name. "The whole village," writes Membré to his superior, "came down to the shore to meet us, except the women, who had run off. I cannot tell you the civility and kindness we received from these barbarians, who brought us poles to make huts, supplied us with firewood during the three days we were among them, and took turns in feasting us. But, my Reverend Father, this gives no idea of the good qualities of these savages, who are gay, civil, and free-hearted. The young men, though the most alert and spirited we had seen, are nevertheless so modest that not one of them would take the liberty to enter our hut, but all stood quietly at the door. They are so well formed that we were in admiration at their beauty. We did not lose the value of a pin while we were among them."

Various were the dances and ceremonies with which they entertained the strangers, who, on their part, responded with a solemnity which their hosts would have liked less if they had understood it better. La Salle and Tonty, at the head of their followers, marched to the open area in the midst of the village. Here, to the admiration of the gazing crowd of warriors, women, and children, a cross was raised bearing the arms of France. Mem-bré, in canonicals, sang a hymn; the men shouted *Vive le Roi*; and La Salle, in the King's name, took formal possession of the country. The friar, not, he flatters himself, without success, labored to expound by signs the mysteries of the Faith; while La Salle, by methods equally satisfactory, drew from the chief an acknowledgment of fealty to Louis XIV.

After touching at several other towns of this people, the voyagers resumed their course, guided by two of the Arkansas; passed the sites, since become historic, of Vicksburg and Grand Gulf; and, about three hundred miles below the Arkansas, stopped by the edge of a swamp on the western side of the river.[8] Here, as their two guides told them, was the path to the great town of the Taensas. Tonty and Membré were sent to visit it. They and their men shouldered their birch canoe through the swamp, and launched it on a lake which had once formed a portion of the channel of the river. In two hours, they reached the town; and Tonty gazed at it with astonishment. He had seen nothing like it in America,—large square dwellings, built of sun-baked mud mixed with straw, arched over with a dome-shaped roof of canes, and placed in regular order around an open area. Two of them were larger and better than the rest. One was the lodge of the chief; the other was the temple, or house of the Sun. They entered the former, and found a single room, forty feet square, where, in the dim light,—for there was no opening but the door,—the chief sat awaiting them on a sort of bedstead, three of his wives at his side; while sixty old men, wrapped in white cloaks woven of mulberry-bark, formed his divan.[9] When he spoke, his wives howled to do him honor; and the assembled councillors listened with the reverence due to a potentate for whom, at his death, a hundred victims were to be sacrificed. He received the visitors graciously, and joyfully accepted the gifts which Tonty laid before him. This interview over, the Frenchmen repaired to the temple, wherein were kept the bones of the departed chiefs. In construction, it was much like the royal dwelling. Over it were rude wooden figures, representing three eagles turned towards the east. A strong mud wall surrounded it, planted with stakes, on which were stuck the skulls of enemies sacrificed to the Sun; while before the door was a block of wood, on which lay a large shell surrounded with the braided hair of the victims. The interior was rude as a barn, dimly lighted from the doorway, and full of smoke. There was a structure in the middle which Membré thinks was a kind of altar; and before it burned a perpetual fire, fed with three logs laid end to end, and watched by two old men devoted to this sacred office. There was a mysterious recess, too, which the strangers were forbidden to explore, but which, as Tonty was told, contained the riches of the nation, consisting of pearls from the Gulf, and trinkets obtained, probably through other tribes, from the Spaniards and other Europeans.

The chief condescended to visit La Salle at his camp,—a favor which he would by no means have granted, had the visitors been Indians. A master of ceremonies and six attendants preceded him, to clear the path and prepare the place of meeting. When all was ready, he was seen advancing, clothed in a white robe and preceded by two men bearing white fans, while a third displayed a disk of burnished copper,—doubtless to represent the Sun, his ancestor, or, as others will have it, his elder brother. His aspect was marvel-

8. In Tensas County, Louisiana. Tonty's estimates of distance are here much too low. They seem to be founded on observations of latitude, without reckoning the windings of the river. It may interest sportsmen to know that the party killed several large alligators on their way. Membré is much astonished that such monsters should be born of eggs like chickens. [Parkman's note]

9. Council of state.

lously grave, and he and La Salle met with gestures of ceremonious courtesy. The interview was very friendly; and the chief returned well pleased with the gifts which his entertainer bestowed on him, and which, indeed, had been the principal motive of his visit.

On the next morning, as they descended the river, they saw a wooden canoe full of Indians; and Tonty gave chase. He had nearly overtaken it, when more than a hundred men appeared suddenly on the shore, with bows bent to defend their countrymen. La Salle called out to Tonty to withdraw. He obeyed; and the whole party encamped on the opposite bank. Tonty offered to cross the river with a peace-pipe, and set out accordingly with a small party of men. When he landed, the Indians made signs of friendship by joining their hands,—a proceeding by which Tonty, having but one hand, was somewhat embarrassed; but he directed his men to respond in his stead. La Salle and Membré now joined him, and went with the Indians to their village, three leagues distant. Here they spent the night. "The Sieur de la Salle," writes Membré, "whose very air, engaging manners, tact, and address attract love and respect alike, produced such an effect on the hearts of these people that they did not know how to treat us well enough."

The Indians of this village were the Natchez; and their chief was brother of the great chief, or Sun, of the whole nation. His town was several leagues distant, near the site of the city of Natchez; and thither the French repaired to visit him. They saw what they had already seen among the Taensas,—a religious and political despotism, a privileged caste descended from the sun, a temple, and a sacred fire.[1] La Salle planted a large cross, with the arms of France attached, in the midst of the town; while the inhabitants looked on with a satisfaction which they would hardly have displayed had they understood the meaning of the act.

The French next visited the Coroas, at their village two leagues below; and here they found a reception no less auspicious. On the thirty-first of March, as they approached Red River, they passed in the fog a town of the Oumas, and three days later discovered a party of fishermen, in wooden

---

1. The Natchez and the Taensas, whose habits and customs were similar, did not, in their social organization, differ radically from other Indians. The same principle of clanship, or *totemship*, so widely spread, existed in full force among them, combined with their religious ideas, and developed into forms of which no other example, equally distinct, is to be found. (For Indian clanship, see "The Jesuits in North America," *Introduction.*) Among the Natchez and Taensas, the principal clan formed a ruling caste; and its chiefs had the attributes of demi-gods. As descent was through the female, the chief's son never succeeded him, but the son of one of his sisters; and as she, by the usual totemic law, was forced to marry in another clan,—that is, to marry a common mortal,—her husband, though the destined father of a demi-god, was treated by her as little better than a slave. She might kill him, if he proved unfaithful; but he was forced to submit to her infidelities in silence.

The customs of the Natchez have been described by Du Pratz, Le Petit, Penicaut, and others. Charlevoix visited their temple in 1721, and found it in a somewhat shabby condition. At this time, the Taensas were extinct. In 1729 the Natchez, enraged by the arbitrary conduct of a French commandant, massacred the neighboring settlers, and were in consequence expelled from their country and nearly destroyed. A few still survive, incorporated with the Creeks; but they have lost their peculiar customs. [Parkman's note]

canoes, among the canes along the margin of the water. They fled at sight of the Frenchmen. La Salle sent men to reconnoitre, who, as they struggled through the marsh, were greeted with a shower of arrows; while from the neighboring village of the Quinipissas,[2] invisible behind the canebrake, they heard the sound of an Indian drum and the whoops of the mustering warriors. La Salle, anxious to keep the peace with all the tribes along the river, recalled his men, and pursued his voyage. A few leagues below they saw a cluster of Indian lodges on the left bank, apparently void of inhabitants. They landed, and found three of them filled with corpses. It was a village of the Tangibao, sacked by their enemies only a few days before.

And now they neared their journey's end. On the sixth of April the river divided itself into three broad channels. La Salle followed that of the west, and Dautray that of the east; while Tonty took the middle passage. As he drifted down the turbid current, between the low and marshy shores, the brackish water changed to brine, and the breeze grew fresh with the salt breath of the sea. Then the broad bosom of the great Gulf opened on his sight, tossing its restless billows, limitless, voiceless, lonely as when born of chaos, without a sail, without a sign of life.

La Salle, in a canoe, coasted the marshy borders of the sea; and then the reunited parties assembled on a spot of dry ground, a short distance above the mouth of the river. Here a column was made ready, bearing the arms of France, and inscribed with the words, "LOUIS LE GRAND, ROY DE FRANCE ET DE NAVARRE, RÈGNE; LE NEUVIÈME AVRIL, 1682."

The Frenchmen were mustered under arms; and while the New England Indians and their squaws looked on in wondering silence, they chanted the *Te Deum*, the *Exaudiat*, and the *Domine salvum fac Regem*.[3] Then, amid volleys of musketry and shouts of *Vive le Roi*, La Salle planted the column in its place, and, standing near it, proclaimed in a loud voice,—

"In the name of the most high, mighty, invincible, and victorious Prince, Louis the Great, by the grace of God King of France and of Navarre, Fourteenth of that name, I, this ninth day of April, one thousand six hundred and eighty-two, in virtue of the commission of his Majesty, which I hold in my hand, and which may be seen by all whom it may concern, have taken, and do now take, in the name of his Majesty and of his successors to the crown, possession of this country of Louisiana, the seas, harbors, ports, bays, adjacent straits, and all the nations, peoples, provinces, cities, towns, villages, mines, minerals, fisheries, streams, and rivers, within the extent of the said Louisiana, from the mouth of the great river St. Louis, otherwise called the Ohio, . . . as also along the river Colbert, or Mississippi, and the rivers which discharge themselves thereinto, from its source beyond the country of the Nadouessioux . . . as far as its mouth at the sea, or Gulf of Mexico, and also to the mouth of the River of Palms, upon the assurance we have had from the natives of these countries that we are the first Europeans who have

---

2. In St. Charles County, on the left bank, not far above New Orleans. [Parkman's note]

3. Latin hymns in praise of God and the king.

descended or ascended the said river Colbert; hereby protesting against all who may hereafter undertake to invade any or all of these aforesaid countries, peoples, or lands, to the prejudice of the rights of his Majesty, acquired by the consent of the nations dwelling herein. Of which, and of all else that is needful, I hereby take to witness those who hear me, and demand an act of the notary here present.[4]

Shouts of *Vive le Roi* and volleys of musketry responded to his words. Then a cross was planted beside the column, and a leaden plate buried near it, bearing the arms of France, with a Latin inscription, *Ludovicus Magnus regnat.*[5] The weather-beaten voyagers joined their voices in the grand hymn of the *Vexilla Regis*[6]:—

> "The banners of Heaven's King advance,
> The mystery of the Cross shines forth;"

and renewed shouts of *Vive le Roi* closed the ceremony.

On that day, the realm of France received on parchment a stupendous accession. The fertile plains of Texas; the vast basin of the Mississippi, from its frozen northern springs to the sultry borders of the Gulf; from the woody ridges of the Alleghanies to the bare peaks of the Rocky Mountains,—a region of savannas and forests, sun-cracked deserts, and grassy prairies, watered by a thousand rivers, ranged by a thousand warlike tribes, passed beneath the sceptre of the Sultan of Versailles; and all by virtue of a feeble human voice, inaudible at half a mile.

---

4. In the passage omitted above, for the sake of brevity, the Ohio is mentioned as being called also the *Olighin-* (Alleghany) *Sipou,* and *Chukagoua;* and La Salle declares that he takes possession of the country with the consent of the nations dwelling in it, of whom he names the Chaouanons (Shawanoes), Kious, or Nadouessious (Sioux), Chikachas (Chickasaws), Motantees (?), Illinois, Mitchigamias, Arkansas, Natchez, and Koroas. This alleged consent is, of course, mere farce. If there could be any doubt as to the meaning of the words of La Salle, as recorded in the *Procès Verbal de la Prise de Possession de la Louisiane,* it would be set at rest by Le Clerc, who says: "Le Sieur de la Salle prit au nom de sa Majesté possession de ce fleuve, *de toutes les rivières qui y entrent, et de tous les pays qu'elles arrosent.*" These words are borrowed from the report of La Salle (see Thomassy, 14). A copy of the original *Procès Verbal* is before me. It bears the name of Jacques de la Metairie, Notary of Fort Frontenac, who was one of the party. [Parkman's note]

5. Ruled by Louis the Great.

6. Banner (or flag) of the king.

Rebecca Harding Davis
(1831–1910)

Rebecca Harding was brought up in the riverside mill town of Wheeling, Virginia, returning to her birthplace of Washington, Pennsylvania, for her only formal education. Her English immigrant father, a successful businessman and city official, considered American life "vulgar" and devoted his evenings to English literature, especially the works of Shakespeare. Distant and authoritarian, he was the centerpiece of a household dedicated to his needs and comforts. Rebecca, the eldest child, was taught by her mother at home; there were no public schools, and the family hired tutors only to teach her younger brothers.

At fourteen she was sent to a ladies' seminary, from which she graduated as valedictorian. Washington was also home to a college for men and a stop on the national lecture circuit. The town physician, Francis LeMoyne, was a radical reformer who had been the vice presidential candidate on the Abolitionist Party ticket in 1840. Thus, despite the inadequacies of single-sex "finishing school" education, Harding had access, during her three years away from home, to a variety of current reading materials and ideas; it was to be the sole outside influence of her youth. She could not attend the only college in the nation that accepted women at that time, Oberlin, because its liberal attitudes were not acceptable to her family.

Leaving school, Harding retreated once again into the protective family circle, where she found little intellectual companionship. Her enthusiasm for native American writing was not shared by her father, and her family was indifferent, if not hostile, to new ideas such as abolition, women's rights, or relief for overworked laborers. She followed her brother's college course of study, but described this self-education as "a curse" because she could not use it. Her most important asset was her close observation of life around her, carried on despite the severe restrictions imposed on middle-class Victorian women.

Life in the Iron Mills, *her first publication, appeared after thirteen years of this intellectual exile. The* Atlantic Monthly, *to which she submitted the piece, was the nation's most prestigious magazine, and she was so sure of rejection that she carried publisher James T. Fields's acceptance letter around for "a half a day without opening it." With its April 1861 publi-*

cation, Iron Mills *drew an enthusiastic response from critics and the reading public as well as a note of encouragement from Nathaniel Hawthorne, whose stories of American life had been so important to Harding as a young reader.*

The advent of the Civil War strained her city—now the capital of a separate pro-Union state, West Virginia—and her family, sympathetic to the idea of secession. Harding also struggled with inner conflict between the newer ideals epitomized by Dr. LeMoyne and the certainties expounded by her father. She dramatized her ideological struggle in Margret Howth: A Story of Today. *Fields at first refused the work, judging it too depressing, but accepted the revised version for serial publication beginning in October 1861. "John Lamar," depicting philosophical divisions in her home area, appeared in the April 1862 issue.*

Harding had been corresponding with Annie Fields, the publisher's wife, and L. Clarke Davis, a correspondent for Peterson's Magazine. *Both urged her to take a trip North, and in June 1862 Harding traveled to Boston, Concord, New York, and Philadelphia, where she met Oliver Wendell Holmes, Ralph Waldo Emerson, Louisa May Alcott, and Henry Ward Beecher and renewed her friendship with John Charles and Jessie Fremont. In Concord she stayed with the Hawthornes and shared with the novelist a memorable day's ramble.*

Within a week of meeting Davis, who had been her correspondent for over a year, she agreed to marry him. The wedding took place in March 1863, and the couple moved immediately into Davis's sister's Philadelphia home. Harding's first child, named Richard Harding Davis to honor her deceased father, was born in April 1864. He was destined to achieve, in his time, a greater reputation as a writer than his mother. A second son and a daughter were born, but Rebecca Harding Davis wrote steadily until her last years. Waiting for the Verdict, *a study of the problems facing the country after the abolition of slavery appeared in 1868, followed by* John Andross *(1874) on political corruption.* Silhouettes of American Life *(1892), a story collection, was both a critical and a popular success. Despite her extensive output, Harding never achieved the promise of her first publication, and when she died at age seventy-nine, her work was nearly forgotten. Obituary notices identified her only as the mother of Richard Harding Davis.*

"John Lamar" is taken from *The Atlantic Monthly* (April 1862).

John Lamar

THE GUARD-HOUSE was, in fact, nothing but a shed in the middle of a stubble-field. It had been built for a cider-press last summer; but since Captain Dorr had gone into the army, his regiment had camped over half his plantation, and the shed was boarded up, with heavy wickets at either end, to hold whatever prisoners might fall into their hands from Floyd's[1] forces. It was a strong point for the Federal troops, his farm,—a sort of wedge in the Rebel Cheat counties of Western Virginia. Only one prisoner was in the guard-house now. The sentry, a raw boat-hand from Illinois, gaped incessantly at him through the bars, not sure if the "Secesh" were limbed and headed like other men; but the November fog was so thick that he could discern nothing but a short, squat man, in brown clothes and white hat, heavily striding to and fro. A negro was crouching outside, his knees cuddled in his arms to keep warm: a field-hand, you could be sure from the face, a grisly patch of flabby black, with a dull eluding word of something, you could not tell what, in the points of eyes,—treachery or gloom. The prisoner stopped, cursing him about something: the only answer was a lazy rub of the heels.

"Got any 'baccy, Mars' John?" he whined, in the middle of the hottest oath.

The man stopped abruptly, turning his pockets inside out.

"That's all, Ben," he said, kindly enough. "Now begone, you black devil!"

"Dem's um, Mars'! Goin' 'mediate,"—catching the tobacco, and lolling down full length as his master turned off again.

Dave Hall, the sentry, stared reflectively, and sat down.

"Ben? Who air you next?"—nursing his musket across his knees, baby-fashion.

Ben measured him with one eye, polished the quid in his greasy hand, and looked at it.

"Pris'ner o' war," he mumbled, finally,—contemptuously; for Dave's trousers were in rags like his own, and his chilblained toes stuck through the shoe-tops. Cheap white trash, clearly.

"Yer master's some at swearin'. Heow many, neow, hes he like you, down to Georgy?"

The boatman's bony face was gathering a woful pity. He had enlisted to free the Uncle Toms, and carry God's vengeance to the Legrees.[2] Here they were, a pair of them.

---

1. General John Buchanan Floyd (1807–1863), U.S. Secretary of War (1857–1860) and Confederate Brigadier General.

2. Uncle Tom was a sympathetic black character and Simon Legree a vicious white one in Harriet Beecher Stowe's popular novel *Uncle Tom's Cabin* (1852).

Ben squinted another critical survey of the "miss'able Linkinite."[3]

"How many wells hev *yer* poisoned since yer set out?" he muttered.

The sentry stopped.

"How many 'longin' to de Lamars? 'Bout as many as der's dam' Yankees in Richmond 'baccy-houses!"

Something in Dave's shrewd, whitish eye warned him off.

"Ki yi! yer white nigger, yer!" he chuckled, shuffling down the stubble.

Dave clicked his musket,—then, choking down an oath into a grim Methodist psalm, resumed his walk, looking askance at the coarse-moulded face of the prisoner peering through the bars, and the diamond studs in his shirt,—bought with human blood, doubtless. The man was the black curse of slavery itself in the flesh, in his thought somehow, and he hated him accordingly. Our men of the Northwest have enough brawny Covenanter[4] muscle in their religion to make them good haters for opinion's sake.

Lamar, the prisoner, watched him with a lazy drollery in his sluggish black eyes. It died out into sternness, as he looked beyond the sentry. He had seen this Cheat country before; this very plantation was his grandfather's a year ago, when he had come up from Georgia here, and loitered out the summer months with his Virginia cousins, hunting. That was a pleasant summer! Something in the remembrance of it flashed into his eyes, dewy, genial; the man's leather-covered face reddened like a child's. Only a year ago,—and now——The plantation was Charley Dorr's now, who had married Ruth. This very shed he and Dorr had planned last spring, and now Charley held him a prisoner in it. The very thought of Charley Dorr warmed his heart. Why, he could thank God there were such men. True grit, every inch of his little body! There, last summer, how he had avoided Ruth until the day when he (Lamar) was going away!—then he told him he meant to try and win her. "She cared most for you always," Lamar had said, bitterly; "why have you waited so long?" "You loved her first, John, you know." That was like a man! He remembered that even that day, when his pain was breathless and sharp, the words made him know that Dorr was fit to be her husband.

Dorr was his friend. The word meant much to John Lamar. He thought less meanly of himself, when he remembered it. Charley's prisoner! An odd chance! Better that than to have met in battle. He thrust back the thought, the sweat oozing out on his face,—something within him muttering, "For Liberty! I would have killed him, so help me God!"

He had brought despatches to General Lee, that he might see Charley, and the old place, and—Ruth again; there was a gnawing hunger in his heart to see them. Fool! what was he to them? The man's face grew slowly pale, as that of a savage or an animal does, when the wound is deep and inward.

The November day was dead, sunless: since morning the sky had had only enough life in it to sweat out a few muddy drops, that froze as they fell:

---

3. Follower of Abraham Lincoln.

4 Scotch Presbyterian; many adherents of that faith were martyred in the mid-seventeenth century.

the cold numbed his mouth as he breathed it. This stubbly slope was where he and his grandfather had headed the deer: it was covered with hundreds of dirty, yellow tents now. Around there were hills like uncouth monsters, swathed in ice, holding up the soggy sky; shivering pine-forests; unmeaning, dreary flats; and the Cheat, coiled about the frozen sinews of the hills, limp and cold, like a cord tying a dead man's jaws. Whatever outlook of joy or worship this region had borne on its face in time gone, it turned to him to-day nothing but stagnation, a great death. He wondered idly, looking at it, (for the old Huguenot[5] brain of the man was full of morbid fancies,) if it were winter alone that had deadened color and pulse out of these full-blooded hills, or if they could know the colder horror crossing their threshold, and forgot to praise God as it came.

Over that farthest ridge the house had stood. The guard (he had been taken by a band of Snake-hunters,[6] back in the hills) had brought him past it. It was a heap of charred rafters. "Burned in the night," they said, "when the old Colonel was alone." They were very willing to show him this, as it was done by his own party, the Secession "Bush-whackers"; took him to the wood-pile to show him where his grandfather had been murdered, (there was a red mark,) and buried, his old hands above the ground. "Colonel said 't was a job fur us to pay up; so we went to the village an' hed a scrimmage,"—pointing to gaps in the hedges where the dead Bush-whackers yet lay unburied. He looked at them, and at the besotted faces about him, coolly. Snake-hunters and Bush-whackers, he knew, both armies used in Virginia as tools for rapine and murder: the sooner the Devil called home his own, the better. And yet, it was not God's fault, surely, that there were such tools in the North, any more than that in the South Ben was—Ben. Something was rotten in freer States than Denmark, he thought.

One of the men went into the hedge, and brought out a child's golden ringlet as a trophy. Lamar glanced in, and saw the small face in its woollen hood, dimpled yet, though dead for days. He remembered it. Jessy Birt, the ferryman's little girl. She used to come up to the house every day for milk. He wondered for which flag *she* died. Ruth was teaching her to write. *Ruth!* Some old pain hurt him just then, nearer than even the blood of the old man or the girl crying to God from the ground. The sergeant mistook the look. "They'll be buried," he said, gruffly. "Ye brought it on yerselves." And so led him to the Federal camp.

The afternoon grew colder, as he stood looking out of the guard-house. Snow began to whiten through the gray. He thrust out his arm through the wicket, his face kindling with childish pleasure, as he looked closer at the fairy stars and crowns on his shaggy sleeve. If Floy were here! She never had seen snow. When the flakes had melted off, he took a case out of his pocket to look at Floy. His sister,—a little girl who had no mother, nor father, nor lover, but Lamar. The man among his brother officers in Richmond was coarse, arrogant, of dogged courage, keen palate at the table, as

---

5. French Protestant sect of the sixteenth and seventeenth centuries.
6. Union guerrillas.

keen eye on the turf. Sickly little Floy, down at home, knew the way to
something below all this: just as they of the Rommany[7] blood see below the
muddy boulders of the streets the enchanted land of Boabdil bare beneath.
Lamar polished the ivory painting with his breath, remembering that he
had drunk nothing for days. A child's face, of about twelve, delicate,—a
breath of fever or cold would shatter such weak beauty; big, dark eyes, (her
mother was pure Castilian,) out of which her little life looked irresolute into
the world, uncertain what to do there. The painter, with an unapt fancy, had
clustered about the Southern face the Southern emblem, buds of the mag-
nolia, unstained, as yet, as pearl. It angered Lamar, remembering how the
creamy whiteness of the full-blown flower exhaled passion of which the
crimsonest rose knew nothing,—a content, ecstasy, in animal life. Would
Floy——Well, God help them both! they needed help. Three hundred souls
was a heavy weight for those thin little hands to hold sway over,—to lead to
hell or heaven. Up North they could have worked for her, and gained only
her money. So Lamar reasoned, like a Georgian: scribbling a letter to "My
Baby" on the wrapper of a newspaper,—drawing the shapes of the snowflakes,—telling her he had reached their grandfather's plantation, but "have
not seen our Cousin Ruth yet, of whom you may remember I have told
you, Floy. When you grow up, I should like you to be just such a woman; so
remember, my darling, if I"——He scratched the last words out: why
should he hint to her that he could die? Holding his life loose in his hand,
though, had brought things closer to him lately,—God and death, this war,
the meaning of it all. But he would keep his brawny body between these
terrible realities and Floy, yet awhile. "I want you," he wrote, "to leave the
plantation, and go with your old maumer to the village. It will be safer
there." He was sure the letter would reach her. He had a plan to escape to-
night, and he could put it into a post inside the lines. Ben was to get a small
hand-saw that would open the wicket; the guards were not hard to elude.
Glancing up, he saw the negro stretched by a camp-fire, listening to the
gaunt boatman, who was off duty. Preaching Abolitionism, doubtless: he
could hear Ben's derisive shouts of laughter. "And so, good bye, Baby Florence!" he scrawled. "I wish I could send you some of this snow, to show
you what the floor of heaven is like."

While the snow fell faster without, he stopped writing, and began idly
drawing a map of Georgia on the tan-bark with a stick. Here the Federal
troops could effect a landing: he knew the defences at that point. If they did?
He thought of these Snake-hunters who had found in the war a peculiar
road for themselves downward with no gallows to stumble over, fancied he
saw them skulking through the fields at Cedar Creek, closing around the
house, and behind them a mass of black faces and bloody bayonets. Floy
alone, and he here,—like a rat in a trap! "God keep my little girl!" he wrote,
unsteadily. "God bless you, Floy!" He gasped for breath, as if he had been
writing with his heart's blood. Folding up the paper, he hid it inside his shirt

---

7. Gypsy.

and began his dogged walk, calculating the chances of escape. Once out of this shed, he could baffle a blood-hound, he knew the hills so well.

His head bent down, he did not see a man who stood looking at him over the wicket. Captain Dorr. A puny little man, with thin yellow hair, and womanish face: but not the less the hero of his men,—they having found out, somehow, that muscle was not the solidest thing to travel on in wartimes. Our regiments of "roughs" were not altogether crowned with laurel at Manassas![8] So the men built more on the old Greatheart soul in the man's blue eyes: one of those souls born and bred pure, sent to teach, that can find breath only in the free North. His hearty "Hillo!" startled Lamar.

"How are you, old fellow?" he said, unlocking the gate and coming in.

Lamar threw off his wretched thoughts, glad to do it. What need to borrow trouble? He liked a laugh,—had a lazy, jolly humor of his own. Dorr had finished drill, and come up, as he did every day, to freshen himself with an hour's talk to this warm, blundering fellow. In this dismal war-work, (though his whole soul was in that, too,) it was like putting your hands to a big blaze. Dorr had no near relations; Lamar—they had played marbles together—stood to him where a younger brother might have stood. Yet, as they talked, he could not help his keen eye seeing him just as he was.

Poor John! he thought: the same uncouth-looking effort of humanity that he had been at Yale. No wonder the Northern boys jeered him, with his slothways, his mouthed English, torpid eyes, and brain shut up in that worst of mud-moulds,—belief in caste. Even now, going up and down the tan-bark, his step was dead, sodden, like that of a man in whose life God had not yet wakened the full live soul. It was wakening, though, Dorr thought. Some pain or passion was bringing the man in him out of the flesh, vigilant, alert, aspirant. A different man from Dorr.

In fact, Lamar was just beginning to think for himself, and of course his thoughts were defiant, intolerant. He did not comprehend how his companion could give his heresies such quiet welcome, and pronounce sentence of death on them so coolly. Because Dorr had gone farther up the mountain, had he the right to make him follow in the same steps? The right,—that was it. By brute force, too? Human freedom, eh? Consequently, their talks were stormy enough. To-day, however, they were on trivial matters.

"I've brought the General's order for your release at last, John. It confines you to this district, however."

Lamar shook his head.

"No parole for me! My stake outside is too heavy for me to remain a prisoner on anything but compulsion. I mean to escape, if I can. Floy has nobody but me, you know, Charley."

There was a moment's silence.

"I wish," said Dorr, half to himself, "the child was with her cousin Ruth. If she could make her a woman like herself!"

---

8. A town in northeast Virgina. The battles of Bull Run were fought there. The first battle (July 21, 1861) ended in a panicked retreat by the Union Army. The second battle of Bull Run (August 29–30, 1862) was also a Confederate victory.

"You are kind," Lamar forced out, thinking of what might have been a year ago.

Dorr had forgotten. He had just kissed little Ruth at the door-step, coming away: thinking, as he walked up to camp, how her clear thought, narrow as it was, was making his own higher, more just; wondering if the tears on her face last night, when she got up from her knees after prayer, might not help as much in the great cause of truth as the life he was ready to give. He was so used to his little wife now, that he could look to no hour of his past life, nor of the future coming ages of event and work, where she was not present,—very flesh of his flesh, heart of his heart. A gulf lay between them and the rest of the world. It was hardly probable he could see her as a woman towards whom another man looked across the gulf, dumb, hopeless, defrauded of his right.

"She sent you some flowers, by the way, John,—the last in the yard,— and bade me be sure and bring you down with me. Your own colors, you see?—to put you in mind of home,"—pointing to the crimson asters flaked with snow.

The man smiled faintly: the smell of the flowers choked him: he laid them aside. God knows he was trying to wring out this bitter old thought: he could not look in Dorr's frank eyes while it was there. He must escape to-night: he never would come near them again, in this world, or beyond death,—never! He thought of that like a man going to drag through eternity with half his soul gone. Very well: there was man enough left in him to work honestly and bravely, and to thank God for that good pure love he yet had. He turned to Dorr with a flushed face, and began talking of Floy in hearty earnest,—glancing at Ben coming up the hill, thinking that escape depended on him.

"I ordered your man up," said Captain Dorr. "Some canting Abolitionist had him open-mouthed down there."

The negro came in, and stood in the corner, listening while they talked. A gigantic fellow, with a gladiator's muscles. Stronger than that Yankee captain, he thought,—than either of them: better breathed,—drawing the air into his brawny chest. "A man and a brother." Did the fool think he didn't know that before? He had a contempt for Dave and his like. Lamar would have told you Dave's words were true, but despised the man as a crude, unlicked bigot. Ben did the same, with no words for the idea. The negro instinct in him recognized gentle blood by any of its signs,—the transparent animal life, the reticent eye, the mastered voice: he had better men than Lamar at home to learn it from. It is a trait of serfdom, the keen eye to measure the inherent rights of a man to be master. A negro or a Catholic Irishman does not need "Sartor Resartus"[9] to help him to see through any clothes. Ben leaned, half-asleep, against the wall, some old thoughts creeping

---

9. Essay by Thomas Carlyle (1795–1881) published in *Frazer's Magazine* (1833–1834) and in Boston in 1836. The theme is that worldly things are merely cover-ups of the spiritual. The Latin title means "the tailor re-patched."

out of their hiding-places through the torpor, like rats to the sunshine: the boatman's slang had been hot and true enough to rouse them in his brain.

"So, Ben," said his master, as he passed once, "your friend has been persuading you to exchange the cotton-fields at Cedar Creek for New-York alleys, eh?"

"Ki!" laughed Ben, "white darkey. Mind ole dad, Mars' John, as took off in der swamp? Um asked dat Linkinite ef him saw dad up Norf. Guess him's free now. Ki! ole dad!"

"The swamp was the place for him," said Lamar. "I remember."

"Dunno," said the negro, surlily: "him 's dad, af'er all: tink him's free now,"—and mumbled down into a monotonous drone about

Oh yo, bredern, is yer gwine ober Jordern?

Half-asleep, they thought,—but with dull questionings at work in his brain, some queer notions about freedom, of that unknown North, mostly mixed with his remembrance of his father, a vicious old negro, that in Pennsylvania would have worked out his salvation in the under cell of the penitentiary, but in Georgia, whipped into heroism, had betaken himself into the swamp, and never returned. Tradition among the Lamar slaves said he had got off to Ohio, of which they had as clear an idea as most of us have of heaven. At any rate, old Kite became a mystery, to be mentioned with awe at fish-bakes and barbecues. He was this uncouth wretch's father,—do you understand? The flabby-faced boy, flogged in the cotton-field for whining after his dad, or hiding away part of his flitch and molasses for months in hopes the old man would come back, was rather a comical object, you would have thought. Very different his, from the feeling with which you left your mother's grave,—though as yet we have not invented names for the emotions of those people. We'll grant that it hurt Ben a little, however. Even the young polypus, when it is torn from the old one, bleeds a drop or two, they say. As he grew up, the great North glimmered through his thought, a sort of big field,—a paradise of no work, no flogging, and white bread every day, where the old man sat and ate his fill.

The second point in Ben's history was that he fell in love. Just as you did,—with the difference, of course: though the hot sun, or the perpetual foot upon his breast, does not make our black Prometheus[1] less fierce in his agony of hope or jealousy than you, I am afraid. It was Nan, a pale mulatto house-servant, that the field-hand took into his dull, lonesome heart to make life of, with true-love defiance of caste. I think Nan liked him very truly. She was lame and sickly, and if Ben was black and a picker, and stayed in the quarters, he was strong, like a master to her in some ways: the only thing she could call hers in the world was the love the clumsy boy gave her. White women feel in that way sometimes, and it makes them very tender to men not their equals. However, old Mrs. Lamar, before she died, gave her house-servants their free papers, and Nan was among them. So she set off,

---

1. A figure of Greek mythology who stole fire from Olympus in defiance of Zeus.

with all the finery little Floy could give her: went up into that great, dim North. She never came again.

The North swallowed up all Ben knew or felt outside of his hot, hated work, his dread of a lashing on Saturday night. All the pleasure left him was 'possum and hominy for Sunday's dinner. It did not content him. The spasmodic religion of the field-negro does not teach endurance. So it came, that the slow tide of discontent ebbing in everybody's heart towards some unreached sea set in his ignorant brooding towards that vague country which the only two who cared for him had found. If he forgot it through the dogged, sultry days, he remembered it when the overseer scourged the dull tiger-look into his eyes, or when, husking corn with the others at night, the smothered negro-soul, into which their masters dared not look, broke out in their wild, melancholy songs. Aimless, unappealing, yet no prayer goes up to God more keen in its pathos. You find, perhaps, in Beethoven's seventh symphony the secrets of your heart made manifest, and suddenly think of a Somewhere to come, where your hope waits for you with late fulfilment. Do not laugh at Ben, then, if he dully told in his song the story of all he had lost, or gave to his heaven a local habitation and a name.

From the place where he stood now, as his master and Dorr walked up and down, he could see the purplish haze beyond which the sentry had told him lay the North. The North! Just beyond the ridge. There was a pain in his head, looking at it; his nerves grew cold and rigid, as yours do when something wrings your heart sharply: for there are nerves in these black carcasses, thicker, more quickly stung to madness than yours. Yet if any savage longing, smouldering for years, was heating to madness now in his brain, there was no sign of it in his face. Vapid, with sordid content, the huge jaws munching tobacco slowly, only now and then the beady eye shot a sharp glance after Dorr. The sentry had told him the Northern army had come to set the slaves free; he watched the Federal officer keenly.

"What ails you, Ben?" said his master. "Thinking over your friend's sermon?"

Ben's stolid laugh was ready.

"Done forgot dat, Mars'. Would n't go, nohow. Since Mars' sold dat cussed Joe, gorry good times 't home. Dam' Abolitioner say we ums all goin' Norf,"—with a stealthy glance at Dorr.

"That's more than your philanthropy bargains for, Charley," laughed Lamar.

The men stopped; the negro skulked nearer, his whole senses sharpened into hearing. Dorr's clear face was clouded.

"This slave question must be kept out of the war. It puts a false face on it."

"I thought one face was what it needed," said Lamar. "You have too many slogans. Strong government, tariff, Sumter,[2] a bit of bunting, eleven

---

2. The bombardment of Fort Sumter, in the harbor of Charleston, South Carolina, by Confederate guns on April 12, 1861 was the incident that opened the Civil War.

dollars a month. It ought to be a vital truth that would give soul and *vim* to a body with the differing members of your army. You, with your ideal theory, and Billy Wilson with his 'Blood and Baltimore!' Try human freedom. That's high and sharp and broad."

Ben drew a step closer.

"You are shrewd, Lamar. I am to go below all constitutions or expediency or existing rights, and tell Ben here that he is free? When once the Government accepts that doctrine, you, as a Rebel, must be let alone."

The slave was hid back in the shade.

"Dorr," said Lamar, "you know I'm a groping, ignorant fellow, but it seems to me that prating of constitutions and existing rights is surface talk; there is a broad common-sense underneath, by whose laws the world is governed, which your statesmen don't touch often. You in the North, in your dream of what shall be, shut your eyes to what is. You want a republic where every man's voice shall be heard in the council, and the majority shall rule. Granting that the free population are educated to a fitness for this,— (God forbid I should grant it with the Snake-hunters before my eyes!)— look here!"

He turned round, and drew the slave out into the light: he crouched down, gaping vacantly at them.

"There is Ben. What, in God's name, will you do with him? Keep him a slave, and chatter about self-government? Pah! The country is paying in blood for the lie, to-day. Educate him for freedom, by putting a musket in his hands? We have this mass of heathendom drifted on our shores by your will as well as mine. Try to bring them to a level with the whites by a wrench, and you'll waken out of your dream to a sharp reality. Your Northern philosophy ought to be old enough to teach you that spasms in the body-politic shake off no atom of disease,—that reform, to be enduring, must be patient, gradual, inflexible as the Great Reformer. 'The mills of God,' the old proverb says, 'grind surely.' But, Dorr, they grind exceeding slow!"

Dorr watched Lamar with an amused smile. It pleased him to see his brain waking up, eager, vehement. As for Ben, crouching there, if they talked of him like a clod, heedless that his face deepened in stupor, that his eyes had caught a strange, gloomy treachery,—we all do the same, you know.

"What is your remedy, Lamar? You have no belief in the right of Secession, I know," said Dorr.

"It's a bad instrument for a good end. Let the white Georgian come out of his sloth, and the black will rise with him. Jefferson Davis[3] may not intend it, but God does. When we have our Lowell,[4] our New York, when we are a self-sustaining people instead of lazy land-princes, Ben here will have

---

3. Jefferson Davis (1808–1889) was elected President of the Confederacy and inaugurated in February 1861.

4. James Russell Lowell (1819–1891), New England poet, Harvard professor, and abolitionist.

climbed the second of the great steps of Humanity. Do you laugh at us?"
said Lamar, with a quiet self-reliance. "Charley, it needs only work and
ambition to cut the brute away from my face, and it will leave traits very
like your own. Ben's father was a Guinea[5] fetich-worshipper; when we stand
where New England does, Ben's son will be ready for his freedom."

"And while you theorize," laughed Dorr, "I hold you a prisoner, John,
and Ben knows it is his right to be free. He will not wait for the grinding of
the mill, I fancy."

Lamar did not smile. It was womanish in the man, when the life of great
nations hung in doubt before them, to go back so constantly to little Floy
sitting in the lap of her old black maumer. But he did it,—with the quick
thought that to-night he must escape, that death lay in delay.

While Dorr talked, Lamar glanced significantly at Ben. The negro was
not slow to understand,—with a broad grin, touching his pocket, from which
projected the dull end of a hand-saw. I wonder what sudden pain made the
negro rise just then, and come close to his master, touching him with a
strange affection and remorse in his tired face, as though he had done him
some deadly wrong.

"What is it, old fellow?" said Lamar, in his boyish way. "Homesick, eh?
There's a little girl in Georgia that will be glad to see you and your master,
and take precious good care of us when she gets us safe again. That's true,
Ben!" laying his hand kindly on the man's shoulder, while his eyes went
wandering off to the hills lying South.

"Yes, Mars'," said Ben, in a low voice, suddenly bringing a blacking-
brush, and beginning to polish his master's shoes,—thinking, while he did
it, of how often Mars' John had interfered with the overseers to save him
from a flogging,—(Lamar, in his lazy way, was kind to his slaves,)—thinking of little Mist' Floy with an odd tenderness and awe, as a gorilla might of
a white dove: trying to think thus,—the simple, kindly nature of the negro
struggling madly with something beneath, new and horrible. He understood enough of the talk of the white men to know that there was no help
for him,—none. Always a slave. Neither you nor I can ever know what
those words meant to him. The pale purple mist where the North lay was
never to be passed. His dull eyes turned to its constantly,—with a strange
look, such as the lost women might have turned to the door, when Jesus
shut it: they forever outside. There was a way to help himself? The stubby
black fingers holding the brush grew cold and clammy,—noting withal, the
poor wretch in his slavish way, that his master's clothes were finer than the
Northern captain's, his hands whiter, and proud that it was so,—holding
Lamar's foot daintily, trying to see himself in the shoe, smoothing down
the trousers with a boorish, affectionate touch,—with the same fierce whisper in his ear, Would the shoes ever be cleaned again? would the foot move
to-morrow?

---

5. Coastal area of West Africa.

It grew late. Lamar's supper was brought up from Captain Dorr's, and placed on the bench. He poured out a goblet of water.

"Come, Charley, let's drink. To Liberty! It is a war-cry for Satan or Michael."

They drank, laughing, while Ben stood watching. Dorr turned to go, but Lamar called him back,—stood resting his hand on his shoulder: he never thought to see him again, you know.

"Look at Ruth, yonder," said Dorr, his face lighting. "She is coming to meet us. She thought you would be with me."

Lamar looked gravely down at the low field-house and the figure at the gate. He thought he could see the small face and earnest eyes, though it was far off, and night was closing.

"She is waiting for you, Charley. Go down. Good night, old chum!"

If it cost any effort to say it, Dorr saw nothing of it.

"Good night, Lamar! I'll see you in the morning."

He lingered. His old comrade looked strangely alone and desolate.

"John!"

"What is it, Dorr?"

"If I could tell the Colonel you would take the oath? For Floy's sake."

The man's rough face reddened.

"You should know me better. Good bye."

"Well, well, you are mad. Have you no message for Ruth?"

There was a moment's silence.

"Tell her I say, God bless her!"

Dorr stopped and looked keenly in his face,—then, coming back, shook hands again, in a different way from before, speaking in a lower voice,—

"God help us all, John! Good night!"—and went slowly down the hill.

It was nearly night, and bitter cold. Lamar stood where the snow drifted in on him, looking out through the horizonless gray.

"Come out o' dem cold, Mars' John," whined Ben, pulling at his coat.

As the night gathered, the negro was haunted with a terrified wish to be kind to his master. Something told him that the time was short. Here and there through the far night some tent-fire glowed in a cone of ruddy haze, through which the thick-falling snow shivered like flakes of light. Lamar watched only the square block of shadow where Dorr's house stood. The door opened at last, and a broad, cheerful gleam shot out red darts across the white waste without; then he saw two figures go in together. They paused a moment; he put his head against the bars, straining his eyes, and saw that the woman turned, shading her eyes with her hand, and looked up to the side of the mountain where the guard-house lay,—with a kindly look, perhaps, for the prisoner out in the cold. A kind look: that was all. The door shut on them. Forever: so, good night, Ruth!

He stood there for an hour or two, leaning his head against the muddy planks, smoking. Perhaps, in his coarse fashion, he took the trouble of his manhood back to the same God he used to pray to long ago. When he turned at last, and spoke, it was with a quiet, strong voice, like one who would fight through life in a manly way. There was a grating sound at the back of the shed: it was Ben, sawing through the wicket, the guard having lounged off to supper. Lamar watched him, noticing that the negro was unusually silent. The plank splintered, and hung loose.

"Done gone, Mars' John, now,"—leaving it, and beginning to replenish the fire.

"That's right, Ben. We'll start in the morning. That sentry at two o'clock sleeps regularly."

Ben chuckled, heaping up the sticks.

"Go on down to the camp, as usual. At two, Ben, remember! We will be free to-night, old boy!"

The black face looked up from the clogging smoke with a curious stare.

"Ki! we'll be free to-night, Mars'!"—gulping his breath.

Soon after, the sentry unlocked the gate, and he shambled off out into the night. Lamar, left alone, went closer to the fire, and worked busily at some papers he drew from his pocket: maps and schedules. He intended to write until two o'clock; but the blaze dying down, he wrapped his blanket about him, and lay down on the heaped straw, going on sleepily, in his brain, with his calculations.

The negro, in the shadow of the shed, watched him. A vague fear beset him,—of the vast, white cold,—the glowering mountains,—of himself; he clung to the familiar face, like a man drifting out into an unknown sea, clutching some relic of the shore. When Lamar fell asleep, he wandered uncertainly towards the tents. The world had grown new, strange; was he Ben, picking cotton in the swamp-edge?—plunging his fingers with a shudder in the icy drifts. Down in the glowing torpor of the Santilla flats, where the Lamar plantations lay, Ben had slept off as maddening hunger for life and freedom as this of to-day; but here, with the winter air stinging every nerve to life, with the perpetual mystery of the mountains terrifying his bestial nature down, the strength of the man stood up: groping, blind, malignant, it may be; but whose fault was that? He was half-frozen: the physical pain sharpened the keen doubt conquering his thought. He sat down in the crusted snow, looking vacantly about him, a man, at last,—but wakening, like a new-born soul, into a world of unutterable solitude. Wakened dully, slowly; sitting there far into the night, pondering stupidly on his old life; crushing down and out the old parasite affection for his master, the old fears, the old weight threatening to press out his thin life; the muddy blood heating, firing with the same heroic dream that bade Tell and Garibaldi⁶ lift up their hands to God, and cry aloud that they were men and free: the same,—God-given, burning in the imbruted veins of a Guinea slave. To what end? May God be merciful to America while she answers the question! He sat, rubbing his cracked, bleeding feet, glancing stealthily at the southern hills. Beyond them lay all that was past; in an hour he would follow Lamar back to—what? He lifted his hands up to the sky, in his silly

---

6. William Tell, legendary Swiss patriot; Giuseppe Garibaldi (1807–1882), Italian revolutionary.

way sobbing hot tears. "Gor-a'mighty, Mars' Lord, I 'se tired," was all the prayer he made. The pale purple mist was gone from the North; the ridge behind which love, freedom waited, struck black across the sky, a wall of iron. He looked at it drearily. Utterly alone: he had always been alone. He got up at last, with a sigh.

"It's a big world,"—with a bitter chuckle,—"but der's no room in it fur poor Ben."

He dragged himself through the snow to a light in a tent where a voice in a wild drone, like that he had heard at negro camp-meetings, attracted him. He did not go in: stood at the tent-door, listening. Two or three of the guard stood around, leaning on their muskets; in the vivid fire-light rose the gaunt figure of the Illinois boatman, swaying to and fro as he preached. For the men were honest, God-fearing souls, members of the same church, and Dave, in all integrity of purpose, read aloud to them,—the cry of Jeremiah[7] against the foul splendors of the doomed city,—waving, as he spoke, his bony arm to the South. The shrill voice was that of a man wrestling with his Maker. The negro's fired brain caught the terrible meaning of the words,—found speech in it: the wide, dark night, the solemn silence of the men, were only fitting audience.

The man caught sight of the slave, and, laying down his book, began one of those strange exhortations in the manner of his sect. Slow at first, full of unutterable pity. There was room for pity. Pointing to the human brute crouching there, made once in the image of God,—the saddest wreck on His green footstool: to the great stealthy body, the revengeful jaws, the foreboding eyes. Soul, brains,—a man, wifeless, homeless, nationless, hawked, flung from trader to trader for a handful of dirty shinplasters. "Lord God of hosts," cried the man, lifting up his trembling hands, "lay not this sin to our charge!" There was a scar on Ben's back where the lash had buried itself: it stung now in the cold. He pulled his clothes tighter, that they should not see it; the scar and the words burned into his heart: the childish nature of the man was gone; the vague darkness in it took a shape and name. The boatman had been praying for him; the low words seemed to shake the night:—

"Hear the prayer of Thy servant, and his supplications! Is not this what Thou hast chosen: to loose the bands, to undo the heavy burdens, and let the oppressed go free? O Lord, hear! O Lord, hearken and do! Defer not for Thine own sake, O my God!"

"What shall I do?" said the slave, standing up.

The boatman paced slowly to and fro, his voice chording in its dull monotone with the smothered savage muttering in the negro's brain.

"The day of the Lord cometh; it is night at hand. Who can abide it? What saith the prophet Jeremiah? 'Take up a burden against the South. Cry aloud, spare not. Woe unto Babylon, for the day of her vengeance is come, the day of her visitation! Call together the archers against Babylon; camp

---

7. Old Testament prophet.

against it round about; let none thereof escape. Recompense her: as she hath done unto my people, be it done unto her. A sword is upon Babylon: it shall break in pieces the shepherd and his flock, the man and the woman, the young man and the maid. I will render unto her the evil she hath done in my sight, saith the Lord.'"

It was the voice of God: the scar burned fiercer; the slave came forward boldly,—

"Mars'er, what shall I do?"

"Give the poor devil a musket," said one of the men. "Let him come with us, and strike a blow for freedom."

He took a knife from his belt, and threw it to him, then sauntered off to his tent.

"A blow for freedom?" mumbled Ben, taking it up.

"Let us sing to the praise of God," said the boatman, "the sixty-eighth psalm," lining it out while they sang,—the scattered men joining, partly to keep themselves awake. In old times David's harp charmed away the demon from a human heart. It roused one now, never to be laid again. A dull, droning chant, telling how the God of Vengeance rode upon the wind, swift to loose the fetters of the chained, to make desert the rebellious land; with a chorus, or refrain, in which Ben's wild, melancholy cry sounded like the wail of an avenging spirit:—

> That in the blood of enemies
> Thy foot imbrued may be:
> And of thy dogs dipped in the same
> The tongues thou mayest see.

The meaning of that was plain; he sang it lower and more steadily each time, his body swaying in cadence, the glitter in his eye more steely.

Lamar, asleep in his prison, was wakened by the far-off plaintive song: he roused himself, leaning on one elbow, listening with a half-smile. It was Naomi they sang, he thought,—an old-fashioned Methodist air that Floy had caught from the negroes, and used to sing to him sometimes. Every night, down at home, she would come to his parlor-door to say good-night: he thought he could see the little figure now in its white nightgown, and hear the bare feet pattering on the matting. When he was alone, she would come in, and sit on his lap awhile, and kneel down before she went away, her head on his knee, to say her prayers, as she called it. Only God knew how many times he had remained alone after hearing those prayers, saved from nights of drunken debauch. He thought he felt Floy's pure little hand on his forehead now, as if she were saying her usual "Good night, Bud." He lay down to sleep again, with a genial smile on his face, listening to the hymn.

"It's the same God," he said,—"Floy's and theirs."

Outside, as he slept, a dark figure watched him. The song of the men ceased. Midnight, white and silent, covered the earth. He could hear only the slow breathing of the sleeper. Ben's black face grew ashy pale, but he did not tremble, as he crept, cat-like, up to the wicket, his blubber lips apart, the white teeth clenched.

"It's for Freedom, Mars' Lord!" he gasped, looking up to the sky, as if he expected an answer. "Gor-a'mighty, it 's for Freedom!" And went in.

A belated bird swooped through the cold moonlight into the valley, and vanished in the far mountain-cliffs with a low, fearing cry, as though it had passed through Hades.

They had broken down the wicket: he saw them lay the heavy body on the lumber outside, the black figures hurrying over the snow. He laughed low, savagely, watching them. Free now! The best of them despised him; the years past of cruelty and oppression turned back, fused in a slow, deadly current of revenge and hate, against the race that had trodden him down. He felt the iron muscles of his fingers, looked close at the glittering knife he held, chuckling at the strange smell it bore. Would the Illinois boatman blame him, if it maddened him? And if Ben took the fancy to put it to his throat, what right has he to complain? Has not he also been a dweller in Babylon? He hesitated a moment in the cleft of the hill, choosing his way, exultantly. He did not watch the North now; the quiet old dream of content was gone; his thick blood throbbed and surged with passions of which you and I know nothing: he had a lost life to avenge. His native air, torrid, heavy with latent impurity, drew him back: a fitter breath than this cold snow for the animal in his body, the demon in his soul, to triumph and wallow in. He panted, thinking of the saffron hues of the Santilla flats, of the white, stately dwellings, the men that went in and out from them, quiet, dominant,—feeling the edge of his knife. It was his turn to be master now! He ploughed his way doggedly through the snow,—panting, as he went,—a hotter glow in his gloomy eyes. It was his turn for pleasure now: he would have his fill! Their wine and their gardens and——He did not need to choose a wife from his own color now. He stopped, thinking of little Floy, with her curls and great listening eyes, watching at the door for her brother. He had watched her climb up into his arms and kiss his cheek. She never would do that again! He laughed aloud, shrilly. By God! she should keep the kiss for other lips! Why should he not say it?

Up on the hill the night-air throbbed colder and holier. The guards stood about in the snow, silent, troubled. This was not like a death in battle: it put them in mind of home, somehow. All that the dying man said was, "Water," now and then. He had been sleeping, when struck, and never had thoroughly wakened from his dream. Captain Poole, of the Snake-hunters, had wrapped him in his own blanket, finding nothing more could be done. He went off to have the Colonel summoned now, muttering that it was "a damned shame." They put snow to Lamar's lips constantly, being hot and parched; a woman, Dorr's wife, was crouching on the ground beside him, chafing his hands, keeping down her sobs for fear they would disturb him. He opened his eyes at last, and knew Dorr, who held his head.

"Unfasten my coat, Charley. What makes it so close here?"

Dorr could not speak.

"Shall I lift you up, Captain Lamar?" asked Dave Hall, who stood leaning on his rifle.

He spoke in a subdued tone, Babylon being far off for the moment. Lamar dozed again before he could answer.

"Don't try to move him,—it is too late," said Dorr, sharply.

The moonlight steeped mountain and sky in a fresh whiteness. Lamar's face, paling every moment, hardening, looked in it like some solemn work of an untaught sculptor. There was a breathless silence. Ruth, kneeling beside him, felt his hand grow slowly colder than the snow. He moaned, his voice going fast,—

"At two, Ben, old fellow! We'll be free to-night!"

Dave, stooping to wrap the blanket, felt his hand wet: he wiped it with a shudder.

"As he hath done unto My people, be it done unto him!" he muttered, but the words did not comfort him.

Lamar moved, half-smiling.

"That's right, Floy. What is it she says? 'Now I lay me down'———I forget. Good night. Kiss me, Floy."

He waited,—looked up uneasily. Dorr looked at his wife: she stooped, and kissed his lips. Charley smoothed back the hair from the damp face with as tender a touch as a woman's. Was he dead? The white moonlight was not more still than the calm face.

Suddenly the night-air was shattered by a wild, revengeful laugh from the hill. The departing soul rushed back, at the sound, to life, full consciousness. Lamar started from their hold,—sat up.

"It was Ben," he said, slowly.

In that dying flash of comprehension, it may be, the wrongs of the white man and the black stood clearer to his eyes than ours: the two lives trampled down. The stern face of the boatman bent over him: he was trying to stanch the flowing blood. Lamar looked at him: Hall saw no bitterness in the look,—a quiet, sad question rather, before which his soul lay bare. He felt the cold hand touch his shoulder, saw the pale lips move.

"Was this well done?" they said.

Before Lamar's eyes the rounded arch of gray receded, faded into dark; the negro's fierce laugh filled his ear: some woful thought at the sound wrung his soul, as it halted at the gate. It caught at the simple faith his mother taught him.

"Yea," he said aloud, "though I walk through the valley of the shadow of death, I will fear no evil: for Thou art with me."[8]

Dorr gently drew down the uplifted hand. He was dead.

"It was a manly soul," said the Northern captain, his voice choking, as he straightened the limp hair.

"He trusted in God? A strange delusion!" muttered the boatman.

Yet he did not like that they should leave him alone with Lamar, as they did, going down for help. He paced to and fro, his rifle on his shoulder, arming his heart with strength to accomplish the vengeance of the Lord against

---

8. Psalm 23:4.

Babylon. Yet he could not forget the murdered man sitting there in the calm moonlight, the dead face turned towards the North,—the dead face, whereon little Floy's tears should never fall. The grave, unmoving eyes seemed to the boatman to turn to him with the same awful question. "Was this well done?" they said. He thought in eternity they would rise before him, sad, unanswered. The earth, he fancied, lay whiter, colder,—the heaven farther off; the war, which had become a daily business, stood suddenly before him in all its terrible meaning. God, he thought, had met in judgment with His people. Yet he uttered no cry of vengeance against the doomed city. With the dead face before him, he bent his eyes to the ground, humble, uncertain,— speaking out of the ignorance of his own weak, human soul.

"The day of the Lord is nigh," he said; "it is at hand; and who can abide it?"

George Washington Cable
(1844–1925)

Born in New Orleans, George Washington Cable became the first writer of major talent to portray that city in all its multicultural diversity. With his father from Virginia and his mother from New England, he inherited some of the advantages of an outside observer in a land marked by contradictions and a time wracked by the tragedy of the Civil War and its aftermath. When he was fourteen, his father died, and he went to work to support his mother and sisters. A few years later, the war broke out; when New Orleans fell to the North, Cable joined the Confederate cavalry. A twice-wounded veteran at twenty-one, when the war ended, he clerked in a cotton ware-house and wrote sketches for the New Orleans Picayune. *His first national publication came with the story "'Sieur George," in* Scribner's Monthly *in 1873. This and other sketches gathered in* Old Creole Days *(1879) launched a career that lasted forty years and placed him among the most acclaimed authors of his day.*

Cable's best subject was Creole New Orleans in all its permutations, from those Creoles who were in the strictest sense pure-blooded descen-dants of French or Spanish immigrants to Creole slaves, Creole free Negroes, and people of mixed blood. French was the dominant culture and language. Occasionally, he wrote also of the poorer Cajuns, or Acadians, exiled by the English from Nova Scotia in 1755 to settle in the lowlands of southwestern Louisiana. Few areas have been so thoroughly covered in the work of one writer. Popular in the North, Cable's work was not always appreciated in the South, and when he turned increasingly to the rights of freed blacks, he found himself the target of such hostility in his native state that he moved in 1885 to Northampton, Massachusetts.

Among Cable's later books, The Grandissimes *(1880), a novel, tells of a conflict between Creole families, and* Madame Delphine *(1881) is a story of a New Orleans quadroon.* The Silent South *(1885) and* The Negro Question *(1890) are nonfiction.*

Studies include Arlin Turner, *George W. Cable: A Biography* (1956) and Louis D. Rubin, *George W. Cable: The Life and Times of a Southern Heretic* (1969).

"Posson Jone'"[1]

To Jules St.-Ange—elegant little heathen—there yet remained at manhood a remembrance of having been to school, and of having been taught by a stony-headed Capuchin that the world is round—for example, like a cheese. This round world is a cheese to be eaten through, and Jules had nibbled quite into his cheese-world already at twenty-two.

He realized this as he idled about one Sunday morning where the intersection of Royal and Conti Streets some seventy years ago[2] formed a central corner of New Orleans. Yes, yes, the trouble was he had been wasteful and honest. He discussed the matter with that faithful friend and confidant, Baptiste, his yellow body-servant. They concluded that, papa's patience and *tante's* pin-money having been gnawed away quite to the rind, there were left open only these few easily-enumerated resorts: to go to work—they shuddered; to join Major Innerarity's filibustering expedition; or else—why not?—to try some games of confidence. At twenty-two one must begin to be something. Nothing else tempted; could that avail? One could but try. It is noble to try; and, besides, they were hungry. If one could "make the friendship" of some person from the country, for instance, with money, not expert

---

1. Text from the 1883 edition of *Old Creole Days.*

2. Seventy years before the story's first publication, in *Appleton's Journal*, April 1, 1876, would date the events as in 1806.

at cards or dice, but, as one would say, willing to learn, one might find cause
to say some "Hail Marys."

The sun broke through a clearing sky, and Baptiste pronounced it good
for luck. There had been a hurricane in the night. The weed-grown tile-roofs
were still dripping, and from lofty brick and low adobe walls a rising steam
responded to the summer sunlight. Up-street, and across the Rue du Canal,
one could get glimpses of the gardens in Faubourg Ste.-Marie standing in
silent wretchedness, so many tearful Lucretias, tattered victims of the storm.
Short remnants of the wind now and then came down the narrow street in
erratic puffs heavily laden with odors of broken boughs and torn flowers,
skimmed the little pools of rain-water in the deep ruts of the unpaved street,
and suddenly went away to nothing, like a juggler's butterflies or a young
man's money.

It was very picturesque, the Rue Royale. The rich and poor met
together. The locksmith's swinging key creaked next door to the bank; across
the way, crouching, mendicant-like, in the shadow of a great importing-
house, was the mud laboratory of the mender of broken combs. Light balconies overhung the rows of showy shops and stores open for trade this
Sunday morning, and pretty Latin faces of the higher class glanced over
their savagely-pronged railings upon the passers below. At some windows
hung lace curtains, flannel duds at some, and at others only the scraping and
sighing one-hinged shutter groaning toward Paris after its neglectful master.

M. St.-Ange stood looking up and down the street for nearly an hour.
But few ladies, only the inveterate mass-goers, were out. About the entrance
of the frequent *cafés* the masculine gentility stood leaning on canes, with
which now one and now another beckoned to Jules, some even adding pan-
tomimic hints of the social cup.

M. St.-Ange remarked to his servant without turning his head that
somehow he felt sure he should soon return those *bons* that the mulatto had
lent him.

"What will you do with them?"

"Me!" said Baptiste, quickly; "I will go and see the bull-fight in the
Place Congo."

"There is to be a bull-fight? But where is M. Cayetano?"

"Ah, got all his affairs wet in the tornado. Instead of his circus, they are
to have a bull-fight—not an ordinary bull-fight with sick horses, but a buf-
falo-and-tiger fight. I would not miss it"—

Two or three persons ran to the opposite corner, and commenced striking at something with their canes. Others followed. Can M. St.-Ange and
servant, who hasten forward—can the Creoles, Cubans, Spaniards, San
Domingo refugees, and other loungers—can they hope it is a fight? They
hurry forward. Is a man in a fit? The crowd pours in from the side-streets.
Have they killed a so-long snake? Bareheaded shopmen leave their wives,
who stand upon chairs. The crowd huddles and packs. Those on the outside
make little leaps into the air, trying to be tall.

"What is the matter?"

"Have they caught a real live rat?"

Who is hurt?" asks some one in English.

"*Personne*," replies a shopkeeper; "a man's hat blow' in the gutter; but he has it now. Jules pick' it. See, that is the man, head and shoulders on top the res'."

"He in the homespun?" asks a second shopkeeper. "Humph! an *Améri-cain*—a West-Floridian; bah!"

"But wait; 'st! he is speaking; listen!"

"To who is he speak——?"

"Sh-sh-sh! to Jules."

"Jules who?"

"Silence, you! To Jules St.-Ange, what howe me a bill since long time. Sh-sh-sh!"

Then the voice was heard.

Its owner was a man of giant stature, with a slight stoop in his shoulders, as if he was making a constant, good-natured attempt to accommodate himself to ordinary doors and ceilings. His bones were those of an ox. His face was marked more by weather than age, and his narrow brow was bald and smooth. He had instantaneously formed an opinion of Jules St.-Ange, and the multitude of words, most of them lingual curiosities, with which he was rasping the wide-open ears of his listeners, signified, in short, that, as sure as his name was Parson Jones, the little Creole was a "plum gentleman."

M. St.-Ange bowed and smiled, and was about to call attention, by both gesture and speech, to a singular object on top of the still uncovered head, when the nervous motion of the *Américain* anticipated him, as, throwing up an immense hand, he drew down a large roll of bank-notes. The crowd laughed, the West-Floridian joining, and began to disperse.

"Why, that money belongs to Smyrny Church," said the giant.

"You are very dengerous to make your money expose like that, Misty Posson Jone'," said St.-Ange, counting it with his eyes.

The countryman gave a start and smile of surprise.

"How d'dyou know my name was Jones?" he asked; but, without pausing for the Creole's answer, furnished in his reckless way some further specimens of West-Floridian English; and the conciseness with which he presented full intelligence of his home, family, calling, lodging-house, and present and future plans, might have passed for consummate art, had it not been the most run-wild nature. "And I've done been to Mobile, you know, on business for Bethesdy Church. It's the on'yest time I ever been from home; now you wouldn't of believed that, would you? But I admire to have saw you, that's so. You've got to come and eat with me. Me and my boy ain't been fed yit. What might one call yo' name? Jools? Come on, Jools. Come on, Colossus. That's my niggah—his name's Colossus of Rhodes. Is that yo' yallah boy, Jools? Fetch him along, Colossus. It seems like a special provi-dence.—Jools, do you believe in a special provi*dence*?"

Jules said he did.

The new-made friends moved briskly off, followed by Baptiste and a short, square, old negro, very black and grotesque, who had introduced himself to the mulatto, with many glittering and cavernous smiles, as "d'body-sarvant of d'Rev'n' Mr. Jones."

Both pairs enlivened their walk with conversation. Parson Jones descanted upon the doctrine he had mentioned, as illustrated in the perplexities of cotton-growing, and concluded that there would always be "a special provi*dence* again' cotton untell folks quits apressin' of it and haulin' of it on Sundays!"

"*Je dis,*"[3] said St.-Ange, in response, "I thing you is juz right. I believe, me, strong-strong in the improvidence, yes. You know my papa he hown a sugah-plantation, you know. 'Jules, me son,' he say one time to me, 'I goin' to make one baril sugah to fedge the moze high price in New Orleans.' Well, he take his bez baril sugah—I nevah see a so careful man like me papa always to make a so beautiful sugah *et sirop*. 'Jules, go at Father Pierre an' ged this lill pitcher fill with holy-water, an' tell him sen' his tin bucket, and I will make it fill with *quitte*.' I ged the holy-water; my papa sprinkle it over the baril, an' make one cross on the 'ead of the baril."

"Why, Jools," said Parson Jones, "that didn't do no good."

"Din do no good! Id broughd the so great value! You can strike me dead if thad baril sugah din fedge the more high cost than any other in the city. *Parce-que*, the man what buy that baril sugah he make a mistake of one hundred pound"—falling back—"*Mais* certainlee!"

"And you think that was growin' out of the holy-water?" asked the parson.

"*Mais*, what could make it else? Id could not be the *quitte*, because my papa keep the bucket, an' forget to sen' the *quitte* to Father Pierre."

Parson Jones was disappointed.

"Well, now, Jools, you know, I don't think that was right. I reckon you must be a plum Catholic."

M. St.-Ange shrugged. He would not deny his faith.

"I am a *Catholique, mais*"—brightening as he hoped to recommend himself anew—"not a good one."

"Well, you know," said Jones—"where's Colossus? Oh! all right. Colossus strayed off a minute in Mobile, and I plum lost him for two days. Here's the place; come in. Colossus and this boy can go to the kitchen.—Now, Colossus, what *air* you a-beck-onin' at me faw?"

He let his servant draw him aside and address him in a whisper.

"Oh, go 'way!" said the parson with a jerk. "Who's goin' to throw me? What? Speak louder. Why, Colossus, you shayn't talk so, saw. 'Pon my soul, you're the mightiest fool I ever taken up with. Jest you go down that alley-way with this yalla boy, and don't show yo' face untell yo' called!"

The negro begged; the master wrathily insisted.

"Colossus, will you do ez I tell you, or shell I hev' to strike you, saw?"

---

3. "I say."

"O Mahs Jimmy, I—I's gwine; but"—he ventured nearer—"don't on no account drink nothin', Mahs Jimmy."

Such was the negro's earnestness that he put one foot in the gutter, and fell heavily against his master. The parson threw him off angrily.

"Thar, now! Why, Colossus, you most of been dosted with sumthin'; yo' plum crazy.—Humph, come on, Jools, let's eat! Humph! to tell me that when I never taken a drop, exceptin' for chills, in my life—which he knows so as well as me!"

The two masters began to ascend a stair.

"*Mais*, he is a sassy; I would sell him, me," said the young Creole.

"No, I wouldn't do that," replied the parson; "though there is people in Bethesdy who says he is a rascal. He's a powerful smart fool. Why, that boy's got money, Jools; more money than religion, I reckon. I'm shore he fallen into mighty bad company"—they passed beyond earshot.

Baptise and Colossus, instead of going to the tavern kitchen, passed to the next door and entered the dark rear corner of a low grocery, where, the law notwithstanding, liquor was covertly sold to slaves. There, in the quiet company of Baptiste and the grocer, the colloquial powers of Colossus, which were simply prodigious, began very soon to show themselves.

"For whilst," said he, "Mahs Jimmy has eddication, you know—whilst he has eddication, I has 'scretion. He has eddication and I has 'scretion, an' so we gits along."

He drew a black bottle down the counter, and, laying half his length upon the damp board, continued:

"As a p'inciple I discredits de imbimin' of awjus liquors. De imbimin' of awjus liquors, de wiolution of de Sabbaf, de playin' of de fiddle, and de usin' of by-words, dey is de fo' sins of de conscience; an' if any man sin de fo' sins of de conscience, de debble done sharp his fork fo' dat man.—Ain't that so, boss?"

The grocer was sure it was so.

"Neberdeless, mind you"—here the orator brimmed his glass from the bottle and swallowed the contents with a dry eye—"mind you, a roytious man, sech as ministers of de gospel and dere body-sarvants, can take a *leetle* for de weak stomach."

But the fascinations of Colossus's eloquence must not mislead us; this is the story of a true Christian; to wit, Parson Jones.

The parson and his new friend ate. But the coffee M. St.-Ange declared he could not touch; it was too wretchedly bad. At the French Market, near by, there was some noble coffee. This, however, would have to be bought, and Parson Jones had scruples.

"You see, Jools, every man has his conscience to guide him, which it does so in"—

"Oh, yes!" cried St.-Ange, "conscien'; thad is the bez, Posson Jone'. Certainlee! I am a *Catholique*, you is a *schismatique*; you thing it is wrong to dring some coffee—well, then, it *is* wrong; you thing it is wrong to make the sugah to ged the so large price—well, then, it *is* wrong; I thing it is right—well, then, it *is* right; it is all 'abit; *c'est tout*. What a man thing is right, *is right*; 'tis all 'abit. A man muz nod go again' his conscien'. My faith! do you thing I would go again' my conscien'? *Mais allons*, led us go and ged some coffee."

"Jools."

"W'at?"

"Jools, it ain't the drinkin' of coffee, but the buyin' of it on a Sabbath. You must really excuse me, Jools, it's again' conscience, you know."

"Ah!" said St.-Ange, "*c'est* very true. For you it would be a sin, *mais* for me it is only 'abit. Rilligion is a very strange; I know a man one time, he thing it was wrong to go to cock-fight Sunday evening. I thing it is all 'abit. *Mais*, come, Posson Jone'; I have got one friend, Miguel; led us go at his house and ged some coffee. Come; Miguel have no familie; only him and Joe—always like to see friend; *allons*, led us come yonder."

"Why, Jools, my dear friend, you know," said the shamefaced parson, "I never visit on Sundays."

"Never w'at?" asked the astounded Creole.

"No," said Jones, smiling awkwardly.

"Never visite?"

"Exceptin' sometimes amongst church-members," said Parson Jones.

"*Mais*," said the seductive St.-Ange, "Miguel and Joe is church-member'—certainlee! They love to talk about rilligion. Come at Miguel and talk about some rilligion. I am nearly expire for me coffee."

Parson Jones took his hat from beneath his chair and rose up.

"Jools," said the weak giant, "I ought to be in church right now."

"*Mais*, the church is right yonder at Miguel', yes. Ah!" continued St.-Ange, as they descended the stairs, "I thing every man muz have the rilligion he like' the bez—me, I like the *Catholique* rilligion the bez—for me it *is* the bez. Every man will sure go to heaven if he like his rilligion the bez."

"Jools," said the West-Floridian, laying his great hand tenderly upon the Creole's shoulder, as they stepped out upon the *banquette*, "do you think you have any shore hopes of heaven?"

"Yass!" replied St.-Ange; "I am sure-sure. I thing everybody will go to heaven. I thing you will go, *et* I thing Miguel will go, *et* Joe—everybody, I thing—*mais*, hof course, not if they not have been christen'. Even I thing some niggers will go."

"Jools," said the parson, stopping in his walk—"Jools, I *don't* want to lose my niggah."

"You will not loose him. With Baptiste he *cannot* ged loose."

But Colossus's master was not re-assured.

"Now," said he, still tarrying, "this is jest the way; had I of gone to church"—

"Posson Jone'," said Jules.

"What?"

"I tell you. We goin' to church!"

"Will you?" asked Jones, joyously.

"*Allons*, come along," said Jules, taking his elbow.

They walked down the Rue Chartres, passed several corners, and by and by turned into a cross street. The parson stopped an instant as they were turning, and looked back up the street.

"W'at you lookin'?" asked his companion.

"I thought I saw Colossus," answered the parson, with an anxious face; "I reckon 'twa'n't him, though." And they went on.

The street they now entered was a very quiet one. The eye of any chance passer would have been at once drawn to a broad, heavy, white brick edifice on the lower side of the way, with a flag-pole standing out like a bowsprit from one of its great windows, and a pair of lamps hanging before a large closed entrance. It was a theatre, honey-combed with gambling-dens. At this morning hour all was still, and the only sign of life was a knot of little barefoot girls gathered within its narrow shade, and each carrying an infant relative. Into this place the parson and M. St.-Ange entered, the little nurses jumping up from the sills to let them pass in.

A half-hour may have passed. At the end of that time the whole juvenile company were laying alternate eyes and ears to the chinks, to gather what they could of an interesting quarrel going on within.

"I did not, saw! I given you no cause of offence, saw! It's not so, saw! Mister Jools simply mistaken the house, thinkin' it was a Sabbath-school! No such thing, saw; I *ain't* bound to bet! Yes, I kin git out! Yes, without bettin'! I hev a right to my opinion; I reckon I'm *a white man*, saw! No saw! I on'y said I didn't think you could get the game on them cards. 'Sno such thing, saw! I do *not* know how to play! I wouldn't hev a rascal's money ef I should win it! Shoot, ef you dare! You can kill me, but you cayn't scare me! No, I shayn't bet! I'll die first! Yes, saw; Mr. Jools can bet for me if he admires to; I ain't his mostah."

Here the speaker seemed to direct his words to St.-Ange.

"Saw, I don't understand you, saw. I never said I'd loan you money to bet for me. I didn't suspicion this from you, saw. No, I won't take any more lemonade; it's the most notorious stuff I ever drank, saw!"

M. St.-Ange's replies were in *falsetto* and not without effect; for presently the parson's indignation and anger began to melt. "Don't ask me, Jools, I can't help you. It's no use; it's a matter of conscience with me, Jools."

"*Mais oui!* 'tis a matt' of conscien' wid me, the same."

"But, Jools, the money's none o' mine, nohow; it belongs to Smyrny, you know."

"If I could make jus' *one* bet," said the persuasive St.-Ange, "I would leave this place, fas'-fas', yes. If I had thing—*mais* I did not soupspicion this from you, Posson Jone'"—

"Don't, Jools, don't!"

"No! Posson Jone'."

"You're bound to win?" said the parson, wavering.

"*Mais certainement!* But it is not to win that I want; 'tis me conscien'—me honor!"

"Well, Jools, I hope I'm not a-doin' no wrong. I'll loan you some of this money if you say you'll come right out 'thout takin' your winnin's."

All was still. The peeping children could see the parson as he lifted his hand to his breast-pocket. There it paused a moment in bewilderment, then plunged to the bottom. It came back empty, and fell lifelessly at his side. His head dropped upon his breast, his eyes were for a moment closed, his broad palms were lifted and pressed against his forehead, a tremor seized him, and he fell all in a lump to the floor. The children ran off with their infant-loads, leaving Jules St.-Ange swearing by all his deceased relatives, first to Miguel and Joe, and then to the lifted parson, that he did not know what had become of the money "except if" the black man had got it.

In the rear of ancient New Orleans, beyond the sites of the old rampart, a trio of Spanish forts, where the town has since sprung up and grown old, green with all the luxuriance of the wild Creole summer, lay the Congo Plains. Here stretched the canvas of the historic Cayetano, who Sunday after Sunday sowed the sawdust for his circus-ring.

But to-day the great showman had fallen short of his printed promise. The hurricane had come by night, and with one fell swash had made an irretrievable sop of every thing. The circus trailed away its bedraggled magnificence, and the ring was cleared for the bull.

Then the sun seemed to come out and work for the people. "See," said the Spaniards, looking up at the glorious sky with its great, white fleets drawn off upon the horizon—"see—heaven smiles upon the bull-fight!"

In the high upper seats of the rude amphitheatre sat the gayly-decked wives and daughters of the Gascons, from the *métaries* along the Ridge, and the chattering Spanish women of the Market, their shining hair unbonneted to the sun. Next below were their husbands and lovers in Sunday blouses, milkmen, butchers, bakers, black-bearded fishermen, Sicilian fruiterers; swarthy Portuguese sailors, in little woollen caps, and strangers of the graver sort; mariners of England, Germany, and Holland. The lowest seats were full of trappers, smugglers, Canadian *voyageurs*, drinking and singing; *Américains*, too—more's the shame—from the upper rivers—who will not keep their seats—who ply the bottle, and who will get home by and by and tell how wicked Sodom is; broad-brimmed, silver-braided Mexicans, too, with their copper cheeks and bat's eyes, and their tinkling spurred heels. Yonder, in that quieter section, are the quadroon women in their black lace shawls—and there is Baptiste; and below them are the turbaned black women, and there is—but he vanishes—Colossus.

The afternoon is advancing, yet the sport, though loudly demanded, does not begin. The *Américains* grow derisive and find pastime in gibes and raillery. They mock the various Latins with their national inflections, and answer their scowls with laughter. Some of the more aggressive shout pretty French greetings to the women of Gascony, and one bargeman, amid peals of applause, stands on a seat and hurls a kiss to the quadroons. The mariners of England, Germany, and Holland, as spectators, like the fun, while the

Spaniards look black and cast defiant imprecations upon their persecutors. Some Gascons, with timely caution, pick their women out and depart, running a terrible fire of gallantries.

In hope of truce, a new call is raised for the bull: "The bull, the bull!—hush!"

In a tier near the ground a man is standing and calling—standing head and shoulders above the rest—calling in the *Américaine* tongue. Another man, big and red, named Joe, and a handsome little Creole in elegant dress and full of laughter, wish to stop him, but the flat-boatmen, ha-ha-ing and cheering, will not suffer it. Ah, through some shameful knavery of the men, into whose hands he has fallen, he is drunk! Even the women can see that; and now he throws his arms wildly and raises his voice until the whole great circle hears it. He is preaching!

Ah! kind Lord, for a special providence now! The men of his own nation—men from the land of the open English Bible and temperance cup and song are cheering him on to mad disgrace. And now another call for the appointed sport is drowned by the flat-boatmen singing the ancient tune of Mear. You can hear the words—

> Old Grimes is dead, that good old soul

—from ribald lips and throats turned brazen with laughter, from singers who toss their hats aloft and roll in their seats; the chorus swells to the accompaniment of a thousand brogans—

> He used to wear an old gray coat
> All buttoned down before.

A ribboned man in the arena is trying to be heard, and the Latins raise one mighty cry for silence. The big red man gets a hand over the parson's mouth, and the ribboned man seizes his moment.

"They have been endeavoring for hours," he says, "to draw the terrible animals from their dens, but such is their strength and fierceness, that"—

His voice is drowned. Enough has been heard to warrant the inference that the beasts cannot be whipped out of the storm-drenched cages to which menagerie-life and long starvation have attached them, and from the roar of indignation the man of ribbons flies. The noise increases. Men are standing up by hundreds, and women are imploring to be let out of the turmoil. All at once, like the bursting of a dam, the whole mass pours down into the ring. They sweep across the arena and over the showman's barriers. Miguel gets a frightful trampling. Who cares for gates or doors? They tear the beasts' houses bar from bar, and, laying hold of the gaunt buffalo, drag him forth by feet, ears, and tail; and in the midst of the *mêlée*, still head and shoulders above all, wilder, with the cup of the wicked, than any beast, is the man of God from the Florida parishes!

In his arms he bore—and all the people shouted at once when they saw it—the tiger. He had lifted it high up with its back to his breast, his arms clasped under its shoulders; the wretched brute had curled up caterpillar-wise, with its long tail against its belly, and through its filed teeth grinned a fixed and impotent wrath. And Parson Jones was shouting:

"The tiger and the buffler *shell* lay down together![4] You dah to say they shayn't and I'll comb you with this varmint from head to foot! The tiger and the buffler *shell* lay down together. They *shell*! Now, you, Joe! Behold! I am here to see it done. The lion and the buffler *shell* lay down together!"

Mouthing these words again and again, the parson forced his way through the surge in the wake of the buffalo. This creature the Latins had secured by a lariat over his head, and were dragging across the old rampart and into a street of the city.

The northern races were trying to prevent, and there was pommelling and knocking down, cursing and knife-drawing, until Jules St.-Ange was quite carried away with the fun, laughed, clapped his hands, and swore with delight, and ever kept close to the gallant parson.

Joe, contrariwise, counted all this child's-play an interruption. He had come to find Colossus and the money. In an unlucky moment he made bold to lay hold of the parson, but a piece of the broken barriers in the hands of a flat-boatman felled him to the sod, the terrible crowd swept over him, the lariat was cut and the giant parson hurled the tiger upon the buffalo's back. In another instant both brutes were dead at the hands of the mob; Jones was lifted from his feet, and prating of Scripture and the millennium, of Paul at Ephesus and Daniel in the "buffler's" den, was borne aloft upon the shoulders of the huzzaing *Américains*. Half an hour later he was sleeping heavily on the floor of a cell in the *calaboza*.

When Parson Jones awoke, a bell was somewhere tolling for midnight. Somebody was at the door of his cell with a key. The lock grated, the door swung, the turnkey looked in and stepped back, and a ray of moonlight fell upon M. Jules St.-Ange. The prisoner sat upon the empty shackles and ringbolt in the centre of the floor.

"Misty Posson Jone'," said the visitor, softly.

"O Jools!"

"*Mais*, w'at de matter, Posson Jone'?"

"My sins, Jools, my sins!"

"Ah! Posson Jone', is that something to cry, because a man get sometime a litt' bit intoxicate? *Mais*, if a man keep *all the time* intoxicate, I think that is again' the conscien'."

"Jools, Jools, your eyes is darkened—oh! Jools, where's my pore old niggah?"

"Posson Jone', never min'; he is wid Baptiste."

"Where?"

"I don' know w'ere—*mais* he is wid Baptiste. Baptiste is a beautiful to take care of somebody."

---

4 According to Isaiah 11:6, "The wolf also shall dwell with the lamb, and the leopard shall lie down with the kid; and the calf and the young lion and the fatling together; and a little child shall lead them."

"Is he as good as you, Jools?" asked Parson Jones, sincerely.

Jules was slightly staggered.

"You know, Posson Jone', you know, a nigger cannot be good as a w'ite man—*mais* Baptiste is a good nigger."

The parson moaned and dropped his chin into his hands.

"I was to of left for home to-morrow, sun-up, on the Isabella schooner. Pore Smyrny!" He deeply sighed.

"Posson Jone'," said Jules, leaning against the wall and smiling, "I swear you is the moz funny man I ever see. If I was you I would say, me, 'Ah! 'ow I am lucky! the money I los', it was not mine, anyhow!' My faith! shall a man make hisse'f to be the more sorry because the money he los' is not his? Me, I would say, 'it is a specious providence.'

"Ah! Misty Posson Jone'," he continued, "you make a so droll sermon ad the bull-ring. Ha! ha! I swear I thing you can make money to preach thad sermon many time ad the theatre St. Philippe. Hah! you is the moz brave dat I never see, *mais* ad the same time the moz rilligious man. Where I'm going' to fin' one priest to make like dat? *Mais*, why you can't cheer up an' be 'appy? Me, if I should be miserabl' like that I would kill meself."

The countryman only shook his head.

"*Bien*, Posson Jone', I have the so good news for you."

The prisoner looked up with eager inquiry.

"Las' evening when they lock' you, I come right off at M. De Blanc's house to get you let out of de calaboose; M. De Blanc he is the judge. So soon I was entering—'Ah! Jules, me boy, juz the man to make complete the game!' Posson Jone', it was a specious providence! I win in t'ree hours more dan six hundred dollah! Look." He produced a mass of bank-notes, *bons*, and due-bills.

"And you got the pass?" asked the parson, regarding the money with a sadness incomprehensible to Jules.

"It is here; it take the effect so soon the daylight."

"Jools, my friend, your kindness is in vain."

The Creole's face became a perfect blank.

"Because," said the parson, "for two reasons: firstly, I have broken the laws, and ought to stand the penalty; and secondly—you must really excuse me, Jools, you know, but the pass has been got on-fairly, I'm afeerd. You told the judge I was innocent; and in neither case it don't become a Christian (which I hope I can still say I am one) to 'do evil that good may come.' I muss stay."

M. St.-Ange stood up aghast, and for a moment speechless, at this exhibition of moral heroism; but an artifice was presently hit upon. "*Mais*, Posson Jone'!"—in his old *falsetto*—"de order—you cannot read it, it is in French—compel you to go hout, sir!"

"Is that so?" cried the parson, bounding up with radiant face—"is that so, Jools?"

The young man nodded, smiling; but, though he smiled, the fountain of his tenderness was opened. He made the sign of the cross as the parson knelt in prayer, and even whispered "Hail Mary," etc., quite through, twice over.

Morning broke in summer glory upon a cluster of villas behind the city, nestled under live-oaks and magnolias on the banks of a deep bayou, and known as Suburb St. Jean.

With the first beam came the West-Floridian and the Creole out upon the bank below the village. Upon the parson's arm hung a pair of antique saddle-bags. Baptiste limped wearily behind; both his eyes were encircled with broad, blue rings, and one cheek-bone bore the official impress of every knuckle of Colossus's left hand. The "beautiful to take care of somebody" had lost his charge. At mention of the negro he became wild, and, half in English, half in the "gumbo" dialect, said murderous things. Intimidated by Jules to calmness, he became able to speak confidently on one point; he could, would, and did swear that Colossus had gone home to the Florida parishes; he was almost certain; in fact, he thought so.

There was a clicking of pulleys as the three appeared upon the bayou's margin, and Baptiste pointed out, in the deep shadow of a great oak, the Isabella, moored among the bulrushes, and just spreading her sails for departure. Moving down to where she lay, the parson and his friend paused on the bank, loath to say farewell.

"O Jools!" said the parson, "supposin' Colossus ain't gone home! O Jools, if you'll look him out for me, I'll never forget you—I'll never forget you, nohow, Jools. No, Jools, I never will believe he taken that money. Yes, I know all niggahs will steal"—he set foot upon the gang-plank—"but Colossus wouldn't steal from me. Good-by."

"Misty Posson Jone'," said St.-Ange, putting his hand on the parson's arm with genuine affection, "hol' on. You see dis money—w'at I win las' night? Well, I win' it by a specious providence, ain't it?"

"There's no tellin'," said the humbled Jones. "Providence

Moves in a mysterious way
His wonders to perform.

"Ah!" cried the Creole, "*c'est* very true. I ged this money in the mysterieuze way. *Mais,* if I keep dis money, you know where it goin' be to-night?"

"I really can't say," replied the parson.

"Goin' to de dev'," said the sweetly-smiling young man.

The schooner-captain, leaning against the shrouds, and even Baptiste, laughed outright.

"O Jools, you mustn't!"

"Well, den, w'at I shall do wid *it*"

"Any thing!" answered the parson; "better donate it away to some poor man"—

"Ah! Misty Posson Jone', dat is w'at I want. You los' five hondred dollar'—'twas me fault."

"No, it wa'n't, Jools."

"*Mais*, it was!"

"No!"

"It *was* me fault! I *swear* it was me fault! *Mais*, here is five hondred dollar'; I wish you shall take it. Here! I don't got no use for money.—Oh, my faith! Posson Jone', you must not begin to cry some more."

Parson Jones was choked with tears. When he found voice he said:

"O Jools, Jools, Jools! my pore, noble, dear, misguidened friend! ef you hed of hed a Christian raisin'! May the Lord show you your errors better'n I kin, and bless you for your good intentions—oh, no! I cayn't touch that money with a ten-foot pole; it wa'n't rightly got; you must really excuse me, my dear friend, but I cayn't touch it."

St.-Ange was petrified.

"Good-by, dear Jools," continued the parson. "I'm in the Lord's haynds, and he's very merciful, which I hope and trust you'll find it out. Good-by!"—the schooner swang slowly off before the breeze—"good-by!"

St.-Ange roused himself.

"Posson Jone'! make me hany'ow *dis* promise: you never, never, *never* will come back to New Orleans."

"Ah, Jools, the Lord willin', I'll never leave home again!"

"All right!" cried the Creole; "I thing he's willin'. Adieu, Posson Jone'. My faith'! you are the so fighting an' moz rilligious man as I never saw! Adieu! Adieu!"

Baptiste uttered a cry and presently ran by his master toward the schooner, his hands full of clods.

St.-Ange looked just in time to see the sable form of Colossus of Rhodes emerge from the vessel's hold, and the pastor of Smyrna and Bethesda seize him in his embrace.

"O Colossus! you outlandish old nigger! Thank the Lord! Thank the Lord!"

The little Creole almost wept. He ran down the tow-path, laughing and swearing, and making confused allusion to the entire *personnel* and furniture of the lower regions.

By odd fortune, at the moment that St.-Ange further demonstrated his delight by tripping his mulatto into a bog, the schooner came brushing along the reedy bank with a graceful curve, the sails flapped, and the crew fell to poling her slowly along.

Parson Jones was on the deck, kneeling once more in prayer. His hat had fallen before him; behind him knelt his slave. In thundering tones he was confessing himself "a plum fool," from whom "the conceit had been jolted out," and who had been made to see that even his "nigger had the longest head of the two."

Colossus clasped his hands and groaned.

The parson prayed for a contrite heart.

"Oh, yes!" cried Colossus.

The master acknowledged countless mercies.

"Dat's so!" cried the slave.

The master prayed that they might still be "piled on."

"Glory!" cried the black man, clapping his hands; "pile on!"

"An' now," continued the parson, "bring this pore, backslidin' jackace of a parson and this pore ole fool nigger back to thar home in peace!"

"Pray fo' de money!" called Colossus.

But the parson prayed for Jules.

"Pray fo' de *money!*" repeated the negro.

"And oh, give thy servant back that there lost money!"

Colossus rose stealthily, and tiptoed by his still shouting master. St.-Ange, the captain, the crew, gazed in silent wonder at the strategist. Pausing but an instant over the master's hat to grin an acknowledgment of his beholder's speechless interest, he softly placed in it the faithfully-mourned and honestly-prayed-for Smyrna fund; then, saluted by the gesticulative, silent applause of St.-Ange and the schoonermen, he resumed his first attitude behind his roaring master.

"Amen!" cried Colossus, meaning to bring him to a close.

"Onworthy though I be"—cried Jones.

"*Amen!*" reiterated the negro.

"A-a-amen!" said Parson Jones.

He rose to his feet, and, stooping to take up his hat, beheld the well-known roll. As one stunned, he gazed for a moment upon his slave, who still knelt with clasped hands and rolling eyeballs; but when he became aware of the laughter and cheers that greeted him from both deck and shore, he lifted eyes and hands to heaven, and cried like the veriest babe. And when he looked at the roll again, and hugged and kissed it, St.-Ange tried to raise a second shout, but choked, and the crew fell to their poles.

And now up runs Baptiste, covered with slime, and prepares to cast his projectiles. The first one fell wide of the mark; the schooner swung round into a long reach of water, where the breeze was in her favor; another shout of laughter drowned the maledictions of the muddy man; the sails filled; Colossus of Rhodes, smiling and bowing as hero of the moment, ducked as the main boom swept round, and the schooner, leaning slightly to the pleasant influence, rustled a moment over the bulrushes, and then sped far away down the rippling bayou.

M. Jules St.-Ange stood long, gazing at the receding vessel as it now disappeared, now re-appeared beyond the tops of the high undergrowth; but, when an arm of the forest hid it finally from sight, he turned townward, followed by that fagged-out spaniel, his servant, saying, as he turned, "Baptiste."

"*Miché?*"

"You know w'at I goin' do wid dis money?"

"*Non, m'sieur.*"

"Well, you can strike me dead if I don't goin' to pay hall my debts! *Allons!*"

He began a merry little song to the effect that his sweetheart was a wine-bottle, and master and man, leaving care behind, returned to the picturesque Rue Royale. The ways of Providence are indeed strange. In all Parson Jones's after-life, amid the many painful reminiscences of his visit to the City of the Plain, the sweet knowledge was withheld from him that by the light of the Christian virtue that shone from him even in his great fall, Jules St.-Ange arose, and went to his father an honest man.

Sarah Winnemucca Hopkins
(1844–1891)

Sarah Winnemucca, the descendant and sister of Paiute chiefs, was born in the Great Basin area of Nevada. Her people spoke a Shoshonean dialect of the Uto-Aztecan language family, encompassing tribes from Central America to Idaho. The Paiutes were part of that group of people, resident in a hostile climate, who subsisted on plants and small game and were designated by white settlers as "digger Indians." From an early age Hopkins was fluent in English and acted as an intermediary between her tribe and Indian agents, military officers, and settlers. In that role, she had ample opportunity to observe the abuses of federal policy practiced by greedy government appointees who forced Indians to work but refused them the fruits of their labors, kept for themselves the supplies they were supposed to distribute to the tribes, and sold off grazing and mineral rights to reservation lands.

After the Bannock War of 1878, she went East where she delivered over three hundred lectures in an effort to influence public opinion and bring about changes in federal policy toward Native Americans. In meetings with Secretary of the Interior Carl Schurz and President Rutherford B. Hayes, she pleaded for the repatriation of a group of her people who had been forcibly removed to the Yakima River area of Washington. In July 1880 Secretary Schurz issued a directive allowing the tribe to return to its hereditary lands and alloting to each family and adult male 160 acres of land for cultivation. Like so many other government promises, these were not kept.

Her publication of Life among the Piutes: Their Wrongs and Claims *(1883) was also an attempt to bring her people's plight to public attention. In it she describes the first meetings between white settlers and the Paiutes, customs of child rearing, courtship and death, good and bad Indian agents, relations with the military officers assigned to the area, conflicts between the tribe and its neighbors, and the removal to Yakima. Mary Peabody Mann, who edited and introduced the publication, helped organize a peti-*

tion drive for restitution of the hereditary lands, and a measure on behalf of the displaced people was introduced in Congress, but no equitable settlement was made.

Discouraged, Hopkins retired to her brother's farm. Together they founded a school for Paiute children and operated it until financial hardship and Sarah's ill health forced its closure in 1887.

[From] Life among the Piutes

CHAPTER I. FIRST MEETING OF PIUTES AND WHITES

I WAS BORN SOMEWHERE NEAR 1844, but am not sure of the precise time. I was a very small child when the first white people came into our country. They came like a lion, yes, like a roaring lion, and have continued so ever since, and I have never forgotten their first coming. My people were scattered at that time over nearly all the territory now known as Nevada. My grandfather was chief of the entire Piute nation, and was camped near Humboldt Lake, with a small portion of his tribe, when a party travelling eastward from California was seen coming. When the news was brought to my grandfather, he asked what they looked like? When told that they had hair on their faces, and were white, he jumped up and clasped his hands together, and cried aloud,—

"My white brothers,—my long-looked for white brothers have come at last!"

He immediately gathered some of his leading men, and went to the place where the party had gone into camp. Arriving near them, he was commanded to halt in a manner that was readily understood without an interpreter. Grandpa at once made signs of friendship by throwing down his robe and throwing up his arms to show them he had no weapons; but in vain,— they kept him at a distance. He knew not what to do. He had expected so much pleasure in welcoming his white brothers to the best in the land, that after looking at them sorrowfully for a little while, he came away quite unhappy. But he would not give them up so easily. He took some of his most trustworthy men and followed them day after day, camping near them at night, and travelling in sight of them by day, hoping in this way to gain their confidence. But he was disappointed, poor dear old soul!

I can imagine his feelings, for I have drank deeply from the same cup. When I think of my past life, and the bitter trials I have endured, I can scarcely believe I live, and yet I do; and, with the help of Him who notes the sparrow's fall, I mean to fight for my down-trodden race while life lasts.

Seeing they would not trust him, my grandfather left them, saying, "Perhaps they will come again next year." Then he summoned his whole people, and told them this tradition:—

"In the beginning of the world there were only four, two girls and two boys. Our forefather and mother were only two, and we are their children. You all know that a great while ago there was a happy family in this world. One girl and one boy were dark and the others were white. For a time they got along together without quarrelling, but soon they disagreed, and there was trouble. They were cross to one another and fought, and our parents were very much grieved. They prayed that their children might learn better, but it did not do any good; and afterwards the whole household was made so unhappy that the father and mother saw that they must separate their children; and then our father took the dark boy and girl, and the white boy and girl, and asked them, 'Why are you so cruel to each other?' They hung down their heads, and would not speak. They were ashamed. He said to them, 'Have I not been kind to you all, and given you everything your hearts wished for? You do not have to hunt and kill your own game to live upon. You see, my dear children, I have power to call whatsoever kind of game we want to eat; and I also have the power to separate my dear children, if they are not good to each other.' So he separated his children by a word. He said, 'Depart from each other, you cruel children;—go across the mighty ocean and do not seek each other's lives.'

"So the light girl and boy disappeared by that one word, and their parents saw them no more, and they were grieved, although they knew their children were happy. And by-and-by the dark children grew into a large nation; and we believe it is the one we belong to, and that the nation that sprung from the white children will some time send some one to meet us and heal all the old trouble. Now, the white people we saw a few days ago must certainly be our white brothers, and I want to welcome them. I want to love them as I love all of you. But they would not let me; they were afraid. But they will come again, and I want you one and all to promise that, should I not live to welcome them myself, you will not hurt a hair on their heads, but welcome them as I tried to do."

How good of him to try and heal the wound, and how vain were his efforts! My people had never seen a white man, and yet they existed, and were a strong race. The people promised as he wished, and they all went back to their work.

The next year came a great emigration, and camped near Humboldt

Lake. The name of the man in charge of the trains was Captain Johnson, and they stayed three days to rest their horses, as they had a long journey before them without water. During their stay my grandfather and some of his people called upon them, and they all shook hands, and when our white brothers were going away they gave my grandfather a white tin plate. Oh, what a time they had over that beautiful gift,—it was so bright! They say that after they left, my grandfather called for all his people to come together, and he then showed them the beautiful gift which he had received from his white brothers. Everybody was so pleased; nothing like it was ever seen in our country before. My grandfather thought so much of it that he bored holes in it and fastened it on his head, and wore it as his hat. He held it in as much admiration as my white sisters hold their diamond rings or a sealskin jacket. So that winter they talked of nothing but their white brothers. The following spring there came great news down the Humboldt River, saying that there were some more of the white brothers coming, and there was something among them that was burning all in a blaze. My grandfather asked them what it was like. They told him it looked like a man; it had legs and hands and a head, but the head had quit burning, and it was left quite black. There was the greatest excitement among my people everywhere about the men in a blazing fire. They were excited because they did not know there were any people in the world but the two,—that is, the Indians and the whites; they thought that was all of us in the beginning of the world, and, of course, we did not know where the others had come from, and we don't know yet. Ha! ha! oh, what a laughable thing that was! It was two negroes wearing red shirts!

The third year more emigrants came, and that summer Captain Fremont, who is now General Fremont.

My grandfather met him, and they were soon friends. They met just where the railroad crosses Truckee River, now called Wadsworth, Nevada. Captain Fremont gave my grandfather the name of Captain Truckee, and he also called the river after him. Truckee is an Indian word; it means *all right*, or *very well*. A party of twelve of my people went to California with Captain Fremont. I do not know just how long they were gone.

* * *

When my grandfather went to California he helped Captain Fremont fight the Mexicans. When he came back he told the people what a beautiful country California was. Only eleven returned home, one having died on the way back.

They spoke to their people in the English language, which was very strange to them all.

Captain Truckee, my grandfather, was very proud of it, indeed. They all brought guns with them. My grandfather would sit down with us for hours, and would say over and over again, "Goodee gun, goodee, goodee gun, heap shoot." They also brought some of the soldiers' clothes with all their brass buttons, and my people were very much astonished to see the clothes, and all that time they were peaceable toward their white brothers. They had learned to love them, and they hoped more of them would come. Then my people were less barbarous than they are nowadays.

That same fall, after my grandfather came home, he told my father to take charge of his people and hold the tribe, as he was going back to California with as many of his people as he could get to go with him. So my father took his place as Chief of the Piutes, and had it as long as he lived. Then my grandfather started back to California again with about thirty families. That same fall, very late, the emigrants kept coming. It was this time that our white brothers first came amongst us. They could not get over the mountains, so they had to live with us. It was on Carson River, where the great Carson City stands now. You call my people bloodseeking. My people did not seek to kill them, nor did they steal their horses,—no, no, far from it. During the winter my people helped them. They gave them such as they had to eat. They did not hold out their hands and say:—

"You can't have anything to eat unless you pay me." No,—no such word was used by us savages at that time; and the persons I am speaking of are living yet; they could speak for us if they choose to do so.

The following spring, before my grandfather returned home, there was a great excitement among my people on account of fearful news coming from different tribes, that the people whom they called their white brothers were killing everybody that came in their way, and all the Indian tribes had gone into the mountains to save their lives. So my father told all his people to go into the mountains and hunt and lay up food for the coming winter. Then we all went into the mountains. There was a fearful story they told us children. Our mothers told us that the whites were killing everybody and eating them. So we were all afraid of them. Every dust that we could see blowing in the valleys we would say it was the white people. In the late fall my father told his people to go to the rivers and fish, and we all went to Humboldt River, and the women went to work gathering wild seed, which they grind between the rocks. The stones are round, big enough to hold in the hands. The women did this when they got back, and when they had gathered all they could they put it in one place and covered it with grass, and then over the grass mud. After it is covered it looks like an Indian wigwam.

Oh, what a fright we all got one morning to hear some white people were coming. Every one ran as best they could. My poor mother was left with my little sister and me. Oh, I never can forget it. My poor mother was carrying my little sister on her back, and trying to make me run; but I was so frightened I could not move my feet, and while my poor mother was trying to get me along my aunt overtook us, and she said to my mother: "Let us bury our girls, or we shall all be killed and eaten up." So they went to work and buried us, and told us if we heard any noise not to cry out, for if we did they would surely kill us and eat us. So our mothers buried me and my cousin, planted sage bushes over our faces to keep the sun from burning them, and there we were left all day.

Oh, can any one imagine my feelings *buried alive*, thinking every minute that I was to be unburied and eaten up by the people that my grandfather loved so much? With my heart throbbing, and not daring to breathe, we lay there all day. It seemed that the night would never come. Thanks be to God! the night came at last. Oh, how I cried and said: "Oh, father, have you forgotten me? Are you never coming for me?" I cried so I thought my very heartstrings would break.

At last we heard some whispering. We did not dare to whisper to each other, so we lay still. I could hear their footsteps coming nearer and nearer. I thought my heart was coming right out of my mouth. Then I heard my mother say, "'T is right here!" Oh, can any one in this world ever imagine what were my feelings when I was dug up by my poor mother and father? My cousin and I were once more happy in our mothers' and fathers' care, and we were taken to where all the rest were.

I was once buried alive; but my second burial shall be for ever, where no father or mother will come and dig me up. It shall not be with throbbing heart that I shall listen for coming footsteps. I shall be in the sweet rest of peace,—I, the chieftain's weary daughter.

Well, while we were in the mountains hiding, the people that my grandfather called our white brothers came along to where our winter supplies were. They set everything we had left on fire. It was a fearful sight. It was all we had for the winter, and it was all burnt during that night. My father took some of his men during the night to try and save some of it, but they could not; it had burnt down before they got there.

These were the last white men that came along that fall. My people talked fearfully that winter about those they called our white brothers. My people said they had something like awful thunder and lightning, and with that they killed everything that came in their way.

This whole band of white people perished in the mountains, for it was too late to cross them. We could have saved them, only my people were afraid of them. We never knew who they were, or where they came from. So, poor things, they must have suffered fearfully, for they all starved there. The snow was too deep.

Early in the following spring, my father told all his people to go to the mountains, for there would be a great emigration that summer. He told them he had had a wonderful dream, and wanted to tell them all about it.

He said, "Within ten days come together at the sink of Carson, and I will tell you my dream."

The sub-chiefs went everywhere to tell their people what my father had told them to say; and when the time came we all went to the sink of Carson.

Just about noon, while we were on the way, a great many of our men came to meet us, all on their horses. Oh, what a beautiful song they sang for my father as they came near us! We passed them, and they followed us, and as we came near to the encampment, every man, woman, and child were out looking for us. They had a place all ready for us. Oh, how happy everybody was! One could hear laughter everywhere, and songs were sung by happy women and children.

My father stood up and told his people to be merry and happy for five

days. It is a rule among our people always to have five days to settle anything. My father told them to dance at night, and that the men should hunt
rabbits and fish, and some were to have games of football, or any kind of
sport or playthings they wished, and the women could do the same, as they
had nothing else to do. My people were so happy during the five days,—the
women ran races, and the men ran races on foot and on horses.

My father got up very early one morning, and told his people the time
had come,—that we could no longer be happy as of old, as the white people
we called our brothers had brought a great trouble and sorrow among us
already. He went on and said,—

"These white people must be a great nation, as they have houses that
move. It is wonderful to see them move along. I fear we will suffer greatly
by their coming to our country; they come for no good to us, although my
father said they were our brothers, but they do not seem to think we are like
them. What do you all think about it? Maybe I am wrong. My dear children,
there is something telling me that I am not wrong, because I am sure they
have minds like us, and think as we do; and I know that they were doing
wrong when they set fire to our winter supplies. They surely knew it was
our food."

And this was the first wrong done to us by our white brothers.

Now comes the end of our merrymaking.

Then my father told his people his fearful dream, as he called it. He
said,—

"I dreamt this same thing three nights,—the very same. I saw the greatest emigration that has yet been through our country. I looked North and
South and East and West, and saw nothing but dust, and I heard a great
weeping. I saw women crying, and I also saw my men shot down by the
white people. They were killing my people with something that made a
great noise like thunder and lightning, and I saw the blood streaming from
the mouths of my men that lay all around me. I saw it as if it was real. Oh,
my dear children! You may all think it is only a dream,—nevertheless, I feel
that it will come to pass. And to avoid bloodshed, we must all go to the
mountains during the summer, or till my father comes back from California.
He will then tell us what to do. Let us keep away from the emigrant roads
and stay in the mountains all summer. There are to be a great many pine-
nuts this summer, and we can lay up great supplies for the coming winter,
and if the emigrants don't come too early, we can take a run down and fish
for a month, and lay up dried fish. I know we can dry a great many in a
month, and young men can go into the valleys on hunting excursions, and
kill as many rabbits as they can. In that way we can live in the mountains all
summer and all winter too."

So ended my father's dream. During that day one could see old women
getting together talking over what they had heard my father say. They
said,—

"It is true what our great chief has said, for it was shown to him by a
higher power. It is not a dream. Oh, it surely will come to pass. We shall no

longer be a happy people, as we now are; we shall no longer go here and there as of old; we shall no longer build our big fires as a signal to our friends, for we shall always be afraid of being seen by those bad people."

"Surely they don't eat people?"

"Yes, they do eat people, because they ate each other up in the mountains last winter."[1]

This was the talk among the old women during the day.

"Oh, how grieved we are! Oh, where will it end?"

Kate Chopin
(1851–1904)

Katherine O'Flaherty was born in St. Louis. When she was four years old, her well-to-do Irish immigrant father was killed in a railroad accident. She was raised by her French-speaking mother, grandmother, and great-grandmother and educated in a bilingual parochial school. By the time she was fifteen, both her brothers and her maternal great-grandmother, a favorite storyteller, were also dead.

She first visited New Orleans as a girl of eighteen, returning two years later as the bride of Oscar Chopin, a Creole cotton trader. Between 1871 and 1880, Chopin gave birth to six children. When Oscar's cotton business failed, the family moved to the Cane River region of Natchitoches parish, where he managed a general store and several of their small plantations.

During her brief time there, Chopin came to know the region's Creoles, Cajuns, and freed Negroes. Nearly two thirds of her stories are set in Louisiana, most of them in the bayou area. After her husband died of swamp fever in 1882, Chopin stayed on briefly before returning with her children to St. Louis. Her mother died there in 1885, and the author was left alone with her young family. Her daughter observed that all the deaths in Chopin's young life, "left a stamp of sadness on her that was never lost."

Chopin began to write for publication five years after the death of her husband, with stories set on a plantation very like their Cloutierville home.

---

1. In the winter of 1846–1847 a group of emigrants to California were caught in the Sierra Nevada Mountains in a snowstorm. Later named the Donner party after two prominent families in the group, they resorted to cannibalism. Only about half the original eighty-seven members of the group survived.

Since she usually wrote surrounded by her children, her tales were often completed in one attempt. She complained that revision "has always proved disastrous to my work, and I avoid it, preferring the integrity of crudities to artificialities."

Her first story was published when she was thirty-eight years old; a novel, At Fault, *followed, and in succeeding years, Chopin was successful in selling work to some of the nation's leading periodicals. These local color tales, collected in* Bayou Folk *in 1894 and* A Night in Acadie *in 1897, portray the people of the Cane River region with sympathy and humor. Influenced by such French writers as Guy de Maupassant and Gustave Flaubert and American models Sarah Orne Jewett and Mary E. Wilkins Freeman, Chopin unrolled her tales with economy and realistic observation. The influence of Walt Whitman is also apparent in her choice of phrase and image. Chopin portrays skillfully the various Louisiana dialects and the atmosphere of the bayou. Often the subject of her fiction is love, ranging from the noble self-sacrifice of characters in "A No-Account Creole" or "Nég Créol" to the destructive possessiveness of the mistress in "La Belle Zoraïde."*

Themes of female independence and sexuality and revolt against patriarchal society, treated in such tales as "A Respectable Woman" and "Athénaise," are dealt with more fully in her masterwork, The Awakening. *The account of the matron Edna Pontellier's self-realization and sexual expression, her affair with a younger man, and her subsequent suicide shocked readers of her day; they were not ready for the boldness of that work—particularly from a woman writer. It was roundly condemned when it appeared in April 1899. Critics found* The Awakening *indelicate and—not denying that such incidents might take place "behind the mask"—deplored their exposure in print. Chopin, impatient with the restrictions of her day, and discouraged by such critical timidity, wrote and published little in her few remaining years.*

Chopin's writings, including several pieces unpublished in her lifetime, appear in *The Complete Works of Kate Chopin*, 2 volumes, edited by Per Seyersted (1969). Studies include Per Seyersted, *Kate Chopin: A Critical Biography* (1969); Peggy Skaggs, *Kate Chopin* (1985); and Barbara C. Elwell, *Kate Chopin* (1986).

La Belle Zoraïde[1]

THE SUMMER NIGHT was hot and still; not a ripple of air swept over the marais.[2] Yonder, across Bayou St. John, lights twinkled here and there in the darkness, and in the dark sky above a few stars were blinking. A lugger that had come out of the lake was moving with slow, lazy motion down the bayou. A man in the boat was singing a song.

The notes of the song came faintly to the ears of old Manna Loulou, herself as black as the night, who had gone out upon the gallery to open the shutters wide.

Something in the refrain reminded the woman of an old, half-forgotten Creole romance, and she began to sing it low to herself while she threw the shutters open:—

> Lisett' to kité la plaine,
> Mo perdi bonhair à moué;
> Ziés à moué semblé fontaine,
> Dépi mo pa miré toué.[3]

And then this old song, a lover's lament for the loss of his mistress, floating into her memory, brought with it the story she would tell to Madame, who lay in her sumptuous mahogany bed, waiting to be fanned and put to sleep to the sound of one of Manna Loulou's stories. The old negress had already bathed her mistress's pretty white feet and kissed them lovingly, one, then the other. She had brushed her mistress's beautiful hair, that was as soft and shining as satin, and was the color of Madame's wedding-ring. Now, when she reëntered the room, she moved softly toward the bed, and seating herself there began gently to fan Madame Delisle.

Manna Loulou was not always ready with her story, for Madame would hear none but those which were true. But to-night the story was all there in Manna Loulou's head—the story of la belle Zoraïde—and she told it to her mistress in the soft Creole patois, whose music and charm no English words can convey.

"La belle Zoraïde had eyes that were so dusky, so beautiful, that any man who gazed too long into their depths was sure to lose his head, and even his heart sometimes. Her soft, smooth skin was the color of *café-au-lait*. As for her elegant manners, her *svelte* and graceful figure, they were the envy of half the ladies who visited her mistress, Madame Delarivière.

---

1. "La Belle Zoraïde" was first collected in *Bayou Folk* (1894), the source of the present text.

2. Marsh, swamp.

3. Lisette, you have left the plain.
   I have lost my happiness;
   My eyes resemble a fountain
   When I cannot see you.

"No wonder Zoraïde was as charming and as dainty as the finest lady of la rue Royale:[4] from a toddling thing she had been brought up at her mistress's side; her fingers had never done rougher work than sewing a fine muslin seam; and she even had her own little black servant to wait upon her. Madame, who was her godmother as well as her mistress, would often say to her:—

"'Remember, Zoraïde, when you are ready to marry, it must be in a way to do honor to your bringing up. It will be at the Cathedral. Your wedding gown, your corbeille,[5] all will be of the best; I shall see to that myself. You know, M'sieur Ambroise is ready whenever you say the word; and his master is willing to do as much for him as I shall do for you. It is a union that will please me in every way.'

M'sieur Ambroise was then the body servant of Doctor Langlé. La belle Zoraïde detested the little mulatto, with his shining whiskers like a white man's, and his small eyes, that were cruel and false as a snake's. She would cast down her own mischievous eyes, and say:—

"'Ah, nénaine,[6] I am so happy, so contented here at your side just as I am. I don't want to marry now; next year, perhaps, or the next.' And Madame would smile indulgently and remind Zoraïde that a woman's charms are not everlasting.

"But the truth of the matter was, Zoraïde had seen le beau Mézor dance the Bamboula[7] in Congo Square. That was a sight to hold one rooted to the ground. Mézor was as straight as a cypress-tree and as proud looking as a king. His body, bare to the waist, was like a column of ebony and it glistened like oil.

"Poor Zoraïde's heart grew sick in her bosom with love for le beau Mézor from the moment she saw the fierce gleam of his eye, lighted by the inspiring strains of the Bamboula, and beheld the stately movements of his splendid body swaying and quivering through the figures of the dance.

"But when she knew him later, and he came near her to speak with her, all the fierceness was gone out of his eyes, and she saw only kindness in them and heard only gentleness in his voice; for love had taken possession of him also, and Zoraïde was more distracted than ever. When Mézor was not dancing Bamboula in Congo Square, he was hoeing sugar-cane, barefooted and half naked, in his master's field outside of the city. Doctor Langlé was his master as well as M'sieur Ambroise's.

"One day, when Zoraïde kneeled before her mistress, drawing on Madame's silken stockings, that were of the finest, she said:

"'Nénaine, you have spoken to me often of marrying. Now, at last, I have chosen a husband, but it is not M'sieur Ambroise; it is le beau Mézor that I want and no other.' And Zoraïde hid her face in her hands when she had said that, for she guessed, rightly enough, that her mistress would be very angry. And, indeed, Madame Delarivière was at first speechless with rage. When she finally spoke it was only to gasp out, exasperated:—

---

4. A fashionable street in New Orleans.

5. Trousseau.

6. Term of endearment.

7. A lively dance performed to the sound of a drum with the same name.

"'That negro! that negro! Bon Dieu Seigneur,[8] but this is too much!'

"'Am I white, nénaine?' pleaded Zoraïde.

"'You white! *Malheureuse!*[9] You deserve to have the lash laid upon you like any other slave; you have proven yourself no better than the worst.'

"'I am not white,' persisted Zoraïde, respectfully and gently. 'Doctor Langlé gives me his slave to marry, but he would not give me his son. Then, since I am not white, let me have from out of my own race the one whom my heart has chosen.'

"However, you may well believe that Madame would not hear to that. Zoraïde was forbidden to speak to Mézor, and Mézor was cautioned against seeing Zoraïde again. But you know how the negroes are, Ma'zélle Titite," added Manna Loulou, smiling a little sadly. "There is no mistress, no master, no king nor priest who can hinder them from loving when they will. And these two found ways and means.

"When months had passed by, Zoraïde, who had grown unlike herself,—sober and preoccupied,—said again to her mistress:—

"'Nénaine, you would not let me have Mézor for my husband; but I have disobeyed you, I have sinned. Kill me if you wish, nénaine: forgive me if you will; but when I heard le beau Mézor say to me, "Zoraïde, mo l'aime toi,"[1] I could have died, but I could not have helped loving him.'

"This time Madame Delarivière was so actually pained, so wounded at hearing Zoraïde's confession, that there was no place left in her heart for anger. She could utter only confused reproaches. But she was a woman of action rather than of words, and she acted promptly. Her first step was to induce Doctor Langlé to sell Mézor. Doctor Langlé, who was a widower, had long wanted to marry Madame Delarivière, and he would willingly have walked on all fours at noon through the Place d'Armes if she wanted him to. Naturally he lost no time in disposing of le beau Mézor, who was sold away into Georgia, or the Carolinas, or one of those distant countries far away, where he would no longer hear his Creole tongue spoken, nor dance Calinda, nor hold la belle Zoraïde in his arms.

"The poor thing was heartbroken when Mézor was sent away from her, but she took comfort and hope in the thought of her baby that she would soon be able to clasp to her breast.

"La belle Zoraïde's sorrows had now begun in earnest. Not only sorrows but sufferings, and with the anguish of maternity came the shadow of death. But there is no agony that a mother will not forget when she holds her firstborn to her heart, and presses her lips upon the baby flesh that is her own, yet far more precious than her own.

"So, instinctively, when Zoraïde came out of the awful shadow she gazed questioningly about her and felt with her trembling hands upon either side of her. 'Où li, mo piti a moin? where is my little one?' she asked imploringly. Madame who was there and the nurse who was there both told her in

---

8. "Good Lord God!"

9. "Unfortunate!"

1. "Zoraïde, I love you."

turn, 'To piti á toi, li mouri' ('Your little one is dead'), which was a wicked falsehood that must have caused the angels in heaven to weep. For the baby was living and well and strong. It had at once been removed from its mother's side, to be sent away to Madame's plantation, far up the coast. Zoraïde could only moan in reply, 'Li mouri, li mouri,' and she turned her face to the wall.

"Madame had hoped, in thus depriving Zoraïde of her child, to have her young waiting-maid again at her side free, happy, and beautiful as of old. But there was a more powerful will than Madame's at work—the will of the good God, who had already designed that Zoraïde should grieve with a sorrow that was never more to be lifted in this world. La belle Zoraïde was no more. In her stead was a sad-eyed woman who mourned night and day for her baby. 'Li mouri, li mouri,' she would sigh over and over again to those about her, and to herself when others grew weary of her complaint.

"Yet, in spite of all, M'sieur Ambroise was still in the notion to marry her. A sad wife or a merry one was all the same to him so long as that wife was Zoraïde. And she seemed to consent, or rather submit, to the approaching marriage as though nothing mattered any longer in this world.

"One day, a black servant entered a little noisily the room in which Zoraïde sat sewing. With a look of strange and vacuous happiness upon her face, Zoraïde arose hastily. 'Hush, hush,' she whispered, lifting a warning finger, 'my little one is asleep; you must not awaken her.'

"Upon the bed was a senseless bundle of rags shaped like an infant in swaddling clothes. Over this dummy the woman had drawn the mosquito bar, and she was sitting contentedly beside it. In short, from that day Zoraïde was demented. Night nor day did she lose sight of the doll that lay in her bed or in her arms.

"And now was Madame stung with sorrow and remorse at seeing this terrible affliction that had befallen her dear Zoraïde. Consulting with Doctor Langlé, they decided to bring back to the mother the real baby of flesh and blood that was now toddling about, and kicking its heels in the dust yonder upon the plantation.

"It was Madame herself who led the pretty, tiny little "griffe"[2] girl to her mother. Zoraïde was sitting upon a stone bench in the courtyard, listening to the soft splashing of the fountain, and watching the fitful shadows of the palm leaves upon the broad, white flagging.

"'Here,' said Madame, approaching, 'here, my poor dear Zoraïde, is your own little child. Keep her; she is yours. No one will ever take her from you again.'

"Zoraïde looked with sullen suspicion upon her mistress and the child before her. Reaching out a hand she thrust the little one mistrustfully away from her. With the other hand she clasped the rag bundle fiercely to her breast; for she suspected a plot to deprive her of it.

"Nor could she ever be induced to let her own child approach her; and

---

2. Child of a Negro and a mulatto, one of the legally defined categories of mixed blood.

finally the little one was sent back to the plantation, where she was never to know the love of mother or father.

"And now this is the end of Zoraïde's story. She was never known again as la belle Zoraïde, but ever after as Zoraïde la folle,[3] whom no one ever wanted to marry—not even M'sieur Ambroise. She lived to be an old woman, whom some people pitied and others laughed at—always clasping her bundle of rags—her 'piti.'[4]

"Are you asleep, Ma'zélle Titite?"

"No, I am not asleep; I was thinking. Ah, the poor little one, Man Loulou, the poor little one! better had she died!"

But this is the way Madame Delisle and Manna Loulou really talked to each other:—

"Von pré droumi, Ma'zélle Titite?"

"Non, pa pré droumi; mo yapré zongler. Ah, la pauv' piti, Man Loulou. La pauv' piti! Mieux li mouri!"

Charles W. Chesnutt
(1858–1932)

Born in Cleveland, Ohio, Charles Waddell Chesnutt was the son of free blacks from North Carolina. His father served in the Union army, then moved the family back South after the war. The future writer grew up in Fayetteville, North Carolina, taught in North Carolina schools beginning at fourteen, and began a rigorous campaign of self-education, studying French, German, and Greek and reading in Shakespeare, Molière, Dickens, and Dumas, père as well as Harriet Beecher Stowe. By twenty-two he was ready to declare that if he became a writer, "The object of my writings would be not so much the elevation of the colored people as the elevation of the whites—for I consider the unjust spirit of caste which is so insidious as to pervade a whole nation and so powerful as to subject a whole race and all connected with it to scorn and social ostracism—I consider this a barrier to the moral progress of the American people."

White enough to pass for white had he chosen to do so, Chesnutt became familiar with the color line in both North and South. At twenty-five, he left North Carolina to live briefly in New York before settling in

---

3. The mad.

4. Petite, "little one."

Cleveland, where he remained. He worked as a lawyer and court stenographer, and in the 1880s began publishing his stories for a national audience, first in newspapers through the McClure syndicate and in magazines like Puck and Youth's Companion, then in the Atlantic Monthly. In 1899 he published his first collection, The Conjure Woman, dialect stories told by an old black gardener to his northern employer. Then in rapid succession appeared The Wife of His Youth and Other Stories of the Color Line and a brief Life of Frederick Douglass. Turning to writing full time, Chesnutt quickly produced two novels, The House Behind the Cedars (1900) and The Marrow of Tradition (1901). These were not well received, however, and Chesnutt returned to court stenography. His last book published during his lifetime was a novel, The Colonel's Dream (1905). For much of his later life he was in ill health. In 1928 the NAACP awarded him the Spingarn Medal for his "pioneer work as a literary artist depicting the life and struggles of Americans of Negro descent."

Studies include Helen W. Chesnutt, *Charles Waddell Chesnutt: Pioneer of the Color Line* (1952); J. Noel Heermance, *Charles W. Chesnutt: America's First Great Black Novelist* (1974); William L. Andrews, *The Literary Career of Charles W. Chesnutt* (1980); and Sylvia L. Render, *Charles W. Chesnutt* (1980).

——

The Sheriff's Children[1]

BRANSON COUNTY, NORTH CAROLINA, is in a sequestered district of one of the staidest and most conservative States of the Union. Society in Branson County is almost primitive in its simplicity. Most of the white people own the farms they till, and even before the war there were no very wealthy families to force their neighbors, by comparison, into the category of "poor whites."

To Branson County, as to most rural communities in the South, the war is the one historical event that overshadows all others. It is the era from which all local chronicles are dated,—births, deaths, marriages, storms, freshets. No description of the life of any Southern community would be perfect that failed to emphasize the all pervading influence of the great conflict.

---

1. First collected in *The Wife of His Youth and Other Stories of the Color Line* (1899), the source of the present text.

Yet the fierce tide of war that had rushed through the cities and along the great highways of the country had comparatively speaking but slightly disturbed the sluggish current of life in this region, remote from railroads and navigable streams. To the north in Virginia, to the west in Tennessee, and all along the seaboard the war had raged; but the thunder of its cannon had not disturbed the echoes of Branson County, where the loudest sounds heard were the crack of some hunter's rifle, the baying of some deep-mouthed hound, or the yodel of some tuneful negro on his way through the pine forest. To the east, Sherman's army had passed on its march to the sea; but no straggling band of "bummers" had penetrated the confines of Branson County. The war, it is true, had robbed the county of the flower of its young manhood; but the burden of taxation, the doubt and uncertainty of the conflict, and the sting of ultimate defeat, had been borne by the people with an apathy that robbed misfortune of half its sharpness.

The nearest approach to town life afforded by Branson County is found in the little village of Troy, the county seat, a hamlet with a population of four or five hundred.

Ten years make little difference in the appearance of these remote Southern towns. If a railroad is built through one of them, it infuses some enterprise; the social corpse is galvanized by the fresh blood of civilization that pulses along the farthest ramifications of our great system of commercial highways. At the period of which I write, no railroad had come to Troy. If a traveler, accustomed to the bustling life of cities, could have ridden through Troy on a summer day, he might easily have fancied himself in a deserted village. Around him he would have seen weather-beaten houses, innocent of paint, the shingled roofs in many instances covered with a rich growth of moss. Here and there he would have met a razor-backed hog lazily rooting his way along the principal thoroughfare; and more than once he would probably have had to disturb the slumbers of some yellow dog, dozing away the hours in the ardent sunshine, and reluctantly yielding up his place in the middle of the dusty road.

On Saturdays the village presented a somewhat livelier appearance, and the shade trees around the court house square and along Front Street served as hitching-posts for a goodly number of horses and mules and stunted oxen, belonging to the farmer-folk who had come in to trade at the two or three local stores.

A murder was a rare event in Branson County. Every well-informed citizen could tell the number of homicides committed in the county for fifty years back, and whether the slayer, in any given instance, had escaped, either by flight or acquittal, or had suffered the penalty of the law. So, when it became known in Troy early one Friday morning in summer, about ten years after the war, that old Captain Walker, who had served in Mexico under Scott, and had left an arm on the field of Gettysburg, had been foully murdered during the night, there was intense excitement in the village. Business was practically suspended, and the citizens gathered in little groups to discuss the murder, and speculate upon the identity of the murderer. It transpired from testimony at the coroner's inquest, held during the morning, that a strange mulatto had been seen going in the direction of Captain Walker's house the night before, and had been met going away from Troy early Friday morning, by a farmer on his way to town. Other circumstances seemed to connect the stranger with the crime. The sheriff organized a posse to search for him, and early in the evening, when most of the citizens of Troy were at supper, the suspected man was brought in the lodged in the county jail.

By the following morning the news of the capture had spread to the farthest limits of the county. A much larger number of people than usual came to town that Saturday,—bearded men in straw hats and blue homespun shirts, and butternut trousers of great amplitude of material and vagueness of outline; women in homespun frocks and slat-bonnets, with faces as expressionless as the dreary sandhills which gave them a meagre sustenance.

The murder was almost the sole topic of conversation. A steady stream of curious observers visited the house of mourning, and gazed upon the rugged face of the old veteran, now stiff and cold in death; and more than one eye dropped a tear at the remembrance of the cheery smile, and the joke—sometimes superannuated, generally feeble, but always good-natured—with which the captain had been wont to greet his acquaintances. There was a growing sentiment of anger among these stern men, toward the murderer who had thus cut down their friend, and a strong feeling that ordinary justice was too slight a punishment for such a crime.

Toward noon there was an informal gathering of citizens in Dan Tyson's store.

"I hear it 'lowed that Square Kyahtah's too sick ter hol' co'te this evenin'," said one, "an' that the purlim'nary hearin' 'll haf ter go over 'tel nex' week."

A look of disappointment went round the crowd.

"Hit's the durndes', meanes' murder ever committed in this caounty," said another, with moody emphasis.

"I s'pose the nigger 'lowed the Cap'n had some greenbacks," observed a third speaker.

"The Cap'n," said another, with an air of superior information, "has left two bairls of Confedrit money, which he 'spected 'ud be good some day er nuther."

This statement gave rise to a discussion of the speculative value of Confederate money; but in a little while the conversation returned to the murder.

"Hangin' air too good fer the murderer," said one; "he oughter be burnt, stidier bein' hung."

There was an impressive pause at this point, during which a jug of moonlight whiskey went the round of the crowd.

"Well," said a round-shouldered farmer, who, in spite of his peaceable expression and faded gray eye, was known to have been one of the most daring followers of a rebel guerrilla chieftain, "what air yer gwine ter do about it? Ef you fellers air gwine ter set down an' let a wuthless nigger kill the bes' white man in Branson, an' not say nuthin' ner do nuthin', *I'll* move outen the caounty."

This speech gave tone and direction to the rest of the conversation. Whether the fear of losing the round-shouldered farmer operated to bring about the result or not is immaterial to this narrative; but, at all events, the crowd decided to lynch the negro. They agreed that this was the least that could be done to avenge the death of their murdered friend, and that it was a becoming way in which to honor his memory. They had some vague notions of the majesty of the law and the rights of the citizen, but in the passion of the moment these sunk into oblivion; a white man had been killed by a negro.

"The Cap'n was an ole sodger," said one of his friends solemnly. "He'll sleep better when he knows that a co'te-martial has be'n hilt an' jestice done."

By agreement the lynchers were to meet at Tyson's store at five o'clock in the afternoon, and proceed thence to the jail, which was situated down the Lumberton Dirt Road (as the old turnpike antedating the plank-road was called), about half a mile south of the court-house. When the preliminaries of the lynching had been arranged, and a committee appointed to manage the affair, the crowd dispersed, some to go to their dinners, and some to secure recruits for the lynching party.

It was twenty minutes to five o'clock, when an excited negro, panting and perspiring, rushed up to the back door of Sheriff Campbell's dwelling, which stood at a little distance from the jail and somewhat farther than the latter building from the court-house. A turbaned colored woman came to the door in response to the negro's knock.

"Hoddy, Sis' Nance."

"Hoddy, Brer Sam."

"Is de shurff in," inquired the negro.

"Yas, Brer Sam, he's eatin' his dinner," was the answer.

"Will yer ax 'im ter step ter de do' a minute, Sis' Nance?"

The woman went into the dining-room, and a moment later the sheriff came to the door. He was a tall, muscular man, of a ruddier complexion than is usual among Southerners. A pair of keen, deep-set gray eyes looked out from under bushy eyebrows, and about his mouth was a masterful expression, which a full beard, once sandy in color, but now profusely sprinkled with gray, could not entirely conceal. The day was hot; the sheriff had discarded his coat and vest, and had his white shirt open at the throat.

"What do you want, Sam?" he inquired of the negro, who stood hat in hand, wiping the moisture from his face with a ragged shirt-sleeve.

"Shurff, dey gwine ter hang de pris'ner w'at's lock' up in de jail. Dey're comin' dis a-way now. I wuz layin' down on a sack er corn down at de sto', behine a pile er flour-bairls, w'en I hearn Doc' Cain en Kunnel Wright talkin' erbout it. I slip' outen de back do', en run here as fas' as I could. I hearn you say down ter de sto' once't dat you wouldn't let nobody take a pris'ner 'way fum you widout walkin' over yo' dead body, en I thought I'd let you know 'fo' dey come, so yer could pertec' de pris'ner."

The sheriff listened calmly, but his face grew firmer, and a determined gleam lit up his gray eyes. His frame grew more erect, and he unconsciously assumed the attitude of a soldier who momentarily expects to meet the enemy face to face.

"Much obliged, Sam," he answered. "I'll protect the prisoner. Who's coming?"

"I dunno who-all *is* comin'," replied the negro. "Dere's Mistah McSwayne, en Doc' Cain, en Maje' McDonal', en Kunnel Wright, en a heap er yuthers. I wuz so skeered I done furgot mo' d'n half un em. I spec' dey mus' be mos' here by dis time, so I'll git outen de way, fer I don' want nobody fer ter think I wuz mix' up in dis business." The negro glanced nervously down the road toward the town, and made a movement as if to go away.

"Won't you have some dinner first?" asked the sheriff.

The negro looked longingly in at the open door, and sniffed the appetizing odor of boiled pork and collards.

"I ain't got no time fer ter tarry, Shurff," he said, "but Sis' Nance mought gin me sump'n I could kyar in my han' en eat on de way."

A moment later Nancy brought him a huge sandwich of split corn-pone, with a thick slice of fat bacon inserted between the halves, and a couple of baked yams. The negro hastily replaced his ragged hat on his head, dropped the yams in the pocket of his capacious trousers, and, taking the sandwich in his hand, hurried across the road and disappeared in the woods beyond.

The sheriff reentered the house, and put on his coat and hat. He then took down a double-barreled shotgun and loaded it with buckshot. Filling the chambers of a revolver with fresh cartridges, he slipped it into the pocket of the sack-coat which he wore.

A comely young woman in a calico dress watched these proceedings with anxious surprise.

"Where are you going, father?" she asked. She had not heard the conversation with the negro.

"I am goin' over to the jail," responded the sheriff. "There's a mob comin' this way to lynch the nigger we've got locked up. But they won't do it," he added, with emphasis.

"Oh, father! don't go!" pleaded the girl, clinging to his arm; "they'll shoot you if you don't give him up."

"You never mind me, Polly," said her father reassuringly, as he gently unclasped her hands from his arm. "I'll take care of myself and the prisoner, too. There ain't a man in Branson County that would shoot me. Besides, I have faced fire too often to be scared away from my duty. You keep close in the house," he continued, "and if any one disturbs you just use the old horse-pistol in the top bureau drawer. It's a little old-fashioned, but it did good work a few years ago."

The young girl shuddered at this sanguinary allusion, but made no further objection to her father's departure.

The sheriff of Branson was a man far above the average of the community in wealth, education, and social position. His had been one of the few families in the county that before the war had owned large estates and numerous slaves. He had graduated at the State University at Chapel Hill, and had kept up some acquaintance with current literature and advanced thought. He had traveled some in his youth, and was looked up to in the county as an authority on all subjects connected with the outer world. At first an ardent supporter of the Union, he had opposed the secession movement in his native State as long as opposition availed to stem the tide of public opinion. Yielding at last to the force of circumstances, he had entered the Confederate service rather late in the war, and served with distinction through several campaigns, rising in time to the rank of colonel. After the war he had taken the oath of allegiance, and had been chosen by the people as the most available candidate for the office of sheriff, to which he had been elected without opposition. He had filled the office for several terms, and was universally popular with his constituents.

Colonel or Sheriff Campbell, as he was indifferently called, as the military or civil title happened to be most important in the opinion of the person addressing him, had a high sense of the responsibility attaching to his office. He had sworn to do his duty faithfully, and he knew what his duty was, as sheriff, perhaps more clearly than he had apprehended it in other passages of his life. It was, therefore, with no uncertainty in regard to his course that he prepared his weapons and went over to the jail. He had no fears for Polly's safety.

The sheriff had just locked the heavy front door of the jail behind him when a half dozen horsemen, followed by a crowd of men on foot, came round a bend in the road and drew near the jail. They halted in front of the picket fence that surrounded the building, while several of the committee of arrangements rode on a few rods farther to the sheriff's house. One of them dismounted and rapped on the door with his riding-whip.

"Is the sheriff at home?" he inquired.

"No, he has just gone out," replied Polly, who had come to the door.

"We want the jail keys," he continued.

"They are not here," said Polly. "The sheriff has them himself." Then she added, with assumed indifference, "He is at the jail now."

The man turned away, and Polly went into the front room, from which she peered anxiously between the slats of the green blinds of a window that looked toward the jail. Meanwhile the messenger returned to his companions and announced his discovery. It looked as though the sheriff had learned of their design and was preparing to resist it.

One of them stepped forward and rapped on the jail door.

"Well, what is it?" said the sheriff, from within.

"We want to talk to you, Sheriff," replied the spokesman.

There was a little wicket in the door; this the sheriff opened, and answered through it.

"All right, boys, talk away. You are all strangers to me, and I don't know what business you can have." The sheriff did not think it necessary to recognize anybody in particular on such an occasion; the question of identity sometimes comes up in the investigation of these extra-judicial executions.

"We're a committee of citizens and we want to get into the jail."

"What for? It ain't much trouble to get into jail. Most people want to keep out."

The mob was in no humor to appreciate a joke, and the sheriff's witticism fell dead upon an unresponsive audience.

"We want to have a talk with the nigger that killed Cap'n Walker."

"You can talk to that nigger in the courthouse, when he's brought out for trial. Court will be in session here next week. I know what you fellows want, but you can't get my prisoner to-day. Do you want to take the bread out of a poor man's mouth? I get seventy-five cents a day for keeping this prisoner, and he's the only one in jail. I can't have my family suffer just to please you fellows."

One or two young men in the crowd laughed at the idea of Sheriff Campbell's suffering for want of seventy-five cents a day; but they were frowned into silence by those who stood near them.

"Ef yer don't let us in," cried a voice, "we'll bu's' the do' open."

"Bust away," answered the sheriff, raising his voice so that all could hear. "But I give you fair warning. The first man that tries it will be filled with buckshot. I'm sheriff of this county; I know my duty, and I mean to do it."

"What's the use of kicking, Sheriff?" argued one of the leaders of the mob. "The nigger is sure to hang anyhow; he richly deserves it; and we've got to do something to teach the niggers their places, or white people won't be able to live in the county."

"There's no use talking, boys," responded the sheriff. "I'm a white man outside, but in this jail I'm sheriff; and if this nigger's to be hung in this county, I propose to do the hanging. So you fellows might as well right-about-face, and march back to Troy. You've had a pleasant trip, and the exercise will be good for you. You know *me*. I've got powder and ball, and I've faced fire before now, with nothing between me and the enemy, and I don't mean to surrender this jail while I'm able to shoot." Having thus announced his determination, the sheriff closed and fastened the wicket, and looked around for the best position from which to defend the building.

The crowd drew off a little, and the leaders conversed together in low tones.

The Branson County jail was a small, two-story brick building, strongly constructed, with no attempt at architectural ornamentation. Each story was divided into two large cells by a passage running from front to rear. A grated iron door gave entrance from the passage to each of the four cells. The jail seldom had many prisoners in it, and the lower windows had been boarded up. When the sheriff had closed the wicket, he ascended the steep wooden stairs to the upper floor. There was no window at the front of the upper passage, and the most available position from which to watch the movements of the crowd below was the front window of the cell occupied by the solitary prisoner.

The sheriff unlocked the door and entered the cell. The prisoner was crouched in a corner, his yellow face, blanched with terror, looking ghastly in the semi-darkness of the room. A cold perspiration had gathered on his forehead, and his teeth were chattering with affright.

"For God's sake, Sheriff," he murmured hoarsely, "don't let 'em lynch me; I didn't kill the old man."

The sheriff glanced at the cowering wretch with a look of mingled contempt and loathing.

"Get up," he said sharply. "You will probably be hung sooner or later, but it shall not be to-day, if I can help it. I'll unlock your fetters, and if I can't hold the jail, you'll have to make the best fight you can. If I'm shot, I'll consider my responsibility at an end."

There were iron fetters on the prisoner's ankles, and handcuffs on his wrists. These the sheriff unlocked, and they fell clanking to the floor.

"Keep back from the window," said the sheriff. "They might shoot if they saw you."

The sheriff drew toward the window a pine bench which formed a part of the scanty furniture of the cell, and laid his revolver upon it. Then he took his gun in hand, and took his stand at the side of the window where he could with least exposure of himself watch the movements of the crowd below.

The lynchers had not anticipated any determined resistance. Of course they had looked for a formal protest, and perhaps a sufficient show of opposition to excuse the sheriff in the eye of any stickler for legal formalities. They had not however come prepared to fight a battle, and no one of them seemed willing to lead an attack upon the jail. The leaders of the party conferred together with a good deal of animated gesticulation, which was visible to the sheriff from his outlook, though the distance was too great for him to hear what was said. At length one of them broke away from the group, and rode back to the main body of the lynchers, who were restlessly awaiting orders.

"Well, boys," said the messenger, "we'll have to let it go for the present. The sheriff says he'll shoot, and he's got the drop on us this time. There ain't any of us that want to follow Cap'n Walker jest yet. Besides, the sheriff is a good fellow, and we don't want to hurt 'im. But," he added, as if to reassure the crowd, which began to show signs of disappointment, "the nigger might as well say his prayers, for he ain't got long to live."

There was a murmur of dissent from the mob, and several voices insisted that an attack be made on the jail. But pacific counsels finally prevailed, and the mob sullenly withdrew.

The sheriff stood at the window until they had disappeared around the bend in the road. He did not relax his watchfulness when the last one was out of sight. Their withdrawal might be a mere feint, to be followed by a further attempt. So closely, indeed, was his attention drawn to the outside, that he neither saw nor heard the prisoner creep stealthily across the floor, reach out his hand and secure the revolver which lay on the bench behind the sheriff, and creep as noiselessly back to his place in the corner of the room.

A moment after the last of the lynching party had disappeared there was a shot fired from the woods across the road; a bullet whistled by the window and buried itself in the wooden casing a few inches from where the sheriff was standing. Quick as thought, with the instinct born of a semi-guerrilla army experience, he raised his gun and fired twice at the point from which a faint puff of smoke showed the hostile bullet to have been sent. He stood a moment watching, and then rested his gun against the window, and reached behind him mechanically for the other weapon. It was not on the bench. As the sheriff realized this fact, he turned his head and looked into the muzzle of the revolver.

"Stay where you are, Sheriff," said the prisoner, his eyes glistening, his face almost ruddy with excitement.

The sheriff mentally cursed his own carelessness for allowing him to be caught in such a predicament. He had not expected anything of the kind. He had relied on the negro's cowardice and subordination in the presence of an armed white man as a matter of course. The sheriff was a brave man, but realized that the prisoner had him at an immense disadvantage. The two men stood thus for a moment, fighting a harmless duel with their eyes.

"Well, what do you mean to do?" asked the sheriff with apparent calmness.

"To get away, of course," said the prisoner, in a tone which caused the sheriff to look at him more closely, and with an involuntary feeling of apprehension; if the man was not mad, he was in a state of mind akin to madness, and quite as dangerous. The sheriff felt that he must speak the prisoner fair, and watch for a chance to turn the tables on him. The keen-eyed, desperate man before him was a different being altogether from the groveling wretch who had begged so piteously for life a few minutes before.

At length the sheriff spoke:—

"Is this your gratitude to me for saving your life at the risk of my own? If I had not done so, you would now be swinging from the limb of some neighboring tree."

"True," said the prisoner, "you saved my life, but for how long? When you came in, you said Court would sit next week. When the crowd went away they said I had not long to live. It is merely a choice of two ropes."

"While there's life there's hope," replied the sheriff. He uttered this commonplace mechanically, while his brain was busy in trying to think out some way of escape. "If you are innocent you can prove it."

The mulatto kept his eye upon the sheriff. "I did n't kill the old man," he replied; "but I shall never be able to clear myself. I was at his house at nine o'clock. I stole from it the coat that was on my back when I was taken. I would be convicted, even with a fair trial, unless the real murderer were discovered beforehand."

The sheriff knew this only too well. While he was thinking what argument next to use, the prisoner continued:—

"Throw me the keys—no, unlock the door."

The sheriff stood a moment irresolute. The mulatto's eye glittered ominously. The sheriff crossed the room and unlocked the door leading into the passage.

"Now go down and unlock the outside door."

The heart of the sheriff leaped within him. Perhaps he might make a dash for liberty, and gain the outside. He descended the narrow stairs, the prisoner keeping close behind him.

The sheriff inserted the huge iron key into the lock. The rusty bolt yielded slowly. It still remained for him to pull the door open.

"Stop!" thundered the mulatto, who seemed to divine the sheriff's purpose. "Move a muscle, and I'll blow your brains out."

The sheriff obeyed; he realized that his chance had not yet come.

"Now keep on that side of the passage, and go back upstairs."

Keeping the sheriff under cover of the revolver, the mulatto followed him up the stairs. The sheriff expected the prisoner to lock him into the cell and make his own escape. He had about come to the conclusion that the best thing he could do under the circumstances was to submit quietly, and take his chances of recapturing the prisoner after the alarm had been given. The sheriff had faced death more than once upon the battlefield. A few minutes before, well armed, and with a brick wall between him and them he had dared a hundred men to fight; but he felt instinctively that the desperate man confronting him was not to be trifled with, and he was too prudent a man to risk his life against such heavy odds. He had Polly to look after, and there was a limit beyond which devotion to duty would be quixotic and even foolish.

"I want to get away," said the prisoner, "and I don't want to be captured; for if I am I know I will be hung on the spot. I am afraid," he added somewhat reflectively, "that in order to save myself I shall have to kill you."

"Good God!" exclaimed the sheriff in involuntary terror; "you would not kill the man to whom you owe your own life."

"You speak more truly than you know," replied the mulatto. "I indeed owe my life to you."

The sheriff started. He was capable of surprise, even in that moment of extreme peril. "Who are you?" he asked in amazement.

"Tom, Cicely's son," returned the other. He had closed the door and stood talking to the sheriff through the grated opening. "Don't you remember Cicely—Cicely whom you sold, with her child, to the speculator on his way to Alabama?"

The sheriff did remember. He had been sorry for it many a time since. It had been the old story of debts, mortgages, and bad crops. He had quarreled with the mother. The price offered for her and her child had been unusually large, and he had yielded to the combination of anger and pecuniary stress.

"Good God!" he gasped, "you would not murder your own father?"

"My father?" replied the mulatto. "It were well enough for me to claim the relationship, but it comes with poor grace from you to ask anything by reason of it. What father's duty have you ever performed for me? Did you give me your name, or even your protection? Other white men gave their colored sons freedom and money, and sent them to the free States. *You* sold *me* to the rice swamps."

"I at least gave you the life you cling to," murmured the sheriff.

"Life?" said the prisoner, with a sarcastic laugh. "What kind of a life?

You gave me your own blood, your own features,—no man need look at us together twice to see that,—and you gave me a black mother. Poor wretch! She died under the lash, because she had enough womanhood to call her soul her own. You gave me a white man's spirit, and you made me a slave, and crushed it out."

"But you are free now," said the sheriff. He had not doubted, could not doubt, the mulatto's word. He knew whose passions coursed beneath that swarthy skin and burned in the black eyes opposite his own. He saw in this mulatto what he himself might have become had not the safeguards of parental restraint and public opinion been thrown around him.

"Free to do what?" replied the mulatto. "Free in name, but despised and scorned and set aside by the people to whose race I belong far more than to my mother's."

"There are schools," said the sheriff. "You have been to school." He had noticed that the mulatto spoke more eloquently and used better language than most Branson County people.

"I have been to school, and dreamed when I went that it would work some marvelous change in my condition. But what did I learn? I learned to feel that no degree of learning or wisdom will change the color of my skin and that I shall always wear what in my own country is a badge of degradation. When I think about it seriously I do not care particularly for such a life. It is the animal in me, not the man, that flees the gallows. I owe you nothing," he went on, "and expect nothing of you; and it would be no more than justice if I should avenge upon you my mother's wrongs and my own. But still I hate to shoot you; I have never yet taken human life—for I did *not* kill the old captain. Will you promise to give no alarm and make no attempt to capture me until morning, if I do not shoot?"

So absorbed were the two men in their colloquy and their own tumultuous thoughts that neither of them had heard the door below move upon its hinges. Neither of them had heard a light step come stealthily up the stairs, nor seen a slender form creep along the darkening passage toward the mulatto.

The sheriff hesitated. The struggle between his love of life and his sense of duty was a terrific one. It may seem strange that a man who could sell his own child into slavery should hesitate at such a moment, when his life was trembling in the balance. But the baleful influence of human slavery poisoned the very fountains of life, and created new standards of right. The sheriff was conscientious; his conscience had merely been warped by his environment. Let no one ask what his answer would have been; he was spared the necessity of a decision.

"Stop," said the mulatto, "you need not promise. I could not trust you if you did. It is your life for mine; there is but one safe way for me; you must die."

He raised his arm to fire, when there was a flash—a report from the passage behind him. His arm fell heavily at his side, and the pistol dropped at his feet.

The sheriff recovered first from his surprise, and throwing open the door secured the fallen weapon. Then seizing the prisoner he thrust him into the cell and locked the door upon him; after which he turned to Polly, who leaned half-fainting against the wall, her hands clasped over her heart.

"Oh, father, I was just in time!" she cried hysterically, and, wildly sobbing, threw herself into her father's arms.

"I watched until they all went away," she said. "I heard the shot from the woods and I saw you shoot. The when you did not come out I feared something had happened, that perhaps you had been wounded. I got out the other pistol and ran over here. When I found the door open, I knew something was wrong, and when I heard voices I crept upstairs, and reached the top just in time to hear him say he would kill you. Oh, it was a narrow escape!"

When she had grown somewhat calmer, the sheriff left her standing there and went back into the cell. The prisoner's arm was bleeding from a flesh wound. His bravado had given place to a stony apathy. There was no sign in his face of fear of fear or disappointment or feeling of any kind. The sheriff sent Polly to the house for cloth, and bound up the prisoner's wound with a rude skill acquired during his army life.

"I'll have a doctor come and dress the wound in the morning," he said to the prisoner. "It will do very well until then, if you will keep quiet. If the doctor asks you how the wound was caused, you can say that you were struck by the bullet fired from the woods. It would do you no good to have it known that you were shot while attempting to escape."

The prisoner uttered no word of thanks or apology, but sat in sullen silence. When the wounded arm had been bandaged, Polly and her father returned to the house.

The sheriff was in an unusually thoughtful mood that evening. He put salt in his coffee at supper, and poured vinegar over his pancakes. To many of Polly's questions he returned random answers. When he had gone to bed he lay awake for several hours.

In the silent watches of the night, when he was alone with God, there came into his mind a flood of unaccustomed thoughts. An hour or two before, standing face to face with death, he had experienced a sensation similar to that which drowning men are said to feel—a kind of clarifying of the moral faculty, in which the veil of the flesh, with its obscuring passions and prejudices, is pushed aside for a moment, and all the acts of one's life stand out, in the clear light of truth, in their correct proportions and relations,—a state of mind in which one sees himself as God may be supposed to see him. In the reaction following his rescue, this feeling had given place for a time to far different emotions. But now, in the silence of midnight, something of this clearness of spirit returned to the sheriff. He saw that he had owed some duty to this son of his,—that neither law nor custom could destroy a responsibility inherent in the nature of mankind. He could not thus, in the eyes of God at least, shake off the consequences of his sin. Had he never sinned, this wayward spirit would never have come back from the vanished past to haunt him. As these thoughts came, his anger against the mulatto died away, and in its place there sprang up a great pity. The hand of parental authority might have restrained the passions he had seen burning in the prisoner's eyes when the desperate man spoke the words which had seemed to doom his father to death. The sheriff felt that he might have saved this fiery spirit from the slough of slavery; that he might have sent him to the free North, and given him there, or in some other land, an opportunity to turn to usefulness and honorable pursuits the talents that had run to crime, perhaps to madness; he might, still less, have given this son of his the poor simulacrum of liberty which men of his caste could possess in a slave-holding community; or least of all, but still something, he might have kept the boy on the plantation, where the burdens of slavery would have fallen lightly upon him.

The sheriff recalled his own youth. He had inherited an honored name to keep untarnished; he had had a future to make; the picture of a fair young bride had beckoned him on to happiness. The poor wretch now stretched upon a pallet of straw between the brick walls of the jail had had none of these things,—no name, no father, no mother—in the true meaning of motherhood,—and until the past few years no possible future, and then one vague and shadowy in its outline, and dependent for form and substance upon the slow solution of a problem in which there were many unknown quantities.

From what he might have done to what he might yet do was an easy transition for the awakened conscience of the sheriff. It occurred to him, purely as a hypothesis, that he might permit his prisoner to escape; but his oath of office, his duty as sheriff, stood in the way of such a course, and the sheriff dismissed the idea from his mind. He could, however, investigate the circumstances of the murder, and move Heaven and earth to discover the real criminal, for he no longer doubted the prisoner's innocence; he could employ counsel for the accused, and perhaps influence public opinion in his favor. An acquittal once secured, some plan could be devised by which the sheriff might in some degree atone for his crime against this son of his— against society—against God.

When the sheriff had reached this conclusion he fell into an unquiet slumber, from which he awoke late the next morning.

He went over to the jail before breakfast and found the prisoner lying on his pallet, his face turned to the wall; he did not move when the sheriff rattled the door.

"Good-morning," said the latter, in a tone intended to waken the prisoner.

There was no response. The sheriff looked more keenly at the recumbent figure; there was an unnatural rigidity about its attitude.

He hastily unlocked the door and, entering the cell, bent over the prostrate form. There was no sound of breathing; he turned the body over—it was cold and stiff. The prisoner had torn the bandage from his wound and bled to death during the night. He had evidently been dead several hours.

Abraham Cahan
(1860–1951)

Born in a Lithuanian village near Vilna, Abraham Cahan was the son of a Hebrew teacher and was educated in both Hebrew and Russian schools. As a young socialist revolutionary wanted by the police, he fled from Russia, arriving in the United States in 1882. Becoming a socialist journalist and editor in New York, he helped found the Yiddish Forverts *(the Jewish Daily Forward) in 1897 and then edited it from 1902 until his death. Boasting a circulation of a quarter of a million at its peak, the* Forward *published most of the notable Yiddish writers, helping to raise Yiddish from a primarily vernacular language to a medium of distinguished literary accomplishment. Modeling his own writing on the Russian realism of Tolstoy and Chekhov, he caught the eye of William Dean Howells, who championed his career, as he did the career of many another young writer in assisting American literature toward its marked diversification around the turn of the century.*

Cahan's subject was the Jewish life of New York's old East Side. Here, from Henry Street north to Tenth Street and from the Bowery toward the East River, Russian and Polish Jews had begun to settle before the Civil War, augmenting the numbers of German Jews who had begun to arrive in the United States still earlier. As many as 150,000 immigrants and their descendants inhabited the tenements of the area, struggling to keep alive their traditions and to adapt to American life. In Yekl, a Tale of the New York Ghetto *(1896), Cahan wrote of a married couple feeling the stress of the new life. In the stories collected in* The Imported Bridegroom and Other Stories of the New York Ghetto *(1898), he treated similar material, always with a keen eye to the conflicts of cultural traditions. His most celebrated work, the novel* The Rise of David Levinsky *(1917), is an account of life in the old country, immigration, and adaptation to the world of American business, told in the first person by a man who in some ways questions the value of his ultimate success.*

Circumstances[1]

I

Tatyana Markovna Lurie had just received the July number of "Russian Thought," and was in a flurry. She felt like devouring all the odd dozen of articles in the voluminous book at once; and the patience failing her to cut the leaves, she fell to prying between them on the rocking-chair which she had drawn up close to one of the two windows of the best room.

Altogether, the residence of the Luries consisted of three small uncarpeted and scantily furnished apartments, and occupied a fourth of the top floor of a veteran tenement house on Madison Street.

Ultimately, Tatyana Markovna settled on an extensive review of a new translation of Guy de Maupassant's stories.[2] But here again she was burning to glance over the beginning, the middle, and the end of the article simultaneously. And so she sat, feverishly skipping and hopping over the lines, until a thought expressed by the critic, and which struck her as identical with one she had set forth in a recent discussion with her husband, finally fixed her attention and overspread her youthful little face with radiance. She was fore-relishing her triumph when, upon Boris's return from work, she would show him the passage; for in their debate he had made light of her contention, and met her irresolute demurrer with the patronizing and slightly ironical tone which he usually took while discussing book questions with her.

But at the thought of Boris she suddenly remembered her soup, and growing pale she put the magazine aside, and darted into the semi-obscurity of the kitchen.

Tatyana, or Tanya, as her husband would fondly call her, was the daughter of a merchant and Hebrew writer in Kieff, who usually lost upon his literary ventures what he would save from his business. It was not long after she had graduated from one of the female gymnasiums[3] of her native city that she met Boris Lurie, then a law student at the University of St. Vladimir.

He was far from being what Russian college girls would call "a dear little soul;" for he was tall and lank, awkwardly nearsighted, and rather plain of feature, and the scar over his left eyebrow, too, added anything but beauty

---

1. From *The Imported Bridegroom and Other Stories of the New York Ghetto* (1898), the source of the present text.

2. Guy de Maupassant (1850–1893), French short story writer and novelist.

3. High schools.

to his looks. But for all that, the married young women of his circle voted him decidedly interesting.

Tanya was attracted by his authoritative tone and rough sort of impetuosity upon discussing social or literary topics; by his reputation of being one of the best-read men at the university, as well as a leading spirit in student "circles," and by the perfect Russian way in which his coal-black hair fell over his commanding forehead. As to him, he was charmed by that in her which had charmed many a student before him: the delicate freshness of her pink complexion, which, by the time we first find her in the Madison Street tenement, had only partially faded; the enthusiastic smile beaming from her every feature as she spoke; and the way her little nose, the least bit retrousseé, would look upward, and her beautiful hazel eyes would assume a look of childlike curiosity, while she was listening to her interlocutor.

They were married immediately after his graduation, with the intention of settling in Kremenchug, where he had every prospect of a large practice. But when he presented himself for admission to the bar, as a "private attorney," he encountered obstacle after obstacle. He tried another district, but with no better success. By that time it had become clear that the government was bent upon keeping the Jews out of the forensic profession, although it had not officially placed it upon the list of vocations proscribed to their race.

After a year of peregrination and petitioning he came, a bundle of nerves, to Jitomir to make a last attempt in the province of Volyn.

A high judiciary officer who received him rather politely, made, in the course of their interview, the semi-jocular remark that the way to the bar lay through the baptismal font.

"Villain!" Lurie thundered, his fists clenched and his eyes flashing.

Luckily the functionary was a cool-headed old man who knew how to avoid unsavory publicity. And so, when Lurie defiantly started to stalk out of the room, he was not stopped.

A month or two later, Boris and Tanya arrived in New York.

It was near seven o'clock when Boris came from the pearl-button factory where he earned, at piece-work, from six to seven dollars a week. As Tanya heard his footsteps through the door she sprang to her feet and, with a joyous gleam in her eye, she ran out to meet him at the head of the stairs. In her delight she at once forgot the Maupassant article.

After an affectionate greeting she said, with burlesque supplication:—

"Don't get angry, Borya, but I am afraid I have flunked on my soup again."

His fatigued smile expanded.

"The worst of it," she pursued, "is the fact that this time my negligence resulted from something which is against you. Yes, I have something that will show you that Mr. Boris has not monopolized all the wisdom in the world; that other people know something, too. Yes, sir!" she beamingly concluded, in English.

"You must have received the July number, have you?" he burst out, flushing with anticipated delight.

"Not your booseeness" (business), she replied in English, playfully pronouncing the words as in Russian. "You know you can't get it before supper is over; so what is the use asking?" she added, in the tongue of her native country. With which she briskly busied herself about the table and the stove, glowing with happiness, every inch of her a woman in the long-awaited presence of the man she loves.

Boris's shabby working clothes, his few days' growth of beard and general appearance of physical exhaustion vainly combined, as it were, to extinguish the light of culture and intellectuality from his looks; they only succeeded in adding the tinge of martyrdom to them. As to Tatyana, she had got so far habituated to the change that she was only occasionally aware of it. And when she was, it would move her to pity and quicken her love for him. At such moments his poor workaday clothes would appear to her as something akin to the prison garb of the exiled student in Siberia.

"Let me just take a glance at the table of contents," he begged, brokenly, washing himself at the sink.

"After supper."

"Then do you tell me what there is to read. Anything interesting?"

"After supper."

"Or is it that you begrudge me the few minutes' talk we have together?" she resumed more earnestly, after a slight pause. "The whole day I am all alone, and when he comes he plunges into some book or other or falls asleep like a murdered man. All there remains is the half hour at supper; so that, too, he would willingly deprive me of."

It was Tanya's standing grievance, and she would deliver himself of it on the slightest provocation, often quite irrelevantly.

After supper she read to him the passage which she regarded as an indorsement of her view upon Maupassant. When she had finished and turned to him a face full of triumphant inquiry, she was rather disappointed by the lukewarm readiness of his surrender.

"Oh, I see. It is rather an interesting point," he remarked lazily.

He was reclining on the stiff carpet-covered lounge in the front room, while she was seated in the rocker, in front of him. It flashed across her mind that such unusual tractability in him might augur some concession to be exacted from her. She flew into a mild little passion in advance, but made no inquiries, and only said, with good-natured sarcasm:—

"Of course, once it is printed in 'Russian Thought,' it is 'rather an interesting point,' but when it was only Tanya who made it, why then it was mere rubbish."

"You know I never said it was rubbish, Tanya," he returned deprecatingly.

After a slight pause, he resumed listlessly:—

"Besides, I am sick of these 'interesting points.' They have been the ruin of us, Tanychka; they eat us up alive, these 'interesting points'—the deuce grab them. If I cared less about 'interesting points'"—he articulated the two words with venomous relish—"and a little more about your future and mine, I might not now have to stick in a button factory."

She listened to him with an amused air, and when he paused, she said flippantly":—

"We have heard it before."

"So much the worse for both of us. If you at least took a more sober view of things! Seriously, Tanya, you ought to make life a burden to me until I begin to do something to get out of this devilish—of this villainous, unpardonable position."

"You should have married Cecilia Trotzky, then," she said, laughing.

Cecilia Trotzky was the virago among the educated Russo-Jewish immigrants, who form a numerous colony within a colony in the Ghetto of New York. She was described as a woman who had placed her husband in a medical college, then made a point of sending him supperless to bed every time he failed to study his lessons, and later, when he was practicing, fixed the fees with his patients.

"Well, what is the use of joking?" he said gloomily, suppressing a smile. "Every illiterate nonentity," he went on, letting the words filter through his teeth with languid bitterness, "every shop clerk, who at home hardly knew there was such a thing as a university in the world, goes to college here; and I am serving the community by supplying it with pearl buttons for six dollars a week. Would this were regular, at least! But it is not. I forgot to tell you, but we may again have a slack season, Tanya. Oh! I will not let things go on like this. If I don't begin to do something at once, I shall send a bullet through my forehead. You may laugh, but this time it is not idle talk. From this day on I shall be a different man. I have a plan; I have considered everything carefully. If we wish to get rid of our beggarly position, of this terrible feeling of insecurity and need," he proceeded, as he raised himself to a sitting posture, his voice gathering energy and his features becoming contorted with an expression of disgust; "if we really mean to free ourselves from this constant trembling lest I lose my job, from these excursions to the pawn shops—laugh away! laugh away!—but, as I say, if we seriously wish to make it possible for me to enter some college here, we must send all literature and magazines and all gush about Russia to the deuce, and do as others do. I have a splendid plan. Everything depends upon you, Tanya."

At this the childlike look of curiosity came into her face. But he seemed in no hurry to come to the point.

"People who hang about pawn shops have no right to 'interesting points' and Guy de Maupassant and that sort of luxury. Poverty *is* a crime! Well, but from now on, everything will be different. Listen, Tanychka; the greatest trouble is the rent, is it not? It eats up the larger part of my wages—that is, provided I work full time; and you know how we tremble and are on the verge of insanity each time the first of the month is drawing near. If we wish to achieve something, we must be satisfied to pinch ourselves and to put up with some inconvenience. Above all, we must not forget that I am a common workingman. Well, every workingman's family around here keeps a boarder or two; let us also take one. There is no way out of it, Tanya."

He uttered the concluding words with studied nonchalance, but without daring to look her in the face.

"Bor-ya!" she exclaimed, with a bewildered air.

Her manner angered him.

"There, now! I expected as much!" he said irascibly. And continuing in softer accents, he forced her to listen to the details of his project. The boarder's pay would nearly come up to their rent. If they lived more economically than now they could save up enough for his first year's tuition at a New York college, or, as a stepping-stone, for a newspaper stand. Free from worry about their rent, he would be in a fitter mood to study English after work. In course of time he would know the language enough to teach it to the uneducated workingmen of the Jewish quarter; and so he would be liberated from his factory yoke, as many an immigrant of his class had been. Dalsky, a friend of theirs, and a former classmate of Boris's, who was studying medicine, earned his living by giving such lessons in English, and, by the way, he was now looking for a lodging. Why should they not offer him their parlor? They could do with the kitchen and the bedroom. Besides, Dalsky would be one of the family, and would have only partial use of the parlor.

As the plan assumed a personified form in her mind—the face of a definite boarder—her realization of its horrors was so keen that she shut her ears and begged Boris to take pity on her and desist. Whereupon he flew into a rage and charged her with nursing aristocratic instincts which in their present position they could not afford. She retorted, tearfully, that she was ready to put up with any amount of additional work and discomfort, but that she did not care to have a "constant cataract on the eye."

"God knows you give me little enough of your company, as it is. I must have tired you capitally, if you seek somebody to talk to and to save you from being alone with me."

"You know it is the rankest nonsense you are saying!" he flamed out. "And what is the use crying like that? As if I took a delight in the whole affair! Cry to our circumstances, not to me. Circumstances, circumstances, Tanya!" he repeated, with pleading vehemence.

Little by little he relented, however, and eventually he promised never to mention the matter again, although inwardly both of them felt that he would. He sat by her side on the lounge, fondling her little hands and murmuring love, when suddenly bending upon him an imploring face, she said, in a tremulous, tearful voice: "Borinka, dear! I shall also go to some factory. We will get along without boarders," with which she fell upon his shoulder in a fit of heart-rending sobbing.

He clasped her to him, whispering: "You know, my angel, that I would commit suicide before letting you go to work. Don't worry, my joy, we *will* get along without boarders."

"I want no strangers to hang around the house all the time; I want to be with you alone, I want nobody, nobody, nobody else in the world!" she said, pressing him tightly to her heart.

III

On the following evening, as Boris was musingly trudging on his way home, after work, it suddenly came over him that his manner with the foreman of the shop was assuming a rather obsequious nature. Work was scarce, and the distribution of it was, to a considerable extent, a matter of favoritism. He recalled how the Czech foreman, half tipsy with beer, had been making some stupid efforts at being witty, and how he, Boris Lurie; standing by, in greedy expectation of work, had smiled a broad, ingratiating smile of approbation. At the moment he had been so far merged in the surroundings and in his anxiety about work that he had not been aware of doing anything unnatural. But now, as it all came back to him, with inexorable vividness, and he beheld his own wretched, artificial smile, he was overcome with disgust. "Vil-lain!" he broke out at himself, gnashing his teeth; and at the next moment he was at the point of bursting into tears for self-pity. To think of him, who had not hesitated to call the president of a Russian court "rogue" to his face, simpering like a miserable time-server at every stupidity and nastiness of a drunken brute! Is that what circumstances had made of him?

He reached home out of temper, and before supper was well over he reopened the discussion of his scheme. It again led to a slight quarrel, which was again made up by his surrender, as in the previous instance.

A few days later he was "laid off" for a fortnight.

To eke out their rent they had to forego meat. For several consecutive days they lived on bread and butter and coffee. Boris grew extremely nervous and irritable.

One morning, coming back from the pawn shops, Boris, pale and solemn, quietly laid on the kitchen table the package which he had under his arm.

"They wouldn't take it," he said almost in a whisper. "It is not worth anything, they say."

Tanya only raised at him a meek glance, and went on with her work. Boris fell to pacing the front room. They could not speak.

Presently she stepped up to his side and said, with rueful tenderness:—

"Well, what is the good of grieving, Borya?"

Their hands clasped tightly, and their eyes fixed themselves forlornly on the floor.

"I have promised Dalsky an answer," he said, after a little.

"Let him move in," she returned lugubriously, with a slight shrug of her shoulder, as if submitting to fate.

IV

It was about nine in the morning, and Dalsky, slowly pacing the front room, "Quiz-Compend" in hand, was reviewing his lesson. He had a certain dignity and nobleness of feature which consorted well with the mysterious pallor of his oval face, and to which, by the way, his moral complexion gave him perfect right. Then, too, his middle-sized form was exceedingly well proportioned. But for the rest, his looks, like everything else about him, presented nothing to produce an impression.

Presently he deliberately closed the book, carefully placed it on his whatnot, and, his eye falling upon the little flower-pot on the window, he noiselessly stepped into the kitchen, where Tanya was ironing some trifles on the dining-table.

"What are you looking for, Monsieur Dalsky?" she inquired amiably, turning her flushed face to the boarder, who was then gazing about the kitchen.

"Nothing—do not trouble yourself, Tatyana Markovna—I have got it," he answered politely, resting the soft look of his good gray eyes at her, and showing the enameled cup which he was carrying to the water-tap.

"It is high time to give my flower-pot its breakfast; it must have grown hungry," he remarked unobtrusively, retracing his steps to the front room, with the cup half filled with water.

"It gets good board with you, your little flower-pot," Tanya returned, in her plaintive soprano, speaking through the open window, which sometimes served to separate and sometimes to connect the kitchen and the front room. "By the way, it is time for its master to have its breakfast too. Shall I set the table, Monsieur Dalsky?"

"All rightissimo!" answered the student jestingly, with the remotest suggestion of a chivalrous smile and a bow of his head.

As he ate, she made a playful attempt at reading the portly text-book, which he had brought with him. Whenever she happened to mispronounce an English word, he would set her right, in a matter-of-fact way; whereupon she accepted his correction with a slight blush and a smile, somewhat bashful and somewhat humorous.

Hardly a fortnight had elapsed since Dalsky had installed himself and his scanty effects at the Luries', yet he seemed to have grown into the family, and the three felt as if they had dwelt together all their lives. His presence in the house produced a change that was at once striking and imperceptible. When free from college and from teaching, an hour or two in the morning and a few hours during the afternoon, he would stay at home studying or reading, humming, between whiles, some opera tune, or rolling up a cigarette and smoking it as he paced up and down the floor—all of which he did softly, unobtrusively, with a sort of pleasing fluency. Often he would bring from the street some useful or decorative trifle—a match-box, a towel-ring, a bit of bric-a-brac for the mantelpiece, a flower-pot. At supper he, Boris and Tanya would have a friendly chat over the contents of the newspapers, or the gossip of the colony, or some Russian book, although Boris was apt to monopolize the time for his animadversions upon the occurrences in the pearl-button shop, which both Tanya and Dalsky were beginning to think rather too minute and uninteresting. "Poor fellow; the pearl-button environment *has* eaten him up," the medical student would say to himself, with heartfelt commiseration. As to his own college, he would scarcely ever refer to it. After supper he usually left for his private lessons, after which he would perhaps drop in at the Russian Students' Club; and altogether his presence did not in the least encroach upon the privacy of the Luries' life, while, on the other hand, it seemed to have breathed an easier and pleasanter atmosphere into their home.

"Well, was there any ground for making so much ado?" Boris once said triumphantly. "We are as much alone as ever, and you are not lonely all day, into the bargain."

Dalsky had come to America with the definite purpose of studying and then practicing medicine. He had landed penniless, yet in a little over two years, and before his friends in the colony had noticed it, he was in a position to pay his first year's tuition and to meet all the other bills of his humble, but well ordered and, to him, gratifying living.

He was a normally constituted and well-regulated young man of twenty-five, a year or two Lurie's junior. There was nothing bright nor deep about him, but he was seldom guilty of a gross want of tact. He would be the last man to neglect his task on account of a ball or an interesting book, yet he was never classed among the "grinds." He was endowed with a light touch for things as well as for men, and with that faculty for ranking high in his class, which, as we all know, does not always precede distinction in the school of life. This sort of people give the world very little, ask of it still less, but get more than they give.

As he neither intruded too far into other people's souls, nor allowed others too deep into his own confidence, he was at peace with himself and everybody else in the colony.

V

Three months more had passed. The button factory was busy. Boris's hard, uncongenial toil was deepening its impress upon him. When he came from work he would be so completely fagged out that an English grammar was out of the question.

He grew more morose every day.

Tanya was becoming irritable with him.

One afternoon after six she was pensively rocking and humming a Russian folk-song, one of her little white hands resting on an open Russian book in her lap. Dalsky was out, for it was one of those days when he would stay at college until six and come home at about the same time as Boris.

Presently she was awakened from her reverie by the sound of footsteps. The door opened before she had time to make out whose they were, and as her eye fell upon Boris, a shadow of disappointment flitted across her brow.

Still, at the sight of his overworked face, her heart was wrung with pity, and she greeted him with a commiserating, nervous, exaggerated sort of cordiality.

After a little he took to expounding a plan, bearing upon their affairs, which he had conceived while at work. She started to listen with real interest, but her attention soon wandered away, and as he went on she gazed at him blankly and nodded irrelevant assent.

"What is the use of talking, since you are not listening anyway?" he said, mildly.

She was about to say softly, "Excuse me, Borya, say it again, I'll listen," but she said resentfully, "Suit yourself!"

His countenance fell.

"Any letters from home?" he demanded, after a while, to break an awkward stillness.

"No," she replied, with an impatient jerk of her shoulder.

He gave a perplexed shrug, and took up his grammar.

When Dalsky came he found them plainly out of sorts with each other. Tanya returned his "Good health to you," only partly relaxing the frown on her face. Boris raised his black head from his book; his brusque 'Good health, Dalsky!" had scarcely left his lips when his short-sighted eyes again nearly touched the open grammar.

"You must excuse me; I am really sorry to have kept you waiting," the boarder apologized, methodically taking off his overcoat and gently brushing its velvet collar before hanging it up, "but I was unavoidably detained at the lecture, and then I met Stern, and you know how hard it is to shake oneself free from him."

"It is not late at all," Tanya observed, unnecessarily retaining a vestige of the cloud upon her countenance. "What does he want, Stern? Some new scheme again?"

"You hit it there, Tatyana Markovna; and, by the way, you two are to play first violin in it."

"I?" asked Tanya, her countenance suddenly blazing up with confused animation. "What is it?" Boris laid down his book and pricked up his ears.

"He has unearthed some remarkable dialogue in Little Russian,—you know everything Stern comes across is remarkable. Well, and he wants the two of you to recite it or act it—that's your business—at the New Year's gathering."

"What an idiotic plan!" was Boris's verdict, which his countenance belied unceremoniously.

"Who else is going to participate?" inquired Tanya.

Fixing his mild gray eyes on his youthful landlady, Dalsky proceeded to describe the prospective entertainment in detail. Presently he grew absent-minded and lost the thread of a sentence. He noticed that, as his listener's eyes met his, her gaze became unsteady, wandering, as though she were looked out of countenance.

She confusedly transferred her glance to his fresh, clean-shaven face and then to his neatly tied scarf and immaculate shirt front.

Boris wore a blue flannel shirt, and, as usual in the middle of the week, his face was overgrown with what he jocosely called underbrush. As he had warmed up to Dalsky's subject and rose to his feet to ply him with questions, the contrast which the broad, leaf-shaped gas flame illuminated was striking. It was one between a worn, wretched workingman and a trim, fresh-looking college student.

Supper passed in animated conversation, as usual. When it was over and the boarder was gone to his pupils, Boris, reclining on the lounge, took up his "Dombey and Son"[4] and Alexandroff's Dictionary. In a quarter of an hour he was fast asleep and snoring. It attracted the attention of Tanya, who sat near by, reading her Russian novel. She let the book rest on her lap and fell to contemplating her husband. His sprawling posture and his snores at once revolted her and filled her with pity. She looked at the scar over his eyebrow, and it pained her; and yet, somehow, she could not divert her eyes from it. At the same time she felt a vague reminiscence stirring in her mind. What was it? She seemed to have seen or heard or read something somewhere which had a certain bearing upon the painful feeling which she was now nursing, in spite of herself, as she was eyeing the scar over Boris's eyebrow. What could it be?

A strenuous mental effort brought to her mind the passage in Tolstoi's novel[5] where Anna Karenina, after having fallen under Vronsky's charm, is met by her husband upon her return to St. Petersburg, whereupon the first thing that strikes her about him is the uncouth hugeness of his ears.

It was not the first time her thoughts had run in this direction. She had repeatedly caught herself dwelling upon such apparently silly subjects as the graceful trick which Dalsky had in knocking off the ashes of his cigarette, or the way he would look about the cupboard for the cup with which he watered his plant, or, again, the soft ring of his voice as he said, "Tatyana Markovna!"—the thoroughly Russian form of address, not much in vogue in the colony. Once, upon touching his flower on the window sill, she

---

4. A novel by Charles Dickens (1812–1870).

5. *Anna Karenina*, by Leo Tolstoy (1828–1910).

became conscious of a thrill, deliciously disquieting and as if whispering something to her. And yet, as the case of Anna Karenina now came to her mind, as an illustration of her own position, it smote her consciousness as a startling discovery.

"And so I am a married woman in love with another man!" was her first thought; and with her soul divided between a benumbing terror and the sweet titillation produced by a sense of tasting forbidden fruit, she involuntarily repeated the mental exclamation:—

"Yes, I am a married woman in love with another man!"

And with a painful, savage sort of relish she went on staring at her husband's scar and listening to his fatigued breathing. There was a moment when a wave of sympathy suddenly surged to her heart and nearly moved her to tears; but at the next moment it came back to her that it was at Boris's insistance, and in spite of her sobs, that the boarder had been taken into the house; whereupon her heart swelled with a furious sense of revenge. The image of Dalsky floated past her mental vision and agitated her soul with a novel feeling. When a moment or two after she threw a glance at the looking-glass she seemed a stranger to herself.

"Is this Tanya? Is this the respectable, decorous young woman that she has been?" she seemed to soliloquize. "What nonsense; why not? What have I done? Dalsky himself does not even suspect anything." It seemed as if she were listening to the depth of her own soul for a favorable answer to her question, and as if the favorable answer did not come.

She became fearful of herself, and, with another sudden flow of affection for her husband, she stepped up to his side to wake him; but as she came into close contact with him, the wave of tenderness ebbed away and she left the room.

"It *is* nonsense," she decided; "still, I must invent some pretext for insisting upon his removal. Then I'll forget him, anyway."

Whether she would have had the courage to carry out her resolve or not, is not known, for the task soon became superfluous.

A few days later, as Dalsky was drawing on his overcoat to leave for his lessons, he said, rather awkwardly, addressing himself to both, while looking at Boris:—

"By the way, I have to tell you something. I am afraid that devilish college will make it impossible for me to live downtown."

Both Boris and Tanya grew pale.

"You see," Dalsky pursued, "the lectures and the work in the dissecting-room are so scattered throughout the day that I don't see my way out unless I get a room in the neighborhood of the college." And to talk himself out of the embarrassing position, he went on to explain college affairs with unnecessary detail.

As a matter of fact, however, his whole explanation, although not based on an untruth, was not the real cause of his determination to leave the Luries. He had known Boris in his better days, and now sympathized with him and Tanya keenly. The frequent outbreaks of temper between husband

and wife, and the cloud which now almost constantly hung over the house, heavily bore down upon him as a friend, and made his life there extremely uncomfortable. At last he had perceived the roving, nonplussed look in her eyes as their glances met. Once become observant in this direction, he noticed a thousand and one other little things which seemed to confirm his suspicion. "Can it be that she is interested in me?" he said to himself. For a moment the thought caressed his vanity and conjured up the image of Tanya in a novel aspect, which lured him and spoke of the possibility of reciprocating her feeling—of an adventure.

It was on the very next day that he announced his intention to move.

VI

The house became so dreary to Tanya that her loneliness during the day frightened her, though the presence of Boris irritated her more than ever. She felt as if some member of the household had died. Wherever she turned she beheld some trace of the student; worse than anything else was the window-plant, which Dalsky had left behind him. She avoided looking at it, lest it should thrill her with a crushing sense of her desolation, of her bereavement, as it were. Yet, when she was about to remove it, she had not the heart to do it. She strayed about like a shadow, and often felt as though it were enough to touch her to make her melt away in tears.

One evening, after an unbearable silence, succeeding a sharp altercation, Boris asked, pleadingly:—

"What has become of you, Tanya? I simply fail to recognize you."

"If you understand, then it is foolish to ask," she retorted, with a smile of mild sarcasm, eyeing the floor.

"I understand nothing." But as the words left his lips, something suddenly dawned upon him which made his blood run cold. An array of situations which had produced an impression upon him, but which had been lost upon his consciousness, now uprose in his mind. He grew ashen pale.

"Well, so much the worse," said she.

"Tell me, and I will know," he rejoined, with studied irony, while in his heart he was praying Heaven that his misgivings might prove baseless.

"Oh! I think you do understand; you are not so blind." Her voice now sounded alien in his ears, and she herself seemed to him suddenly changed—as if she had in one moment become transmuted into an older, wiser, sterner, and more beautiful, fiercely beautiful, woman.

"I swear to you that I do not know anything."

"Very well, then; I shall write it," she said, with a sudden determination, rising to produce paper, pen, and ink.

"All right," he said, in abject cowardice, with a meaningless smile.

She wrote:—

"I am your best friend in the world. I have been thinking, and thinking, and have arrived at the conclusion that the best thing for us to do is to part for a time. I do not blame anybody but myself, but I cannot help it. I have no moral right to live with you as long as my mind is constantly occupied with somebody else. I have struggled hard to keep out the thoughts of him, but it is of no avail."

The phlegmatic ticking of the cheap alarm clock was singing a solemn accompaniment to the impressive stillness of the surroundings. Boris, gazing at the corner of the room with a faint, stolid smile, was almost trembling. Tanya's face was burning with excitement. She went on:—

"I repeat, I have only myself to blame, and I am doing my best to struggle out of this state of mind. But while it lasts, my false, my dishonest position in this house aggravates things. I wish to be alone, for a while, at least. Then, under new conditions, I hope I shall soon get over it. For the sake of everything that is good, do not attempt to persuade me to stay. It is all thought out and decided. Nor do you need offer to support me. I have no right to it, and will not accept it under any circumstances. I can work and earn my own living. I am prepared to bear the cross. Besides, shall I be the only Russian college woman to work in an American factory? Above all, do not let anybody know anything—the person to whom I have referred not excluded, *of course*. I am sure he does not suspect anything. Do not let him surmise the cause of it all, if you do not wish to see my corpse. We can invent some explanation."

VII

It was the early part of a bleak wintry evening. The interior of Silberman's shop, crowded with men and women and their sewing-machines, every bit of space truckled up with disorderly piles of finished shirts or bundles of stuff, was dappled with cheerless gaslight. The spacious, barn-like loft rang and trembled with a chaos of mournful and merry song, vying with the insolent rattle of the machines. There were synagogue airs in the chorus and airs of the Jewish stage; popular American airs, airs from the dancing schools, and time-honored airs imported from Russia, Poland, Galicia, Roumania, Hungary.

Only Tanya was not singing. Bent upon her machine, in a remote corner, she was practicing a straight stitch upon some cuttings. She was making marked progress, and, flushed with her success, had almost grown oblivious of the heavy lump at her heart, and the pricking pain which seemed to fill her every limb. Presently the girl next her, who had been rapturously singing "I have a girl in Baltimore" in a sort of crosstune between the song's own melody and the highly melancholy strains of a Hebrew prayer, suddenly switched off into one of the most Russian of Russian folk-songs,—

> By the little brook,
> By the little bridge,
> Grass was growing

This she sang with such an un-Russian flavor, and pronounced the words with such a strong Yiddish accent, and so illiterately, that Tanya gnashed her teeth as if touched to the quick, and closed her eyes and ears. The surroundings again grew terrible to her. Commencement Day at the Kieff Gymnasium loomed before her imagination, and she beheld herself one of a group of blooming young maidens, all in fresh brown dresses with black aprons, singing that very song, but in sturdy, ringing, charming Russian. A cruel anguish choked her. Everybody and everything about her was so strange, so hideously hostile, so exile-like! She once more saw the little home where she had recently reigned. "How do I happen here?" she asked herself. She thought of Boris, and was tempted to run back to him, to fly into his arms and beg him to establish a home again. But presently came the image of Dalsky, neat, polite, dignified, and noiseless; and she once more fell to her machine, and with a furious cruelty for herself, she went on working the treadle. Whereupon her mind gradually occupied itself with the New Year's entertainment, with the way the crowd would be commenting upon her separation, and above all, with her failure to appear on the platform to recite in Little Russian and to evoke a storm of applause in the presence of Dalsky.

At that time Boris was on his way from work, in the direction of Madison Street. It was the second day after he had cleared the rooms by selling the furniture and cooking utensils to the neighbors, who rushed at them like flies at a drop of molasses. But he still had his books and some other effects to remove. When he entered the rooms, there was light enough from the street to show the unwonted darkness in them. A silvery streak fell upon the black aperture which had the day before been filled with the pipe of a little parlor stove. This and the weird gloom of the rest of the apartment overwhelmed him with distress and terror. He hastened to light the gas. The dead emptiness of the three rooms which so recently had been full of life, the floors littered with traces of Tanya and their life together—every corner and recess had a look of doleful, mysterious reproach.

For the first time he seemed to realize what had befallen him; and for the first time in many years he burst into tears. Hot tears they were, and they fell in vehement drops, as, leaning his wearied form against the doorpost and burying his face in his arm, he whispered brokenly, "Tanychka! Tanychka!"

Edith Maud Eaton (Sui Sin Far)
(1865–1914)

Edith Maud Eaton was the eldest daughter of a Chinese mother and an English father. She was one of fourteen children, raised in a culturally rich family, and living at various times in England, Canada, and the United States. Eaton noted in her autobiographical essay "Leaves from the Mental Portfolio of an Eurasian" that her facial features did not look Chinese. Faced with bigotry in childhood, she declared, "I'd rather be Chinese than anything else in the world," and throughout her life, she always asserted her Chinese identity and searched out Chinese settlements in each city where she lived. Her tombstone in the Protestant cemetery in Montreal bears the inscription in Chinese characters "Yi bu wong hua" (the righteous one does not forget her country).

Under the pen name Sui Sin Far, Chinese for "waterlily," Eaton wrote a series of realistic narratives about the lives of Chinese immigrants in the United States and Canada. The stories began appearing in national publications such as Overland, Century, The Chautauquan, Good Housekeeping, *and the* New England Magazine *in the late 1880s. Eaton was the first person of Chinese ancestry to write in defense of a group subjected to bigotry, violence, and repressive immigration policies, culminating in the Chinese Exclusion Act of 1882.*

The following piece was first published in the New York magazine *Independent* (September 2, 1909) and was collected with other stories in *Mrs. Spring Fragrance* (1912).

In the Land of the Free

I

"See, Little One—the hills in the morning sun. There is thy[1] home for years to come. It is very beautiful and thou wilt be very happy there."

The Little One looked up into his mother's face in perfect faith. He was engaged in the pleasant occupation of sucking a sweetmeat; but that did not prevent him from gurgling responsively.

"Yes, my olive bud; there is where thy father is making a fortune for thee. Thy father! Oh, wilt thou not be glad to behold his dear face. 'Twas for thee I left him."

The Little One ducked his chin sympathetically against his mother's knee. She lifted him on to her lap. He was two years old, a round, dimple-cheeked boy with bright brown eyes and a sturdy little frame.

"Ah! Ah! Ah! Ooh! Ooh! Ooh!" puffed he, mocking a tugboat steaming by.

San Francisco's waterfront was lined with ships and steamers, while other craft, large and small, including a couple of white transports from the Philippines, lay at anchor here and there off shore. It was some time before the *Eastern Queen* could get docked, and even after that was accomplished, a lone Chinaman who had been waiting on the wharf for an hour was detained that much longer by men with the initials U.S.C.[2] on their caps, before he could board the steamer and welcome his wife and child.

"This is thy son," announced the happy Lae Choo.

Hom Hing lifted the child, felt of his little body and limbs, gazed into his face with proud and joyous eyes; then turned inquiringly to a customs officer at his elbow.

"That's a fine boy you have there," said the man. "Where was he born?"

"In China," answered Hom Hing, swinging the Little One on his right shoulder, preparatory to leading his wife off the steamer.

"Ever been to America before?"

"No, not he," answered the father with a happy laugh.

The customs officer beckoned to another.

"This little fellow," said he, "is visiting America for the first time."

---

1. The use of "thee" and "thou" is intended to suggest that the mother is speaking to her small child in Chinese dialect.

2. U.S. Customs.

The other customs officer stroked his chin reflectively.

"Good day," said Hom Hing.

"Wait!" commanded one of the officers. "You cannot go just yet."

"What more now?" asked Hom Hing.

"I'm afraid," said the first customs officer, "that we cannot allow the boy to go ashore. There is nothing in the papers that you have shown us— your wife's papers and your own—having any bearing upon the child."

"There was no child when the papers were made out," returned Hom Hing. He spoke calmly; but there was apprehension in his eyes and in his tightening grip on his son.

"What is it? What is it?" quavered Lae Choo, who understood a little English.

The second customs officer regarded her pityingly.

"I don't like this part of the business," he muttered.

The first officer turned to Hom Hing and in an official tone of voice, said:

"Seeing that the boy has no certificate entitling him to admission to this country you will have to leave him with us."

"Leave my boy!" exclaimed Hom Hing.

"Yes; he will be well taken care of, and just as soon as we can hear from Washington he will be handed over to you."

"But," protested Hom Hing, "he is my son."

"We have no proof," answered the man with a shrug of his shoulders; "and even if so we cannot let him pass without orders from the Government."

"He is my son," reiterated Hom Hing, slowly and solemnly. "I am a Chinese merchant and have been in business in San Francisco for many years. When my wife told to me one morning that she dreamed of a green tree with spreading branches and one beautiful red flower growing thereon, I answered her that I wished my son to be born in our country, and for her to prepare to go to China. My wife complied with my wish. After my son was born my mother fell sick and my wife nursed and cared for her; then my father, too, fell sick, and my wife also nursed and cared for him. For twenty moons my wife care for and nurse the old people, and when they die they bless her and my son, and I send for her to return to me. I had no fear of trouble. I was a Chinese merchant and my son was my son."

"Very good, Hom Hing," replied the first officer. "Nevertheless, we take your son."

"No, you not take him; he my son too."

It was Lae Choo. Snatching the child from his father's arms she held and covered him with her own.

The officers conferred together for a few moments; then one drew Hom Hing aside and spoke in his ear.

Resignedly Hom Hing bowed his head, then approached his wife. "'Tis the law," said he, speaking in Chinese, "and 'twill be but for a little while— until tomorrow's sun arises."

"You, too," reproached Lae Choo in a voice eloquent with pain. But accustomed to obedience she yielded the boy to her husband, who in turn delivered him to the first officer. The Little One protested lustily against the transfer; but his mother covered her face with her sleeve and his father silently led her away. Thus was the law of the land complied with.

II

Day was breaking. Lae Choo, who had been awake all night, dressed herself, then awoke her husband.

"'Tis the morn," she cried. "Go, bring our son."

The man rubbed his eyes and arose upon his elbow so that he could see out of the window. A pale star was visible in the sky. The petals of a lily in a bowl on the windowsill were unfurled.

"'Tis not yet time," said he, laying his head down again.

"Not yet time. Ah, all the time that I lived before yesterday is not so much as the time that has been since my little one was taken from me."

The mother threw herself down beside the bed and covered her face.

Hom Hing turned on the light, and touching his wife's bowed head with a sympathetic hand inquired if she had slept.

"Slept!" she echoed, weepingly. "Ah, how could I close my eyes with my arms empty of the little body that has filled them every night for more than twenty moons! You do not know—man—what it is to miss the feel of the little fingers and the little toes and the soft round limbs of your little one. Even in the darkness his darling eyes used to shine up to mine, and often have I fallen into slumber with his pretty babble at my ear. And now, I see him not; I touch him not; I hear him not. My baby, my little fat one!"

"Now! Now! Now!" consoled Hom Hing, patting his wife's shoulder reassuringly; "there is no need to grieve so; he will soon gladden you again. There cannot be any law that would keep a child from its mother!"

Lae Choo dried her tears.

"You are right, my husband," she meekly murmured. She arose and stepped about the apartment, setting things to rights. The box of presents she had brought for her California friends had been opened the evening before; and silks, embroideries, carved ivories, ornamental lacquer-ware, brasses, camphorwood boxes, fans, and chinaware were scattered around in confused heaps. In the midst of unpacking the thought of her child in the hands of strangers had overpowered her, and she had left everything to crawl into bed and weep.

Having arranged her gifts in order she stepped out on to the deep balcony.

The star had faded from view and there were bright streaks in the western sky. Lae Choo looked down the street and around. Beneath the flat occupied by her and her husband were quarters for a number of bachelor Chinamen, and she could hear them from where she stood, taking their early morning breakfast. Below their dining-room was her husband's grocery store. Across the way was a large restaurant. Last night it had been resplendent with gay colored lanterns and the sound of music. The rejoicings over "the completion of the moon," by Quong Sum's first-born, had been long and loud, and had caused her to tie a handkerchief over her ears. She, a bereaved mother, had it not in her heart to rejoice with other parents. This morning the place was more in accord with her mood. It was still and quiet. The revellers had dispersed or were asleep.

A roly-poly woman in black sateen, with long pendant earrings in her ears, looked up from the street below and waved her a smiling greeting. It was her old neighbor, Kuie Hoe, the wife of the gold embosser, Mark Sing. With her was a little boy in yellow jacket and lavender pantaloons. Lae Choo remembered him as a baby. She used to like to play with him in those days when she had no child of her own. What a long time ago that seemed! She caught her breath in a sigh, and laughed instead.

"Why are you so merry?" called her husband from within.

"Because my Little One is coming home," answered Lae Choo. "I am a happy mother—a happy mother."

She pattered into the room with a smile on her face.

The noon hour had arrived. The rice was steaming in the bowls and a fragrant dish of chicken and bamboo shoots was awaiting Hom Hing. Not for one moment had Lae Choo paused to rest during the morning hours; her activity had been ceaseless. Every now and again, however, she had raised her eyes to the gilded clock on the curiously carved mantelpiece. Once, she had exclaimed:

"Why so long, oh! why so long?" Then apostrophizing herself: "Lae Choo, be happy. The Little One is coming! The Little One is coming!" Several times she burst into tears and several times she laughed aloud.

Hom Hing entered the room; his arms hung down by his side.

"The Little One!" shrieked Lae Choo.

"They bid me call tomorrow."

With a moan the mother sank to the floor.

The noon hour passed. The dinner remained on the table.

III

The winter rains were over: the spring had come to California, flushing the hills with green and causing an ever-changing pageant of flowers to pass over them. But there was no spring in Lae Choo's heart, for the Little One remained away from her arms. He was being kept in a mission. White women were caring for him, and though for one full moon he had pined for his mother and refused to be comforted he was now apparently happy and contented. Five moons or five months had gone by since the day he had passed with Lae Choo through the Golden Gate; but the great Government at Washington still delayed sending the answer which would return him to his parents.

Hom Hing was disconsolately rolling up and down the balls in his abacus box when a keen-faced young man stepped into his store.

"What news?" asked the Chinese merchant.

"This!" The young man brought forth a typewritten letter. Hom Hing read the words:

"Re Chinese child, alleged to be the son of Hom Hing, Chinese merchant, doing business at 425 Clay street, San Francisco.

"Same will have attention as soon as possible."

Hom Hing returned the letter, and without a word continued his manipulation of the counting machine.

"Have you anything to say?" asked the young man.

"Nothing. They have sent the same letter fifteen times before. Have you not yourself showed it to me?"

"True!" The young man eyed the Chinese merchant furtively. He had a proposition to make and he was pondering whether or not the time was opportune.

"How is your wife?" he inquired solicitously—and diplomatically.

Hom Hing shook his head mournfully.

"She seems less every day," he replied. "Her food she takes only when I bid her and her tears fall continually. She finds no pleasure in dress or flowers and cares not to see her friends. Her eyes stare all night. I think before another moon she will pass into the land of spirits."

"No!" exclaimed the young man, genuinely startled.

"If the boy not come home I lose my wife sure," continued Hom Hing with bitter sadness.

"It's not right," cried the young man indignantly. Then he made his proposition.

The Chinese father's eyes brightened exceedingly.

"Will I like you to go to Washington and make them give you the paper to restore my son?" cried he. "How can you ask when you know my heart's desire?"

"Then," said the young fellow, "I will start next week. I am anxious to see this thing through if only for the sake of your wife's peace of mind."

"I will call her. To hear what you think to do will make her glad," said Hom Hing.

He called a message to Lae Choo upstairs through a tube in the wall.

In a few moments she appeared, listless, wan, and hollow-eyed; but when her husband told her the young lawyer's suggestion she became as one electrified; her form straightened, her eyes glistened; the color flushed to her cheeks.

"Oh," she cried, turning to James Clancy, "You are a hundred man good!"

The young man felt somewhat embarrassed; his eyes shifted a little under the intense gaze of the Chinese mother.

"Well, we must get your boy for you," he responded. "Of course"—turning to Hom Hing—"it will cost a little money. You can't get fellows to hurry the Government for you without gold in your pocket."

Hom Hing stared blankly for a moment. Then: "How much do you want, Mr. Clancy?" he asked quietly.

"Well, I will need at least five hundred to start with."

Hom Hing cleared his throat.

"I think I told to you the time I last paid you for writing letters for me and seeing the Custom boss here that nearly all I had was gone!"

"Oh, well then we won't talk about it, old fellow. It won't harm the boy to stay where he is, and your wife may get over it all right."

"What that you say?" quavered Lae Choo.

James Clancy looked out of the window.

"He says," explained Hom Hing in English, "that to get our boy we have to have much money."

"Money! Oh, yes."

Lae Choo nodded her head.

"I have not got the money to give him."

For a moment Lae Choo gazed wonderingly from one face to the other; then, comprehension dawning upon her, with swift anger, pointing to the lawyer, she cried: "You not one hundred man good; you just common white man."

"Yes, ma'am," returned James Clancy, bowing and smiling ironically.

Hom Hing pushed his wife behind him and addressed the lawyer again: "I might try," said he, "to raise something; but five hundred—it is not possible."

"What about four?"

"I tell you I have next to nothing left and my friends are not rich."

"Very well!"

The lawyer moved leisurely toward the door, pausing on its threshold to light a cigarette.

"Stop, white man; white man, stop!"

Lae Choo, panting and terrified, had started forward and now stood beside him, clutching his sleeve excitedly.

"You say you can go to get paper to bring my Little One to me if Hom Hing give you five hundred dollars?"

The lawyer nodded carelessly; his eyes were intent upon the cigarette which would not take the fire from the match.

"Then you go get paper. If Hom Hing not can give you five hundred dollars—I give you perhaps what more that much."

She slipped a heavy gold bracelet from her wrist and held it out to the man. Mechanically he took it.

"I go get more!"

She scurried away, disappearing behind the door through which she had come.

"Oh, look here, I can't accept this," said James Clancy, walking back to Hom Hing and laying down the bracelet before him.

"It's all right," said Hom Hing, seriously, "pure China gold. My wife's parent give it to her when we married."

"But I can't take it anyway," protested the young man.

"It is all same as money. And you want money to go to Washington," replied Hom Hing in a matter of fact manner.

"See, my jade earrings—my gold buttons—my hairpins—my comb of pearl and my rings—one, two, three, four, five rings; very good—very good—all same much money. I give them all to you. You take and bring me paper for my Little One."

Lae Choo piled up her jewels before the lawyer.

Hom Hing laid a restraining hand upon her shoulder. "Not all, my wife," he said in Chinese. He selected a ring—his gift to Lae Choo when she dreamed of the tree with the red flower. The rest of the jewels he pushed toward the white man.

"Take them and sell them," said he. "They will pay your fare to Washington and bring you back with the paper."

For one moment James Clancy hesitated. He was not a sentimental man; but something within him arose against accepting such payment for his services.

"They are good, good," pleadingly asserted Lae Choo, seeing his hesitation.

Whereupon he seized the jewels, thrust them into his coat pocket, and walked rapidly away from the store.

IV

Lae Choo followed after the missionary woman through the mission nursery school. Her heart was beating so high with happiness that she could scarcely breathe. The paper had come at last—the precious paper which gave Hom Hing and his wife the right to the possession of their own child. It was ten months now since he had been taken from them—ten months since the sun had ceased to shine for Lae Choo.

The room was filled with children—most of them wee tots, but none so wee as her own. The mission woman talked as she walked. She told Lae Choo that little Kim, as he had been named by the school, was the pet of the place, and that his little tricks and ways amused and delighted every one. He had been rather difficult to manage at first and had cried much for his mother; "but children so soon forget, and after a month he seemed quite at home and played around as bright and happy as a bird."

"Yes," responded Lae Choo. "Oh, yes, yes!"

But she did not hear what was said to her. She was walking in a maze of anticipatory joy.

"Wait here, please," said the mission woman, placing Lae Choo in a chair. "The very youngest ones are having their breakfast."

She withdrew for a moment—it seemed like an hour to the mother—then she reappeared leading by the hand a little boy dressed in blue cotton overalls and white-soled shoes. The little boy's face was round and dimpled and his eyes were very bright.

"Little One, ah, my Little One!" cried Lae Choo.

She fell on her knees and stretched her hungry arms toward her son.

But the Little One shrunk from her and tried to hide himself in the folds of the white woman's skirt.

"Go'way, go'way!" he bade his mother.

Ole Rölvaag
(1876–1931)

Born in a fishing village on the Norwegian island of Dönna near the Arctic Circle, Ole Rölvaag emigrated at age twenty. He took his surname from a cove near his home; in Norway, he would have been called Pedersen because his father's name was Peder. He left school at fourteen, but read intensively in the local library—the novels of James Fenimore Cooper, Charles Dickens, Captain Frederick Marryat, and Edward Bulwer-Lytton as well as work by Scandinavian authors. He went out as a fisherman first when he was fifteen. When several of his friends were killed in a severe winter storm in 1893, Rölvaag wrote a letter to an uncle in South Dakota asking for a ticket to the United States.

Rölvaag described his trip in Amerika-Breve (Letters from America), *published under the pseudonym Paal Morck in 1912. During the three-day train trip from New York, he lived on one loaf of bread. Speaking no English and unmet at the station, he walked across the prairie half the night until he found a Norwegian speaker who could direct him to his uncle's farm. He tried farming and other work before entering Augustana College—a preparatory school—in 1899, going from there to St. Olaf's College in Minnesota. At age twenty-eight he graduated with honors and borrowed money for a year of study at the University of Oslo, returning to take a faculty position teaching Norwegian literature at St. Olaf's in 1906.*

Rölvaag's first novel, To Tulliger (Two Fools, 1920; *English version* Pure

Gold, *1930), about a boorish pair of immigrants who attain financial success and hoard their wealth, created a sensation among Norwegian Americans. The more poetic and tragic* Laengselens Baat (Ship of Longing)
followed in 1922.

*Hearing that the novelist Johan Bojer was planning a book on the life of
Norwegian immigrants, Rölvaag decided that only one who had actually
lived the experience could do justice to the theme. He took a year's leave of
absence, revisited North Dakota, and met with Bojer in Norway before
writing the first book of* Giants in the Earth. *It appeared in Norway as* I De
Dage (In Those Days, *1924) one month before Bojer's novel, entitled in
English* The Emigrants. *The second volume,* Riket Grundlaegges (Founding
the Kingdom), *appeared a year later. All of these works were first written in
Norwegian. In cooperation with several translators, especially Lincoln Col-
cord, Rölvaag prepared a one-volume English version published in 1927.
The sequel,* Peder Victorious, *appeared in 1929. These tales of hardship and
determination among the settlers of the Great Plains are classics of the
American experience.*

[From] Giants in the Earth

II. Home-founding

I

ON THE SIDE of a hill, which sloped gently away toward the southeast and
followed with many windings a creek that wormed its way across the prairie,
stood Hans Olsa, laying turf. He was building a sod house. The walls had
now risen breast-high; in its half-finished condition, the structure resembled
more a bulwark against some enemy than anything intended to be a human
habitation. And the great heaps of cut sod, piled up in each corner, might
well have been the stores of ammunition for defence of the stronghold.

For a man of his strength and massive build, his motions were unusually quick and agile; but he worked by fits and starts to-day. At times he
stopped altogether; in these pauses he would straighten himself up and draw
his sleeve with a quick stroke across his troubled face; with each stroke the

sleeve would come away damper; and standing so, he would fix his gaze intently on the prairie to the eastward. His eyes had wandered so often now over the stretch of land lying before them, that they were familiar with every tussock and hollow. . . . No—nothing in sight yet! . . . He would resume his task, as if to make up for lost time, and work hard for a spell; only to forget himself once more, pause involuntarily, and stand inert and abstracted, gazing off into the distance.

Beyond the house a tent had been pitched; a wagon was drawn up close beside it. On the ground outside of the tent stood a stove, a couple of chairs, and a few other rough articles of furniture. A stout, healthy-looking woman, whose face radiated an air of simple wisdom and kindliness, was busy preparing the midday meal. She sang to herself as she worked. A ten year-old girl, addressed by the woman as Sofie, was helping her. Now and then the girl would take up the tune and join in the singing.

Less than a quarter of a mile away, in a southeasterly direction, a finished sod house rose on the slope of the hill. Smoke was winding up from it at this moment. This house, which had been built the previous fall, belonged to Syvert Tönseten.

Some distance north from the place where Hans Olsa had located, two other sod houses were under construction; but a hillock lay between, so that he could not see them from where he stood. There the two Solum boys had driven down their stakes and had begun building. Tönseten's completed house, and the other three half-finished ones, marked the beginning of the settlement on Spring Creek.

The woman who had been bustling about preparing the meal, now called to her husband that dinner was ready—he must come at once! He answered her, straightened up for the hundredth time, wiped his hands on his trousers, and stood for a moment gazing off eastward. . . . No use to look—not a soul in sight yet! . . . He sighed heavily, and walked with slow steps toward the tent, his eyes on the ground.

It was light and airy inside the tent, but stifling hot, because of the unobstructed sunlight beating down upon it. Two beds were ranged along the wall, both of them homemade; a big emigrant chest stood at the head of each. Nails had been driven into the centre pole of the tent, on which hung clothing; higher up a crosspiece, securely fastened, was likewise hung with clothes. Two of the walls were lined with furniture; on these pieces the dishes were displayed, all neatly arranged.

A large basin of water stood on a chair just inside the tent door. Hans Olsa washed his face and hands; then he came out and sat down on the ground, where his wife had spread the table. It was so much cooler outside. The meal was all ready; both mother and daughter had been waiting for him.

"I suppose you haven't seen any signs of them yet?" his wife asked at last.

"No—nothing at all!"

"Can you imagine what has become of them?"

"The Lord forgive us—if I only knew!"

Her husband looked so anxious that she asked no more questions. Out of her kind heart rose a hopeful, "Don't worry, they'll get her all right!" . . . But in spite of the cheerfulness of the words, she could not give them that ring of buoyant confidence which she would have liked to show. . . . "Of course!" said the girl with a laugh. "Store-Hans and Ola have two good pairs of eyes. Leave it to them—they'll find us!"

The father gave her a stern glance; he didn't tell her in words to stop her foolish chatter—but she said no more. Without speaking once, he ate his dinner. As soon as he had finished, he tossed his spoon on the blanket, thanked them for the food, got up gloomily, and went back to the half-completed wall. There he sat down awhile, as if lost in thought . . . gazing eastward. His large, rugged features were drawn and furrowed with anxiety. . . . "God Almighty!" he sighed, and folded his big hands. "What can have become of Per Hansa?"

His wife was watching him closely as he sat there on the wall. By and by she told her daughter to finish washing the dishes, and started to go over where he was. When he saw her coming, he tried to begin working as if there were nothing on his mind.

"Hans," she said, quickly, when she had reached his side, "I think you ought to go out and look for them!"

He waited until he had got a strip of sod in place before he answered: "Easier said than done . . . when we haven't the faintest idea where to look . . . on such stretches of prairie!"

"Yes, I know; but it would make us all feel better, anyway . . . as if we were doing something."

Hans Olsa laid another strip of turf; then he stopped, let his hands fall to his sides, and began thinking aloud as he gazed off into the distance. . . .

"I know this much—you don't often find a smarter fellow than Per Hansa. . . . That's what makes it so queer! I don't suppose he's able to get much speed out of his oxen; but one thing I'm certain of—he has been hurrying as fast as he could. And we surely didn't come along very fast . . . but now it's the fifth day since we arrived here! If he made use of these bright moonlight nights, as he probably did, I begin to be afraid that he's gone on west of us somewhere, instead of being still to the eastward. . . . It's certainly no child's play to start looking for him!"

Hans Olsa slumped down on the wall, the picture of dejection. His wife quickly found a place beside him. Together they sat there in silence. The same fear that she felt him struggling with, a fear thrown into sharp relief by the things he had just been saying, had long since gripped her heart also.

"I feel so sorry for Beret, poor thing . . . and the children. You must remember, though, that he couldn't go very fast on account of her condition. . . . I think she is with child again!" She paused. "I dreamed about them last night . . . a bad dream. . . ."

Her husband glanced sidewise at her. "We mustn't pay attention to such things. A bad dream is a good sign, anyway—that's what my mother always said. . . . But I suppose I'll never forgive myself for not waiting for him." He got up heavily and laid another strip of turf. "He's always been like that, Per Hansa; he never would take help from any man. But this time he's carried it a little too far!"

His wife made no answer. She was watching a short stout man with a reddish beard who had started up the slope from the direction of the house to the south of them. He had cheeks like two rosy apples, a quick step, and eyes that flitted all about; he was noted among them for his glib tongue and the flood of his conversation. With hands stuck into the waistband of his trousers, and elbows out akimbo, the man looked half as broad again as he really was.

"Here comes Tönseten," said the woman. "Why don't you talk it over with him? I really think you ought to go out and look for them."

"Seen anything of them yet, Hans Olsa?" asked the man, without further greeting, as soon as he arrived. . . . "Well, well! this looks fine! Ha, ha! It's a warm house, you know, that's built by the aid of a woman's hand."

Hans Olsa wheeled on him. "You haven't caught sight of them yourself, Syvert, have you?"

"Caught sight of them? Why, man alive, that's just what I've come up here to tell you! I've had them in sight for over an hour now. Seems to me you ought to be able to see them easy enough—you who carry your eyes so high up in the air! . . . Good Lord! it won't be long before they arrive here, at the rate they're coming!"

"What's that you say?" the others burst out with one voice. . . . "Where are they?" . . .

"I reckon Per Hansa must have got off his course a little. Maybe the oxen didn't steer well, or maybe he didn't figure the current right. . . . Look to the westward, neighbours! Look over there about west-northwest, and you'll see him plain enough. . . . No need to worry. That fellow never would drown in such shallow water as this! . . . I wonder, now, how far west he's really been?"

Hans Olsa and his wife faced around in the direction that Tönseten had indicated. Sure enough, out of the west a little caravan was crawling up toward them on the prairie.

"Can that be them? . . . I really believe it is!" said Hans Olsa in a half whisper, as if hardly daring yet to give vent to his joy.

"*Of course* it is!" cried his wife, excitedly. . . . "Thank God!"

"Not the least doubt of it," Tönseten assured them. "You might as well go and put your coffeepot on the stove, Mother Sörrina! That Kjersti of mine is coming over pretty soon, she'll probably have something good tucked under her apron. . . . In half an hour we'll have the lost sheep back in the fold!"

"Yes! Heavens and earth, Sörrina!" cried Hans Olsa, "fetch out the best you've got! . . . Per, Per, is it really you, old boy? . . . But why are you coming from the west, I'd like to know?"

Tönseten coughed, and gave the woman a sly wink.

"Look here, Mother Sörrina," he said with a twinkle in his eyes, "won't you be good enough, please, to take a peek at Hans Olsa's Sunday bottle? . . . Not that *I* want anything to drink, you understand—I should say not. Good Lord, no! But think of that poor woman out there, who has been suffering all this time without a drop! And I'd be willing to bet that Per Hansa wouldn't object to having his stomach warmed up a little, too!"

At that they burst out laughing, from mingled joy and relief; but Tönseten's laughter at his own joke was the loudest of all. . . . Work was resumed at once; Syvert began to carry the sods for Hans Olsa to lay up, while Mother Sörrina went off in a happy frame of mind, to make her preparations for the reception of the wanderers.

Before the half hour allotted by Tönseten had passed, the caravan came slowly crawling up the slope. Per Hansa still strode in the van, with Store-Hans at his side; Ole walked abreast of the oxen, driving them with the goad. Beret and And-Ongen sat in the wagon. Rosie came jogging along behind at her own gait; she gave a loud, prolonged "moo-o-o-o" as she discovered the other animals across the prairie.

Both families stood ready to receive them; Hans Olsa and Sörine, Tönseten and his Kjersti, all watching intently the movements of the approaching company; but the girl couldn't possess her patience any longer, and ran down to meet the new arrivals. She took Store-Hans by the hand and fell in beside him; the first question she asked was whether he hadn't been terribly scared at night? . . .

As the slope of the hill grew steeper, the oxen had to bend to the yoke.

"Hey, there, folks!" shouted Per Hansa, boisterously "Don't be standing around loafing, now! It's only the middle of the afternoon. Haven't you got anything to do around here?"

"Coffee time, coffee time, Per Hansa . . . ha, ha, ha!" Tönseten was bubbling over with good spirits. "We thought we might as well wait a little while for you, you know."

. . . "You've found us at last!" said Hans Olsa, with a deep, happy chuckle. . . . He didn't seem able to let go of Per Hansa's hand.

"Found you? Why, devil take it, it's no trick to follow a course out here! You just have to keep on steering straight ahead. And you had marked the trail pretty well, all the way along. I found plenty of traces of you. . . . I guess we stood a little too far to the westward, between Sioux Falls and here; that's how it happened. . . . So *this* is the place, is it? . . . The pastures of Goshen in the land of Egypt—eh?"[1]

"Just so, just so!" cried Tönseten, nodding and laughing. "Pastures of Goshen—right you are! That's exactly what we are going to call the place— Goshen—if only you haven't sailed in to mix things up for us!" . . .

Beret and the child had now got down from the wagon; the other two women hovered around her, drawing her toward the tent. But she hung back for a moment; she wanted to stop and look around.

. . . Was this the place? . . . *Here!* . . . Could it be possible? . . . She stole a

---

1. Goshen was a pastoral region of Lower Egypt where the Israelites lived before the Exodus (see Genesis 45:10).

glance at the others, at the half-completed hut, then turned to look more closely at the group standing around her; and suddenly it struck her that *here something was about to go wrong.* . . . For several days she had sensed this same feeling; she could not seem to tear herself loose from the grip of it. . . . A great lump kept coming up in her throat; she swallowed hard to keep it back, and forced herself to look calm. Surely, surely, she mustn't give way to her tears now, in the midst of all this joy. . . .

Then she followed the other two women into the tent; seeing a chair, she sank down in it, as if her strength had gone!

Sörine was patting her on the shoulder. . . . "Come, get your things off, Beret. You ought to loosen up your clothes, you know. Just throw this dress of mine around you. . . . Here's the water to wash yourself in. Let down your hair, and take your time about it. . . . Don't mind Kjersti and me being around."

After they had bustled about for a little while the others left her. The moment they had gone she jumped up and crossed the tent, to look out of the door. . . . How will human beings be able to endure this place? she thought. Why, there isn't even a thing that one can *hide behind!* . . . Her sensitive, rather beautiful face was full of blank dismay; she turned away from the door and began to loosen her dress; then her eyes fell on the centre pole with its cross-piece, hung with clothes, and she stood a moment irresolute, gazing at it in startled fright. . . . It looked like the giants she had read about as a child; for a long while she was unable to banish the picture from her mind.

Outside the tent, Ole stood with his hand resting on one of the oxen. He was disgusted; the older people seemed to have clean forgotten his existence. They never would get done talking—when he, too, might have had a word to put in! . . .

"Hadn't we better unhitch the oxen, Dad?"

"Yes, yes—that's right, Ola. We might as well camp down here for the night, since we've run across some folks we used to know. . . . How about it, you fellows?" He turned to the other two. "I suppose there's a little more land left around here, isn't there, after you've got through?"

"*Land?* Good God! Per Hansa, what are you talking about? Take whatever you please, from here to the Pacific Ocean!" Tönseten's enthusiasm got so far away with him that he had to pull one of his hands out of his waistband and make a sweeping circle with it in the air.

"You must take a look around as soon as you can," Hans Olsa said, "and see if you find anything better that meets your fancy. In the meanwhile I've put down a stake for you on the quarter section[2] that lies north of mine. We'll go over and have a look at it pretty soon. Sam Solum wanted it, but I told him he'd better leave it till you came.. . . . You see, you would be next to the creek there; and then you and I would be the nearest neighbours, just as we've always planned. It makes no particular difference to Sam; he can take the quarter alongside his brother's."

---

2. A square tract—1/2 mile on a side—containing 160 acres.

Per Hansa drew a deep breath, as if filling himself with life's great goodness. . . . Here Hans Olsa had been worrying about him, and with kindly forethought had arranged everything to his advantage! . . . "Well, well, we'll have to settle all that later, Hans Olsa. For the present, I can only say that I'm deeply thankful to you! . . . Unhitch the beasts, there, Ola! . . . And now, if you folks have got anything handy, to either eat or drink, I'll accept it with pleasure."

. . . "Or *both*, Per Hansa!" put in Tönseten, excitedly.

"Yes, both, Syvert. I won't refuse!"

Soon they were all gathered around a white cloth which Mother Sörine had spread on the ground. On one side of it lay a whole leg of dried mutton; on the other a large heap of *flatbröd*, with cheese, bread, and butter; in the centre of the cloth stood a large bowl of sweet milk, and from the direction of the stove the breeze wafted to them a pleasant odour of fried bacon and strong coffee. Mother Sörine herself took charge of the ceremony, bringing the food and urging them all to sit down. The stocky figure of Per Hansa rocked back and forth in blissful delight as he squatted there with his legs crossed under him.

"Come, Sörrina, sit down!" he cried. "I guess we've fallen in with gentlefolks, by the looks of things around here. . . . I suppose you think you're old Pharaoh himself—eh, Hans Olsa?"

"Who do you call me, then?" inquired Tönseten.

"You, Syvert? Well, now, I really don't know what to say. Of course you'd like to be His Majesty's butler, but you mustn't be encouraged— remember what happened to that poor fellow![3] . . . I think we'd better make you the baker—it might be safer, all around. What's your idea, Hans Olsa?"

By this time they were all laughing together.

In the midst of the jollification came Sörine, carrying a plate with a large bottle and a dram glass on it. . . . "Here, take this off my hands, Hans Olsa— you will know what to do with it!"

Tönseten fairly bubbled over in his admiration for her:

"Oh, you sweet Sörrina-girl!—you're dearer to my heart than a hundred women! . . . What a blessing it must be, to have a wife like that!"

"Stop your foolishness!" said Kjersti, but her voice didn't sound too severe.

For a long while they continued to sit around the cloth, chatting, eating, and drinking, and thoroughly enjoying themselves. Hans Olsa seemed like a different man from the one who had eaten here at noon. His loud voice led the cheerful talk; his ponderous bulk was always the centre of the merriment; it seemed as if he would never tire of gazing into that bearded, roguish face of Per Hansa's.

Once, as Per Hansa was slicing off a piece of mutton, he regarded the cut thoughtfully, and asked:

"I suppose you brought all your supplies through safe enough?"

---

3. References are to the Old Testament story of Joseph and the coat of many colors. (See Genesis 37–48.)

"Oh, sure," answered Hans Olsa, innocently. "We had no trouble at all—didn't lose anything; that is, except for the leg that we left behind somewhere, east on the prairie. But that's hardly worth mentioning."

Per Hansa paused with the piece of meat halfway to his mouth, and looked at Sörine with an expression of deep concern:

"The devil you say! Did you lose one of your legs . . .?"

Mother Sörine laughed heartily at him. "Oh no—not quite so bad as that. . . . But a leg of mutton might come in handy later on, I'll tell you; there aren't too many of them to be had around here."

Per Hansa chewed away on the meat and looked very serious. At last he said:

"That's always the way with folks who have more of the world's goods than they can take care. . . . But I'll promise you one thing, Sörrina: if I can get my old blunderbuss to work, you're going to have your lost leg back again. . . . How about it, fellows? Have you seen any game that's fit to eat out here?"

III

They sat on until the first blue haze of evening began to spread eastward over the plain. The talk had now drifted to questions of a more serious nature, mostly concerned with how they should manage things out here; of their immediate prospects; of what the future might hold in store for them; of land and crops, and of the new kingdom which they were about to found. . . . No one put the thought into words, but they all felt it strongly; now they had gone back to the very beginning of things. . . .

As the evening shadows deepened the conversation gradually died away into silence. A peculiar mood came drifting in with the dusk. It seemed to float on the evening breeze, to issue forth out of the heart of the untamed nature round about them; it lurked in the very vastness and endlessness surrounding them on every hand; it even seemed to rise like an impalpable mist out of the ground on which they sat.

This mood brought vague premonitions to them, difficult to interpret. . . . No telling what might happen out here . . . for almost anything *could* happen! . . .

They were so far from the world . . . cut off from the haunts of their fellow beings . . . so terribly far! . . .

The faces that gazed into one another were sober now, as silence claimed the little company; but lines of strength and determination on nearly every countenance told of an inward resolve to keep the mood of depression from gaining full control.

Per Hansa was the first to rouse himself and throw off the spell. He jumped up with nervous energy; a shiver passed over him, as if he were having a chill.

"What is it—are you cold?" asked his wife. She had instinctively sensed his mood as she looked at him—and loved him better for it. Until that moment, she had supposed that she herself was the only one who felt this peculiar influence.

"Such crazy talk!" he burst out. "I believe we've all lost our senses, every last one of us! Here we sit around celebrating in broad daylight, in the middle of summer, as if it was the Christmas holidays! . . . Come on, woman, let's go over to our new home!"

Everyone got up.

"You must do exactly as you please about it, Per Hansa," spoke up Hans Olsa with an apologetic air. "Don't feel that you must take this quarter if you don't like it. But as far as I can see, it's as good a piece of land as you could find anywhere around—every square foot of it plowland, except the hill over there. Plenty of water for both man and beast. . . . As for my part, if I can only sit here between you and Syvert, I certainly won't be kicking about my neighbours. . . . But I don't want you to feel that you have to take this quarter on my account, you understand. . . . If you do take it, though, we must get one of the Solum boys to go down to Sioux Falls with you the first thing to-morrow, so that you can file your claim. You'll have to do that in any case, you know, whichever quarter you take. . . . There's likely to be a lot of people moving into this region before the snow flies; we five oughtn't to part company or let anyone get in between us. . . . You've heard my best advice, anyway."

"Now, that's the talk!" Tönseten chimed in, briskly. "And considering the size of the head it comes from, it isn't half bad, either. You're damned well right, Hans Olsa. Before the snow flies you're going to see such a multitude swarming around these parts, that the thundering place won't be fit to live in! Remember what I say, boys, in times to come—bear it in mind that those were Syvert's very words! . . . You've got to go straight to Sioux Falls tomorrow morning, Per Hansa, and no two ways about it! If one of the Solum boys can't go along to do the talking for you, why, I shall have to buckle down to the job myself."

Once more Per Hansa's heart filled with a deep sense of peace and contentment as he realized how matters were being smoothed out for him. They seemed to move of their own accord but he knew better. . . . Was he really to own it? Was it really to become his possession, this big stretch of fine land that spread here before him? Was he really to have his friends for neighbours, both to the north and to the south—folks who cared for him and wanted to help him out in every way? . . .

He was still chuckling with the rare pleasure of it as he asked. "You haven't discovered any signs of life since you came?"

"Devil, no!" Tönseten assured him. "Neither Israelites nor Canaanites! I was the first one to find this place, you know. . . . But there's no telling how soon the drift will loosen, the way folks were talking back East last winter.

And now the land office for this whole section of country has been moved to Sioux Falls, too. That means business; the government, you may be certain, has good reason for doing such a thing." Tönseten spoke with all the importance of a man who has inside knowledge.

Per Hansa looked at him, and a bantering tone came into his voice:

"I see it clearly. Syvert—it would never do to keep you around here as a mere baker! We'll have to promote you to a higher office, right away. . . . Now, boys, I'm going over to see this empire that you two have set aside for me. Ola, you hitch up the oxen again and bring the wagons along."

With these commands he walked rapidly away; the others had almost to run in order to keep up with him. Strong emotions surged through him as he strode on. . . .

"It lies high," he observed after a while, when they had looked all the plowland over. . . . "There must be a fine view from the top of that hill."

They were bending their steps in this direction, and soon had reached the highest point. It seemed so spacious and beautiful to stand high above the prairie and look around, especially now, when the shades of evening were falling. . . . Suddenly Per Hansa began to step more cautiously; he sniffed the air like an animal; in a moment he stopped beside a small depression in the ground, and stood gazing at it intently for quite a while; then he said, quietly:

"There are people buried here. . . . That is a grave!"

"Oh no, Per Hansa! It can't be possible."

"No doubt about it," he said in the same subdued but positive tone.

Tönseten and Hans Olsa were so astonished that they could hardly credit the fact; they came over at once to where Per Hansa stood, and gazed down into the hollow.

Hans Olsa bent over and picked up a small stone that his eyes had lighted on; he turned it around in his hand several times. . . . "That's a queer-looking piece of stone! I almost believe people have shaped it for some use. . . . Here, see what you make of it, Syvert."

Tönseten's ruddy face grew sober and thoughtful as he examined the object.

"By thunder! It certainly looks as if the Indians had been here! . . . Now isn't that rotten luck?" . . .

"I'm afraid so," said Per Hansa, with a vigorous nod. Then he added, sharply, "But we needn't shout the fact from the house-tops, you know! . . . It takes so very little to scare some folks around here."

He waited no longer but walked hastily down the hill; at the foot he called to Ole, telling him not to drive any farther; but first he turned to Hans Olsa to find out whether they were well across the line between the two quarters.

"No use in building farther away from you than is absolutely necessary," he said. "It's going to be lonesome for the women-folks at times." . . .

. . . Awhile later, Tönseten was dragging his way homeward. For reasons that he wouldn't admit even to himself, he walked a good deal heavier now than when he had climbed the slope that afternoon.

Per Hansa returned with his other neighbour to the wagons, where Beret and the children were waiting. Again he inquired about the line between the two quarters; then asked Beret and Hans Olsa to help pick the best building place; his words, though few and soberly spoken, had in them an unmistakable ring of determination. . . . This vast stretch of beautiful land was to be his—yes, *his*—and no ghost of a dead Indian would drive him away! . . . His heart began to expand with a mighty exaltation. An emotion he had never felt before filled him and made him walk erect. . . . "Good God!" he panted. "This kingdom is going to be *mine*!"

IV

Early the next morning Per Hansa and one of the Solum boys set out on the fifty-two-mile journey to Sioux Falls, where Per Hansa filed an application for the quarter-section of land which lay to the north of Hans Olsa's. To confirm the application, he received a temporary deed to the land. The deed was made out in the name of *Peder Benjamin Hansen*; it contained a description of the land, the conditions which he agreed to fulfil in order to become the owner, and the date, *June 6, 1873*.

Sörine wanted Beret and the children to stay with her during the two days that her husband would be away; but she refused the offer with thanks. If they were to get ready a home for the summer, she said, she would have to take hold of matters right away.

. . . "For the summer?" exclaimed the other woman, showing her astonishment. "What about the winter, then?"

Beret saw that she had uttered a thought which she ought to have kept to herself; she evaded the question as best she could.

During the first day, both she and the boys found so much to do that they hardly took time to eat. They unloaded both the wagons, set up the stove, and carried out the table. Then Beret arranged their bedroom in the larger wagon. With all the things taken out it was quite roomy in there; it made a tidy bedroom when everything had been put in order. The boys thought this work great fun, and she herself found some relief in it for her troubled mind. But something vague and intangible hovering in the air would not allow her to be wholly at ease; she had to stop often and look about, or stand erect and listen. . . . Was that a sound she heard? . . . All the while, the thought that had struck her yesterday when she had first got down from the wagon, stood vividly before her mind: here there was nothing even to hide behind! . . . When the room was finished, and a blanket had been hung up to serve as a door, she seemed a little less conscious of this feeling. But back in the recesses of her mind it still was there. . . .

After they had milked the cow, eaten their evening porridge, and talked awhile to the oxen, she took the boys and And-Ongen and strolled away from camp. With a common impulse, they went toward the hill; when they had reached the summit, Beret sat down and let her gaze wander aimlessly around. . . . In a certain sense, she had to admit to herself, it was lovely up here. The broad expanse stretching away endlessly in every direction, seemed almost like the ocean—especially now, when darkness was falling. It reminded her strongly of the sea, and yet it was very different . . . . This formless prairie had no heart that beat, no waves that sang, no soul that could be touched . . . or cared. . . .

The infinitude surrounding her on every hand might not have been so oppressive, might even have brought her a measure of peace, if it had not been for the deep silence, which lay heavier here than in a church. Indeed, what was there to break it? She had passed beyond the outposts of civilization; the nearest dwelling places of men were far away. Here no warbling of birds rose on the air, no buzzing of insects sounded:[4] even the wind had died away; the waving blades of grass that trembled to the faintest breath now stood erect and quiet, as if listening, in the great hush of the evening. . . . All along the way, coming out, she had noticed this strange thing: the stillness had grown deeper, the silence more depressing, the farther west they journeyed; it must have been over two weeks now since she had heard a bird sing! Had they travelled into some nameless, abandoned region? Could no living thing exist out here, in the empty, desolate, endless wastes of green and blue? . . . How *could* existence go on, she thought, desperately? If life is to thrive and endure, it must at least have something to hide behind! . . .

The children were playing boisterously a little way off. What a terrible noise they made! But she had better let them keep on with their play, as long as they were happy. . . . She sat perfectly quiet, thinking of the long, oh, so interminably long march that they would have to make, back to the place where human beings dwelt. It would be small hardship for her, of course, sitting in the wagon; but she pitied Per Hansa and the boys—and then the poor oxen! . . . He certainly would soon find out for himself that a home for men and women and children could never be established in this wilderness. . . . And how could she bring new life into the world out here! . . .

Slowly her thoughts began to centre on her husband; they grew warm and tender as they dwelt on him. She trembled as they came. . . .

But only for a brief while. As her eyes darted nervously here and there, flitting from object to object and trying to pierce the purple dimness that was steadily closing in, a sense of desolation so profound settled upon her that she seemed unable to think at all. It would not do to gaze any longer at the terror out there, where everything was turning to grim and awful darkness. . . . She threw herself back in the grass and looked up into the heavens.

---

4. Early settlers found no birds or insects when they first arrived on the prairie.

But darkness and infinitude lay there, also—the sense of utter desolation still remained. . . . Suddenly, for the first time, she realized the full extent of her loneliness, the dreadful nature of the fate that had overtaken her. Lying there on her back, and staring up into the quiet sky across which the shadows of night were imperceptibly creeping, she went over in her mind every step of their wanderings, every mile of the distance they had travelled since they had left home. . . .

First they had boarded the boat at Sandnessjöen. . . . This boat had carried them southward along the coast. . . . In Namsos there had been a large ship with many white sails, that had taken her, with her dear ones, and sailed away—that had carried them off relentlessly, farther and farther from the land they knew. In this ship they had sailed for weeks; the weeks had even grown into months; they had seemed to be crossing an ocean which had no end. . . . There had been something almost laughable in this blind course, steadily fixed on the sunset! When head winds came, they beat up against them; before sweeping fair breezes they scudded along; but always they were westering! . . .

. . . At last they had landed in Quebec. There she had walked about the streets, confused and bewildered by a jargon of unintelligible sounds that did not seem like the speech of people. . . . Was this the Promised Land? Ah no—it was only the beginning of the real journey. . . . Then something within her had risen up in revolt: I will go no farther! . . .

. . . But they had kept on, just the same—had pushed steadily westward, over plains, through deserts, into towns, and out of them again. . . . One fine day they had stood in Detroit, Michigan. This wasn't the place, either, it seemed. . . . Move on! . . . Once more she had felt the spirit of revolt rising to shout aloud: I will go no farther! . . . But it had been as if a resistless flood had torn them loose from their foundations and was carrying them helplessly along on its current—flinging them here and there, hurling them madly onward, with no known destination ahead.

Farther and farther onward . . . always west. . . . For a brief while there had been a chance to relax once more; they had travelled on water again, and she could hear the familiar splash of waves against the ship's side. This language she knew of old, and did not fear; it had lessened the torture of that section of the journey for her, though they had been subjected to much ill-treatment and there had been a great deal of bullying and brawling on board.

At last the day had arrived when they had landed in Milwaukee. But here they were only to make a new start—to take another plunge into the unknown. . . . Farther, and always farther. . . . The relentless current kept whirling them along. . . . Was it bound nowhere, then? . . . Did it have no end? . . .

In the course of time they had come jogging into a place called Prairie du Chien. . . . Had that been in Wisconsin, or some other place named after savages? . . . It made no difference—they had gone on. They had floundered along to Lansing, in Iowa. . . . Onward again. Finally they had reached Fillmore County, in Minnesota. . . . But even that wasn't the place, it seemed! . . .

. . . Now she was lying here on a little green hillock, surrounded by the open, endless prairie, far off in a spot from which no road led back! . . . It seemed to her that she had lived many lives already, in each one of which she had done nothing but wander and wander, always straying farther away from the home that was dear to her.

She sat up at last, heaved a deep sigh, and glanced around as if waking from a dream. . . . The unusual blending of the gentle and forceful in her features seemed to be thrown into relief by the scene in which she sat and the twilight hovering about her, as a beautiful picture is enhanced by a well-chosen frame.

The two boys and their little sister were having great fun up here. So many queer things were concealed under the tufts of grass. Store-Hans came running, and brought a handful of little flat, reddish chips of stone that looked as though they had been carved out of the solid rock; they were pointed at one end and broadened out evenly on both sides, like the head of a spear. The edges were quite sharp; in the broad end a deep groove had been filed. Ole brought more of them, and gave a couple to his little sister to play with. . . . The mother sat for a while with the stones in her lap, where the children had placed them; at last she took them up, one by one, and examined them closely. . . . These must have been formed by human hands, she thought.

Suddenly Ole made another rare discovery. He brought her a larger stone, that looked like a sledge hammer; in this the groove was deep and broad.

The mother got up hastily.

"Where are you finding these things?"

The boys at once took her to the place; in a moment she, too, was standing beside the little hollow at the brow of the hill, which the men had discovered the night before; the queer stones that the children had been bringing her lay scattered all around.

"Ola says that the Indians made them!" cried Store-Hans, excitedly. "Is it true, mother? . . . Do you suppose they'll ever come back?"

"Yes, maybe—if we stay here long enough. . . ." She remained standing awhile beside the hollow; the same thought possessed her that had seized hold of her husband when he had first found the spot—here a human being lay buried. Strangely enough, it did not frighten her; it only showed her more plainly, in a stronger, harsher light, how unspeakably lonesome this place was.

The evening dusk had now almost deepened into night. It seemed to gather all its strength around her, to close in on every side, to have its center in the spot where she stood. The wagons had become only a dim speck in the darkness, far, far away; the tent at Hans Olsa's looked like a tuft of grass that had whitened at the top; Tönseten's sod house she was unable to make out at all. . . . She could not bring herself to call aloud to the boys; instead, she walked around the hollow, spoke to them softly, and said that it was time to go home. . . . No, no, they mustn't take the stones with them to-night! But to-morrow they might come up here again to play.

. . . Beret could not go to sleep for a long time that night. At last she grew thoroughly angry with herself; her nerves were taut as bowstrings; her head kept rising up from the pillow to listen—but there was nothing to hear . . . nothing except the night wind, which now had begun to stir.

. . . It stirred with so many unknown things! . . .

V

Per Hansa came home late the following afternoon; he had so many words of praise for what she and the boys had accomplished while he had been gone, that he fairly bewildered her. Now it had taken possession of him again—that indomitable, conquering mood which seemed to give him the right of way wherever he went, whatever he did. Outwardly, at such times, he showed only a buoyant recklessness, as if wrapped in a cloak of gay, wanton levity; but down beneath all this lay a stern determination of purpose, a driving force, so strong that she shrank back from the least contact with it.

To-day he was talking in a steady stream.

"Here is the deed to our kingdom, Beret-girl! See to it that you take good care of the papers. . . . Isn't it stranger than a fairy tale, that a man can have such things here just for the taking? . . . Yes—and years after he won the princess, too!" He cocked his head on one side. "I'll tell you what, it seems so impossible and unheard of, that I can't quite swallow it all yet. . . . What do you say, my Beret-girl?"

Beret stood smiling at him, with tears in her eyes, beside the improvised house that she had made; there was little for her to say. And what would be the use of speaking now? He was so completely wrapped up in his own plans that he would not listen nor understand. It would be wrong, too, to trouble him with her fears and misgivings. . . . When he felt like this he was so tender to her, so cheerful, so loving and kind. . . . How well she knew Per Hansa! . . .

"What are you thinking about it all, my Beret-girl?" He flung his arm around her, whirled her off her feet, and drew her toward him.

"Oh, Per, it's only this—I'm so afraid out here!" She snuggled up against him, as if trying to hide herself. "It's all so big and open . . . so empty. . . . Oh, Per! Not another human being from here to the end of the world!"

Per Hansa laughed loud and long, so that she winced under the force and meaning of it. "There'll soon be more people, girl . . . never you fear. . . . By God! there'll soon be more people here!"

But suddenly another idea took hold of him. He led her over to the large chest, made her sit down, and stood in front of her with a swaggering air:

"Now let me tell you what came into my mind yesterday, after I had got the papers. I went right out and bought ten sacks of potatoes! I felt so good, Beret—and you know how we men from Nordland like potatoes!" he added with a laugh. "This is the point of it: we're not going to start right in with building a house. The others are just foolish to do it." His voice grew low and eager. "They're beginning at the wrong end, you see. For my part, I'm going over to Hans Olsa's this very night and borrow his plow—and to-morrow morning I shall start breaking my ground! Yes, sir! I tell you those potatoes have got to go into the ground at once. Do you hear me, Beret-girl? If the soil out here is half as good as it's cracked up to be, we'll have a fine crop the very first fall! . . . Then I can build later in the summer, you know, when I am able to take my time about it. . . . Just wait, my girl, just wait. It's going to be wonderful; you'll see how wonderful I can make it for you, this kingdom of ours!" He laughed until his eyes were drawn out in two narrow slits. "And no old worn-out, thin-shanked, pot-bellied king is going to come around and tell me what I have to do about it, either!"

He explained to her at great length how he intended to arrange everything and how success would crown his efforts, she sitting there silently on the chest, he standing in front of her, waving his arms; while about them descended the grandeur of the evening. But with all his strength and enthusiasm, and with all her love, he didn't succeed in winning her heart over altogether—no, not altogether. She had heard with her own ears how no bird sang out here; she had seen with her own eyes how, day after day as they journeyed, they had left the abodes of men farther and farther behind. Wasn't she sitting here now, gazing off into an endless blue-green solitude that had neither heart nor soul? . . .

"Do you know," she said, quietly, as she got up once more and leaned close against him, "I believe there is a grave over there on the hill?"

"Why, Beret! Did you find it? Have you been going around brooding over that, too? . . . Don't worry, girl. He'll bring us nothing but good luck, the fellow who lies up there."

"Perhaps. . . . But it seems so strange that some one lies buried in unconsecrated ground right at our very door. How quiet it must be there! . . . The children found so many things to play with, while we were up on the hill last night, that I let them go again to-night. Come, we had better begin to look for them. . . . It is beautiful up there." She sighed, and moved away.

They climbed the hill together, holding each other's hands. There was something in that sad resignation of hers which he was powerless against. As he walked beside her and held her hand, he felt as if he could laugh and cry in the same breath. . . . She was so dear, so dear to him. Why could he never make her understand it fully? It was a strange, baffling thing! But perhaps the reason for it lay in this: she was not built to wrestle with fortune—she was too fine-grained. . . . Oh, well—he knew one person, at any rate, who stood ready to do the fighting for her!

Per Hansa had so much to think about that night that a long time passed before he could get to sleep. Now was a good chance to make his plans, while Beret lay at his side, sleeping safe and sound; he must utilize every moment now; he didn't feel very tired, either.

There seemed to be no end to the things he needed. But thirty dollars was all the money he had in the world; and when he thought of what would have to be bought in the near future, and of everything that waited to be done, the list grew as long as the distance they had travelled. . . . First of all, house and barn; that would need doors and windows. Then food and tobacco; shoes and clothing; and implements—yes, farming implements! If he only had horses and the necessary implements, the whole quarter-section would soon blossom like a garden. . . . The horses he would have to do without, to begin with. But he ought to get at least one more cow before fall came—no dodging that fact. . . . And pigs—he absolutely had to have some pigs for winter! . . . If the potatoes turned out well, there would be plenty to feed them on. . . . Then he would buy some chickens, as soon as he could run across any folks who had chickens to sell. Things like that would only be pleasant diversions for Beret. . . . There certainly seemed to be no end to all that he needed.

. . . But now came the main hitch in his calculations. Beret was going to have a baby again. . . . Only a blessing, of course—but what a lot of their time it would take up, just now! . . . Oh, well, she would have to bear the brunt of it herself, as the woman usually did. A remarkably brave and clever wife, that she was . . . a woman of tender kindness, of deep, fine fancies— one whom you could not treat like an ordinary clod.

. . . How hard he would strive to make life pleasant for her out here! Her image dominated all the visions which now seemed to come to him of their own accord. . . . The whole farm lay there before him, broken and under cultivation, yielding its fruitful harvests; there ran many horses and cows, both young and grown. And over on the location where to-day he was about to build the sod hut should stand a large dwelling . . . a *white* house, it would be! Then it would gleam so beautifully in the sun, white all over— but the cornices should be bright green! . . .

When, long ago, Per Hansa had had his first vision of the house, it had been painted white, with green cornices; and these colours had belonged to it in his mind ever since. But the stable, the barn, and all the rest of the out-houses should be painted red, with white cornices—for that grave such a fine effect! . . . Oh yes, that Beret-girl of his should certainly have a royal mansion for herself and her little princess! . . .

Mary Antin
(1881–1949)

Mary Antin was born in Polotsk, Russia, "Within the Pale," as she expresses it in the first chapter of The Promised Land: *"within this area the Czar commanded me to stay, with my father and mother and friends, and all other people like us. We must not be found outside the Pale, because we were Jews." She describes the world of her youth in the early chapters of* The Promised Land: *the struggle for a living, ironclad religious and social traditions, Hebrew school for the boys, the kitchen and their mother's instruction for the girls, the pleasures of the child turning into the duties of the adult, the marriage broker, the cycle begun again.*

"We are not born all at once," she wrote, "but by bits." At fourteen, with her mother and sister, she came to America to join her father, who had gone ahead. Breaking with tradition, the family had given her some education in Russia. With that, and her American schooling, she was ready at eighteen to publish her first book, From Plotzk to Boston *(1899), letters to an uncle in Russia, written in Yiddish but translated into English for publication. She married a Columbia University professor and attended college at Columbia before returning to Boston and settlement work at Hale House.* The Promised Land *(1912) was one of the most popular descriptions of the American immigration experience ever written; by 1930 it had gone through twenty-nine printings. Antin used the platform of her success to argue for an open immigration policy in* They Who Knock at Our Gates: A Complete Gospel of Immigration *(1914), but wrote little in later life.*

[From] The Promised Land

CHAPTER IX. THE PROMISED LAND

HAVING MADE SUCH GOOD TIME across the ocean, I ought to be able to proceed no less rapidly on *terra firma*, where, after all, I am more at home. And yet here is where I falter. Not that I hesitated, even for the space of a breath, in my first steps in America. There was no time to hesitate. The most ignorant immigrant, on landing, proceeds to give and receive greetings, to eat, sleep, and rise, after the manner of his own country; wherein he is corrected, admonished, and laughed at, whether by interested friends or the most indifferent strangers; and his American experience is thus begun. The process is spontaneous on all sides, like the education of the child by the family circle. But while the most stupid nursery maid is able to contribute her part toward the result, we do not expect an analysis of the process to be furnished by any member of the family, least of all by the engaging infant. The philosophical maiden aunt alone, or some other witness equally psychological and aloof, is able to trace the myriad efforts by which the little Johnnie or Nellie acquires a secure hold on the disjointed parts of the huge plaything, life.

Now I was not exactly an infant when I was set down, on a May day some fifteen years ago, in this pleasant nursery of America. I had long since acquired the use of my faculties, and had collected some bits of experience, practical and emotional, and had even learned to give an account of them. Still, I had very little perspective, and my observations and comparisons were superficial. I was too much carried away to analyze the forces that were moving me. My Polotzk I knew well before I began to judge it and experiment with it. America was bewilderingly strange, unimaginably complex, delightfully unexplored. I rushed impetuously out of the cage of my provincialism and looked eagerly about the brilliant universe. My question was, What have we here?—not, What does this mean? That query came much later. When I now become retrospectively introspective, I fall into the predicament of the centipede in the rhyme, who got along very smoothly until he was asked which leg came after which, whereupon he became so rattled that he could n't take a step. I know I have come on a thousand feet, on wings, winds, and American machines,—I have leaped and run and climbed and crawled,—but to tell which step came after which I find a puzzling matter. Plenty of maiden aunts were present during my second infancy, in the guise of immigrant officials, school-teachers, settlement workers, and sundry other unprejudiced and critical observers. Their statistics I might properly borrow to fill the gaps in my recollections, but I am prevented by my sense of harmony. The individual, we know, is a creature unknown to the statistician, whereas I undertook to give the personal view of everything. So I am bound to unravel, as well as I can, the tangle of events, outer and inner, which made up the first breathless years of my American life.

During his three years of probation, my father had made a number of false starts in business. His history for that period is the history of thousands who come to America, like him, with pockets empty, hands untrained to the use of tools, minds cramped by centuries of repression in their native land. Dozens of these men pass under your eyes every day, my American friend, too absorbed in their honest affairs to notice the looks of suspicion which you cast at them, the repugnance with which you shrink from their touch. You see them shuffle from door to door with a basket of spools and buttons, or bending over the sizzling irons in a basement tailor shop, or rummaging in your ash can, or moving a pushcart from curb to curb, at the command of the burly policeman. "The Jew peddler!" you say, and dismiss him from your premises and from your thoughts, never dreaming that the sordid drama of his days may have a moral that concerns you. What if the creature with the untidy beard carries in his bosom his citizenship papers? What if the cross-legged tailor is supporting a boy in college who is one day going to mend your state constitution for you? What if the ragpicker's daughters are hastening over the ocean to teach your children in the public schools? Think, every time you pass the greasy alien on the street, that he was born thousands of years before the oldest native American; and he may have something to communicate to you, when you two shall have learned a common language. Remember that his very physiognomy is a cipher the key to which it behooves you to search for most diligently.

By the time we joined my father, he had surveyed many avenues of approach toward the coveted citadel of fortune. One of these, heretofore untried, he now proposed to essay, armed with new courage, and cheered on by the presence of his family. In partnership with an energetic little man who had an English chapter in his history, he prepared to set up a refreshment booth on Crescent Beach. But while he was completing arrangements at the beach we remained in town, where we enjoyed the educational advantages of a thickly populated neighborhood; namely, Wall Street, in the West End of Boston.

Anybody who knows Boston knows that the West and North Ends are the wrong ends of that city. They form the tenement district, or, in the newer phrase, the slums of Boston. Anybody who is acquainted with the slums of any American metropolis knows that that is the quarter where poor immigrants foregather, to live, for the most part, as unkempt, half-washed, toiling, unaspiring foreigners; pitiful in the eyes of social missionaries, the despair of boards of health, the hope of ward politicians, the touchstone of American democracy. The well-versed metropolitan knows the slums as a sort of house of detention for poor aliens, where they live on probation till they can show a certificate of good citizenship.

He may know all this and yet not guess how Wall Street, in the West

End, appears in the eyes of a little immigrant from Polotzk. What would the sophisticated sight-seer say about Union Place, off Wall Street, where my new home waited for me? He would say that it is no place at all, but a short box of an alley. Two rows of three-story tenements are its sides, a stingy strip of sky is its lid, a littered pavement is the floor, and a narrow mouth its exit.

But I saw a very different picture on my introduction to Union Place. I saw two imposing rows of brick buildings, loftier than any dwelling I had ever lived in. Brick was even on the ground for me to tread on, instead of common earth or boards. Many friendly windows stood open, filled with uncovered heads of women and children. I thought the people were interested in us, which was very neighborly. I looked up to the topmost row of windows, and my eyes were filled with the May blue of an American sky!

In our days of affluence in Russia we had been accustomed to upholstered parlors, embroidered linen, silver spoons and candlesticks, goblets of gold, kitchen shelves shining with copper and brass. We had featherbeds heaped halfway to the ceiling; we had clothes presses dusky with velvet and silk and fine woollen. The three small rooms into which my father now ushered us, up one flight of stairs, contained only the necessary beds, with lean mattresses; a few wooden chairs; a table or two; a mysterious iron structure, which later turned out to be a stove; a couple of unornamental kerosene lamps; and a scanty array of cooking-utensils and crockery. And yet we were all impressed with our new home and its furniture. It was not only because we had just passed through our seven lean years, cooking in earthen vessels, eating black bread on holidays and wearing cotton; it was chiefly because these wooden chairs and tin pans were American chairs and pans that they shone glorious in our eyes. And if there was anything lacking for comfort or decoration we expected it to be presently supplied—at least, we children did. Perhaps my mother alone, of us newcomers, appreciated the shabbiness of the little apartment, and realized that for her there was as yet no laying down of the burden of poverty.

Our initiation into American ways began with the first step on the new soil. My father found occasion to instruct or correct us even on the way from the pier to Wall Street, which journey we made crowded together in a rickety cab. He told us not to lean out of the windows, not to point, and explained the word "greenhorn." We did not want to be "greenhorns," and gave the strictest attention to my father's instructions. I do not know when my parents found opportunity to review together the history of Polotzk in the three years past, for we children had no patience with the subject; my mother's narrative was constantly interrupted by irrelevant questions, interjections, and explanations.

The first meal was an object lesson of much variety. My father produced several kinds of food, ready to eat, without any cooking, from little tin cans that had printing all over them. He attempted to introduce us to a queer, slippery kind of fruit, which he called "banana," but had to give it up for the time being. After the meal, he had better luck with a curious piece of furniture on runners, which he called "rocking-chair." There were five of us new-comers, and we found five different ways of getting into the American machine of perpetual motion, and as many ways of getting out of it. One born and bred to the use of a rocking-chair cannot imagine how ludicrous people can make themselves when attempting to use it for the first time. We laughed immoderately over our various experiments with the novelty, which was a wholesome way of letting off steam after the unusual excitement of the day.

In our flat we did not think of such a thing as storing the coal in the bathtub. There was no bathtub. So in the evening of the first day my father conducted us to the public baths. As we moved along in a little procession, I was delighted with the illumination of the streets. So many lamps, and they burned until morning, my father said, and so people did not need to carry lanterns. In America, then, everything was free, as we had heard in Russia. Light was free; the streets were as bright as a synagogue on a holy day. Music was free; we had been serenaded to our gaping delight, by a brass band of many pieces, soon after our installation on Union Place.

Education was free. That subject my father had written about repeatedly, as comprising his chief hope for us children, the essence of American opportunity, the treasure that no thief could touch, not even misfortune or poverty. It was the one thing that he was able to promise us when he sent for us; surer, safer than bread or shelter. On our second day I was thrilled with the realization of what this freedom of education meant. A little girl from across the alley came and offered to conduct us to school. My father was out, but we five between us had a few words of English by this time. We knew the word school. We understood. This child, who had never seen us till yesterday, who could not pronounce our names, who was not much better dressed than we, was able to offer us the freedom of the schools of Boston! No application made, no questions asked, no examinations, rulings, exclusions; no machinations, no fees. The doors stood open for every one of us. The smallest child could show us the way.

This incident impressed me more than anything I had heard in advance of the freedom of education in America. It was a concrete proof—almost the thing itself. One had to experience it to understand it.

It was a great disappointment to be told by my father that we were not to enter upon our school career at once. It was too near the end of the term, he said, and we were going to move to Crescent Beach in a week or so. We had to wait until the opening of the schools in September. What a loss of precious time—from May till September!

Not that the time was really lost. Even the interval on Union Place was crowded with lessons and experiences. We had to visit the stores and be dressed from head to foot in American clothing; we had to learn the mysteries of the iron stove, the washboard, and the speaking-tube; we had to learn to trade with the fruit peddler through the window, and not to be afraid of the policeman; and, above all, we had to learn English.

The kind people who assisted us in these important matters form a group by themselves in the gallery of my friends. If I had never seen them from those early days till now, I should still have remembered them with gratitude. When I enumerate the long list of my American teachers, I must begin with those who came to us on Wall Street and taught us our first steps. To my mother, in her perplexity over the cookstove, the woman who showed her how to make the fire was an angel of deliverance. A fairy god-mother to us children was she who led us to a wonderful country called "uptown," where, in a dazzlingly beautiful palace called a "department store," we exchanged our hateful homemade European costumes, which pointed us out as "greenhorns" to the children on the street, for real American machine-made garments, and issued forth glorified in each other's eyes.

With our despised immigrant clothing we shed also our impossible Hebrew names. A committee of our friends, several years ahead of us in American experience, put their heads together and concocted American names for us all. Those of our real names that had no pleasing American equivalents they ruthlessly discarded, content if they retained the initials. My mother, possessing a name that was not easily translatable, was punished with the undignified nickname of Annie. Fetchke, Joseph, and Deborah issued as Frieda, Joseph, and Dora, respectively. As for poor me, I was simply cheated. The name they gave me was hardly new. My Hebrew name being Maryashe in full, Mashke for short, Russianized into Marya (*Mar-ya*), my friends said that it would hold good in English as *Mary*; which was very disappointing, as I longed to possess a strange-sounding American name like the others.

I am forgetting the consolation I had, in this matter of names, from the use of my surname, which I have had no occasion to mention until now. I found on my arrival that my father was "Mr. Antin" on the slightest provocation, and not, as in Polotzk, on state occasions alone. And so I was "Mary Antin," and I felt very important to answer to such a dignified title. It was just like America that even plain people should wear their surnames on week days.

As a family we were so diligent under instruction, so adaptable, and so clever in hiding our deficiencies, that when we made the journey to Crescent Beach, in the wake of our small wagon-load of household goods, my father had very little occasion to admonish us on the way, and I am sure he was not ashamed of us. So much we had achieved toward our Americanization during the two weeks since our landing.

Crescent Beach is a name that is printed in very small type on the maps of the environs of Boston, but a life-size strip of sand curves from Winthrop to Lynn; and that is historic ground in the annals of my family. The place is now a popular resort for holiday crowds, and is famous under the name of Revere Beach. When the reunited Antins made their stand there, however, there were no boulevards, no stately bath-houses, no hotels, no gaudy amusement places, no illuminations, no showmen, no tawdry rabble. There was only the bright clean sweep of sand, the summer sea, and the summer sky. At high tide the whole Atlantic rushed in, tossing the seaweeds in his mane; at low tide he rushed out, growling and gnashing his granite teeth. Between tides a baby might play on the beach, digging with pebbles and shells, till it lay asleep on the sand. The whole sun shone by day, troops of stars by night, and the great moon in its season.

Into this grand cycle of the seaside day I came to live and learn and play. A few people came with me, as I have already intimated; but the main thing was that *I* came to live on the edge of the sea—I, who had spent my life inland, believing that the great waters of the world were spread out before me in the Dvina.[1] My idea of the human world had grown enormously during the long journey; my idea of the earth had expanded with every day at sea; my idea of the world outside the earth now budded and swelled during my prolonged experience of the wide and unobstructed heavens.

Not that I got any inkling of the conception of a multiple world. I had had no lessons in cosmogony, and I had no spontaneous revelation of the true position of the earth in the universe. For me, as for my fathers, the sun set and rose, and I did not feel the earth rushing through space. But I lay stretched out in the sun, my eyes level with the sea, till I seemed to be absorbed bodily by the very materials of the world around me; till I could not feel my hand as separate from the warm sand in which it was buried. Or I crouched on the beach at full moon, wondering, wondering, between the two splendors of the sky and the sea. Or I ran out to meet the incoming storm, my face full in the wind, my being a-tingle with an awesome delight to the tips of my fog-matted locks flying behind; and stood clinging to some stake or upturned boat, shaken by the roar and rumble of the waves. So clinging, I pretended that I was in danger, and was deliciously frightened; I held on with both hands, and shook my head, exulting in the tumult around me, equally ready to laugh or sob. Or else I sat, on the stillest days, with my back to the sea, not looking at all, but just listening to the rustle of the waves on the sand; not thinking at all, but just breathing with the sea.

Thus courting the influence of sea and sky and variable weather, I was bound to have dreams, hints, imaginings. It was no more than this, perhaps: that the world as I knew it was not large enough to contain all that I saw and felt; that the thoughts that flashed through my mind, not half understood, unrelated to my utterable thoughts, concerned something for which I had as yet no name. Every imaginative growing child has these flashes of intuition, especially one that becomes intimate with some one aspect of nature. With me it was the growing time, that idle summer by the sea, and I grew all the faster because I had been so cramped before. My mind, too, had so recently been worked upon by the impressive experience of a change of country that I was more than commonly alive to impressions, which are the seeds of ideas.

Let no one suppose that I spent my time entirely, or even chiefly, in inspired solitude. By far the best part of my day was spent in play—frank,

---

1. River flowing through Polotsk.

hearty, boisterous play, such as comes natural to American children. In Polotzk I had already begun to be considered too old for play, excepting set games or organized frolics. Here I found myself included with children who still played, and I willingly returned to childhood. There were plenty of playfellows. My father's energetic little partner had a little wife and a large family. He kept them in the little cottage next to ours; and that the shanty survived the tumultuous presence of that brood is a wonder to me to-day. The young Wilners included an assortment of boys, girls, and twins, of every possible variety of age, size, disposition, and sex. They swarmed in and out of the cottage all day long, wearing the door-sill hollow, and trampling the ground to powder. They swung out of windows like monkeys, slid up the roof like flies, and shot out of trees like fowls. Even a small person like me could n't go anywhere without being run over by a Wilner; and I could never tell which Wilner it was because none of them ever stood still long enough to be identified; and also because I suspected that they were in the habit of interchanging conspicuous articles of clothing, which was very confusing.

You would suppose that the little mother must have been utterly lost, bewildered, trodden down in this horde of urchins; but you are mistaken. Mrs. Wilner was a positively majestic little person. She ruled her brood with the utmost coolness and strictness. She had even the biggest boy under her thumb, frequently under her palm. If they enjoyed the wildest freedom outdoors, indoors the young Wilners lived by the clock. And so at five o'clock in the evening, on seven days in the week, my father's partner's children could be seen in two long rows around the supper table. You could tell them apart on this occasion, because they all had their faces washed. And this is the time to count them: there are twelve little Wilners at table.

I managed to retain my identity in this multitude somehow, and while I was very much impressed with their numbers, I even dared to pick and choose my friends among the Wilners. One or two of the smaller boys I liked best of all, for a game of hide-and-seek or a frolic on the beach. We played in the water like ducks, never taking the trouble to get dry. One day I waded out with one of the boys, to see which of us dared go farthest. The tide was extremely low, and we had not wet our knees when we began to look back to see if familiar objects were still in sight. I thought we had been wading for hours, and still the water was so shallow and quiet. My companion was marching straight ahead, so I did the same. Suddenly a swell lifted us almost off our feet, and we clutched at each other simultaneously. There was a lesser swell, and little waves began to run, and a sigh went up from the sea. The tide was turning—perhaps a storm was on the way—and we were miles, dreadful miles from dry land.

Boy and girl turned without a word, four determined bare legs ploughing through the water, four scared eyes straining toward the land. Through an eternity of toil and fear they kept dumbly on, death at their heels, pride still in their hearts. At last they reach high-water mark—six hours before full tide.

Each has seen the other afraid, and each rejoices in the knowledge. But only the boy is sure of his tongue.

"You was scared, war n't you?" he taunts.

The girl understands so much, and is able to reply:—

"You can schwimmen, I not."

"Betcher life I can schwimmen," the other mocks.

And the girl walks off, angry and hurt.

"An' I can walk on my hands," the tormentor calls after her. "Say, you greenhorn, why don'tcher look?"

The girl keeps straight on, vowing that she would never walk with that rude boy again, neither by land nor sea, not even though the waters should part at his bidding.

I am forgetting the more serious business which had brought us to Crescent Beach. While we children disported ourselves like mermaids and mermen in the surf, our respective fathers dispensed cold lemonade, hot peanuts, and pink popcorn, and piled up our respective fortunes, nickel by nickel, penny by penny. I was very proud of my connection with the public life of the beach. I admired greatly our shining soda fountain, the rows of sparkling glasses, the pyramids of oranges, the sausage chains, the neat white counter, and the bright array of tin spoons. It seemed to me that none of the other refreshment stands on the beach—there were a few—were half so attractive as ours. I thought my father looked very well in a long white apron and shirt sleeves. He dished out ice cream with enthusiasm, so I supposed he was getting rich. It never occurred to me to compare his present occupation with the position for which he had been originally destined; or if I thought about it, I was just as well content, for by this time I had by heart my father's saying, "America is not Polotzk." All occupations were respectable, all men were equal, in America.

If I admired the soda fountain and the sausage chains, I almost worshipped the partner, Mr. Wilner. I was content to stand for an hour at a time watching him make potato chips. In his cook's cap and apron, with a ladle in his hand and a smile on his face, he moved about with the greatest agility, whisking his raw materials out of nowhere, dipping into his bubbling kettle with a flourish, and bringing forth the finished product with a caper. Such potato chips were not to be had anywhere else on Crescent Beach. Thin as tissue paper, crisp as dry snow, and salt as the sea—such thirst-producing, lemonade-selling, nickel-bringing potato chips only Mr. Wilner could make. On holidays, when dozens of family parties came out by every train from town, he could hardly keep up with the demand for his potato chips. And with a waiting crowd around him our partner was at his best. He was as voluble as he was skilful, and as witty as he was voluble; at least so I guessed from the laughter that frequently drowned his voice. I could not understand his jokes, but if I could get near enough to watch his lips and his smile and his merry eyes, I was happy. That any one could talk so fast, and in English, was marvel enough, but that this prodigy should belong to *our* establishment was a fact to thrill me. I had never seen anything like Mr. Wilner, except a wedding jester; but then he spoke common Yiddish. So proud was I of the talent and good taste displayed at our stand that if my father beckoned to me in the crowd and sent me on an errand, I hoped the people noticed that I, too, was connected with the establishment.

And all this splendor and glory and distinction came to a sudden end. There was some trouble about a license—some fee or fine—there was a storm in the night that damaged the soda fountain and other fixtures—there was talk and consultation between the houses of Antin and Wilner—and the promising partnership was dissolved. No more would the merry partner gather the crowd on the beach; no more would the twelve young Wilners gambol like mermen and mermaids in the surf. And the less numerous tribe of Antin must also say farewell to the jolly seaside life; for men in such humble business as my father's carry their families, along with their other earthly goods, wherever they go, after the manner of the gypsies. We had driven a feeble stake into the sand. The jealous Atlantic, in conspiracy with the Sunday law, had torn it out. We must seek our luck elsewhere.

In Polotzk we had supposed that "America" was practically synonymous with "Boston." When we landed in Boston, the horizon was pushed back, and we annexed Crescent Beach. And now, espying other lands of promise, we took possession of the province of Chelsea, in the name of our necessity.

In Chelsea, as in Boston, we made our stand in the wrong end of the town. Arlington Street was inhabited by poor Jews, poor Negroes, and a sprinkling of poor Irish. The side streets leading from it were occupied by more poor Jews and Negroes. It was a proper locality for a man without capital to do business. My father rented a tenement with a store in the basement. He put in a few barrels of flour and of sugar, a few boxes of crackers, a few gallons of kerosene, an assortment of soap of the "save the coupon" brands; in the cellar, a few barrels of potatoes, and a pyramid of kindling-wood; in the showcase, an alluring display of penny candy. He put out his sign, with a gilt-lettered warning of "Strictly Cash," and proceeded to give credit indiscriminately. That was the regular way to do business on Arlington Street. My father, in his three years' apprenticeship, had learned the tricks of many trades. He knew when and how to "bluff." The legend of "Strictly Cash" was a protection against notoriously irresponsible customers; while none of the "good" customers, who had a record for paying regularly on Saturday, hesitated to enter the store with empty purses.

If my father knew the tricks of the trade, my mother could be counted on to throw all her talent and tact into the business. Of course she had no English yet, but as she could perform the acts of weighing, measuring, and mental computation of fractions mechanically, she was able to give her whole attention to the dark mysteries of the language, as intercourse with her customers gave her opportunity. In this she made such rapid progress that she soon lost all sense of disadvantage, and conducted herself behind the counter very much as if she were back in her old store in Polotzk. It was far more cosey than Polotzk—at least, so it seemed to me; for behind the store was the kitchen, where, in the intervals of slack trade, she did her cooking and washing. Arlington Street customers were used to waiting while the storekeeper salted the soup or rescued a loaf from the oven.

Once more Fortune favored my family with a thin little smile, and my father, in reply to a friendly inquiry, would say, "One makes a living," with a shrug of the shoulders that added "but nothing to boast of." It was characteristic of my attitude toward bread-and-butter matters that this contented me, and I felt free to devote myself to the conquest of my new world. Looking back to those critical first years, I see myself always behaving like a child let loose in a garden to play and dig and chase the butterflies. Occasionally, indeed, I was stung by the wasp of family trouble; but I knew a healing ointment—my faith in America. My father had come to America to make a living. America, which was free and fair and kind, must presently yield him what he sought. I had come to America to see a new world, and I followed my own ends with the utmost assiduity; only as I ran out to explore, I would look back to see if my house were in order behind me—if my family still kept its head above water.

In after years, when I passed as an American among Americans, if I was suddenly made aware of the past that lay forgotten,—if a letter from Russia, or a paragraph in the newspaper, or a conversation overheard in the streetcar, suddenly reminded me of what I might have been,—I thought it miracle enough that I, Mashke, the granddaughter of Raphael the Russian, born to a humble destiny, should be at home in an American metropolis, be free to fashion my own life, and should dream my dreams in English phrases. But in the beginning my admiration was spent on more concrete embodiments of the splendors of America; such as fine houses, gay shops, electric engines and apparatus, public buildings, illuminations, and parades. My early letters to my Russian friends were filled with boastful descriptions of these glories of my new country. No native citizen of Chelsea took such pride and delight in its institutions as I did. It required no fife and drum corps, no Fourth of July procession, to set me tingling with patriotism. Even the common agents and instruments of municipal life, such as the letter carrier and the fire engine, I regarded with a measure of respect. I know what I thought of people who said that Chelsea was a very small, dull, unaspiring town, with no discernible excuse for a separate name or existence.

The apex of my civic pride and personal contentment was reached on the bright September morning when I entered the public school. That day I must always remember, even if I live to be so old that I cannot tell my name. To most people their first day at school is a memorable occasion. In my case the importance of the day was a hundred times magnified, on account of the years I had waited, the road I had come, and the conscious ambitions I entertained.

I am wearily aware that I am speaking in extreme figures, in superlatives. I wish I knew some other way to render the mental life of the immigrant child of reasoning age. I may have been ever so much an exception in acuteness of observation, powers of comparison, and abnormal self-consciousness; none the less were my thoughts and conduct typical of the attitude of the intelligent immigrant child toward American institutions. And what the child thinks and feels is a reflection of the hopes, desires, and purposes of the parents who brought him overseas, no matter how precocious and independent the child may be. Your immigrant inspectors will tell you what poverty the foreigner brings in his baggage, what want in his pockets. Let the overgrown boy of twelve, reverently drawing his letters in the baby class, testify to the noble dreams and high ideals that may be hidden beneath the greasy caftan of the immigrant. Speaking for the Jews, at least, I know I am safe in inviting such an investigation.

Who were my companions on my first day at school? Whose hand was in mine, as I stood, overcome with awe, by the teacher's desk, and whispered my name as my father prompted? Was it Frieda's steady, capable hand? Was it her loyal heart that throbbed, beat for beat with mine, as it had done through all our childish adventures? Frieda's heart did throb that day, but not with my emotions. My heart pulsed with joy and pride and ambition; in her heart longing fought with abnegation. For I was led to the schoolroom, with its sunshine and its singing and the teacher's cheery smile; while she was led to the workshop, with its foul air, care-lined faces, and the foreman's stern command. Our going to school was the fulfilment of my father's best promises to us, and Frieda's share in it was to fashion and fit the calico frocks in which the baby sister and I made our first appearance in a public schoolroom.

I remember to this day the gray pattern of the calico, so affectionately did I regard it as it hung upon the wall—my consecration robe awaiting the beatific day. And Frieda, I am sure, remembers it, too, so longingly did she regard it as the crisp, starchy breadths of it slid between her fingers. But whatever were her longings, she said nothing of them; she bent over the sewing-machine humming an Old-World melody. In every straight, smooth seam, perhaps, she tucked away some lingering impulse of childhood; but she matched the scrolls and flowers with the utmost care. If a sudden shock of rebellion made her straighten up for an instant, the next instant she was bending to adjust a ruffle to the best advantage. And when the momentous day arrived, and the little sister and I stood up to be arrayed, it was Frieda herself who patted and smoothed my stiff new calico; who made me turn round and round, to see that I was perfect; who stooped to pull out a disfiguring basting-thread. If there was anything in her heart besides sisterly love and pride and good-will, as we parted that morning, it was a sense of loss and a woman's acquiescence in her fate; for we had been close friends, and now our ways would lie apart. Longing she felt, but no envy. She did not grudge me what she was denied. Until that morning we had been children together, but now, at the fiat of her destiny, she became a woman, with all a woman's cares; whilst I, so little younger than she, was bidden to dance at the May festival of untroubled childhood.

I wish, for my comfort, that I could say that I had some notion of the difference in our lots, some sense of the injustice to her, of the indulgence to me. I wish I could even say that I gave serious thought to the matter. There had always been a distinction between us rather out of proportion to the dif-

ference in our years. Her good health and domestic instincts had made it
natural for her to become my mother's right hand, in the years preceding
the emigration, when there were no more servants or dependents. Then
there was the family tradition that Mary was the quicker, the brighter of the
two, and that hers could be no common lot. Frieda was relied upon for help,
and her sister for glory. And when I failed as a milliner's apprentice, while
Frieda made excellent progress at the dressmaker's, our fates, indeed, were
sealed. It was understood, even before we reached Boston, that she would go
to work and I to school. In view of the family prejudices, it was the
inevitable course. No injustice was intended. My father sent us hand in hand
to school, before he had ever thought of America. If, in America, he had
been able to support his family unaided, it would have been the culmination
of his best hopes to see all his children at school, with equal advantages at
home. But when he had done his best, and was still unable to provide even
bread and shelter for us all, he was compelled to make us children self-supporting as fast as it was practicable. There was no choosing possible; Frieda
was the oldest, the strongest, the best prepared, and the only one who was of
legal age to be put to work.

My father has nothing to answer for. He divided the world between his
children in accordance with the laws of the country and the compulsion of
his circumstances. I have no need of defending him. It is myself that I would
like to defend, and I cannot. I remember that I accepted the arrangements
made for my sister and me without much reflection, and everything that
was planned for my advantage I took as a matter of course. I was no heartless monster, but a decidedly self-centred child. If my sister had seemed
unhappy it would have troubled me; but I am ashamed to recall that I did
not consider how little it was that contented her. I was so preoccupied with
my own happiness that I did not half perceive the splendid devotion of her
attitude towards me, the sweetness of her joy in my good luck. She not only
stood by approvingly when I was helped to everything; she cheerfully
waited on me herself. And I took everything from her hand as if it were my
due.

The two of us stood a moment in the doorway of the tenement house on
Arlington Street, that wonderful September morning when I first went to
school. It was I that ran away, on winged feet of joy and expectation; it was
she whose feet were bound in the treadmill of daily toil. And I was so blind
that I did not see that the glory lay on her, and not on me.

Father himself conducted us to school. He would not have delegated that
mission to the President of the United States. He had awaited the day with
impatience equal to mine, and the visions he saw as he hurried us over the
sun-flecked pavements transcended all my dreams. Almost his first act on
landing on American soil, three years before, had been his application for
naturalization. He had taken the remaining steps in the process with eager
promptness, and at the earliest moment allowed by the law, he became a citizen of the United States. It is true that he had left home in search of bread

for his hungry family, but he went blessing the necessity that drove him to America. The boasted freedom of the New World meant to him far more than the right to reside, travel, and work wherever he pleased; it meant the freedom to speak his thoughts, to throw off the shackles of superstition, to test his own fate, unhindered by political or religious tyranny. He was only a young man when he landed—thirty-two; and most of his life he had been held in leading-strings. He was hungry for his untasted manhood.

Three years passed in sordid struggle and disappointment. He was not prepared to make a living even in America, where the day laborer eats wheat instead of rye. Apparently the American flag could not protect him against the pursuing Nemesis of his limitations; he must expiate the sins of his fathers who slept across the seas. He had been endowed at birth with a poor constitution, a nervous, restless temperament, and an abundance of hindering prejudices. In his boyhood his body was starved, that his mind might be stuffed with useless learning. In his youth this dearly gotten learning was sold, and the price was the bread and salt which he had not been trained to earn for himself. Under the wedding canopy he was bound for life to a girl whose features were still strange to him; and he was bidden to multiply himself, that sacred learning might be perpetuated in his sons, to the glory of the God of his fathers. All this while he had been led about as a creature without a will, a chattel, an instrument. In his maturity he awoke, and found himself poor in health, poor in purse, poor in useful knowledge, and hampered on all sides. At the first nod of opportunity he broke away from his prison, and strove to atone for his wasted youth by a life of useful labor; while at the same time he sought to lighten the gloom of his narrow scholarship by freely partaking of modern ideas. But his utmost endeavor still left him far from his goal. In business, nothing prospered with him. Some fault of hand or mind or temperament led him to failure where other men found success. Wherever the blame for his disabilities be placed, he reaped their bitter fruit. "Give me bread!" he cried to America. "What will you do to earn it?" the challenge came back. And he found that he was master of no art, of no trade; that even his precious learning was of no avail, because he had only the most antiquated methods of communicating it.

So in his primary quest he had failed. There was left him the compensation of intellectual freedom. That he sought to realize in every possible way. He had very little opportunity to prosecute his education, which, in truth, had never been begun. His struggle for a bare living left him no time to take advantage of the public evening school; but he lost nothing of what was to be learned through reading, through attendance at public meetings, through exercising the rights of citizenship. Even here he was hindered by a natural inability to acquire the English language. In time, indeed, he learned to read, to follow a conversation or lecture; but he never learned to write correctly, and his pronunciation remains extremely foreign to this day.

If education, culture, the higher life were shining things to be worshipped from afar, he had still a means left whereby he could draw one step nearer to them. He could send his children to school, to learn all those things that he knew by fame to be desirable. The common school, at least, perhaps high school; for one or two, perhaps even college! His children should be students, should fill his house with books and intellectual company; and thus he would walk by proxy in the Elysian Fields of liberal learning. As for the children themselves, he knew no surer way to their advancement and happiness.

So it was with a heart full of longing and hope that my father led us to school on that first day. He took long strides in his eagerness, the rest of us running and hopping to keep up.

At last the four of us stood around the teacher's desk; and my father, in his impossible English, gave us over in her charge, with some broken word of his hopes for us that his swelling heart could no longer contain. I venture to say that Miss Nixon was struck by something uncommon in the group we made, something outside of Semitic features and the abashed manner of the alien. My little sister was as pretty as a doll, with her clear pink-and-white face, short golden curls, and eyes like blue violets when you caught them looking up. My brother might have been a girl, too, with his cherubic contours of face, rich red color, glossy black hair, and fine eyebrows. Whatever secret fears were in his heart, remembering his former teachers, who had taught with the rod, he stood up straight and uncringing before the American teacher, his cap respectfully doffed. Next to him stood a starved-looking girl with eyes ready to pop out, and short dark curls that would not have made much of a wig for a Jewish bride.

All three children carried themselves rather better than the common run of "green" pupils that were brought to Miss Nixon. But the figure that challenged attention to the group was the tall, straight father, with his earnest face and fine forehead, nervous hands eloquent in gesture, and a voice full of feeling. This foreigner, who brought his children to school as if it were an act of consecration, who regarded the teacher of the primer class with reverence, who spoke of visions, like a man inspired, in a common schoolroom, was not like other aliens, who brought their children in dull obedience to the law; was not like the native fathers, who brought their unmanageable boys, glad to be relieved of their care. I think Miss Nixon guessed what my father's best English could not convey. I think she divined that by the simple act of delivering our school certificates to her he took possession of America.

Zora Neale Hurston
(1891–1960)

The all-black town of Eatonville, Florida, near Orlando, was Zora Neale Hurston's birthplace and formative home. There she learned the folktales and traditions that formed the basis of her work as a writer and anthropologist. After the death of her encouraging and influential mother, Lucy, Hurston was shunted from one relative to another until she left home for work and schooling.

She attended Howard University and, as a student at Barnard College in New York City, became the protegée of Professor Frank Boas, the well-known Columbia University anthropologist. With the encouragement of Boas and financial support provided by a wealthy white woman, Hurston went back home in 1927 to collect folk materials. Jonah's Gourd Vine (1934), her first novel, is grounded in the life of Eatonville and loosely parallels the lives of her parents. Lucy Pearson, the preacher's wife of the story, bequeaths to her daughter Isis the spirit to strive and "never be de tail uh nothin'."

Other titles followed quickly: Mules and Men, fictions based on folklore, was published in 1935; two years later her best-known novel, Their Eyes Were Watching God, appeared. Tell My Horse (1938), a gathering of folktales, Moses, Man of the Mountain (1941), a retelling of the biblical story with black characters, and Dust Tracks on the Road (1942), a fictionalized autobiography, all show evidence of Hurston's folklore research. Seraph on the Suwanee (1948), a novel about poor rural whites, was less successful.

Hurston, a key figure in the twenties coterie of artists known as "the Harlem Renaissance" became the object of severe criticism by other black writers in the forties and fifties. Richard Wright questioned Hurston's seriousness as a black artist; he dismissed Their Eyes Were Watching God as just "a minstrel technique" designed to amuse white people. Langston Hughes attacked her relations to wealthy whites by saying "some of them simply paid her just to sit around and represent the Negro race for them, she did it in such a racy fashion." Her criticism of the 1954 Supreme Court decision outlawing segregation in public schools outraged many, and her reputation suffered.

During the last years of her life Hurston was in ill health and chronically short of money. Some of her writing was rejected by her publisher, and she fell back on journalism and work as a librarian and substitute teacher. At the end of 1959, having suffered a stroke and nearly penniless, she entered the county welfare home where she died three months later.

Her celebration of black experience gained new appreciation in the 1970s. Hurston's posthumous reputation far outshines the level of appreciation she enjoyed in life, and more of her work is in print today than when she was writing.

Robert Hemenway's biographical study *Zora Neale Hurston: A Literary Biography* appeared in 1977.

———

[From] Dust Tracks on a Road

CHAPTER 3. I GET BORN

THIS IS ALL HEAR-SAY. Maybe some of the details of my birth as told me might be a little inaccurate, but it is pretty well established that I really did get born.

The saying goes like this. My mother's time had come and my father was not there. Being a carpenter, successful enough to have other helpers on some jobs, he was away often on building business, as well as preaching. It seems that my father was away from home for months this time. I have never been told why. But I did hear that he threatened to cut his throat when he got the news. It seems that one daughter was all that he figured he could stand. My sister, Sarah, was his favorite child, but that one girl was enough. Plenty more sons, but no more girl babies to wear out shoes and bring in nothing. I don't think he ever got over the trick he felt that I played on him by getting born a girl, and while he was off from home at that. A little of my sugar used to sweeten his coffee right now. That is a Negro way of saying his patience was short with me. Let me change a few words with him—and I am of the word-changing kind—and he was ready to change ends. Still and all, I looked more like him than any child in the house. Of course, by the time I got born, it was too late to make any suggestions, so the old man had to put up with me. He was nice about it in a way. He didn't tie me in a sack and drop me in the lake, as he probably felt like doing.

People were digging sweet potatoes, and then it was hog-killing time. Not at our house, but it was going on in general over the country like, being January and a bit cool. Most people were either butchering for themselves, or off helping other folks do their butchering, which was almost just as good. It is a gay time. A big pot of hasslits cooking with plenty of seasoning, lean slabs of fresh-killed pork frying for the helpers to refresh themselves after the work is done. Over and above being neighborly and giving aid, there is the food, the drinks and the fun of getting together.

So there was no grown folks close around when Mama's water broke. She sent one of the smaller children to fetch Aunt Judy, the mid-wife, but she was gone to Woodbridge, a mile and a half away, to eat at a hog-killing. The child was told to go over there and tell Aunt Judy to come. But nature, being indifferent to human arrangements, was impatient. My mother had to make it alone. She was too weak after I rushed out to do anything for herself, so she just was lying there, sick in the body, and worried in mind, wondering what would become of her, as well as me. She was so weak, she couldn't even reach down to where I was. She had one consolation. She knew I wasn't dead, because I was crying strong.

Help came from where she never would have thought to look for it. A white man of many acres and things, who knew the family well, had butchered the day before. Knowing that Papa was not at home, and that consequently there would be no fresh meat in our house, he decided to drive the five miles and bring a half of a shoat, sweet potatoes, and other garden stuff along. He was there a few minutes after I was born. Seeing the front door standing open, he came on in, and hollered, "Hello, there! Call your dogs!" That is the regular way to call in the country because nearly everybody who has anything to watch has biting dogs.

Nobody answered, but he claimed later that he heard me spreading my lungs all over Orange County, so he shoved the door open and bolted on into the house.

He followed the noise and then he saw how things were, and, being the kind of a man he was, he took out his Barlow Knife and cut the navel cord, then he did the best he could about other things. When the mid-wife, locally known as a granny, arrived about an hour later, there was a fire in the stove and plenty of hot water on. I had been sponged off in some sort of a way, and Mama was holding me in her arms.

As soon as the old woman got there, the white man unloaded what he had brought, and drove off cussing about some blankety-blank people never being where you could put your hands on them when they were needed.

He got no thanks from Aunt Judy. She grumbled for years about it. She complained that the cord had not been cut just right, and the belly-band had not been put on tight enough. She was mighty scared I was going to have a weak back, and that I would have trouble holding my water until I reached puberty. I did.

The next day or so a Mrs. Neale, a friend of Mama's, came in and reminded her that she had promised to let her name the baby in case it was a girl. She had picked up a name somewhere which she thought was very pretty. Perhaps she had read it somewhere, or somebody back in those woods was smoking Turkish cigarettes. So I became Zora Neale Hurston.

There is nothing to make you like other human beings so much as doing things for them. Therefore, the man who grannied me was back next day to see how I was coming along. Maybe it was pride in his own handiwork, and his resourcefulness in a pinch, that made him want to see it through. He remarked that I was a God-damned fine baby, fat and plenty of lung-power. As time went on, he came infrequently, but somehow kept a pinch of interest in my welfare. It seemed that I was spying noble, growing like a gourd vine, and yelling bass like a gator. He was the kind of a man that had no use for puny things, so I was all to the good with him. He thought my mother was justified in keeping me.

But nine months rolled around, and I just would not get on with the walking business. I was strong, crawling well, but showed no inclination to use my feet. I might remark in passing, that I still don't like to walk. Then I was over a year old, but still I would not walk. They made allowances for my weight, but yet, that was no real reason for my not trying.

They tell me that and old sow-hog taught me how to walk. That is, she didn't instruct me in detail, but she convinced me that I really ought to try.

It was like this. My mother was going to have collard greens for dinner, so she took the dishpan and went down to the spring to wash the greens. She left me sitting on the floor, and gave me a hunk of cornbread to keep me quiet. Everything was going along all right, until the sow with her litter of pigs in convoy came abreast of the door. She must have smelled the cornbread I was messing with and scattering crumbs about the floor. So, she came right on in, and began to nuzzle around.

My mother heard my screams and came running. Her heart must have stood still when she saw the sow in there, because hogs have been known to eat human flesh.

But I was not taking this thing sitting down. I had been placed by a chair, and when my mother got inside the door, I had pulled myself up by that chair and was getting around it right smart.

As for the sow, poor misunderstood lady, she had no interest in me except my bread. I lost that in scrambling to my feet and she was eating it. She had much less intention of eating Mama's baby, than Mama had of eating hers.

With no more suggestions from the sow or anybody else, it seems that I just took to walking and kept the thing a-going. The strangest thing about it was that once I found the use of my feet, they took to wandering. I always wanted to go. I would wander off in the woods all alone, following some inside urge to go places. This alarmed my mother a great deal. She used to say that she believed a woman who was an enemy of hers had sprinkled "travel dust" around the doorstep the day I was born. That was the only explanation she could find. I don't know why it never occurred to her to connect my tendency with my father, who didn't have a thing on his mind but this town and the next one. That should have given her a sort of hint. Some children are just bound to take after their fathers in spite of women's prayers.

Chapter 4. The Inside Search

* * *

So I was driven inward. I lived an exciting life unseen. But I had one person who pleased me always. That was the robust, gray-haired white man who had helped me get into the world. When I was quite small, he would come by and tease me and then praise me for not crying. When I got old enough to do things, he used to come along some afternoons and ask to take me with him fishing. He said he hated to bait his own hook and dig worms. It always turned out when we got to some lake back in the woods that he had a full can of bait. He baited his own hooks. In between fishing business, he would talk to me in a way I liked—as if I were as grown as he. He would tell funny stories and swear at every other word. He was always making me tell him things about my doings, and then he would tell me what to do about things. He called me Snidlits, explaining that Zora was a hell of a name to give a child.

"Snidlits, don't be a nigger," he would say to me over and over. "Niggers lie and lie! Any time you catch folks lying, they are skeered of something. Lying is dodging. People with guts don't lie. They tell the truth and then if they have to, they fight it out. You lay yourself open by lying. The other fellow knows right off that you are skeered of him and he's more'n apt to tackle you. If he don't do nothing, he starts to looking down on you from then on. Truth is a letter from courage. I want you to grow guts as you go along. So don't you let me hear of you lying. You'll get 'long all right if you do like I tell you. Nothing can't lick you if you never get skeered."

My face was all scratched up from fighting one time, so he asked me if I had been letting some kid lick me. I told him how Mary Ann and I had started to fighting and I was doing fine until her older sister Janie and her brother Ed, who was about my size, had all doubleteened me.

"Now, Snidlits, this calls for talking. Don't you try to fight three kids at one time unlessen you just can't get around it. Do the best you can, if you have to. But learn right now, not to let your head start more than your behind can stand. Measure out the amount of fighting you can do, and then do it. When you take on too much and get licked, folks will pity you first and scorn you after a while, and that's bad. Use your head!"

"Do de best I can," I assured him, proud for him to think I could.

"That's de ticket, Snidlits. The way I want to hear you talk. And while I'm on the subject, don't you never let nobody spit on you or kick you. Anybody who takes a thing like that ain't worth de powder and shot it takes to kill 'em, hear?"

"Yessir."

"Can't nothing wash that off, but blood. If anybody ever do one of those things to you, kill dead and go to jail. Hear me?"

I promised him I would try and he took out a peanut bar and gave it to me.

"Now, Snidlits, another thing. Don't you never threaten nobody you don't aim to fight. Some folks will back off of you if you put out plenty threats, but you going to meet some that don't care how big you talk, they'll try you. Then, if you can't back your crap with nothing but talk, you'll catch hell. Some folks puts dependence in bluffing, but I ain't never seen one that didn't get his bluff called sooner or later. Give 'em what you promise em and they'll look up to you even if they hate your guts. Don't worry over that part. Somebody is going to hate you anyhow, don't care what you do. My idea is to give 'em a good cause if it's got to be. And don't change too many words if you aim to fight. Lam hell out of 'em with the first lick and keep on lamming. I've seen many a fight finished with the first lick. Most folks can't stand to be hurt. But you must realize that getting hurt is part of fighting. Keep right on. The one that hurts the other one the worst wins the fight. Don't try to win no fights by calling 'em low-down names. You can call 'em all the names you want to, after the fight. That's the best time to do it, anyhow."

I knew without being told that he was not talking about my race when he advised me not to be a nigger. He was talking about class rather than race. He frequently gave money to Negro schools.

These talks went on until I was about ten. Then the hard-riding, hard-drinking, hard-cussing, but very successful man, was thrown from his horse and died. Nobody ever expected him to die in bed, so that part was all right. Everybody said that he had been a useful citizen, just powerful hot under the collar.

He was an accumulating man, a good provider, paid his debts and told the truth. Those were all the virtues the community expected. Any more than that would not have been appreciated. He could ride like a centaur, swim long distances, shoot straight with either pistol or guns, and he allowed no man to give him the lie to his face. He was supposed to be so tough, it was said that once he was struck by lightening and was not even knocked off his feet, but that lightning went off through the woods limping. Nobody found any fault with a man like that in a country where personal strength and courage were the highest virtues. People were supposed to take care of themselves without whining.

* * *

So the old man died in high favor with everybody. He had done his cussing and fighting and drinking as became a man, taken care of his family and accumulated property. Nobody thought anything about his going to the county seat frequently, getting drunk, getting his riding-mule drunk along with him, and coming down the pike yelling and singing while his mule brayed in drunken hilarity. There went a man!

I used to take a seat on top of the gate-post and watch the world go by. One way to Orlando ran past my house, so the carriages and cars would pass before me. The movement made me glad to see it. Often the white travelers would hail me, but more often I hailed them, and asked, "Don't you want me to go a piece of the way with you?"

They always did. I know now that I must have caused a great deal of amusement among them, but my self-assurance must have carried the point, for I was always invited to come along. I'd ride up the road for perhaps a half-mile, then walk back. I did not do this with the permission of my parents, nor with their foreknowledge. When they found out about it later, I usually got a whipping. My grandmother worried about my forward ways a great deal. She had known slavery and to her my brazenness was unthinkable.

"Git down offa dat gate-post! You li'l sow, you! Git down! Setting up dere looking dem white folks right in de face! They's gowine to lynch you, yet. And don't stand in dat door-way gazing out at 'em neither. Youse too brazen to live long."

Nevertheless, I kept right on gazing at them, and "going a piece of the way" whenever I could make it. The village seemed dull to me most of the time. If the village was singing a chorus, I must have missed the tune.

Perhaps a year before the old man died, I came to know two other white people for myself. They were women.

It came about this way. The whites who came down from the North were often brought by their friends to visit the village school. A Negro school was something strange to them, and while they were always sympathetic and kind, curiosity must have been present, also. They came and went, came and went. Always, the room was hurriedly put in order, and we were threatened with a prompt and bloody death if we cut one caper while the visitors were present. We always sang a spiritual, led by Mr. Calhoun himself. Mrs. Calhoun always stood in the back, with a palmetto switch in her hand as a squelcher. We were all little angels for the duration, because we'd better be. She would cut her eyes and give us a glare that meant trouble, then turn her face towards the visitors and beam as much as to say it was a great privilege and pleasure to teach lovely children like us. They couldn't see that palmetto hickory in her hand behind all those benches, but we knew where our angelic behavior was coming from.

Usually, the visitors gave warning a day ahead and we would be cautioned to put on shoes, comb our heads, and see to ears and fingernails. There was a close inspection of every one of us before we marched in that morning. Knotty heads, dirty ears and fingernails got hauled out of line, strapped and sent home to lick the calf over again.

This particular afternoon, the two young ladies just popped in. Mr. Calhoun was flustered, but he put on the best show he could. He dismissed the class that he was teaching up at the front of the room, then called the fifth grade in reading. That was my class.

So we took our readers and went up front. We stood up in the usual line, and opened to the lesson. It was the story of Pluto and Persephone. It was new and hard to the class in general, and Mr. Calhoun was very uncomfortable as the readers stumbled along, spelling out words with their lips, and in mumbling undertones before they exposed them experimentally to the teacher's ears.

Then it came to me. I was fifth or sixth down the line. The story was not new to me, because I had read my reader through from lid to lid, the first week that Papa had bought it for me.

That is how it was that my eyes were not in the book, working out the paragraph which I knew would be mine by counting the children ahead of me. I was observing our visitors, who held a book between them, following the lesson. They had shiny hair, mostly brownish. One had a looping gold chain around her neck. The other one was dressed all over in black and white with a pretty finger ring on her left hand. But the thing that held my eyes were their fingers. They were long and thin, and very white, except up near the tips. There they were baby pink. I had never seen such hands. It was a fascinating discovery for me. I wondered how they felt. I would have given those hands more attention, but the child before me was almost through. My turn next, so I got on my mark, bringing my eyes back to the book and made sure of my place. Some of the stories I had reread several times, and this Greco-Roman myth was one of my favorites. I was exalted by it, and that is the way I read my paragraph.

"Yes, Jupiter had seen her (Persephone). He had seen the maiden picking flowers in the field. He had seen the chariot of the dark monarch pause by the maiden's side. He had seen him when he seized Persephone. He had seen the black horses leap down Mount Aetna's fiery throat. Persephone was now in Pluto's dark realm and he had made her his wife."

The two women looked at each other and then back to me. Mr. Calhoun broke out with a proud smile beneath his bristly moustache, and instead of the next child taking up where I had ended, he nodded to me to go on. So I read the story to the end, where flying Mercury, the messenger of the Gods, brought Persephone back to the sunlit earth and restored her to the arms of Dame Ceres, her mother, that the world might have springtime and summer flowers, autumn and harvest. But because she had bitten the pomegranate while in Pluto's kingdom, she must return to him for three months of each year, and be his queen. Then the world had winter, until she returned to earth.

The class was dismissed and the visitors smiled us away and went into a low-voiced conversation with Mr. Calhoun for a few minutes. They glanced my way once or twice and I began to worry. Not only was I barefooted, but my feet and legs were dusty. My hair was more uncombed than usual, and my nails were not shiny clean. Oh, I'm going to catch it now. Those ladies saw me, too. Mr. Calhoun is promising to 'tend to me. So I thought.

Then Mr. Calhoun called me. I went up thinking how awful it was to get a whipping before company. Furthermore, I heard a snicker run over the room. Hennie Clark and Stell Brazzle did it out loud, so I would be sure to hear them. The smart-aleck was going to get it. I slipped one hand behind me and switched my dress tail at them, indicating scorn.

"Come here, Zora Neale," Mr. Calhoun cooed as I reached the desk. He put his hand on my shoulder and gave me little pats. The ladies smiled and held out those flower-looking fingers towards me. I seized the opportunity for a good look.

"Shake hands with the ladies, Zora Neale," Mr. Calhoun prompted and they took my hand one after the other and smiled. They asked me if I loved school, and I lied that I did. There was *some* truth in it, because I liked geography and reading, and I liked to play at recess time. Whoever it was invented writing and arithmetic got no thanks from me. Neither did I like the arrangement where the teacher could sit up there with a palmetto stem and lick me whenever he saw fit. I hated things I couldn't do anything about. But I knew better than to bring that up right there, so I said yes, I *loved* school.

"I can tell you do," Brown Taffeta gleamed. She patted my head, and was lucky enough not to get sandspurs in her hand. Children who roll and tumble in the grass in Florida, are apt to get sandspurs in their hair. They shook hands with me again and I went back to my seat.

When school let out at three o'clock, Mr. Calhoun told me to wait. When everybody had gone, he told me I was to go to the Park House, that was the hotel in Maitland, the next afternoon to call upon Mrs. Johnstone and Miss Hurd. I must tell Mama to see that I was clean and brushed from head to feet, and I must wear shoes and stockings. The ladies liked me, he said, and I must be on my best behavior.

The next day I was let out of school an hour early, and went home to be stood up in a tub of suds and be scrubbed and have my ears dug into. My sandy hair sported a red ribbon to match my red and white checked gingham dress, starched until it could stand alone. Mama saw to it that my shoes were on the right feet, since I was careless about left and right. Last thing, I was given a handkerchief to carry, warned again about my behavior, and sent off, with my big brother John to go as far as the hotel gate with me.

First thing, the ladies gave me strange things, like stuffed dates and preserved ginger, and encouraged me to eat all that I wanted. Then they showed me their Japanese dolls and just talked. I was then handed a copy of *Scrib-ner's Magazine*, and asked to read a place that was pointed out to me. After a paragraph or two, I was told with smiles, that that would do.

I was led out on the grounds and they took my picture under a palm tree. They handed me what was to me then a heavy cylinder done up in fancy paper, tied with a ribbon, and they told me goodbye, asking me not to open it until I got home.

My brother was waiting for me down by the lake, and we hurried home, eager to see what was in the thing. It was too heavy to be candy or anything like that. John insisted on toting it for me.

My mother made John give it back to me and let me open it. Perhaps, I shall never experience such joy again. The nearest thing to that moment was the telegram accepting my first book. One hundred goldy-new pennies rolled out of the cylinder. Their gleam lit up the world. It was not avarice that moved me. It was the beauty of the thing. I stood on the mountain. Mama let me play with my pennies for a while, then put them away for me to keep.

That was only the beginning. The next day I received an Episcopal hymn-book bound in white leather with a golden cross stamped into the front cover, a copy of The Swiss Family Robinson, and a book of fairy tales.

I set about to commit the song words to memory. There was no music written there, just the words. But there was to my consciousness music in between them just the same. "When I survey the Wondrous Cross" seemed the most beautiful to me, so I committed that to memory first of all. Some of them seemed dull and without life, and I pretended they were not there. If white people liked trashy singing like that, there must be something funny about them that I had not noticed before. I stuck to the pretty ones where the words marched to a throb I could feel.

A month or so after the two young ladies returned to Minnesota, they sent me a huge box packed with clothes and books. The red coat with a wide circular collar and the red tam pleased me more than any of the other things. My chums pretended not to like anything that I had, but even then I knew that they were jealous. Old Smarty had gotten by them again. The clothes were not new, but they were very good. I shone like the morning sun.

But the books gave me more pleasure than the clothes. I had never been too keen on dressing up. It called for hard scrubbings with Octagon soap suds getting in my eyes, and none too gentle fingers scrubbing my neck and gouging in my ears.

In that box were Gulliver's Travels, Grimm's Fairy Tales, Dick Whitting-ton, Greek and Roman Myths, and best of all, Norse Tales. Why did the Norse tales strike so deeply into my soul? I do not know, but they did. I seemed to remember seeing Thor swing his mighty short-handled hammer as he sped across the sky in rumbling thunder, lightning flashing from the tread of his steeds and the wheels of his chariot. The great and good Odin, who went down to the well of knowledge to drink, and was told that the price of a drink from that fountain was an eye. Odin drank deeply, then plucked out one eye without a murmur and handed it to the grizzly keeper, and walked away. That held majesty for me.

Of the Greeks, Hercules moved me most. I followed him eagerly on his tasks. The story of the choice of Hercules as a boy when he met Pleasure and Duty, and put his hand in that of Duty and followed her steep way to the blue hills of fame and glory, which she pointed out at the end, moved me profoundly. I resolved to be like him. The tricks and turns of the other Gods and Goddesses left me cold. There were other thin books about this and that sweet and gentle little girl who gave up her heart to Christ and good works. Almost always they died from it, preaching as they passed. I was utterly indifferent to their deaths. In the first place I could not conceive of death, and in the next place they never had any funerals that amounted to a hill of beans, so I didn't care how soon they rolled up their big, soulful, blue eyes and kicked the bucket. They had no meat on their bones.

But I also met Hans Andersen and Robert Louis Stevenson. They seemed to know what I wanted to hear and said it in a way that tingled me. Just a little below these friends was Rudyard Kipling in his Jungle Books. I loved his talking snakes as much as I did the hero.

I came to start reading the Bible through my mother. She gave me a licking one afternoon for repeating something I had overheard a neighbor telling her. She locked me in her room after the whipping, and the Bible was the only thing in there for me to read. I happened to open to the place where David was doing some mighty smiting, and I got interested. David went here and he went there, and no matter where he went, he smote 'em hip and thigh. Then he sung songs to his harp awhile, and went out and smote some more. Not one time did David stop and preach about sins and things. All David wanted to know from God was who to kill and when. He took care of the other details himself. Never a quiet moment. I liked him a lot. So I read a great deal more in the Bible, hunting for some more active people like David. Except for the beautiful language of Luke and Paul, the New Testament still plays a poor second to the Old Testament for me. The Jews had a God who laid about Him when they needed Him. I could see no use waiting till Judgment Day to see a man who was just crying for a good killing, to be told to go and roast. My idea was to give him a good killing first, and then if he got roasted later on, so much the better.

In searching for more Davids, I came upon Leviticus. In that way I found out a number of things the old folks would not have told me. Not knowing what we were actually reading, we got a lot of praise from our elders for our devotion to the Bible.

Having finished that and scanned the Doctor Book, which my mother thought she had hidden securely from my eyes, I read all the things which children write on privy-house walls. Therefore, I lost my taste for pornographic literature. I think that the people who love it got cheated in the matter of privy-houses when they were children.

In a way this early reading gave me great anguish through all my childhood and adolescence. My soul was with the gods and my body in the village. People just would not act like gods. Stew-beef, fried fat-back and morning grits were no ambrosia from Valhalla. Raking back yards and carrying out chamber-pots, were not the tasks of Thor. I wanted to be away from drabness and to stretch my limbs in some mighty struggle. I was only happy in the woods, and when the ecstatic Florida springtime came strolling from the sea, trance-glorifying the world with its aura. Then I hid out in the tall wild oats that waved like a glinty veil. I nibbled sweet oat stalks and listened to the wind soughing and sighing through the crowns of the lofty pines. I made particular friendship with one huge tree and always played about its roots. I named it "the loving pine," and my chums came to know it by that name.

John Joseph Mathews
(c. 1894–1979)

John Joseph Mathews was a member of the Osage tribe, born in Pawhuska, Oklahoma, which he describes as the "last reservation of the Osages." His tribe, part of the Siouan language family, had been successively relocated to make room for white settlement. Forced to leave Missouri in 1821, the tribe settled along the southern border of Kansas in an area it had formally used as a hunting range. Fifty years later the Osages were required to sell their land in Kansas and move south to the Indian Territories. Since the money from the land sale was well invested and the land they were given in Oklahoma was rich in minerals, by the early twentieth century, they had become a wealthy tribe.

Mathews received his B.A. from the University of Oklahoma in 1920 and went on to study at Oxford University. Wah'Kon-Tah: The Osage and the White Man's Road (1932) is a history of his birthplace from the late nineteenth century to the time in which he was writing—the early thirties. In the epigraph, Mathews explains the title: "That which the children of the earth do not comprehend as they travel the roads of the earth and which becomes clear to them only when they have passed on to the Great Mysteries is Wah'Kon-Tah." The account depicts an evolving society, impacted by government policy and white man's wealth, often to the detriment of individuals caught between competing sets of values. Major Laban J. Miles, the idealistic Indian Agent who came to the Osage in 1878, is the focus of the book. It is his vantage point that is utilized to describe the reservation and its people.

Mathews is also the author of Sundown *(1934), a novel;* Talking to the Moon *(1945), an autobiography; a biography of oilman E.W. Marland (1951); and* The Osages: Children of the Middle Waters *(1961).*

———

[From] Wah' Kon-Tah

CHAPTER FIVE. A VISIT TO CHE-SAH-HUNKA

ONE AFTERNOON a runner came into the office. He said, "In camp of Wah Se Se Gah there is white man."

The Major looked up. "You have not seen this man?"

"I have not seen this man. They said I must tell you."

"What is this man doing?"

"I don't know what he is doing. They said I must tell you."

"Why haven't the police brought this man to me?"

"I don't know."

"Good, tomorrow I shall go there to see about this thing."

The runner left the office and soon disappeared along the road that led across the ford by the Mill.

The next morning the Major set out for the western part of the Reservation. His mules were fresh and alert. He crossed the ford by the Mill and was soon climbing a long hill. Quail ran across the road and the grasshoppers ticked in the grass. The blackjacks stood serene and fresh in the morning air, their eastern halves ashy green where the sun hit them while the other half was dark and cool like some metal with a patina.

It was July. The grass was no longer a vivid green but had taken on a golden cast; there was hint of gold about the whole landscape. Mauve flowers on shaggy stems stood tranquilly in the still air. A squirrel chattered from the fresh shade. As the mules topped the hill the crows were strung out in the flight above the trees, raucously proclaiming to a fresh dewy world the importance of all crows.

The buggy creaked and strained and the harness squeaked; the tires rasped on the rock ledges in the roadbed. One of the mules blew loudly through his nostrils.

The Major thought that life was full. He had eaten a good breakfast, and the lunch that had been prepared for him was at his side and still warm. He had the day before him. He would go to the Big Hill country to see the white man who was trespassing and then on to the camp of Big Chief where he would stay the night. Big Chief had sent a runner to the Agency the day before requesting that the Major come to see him as he had much to talk about. Big Chief's camp was in the southern part of the Reservation on the Arkansas river, across from Cedar islands. It would be a long drive on a hot day, but the Major was always glad to see his friend Che Sah Hunka, whom the traders called Big Chief, because he was chief of the Chesho, a grand division of the tribe. His camp was sanctuary to all races of men. They could come to the camp of Che Sah Hunka, if they were in trouble and there stay until the difficulties were settled, safe from attack by their enemies.

The Major anticipated with pleasure his visits to the camp of Big Chief, and as he drove over the prairie he thought of his friend. He thought of the stern face with eyes that smiled, and those characteristics which had endeared him to his people and to the traders. His gentle humor and his calmness were never taken for weakness by those who knew him. There were many stories about the prowess of Big Chief; many stories of his great sense of humor. The Major recalled an incident during the June dances at the Agency.

The dance had begun, and as usual most of the seats were taken by the women and children, and by the agency employes and mixed-bloods. During this particular dance there were some white visitors at the Agency who sat enthralled upon seeing their first Indian dance. They were occupying several places on the end of one of the benches.

During one of the short intervals, Big Chief, who was not taking part, walked into the dance area. He walked with the dignity of an oriental emperor, his beaver-skin bandeau almost touching the branches of the roof. Behind him with eyes cast modestly to the ground came his wife. He walked straight toward the visitors. As he approached they arose as one from their seats, whereupon Big Chief and his wife sat down.

All eyes were on this magnificent chief but he seemed to see no one, and with Olympian indifference to the people about him he sat there and watched the dancers, without approval or disapproval.

There had been no menace in his approach to the visitors. They had arisen instinctively without thinking; as a soldier comes to attention at a command. The roots of heredity are persistent things. The Major had always believed that Big Chief had enjoyed immensely the humor of this occasion, and he often wondered if there had been forethought.

* * *

On the high prairie a breeze was blowing and the sweat on the flanks of the mules had begun to dry, one of them snorting loudly when a flock of prairie chickens arose one at a time from the side of the road where they had run from their dust-bath. They kept rising after the buggy had passed, alternately sailing and flapping over the rolling green of the prairie.

Monotonously the mules trotted. A mere speck in all this green expanse that suggested something gold washed; on toward the meeting place of the green and the sky—the edge of the world.

To a lonesome man this definite meeting place of the sky and the seemingly endless green would have given assurance that there was an end; that there was relief from this glorious space where the winds whispered and the tires rasped out the miles, but to the Major with his thoughts there was no loneliness. He wasn't really aware that he loved the prairie and the hills; perhaps he had never thought about it, but he was much like the lover who loves all things which remind him of his girl; a glove, a perfumed handkerchief; the street where she lives. He loved the blackjacks and the prairie because they were the home of a people whom he loved and respected. He often thought that the wild prairie with its temperamental changes of weather was a perfect home for the children of Wah'Kon-Tah, the Great Mysteries which was the sun, the wind, the lightning; that which lived in all things which had life. The just, cruel, vengeful god visualized by these people.

To the Major Wah'Kon-Tah was more than the god of a so called primitive people. In his strict consciousness, he had seen, in his contacts with the children of Wah'Kon-Tah, how many of the credos of his own belief of Brotherly Love had become mere form, and without meaning. In his contact with primitive virtues he had realized this. This realization had broadened him and given him tolerance. He was never the monitor, nor did he like to be didactic, but he often thought he would like to hold the worshippers of Wah'Kon-Tah up as an example to some of the people who worshipped as he worshipped. Perhaps it was only the tendency to defend these people who were called savages; to defend them against those who do not understand, with the most human desire to say: "You see?"

But he could not lose himself in a few years. He was European and understanding of the people came slowly. First through his beliefs and then through his broad sympathy with humanity, and later through an intense desire to understand, he had begun to appreciate them, though in fact he was still the agent, still the government official, and there had been too many generations of the stern teachings of Right and Wrong, for the Amer-European iron in his soul to have dissolved so quickly. But he was no simpering sentimentalist, and therein lay the value of his sympathy and understanding.

When he came to trees again he noticed that the shade formed a circle about the roots; he looked at his watch and saw that it was 12 o'clock. Ahead he could see the elms that bordered Salt creek and he became conscious of being hungry. He could see the gleam of the water for some time before he reached the stream. Finally on arrival under the shade of the trees he unhitched his mules and watered them.

He sat by the shaded water and ate his lunch. The cicadas had begun their songs; those monotonous songs that in midsummer give a knife-edge to the heat. For a long time he sat and watched the little water-striders skate here and there over the surface of the cool, shaded water. He had heard that these striders were the symbol of one of the clans, and he immediately decided that he would look it up, or ask some one about it. From the tops of the trees where the prairie breezes played, he heard the discontended voice of the cuckoo.

When the mules were rested he hitched them and drove out onto the prairie again.

An hour later he came into a region where the soil was reddish and the ravines small and dry. There were great tangles of undergrowth; redbuds, wild plums, and dogwood. Then when some large oaks came into view he saw the camp of Wah Se Se Gah. There were some Indians sitting in the shade among the trees. He drove up to the camp, but the Indians seemed not to notice him. He got out and hitched his mules to a tall hickory tree, which had become slick and worn from previous hitchings. He walked over to where several men were sitting and sat down with them. For some time he sat, then he said: "I have come long way. I have come to talk about white man who is here." There was silence. He wondered if they understood him; sometimes he had trouble with the deep guttural sounds of the Osage language. Then again he said: "I have come to talk about white man who is here." Again silence. Suddenly he pointed to a man who was sitting with his back to a tree and said: "You will bring white man here; I have much to talk about with this white man." The man then motioned for a small boy to come to him, and as he came up he said: "Go bring white man here." The boy started toward some lodges at the end of the camp, then he turned around and asked: "Ee Stah Hah?" The man replied "How."

The little group in the hot shade of the trees sat silently. Then the Major noticed the boy coming toward him accompanied by a tall, bearded white man, and as they came near he arose and went to meet them. He thought the man, despite his tattered clothes and his hang-dog expression, had all the characteristics of a cultured person; there was something about the mold of his face and his hands, and there was about him a certain air of carelessness, which was unlike the swagger of the ordinary white barbarian.

When they met the white man said: "Yes sir?"

"I am the agent—have you a permit to be on the Reservation?"

"No sir."

"Do you know that the department demands that everyone living on the Reservation, who is not a member of the tribe must have a permit?"

"Yes, I have heard it."

"We must know who is on the Reservation and their reasons for being here—the department is very strict about these matters."

The man seemed to be dejected, but apparently he was not embarrassed. Suddenly he looked up at the Major with an expression of hopelessness: "Your department would not recognize my reasons," he said, "and I shall not ask for a permit, but in explanation to you I will say that my reasons are at least important to me—and perhaps others. The fact is I have come here as the most likely place for losing myself. I am not sure what power you have here on the Reservation, but if you have the authority to take me down on the creek and have me shot, I should consider it a great favor—in that way I could really lose myself and you would be doing something which I haven't the nerve to do."

For some time they stood and looked at each other. The Indians were pretending that they were not in the least interested in the conversation. The Major saw a log a short distance away from the camp and led the way there, saying: "We can talk over there."

When they reached the log and had sat down the Major said: "Now, do you wish to tell me more, so that I can better consider your case?" The man looked intently at some small boys playing among the trees and said wearily: "Guess it makes no difference one way or the other—might as well—here's the story.

"I lived in the east—name of the state makes no difference either—my name is not necessary to the story. I met a girl of position much above mine—I idolized her and she loved me. Her family raised cain when we were married. I had no money—those things matter in the east—at least it matters to soap makers and needle makers. I heard about the great west, and I came. I lived on a claim for several years and nearly starved to death. Finally my wife died and left me with two little girls—couldn't pay a doctor—she might have lived—that's the hell of it. I couldn't even feed the little girls so I changed their name and put them in an orphan-home. Her family knows nothing about it you see—couldn't tell them after all the things they had said and predicted—you see I couldn't call on them—at least I wouldn't. Well, I changed my name and have been wandering in the Indian country ever since. I like these people—you kinda forget." He paused for a moment and looked at the ground, then as an after-thought he continued: "Now you know the reason why I said that if you would take me down by the creek and have me shot that it would be the best thing that you could do for me."

"Give me some clew as to the name, the where-abouts of your children, or the name of your wife's family—they needn't know that I learned from you." The Major was very much moved by the story.

"No, I'll drift on—no use asking—absolutely no use." He got up and disappeared the way he had come; into the undergrowth of the river bottom. That was the last the Reservation saw of Ee Stah Hah.

The Major walked over to his mules, untied them and climbed into the buggy. As he drove out of the bottoms and through the blackjacks to the camp of Big Chief, he kept thinking of this white man. He believed to a certain extent in pride, but he believed that the man's pride was false, and that he had no sense of duty, and Duty was a sort of stern goddess, unbending, unflinching. Finally he clucked to his mules as though he were suddenly in a great hurry; a defense against the unpleasant thoughts.

It was growing late. The shadows had begun to lengthen and the night-hawks filled the air, dodging here and there in their chase of insects, and the warmth of anticipation came over the Major as he neared the camp.

Suddenly through the half lights of the late afternoon he could see the white dome-shaped lodges, looming white and spectre-like among the dark boles of the trees. The dogs began to bark, and some half-naked boys ran out from among the lodges to see who the visitor might be. But instead of running back to tell their parents, they stood and looked as though they were quite unconcerned.

Before the Major had descended to the camp, Big Chief came out of his lodge and stood waiting, until the buggy was at the bottom of the hill, then he motioned for some of the boys to take the Major's team. He approached and offered his hand; "My friend," he said, "it is good to see you." The two then walked to the front of the lodge, sat down and crossed their legs.

Big Chief's wife appeared at the entrance to the lodge and he told her to prepare some food, then he turned to the Major and said: "Tonight we have some fresh meat, and you will tell my woman how you want it cooked." The Major turned to the waiting woman and said: "My sister, you can cook meat long time for me." The woman said "Good" and turned into the lodge again

The two men sat silently in the darkness. The bullfrogs were croaking down on the muddy banks of a small stream. The night-hawks had almost disappeared, except for a few energetic ones that gulped insects from just over the tops of the lodges, the air that passed the corners of their mouths during their dives making sounds like one blowing in a gun barrel. A few cicadas still buzzed from the tall elms, and a myraid of insects had started their chorus from the grass roots. It seemed that this part of the river bottoms was replete with life; as though here was the pulse of the universe.

The boys were playing some game like "tag." But silently, like greyhounds at play; a silent running and dodging broken occasionally by a slight altercation. All through the encampment forms were moving; women carrying wood and water and men leading horses, but with a silence that made their movements more purposeful than agitated rushing here and there. Swiftly they came and went, not in the manner of performing necessary duties, but as though these movements were a part of their existence; of being alive, like breathing.

Soon Big Chief's wife appeared with the food. There were lily roots, fried bread, a large piece of broiled beef and black coffee. The Major ate heartily as Big Chief sat like a statue, paying no attention to two lean dogs that came sniffing tentatively close to them, but his wife came out of the lodge scolding and waving a large spoon, and as the curs ran off with tails between their legs she scolded menacingly.

When the Major finished he wiped his mouth with a large red handkerchief. He said "My friend that is good; it is good to eat at lodge of Che Sah Hunka." Big Chief answered: "I am glad. Today my mind has been troubled." The Major waited for him to continue. Big Chief moved his position slightly, then began to talk in a deep voice: "My friend, I have said that my mind was troubled. But now my mind is not troubled. You have come to lodge of Che Sah Hunka. I will tell you what troubled my mind.

"Yesterday my people came together to talk about business. When they came together there was nothing for feast. That was bad. They came to me and they said: 'There is nothing for feast.' That is bad, I said, if there is nothing for feast. I remembered that there was cow which was visiting our cows. I said this cow should not be with our cattle. I said this cow does not belong here. I called some young men and I told them this: 'Go get that cow that is visiting our cattle, and kill him for feast.' Then I was worried about this thing. I said the owner might come and there would be trouble. But now my mind is not worried about this thing. Since you have come to lodge of Che Sah Hunka, I am glad and this trouble has left my mind. It was like dark cloud, but it is like clear sky in morning. You have come and it is good. I understand in white man's law that if man ate of meat from cow that had been taken, that it would be bad for him too. Now you have eaten this meat and you have gone against white man's law too, and my trouble that was like cloud is gone. I am glad you have eaten meat of this cow."

The Major smiled and he imagined that he could almost see the eyes of Big Chief smiling in the darkness. He wondered if the cow had really been a stray or if it had been from Big Chief's own herd. In any case he enjoyed the joke that his friend was having at his expense.

In the silence that followed the Major enjoyed the hot, heaviness of the evening. In his deep sense of wellbeing, the thoughts came and went but none stayed to disturb him.

Suddenly he realized that his host was preparing to talk. He saw him pick up a short stick and begin to make marks on the ground in front of him, then as he made little circles with the stick, he said in simple Osage so that the Major would understand: "My people are like these marks. They make their road in circles. They do not know where this road will end. Some day they will take white man's road. I know this; but now they are Indians. They do not know what they want, my people. My mind is troubled about this thing. Some young men try to talk like white man; they try to act like white man. But they talk like white man who talks like crow, and they act like white man who acts bad, I believe. It is not good for young men to talk like white man who talks like crow. They send our young men off to school and there they learn to talk like white man who knows how to talk, I believe. I believe that is good. But at this school they make our young men do things like white man; but he is Indian. At this school they make things of iron, and they make things of wood. This is not good, I believe. I am troubled in my mind about this thing. I do not know if it is good for Indian to learn from white man. Indian knows many things, but white man says that these things are not good. I believe white man does not know many things that Indian knows. One time Navajo came to my camp. He had many blankets, and young men stood around and said: 'that is good.' This Navajo made pictures of horses and dancers and braves, and trees when wind blows, and young men stood around and said: 'tompa, that is good; tompa, that is beautiful.' But my mind is troubled about my people. I think they are like dog who has lost trail; they run in circles saying: 'here is trail, here is trail,' but trail is lost and they sit down like dog that has lost trail, and wait with no thoughts in their heads." Big Chief paused and the Major waited.

Quiet had settled over the camp in the river bottom. Occasionally a horse sneezed, and the hobbled ones could be heard moving with short jumps as they grazed. A barred owl sent his booming call into the night from a nearby tree, and another answered him from up the creek, like an echo; then again, and again the answer. A lone whippoorwill talked like a persistent, petulant child. A nearby insect sent his almost metallic rasping from the grass, and a frog gave one "garumph" and fell silent.

Again the low guttural voice of Big Chief broke the silence: "This mourning dance. I am much troubled about mourning dance; I believe it is not good. Much trouble has come to my people because of this mourning dance, and I am much troubled about this thing. Before white man came it was good to have mourning dance, but now it is bad, I believe. Some day Indian will take white man's road; slowly they will take white man's road, and I think it is good if they do not have mourning dance. Slowly they will leave their customs, my people, and I believe that mourning dance should go now. There has been much trouble between my people and white man because of this mourning dance. I think it is time they should stop mourning dance."

"How," said the Major, "I believe it is good too."

"Some day," continued Big Chief, "I shall go away. Soon, I think I shall go away. My people will say: 'It is Che Sah Hunka who has gone away, and we shall mourn for him.' They will have mourning dance but I do not want this. I want you to say when I am gone: 'There will be no mourning dance for Che Sah Hunka.' Say to my people: 'Che Sah Hunka does not want mourning dance; I am his friend and he told me this thing.'"

A pang came to the Major as he sat in the dark with his friend. Somehow he felt that what Big Chief had said about his death was true. Indians were uncanny about such prophecies. Death to them was a mere matter of transition; there was no doubting it; they had faith and they were not afraid. They spoke of the end as they might speak of going to sleep. Not particularly in anticipation, but as a matter of course; as fate weaving its pattern in which night and sleep followed day and activity. The Major thought of them as fatalists, and he had a feeling that Big Chief's prophecy would come to pass. He said: "My friend you will live long time as councillor to your people."

"I shall go soon," he persisted. "For long time I have wished to do many things for my people. I cannot do these things now. For long time I have wished to be governor of my people, but now I believe it is too late; I have lived long time."

The conversation was ended. Big Chief arose and walked into the lodge and the Major followed. There had been a fire burning in the center, and the bed had been prepared on each side; the Major's bed between the fire and the entrance and Big Chief's bed on the other side of the fire. Big Chief's wife and boys slept back of him in the rear of the lodge.

They were soon rolled into their blankets.

The Major lay for some time listening to the noises of the night, and as he lay, thoughts of his worries as an Indian agent came to him. He thought of the payments, and the trips across the wild prairie to the railroad towns in

Kansas. He decided he would take steps immediately to have this matter adjusted by the department. Then his thoughts came around to the trespasser and his children, and he consoled himself with the thought that he would not give up until he had found the family of this man's wife; until he had brought about the happiness of the people interested. With this determination he felt happier, and he thought of his conversations with Big Chief and became vaguely unhappy again; he told himself that Big Chief would live a long time yet.

The thoughts became less definite, and began to fade as though in the distance, where they merged with haze. He was startled by the long mournful howl of a wolf coming from back among the hills, and instantly every dog in camp barked and howled in a different key. A horse snorted, and from down the river, he heard a woman scolding the dogs and they suddenly became silent. A cool breeze came into the lodge, like a breath that had been grudgingly released from the heat-blanket, and had come wandering up the valley, exploring here and there. Finally the sustained, almost audible hum of the silence faded, and sleep came to the Major; untroubled sleep in the lodge of his friend.

Chapter Thirteen. Death of Che-Sah-Hunka

One cold autumn evening the Major drove from Independence into the Agency. After first sighting the dim red lights it seemed hours before he was finally standing before the stove warming his stiff fingers. There was a knock at the door and he was called. He saw an Indian runner standing there. He was one of the Hominy Indians and though there was no reading his face the Major felt that there was bad news, or perhaps trouble. A thought flashed through his mind that his little mules were too tired to make the trip that night. Then he said, "How." "How," replied the runner.

"You are cold, I believe."

"No, I am not cold."

"You will come into the fire and we will talk—you wish to tell me something?"

"Che-Sah-Hunka is dying they say. I have come to tell you this thing."

"That is bad. I will go." The information staggered him. He said to the runner, "Go to barn and tell man there that I want team that is not tired. Tell him I must go see Che-Sah-Hunka." He went back into the room and sat down to the meal that had been prepared for him. He looked up at his wife. "I shall be gone a day or two—Big Chief is dying."

"Thee is going tonight?"

"Yes, I am going as soon as I can get a team."

"Thee is warm enough."

"I'm all right."

Through the cold night with the wind rattling the leaves of the black-jacks he drove the thirty miles through the wooded hills to the south; across Hominy creek and on to the Arkansas river, to the camp of Big Chief.

He came on the camp suddenly. There were no fires burning and he could only guess at the outlines of the lodges.

He stopped in the darkness. A feeling came into his stomach and he felt that he would like to sit there until dawn. The calm of the camp with the winds moaning in the tall trees of the bottom, gave rise to a queer weakness that seemed suddenly to flood his body. He took out his watch and by the light of a match saw that it was just midnight. He believed that if only the dogs would bark his courage would return. He sat there for some minutes then he began to shiver. He got out of the buggy and felt in the darkness for a tree. Finding one he led the team over to it and tied them; he did this slowly as though to gain time but he wasn't sure why he wished to gain time. He would walk to the camp. It would not be courteous to drive into the camp if death had arrived and he felt sure that death had come to his friend.

Still he hesitated in the darkness, and the winds seemed to scream in the tops of the trees, at times accentuating the cold. Suddenly he made out a dark form moving among the lodges and he walked slowly toward it. The form stopped and he spoke to it as he came up. "It is friend of Che-Sah-Hunka," he said, "I have come." The figure said, "How," and led him to the large lodge which he knew so well. He came to the entrance and thrust in his head. There was the odor of charred wood of the dead fire. Then he heard a movement and the wife of Big Chief came out. She stood in the darkness for a second, then said, "He is gone. We will talk about things he said." He followed her into the lodge and feeling a blanket under his feet he sat down and she sat down beside him. She started to talk but her voice broke and she put her hands to her head and began to chant the Song of Death. Suddenly he was flooded with sympathy for this woman, and his heart went out to her in his emotion. He instinctively put out his hand, touched her shoulder and at this human touch of burning sympathy the stoic, the spartan of the prairie and the blackjacks became a woman and sank down, resting her head on his lap, wailing, and the Major put his hand gently on her head and stared at the entrance of the lodge. He was scarcely aware of the something in his throat and the hot moisture on his cheeks, he allowed to dry.

On hearing her voice the wailing was taken up along the line of lodges and the wind in the tree tops became an accompanying dirge. A cur raised his nose to the cold stars and howled long and heartbreakingly, the vague emotion, the instinct or the dim thoughts in his mind unguessable, but with the wail from the lodges, his voice carried that same questing; that question that has been asked through the ages from the darkness enveloping dwellers on the earth. Others took it up and there was no scolding woman with uplifted arm and menacing, shrill voice to stop them.

The night wore on and the wailing was spasmodic. The wife of Big Chief would be silent for long periods and the Major knew that she was not aware of his presence. She had lost herself in grief. Then suddenly she sat up and remained there motionless staring at the invisible walls of the lodge; with the silence of a statue, the dark, vague outlines of her body expressing more effectively than action or words the grief that tore at her heart.

Just before dawn the camp had become quiet again and then suddenly the long-drawn chant of the Song of Death came from the blackjack hills, carried on the dawn:

> *O-hoooooo, it is I who fall upon them unawares,*
> *It is I who attack them thus.*
> *O-hoooooo, it is I who fall upon them unawares,*
> *It is I who attack them thus,*
> *Ah, hoooooooooooooooooooooooooo.*
>
> *O-hoooooo, it is I who serve them thus,*
> *I who brought these deeds to pass.*
> *A-he the he, Ah, the he.*
> *It is I who cause them to lie blackening on the earth,*
> *I who brought these deeds to pass.*
> *A-he the he, Ah-he the he.*
>
> *It is I who cause them to lie yellowing on the earth, etc.*
> *It is I who takes from them their remaining days, etc.*

Then after awhile the wife of Big Chief seemed to come back to the world of men, as she sat and told the Major of Big Chief's sickness and his death. She told him that he had left a message for his friend. He said that he hoped that his friend's years would be many. He had asked her to tell agent again what he had always felt about the mourning dance and request him to see that there was no mourning dance. He had said that many times they had talked about this thing and they had thought that it was bad for his people, that Osages were always in trouble during mourning dance, that there had been trouble with white man because he had believed that white man because of his power and his tricks was their worst enemy, and when his people were in forgetfulness of mourning dance scalp of white man, their enemy, came to their minds. He said that his people were always in trouble with other tribes during mourning dance. That during forgetfulness of mourning dance people thought of scalp of their ancient enemies—Pawnees and Comanches and Cheyennes. He said they had talked about this thing many times and he desired that there would be no mourning dance after his death; that his people should be true Osages but live in peace with white man and tribes; that they should learn all that white man knows and give white man all they know. In his last talk he had said that he desired this thing and that his wife should tell his friend of these things which he had said.

The Major left the wife of Che-Sah-Hunka and walked out into the cold air. The wind had died slightly but was still blowing through the tree tops and swirling the golden and red leaves before it. It caught the smoke of the fires, twisted and distorted them, lifting them, then pressing them to the ground again. He could hear the voice of a lone dog down the river, probably in the camp of Shon Kah Sabe. It must have been young and excited about something, as surely the older ones were curled up in the shelter of the lodges.

Soon the sun had climbed up above the trees and still he walked about or stood and watched the glittering ribbon of water meandering over a sand-choked bed. The sun felt warm and he stood for some time letting its rays through his clothes. His thoughts would not be concentrated, but he felt vague uneasiness, which he decided was a dread of seeing the ceremony for the burial of his friend. The mourning that tore at your heartstrings; tore your heart because in it was the questing of the ages; the something primitive which stirred the depth of emotion like the screams of a wounded horse; this remonstrance to the Great Mystery.

As the rays of the sun warmed his body he stood and looked out across the sand of the river, and seeing bars and drifts that lay across the bed to the Pawnee side, unbroken except by the glittering, slowly moving ribbon of water, he thought of the time that Big Chief had crossed early one morning to council with the Pawnees. The incident came back to him vividly.

A party of Pawnees had come across the river at flood tide and had taken fifteen head of horses from Big Chief. On learning of the theft Big Chief had immediately crossed over to the Pawnee side and had soon caught up with the band. He had told them in sign language that the horses were his and that he wanted them back. After some talk the Pawnees said that he could have the horses but a young Pawnee who was standing near him suddenly snatched the pistol from Big Chief's saddle and leaping on his horse, ran away toward the Pawnee agency on Black Bear creek.

Big Chief was very angry and rounding up his horses, drove them back to his camp. On arrival he changed horses, rode into the Agency and reported the matter to the agent, the Major's predecessor. After much talk the agent sent word to the agent of the Pawnees that the Osages desired a council and then selected three councillors to accompany Big Chief to the Agency of the Pawnees.

When the party reached the river the yellow waters were in flood, making many channels like fingers among the sand bars. A scout had been sent ahead to find a crossing and he had cut willow sticks and placed them at intervals along the route they were to take in crossing in order that they might avoid quicksand and the deepest water.

They got across but their clothes were wet and they decided to undress and dry them. While they were sitting there an Osage hunter came up and joined them; then another and another, appearing out of the bushes suddenly and silently as In-gro-kah, the panther. And the interpreter had asked Big Chief what these men were doing on the Pawnee side and he said that they were hunters, but when fifty or sixty of these men had joined them the interpreter understood. He told Big Chief that surely he would not take these men to the Pawnee Agency for the council, and Big Chief had replied that they would stay on the bank of the river, but that if he needed them he would send a runner for them. The interpreter could see that they were all young warriors.

At the council Big Chief had given one of his characteristic speeches. The Major could visualize him, rising slowly, pulling his blanket up over his left shoulder and then bringing it together in front under his right arm. He could see him standing there looking over the faces in the council room, announcing gravely that he had come to talk to Pawnees; that he wanted them to listen to words that came from his heart. He told them that Pawnees were great people and that they knew much which Osages did not know; that it would be good if these people could come to visit Osages in friendship. He had said that Osages knew much that Pawnees did not know and that they might visit Pawnees in terms of friendship. It seemed to him that instead of this desire of friendship Pawnees came to take horses from Osages; that certain man had taken horses from him and through guile had taken his pistol which had been given to him by United States cavalry captain who had been his friend. He said that this young man had memory which was very short, he believed; that at one time on plains of west on buffalo hunt he had saved this very man from Cheyennes. He said that he did not believe that Pawnees had short memories but if they did, that it would be bad to have short memories about such things. He said that surely Pawnees knew medicine of Osages. For long time they had fought each other on plains, and Pawnees must surely know about medicine of Osages. He said further that he was peaceful man; that he was Peace Chief, but that he would ask that Pawnees return pistol that had been given him by his friend, captain of United States cavalry.

As he sat down a Pawnee rose and walked quietly out of the council room. Then the Pawnee agent talked for a short time about friendship between the two great tribes and resumed his seat. For a short time no one spoke. There was ominous tenseness in the room.

In this silence a man entered the room and walked up to Big Chief holding out a pistol. Big Chief took it and again there was silence. The agent then said that he believed matters were adjusted and the council was over if there was nothing else to talk about. He said that there would be a feast in the Agency of the Pawnees in honor of the Osages; that the chief of the Pawnees had told him to say this. When he sat down again a head man of the Pawnees got up and made a short talk saying that he wished to be at peace with his neighbors, Great Osages, and to show their friendship Pawnees wanted Osages to attend feast. Without changing the expression on his face, he said that those Osages who were waiting by the river should be told to come to the feast too.

The Major's thought came back again to the gliding, almost imperceptible ribbon of water that ran slowly on through the sand, and above him on the dead top of a sycamore two red headed woodpeckers quarreled with each other about store houses for the winter. The leaves eddied and floated in the chill wind and some fell on the water setting daintily on their voyage and disappearing in the reflected light of the sun. A flock of crows had found a barred owl in the gloom of the tall trees of the bottom, as he dreamed away the day, and were cursing terribly; darting at him or sitting above him, calling him thief and murderer. Life went on around the camps opposite cedar islands the same as when Big Chief walked regally among his people. The Major caught himself wondering why this should be.

There was silence over the camps and the Major knew that they were preparing Big Chief for his long ride to the Happy Hunting Ground and a pang came to his heart and then a queer feeling of dread. If only they would not mourn.

He walked back to the camp and to Big Chief's lodge. There were several people there and he didn't know about the etiquette in such matters. But some force drew him into the lodge. He saw the long body of Big Chief. The painters had finished with him. He was dressed in his best leggings and his best shirt. In his hands he held his eagle wing fan and on his wrists were his bracelets. He had his necklace of bear claws and at his throat was the shell gorget made from the fresh water mussel and representing the sun at noon; the symbol of the god of day. Over his shirt was his bone breastplate with wampum on each side. His face had been painted with red, a symbol of the dawn, symbol of the god of day; the Grandfather. On this were alternating lines of red and black on each side of his face representing the tribe and clan and family and the symbol which designated him as Peace Chief, or chief of the Chesho division of the tribe, the division which represented the sky.

He was gorgeous as he lay there; regal, like some primitive god in austere repose; a sort of oriental gorgeousness like some embalmed pharaoh ready to be taken to his tomb. Somehow this tall figure seemed triumphant and the sorrow which his death had inspired in the Major seemed to disappear as he looked, fascinated by this man dressed for the meeting with Wah'Kon-Tah, the Great Mysteries.

They carried him to the sandstone hill on the back of a pony and placed him in a sitting posture, facing the east, in a cairn of sandstone. They placed in the cairn food for the long journey.

The people followed the body up the hill and stood around in deep grief. The wind whipped their blankets and the prayers of the medicine men were torn from their lips and lost over the wooded hills. The red and yellow leaves floated from the blackjacks on a neighboring hill and drifted past on the quarreling wind that sometimes screamed and at other times sang whining, melancholy songs in the stones of the cairn and carried away the wailing of the mourners.

It took several men to place the United States flag in the top of the cairn where it seemed to take control immediately, as it plopped and crackled occasionally like the report of a gun. It became the dominant sound; above the sobbing of Big Chief's wife; above the wailing of the people; above the chants and the prayers of the medicine man.

The Major looked down the hill and saw three ponies tied to a small tree. He felt sad that these sleekhided ponies should be sacrificed. But Big Chief must have a mount on the long ride. As he looked intently at them he found himself hoping his friend would use the bay as he undoubtedly was the best horse in the Major's opinion.

He began to move down the hill as he did not want to see the killing of the pony. The people had already begun to descend to the feast which was prepared at the camp on the river.

Before sitting down to the feast he held his hands over the smoke of the little cedar fire as others did before him, then found his place among the friends of Big Chief and ate heartily of the beef, lily roots, squash, fried bread and black coffee.

After the feast the sons of Big Chief and his brother-in-law came to the Major saying that they had heard about message that Che Sah Hunka had left concerning mourning dance. They were sorry about this they said. They didn't know what to do about this thing. They said he was greatest of Osages and that they wished to give him greatest mourning dance that had ever been given. The brother-in-law said: "I have fifty ponies. I will spend all of these ponies. I will spend more than fifty ponies for greatest mourning dance that has ever been given any Osage. I will do this in memory of my brother-in-law."

The Major sat and talked to them for a long time. He said he believed that it was best to remember what this great man had said about mourning dance. He said it would show their respect if they remembered what he wished about this thing. "Many times," he said, "he told me this thing. I have listened to him. I said there will be no mourning dance. I have given my word to my friend. He is not here and I cannot take back from him this word which I have given." They could see that this was so, they said, but surely there ought to be mourning dance for Che Sah Hunka. Many people knew that he was great man.

Finally they said that they could not go against wishes of Che Sah Hunka. They had listened to message that Che Sah Hunka had left with his friend.

The Major went to the lodge of his friend but found that the wife was with relatives and he decided not to disturb her. Already he noticed several women with ashes on their heads. He was glad to be leaving. He knew that he could no nothing more.

He watered his mules. As he hitched them they stood hunched and trembling under the cold harness and he had to speak to them many times to get them to stand still. It seemed that they wished to get out of his cheerless bottom too; out into the winds on the upland. Already the shadows had begun to lengthen though it was about mid-afternoon.

The little mules pressed against their collars with desire to go and the whip bending before the wind in the whipsocket was not needed. On the uplands the curtains flapped and the top of the buggy swayed. As he rounded the hill on which Big Chief had been buried the Major looked intently at the cairn of stone with the flag plopping above it. Partly on the piled stones he thought he saw the form of a horse lying there.

The spirit of Big Chief had started on the long ride.

Michael Gold
(1894–1967)

Born Irving Granich on the Lower East Side of Manhattan, he took the name Michael Gold when he began to write. Gold stayed in public school only until he was thirteen, then worked at various jobs from night porter to shipping clerk, mostly in New York but also briefly in Boston.

After the Russian Revolution, he joined the Communist Party and was, from that time, associated with various radical publications. He served as assistant editor of Masses, *founder and editor of* Liberator *(1920–1922), co-founder and editor of* New Masses *(1926–1948), and writer for* The Daily Worker.

*In a well-known essay, "Towards Proletarian Art" (*Liberator, *February 1921), Gold advocated art as a vehicle for social change and with others edited* Proletarian Literature in the United States: An Anthology *(1935). He regarded his own autobiographical novel,* Jews Without Money *(1930), as a prototype of the kind of literature appropriate to a society influenced by the experience of immigrant workers, where "in every American factory there is a dramatic group * * * when mechanics paint in their leisure and farmers write sonnets." The* New Masses *was intended to be an outlet for the literary production of working men and women. His own writing aimed to describe realistically conditions of the working poor, whether in the Lower East Side, Harlem, or Mexico.*

As a dedicated Marxist, Gold always had a political message as the basis for his writing of fiction, plays, or poetry. The Life of John Brown *(1924) and* The Damned Agitator and Other Stories *(1926) were followed by plays such as* Hoboken Blues *(1928),* Fiesta *(1929), and* Money *(1930). Other titles include* 120 Million *(1929),* Change the World! *(1937), and* The Hollow Men *(1941). Two collections are* The Mike Gold Reader *(1954) and* Mike Gold: A Literary Anthology *(1972).*

[From] Jews without Money

Chapter 13. Jews and Christians

1

My mother never learned to like shoes. In Hungary, in her native village, she had rarely worn them, and she could see no reason for wearing them here.

"Does one wear shoes on one's hands?" she would ask. "How can one work in shoes? Shoes are only for people to show off in."

So she paddled about in bare feet whenever she could. This annoyed my father at those times when he was ambitious. To him not wearing shoes was like confessing to the world that one was poor. But my mother had no such false pride, and would even walk barefooted in the street.

Once my father bought her a diamond ring on the installment plan. It was during one of his periods of greatness, when he had earned a big week's pay, and the Boss had hinted at a foreman's job for him.

It was on a Saturday night, and he had been drinking beer with his fellow-workmen. He came home flushed and dramatic. With many flourishes and the hocus-pocus of a magician he extracted the ring from his vest pocket and placed it on my mother's finger.

"At last, Katie!" he said, kissing her with great ceremony, "at last you have a diamond ring! At last you can write home to Hungary that you too are wearing diamonds in America!"

"Pouf!" said my mother angrily, pushing him away. She snatched the ring from her finger as if it burned her. "What foolishness!"

"Foolishness!" my father exclaimed, indignantly. "What! it is foolish to wear diamonds?"

"Yes," said my stubborn mother.

"Every one wears diamonds!" said my father, "every one with a little pride."

"Let others be proud! I am a work horse," said my mother.

My father spat in disgust, and stalked off to find some intelligent males.

The ring remained in the family. It was our only negotiable capital. It was hidden among some towels and sheets in the bureau. In time of need it traveled to the pawnshop, to buy us food and rent. Many East Side families aspired to jewelry for this reason. Money vanished. Jewelry remained. This was the crude credit system of the East Side.

2

My mother was fond of calling herself a work horse. She was proud of the fact that she could work hard. She wanted no diamond rings, no fancy dresses, no decorations. She had a strong sense of reality, and felt that when one was poor, only strength could help one. But my father was a romantic, and dreamed of a bright easy future.

My humble funny little East Side mother! How can I ever forget this dark little woman with bright eyes, who hobbled about all day in bare feet, cursing in Elizabethan Yiddish, using the forbidden words "ladies" do not use, smacking us, beating us, fighting with her neighbors, helping her neighbors, busy from morn to midnight in the tenement struggle for life.

She would have stolen or killed for us. She would have let a railroad train run over her body if it could have helped us. She loved us all with the fierce painful love of a mother-wolf, and scolded us continually like a magpie.

Mother! Momma! I am still bound to you by the cords of birth. I cannot forget you. I must remain faithful to the poor because I cannot be faithless to you! I believe in the poor because I have known you. The world must be made gracious for the poor! Momma, you taught me that!

3

What a hard life she had led. She had known nothing but work since her tenth year. Her father had died then, and she was the oldest child of a large family. She went to work in a bakery, then did a man's labor on a farm.

When she was eighteen, relatives gathered seventy five gulden, and sent her to America as the last hope for her family. She was to work here and send for her brothers and sisters.

The crossing made a deep mark on her mind. She spent seventeen agonized days in the filthy steerage, eating nothing but herrings and potatoes, because there was no *kosher* food.

Her first night in America was spent amid groans and confusion on the floor of a crowded cellar for immigrants. It was called the Nigger House.

A relative found her the next morning. He took her to a job. It was in an East Side restaurant where she was paid five dollars a month, with meals. She slept on a mattress in the evil, greasy kitchen. The working hours were from five to midnight.

In a year she saved enough money to send a ship ticket to her oldest brother.

"Yes, I have had all kinds of good times in America," she would chuckle grimly, when she told us of this time. "Yes, that first year in the restaurant I had lots of fun with the pots and pans.

"It's lucky I'm alive yet. It is a good land, but not for the poor. When the Messiah comes to America, he had better come in a fine automobile, with a dozen servants. If he comes here on a white horse, people will think he is just another poor immigrant. They may set him to work washing dishes in a restaurant."

4

She and my father had married in the old Jewish style; that is, they were brought together by a professional matrimonial broker. He charged them a commission for the service. It is as good a method as any. My parents came to love each other with an emotion deeper than romance; I am sure my father would have died for my mother. But she also made his head ache, and he told her so often.

She was a buttinsky. She tried to "reform" everybody, and fought people because they were "bad." She spoke her mind freely, and told every one exactly where the path of duty lay. She was always engaged in some complicated ethical brawl, and my father had to listen to all the details.

Or she was always finding people in trouble who needed her help. She helped them for days, weeks and months, with money, food, advice and the work of her hands.

She was a midwife in many hasty births, a nurse in sickness, a peacemaker in family battles.

She knew how to make a poultice for boils by chewing bread and mixing it with yellow soap; and how to cure colds with kerosene, and the uses of herbs and other peasant remedies. She was a splendid cook and breadmaker, and shared all these secrets with the neighbors.

When a woman fell sick, the distracted husband appealed to my mother; and for weeks she'd drop in there twice a day, to cook the meals, and scrub the floors, and bathe the children, to joke, gossip, scold, love, to scatter her strength and goodness in the dark home.

It would have shocked her if any one had offered to pay for these services. It was simply something that had to be done for a neighbor.

Once there was a woman on our street who was going crazy. Her cigarmaker husband had deserted her and two children. The woman had spells, and could not sleep at night. She begged my mother to sleep with her. She was afraid she would kill her children during one of her spells.

So my mother slept there every night for more than a month.

How often have I seen my mother help families who were evicted because they could not pay rent. She wrapped herself in her old shawl, and went begging through the tenements for pennies. Puffing with bronchitis, she dragged herself up and down the steep landings of a hundred tenements, telling the sad tale with new emotion each time and begging for pennies.

But this is an old custom on the East Side; whenever a family is to be evicted, the neighboring mothers put on their shawls and beg from door to door.

5

My poor father, worrying over his own load of American troubles, had to listen to the tremendous details of all these tragedies. My mother could discover so many sick people! And so many bad people who needed to be fought! No wonder my father drank beer! No wonder he grabbed his head between his hands, and groaned:

"Stop! you give me a headache! I can't listen any more!"

"It is not your head, but your selfishness!" scoffed my mother.

"One has to be selfish in America," said my father. "It is dog eat dog over here. But you, you neglect your own family to help every passing stranger."

"*Pfui*, what a lie!" my mother spat. "When have my children been neglected?"

"But for God's sake," said my father, "haven't we enough troubles of our own? You're like a man with consumption. It is not enough for him to have this, he has to go skating so that he can break his leg, too."

"*Nu*, I can stand a broken leg," said my mother. "What is a leg when there is so much misery in the world!"

6

My mother was opposed to the Italians, Irish, Germans and every other variety of Christian with whom we were surrounded.

"May eight and eighty black years fall on these *goys!*"[1] she said, her black eyes flashing. "They live like pigs; they have ruined the world. And

---

1. Non-Jews.

they hate and kill Jews. They may seem friendly to us to our faces, but behind our backs they laught at us. I know them well. I have seen them in Hungary."

My father sat one evening at the supper table, drinking beer and reading a Yiddish newspaper. In the hot kitchen my mother was washing the dishes, and humming a Hungarian folk song.

"*Nu, nu!*" my father exclaimed, striking the table with his fist, "another railroad accident! Katie, I have always said it is dangerous to travel on these American railroads!"

"What has happened?" my mother gasped, appearing from the kitchen with steaming hands and face.

"What has happened, you ask?" my father repeated in the important tone of a pedant. "What has happened is that seventeen innocent people were killed in a railroad accident in New Jersey! And whose fault was it? The fault of the rich American railroads!"

My mother was horrified. She wiped her boiling face with her apron and muttered: "God help us and shield us! Were there any Jews among the dead?"

My father glanced rapidly through the list of names. "No," he said, "only Christians were killed."

My mother sighed with relief. She went back into her kitchen. She was no longer interested; Christians did not seem like people to her. They were abstractions. They were the great enemy, to be hated, feared and cursed. In Hungary three Christian peasant girls had once taunted her. Then they had gone in swimming, and had been drowned. This was God's punishment on them for persecuting a Jew. Another peasant had once plucked the beard of an old reverend Jew, and God struck him with lightning a week later. My mother was full of such anecdotes.

The East Side never forgot Europe. We children heard endless tales of the pogroms.[2] Joey Cohen, who was born in Russia, could himself remember one. The Christians had hammered a nail into his uncle's head, and killed him. When we passed a Christian church we were careful to spit three times; otherwise bad luck was sure to befall us. We were obsessed by wild stories of how the Christians loved to kidnap Jewish children, to burn a cross on each cheek with a redhot poker. They also cut off children's ears, and made a kind of soup. Nigger[3] had once seen Jewish ears for sale in the window of a Christian butcher shop.

"In the old days," my mother said, "the Christians hunted the Jews like rabbits. They would gather thousands in a big marketplace, and stuff pork down their throats with swords, and ask the Jews to be baptized. The Jews refused, of course. So they were burnt in great fires, and the Christians laughed, danced and made merry when they saw the poor Jews burning up like candles. Such are the Christians. May they burn some day, too."

---

2. Organized massacres, especially of Jews.

3. The dark-complexioned leader of the narrator's gang of Jewish friends.

These impressions sank into my heart, and in my bad dreams during the hot summer nights, dark Christian ogres the size of tenements moved all around me. They sat on my chest, and clutched my throat with slimy remorseless fingers, shrieking, "Jew, Jew! Jew!"

And I would spend long daylight hours wondering why the Christians hated us so, and form noble plans of how I would lead valiant Jewish armies when I grew up, in defense of the Jews.

7

But my mother was incapable of real hatred. Paradoxically she had many warm friends among the Italian and Irish neighbors. She was always apologetic about this. "These are not like other Christians," she would say, "these are good people." How could she resist another human being in trouble? How could she be indifferent when another was in pain? Her nature was made for universal sympathy, without thought of prejudice. Her hatred of Christians was really the outcry of a motherly soul against the boundless cruelty in life.

Betsy was an Italian woman who lived in the next tenement. She had a long, emaciated face covered with moles, engraved with suffering like an old yellow wood carving. Her coffee-colored eyes always seemed to have a veil over them, as if she were hiding a terrible secret. She avoided people; swathed in her long black scarf she stole down the street furtively, as if conscious of the eyes of the world.

Her husband was in jail for murder. One summer night (I shall never forget it), he burst from the tenement into the street, screaming like a madman. A revolver was in his hand. We were sitting on the stoop, calmly eating ice-cream cones. The spectacle of this wild swarthy Italian in his undershirt, shrieking, and waving a pistol, appalled us like a hallucination. He rushed by us, and dived into a cellar. A crowd gathered. A policeman ran up. He hadn't the nerve to follow the Italian into the cellar, but stood uncertainly on the sidewalk, growling: "Get up out of there, before I shoot yuh." At last the Italian stumbled out, sobbing like a child. His bronzed, rocky face was grotesquely twisted with grief. He wrung his hands, beat his chest, and clawed at his cheeks until the blood spurted. I have never heard such dreadful animal howls, the ferocious and dangerous agony of a dying wolf. He had just killed his brother in a quarrel over a card game.

This passion-blinded assassin was Betsy's husband. She was left with three children, and no friends. She could speak only Italian. My mother visited her, and through sheer sympathy, learned, in the course of several visits, a kind of pigeon-Italian. It was marvelous to hear my mother hold hour-long conversations with this woman, in a polyglot jargon that was a mixture of Italian, Yiddish, Hungarian and English. But the women understood each other.

My mother helped Betsy find a clothing shop that would give her basting work to do at home. My mother helped the Christian in many ways. And Betsy worshipped her. In the midst of her miseries she found time to knit a large wool shawl as a surprise for my mother. She brought it in one night, and cried and jabbered excitedly in Italian, and kissed my mother's hands. And my mother cried, and kissed her, too. We could not understand a word of what they were saying, but my mother kept repeating in Yiddish: "Ach, what a good woman this is! What a dear woman!" My mother treasured this shawl more than anything she owned. She liked to show it to every one, and tell the story of how Betsy had made it.

A shawl like that was worth over ten dollars, more than Betsy earned in a week. It must have taken weeks to knit, many overtime nights under the gaslight after a weary sixteen-hour day at basting clothing. Such gifts are worthy to be treasured; they are knitted in love.

8

There was an Irish family living on the top floor of our tenement. Mr. O'Brien was a truck-driver, a tall gloomy giant with a red face hard as shark-leather. He came home from work at nine and ten o'clock each night. Powerful and hairy in his blue overalls, he stamped ponderously up the stairs. If we children were playing in the halls, he brushed through our games, scowling at us as if he hated children.

"Get the hell out of my way; you're thick as bed-bugs," he muttered, and we scattered from under the feet of the ferocious great Christian.

His wife was also large and red-faced, a soft, sad mountain of flesh waddling around under perpetual baskets of laundry. All Christian ladies did washing, all except the Italians. Mrs. O'Brien was kinder to children than her husband, but we feared her almost as much.

This couple was one of the scandals of the tenement. Night after night, in the restless sleep of our little commune, we heard as in a coöperative nightmare the anguished screams of the Irish mother down the airshaft. Her husband was drunk and was beating her.

"No, no, Jack, don't!" she screamed. "You'll frighten the boy."

This couple had a mysterious child whom nobody had ever seen, and the mother always mentioned him in these brutal midnight scenes.

"Tuh hell with the boy!" roared the man's voice, formidable and deep as a mad bull's. "Tuh hell with everything!"

Crash! he had knocked her down over a table. Windows flew open; heads popped into the airshaft from every side like a shower of curious balloons; the tenement was awake and fascinated. We could hear a child's frightened whimpering, then crash! another powerful blow struck at a soft woman's body.

"Jack, don't! The neighbors will hear!"

"Tuh hell with the kikes! I'll set fire to the damn house and make the sheenies run like rats!"

Bang, crash, scream! The tenement listened with horror. These were the Christians again. No Jew was ever as violent as that. No Jew struck a woman. My mother, ever an agitator, led a campaign against the Irish couple, to force the landlord to put them out. "It is worse than the whores," said my mother, "having Christians in a tenement is worse."

9

But one quiet afternoon, who should burst into my mother's kitchen, pale and stammering with fright, but the Irish washerlady.

"Quick, my boy is choking to death! Help me! Get a doctor, for God's sake!"

My mother, without a superfluous word, sped like a fireman up the stairs, to help the child. It had swallowed a fishbone. My mother, expert and brave in such emergencies, put her finger down his throat and dislodged the bone. Then she had a long intimate talk with the Irish mother.

That night at the supper table, while my work-weary father was trying to eat hamburger steak, and read the Yiddish newspaper, and drink beer, and think about his troubles, and smoke and talk all at the same time, my mother irritated him by sighing profoundly.

"Ach, Herman," she said, "that Irish washerlady has so many misfortunes."

"*Pfui!*" my father spat impatiently, "so have I!"

"She is a good woman," said my mother, "even if she is a Christian. Her husband beats her, but she is sorry for him. He is not a bad man. He is only sad."

"*Gottenu!*" my father groaned in disgust with female logic. "I hope he beats you, too!"

"He was a farmer in Ireland," my mother went on dreamily. "He hates the city life here, but they are too poor to move to the country. And their boy has been sick for years. All their money goes for doctors. That's why he drinks and beats her, but her heart bleeds for him."

"Enough!" said my father, clutching his hair. "Enough, or I will go mad!"

My mother saw that he was really angry, so she took the empty soup plates into the kitchen. There she stirred something in a pot, and opened the stove to take out the noodle pudding. She brought this to the table.

"And, Herman," she said pensively, with the steaming pudding in her hands, "that woman used to gather mushrooms in the forest in Ireland. Just the way I gathered them in Hungary."

10

I was playing with the boys. We had been seized with the impulse to draw horses in chalk on the pavement. Then there was a fight, because Joey Cohen had written under his horse, "NIGGER LOVES LEAH." He also wrote this on an express wagon, on the stoop steps, and on the bock beer sign standing in front of the saloon. Nigger was about ready to punch Joey on the nose, when Mrs. O'Brien shambled up to us, slow, sad and huge, looming above us with the perpetual basket of laundry on her arm.

"Don't fight, boys," she said kindly in her clear Christian speech. "Will one of you do something for me? I will give any boy a nickel who will go up and play with my little boy. He is sick."

We were dumfounded with fear. We stared at her and our mouths fell open. Even Nigger was scared.

Mrs. O'Brien looked right at me. "Will you do it?" she pleaded. I blushed, and suddenly ran off as if I had seen a devil. The other boys scattered. Mrs. O'Brien sighed, picked up her heavy basket, and hobbled on her way.

I told my mother that night. What did it mean? Was the Christian washerlady trying to snare me into her home, where she would burn a cross on my face with a hot poker?

"No," said my mother thoughtfully. "Go up there; it will be a good deed. The Christian child is lonely. Nothing can happen to you."

She took me there herself the next morning. And I found nothing to fear. It was a gray humid morning. In the yellow gloom of a bedroom narrow and damp like a coffin, a child with shrunken face lay in bed. His forehead was pale as marble. It was streaked with blue veins, and altogether too round and large for his head. His head was too large for his body. It dangled clumsily, though supported by a steel brace at the neck.

He looked at me with great mournful eyes. His nose wrinkled like a baby's, and he cried.

"Don't be frightened, Johnnie," said his mother, "this boy is a friend who has come to play with you."

I wound my top and spun it on the floor. He craned his stiff neck to watch. Then I put the top in his hand and tried to teach him to spin it, too. But he was too feeble for this sport. So he wept once more, and I was grieved for him. Was this one of the dreaded Christians?

Jean Toomer
(1894–1967)

Born in Washington, D.C., Jean Toomer grew up in New York and Washington and attended schools in Wisconsin, Massachusetts, Illinois, and New York. Grandson of a prominent black Louisiana politician of the post-Civil War era, he became a spiritual wanderer, unsure of his place in the world. Light-skinned, he was received as a black writer after the success of Cane, *but refused to identify himself as black. Of his ancestry he wrote that "In my body were many bloods, all blended in the fire of six or more generations. I was, then, either a new type of man or the very oldest. In any case I was inescapably myself ∗ ∗ ∗. If I achieved greatness of human stature, then just to the degree that I did I would justify* all *the blood in me."*

Briefly employed in 1921 as a teacher at the Georgia Normal and Industrial Institute in Sparta, he found there the inspiration for Cane *(1923), his major work. A collection of stories, poems, and dramatic fragments,* Cane *is a lyric evocation of the lives of blacks, both northern and southern, with its best passages set in rural Georgia. The success was not repeated.*

Although Toomer wrote other works that mostly remained in manuscript during his life, he turned to other interests. In his search for inner peace, he was for a while a follower of the popular spiritual leader George I. Gurdjieff and later embraced the Quaker religion.

A study is Nellie McKay, *Jean Toomer: Artist* (1984).

Becky[1]

Becky was the white woman who had two Negro sons. She's dead; they've gone away. The pines whisper to Jesus. The Bible flaps its leaves with an aimless rustle on her mound.

BECKY HAD ONE NEGRO SON. Who gave it to her? Damn buck nigger, said the white folks' mouths. She wouldn't tell. Common, God-forsaken, insane white shameless wench, said the white folks' mouths. Her eyes were sunken, her neck stringy, her breasts fallen, till then. Taking their words, they filled her, like a bubble rising—then she broke. Mouth setting in a twist that held her eyes, harsh, vacant, staring. . . Who gave it to her? Low-down nigger with no self-respect, said the black folks' mouths. She wouldnt tell. Poor Catholic poor-white crazy woman, said the black folks' mouths. White folks and black folks built her cabin, fed her and her growing baby, prayed secretly to God who'd put His cross upon her and cast her out.

When the first was born, the white folks said they'd have no more to do with her. And black folks, they too joined hands to cast her out. . . The pines whispered to Jesus. The railroad boss said not to say he said it, but she could live, if she wanted to, on the narrow strip of land between the railroad and the road. John Stone, who owned the lumber and the bricks, would have shot the man who told he gave the stuff to Lonnie Deacon, who stole out there at night and built the cabin. A single room held down to earth. . . O fly away to Jesus . . . by a leaning chimney . . .

Six trains each day rumbled past and shook the ground under her cabin. Fords, and horse- and mule-drawn buggies went back and forth along the road. No one ever saw her. Trainmen, and passengers who'd heard about her, threw out papers and food. Threw out little crumpled slips of paper scribbled with prayers, as they passed her eye-shaped piece of sandy ground. Ground islandized between the road and railroad track. Pushed up where a blue-sheen God with listless eyes could look at it. Folks from the town took turns, unknown, of course, to each other, in bringing corn and meat and sweet potatoes. Even sometimes snuff. . . O thank y Jesus. . . Old David Georgia, grinding cane and boiling syrup, never went her way without some sugar sap. No one ever saw her. The boy grew up and ran around. When he was five years old as folks reckoned it, Hugh Jourdon saw him carrying a baby. "Becky has another son," was what the whole town knew. But nothing was said, for the part of man that says things to the likes of that had told itself that if there was a Becky, that Becky now was dead.

---

1. From *Cane* (1923).

The two boys grew. Sullen and cunning. . . O pines, whisper to Jesus; tell Him to come and press sweet Jesus-lips against their lips and eyes. . . It seemed as though with those two big fellows there, there could be no room for Becky. The part that prayed wondered if perhaps she'd really died, and they had buried her. No one dared ask. They'd beat and cut a man who meant nothing at all in mentioning that they lived along the road. White or colored? No one knew, and least of all themselves. They drifted around from job to job. We, who had cast out their mother because of them, could we take them in? They answered black and white folks by shooting up two men and leaving town. "Godam the white folks; godam the niggers," they shouted as they left town. Becky? Smoke curled up from her chimney; she must be there. Trains passing shook the ground. The ground shook the leaning chimney. Nobody noticed it. A creepy feeling came over all who saw that thin wraith of smoke and felt the trembling of the ground. Folks began to take her food again. They quit it soon because they had a fear. Becky if dead might be a hant, and if alive—it took some nerve even to mention it. . . O pines, whisper to Jesus . . .

It was Sunday. Our congregation had been visiting at Pulverton, and were coming home. There was no wind. The autumn sun, the bell from Ebenezer Church, listless and heavy. Even the pines were stale, sticky, like the smell of food that makes you sick. Before we turned the bend of the road that would show us the Becky cabin, the horses stopped stock-still, pushed back their ears, and nervously whinnied. We urged, then whipped them on. Quarter of a mile away thin smoke curled up from the leaning chimney. . . O pines, whisper to Jesus. . . Goose-flesh came on my skin though there still was neither chill nor wind. Eyes left their sockets for the cabin. Ears burned and throbbed. Uncanny eclipse! fear closed my mind. We were just about to pass. . . Pines shout to Jesus! . . . the ground trembled as a ghost train rumbled by. The chimney fell into the cabin. Its thud was like a hollow report, ages having passed since it went off. Barlo and I were pulled out of our seats. Dragged to the door that had swung open. Through the dust we saw the bricks in a mound upon the floor. Becky, if she was there, lay under them. I thought I heard a groan. Barlo, mumbling something, threw his Bible on the pile. (No one has ever touched it.) Somehow we got away. My buggy was still on the road. The last thing that I remember was whipping old Dan like fury; I remember nothing after that—that is, until I reached town and folks crowded round to get the true word of it.

Becky was the white woman who had two Negro sons. She's dead; they've gone away. The pines whisper to Jesus. The Bible flaps its leaves with an aimless rustle on her mound.

William Faulkner
(1897–1962)

An argument that Faulkner was the greatest American novelist of the twentieth century would be based on the range, depth, and literary quality of his work. Although he focused most of his nearly twenty novels and fifty short stories on the relatively small area of his fictional Yoknapatawpha County, Mississippi, in the end he had written a social history of the county that began with the frontier and encompassed over a century of time, moving well into the Jazz Age and the Great Depression. He wrote of plantation whites, poor whites, slaves, free blacks, Indians, and people of mixed blood, of lawyers, shopkeepers, tenant farmers, convicts, wives, and children, of brilliant minds and simple minds, of courage and cowardice. He wrote comedy and tragedy. He wrote simply, and he wrote with enormous complexity. He wrote, in his own words, of "the human heart in conflict with itself," examining with the precision of a master psychologist the interior confusions of troubled human beings. He wrote also of time's passing, of cultures and of generations in conflict, recording with the encompassing sweep of a master historian the telling events that signify the gap between one age and the next.

Faulkner was born in New Albany and grew up in nearby Oxford in the northern part of Mississippi, where his family had long been settled. The ghost of his great-grandfather, William C. Falkner—plantation owner, colonel in the Confederate army, railroad builder, politician, novelist—was to emerge in his fiction as Colonel Sartoris of Sartoris *(1929),* The Unvanguished *(1938), and other works. Before writing successfully, he served briefly in the Royal Canadian Air Force, attended the University of Mississippi, worked in a post office, and held other odd jobs in Mississippi, New York, and New Orleans. Only after a book of poems and two novels did he find his true subject in* Sartoris. *Faulkner's first great work,* The Sound and the Fury *(1929), followed almost immediately, and then in rapid succession* As I Lay Dying *(1930),* Sanctuary *(1931), and* Light in August *(1932).*

Although he had written some of the major works of his time, Faulkner had not earned a satisfactory living from them, and for many years he wrote for Hollywood, returning regularly, however, to Oxford to continue what he considered to be his true work. Absalom, Absalom! *(1936), one of*

his greatest novels, appeared in the midst of the Depression. At its end, with
The Hamlet *(1940) he began a trilogy on the changing South, continuing
his story of the rise of the unscrupulous Snopes family in* The Town *(1957)*
and The Mansion *(1959). His recognition as a major twentieth-century
novelist came mostly after World War II and was capped by the award of
the Nobel Prize for literature in 1950.*

 *Faulkner's short fiction encapsulates in miniature the themes of his
novels. "A Justice" is one of several in which he portrays the mixed racial
history of Mississippi.*

Collected Stories appeared in 1950. Joseph Blotner edited *Uncollected Stories* (1979).
Earlier collections include *These Thirteen* (1931), *Doctor Martino and Other Stories*
(1934), *Go Down, Moses and Other Stories* (1942), and *Knight's Gambit* (1949).
Biographies include Joseph Blotner, *Faulkner: A Biography* (2 vols., 1974; revised in
one volume, 1984), and frederick R. Karl, *William Faulkner: American Writer*
(1989). Other studies include Cleanth Brooks, *William Faulkner: The Yoknapatawpha Country* (1963), *William Faulkner: Toward Yoknapatawpha and Beyond*
(1978), and *William Faulkner: First Encounters* (1983); David Minter, *William
Faulkner: His Life and Work* (1981); and Stephen B. Oates, *Faulkner; The Man and
the Artist* (1987).

A Justice[1]

I

UNTIL GRANDFATHER DIED, we would go out to the farm every Saturday
afternoon. We would leave home right after dinner in the surrey, I in front
with Roskus, and Grandfather and Caddy and Jason in the back. Grandfather
and Roskus would talk, with the horses going fast, because it was the best
team in the county. They would carry the surrey fast along the levels and up
some of the hills even. But this was in north Mississippi, and on some of the
hills Roskus and I could smell Grandfather's cigar.

---

1. "A Justice" was first collected in *These Thirteen* (1931). The present text is from *Collected Stories*. The story is narrated by Quentin Compson, who also narrates "That Evening Sun" and is a
character in *The Sound and the Fury* and *Absalom, Absalom!*

The farm was four miles away. There was a long, low house in the grove, not painted but kept whole and sound by a clever carpenter from the quarters named Sam Fathers,[2] and behind it the barns and smokehouses, and further still, the quarters themselves, also kept whole and sound by Sam Fathers. He did nothing else, and they said he was almost a hundred years old. He lived with the Negroes and they—the white people; the Negroes called him a blue-gum—called him a Negro. But he wasn't a Negro. That's what I'm going to tell about.

When we got there, Mr. Stokes, the manager, would send a Negro boy with Caddy and Jason to the creek to fish, because Caddy was a girl and Jason was too little, but I wouldn't go with them. I would go to Sam Fathers' shop, where he would be making breast-yokes or wagon wheels, and I would always bring him some tobacco. Then he would stop working and he would fill his pipe—he made them himself, out of creek clay with a reed stem—and he would tell me about the old days. He talked like a nigger—that is, he said his words like niggers do, but he didn't say the same words—and his hair was nigger hair. But his skin wasn't quite the color of a light nigger and his nose and his mouth and chin were not nigger nose and mouth and chin. And his shape was not like the shape of a nigger when he gets old. He was straight in the back, not tall, a little broad, and his face was still all the time, like he might be somewhere else all the while he was working or when people, even white people, talked to him, or while he talked to me. It was just the same all the time, like he might be away up on a roof by himself, driving nails. Sometimes he would quit work with something half-finished on the bench, and sit down and smoke. And he wouldn't jump up and go back to work when Mr. Stokes or even Grandfather came along.

So I would give him the tobacco and he would stop work and sit down and fill his pipe and talk to me.

"These niggers," he said. "They call me Uncle Blue-Gum. And the white folks, they call me Sam Fathers."

"Isn't that your name?" I said.

"No. Not in the old days. I remember. I remember how I never saw but one white man until I was a boy big as you are; a whisky trader that came every summer to the Plantation. It was the Man himself that named me. He didn't name me Sam Fathers, though."

"The Man?" I said.

"He owned the Plantation, the Negroes, my mammy too. He owned all the land that I knew of until I was grown. He was a Choctaw chief. He sold my mammy to your great-grandpappy. He said I didn't have to go unless I wanted to, because I was a warrior too then. He was the one who named me Had-Two-Fathers."

"Had-Two-Fathers?" I said. "That's not a name. That's not anything."

"It was my name once. Listen."

---

2. Part Native American and part black, Sam Fathers earned his name in the manner told in this story. The main events may be dated as around 1810–1820.

II

This is how Herman Basket told it when I was big enough to hear talk. He said that when Doom came back from New Orleans, he brought this woman with him. He brought six black people, though Herman Basket said they already had more black people in the Plantation than they could find use for. Sometimes they would run the black men with dogs, like you would a fox or a cat or a coon. And then Doom brought six more when he came home from New Orleans. He said he won them on the steamboat, and so he had to take them. He got off the steamboat with the six black people, Herman Basket said, and a big box in which something was alive, and the gold box of New Orleans salt about the size of a gold watch. And Herman Basket told how Doom took a puppy out of the box in which something was alive, and how he made a bullet of bread and a pinch of the salt in the gold box, and put the bullet into the puppy and the puppy died.

That was the kind of a man that Doom was, Herman Basket said. He told how, when Doom got off the steamboat that night, he wore a coat with gold all over it, and he had three gold watches, but Herman Basket said that even after seven years, Doom's eyes had not changed. He said that Doom's eyes were just the same as before he went away, before his name was Doom, and he and Herman Basket and my pappy were sleeping on the same pallet and talking at night, as boys will.

Doom's name was Ikkemotubbe then, and he was not born to be the Man, because Doom's mother's brother was the Man, and the Man had a son of his own, as well as a brother. But even then, and Doom no bigger than you are, Herman Basket said that sometimes the Man would look at Doom and he would say: "O Sister's Son, your eye is a bad eye, like the eye of a bad horse."

So the Man was not sorry when Doom got to be a young man and said that he would go to New Orleans, Herman Basket said. The Man was getting old then. He used to like to play mumble-peg and to pitch horseshoes both, but now he just liked mumble-peg. So he was not sorry when Doom went away, though he didn't forget about Doom. Herman Basket said that each summer when the whisky-trader came, the Man would ask him about Doom. "He calls himself David Callicoat now," the Man would say. "But his name is Ikkemotubbe. You haven't heard maybe of a David Callicoat getting drowned in the Big River, or killed in the white man's fight at New Orleans?"

But Herman Basket said they didn't hear from Doom at all until he had been gone seven years. Then one day Herman Basket and my pappy got a written stick from Doom to meet him at the Big River. Because the steamboat didn't come up our river any more then. The steamboat was still in our river, but it didn't go anywhere any more. Herman Basket told how one day during the high water, about three years after Doom went away, the steamboat came and crawled up on a sand-bar and died.

That was how Doom got his second name, the one before Doom. Herman Basket told how four times a year the steamboat would come up our river, and how the People would go to the river and camp and wait to see the steamboat pass, and he said that the white man who told the steamboat where to swim was named David Callicoat. So when Doom told Herman Basket and pappy that he was going to New Orleans, he said, "And I'll tell you something else. From now on, my name is not Ikkemotubbe. It's David Callicoat. And some day I'm going to own a steamboat, too." That was the kind of man that Doom was, Herman Basket said.

So after seven years he sent them the written stick and Herman Basket and pappy took the wagon and went to meet Doom at the Big River, and Doom got off the steamboat with the six black people. "I won them on the steamboat," Doom said. "You and Craw-ford (my pappy's name was Craw-fishford, but usually it was Craw-ford) can divide them."

"I don't want them," Herman Basket said that pappy said.

"Then Herman can have them all," Doom said.

"I don't want them either," Herman Basket said.

"All right," Doom said. Then Herman Basket said he asked Doom if his name was still David Callicoat, but instead of answering, Doom told one of the black people something in the white man's talk, and the black man lit a pine knot. Then Herman Basket said they were watching Doom take the puppy from the box and make the bullet of bread and the New Orleans salt which Doom had in the little gold box, when he said that pappy said:

"I believe you said that Herman and I were to divide these black people."

Then Herman Basket said he saw that one of the black people was a woman.

"You and Herman don't want them," Doom said.

"I wasn't thinking when I said that," pappy said. "I will take the lot with the woman in it. Herman can have the other three."

"I don't want them," Herman Basket said.

"You can have four, then," pappy said. "I will take the woman and one other."

"I don't want them," Herman Basket said.

"I will take only the woman," pappy said. "You can have the other five."

"I don't want them," Herman Basket said.

"You don't want them, either," Doom said to pappy. "You said so yourself."

Then Herman Basket said that the puppy was dead. "You didn't tell us your new name," he said to Doom.

"My name is Doom now," Doom said. "It was given me by a French chief in New Orleans. In French talking, Doo-um; in our talking, Doom."

"What does it mean?" Herman Basket said.

He said how Doom looked at him for a while. "It means the Man," Doom said.

Herman Basket told how they thought about that. He said they stood there in the dark, with the other puppies in the box, the ones that Doom hadn't used, whimpering and scuffing, and the light of the pine knot shining on the eyeballs of the black people and on Doom's gold coat and on the puppy that had died.

"You cannot be the Man," Herman Basket said. "You are only on the sister's side. And the Man has a brother and a son."

"That's right," Doom said. "But if I were the Man, I would give Craw-ford those black people. I would give Herman something, too. For every black man I gave Craw-ford, I would give Herman a horse, if I were the Man."

"Craw-ford only wants this woman," Herman Basket said.

"I would give Herman six horses, anyway," Doom said. "But maybe the Man has already given Herman a horse."

"No," Herman Basket said. "My ghost is still walking."

It took them three days to reach the Plantation. They camped on the road at night. Herman Basket said that they did not talk.

They reached the Plantation on the third day. He said that the Man was not very glad to see Doom, even though Doom brought a present of candy for the Man's son. Doom had something for all his kinsfolk, even for the Man's brother. The Man's brother lived by himself in a cabin by the creek. His name was Sometimes-Wakeup. Sometimes the People took him food. The rest of the time they didn't see him. Herman Basket told how he and pappy went with Doom to visit Sometimes-Wakeup in his cabin. It was at night, and Doom told Herman Basket to close the door. Then Doom took the puppy from pappy and set it on the floor and made a bullet of bread and the New Orleans salt for Sometimes-Wakeup to see how it worked. When they left, Herman Basket said how Sometimes-Wakeup burned a stick and covered his head with the blanket.

That was the first night that Doom was at home. On the next day Herman Basket told how the Man began to act strange at his food, and died before the doctor could get there and burn sticks. When the Willow-Bearer went to fetch the Man's son to be the Man, they found that he had acted strange and then died too.

"Now Sometimes-Wakeup will have to be the Man," pappy said.

So the Willow-Bearer went to fetch Sometimes-Wakeup to come and be the Man. The Willow-Bearer came back soon. "Sometimes-Wakeup does not want to be the Man," the Willow-Bearer said. "He is sitting in his cabin with his head in his blanket."

"Then Ikkemotubbe will have to be the Man," pappy said.

So Doom was the Man. But Herman Basket said that pappy's ghost would not be easy. Herman Basket said he told pappy to give Doom a little time. "I am still walking," Herman Basket said.

"But this is a serious matter with me," pappy said.

He said that at last pappy went to Doom, before the Man and his son had entered the earth, before the eating and the horse-racing were over. "What woman?" Doom said.

"You said that when you were the Man," pappy said. Herman Basket said that Doom looked at pappy but that pappy was not looking at Doom.

"I think you don't trust me," Doom said. Herman Basket said how pappy did not look at Doom. "I think you still believe that that puppy was sick," Doom said. "Think about it."

Herman Basket said that pappy thought.

"What do you think now?" Doom said.

But Herman Basket said that pappy still did not look at Doom. "I think it was a well dog," pappy said.

III

At last the eating and the horse-racing were over and the Man and his son had entered the earth. Then Doom said, "Tomorrow we will go and fetch the steamboat." Herman Basket told how Doom had been talking about the steamboat ever since he became the Man, and about how the House was not big enough. So that evening Doom said, "Tomorrow we will go and fetch the steamboat that died in the river."

Herman Basket said how the steamboat was twelve miles away, and that it could not even swim in the water. So the next morning there was no one in the Plantation except Doom and the black people. He told how it took Doom all that day to find the People. Doom used the dogs, and he found some of the People in hollow logs in the creek bottom. That night he made all the men sleep in the House. He kept the dogs in the House, too.

Herman Basket told how he heard Doom and pappy talking in the dark. "I don't think you trust me," Doom said.

"I trust you," pappy said.

"That is what I would advise," Doom said.

"I wish you could advise that to my ghost," pappy said.

The next morning they went to the steamboat. The women and the black people walked. The men rode in the wagons, with Doom following behind with the dogs.

The steamboat was lying on its side on the sand-bar. When they came to it, there were three white men on it. "Now we can go back home," pappy said.

But Doom talked to the white men. "Does this steamboat belong to you?" Doom said.

"It does not belong to you," the white men said. And though they had guns, Herman Basket said they did not look like men who would own a boat.

"Shall we kill them?" he said to Doom. But he said that Doom was still talking to the men on the steamboat.

"What will you take for it?" Doom said.

"What will you give for it?" the white men said.

"It is dead," Doom said. "It's not worth much."

"Will you give ten black people?" the white men said.

"All right," Doom said. "Let the black people who came with me from the Big River come forward." They came forward, the five men and the woman. "Let four more black people come forward." Four more came forward. "You are now to eat of the corn of those white men yonder," Doom said. "May it nourish you." The white men went away, the ten black people following them. "Now," Doom said, "let us make the steamboat get up and walk."

Herman Basket said that he and pappy did not go into the river with the others, because pappy said to go aside and talk. They went aside. Pappy talked, but Herman Basket said that he said he did not think it was right to kill white men, but pappy said how they could fill the white men with rocks and sink them in the river and nobody would find them. So Herman Basket said they overtook the three white men and the ten black people, then they turned back toward the boat. Just before they came to the steamboat, pappy said to the black men: "Go on to the Man. Go and help make the steamboat get up and walk. I will take this woman on home."

"This woman is my wife," one of the black men said. "I want her to stay with me."

"Do you want to be arranged in the river with rocks in your inside too?" pappy said to the black man.

"Do you want to be arranged in the river yourself?" the black man said to pappy. "There are two of you, and nine of us."

Herman Basket said that pappy thought. Then pappy said, "Let us go to the steamboat and help the Man."

They went to the steamboat. But Herman Basket said that Doom did not notice the ten black people until it was time to return to the Plantation. Herman Basket told how Doom looked at the black people, then looked at pappy. "It seems that the white men did not want these black people," Doom said.

"So it seems," pappy said.

"The white men went away, did they?" Doom said.

"So it seems," pappy said.

Herman Basket told how every night Doom would make all the men sleep in the House, with the dogs in the House too, and how each morning they would return to the steamboat in the wagons. The wagons would not hold everybody, so after the second day the women stayed at home. But it was three days before Doom noticed that pappy was staying at home too. Herman Basket said that the woman's husband may have told Doom. "Craw-ford hurt his back lifting the steamboat," Herman Basket said he told Doom. "He said he would stay at the Plantation and sit with his feet in the Hot Spring so that the sickness in his back could return to the earth."

"That is a good idea," Doom said. "He has been doing this for three days, has he? Then the sickness should be down in his legs by now."

When they returned to the Plantation that night, Doom sent for pappy. He asked pappy if the sickness had moved. Pappy said how the sickness moved very slow. "You must sit in the Spring more," Doom said.

"That is what I think," pappy said.

"Suppose you sit in the Spring at night too," Doom said.

"The night air will make it worse," pappy said.

"Not with a fire there," Doom said. "I will send one of the black people with you to keep the fire burning."

"Which one of the black people?" pappy said.

"The husband of the woman which I won on the steamboat," Doom said.

"I think my back is better," pappy said.

"Let us try it," Doom said.

"I know my back is better," pappy said.

"Let us try it, anyway," Doom said. Just before dark Doom sent four of the People to fix pappy and the black man at the Spring. Herman Basket said the People returned quickly. He said that as they entered the House, pappy entered also.

"The sickness began to move suddenly," pappy said. "It has reached my feet since noon today."

"Do you think it will be gone by morning?" Doom said.

"I think so," pappy said.

"Perhaps you had better sit in the Spring tonight and make sure," Doom said.

"I know it will be gone by morning," pappy said.

IV

When it got to be summer, Herman Basket said that the steamboat was out of the river bottom. It had taken them five months to get it out of the bottom, because they had to cut down the trees to make a path for it. But now he said the steamboat could walk faster on the logs. He told how pappy helped. Pappy had a certain place on one of the ropes near the steamboat that nobody was allowed to take, Herman Basket said. It was just under the front porch of the steamboat where Doom sat in his chair, with a boy with a branch to shade him and another boy with a branch to drive away the flying beasts. The dogs rode on the boat too.

In the summer, while the steamboat was still walking, Herman Basket told how the husband of the woman came to Doom again. "I have done what I could for you," Doom said. "Why don't you go to Craw-ford and adjust this matter yourself?"

The black man said that he had done that. He said that pappy said to adjust it by a cock-fight, pappy's cock against the black man's, the winner to have the woman, the one who refused to fight to lose by default. The black man said he told pappy he did not have a cock, and that pappy said that in that case the black man lost by default and that the woman belonged to pappy. "And what am I to do?" the black man said.

Doom thought. Then Herman Basket said that Doom called to him and asked him which was pappy's best cock and Herman Basket told Doom that pappy had only one. "That black one?" Doom said. Herman Basket said he told Doom that was the one. "Ah," Doom said. Herman Basket told how Doom sat in his chair on the porch of the steamboat while it walked, looking down at the People and the black men pulling the ropes, making the steamboat walk. "Go and tell Craw-ford you have a cock," Doom said to the black man. "Just tell him you will have a cock in the pit. Let it be tomorrow morning. We will let the steamboat sit down and rest." The black man went away. Then Herman Basket said that Doom was looking at him, and that he did not look at Doom. Because he said there was but one better cock in the Plantation than pappy's, and that one belonged to Doom. "I think that that puppy was not sick," Doom said. "What do you think?"

Herman Basket said that he did not look at Doom. "That is what I think," he said.

"That is what I would advise," Doom said.

Herman Basket told how the next day the steamboat sat and rested. The pit was in the stable. The People and the black people were there. Pappy had his cock in the pit. Then the black man put his cock into the pit. Herman Basket said that pappy looked at the black man's cock.

"This cock belongs to Ikkemotubbe," pappy said.

"It is his," the People told pappy. "Ikkemotubbe gave it to him with all to witness."

Herman Basket said that pappy has already picked up his cock. "This is not right," pappy said. "We ought not to let him risk his wife on a cock-fight."

"Then you withdraw?" the black man said.

"Let me think," pappy said. He thought. The People watched. The black man reminded pappy of what he had said about defaulting. Pappy said he did not mean to say that and that he withdrew it. The People told him that he could only withdraw by forfeiting the match. Herman Basket said that pappy thought again. The People watched. "All right," pappy said. "But I am being taken advantage of."

The cocks fought. Pappy's cock fell. Pappy took it up quickly. Herman Basket said it was like pappy had been waiting for his cock to fall so he could pick it quickly up. "Wait," he said. He looked at the People. "Now they have fought. Isn't that true?" The People said that it was true. "So that settles what I said about forfeiting."

Herman Basket said that pappy began to get out of the pit.

"Aren't you going to fight?" the black man said.

"I don't think this will settle anything," pappy said. "Do you?"

Herman Basket told how the black man looked at pappy. Then he quit looking at pappy. He was squatting. Herman Basket said the People looked at the black man looking at the earth between his feet. They watched him take up a clod of dirt, and then they watched the dust come out between the black man's fingers. "Do you think that this will settle anything?" pappy said.

"No," the black man said. Herman Basket said that the People could not hear him very good. But he said that pappy could hear him.

"Neither do I," pappy said. "It would not be right to risk your wife on a cock-fight."

Herman Basket told how the black man looked up, with the dry dust about the fingers of his hand. He said the black man's eyes looked red in the dark pit, like the eyes of a fox. "Will you let the cocks fight again?" the black man said.

"Do you agree that it doesn't settle anything?" pappy said.

"Yes," the black man said.

Pappy put his cock back into the ring. Herman Basket said that pappy's cock was dead before it had time to act strange, even. The black man's cock stood upon it and started to crow, but the black man struck the live cock away and he jumped up and down on the dead cock until it did not look like a cock at all, Herman Basket said.

Then it was fall, and Herman Basket told how the steamboat came to the Plantation and stopped beside the House and died again. He said that for two months they had been in sight of the Plantation, making the steamboat walk on the logs, but now the steamboat was beside the House and the House was big enough to please Doom. He gave an eating. It lasted a week. When it was over, Herman Basket told how the black man came to Doom a third time. Herman Basket said that the black man's eyes were red again, like those of a fox, and that they could hear his breathing in the room. "Come to my cabin," he said to Doom. "I have something to show you."

"I thought it was about that time," Doom said. He looked about the room, but Herman Basket told Doom that pappy had just stepped out. "Tell him to come also," Doom said. When they came to the black man's cabin, Doom sent two of the People to fetch pappy. Then they entered the cabin. What the black man wanted to show Doom was a new man.

"Look," the black man said. "You are the Man. You are to see justice done."

"What is wrong with this man?" Doom said.

"Look at the color of him," the black man said. He began to look around the cabin. Herman Basket said that his eyes went red and then brown and then red, like those of a fox. He said they could hear the black man's breathing. "Do I get justice?" the black man said. "You are the Man."

"You should be proud of a fine yellow man like this," Doom said. He looked at the new man. "I don't see that justice can darken him any," Doom said. He looked about the cabin also. "Come forward, Craw-ford," he said. "This is a man, not a copper snake; he will not harm you." But Herman Basket said that pappy would not come forward. He said the black man's eyes went red and then brown and then red when he breathed. "Yao," Doom said, "this is not right. Any man is entitled to have his melon patch protected from these wild bucks of the woods. But first let us name this man." Doom thought. Herman Basket said the black man's eyes went quieter now, and his breath went quieter too. "We will call him Had-Two-Fathers," Doom said.

V

Sam Fathers lit his pipe again. He did it deliberately, rising and lifting between thumb and forefinger from his forge a coal of fire. Then he came back and sat down. It was getting late. Caddy and Jason had come back from the creek, and I could see Grandfather and Mr. Stokes talking beside the carriage, and at that moment, as though he had felt my gaze, Grandfather turned and called my name.

"What did your pappy do then?" I said.

"He and Herman Basket built the fence," Sam Fathers said. "Herman Basket told how Doom made them set two posts into the ground, with a sapling across the top of them. The nigger and pappy were there. Doom had not told them about the fence then. Herman Basket said it was just like when he and pappy and Doom were boys, sleeping on the same pallet, and Doom would wake them at night and make them get up and go hunting with him, or when he would make them stand up with him and fight with their fists, just for fun, until Herman Basket and pappy would hide from Doom.

"They fixed the sapling across the two posts and Doom said to the nigger: 'This is a fence. Can you climb it?'

"Herman Basket said the nigger put his hand on the sapling and sailed over it like a bird.

"Then Doom said to pappy: 'Climb this fence.'

"'This fence is too high to climb,' pappy said.

"'Climb this fence, and I will give you the woman,' Doom said.

"Herman Basket said pappy looked at the fence a while. 'Let me go under this fence,' he said.

"'No,' Doom said.

"Herman Basket told me how pappy began to sit down on the ground. 'It's not that I don't trust you,' pappy said.

"'We will build the fence this high,' Doom said.

"'What fence?' Herman Basket said.

"'The fence around the cabin of this black man,' Doom said.

"'I can't build a fence I couldn't climb,' pappy said.

"'Herman will help you,' Doom said.

"Herman Basket said it was just like when Doom used to wake them and make them go hunting. He said the dogs found him and pappy about noon the next day, and that they began the fence that afternoon. He told me how they had to cut the saplings in the creek bottom and drag them in by hand, because Doom would not let them use the wagon. So sometimes one post would take them three or four days. 'Never mind,' Doom said. 'You have plenty of time. And the exercise will make Craw-ford sleep at night.'

"He told me how they worked on the fence all that winter and all the next summer, until after the whisky trader had come and gone. Then it was finished. He said that on the day they set the last post, the nigger came out of the cabin and put his hand on the top of a post (it was a palisade fence, the posts set upright in the ground) and flew out like a bird. 'This is a good fence,' the nigger said. 'Wait,' he said. 'I have something to show you.' Herman Basket said he flew back over the fence again and went into the cabin and came back. Herman Basket said that he was carrying a new man and that he held the new man up so they could see it above the fence. 'What do you think about this for color?' he said."

Grandfather called me again. This time I got up. The sun was already down beyond the peach orchard. I was just twelve then, and to me the story did not seem to have got anywhere, to have had point or end. Yet I obeyed Grandfather's voice, not that I was tired of Sam Father's talking, but with that immediacy of children with which they flee temporarily something which they do not quite understand; that, and the instinctive promptness with which we all obeyed Grandfather, not from concern of impatience or reprimand, but because we all believed that he did fine things, that his waking life passed from one fine (if faintly grandiose) picture to another.

They were in the surrey, waiting for me. I got in; the horses moved at once, impatient too for the stable. Caddy had one fish, about the size of a chip, and she was wet to the waist. We drove on, the team already trotting. When we passed Mr. Stokes' kitchen we could smell ham cooking. The smell followed us on to the gate. When we turned onto the road home it was almost sundown. Then we couldn't smell the cooking ham any more. "What were you and Sam talking about?" Grandfather said.

We went on, in that strange, faintly sinister suspension of twilight in which I believed that I could still see Sam Fathers back there, sitting on his wooden block, definite, immobile, and complete, like something looked upon after a long time in a preservative bath in a museum. That was it. I was just twelve then, and I would have to wait until I had passed on and through and beyond the suspension of twilight. Then I knew that I would know. But then Sam Fathers would be dead.

"Nothing, sir," I said. "We were just talking."

Vladimir Nabokov
(1899–1977)

During his childhood and adolescence, Vladimir Nabokov enjoyed a life of privilege in his aristocratic St. Petersburg family. His father, Vladimir Dmitrievich, was a noted jurist and constitutionalist political reformer. Forced by the Bolshevik revolution to flee Russia in 1919, the family settled in Berlin. During the time that Nabokov was a literature student at Trinity College, Cambridge, his father was killed as he shielded a political opponent who was targeted for assassination.

Nabokov had published two books of poetry before leaving Russia; he continued to produce poetry and fiction in Berlin and in Paris, where he moved with his wife and son in 1937. But faced with the rise of Nazism, the Nabokovs emigrated to the United States in 1940.

Becoming an American citizen, Nabokov resolved to write in English. His first novel in that language, The Real Life of Sebastian Knight, was published in 1941. Between 1941 and 1959 Nabokov held posts in creative writing at Wellesley College, comparative zoology at Harvard College, and literature at Cornell University and was awarded two Guggenheim fellowships. Some of his best writing in English, including the novels Lolita (1955) and Pnin, was done during this academic period. When Lolita became a best seller and Nabokov was finally able to give up teaching for full-time writing in English, the Nabokovs took up residence in Switzerland to be near their son who was a student in Italy. Together with his son, Nabokov translated many of his early Russian fictions into English.

Nabokov's work is technically complex, including multilayered plots, virtuoso stylistic touches, literary and historical allusions, and wry humor. Often there are mentions of chess or butterflies, two of his lifelong interests, or attacks on psychology or Sigmund Freud, two of his aversions. Pnin, published in 1957, has all of these features; in it an unnamed fellow immigrant relates Timofey Pnin's gallant struggles with a foreign language, academic politics, a scheming ex-wife, and his Russian memories.

Among works written first in Russian and translated are Mary (1927, trans. 1970); Camera Obscura (1933, trans. as Laughter in the Dark, 1938); and The Enchanter (1986). Fiction written in English includes Bend Sinister

(1947); Pale Fire *(1962);* Ada *(1969); and* Look at the Harlequins! *(1974).* Among story collections are *Nabokov's Dozen (1958) and* Details of a Sunset and Other Stories *(1976).* Speak, Memory *(1952, revised 1966; early title,* Conclusive Evidence, *1951) is a memoir. Nabokov also published poetry collections, a play, and several works of literary criticism.*

Vladimir Nabokov: The Russian Years (1990) by Byron Boyd is the first volume of a definitive biography; critical studies include Leona Toker's *Nabokov: The Mystery of Literary Structures* (1989) and Ellen Pifer's *Nabokov and the Novel* (1980).

———

[From] *Pnin*

Chapter Five. [*Pnin at the Pines*]

1

FROM THE TOP PLATFORM of an old, seldom used lookout tower—a "prospect tower" as it was formerly termed—that stood on a wooded hill eight hundred feet high, called Mount Ettrick, in one of the fairest of New England's fair states, the adventurous summer tourist (Miranda or Mary, Tom or Jim, whose penciled names were almost obliterated on the balustrade) might observe a vast sea of greenery, composed mainly of maple, beech, tacamahac, and pine. Some five miles west, a slender white church steeple marked the spot where nestled the small town of Onkwedo, once famous for its springs. Three miles north, in a riverside clearing at the foot of a grassy knoll, one could distinguish the gables of an ornate house (variously known as Cook's, Cook's Place, Cook's Castle, or The Pines—its initial appellation). Along the south side of Mount Ettrick, a state highway continued east after passing through Onkwedo. Numerous dirt roads and foot trails crisscrossed the timbered plain within the triangle of land limited by the somewhat tortuous hypotenuse of a rural paved road that weaved northeast from Onkwedo to The Pines, the long cathetus of the state highway just mentioned, and the short cathetus of a river spanned by a steel bridge near Mount Ettrick and a wooden one near Cook's.

On a dull warm day in the summer of 1954, Mary or Almira, or, for that matter, Wolfgang von Goethe,[1] whose name had been carved in the balustrade by some old-fashioned wag, might have noticed an automobile that had turned off the highway just before reaching the bridge and was now nosing and poking this way and that in a maze of doubtful roads. It moved warily and unsteadily, and whenever it changed its mind, it would slow down and raise dust behind like a back-kicking dog. At times it might seem, to a less sympathetic soul than our imagined observer, that this pale blue, egg-shaped two-door sedan, of uncertain age and in mediocre condition, was manned by an idiot. Actually its driver was Professor Timofey Pnin, of Waindell College.

Pnin had started taking lessons at the Waindell Driving School early in the year, but "true understanding," as he put it, had come to him only when, a couple of months later, he had been laid up with a sore back and had done nothing but study with deep enjoyment the forty-page *Driver's Manual*, issued by the State Governor in collaboration with another expert, and the article on "Automobile" in the *Encyclopedia Americana*, with illustrations of Transmissions, and Carburetors, and Brakes, and a Member of the Glidden Tour, *circa* 1905, stuck in the mud of a country road among depressing surroundings. Then and only then was the dual nature of his initial inklings transcended at last as he lay on his sickbed, wiggling his toes and shifting phantom gears. During actual lessons with a harsh instructor who cramped his style, issued unnecessary directives in yelps of technical slang, tried to wrestle the wheel from him at corners, and kept irritating a calm, intelligent pupil with expressions of vulgar detraction, Pnin had been totally unable to combine perceptually the car he was driving in his mind and the car he was driving on the road. Now the two fused at last. If he failed the first time he took his driver's-license test, it was mainly because he started an argument with the examiner in an ill-timed effort to prove that nothing could be more humiliating to a rational creature than being required to encourage the development of a base conditional reflex by stopping at a red light when there was not an earthly soul around, heeled or wheeled. He was more circumspect the next time, and passed. An irresistible senior, enrolled in his Russian Language course, Marilyn Hohn, sold him for a hundred dollars her humble old car: she was getting married to the owner of a far grander machine. The trip from Waindell to Onkwedo, with an overnight stop at a tourist home, had been slow and difficult but uneventful. Just before entering Onkwedo, he had pulled up at a gas station and had got out for a breath of country air. An inscrutable white sky hung over a clover field, and from a pile of firewood near a shack came a rooster's cry, jagged and gaudy—a vocal coxcomb. Some chance intonation on the part of this slightly hoarse bird, combined with the warm wind pressing itself against Pnin in search of attention, recognition, anything, briefly reminded him of a dim dead day

---

1. Johann Wolfgang von Goethe (1749–1832), German poet, dramatist, philosopher.

when he, a Petrograd[2] University freshman, had arrived at the small station of a Baltic summer resort, and the sounds, and the smells, and the sadness—

"Kind of muggy," said the hairy-armed attendant, as he started to wipe the windshield.

Pnin took a letter out of his wallet, unfolded the tiny mimeographed-sketch map attached to it, and asked the attendant how far was the church at which one was supposed to turn left to reach Cook's Place. It was really striking how the man resembled Pnin's colleague at Waindell College, Dr. Hagen—one of those random likenesses as pointless as a bad pun.

"Well, there is a better way to get there," said the false Hagen. "The trucks have messed up that road, and besides you won't like the way it winds. Now you just drive on. Drive through the town. Five miles out of Onkwedo, just after you have passed the trail to Mount Ettrick on your left, and just before reaching the bridge, take the first left turn. It's a good gravel road."

He stepped briskly around the hood and lunged with his rag at the windshield from the other side.

"You turn north and go on bearing north at each crossing—there are quite a few logging trails in those woods but you just bear north and you'll get to Cook's in twelve minutes flat. You can't miss it."

Pnin had now been in that maze of forest roads for about an hour and had come to the conclusion that "bear north," and in fact the word "north" itself, meant nothing to him. He also could not explain what had compelled him, a rational being, to listen to a chance busybody instead of firmly following the pedantically precise instructions that his friend, Alexandr Petrovich Kukolnikov (known locally as Al Cook) had sent him when inviting him to spend the summer at his large and hospitable country house. Our luckless car operator had by now lost himself too thoroughly to be able to go back to the highway, and since he had little experience in maneuvering on rutty narrow roads, with ditches and even ravines gaping on either side, his various indecisions and gropings took those bizarre visual forms that an observer on the lookout tower might have followed with a compassionate eye; but there was no living creature in that forlorn and listless upper region except for an ant who had his own troubles, having, after hours of inept perseverance, somehow reached the upper platform and the balustrade (his *autostrada*) and was getting all bothered and baffled much in the same way as that preposterous toy car progressing below. The wind had subsided. Under the pale sky the sea of tree tops seemed to harbor no life. Presently, however, a gun shot popped, and a twig leaped into the sky. The dense upper boughs in that part of the otherwise stirless forest started to move in a receding sequence of shakes or jumps, with a swinging lilt from tree to tree, after which all was still again. Another minute passed, and then everything

---

2. The name given to St. Petersburg in 1914. In 1924 it was changed to Leningrad, and in 1992 the name St. Petersburg was restored to the city.

happened at once: the ant found an upright beam leading to the roof of the tower and started to ascend it with renewed zest; the sun appeared; and Pnin at the height of hopelessness, found himself on a paved road with a rusty but still glistening sign directing wayfarers "To The Pines."

2

Al Cook was a son of Piotr Kukolnikov, wealthy Moscow merchant of Old-Believers[3] antecedents, self-made man, Maecenas[4] and philanthropist—the famous Kukolnikov who under the last Tsar had been twice imprisoned in a fairly comfortable fortress for giving financial assistance to Social-Revolutionary groups (terrorists, mainly), and under Lenin had been put to death as an "Imperialistic spy" after almost a week of medieval tortures in a Soviet jail. His family reached America via Harbin,[5] around 1925, and young Cook by dint of quiet perseverance, practical acumen, and some scientific training, rose to a high and secure position in a great chemical concern. A kindly, very reserved man of stocky build, with a large immobile face that was tied up in the middle by a neat little pince-nez, he looked what he was—a Business Executive, a Mason, a Golfer, a prosperous and cautious man. He spoke beautifully correct, neutral English, with only the softest shadow of a Slavic accent, and was a delightful host, of the silent variety, with a twinkling eye, and a highball in each hand; and only when some very old and beloved Russian friend was his midnight guest would Alexandr Petrovich suddenly start to discuss God, Lermontov,[6] Liberty, and divulge a hereditary streak of rash idealism that would have greatly confused a Marxist eavesdropper.

He married Susan Marshall, the attractive, voluble, blond daughter of Charles G. Marshall, the inventor, and because one could not imagine Alexandr and Susan otherwise than raising a huge healthy family, it came as a shock to me and other well-wishers to learn that as the result of an operation Susan would remain childless all her life. They were still young, loved each other with a sort of old-world simplicity and integrity very soothing to observe, and instead of populating their country place with children and grandchildren, they collected, every even-year summer, elderly Russians (Cook's fathers or uncles, as it were); on odd-year summers they would have

3. Members of one of the sects of dissenters from the Russian Orthodox Church who opposed liturgical reforms of the seventeeth century.

4. Patron of the arts, name taken from Gauis Cilnius Maecena, the Roman statesman (c. 7o–8 B.C.) who supported Horace and Vergil.

5. A city in northeast China.

6. Mikhail Yurievich Lermontov (1814–1841), poet and novelist.

amerikantsī (Americans), Alexandr's business acquaintances or Susan's relatives and friends.

This was the first time Pnin was coming to The Pines but I had been there before. Émigré Russians—liberals and intellectuals who had left Russia around 1920—could be found swarming all over the place. You would find them in every patch of speckled shade, sitting on rustic benches and discussing émigré writers—Bunin, Aldanov, Sirin;[7] lying suspended in hammocks, with the Sunday issue of a Russian-language newspaper over their faces in traditional defense against flies; sipping tea with jam on the veranda; walking in the woods and wondering about the edibility of local toadstools.

Samuil Lvovich Shpolyanski, a large majestically calm old gentleman, and small, excitable, stuttering Count Fyodor Nikitich Poroshin, both of whom, around 1920, had been members of one of those heroic Regional Governments that were formed in the Russian provinces by democratic groups to withstand Bolshevik dictatorship, would pace the avenue of pines and discuss the tactics to be adopted at the next joint meeting of the Free Russia Committee (which they had founded in New York) with another, younger, anti-Communist organization. From a pavilion half smothered by locust trees came fragments of a heated exchange between Professor Bolotov, who taught the History of Philosophy, and Professor Chateau, who taught the Philosophy of History: "Reality is Duration," one voice, Bolotov's, would boom. "It is not!" the other would cry. "A soap bubble is as real as a fossil tooth!"

Pnin and Chateau, both born in the late nineties of the nineteenth century, were comparative youngsters. Most of the other men had seen sixty and had trudged on. On the other hand, a few of the ladies, such as Countess Poroshin and Madam Bolotov, were still in their late forties and, thanks to the hygienic atmosphere of the New World, had not only preserved, but improved, their good looks. Some parents brought their offspring with them—healthy, tall, indolent, difficult American children of college age, with no sense of nature, and no Russian, and no interest whatsoever in the niceties of their parents' backgrounds and pasts. They seemed to live at The Pines on a physical and mental plane entirely different from that of their parents: now and then passing from their own level to ours through a kind of interdimensional shimmer; responding curtly to a well-meaning Russian joke or anxious piece of advice, and then fading away again; keeping always aloof (so that one felt one had engendered a brood of elves), and preferring any Onkwedo store product, any sort of canned goods to the marvelous Russian foods provided by the Kukolnikov household at loud, long dinners on the screened porch. With great distress Poroshin would say of his chil-

---

7. Ivan Alekseevich Bunin (1870–1953), poet, novelist, Nobel Prize 1933; Mark Alexandrovich Aldanov, pseudonym of M. A. Landau (1886–1957), novelist; V. Sirin, one of the pseudonyms used by Nabokov. The Sirin is a mythical bird, and the Sirin publishing house was prominent in prerevolutionary Russia.

dren (Igor and Olga, college sophomores) "My twins are exasperating. When I see them at home during breakfast or dinner and try to tell them most interesting, most exciting things—for instance, about local elective self-government in the Russian Far North in the seventeenth century or, say, something about the history of the first medical schools in Russia— there is, by the way, an excellent monograph by Chistovich on the subject, published in 1883—they simply wander off and turn on the radio in their rooms." Both young people were around the summer Pnin was invited to The Pines. But they stayed invisible; they would have been hideously bored in this out-of-the-way place, had not Olga's admirer, a college boy whose surname nobody seemed to know, arrived from Boston for the weekend in a spectacular car, and had not Igor found a congenial companion in Nina, the Bolotov girl, a handsome slattern with Egyptian eyes and brown limbs, who went to a dancing school in New York.

The household was looked after by Praskovia, a sturdy, sixty-year-old woman of the people with the vivacity of one a score of years younger. It was an exhilarating sight to watch her as she stood on the back porch surveying the chickens, knuckles on hips, dressed in baggy homemade shorts and a matronly blouse with rhinestones. She had nursed Alexandr and his brother when both were children in Harbin and now she was helped in her household duties by her husband, a gloomy and stolid old Cossack whose main passions in life were amateur bookbinding—a self-taught and almost pathological process that he was impelled to inflict upon any old catalogue or pulp magazine that came his way; the making of fruit liqueurs; and the killing of small forest animals.

Of that season's guests, Pnin knew well Professor Chateau, a friend of his youth, with whom he had attended the University of Prague in the early twenties, and he was also well acquainted with the Bolotovs, whom he had last seen in 1949 when he welcomed them with a speech at a formal dinner given them by the Association of Russian Émigré Scholars at the Barbizon-Plaza,[8] upon the occasion of Bolotov's arrival from France. Personally, I never cared much for Bolotov and his philosophical works, which so oddly combine the obscure and the trite; the man's achievement is perhaps a mountain—but a mountain of platitudes; I have always liked, however, Varvara, the seedy philosopher's exuberant buxom wife. When she first visited The Pines, in 1951, she had never seen the New England countryside before. Its birches and bilberries deceived her into placing mentally Lake Onkwedo, not on the parallel of, say, Lake Ohrida in the Balkans, where it belonged, but on that of Lake Onega in northern Russia, where she had spent her first fifteen summers, before fleeing from the Bolsheviks to western Europe, with her aunt Lidia Vinogradov, the well-known feminist and social worker. Consequently the sight of a hummingbird in probing flight, or a catalpa in ample bloom, produced upon Varvara the effect of some unnatural or exotic vision. More fabulous than pictures in a bestiary were to her the tremen-

---

8. A New York hotel.

dous porcupines that came to gnaw at the delicious, gamy old wood of the house, or the elegant, eerie little skunks that sampled the cat's milk in the backyard. She was nonplused and enchanted by the number of plants and creatures she could not identify, mistook Yellow Warblers for stray canaries, and on the occasion of Susan's birthday was known to have brought, with pride and panting enthusiasm, for the ornamentation of the dinner table, a profusion of beautiful poison-ivy leaves, hugged to her pink, freckled breast.

3

The Bolotovs and Madam Shpolyanski, a little lean woman in slacks, were the first people to see Pnin as he cautiously turned into a sandy avenue, bordered with wild lupines, and, sitting very straight, stiffly clutching the steering wheel as if he were a farmer more used to his tractor than to his car, entered, at ten miles an hour and in first gear, the grove of old, disheveled, curiously authentic-looking pines that separated the paved road from Cook's Castle.

Varvara buoyantly rose from the seat of the pavilion—where she and Roza Shpolyanski had just discovered Bolotov reading a battered book and smoking a forbidden cigarette. She greeted Pnin with a clapping of hands, while her husband showed as much geniality as he was capable of by slowly waving the book he had closed on his thumb to mark the place. Pnin killed the motor and sat beaming at his friends. The collar of his green sport shirt was undone; his partly unzipped windbreaker seemed too tight for his impressive torso; his bronzed bald head, with the puckered brow and conspicuous vermicular vein on the temple, bent low as he wrestled with the door handle and finally dived out of the car.

"*Avtomobil,*" *kostyum—nu pryamo amerikanets* (a veritable American), *pryamo Ayzenhauer!*"[9] said Varvara, and introduced Pnin to Roza Abramovna Shpolyanski.

"We had some mutual friends forty years ago," remarked that lady, peering at Pnin with curiosity.

"Oh, let us not mention such astronomical figures," said Bolotov, approaching and replacing with a grass blade the thumb he had been using as a bookmarker. "You know," he continued, shaking Pnin's hand, "I am rereading *Anna Karenin* for the seventh time and I derive as much rapture as I did, not forty, but sixty, years ago, when I was a lad of seven. And, every time, one discovers new things—for instance I notice now that Lyov Nikolaich[1] does not know on what day his novel starts: it seems to be Friday

9. "A veritable Eisenhower!"
1. Leo Tolstoy (1828-1910).

because that is the day the clockman comes to wind up the clocks in the Oblonski house, but it is also Thursday as mentioned in the conversation at the skating rink between Lyovin and Kitty's mother."

"What on earth does it matter," cried Varvara. "Who on earth wants to know the exact day?"

"I can tell you the exact day," said Pnin, blinking in the broken sunlight and inhaling the remembered tang of northern pines. "The action of the novel starts in the beginning of 1872, namely on Friday, February the twenty-third by the New Style. In his morning paper Oblonski reads that Beust is rumored to have proceeded to Wiesbaden. This is of course Count Friedrich Ferdinand von Beust, who had just been appointed Austrian Ambassador to the Court of St. James's. After presenting his credentials, Beust had gone to the continent for a rather protracted Christmas vacation—had spent there two months with his family, and was now returning to London, where, according to his own memoirs in two volumes, preparations were under way for the thanksgiving service to be held in St. Paul's on February the twenty-seventh for the recovering from typhoid fever of the Prince of Wales. However (*odnako*), it really is hot here (*i zharko zhe u vas*)! I think I shall now present myself before the most luminous orbs (*presvetīe ochi*, jocular) of Alexandr Petrovich and then go for a dip (*okupnutsya*, also jocular) in the river he so vividly describes in his letter."

"Alexander Petrovich is away till Monday, on business or pleasure," said Varvara Bolotov, "but I think you will find Susanna Karlovna sun-bathing on her favorite lawn behind the house. Shout before you approach too near."

4

Cook's Castle was a three-story brick-and-timber mansion built around 1860 and partly rebuilt half a century later, when Susan's father purchased it from the Dudley-Greene family in order to make of it a select resort hotel for the richer patrons of the curative Onkwedo Springs. It was an elaborate and ugly building in a mongrel style, with the Gothic bristling through remnants of French and Florentine, and when originally designed might have belonged to the variety which Samuel Sloan, an architect of the time, classified as An Irregular Northern Villa "well adapted to the highest requirements of social life" and called "Northern" because of "the aspiring tendency of its roof and towers." The piquancy of these pinnacles and the merry, somewhat even inebriated air the mansion had of having been composed of several smaller Northern Villas, hoisted into mid-air and knocked together anyhow, with parts of unassimilated roofs, half-hearted gables, cornices, rustic quoins, and other projections sticking out on all sides, had, alas, but briefly attracted tourists. By 1920, the Onkwedo waters had mysteriously lost whatever magic they had contained, and after her father's death Susan had vainly tried to sell The Pines, since they had another more comfortable house in the residential quarter of the industrial city where her husband worked. However, now that they had got accustomed to use the Castle for entertaining their numerous friends, Susan was glad that the meek beloved monster had found no purchaser.

Within, the diversity was as great as without. Four spacious rooms opened from the large hall that retained something of its hostelic stage in the generous dimensions of the grate. The hand rail of the stairs, and at least one of its spindles, dated from 1720, having been transferred to the house, while it was being built, from a far older one, whose very site was no longer exactly known. Very ancient, too, were the beautiful sideboard panels of game and fish in the dining room. In the half a dozen rooms of which each of the upper floors consisted, and in the two wings in the rear, one could discover, among disparate pieces of furniture, some charming satinwood bureau, some romantic rosewood sofa, but also all kinds of bulky and miserable articles, broken chairs, dusty marble-topped tables, morose *étagères* with bits of dark-looking glass in the back as mournful as the eyes of old apes. The chamber Pnin got was a pleasant southeast one on the upper floor: it had remnants of gilt paper on the walls, an army cot, a plain washstand, and all kinds of shelves, brackets, and scrollwork moldings. Pnin shook open the casement, smiled at the smiling forest, again remembered a distant first day in the country, and presently walked down, clad in a new navy-blue bathrobe and wearing on his bare feet a pair of ordinary rubber overshoes, a sensible precaution if one intends to walk through damp and, perhaps, snake-infested grass. On the garden terrace he found Chateau.

Konstantin Ivanich Chateau, a subtle and charming scholar of pure Russian lineage despite his surname (derived, I am told, from that of a Russianized Frenchman who adopted orphaned Ivan), taught at a large New York university and had not seen his very dear Pnin for at least five years. They embraced with a warm rumble of joy. I confess to have been myself, at one time, under the spell of angelic Konstantin Ivanich, namely, when we used to meet every day in the winter of 1935 or 1936 for a morning stroll under the laurels and nettle trees of Grasse, southern France, where he then shared a villa with several other Russian expatriates. His soft voice, the gentlemanly St. Petersburgan burr of his r's, his mild, melancholy caribou eyes, the auburn goatee he continuously twiddled, with a shredding motion of his long, frail fingers—everything about Chateau (to use a literary formula as old-fashioned as he) produced a rare sense of well-being in his friends. Pnin and he talked for a while, comparing notes. As not unusual with firm-principled exiles, every time they met after a separation they not only endeavored to catch up with a personal past, but also to sum up by means of a few rapid passwords—allusions, intonations impossible to render in a foreign language—the course of recent Russian history, thirty-five years of hopeless injustice following a century of struggling justice and glimmering hope. Next, they switched to the usual shop talk of European teachers abroad, sighing and shaking heads over the "typical American college student" who does not know geography, is immune to noise, and thinks education is but a means to get eventually a remunerative job. Then they inquired about each other's work in progress, and both were extremely modest and reticent about their respective researches. Finally, as they walked along a meadow path, brushing against the goldenrod, toward the wood where a rocky river ran, they spoke of their healths: Chateau, who looked so jaunty, with one hand in the pocket of his white flannel trousers and his lustring coat rather rakishly opened on a flannel waistcoat, cheerfully said that in the near future he would have to undergo an exploratory operation of the abdomen, and Pnin said, laughing, that every time *he* was X-rayed, doctors vainly tried to puzzle out what they termed "a shadow behind the heart."

"Good title for a bad novel," remarked Chateau.

As they were passing a grassy knoll just before entering the wood, a pink-faced venerable man in a seersucker suit, with a shock of white hair and a tumefied purple nose resembling a huge raspberry, came striding toward them down the sloping field, a look of disgust contorting his features.

"I have to go back for my hat," he cried dramatically as he drew near.

"Are you acquainted?" murmured Chateau, fluttering his hands introductively. "Timofey Pavlich Pnin, Ivan Ilyich Gramineev."

"*Moyo pochtenie* (My respects)," said both men, bowing to each other over a powerful handshake.

"I thought," resumed Gramineev, a circumstantial narrator, "that the day would continue as overcast as it had begun. By stupidity (*po gluposti*) I came out with an unprotected head. Now the sun is roasting my brains. I have to interrupt my work."

He gestured toward the top of the knoll. There his easel stood in delicate silhouette against the blue sky. From that crest he had been painting a view of the valley beyond, complete with quaint old barn, gnarled apple tree, and kine.

"I can offer you my panama," said kind Chateau, but Pnin had already produced from his bathrobe pocket a large red handkerchief: he expertly twisted each of its corners into a knot.

"Admirable. . . . Most grateful," said Gramineev, adjusting this headgear.

"One moment," said Pnin. "You must tuck in the knots."

This done, Gramineev started walking up the field toward his easel. He was a well-known, frankly academic painter, whose soulful oils—"Mother Volga," "Three Old Friends" (lad, nag, dog), "April Glade," and so forth— still graced a museum in Moscow.

"Somebody told me," said Chateau, as he and Pnin continued to progress riverward, "that Liza's boy has an extraordinary talent for painting. Is that correct?"

"Yes," answered Pnin. "All the more vexing (*tem bolee obidno*) that his mother, who I think is about to marry a third time, took Victor suddenly to California for the rest of the summer, whereas if he had accompanied me here, as had been planned, he would have had the splendid opportunity of being coached by Gramineev."

"You exaggerate the splendor," softly rejoined Chateau.

They reached the bubbling and glistening stream. A concave ledge between higher and lower diminutive cascades formed a natural swimming pool under the alders and pines. Chateau, a non-bather, made himself comfortable on a boulder. Throughout the academic year Pnin had regularly exposed his body to the radiation of a sun lamp; hence, when he stripped down to his bathing trunks, he glowed in the dappled sunlight of the riverside grove with a rich mahogany tint. He removed his cross and his rubbers.

"Look, how pretty," said observant Chateau.

A score of small butterflies, all of one kind, were settled on a damp patch of sand, their wings erect and closed, showing their pale undersides with dark dots and tiny orange-rimmed peacock spots along the hindwing margins; one of Pnin's shed rubbers disturbed some of them and, revealing the celestial hue of their upper surface, they fluttered around like blue snowflakes before settling again.

"Pity Vladimir Vladimirovich is not here," remarked Chateau. "He would have told us all about these enchanting insects."[2]

"I have always had the impression that his entomology was merely a pose."

"Oh no," said Chateau. "You will lose it some day," he added, pointing to the Greek Catholic cross on a golden chainlet that Pnin had removed from his neck and hung on a twig. Its glint perplexed a cruising dragonfly.

"Perhaps I would not mind losing it," said Pnin. "As you well know, I wear it merely from sentimental reasons. And the sentiment is becoming burdensome. After all, there is too much of the physical about this attempt to keep a particle of one's childhood in contact with one's breastbone."

"You are not the first to reduce faith to a sense of touch," said Chateau, who was a practicing Greek Catholic and deplored his friend's agnostic attitude.

A horsefly applied itself, blind fool, to Pnin's bald head, and was stunned by a smack of his meaty palm.

From a smaller boulder than the one upon which Chateau was perched, Pnin gingerly stepped down into the brown and blue water. He noticed he still had his wrist watch—removed it and left it inside one of his rubbers. Slowly swinging his tanned shoulders, Pnin waded forth, the loopy shadows of leaves shivering and slipping down his broad back. He stopped and breaking the glitter and shade around him, moistened his inclined head, rubbed his nape with wet hands, soused in turn each armpit, and then, joining both palms, glided into the water, his dignified breast stroke sending off ripples on either side. Around the natural basin, Pnin swam in state. He swam with a rhythmical splutter—half gurgle, half puff. Rhythmically he opened his legs

---

2. A reference to Vladimir Nabokov's lifelong interest in lepidoptera. His first published article was on Crimean butterflies (1920).

and widened them out at the knees while flexing and straightening out his arms like a giant frog. After two minutes of this, he waded out and sat on the boulder to dry. Then he put on his cross, his wrist watch, his rubbers, and his bathrobe.

5

Dinner was served on the screened porch. As he sat down next to Bolotov and began to stir the sour cream in his red *botvinia* (chilled beet soup), wherein pink ice cubes tinkled, Pnin automatically resumed an earlier conversation.

"You will notice," he said, "that there is a significant difference between Lyovin's spiritual time and Vronski's physical One. In mid-book, Lyovin and Kitty lag behind Vronski and Anna by a whole year. When, on a Sunday evening in May 1876, Anna throws herself under that freight train, she has existed more than four years since the beginning of the novel, but in the case of the Lyovins, during the same period, 1872 to 1876, hardly three years have elapsed. It is the best example of relativity in literature that is known to me."

After dinner, a game of croquet was suggested. These people favored the time-honored but technically illegal setting of hoops, where two of the ten are crossed at the center of the ground to form the so-called Cage or Mousetrap. It became immediately clear that Pnin, who teamed with Madam Bolotov against Shpolyanski and Countess Poroshin, was by far the best player of the lot. As soon as the pegs were driven in and the game started, the man was transfigured. From his habitual, slow, ponderous, rather rigid self, he changed into a terrifically mobile, scampering, mute, sly-visaged hunchback. It seemed to be always his turn to play. Holding his mallet very low and daintily swinging it between his parted spindly legs (he had created a minor sensation by changing into Bermuda shorts expressly for the game), Pnin foreshadowed every stroke with nimble aim-taking oscillations of the mallet head, then gave the ball an accurate tap, and forthwith, still hunched, and with the ball still rolling, walked rapidly to the spot where he had planned for it to stop. With geometrical gusto, he ran it through hoops, evoking cries of admiration from the onlookers. Even Igor Poroshin, who was passing by like a shadow with two cans of beer he was carrying to some private banquet, stopped for a second and shook his head appreciatively before vanishing in the shrubbery. Plaints and protests, however, would mingle with the applause when Pnin, with brutal indifference, croqueted, or rather rocketed, an adversary's ball. Placing in contact with it his own ball, and firmly putting his curiously small foot upon the latter, he would bang at his ball so as to drive the other up the country by the shock of the stroke. When appealed to, Susan said it was completely against the rules, but Madam Shpolyanski insisted it was perfectly acceptable and said that when she was a child her English governess used to call it a Hong Kong.

After Pnin had tolled the stake and all was over, and Varvara accompanied Susan to get the evening tea ready, Pnin quietly retired to a bench under the pines. A certain extremely unpleasant and frightening cardiac sensation, which he had experienced several times throughout his adult life, had come upon him again. It was not pain or palpitation, but rather an awful feeling of sinking and melting into one's physical surroundings—sunset, red boles of trees, sand, still air. Meanwhile Roza Shpolyanski, noticing Pnin sitting alone, and taking advantage of this, walked over to him ("*sidite, sidite!*" don't get up) and sat down next to him on the bench.

"In 1916 or 1917," she said, "you may have had occasion to hear my maiden name—Geller—from some great friends of yours."

"No, I don't recollect," said Pnin.

"It is of no importance, anyway. I don't think we ever met. But you knew well my cousins, Grisha and Mira Belochkin. They constantly spoke of you. He is living in Sweden, I think—and, of course, you have heard of his poor sister's terrible end. . . ."

"Indeed, I have," said Pnin.

"Her husband," said Madam Shpolyanski, "was a most charming man. Samuil Lvovich and I knew him and his first wife, Svetlana Chertok, the pianist, very intimately. He was interned by the Nazis separately from Mira, and died in the same concentration camp as did my elder brother Misha. You did not know Misha, did you? He was also in love with Mira once upon a time."

"*Tshay gotoff* (tea's ready)," called Susan from the porch in her funny functional Russian. "Timofey, Rozochka! *Tshay!*"

Pnin told Madam Shpolyanski he would follow her in a minute, and after she had gone he continued to sit in the first dusk of the arbor, his hands clasped on the croquet mallet he still held.

Two kerosene lamps cozily illuminated the porch of the country house. Dr. Pavel Antonovich Pnin, Timofey's father, an eye specialist, and Dr. Yakov Grigorievich Belochkin, Mira's father, a pediatrician, could not be torn away from their chess game in a corner of the veranda, so Madam Belochkin had the maid serve them there—on a special small Japanese table, near the one they were playing at—their glasses of tea in silver holders, the curd and whey with black bread, the Garden Strawberries, *zemlyanika*, and the other cultivated species, *klubnika* (Hautbois or Green Strawberries), and the radiant golden jams, and the various biscuits, wafers, pretzels, zwiebacks—instead of calling the two engrossed doctors to the main table at the other end of the porch, where sat the rest of the family and guests, some clear, some grading into a luminous mist.

Dr. Belochkin's blind hand took a pretzel; Dr. Pnin's seeing hand took a rook. Dr. Belochkin munched and stared at the hole in his ranks; Dr. Pnin dipped an abstract zwieback into the hole of his tea.

The country house that the Belochkins rented that summer was in the same Baltic resort near which the widow of General N—let a summer cottage to the Pnins on the confines of her vast estate, marshy and rugged, with dark woods hemming in a desolate manor. Timofey Pnin was again the clumsy, shy, obstinate, eighteen-year-old boy, waiting in the dark for Mira— and despite the fact that logical thought put electric bulbs into the kerosene lamps and reshuffled the people, turning them into aging émigrés and securely, hopelessly, forever wire-netting the lighted porch, my poor Pnin, with hallucinatory sharpness, imagined Mira slipping out of there into the garden and coming toward him among tall tobacco flowers whose dull white mingled in the dark with that of her frock. This feeling coincided somehow with the sense of diffusion and dilation within his chest. Gently he laid his mallet aside and, to dissipate the anguish, started walking away from the house, through the silent pine grove. From a car which was parked near the garden tool house and which contained presumably at least two of his fellow guests' children, there issued a steady trickle of radio music.

"Jazz, jazz, they always must have their jazz, those youngsters," muttered Pnin to himself, and turned into the path that led to the forest and river. He remembered the fads of his and Mira's youth, the amateur theatricals, the gypsy ballads, the passion she had for photography. Where were they now, those artistic snapshots she used to take—pets, clouds, flowers, an April glade with shadows of birches on wet-sugar snow, soldiers posturing on the roof of a boxcar, a sunset skyline, a hand holding a book? He remembered the last day they had met, on the Neva embankment in Petrograd, and the tears, and the stars, and the warm rose-red silk lining of her karakul muff. The Civil War of 1918–22 separated them: history broke their engagement. Timofey wandered southward, to join briefly the ranks of Denikin's army, while Mira's family escaped from the Bolsheviks to Sweden and then settled down in Germany, where eventually she married a fur dealer of Russian extraction. Sometime in the early thirties, Pnin, by then married too, accompanied his wife to Berlin, where she wished to attend a congress of psychotherapists, and one night, at a Russian restaurant on the Kurfürstendamm, he saw Mira again. They exchanged a few words, she smiled at him in the remembered fashion, from under her dark brows, with that bashful slyness of hers; and the contour of her prominent cheekbones, and the elongated eyes, and the slenderness of arm and ankle were unchanged, were immortal, and then she joined her husband who was getting his overcoat at the cloakroom, and that was all—but the pang of tenderness remained, akin to the vibrating outline of verses you know you know but cannot recall.

What chatty Madam Shpolyanski mentioned had conjured up Mira's image with unusual force. This was disturbing. Only in the detachment of an incurable complaint, in the sanity of near death, could one cope with this for a moment. In order to exist rationally, Pnin had taught himself, during the last ten years, never to remember Mira Belochkin—not because, in itself, the evocation of a youthful love affair, banal and brief, threatened his peace of mind (alas, recollections of his marriage to Liza were imperious enough to crowd out any former romance), but because, if one were quite sincere with oneself, no conscience, and hence no consciousness, could be expected to subsist in a world where such things as Mira's death were possible. One had to forget—because one could not live with the thought that this graceful, fragile, tender young woman with those eyes, that smile, those gardens and snows in the background, had been brought in a cattle car to an extermination camp and killed by an injection of phenol into the heart, into the gentle heart one had heard beating under one's lips in the dusk of the past. And since the exact form of her death had not been recorded, Mira kept dying a great number of deaths in one's mind, and undergoing a great number of resurrections, only to die again and again, led away by a trained nurse, inoculated with filth, tetanus bacilli, broken glass, gassed in a sham shower bath with prussic acid, burned alive in a pit on a gasoline-soaked pile of beechwood. According to the investigator Pnin had happened to talk to in Washington, the only certain thing was that being too weak to work (though still smiling, still able to help other Jewish women), she was selected to die and was cremated only a few days after her arrival in Buchenwald, in the beautifully wooded Grosser Ettersberg, as the region is resoundingly called. It is an hour's stroll from Weimar, where walked Goethe, Herder, Schiller, Wieland, the inimitable Kotzebue and others.[3] "*Aber warum*—but why—" Dr. Hagen, the gentlest of souls alive, would wail, "why had one to put that horrid camp so near!" for indeed, it was near—only five miles from the cultural heart of Germany—"that nation of universities," as the President of Waindell College, renowned for his use of the *mot juste*, had so elegantly phrased it when reviewing the European situation in a recent Commencement speech, along with the compliment he paid another torture house, "Russia—the country of Tolstoy, Stanislavski, Raskolnikov,[4] and other great and good men."

Pnin slowly walked under the solemn pines. The sky was dying. He did not believe in an autocratic God. He did believe, dimly, in a democracy of ghosts. The souls of the dead, perhaps, formed committees, and these, in continuous session, attended to the destinies of the quick.

The mosquitoes were getting bothersome. Time for tea. Time for a game of chess with Chateau. That strange spasm was over, one could breathe again. On the distant crest of the knoll, at the exact spot where Gramineev's easel had stood a few hours before, two dark figures in profile were silhouetted against the ember-red sky. They stood there closely, facing each other. One could not make out from the road whether it was the Poroshin girl and her beau, or Nina Bolotov and young Poroshin, or merely an emblematic couple placed with easy art on the last page of Pnin's fading day.

---

3. Johann Gottfried von Herder (1744–1803), philosopher and poet; Johann Christophe Friedrich von Schiller (1759–1805), poet, dramatist, historian; Christoph Martin Wieland (1733–1813), poet, novelist, critic; August Friederich Ferdinand von Kotzebue (1761–1819), dramatist.

4. Konstantin Stanislavski, (1863–1938), actor, producer, director; Raskolnikov is the ax murderer in Dostoevsky's *Crime and Punishment*.

James T. Farrell
(1904–1979)

Born in Chicago, James T. Farrell attended the University of Chicago, where he was already writing of Studs Lonigan, his first and best-known hero. Leaving without a degree, he worked at various jobs until the success of Young Lonigan: A Boyhood on the Chicago Streets *(1932) confirmed his vocation as an unparalleled recorder of the life of the Irish Catholics on Chicago's South Side. When* The Young Manhood of Studs Lonigan *(1934) and* Judgment Day *(1935) were combined with the first book as* Studs Lonigan: A Trilogy *(1936), Farrell earned recognition as one of the premier novelists of his generation. Studs was one kind of product of Chicago's South Side; another was his friend Danny O'Neill, who moved out of the Lonigan trilogy into his own series in* A World I Never Made *(1936),* No Star Is Lost *(1938),* Father and Son *(1940),* My Days of Anger *(1943), and* The Face of Time *(1953). Yet another was Bernard Carr (or Clare), hero of* Bernard Clare *(1946),* The Road Between *(1949), and* Yet Other Waters *(1952). Finally, among novels with their roots in Chicago, there were nine in the cycle* A Universe in Time, *about a writer named Eddie Ryan with a career not unlike Farrell's own, published from 1963 to 1978.*

When success came, Farrell moved to New York City, continuing to write of Chicago, but depicting also the lives of people outside his native city. Chicago remained his best subject, however, and youth his most sympathetic period. In the title of A World I Never Made *is expressed much of the naturalistic philosophy that underlies his work. His people are caught in times and places they never chose, trapped between cultures not of their devising.*

Farrell's hundreds of short stories were collected in numerous volumes, beginning with Calico Shoes *(1934). The source of the story below is* The Short Stories of James T. Farrell *(1937), an omnibus volume containing his first three collections.*

Studs[1]

IT IS RAINING OUTSIDE; rain pouring like bullets from countless machine guns; rain spat-spattering on the wet earth and paving in endless silver crystals. Studs' grave out at Mount Olivet will be soaked and soppy, and fresh with the wet, clean odors of watered earth and flowers. And the members of Studs' family will be looking out of the windows of their apartment on the South Side, thinking of the cold, damp grave and the gloomy, muddy cemetery, and of their Studs lying at rest in peaceful acceptance of that wormy conclusion which is the common fate.

At Studs' wake last Monday evening everybody was mournful, sad that such a fine young fellow of twenty-six should go off so suddenly with double pneumonia; blown out of this world like a ripped leaf in a hurricane. They sighed and the women and girls cried, and everybody said that it was too bad. But they were consoled because he'd had the priest and had received Extreme Unction before he died, instead of going off like Sport Murphy who was killed in a saloon brawl. Poor Sport! He was a good fellow, and tough as hell. Poor Studs!

The undertaker (it was probably old man O'Reedy who used to be usher in the old parish church) laid Studs out handsomely. He was outfitted in a sombre black suit and a white silk tie. His hands were folded over his stomach, clasping a pair of black rosary beads. At his head, pressed against the satin bedding, was a spiritual bouquet,[2] set in line with Studs' large nose. He looked handsome, and there were no lines of suffering on his planed face. But the spiritual bouquet (further assurance that his soul would arrive safely in Heaven) was a dirty trick. So was the administration of the last sacraments. For Studs will be miserable in Heaven, more miserable than he was on those Sunday nights when he would hang around the old poolroom at Fifty-eighth and the elevated station, waiting for something to happen. He will find the land of perpetual happiness and goodness dull and boresome, and he'll be resentful. There will be nothing to do in Heaven but to wait in timeless eternity. There will be no can houses, speak-easies, whores (unless they are reformed) and gambling joints; and neither will there be a shortage of plasterers. He will loaf up and down gold-paved streets where there is not even the suggestion of a poolroom, thinking of Paulie Haggerty, Sport Murphy, Arnold Sheehan and Hink Weber, who are possibly in Hell together because there was no priest around to play a dirty trick on them.

I thought of these things when I stood by the coffin, waiting for Tommy Doyle, Red Kelly, Les, and Joe to finish offering a few perfunctory prayers in

---

1. First published in *This Quarter* in 1930, "Studs" was collected in *Guillotine Party and Other Stories* (1935).

2. A list of spiritual favors conferred on one person by the devotional acts of another: for example, a number of rosaries, novenas, or masses.

memory of Studs. When they had showered some Hail Marys and Our Fathers on his already prayer-drenched soul, we went out into the dining room.

Years ago when I was a kid in the fifth grade in the the old parish school, Studs was in the graduating class. He was one of the school leaders, a light-faced, blond kid who was able to fight like sixty and who never took any sass from Tommy Doyle, Red Kelly, or any of those fellows from the Fifty-eighth Street gang. He was quarterback on the school's football team, and liked by the girls.

My first concrete memory of him is of a rainy fall afternoon. Dick Buckford and I were fooling around in front of Helen Shires' house bumping against each other with our arms folded. We never thought of fighting but kept pushing and shoving and bumping each other. Studs, Red O'Connell, Tubby Connell, the Donoghues, and Jim Clayburn came along. Studs urged us into fighting, and I gave Dick a bloody nose. Studs congratulated me, and said that I could come along with them and play tag in Red O'Connell's basement, where there were several trick passageways.

After that day, I used to go around with Studs and his bunch. They regarded me as a sort of mascot, and they kept training me to fight other kids. But any older fellows who tried to pick on me would have a fight on their hands. Every now and then he would start boxing with me.

"Gee, you never get hurt, do you?" he would say.

I would grin in answer, bearing the punishment because of the pride and the glory.

"You must be goofy. You can't be hurt."

"Well, I don't get hurt like other kids."

"You're too good for Morris and those kids. You could trim them with your eyes closed. You're good," he would say, and then he would go on training me.

I arranged for a party on one of my birthdays, and invited Studs and the fellows from his bunch. Red O'Connell, a tall, lanky, cowardly kid, went with my brother, and the two of them convinced my folks that Studs was not a fit person for me to invite. I told Studs what had happened, and he took such an insult decently. But none of the fellows he went with would accept my invitation, and most of the girls also refused. On the day of the party, with my family's permission, I again invited Studs but he never came.

I have no other concrete recollections of Studs while he was in grammar school. He went to Loyola for one year, loafed about for a similar period; and then he became a plasterer for his father. He commenced going round the poolroom. The usual commonplace story resulted. What there was of the boy disappeared in slobbish dissipation. His pleasures became compressed within a hexagonal of whores, movies, pool, alky, poker, and craps. By the time I commenced going into the poolroom (my third year in high school) this process had been completed.

Stud's attitude toward me had also changed to one of contempt. I was a goofy young punk. Often he made cracks about me. Once, when I retaliated by sarcasm, he threatened to bust me, and awed by his former reputation I shut up. We said little to each other, although Studs occasionally condescended to borrow fifty or seventy-five cents from me, or to discuss Curley, the corner imbecile.

Studs' companions were more or less small-time amateur hoodlums. He had drifted away from the Donoghues and George Gogarty, who remained bourgeois young men with such interests as formal dances and shows. Perhaps Slug Mason was his closest friend; a tall, heavy-handed, good-natured, child-minded slugger, who knew the address and telephone number of almost every prostitute on the South Side. Hink Weber, who should have been in the ring and who later committed suicide in an insane asylum, Red Kelly, who was a typical wisecracking corner habitué, Tommy Doyle, a fattening, bull-dozing, half-good-natured moron, Stan Simonsky and Joe Thomas were his other companions.

I feel sure that Studs' family, particularly his sisters, were appalled by his actions. The two sisters, one of whom I loved in an adolescently romantic and completely unsuccessful manner, were the type of middle-class girls who go in for sororities and sensibilities. One Saturday evening, when Studs got drunk earlier than usual, his older sister (who the boys always said was keen) saw him staggering around under the Fifty-eighth Street elevated station. She was with a young man in an automobile, and they stopped. Studs talked loudly to her, and finally they left. Studs reeled after the car, cursing and shaking his fists. Fellows like Johnny O'Brien (who went to the U. of C. to become a fraternity man) talked sadly of how Studs could have been more discriminating in his choice of buddies and liquor; and this, too, must have reached the ears of his two sisters.

Physical decay slowly developed. Studs, always a square-planed, broad person, began getting soft and slightly fat. He played one or two years with the corner football team. He was still an efficient quarterback, but slow. When the team finally disbanded, he gave up athletics. He fought and brawled about until one New Year's Eve he talked out of turn to Jim McGeoghan, who was a boxing champ down at Notre Dame. Jim flattened Stud's nose, and gave him a wicked black eye. Studs gave up fighting.

My associations with the corner gradually dwindled. I went to college, and became an atheist. This further convinced Studs that I wasn't right, and he occasionally remarked about my insanity. I grew up contemptuous of him and the others; and some of this feeling crept into my overt actions. I drifted into other groups and forgot the corner. Then I went to New York, and stories of legendary activities became fact on the corner. I had started a new religion, written poetry, and done countless similar monstrous things. When I returned, I did not see Studs for over a year. One evening, just before the Smith-Hoover election day, I met him as he came out of the I. C. station at Randolph Street with Pat Carrigan and Ike Dugan. I talked to Pat and Ike, but not to Studs.

"Aren't you gonna say hello to me?" he asked in friendly fashion, and he offered me his hand.

I was curious but friendly for several minutes. We talked of Al Smith's chances in an uninformed, unintelligent fashion and I injected one joke about free love. Studs laughed at it; and then they went on.

The next I heard of him, he was dead.

When I went out into the dining room, I found all the old gang there, jabbering in the smoke-thick, crowded room. But I did not have any desire or intention of giving the world for having seen them. They were almost all fat and respectable. Cloddishly, they talked of the tragedy of his death, and then went about remembering the good old days. I sat in the corner and listened.

The scene seemed tragi-comical to me. All these fellows had been the bad boys of my boyhood, and many of them I had admired as proper models. Now they were all of the same kidney. Jackie Cooney (who once stole fifteen bottles of grape juice in one haul from under the eyes of a Greek proprietor over at Sixty-fifth and Stony Island), Monk McCarthy (who lived in a basement on his pool winnings and peanuts for over a year), Al Mumford (the good-natured, dumbly well-intentioned corner scapegoat), Pat Carrigan, the roly-poly fat boy from Saint Stanislaus high school—all as alike as so many cans of tomato soup.

Jim Nolan, now bald-headed, a public accountant, engaged to be married, and student in philosophy at Saint Vincent's evening school, was in one corner with Monk.

"Gee, Monk, remember the time we went to Plantation and I got drunk and went down the alley over-turning garbage cans?" he recalled.

"Yeh, that was some party," Monk said.

"Those were the days," Jim said.

Tubby Connell, whom I recalled as a moody, introspective kid, singled out the social Johnny O'Brien and listened to the latter talk with George Gogarty about Illinois U.

Al Mumford walked about making cracks, finally observing to me, "Jim, get a fiddle and you'll look like Paderwooski."

Red Kelly sat enthroned with Les, Doyle, Simonsky, Bryan, Young Floss Campbell (waiting to be like these older fellows), talking oracularly.

"Yes, sir, it's too bad. A young fellow in the prime of life going like that. It's too bad," he said.

"Poor Studs!" Les said.

"I was out with him a week ago," Bryan said.

"He was all right then," Kelly said.

"Life is a funny thing," Doyle said.

"It's a good thing he had the priest," Kelly said.

"Yeh," Les said.

"Sa-ay, last Saturday I pushed the swellest little baby at Rosy's," Doyle said.

"Was she a blonde?" Kelly said.

"Yeh," Doyle said.

"She's cute. I jazzed her, too," Kelly said.

"Yeh, that night at Plantation was a wow," Jim Nolan said.

"We ought to pull off a drunk some night," Monk said.

"Let's," Nolan said.

"Say, Curley, are you in love?" Mumford asked Curley across the room.

"Now, Duffy," Curley said with imbecilic superiority.

"Remember the time Curley went to Burnham?" Carrigan asked.

Curley blushed.

"What happened, Curley?" Duffy asked.

"Nothing, Al," Curley said, confused.

"Go on, tell him, Curley! Tell him! Don't be bashful now! Don't be bashful! Tell him about the little broad!" Carrigan said.

"Now, Pat, you know me better than that," Curley said.

"Come on, Curley, tell me," Al said.

"Some little girl sat on Curley's knee, and he shoved her off and called her a lousy whore and left the place," Carrigan said.

"Why, Curley, I'm ashamed of you," Al said.

Curley blushed.

"I got to get up at six every morning. But I don't mind it. This not workin' is the bunk. You ain't got any clothes or anything when you ain't got the sheets. I know. No, sir, this loafin' is all crap. You wait around all day for something to happen," Jackie Cooney said to Tommy Rourke.

"Gee, it was tough on Studs," Johnny O'Brien said to George Gogarty.

Gogarty said it was tough, too. Then they talked of some student from Illinois U. Phil Rolfe came in. Phil was professional major-domo of the wake; he was going with Studs' kid sister. Phil used to be a smart Jewboy, misplaced when he did not get into the furrier business. Now he was sorry with everybody, and thanking them for being sorry. He and Kelly talked importantly of pall-bearers. Then he went out. Some fellow I didn't know started telling one of Red Kelly's brothers what time he got up to go to work. Mickey Flannagan, the corner drunk, came in and he, too, said he was working.

They kept on talking, and I thought more and more that they were a bunch of slobs. All the adventurous boy that was in them years ago had been killed. Slobs, getting fat and middle-aged, bragging of their stupid brawls, reciting the commonplaces of their days.

As I left, I saw Studs' kid sister. She was crying so pitifully that she was unable to recognize me. I didn't see how she could ever have been affectionate toward Studs. He was so outside of her understanding. I knew she never mentioned him to me the few times I took her out. But she cried pitifully.

As I left, I thought that Studs had looked handsome. He would have gotten a good break, too, if only they hadn't given him Extreme Unction. For life would have grown into fatter and fatter decay for him, just as it was starting to do with Kelly, Doyle, Cooney and McCarthy. He, too, was a slob; but he died without having to live countless slobbish years. If only they had not sent him to Heaven where there are no whores and poolrooms.

I walked home with Joe, who isn't like the others. We couldn't feel sorry over Studs. It didn't make any difference.

"Joe, he was a slob," I said.

Joe did not care to use the same language, but he did not disagree.

And now the rain keeps falling on Studs' new grave, and his family mournfully watches the leaden sky, and his old buddies are at work wishing that it was Saturday night, and that they were just getting into bed with a naked voluptuous blonde.

William Saroyan
(1908–1981)

William Saroyan, a native of California, spent his early years in an orphanage until his widowed Armenian immigrant mother was financially able to care for her large number of children. He attended Fresno Junior High school until leaving at age twelve to earn money as a telegraph delivery boy.

Saroyan's success as a writer was immediate; the first of his stories to see print was published in an Armenian magazine and selected for the Best Short Stories of 1934 *collection. The* Daring Young Man on the Flying Trapeze *(1934), a gathering of stories in his characteristically impressionistic and enthusiastic style, was well received, and between 1936 and 1939, he published eight story collections. In 1939, he had a hit play,* My Heart's in the Highlands, *on Broadway and another,* The Time of Your Life, *won a Pulitzer Prize.*

Among Saroyan's dozens of other published works are autobiographical works ranging from My Name Is Aram *(1940) to* Chance Meetings *(1978), story collections, plays, and novels. His best-known novel,* The Human Comedy *(1942), centers on a boy who delivers telegrams during World War II.*

Saroyan's fascination with the immigrant experience and his tender amusement toward the human race shine through in all the genres. Often his Armenian relatives and friends appear as characters in his fiction, and references are made to incidents in Armenian history. "Antranik of Armenia," for instance, deals partially with events in 1915, when the Turkish Sultan Abd al-Hamid II accused the Armenians of aiding the Russians. The Armenians rose up against the Turks, and thousands died. In the treaties signed after World War I, Armenia became a Russian republic.

His later writings include *Short Drive, Sweet Chariot* (1966), *Places Where I've Done Time* (1972), and *Obituaries* (1979). The following story was first printed in *My Kind of Crazy Wonderful People* (1936) and then in a collection of works selected by the author, *The Saroyan Special* (1948).

Antranik of Armenia

WHEN MY GRANDMOTHER LUCY came to our house she sang about Antranik the soldier until I knew he was a mountain peasant on a black horse who with only a handful of men was fighting the enemy. That was in 1915, the year of physical pain and spiritual disintegration for the people of my country, and the people of the world, but I was seven and I didn't know. From my own meaningless grief I could imagine something was wrong in the world, but I didn't know what. My grandmother sang in a way that made me begin to find out, chanting mournfully and with great anger in a strong voice, while she worked in the house. I picked up the story of Antranik and Armenia in no time because it was in me in the first place and all I needed to do was hear the words to know the remembrance. I was an Armenian. God damn the Turks for making the trouble. (That is the way it is when you are an Armenian, and it is wrong. It is absurd, but I did not know. I did not know the Turk is a helpless man who does what he is forced to do. I did not know that hating him was the same as hating the Armenian since they were the same. My grandmother didn't know either, and still does not know. I know now, but I don't know what good it is going to do me because there is still idiocy in the world. Everybody in the world knows there is no such thing as nationality, but look at them. Look at Germany, Italy, France, England. Look at Russia. Look at Poland. Just look at all the maniacs. I can't figure out why they won't open their eyes and see that it is all idiocy. I can't figure out why they won't learn to use their strength for life instead of death, but it looks as if they won't. My grandmother is too old to learn, but how about all the people in the world who were born less than thirty years ago? How about all those people? Are they too young to learn? Or is it proper to work only for death?)

In 1915 General Antranik was part of the cause of the trouble in the world, but it wasn't his fault. There was no other way out for him and he was doing only what he had to do. The Turks were killing Armenians and General Antranik and his soldiers were killing Turks, but he wasn't destroying any real criminal because every real criminal was far from the scene of fighting. An eye for an eye, but always the wrong eye. And my grandmother prayed for the triumph and safety of General Antranik, although she knew Turks were good people. She herself said they were.

General Antranik had the same job in Armenia and Turkey that Lawrence of Arabia had in Arabia: to harass the Turkish Army and keep it from being a menace to the armies of Italy and France and England. General Antranik was a simple man who believed the governments of England and France and Italy when these governments told him his people would be given their freedom for making trouble for the Turkish Army. He was not an adventurous and restless English writer who was trying to come to terms with himself as to what was valid in the world for him, and unlike Lawrence of Arabia General Antranik did not know that what he was doing was stupid and futile because after the trouble the governments of England and France and Italy would betray him. He did not know a strong government needs and seeks the friendship of another strong government, and after the war there was nothing in the world for him or the people of Armenia. The strong governments talked about doing something for Armenia, but they never did anything. And the war was over and General Antranik was only a soldier, not a soldier and a diplomat and a writer. He didn't fight the Turkish Army because it would give him something to write about. He didn't write two words about the whole war. He fought the Turkish Army because he was an Armenian. When the war ended and the fine diplomatic negotiating began General Antranik was lost. The Turkish government looked upon him as a criminal and offered a large sum of money for his capture, dead or alive. General Antranik escaped to Bulgaria, but Turkish patriots followed him to Bulgaria, so he came to America.

General Antranik came to my home town. It looked as if all the Armenians in California were at the Southern Pacific depot the day he arrived. I climbed a telephone pole and saw him when he got off the train. He was a man of about fifty in a neat American suit of clothes. He was a little under six feet tall, very solid and very strong. He had an old-style Armenian moustache that was white. The expression of his face was both ferocious and kindly. The people swallowed him up and a committee got him into a great big Cadillac and drove away with him.

I got down from the telephone pole and ran all the way to my uncle's office. That was in 1919 or 1920, and I was eleven or twelve. Maybe it was a year or two later. It doesn't make any difference. Anyway, I was working in my uncle's office as office boy. All I used to do was go out and get him a cold watermelon once in a while which he used to cut in the office, right on his desk. He used to eat the big half and I used to eat the little half. If a client came to see him while he was eating watermelon, I would tell the client my uncle was very busy and ask him to wait in the reception room or come back in an hour. Those were the days for me and my uncle. He was a lawyer with a good practice and I was his nephew, his sister's son, as well as a reader of books. We used to talk in Armenian and English and spit the seeds into the cuspidor.

My uncle was sitting at his desk, smoking a cigarette.

Did you see Antranik? he said in Armenian.

In Armenian we never called him General Antranik, only in English.

I saw him, I said.

My uncle was very excited. Here, he said. Here's a quarter. Go and get a big cold watermelon.

When I came back with the watermelon there were four men in the office, the editor of the *Asbarez*, another lawyer, and two clients, farmers. They were all smoking cigarettes and talking about Antranik. My uncle gave me a dollar and told me to go and get as many more watermelons as I could carry. I came back with a big watermelon under each arm and my uncle cut each melon in half and each of us had half a melon to eat. There were only two big spoons and one butter knife, so the two farmers ate with their fingers, and so did I.

My uncle represented one of the farmers, and the other lawyer represented the other. My uncle's client said he had loaned two hundred dollars to the other farmer three years ago but had neglected to get a note, and the other farmer said he had never borrowed a penny from anybody. That was the argument, but nobody was bothering about it now. We were all eating watermelon and being happy about Antranik. At last the other attorney said, About this little matter?

My uncle squirted some watermelon seeds from his mouth into the cuspidor and turned to the other lawyer's client.

Did Hovsep lend you two hundred dollars three years ago? he said.

Yes, that is true, said the other farmer.

He dug out a big chunk of the heart of the watermelon with his fingers and pushed it into his mouth.

But yesterday, said the other lawyer, you told me he didn't lend you a penny.

That was yesterday, said the farmer. Today I saw Antranik. I have no money now, but I will pay him just as soon as I sell my crop.

Brother, said the farmer named Hovsep to the other farmer, that's all I wanted to know. I loaned you two hundred dollars because you needed the money, and I wanted you to pay me so people wouldn't laugh at me for being a fool. Now it is different. I don't want you to pay me. It is a gift to you. I don't need the money.

No, brother, said the other farmer, a debt is a debt. I insist upon paying.

My uncle swallowed watermelon, listening to the two farmers.

I don't want the money, said the farmer named Hovsep.

I borrowed two hundred dollars from you, didn't I? said the other farmer.

Yes.

Then I must pay you back.

No, brother, I will not accept the money.

But you must.

No.

The other farmer turned to his lawyer bitterly. Can we take the case to court and make him take the money? he said.

The other lawyer looked at my uncle whose mouth was full of watermelon. He looked at my uncle in a way that was altogether comical and Armenian, meaning, Well, what the hell do you call this? and my uncle almost choked with laughter and watermelon and seeds.

Then all of us busted out laughing, even the two farmers.

Countrymen, said my uncle. Go home. Forget this unimportant matter. This is a great day for us. Our hero Antranik has come to us from Hayastan, our native land. Go home and be happy.

The two farmers went away, talking together about the great event.

Every Armenian in California was happy about the arrival of Antranik from the old country.

One day six or seven months later Antranik came to my uncle's office while I was there. I knew he had visited my uncle many times while I was away from the office, in school, but this was the first time I had seen him in the office. I felt very angry because I could see how bewildered and bitter and disappointed he was. Where was the glorious new Armenia he had dreamed of winning for his people?

He came into the office quietly, almost shyly, as only a great man can be quiet and shy, and my uncle jumped up from his desk, loving him more than he loved any other man in the world, and through him loving the lost nation, the multitude dead, and the multitude living in every alien corner of the world. And I with my uncle, jumped up, loving him the same way, but *him* only, Antranik, the great man fallen to nothing, the soldier helpless in a world now full of cheap and false peace, he himself betrayed and his people betrayed, and Armenia only a memory.[1]

He talked quietly for about an hour and then went away, and when I looked at my uncle I saw that tears were in his eyes and his mouth was trembling like the mouth of a small boy who is in great pain but will not let himself cry.

That was what came of our little part in the bad business of 1915, and it will be the same with other nations, great and small, for many years to come because that way is the bad way, and even if your nation is strong enough to win the war, death of one sort or another is the only ultimate consequence, death, not life, is the only end, and it is always people, not nations, because it is all one nation, the living, so why won't they change the way? Why do they want to go on fooling themselves? They know there are a lot of finer ways to be strong than to be strong in numbers, in war, so why don't they cut it out? What do they want to do to the people of every nation in the world? The Turk is the brother of the Armenian and they know it. The German and the Frenchman, the Russian and the Pole, the Japanese and the Chinese. They are all brothers. They are all small tragic entities of mortality. Why do they want them to kill one another? What good does it do anybody?

I cherish the exhilaration that comes from having one's body and mind in opposition to a strong force, but why should that force be one's own brothers instead of something less subject to the agonies of mortality? Why can't the war be a nobler kind of war? Is every noble problem of man solved? Is there nothing more to do but kill? Everybody knows there are other things to do, so why won't they cut out the monkey business?

The governments of strong nations betrayed Antranik and Armenia after the war, but the soldiers of Armenia refused to betray themselves. It was no joke with them. The governments of strong nations were busy with complex diplomatic problems of their own. Their war was ended and the time had come for conversation. For the soldiers of Armenia the time had come for death or great good fortune, and the Armenian is too wise to believe in great good fortune.

---

1. Armenia lost its independent status through the Russo-Turkish Treaty of 1921 and became a Russian republic.

These were the Nationalists, the *Tashnaks*, and they fought for Armenia, for the nation Armenia, because it was the only way they knew how to fight for life and dignity. The world had no other way. It was with guns alone. It was the bad way, but these men were great men and they did what they had to do. They were dead wrong, but it was the only way. Well, they won the war. (No war is ever won: that is a technical term, used solely to save space and time.) Somehow or other the whole people was not annihilated. They were cold and hungry and ill, but these soldiers won their war and Armenia was a nation with a government and a political party, the *Tashnaks*. (That is so sad, that is so pathetic when you think of the thousands who were killed, but I honor the soldiers, those who died and those who still live. These I honor and love, and all who compromised I only love.) It was a mistake, but it was a noble mistake. It was a very small nation of course, a very unimportant nation, surrounded on all sides by enemies, but for two years, for the first time in thousands of years, Armenia was Armenia, and the capital was Erivan.

I know how silly it is to be proud, but I cannot help it, I am proud.

The war was with the Turks of course. The other enemies were less active than the Turks, but watchful. When the time came one of these, in the name of love, not hate, accomplished in no time at all what the Turks, who were more honest, whose hatred was unconcealed, could not accomplish in hundreds of years. These were the Russians. The new ones. They were actually the old ones, but they had a new theory and they said their idea was brotherhood on earth. They made a brother of Armenia at the point of a gun, but even so, if brotherhood was really their idea, that's all right. Very few of the Armenians of Armenia wanted to be brothers to the new Russians, but each of them was hungry and weary of the war and consequently the revolt against the new enemy was brief and tragic. It ended in no time at all. It looked as if the world simply wouldn't let the Armenians have their own country. They just didn't want the Armenians to have their nation. So it turned out that the leaders of the Armenian soldiers were criminals, so they were shot. That's all. The Russian brothers just shot them. Then they told the Armenians not to be afraid, the Turks wouldn't bother them any more. The brotherly Russian soldiers marched through the streets of the cities of Armenia and told everybody not to be afraid. Every soldier had a gun. There was a feeling of great brotherliness in Armenia.

Away out in California I sat in my uncle's office. To hell with it, I said. It's all over. We can begin to forget Armenia now. Antranik is dead. The nation is lost. The strong nations of the world are jumping with new problems. To hell with it. I'm no Armenian. I'm an American.

Well, the truth is I am both and neither. I love Armenia and I love America and I belong to both, but I am only this: an inhabitant of the earth, and so are you, whoever you are.

I tried to forget Armenia but I couldn't do it. My birthplace was California, but I couldn't forget Armenia, so what is one's country? Is it land of the earth, in a specific place? Rivers there? Lakes? The sky there? The way the sun comes up there? And the moon? Is one's country the trees, the vineyards, the grass, the birds, the rocks, the hills and mountains and valleys? Is it the temperature of the place in spring and summer and winter? Is it the animal rhythm of the living there? The huts and houses, the streets of cities, the tables and chairs, and the drinking of tea and talking? Is it the peach ripening in summer heat on the bough? Is it the dead in the earth there? The unborn? Is it the sound of the spoken language in all the places of that country under the sky? The printed word of that language? The picture painted there? The song of that throat and heart? That dance? Is one's country their prayers of thanks for air and water and earth and fire and life? Is it their eyes? Their lips smiling? The grief?

Well, I don't know for sure, but I know it is all these things as remembrance in the blood. It is all these things within one's self, because I have been there, I have been to Armenia and I have seen with my own eyes, and I know. I have been to *that* place. There is no nation there, but that is all the better. And I know this: that there is no nation in the world, no England and France and Italy, and no nation whatsoever. And I know that each who lives upon the earth is no more than a tragic entity of mortality, let him be king or beggar. I would like to see them awaken to this truth and stop killing one another because I believe there are other and finer ways to be great and brave and exhilarated, I believed there are ways whose ends are life instead of death. What difference does it make what the nation is or what political theory governs it? Does that in any way decrease for its subjects the pain and sorrow of mortality? Or in any way increase the strength and delight?

I went to see. To find out. To breathe that air. To be in that place.

The grapes of the Armenian vineyards were not yet ripe, but there were fresh green leaves, and the vines were exactly like the vines of California, and the faces of the Armenians of Armenia were exactly like the faces of the Armenians of California. The rivers Arax and Kura moved slowly through the fertile earth of Armenia in the same way that the rivers Kings and San Joaquin moved through the valley of my birthplace. And the sun was warm and kindly, no less than the sun of California.

And it was nowhere and everywhere. It was different and exactly the same, word for word, pebble for pebble, leaf for leaf, eye for eye and tooth for tooth. It was neither Armenia nor Russia. It was people alive in that place, and not people alone, but all things alive there, animate and inanimate: the vines, the trees, the rocks, the rivers, the streets, the buildings, the whole place, urban and rural. The automobile bounced over the dirt road to the ancient Armenian church at Aitchmiadzin, and the peasants, men and women and children, stood in bare feet on the ancient stone floor, looking up at the cross, bowing their heads, and believing. And the Armenian students of Marx laughed humbly and a little shamefully at the innocent unwisdom and foolish faith of their brothers. And the sadness of Armenia, my country, was so great in me that, sitting in the automobile, returning to Erivan, the only thing I could remember about Armenia was the quiet way General Antranik talked with my uncle many years ago and the tears in my uncle's eyes when he was gone, and the painful way my uncle's lips were trembling.

Richard Wright
(1908–1960)

*Born in rural Mississippi, near Natchez, Richard Wright was the grandson
of slaves. He lived with his mother and other relatives in towns in Mississippi, Arkansas, and Tennessee, almost always in poverty and gaining a
scant education at segregated schools that ended with the ninth grade. His
father, whom he described as "a black peasant who had gone to the city
seeking life, but who had failed in the city," deserted the family when
Wright was six. At fifteen he left home and went from one menial job to
another, leaving Memphis in 1927 for Chicago and the North. Always an
outsider, he had from childhood been driven to inward imaginings and
early decided that he wanted to be a writer, fueling his ambitions with
voracious reading in books obtained under a subterfuge from a whites-only
library in Memphis.*

*Important to Wright's development were the models of critical realism
and naturalistic philosophy found in the works of writers like Theodore
Dreiser, Stephen Crane, and Sinclair Lewis. Becoming active in the Communist Party in the 1930s, he wrote for journals like* New Masses *and* The Daily
Worker, *absorbing the literary tenets of Marxism. Supported from 1935 to
1937 by the Federal Writers Project, he produced his first book,* Uncle Tom's
Children: Four Novellas *(1938), stories of racial oppression in the South.
Well received, this collection led to the strong novel* Native Son *(1940), with
its harrowing tale of Bigger Thomas, a black man driven to murder and
finally condemned to die. Perhaps Wright's greatest achievement, however,
is the autobiographical* Black Boy: A Record of Childhood and Youth *(1945).
Told in direct, spare prose, with few moralistic asides, it details his life from
age four until the time when, "bearing scars, visible and invisible, I headed
North, full of a hazy notion that life could be lived with dignity."*

Convinced by the time of Black Boy *that he could not escape racism
even in the North, Wright moved with his family in 1946 to Paris, where
he died. There he produced two more American novels,* The Outsider *(1953)
and* The Long Dream *(1958), as well as other works of fiction and nonfiction. His legacy is a large body of work capped by the push that* Native Son
and Black Boy *gave to the emergent black American literature of the
decades after 1945.*

Posthumously published works include *Eight Men* (1961), stories; *Lawd Today* (1963), an early novel; and *American Hunger* (1977), a continuation of his autobiography. Earlier nonfiction includes *Twelve Million Black Voices: A Folk History of the Negro in the U.S.* (1941), *Black Power* (1954), *The Color Curtain* (1956), *Pagan Spain* (1957), and *White Man, Listen!* (1957). Studies include Constance Webb, *Richard Wright: A Biography* (1968), Michel Fabre, *The Unfinished Quest of Richard Wright* (1973), and Joyce Ann Joyce, *Richard Wright's Art of Tragedy* (1986).

[From] Black Boy

Chapter XIII. [A New Hunger]

ONE MORNING I arrived early at work and went into the bank lobby where the Negro porter was mopping. I stood at a counter and picked up the Memphis *Commercial Appeal* and began my free reading of the press. I came finally to the editorial page and saw an article dealing with one H. L. Mencken. I knew by hearsay that he was the editor of the *American Mercury*, but aside from that I knew nothing about him. The article was a furious denunciation of Mencken, concluding with one, hot, short sentence: Mencken is a fool.

I wondered what on earth this Mencken had done to call down upon him the scorn of the South. The only people I had ever heard denounced in the South were Negroes, and this man was not a Negro. Then what ideas did Mencken hold that made a newspaper like the *Commercial Appeal* castigate him publicly? Undoubtedly he must be advocating ideas that the South did not like. Were there, then, people other than Negroes who criticized the South? I knew that during the Civil War the South had hated northern whites, but I had not encountered such hate during my life. Knowing no more of Mencken than I did at that moment, I felt a vague sympathy for him. Had not the South, which had assigned me the role of a non-man, cast at him its hardest words?

Now, how could I find out about this Mencken? There was a huge library near the riverfront, but I knew that Negroes were not allowed to patronize its shelves any more than they were the parks and playgrounds of the city. I had gone into the library several times to get books for the white men on the job. Which of them would now help me to get books? And how could I read them without causing concern to the white men with whom I worked? I had so far been successful in hiding my thoughts and feelings from them, but I knew that I would create hostility if I went about this business of reading in a clumsy way.

I weighed the personalities of the men on the job. There was Don, a Jew; but I distrusted him. His position was not much better than mine and I knew that he was uneasy and insecure; he had always treated me in an offhand, bantering way that barely concealed his contempt. I was afraid to ask him to help me to get books; his frantic desire to demonstrate a racial solidarity with the whites against Negroes might make him betray me.

Then how about the boss? No, he was a Baptist and I had the suspicion that he would not be quite able to comprehend why a black boy would want to read Mencken. There were other white men on the job whose attitudes showed clearly that they were Kluxers or sympathizers, and they were out of the question.

There remained only one man whose attitude did not fit into an anti-Negro category, for I had heard the white men refer to him as a "Pope lover." He was an Irish Catholic and was hated by the white Southerners. I knew that he read books, because I had got him volumes from the library several times. Since he, too, was an object of hatred, I felt that he might refuse me but would hardly betray me. I hesitated, weighing and balancing the imponderable realities.

One morning I paused before the Catholic fellow's desk.

"I want to ask you a favor," I whispered to him.

"What is it?"

"I want to read. I can't get books from the library. I wonder if you'd let me use your card?"

He looked at me suspiciously.

"My card is full most of the time," he said.

"I see," I said and waited, posing my question silently.

"You're not trying to get me into trouble, are you, boy?" he asked, staring at me.

"Oh, no, sir."

"What book do you want?"

"A book by H. L. Mencken."

"Which one?"

"I don't know. Has he written more than one?"

"He has written several."

"I didn't know that."

"What makes you want to read Mencken?"

"Oh, I just saw his name in the newspaper," I said.

"It's good of you to want to read," he said. "But you ought to read the right things."

I said nothing. Would he want to supervise my reading?

"Let me think," he said. "I'll figure out something."

I turned from him and he called me back. He stared at me quizzically.

"Richard, don't mention this to the other white men," he said.

"I understand," I said. "I won't say a word."

A few days later he called me to him.

"I've got a card in my wife's name," he said. "Here's mine."

"Thank you, sir."

"Do you think you can manage it?"

"I'll manage fine," I said.

"If they suspect you, you'll get in trouble," he said.

"I'll write the same kind of notes to the library that you wrote when you sent me for books," I told him. "I'll sign your name."

He laughed.

"Go ahead. Let me see what you get," he said.

That afternoon I addressed myself to forging a note. Now, what were the names of books written by H. L. Mencken? I did not know any of them. I finally wrote what I thought would be a fool-proof note: *Dear Madam: Will you please let this nigger boy*—I used the word "nigger" to make the librarian feel that I could not possibly be the author of the note—*have some books by H. L. Mencken?* I forged the white man's name.

I entered the library as I had always done when on errands for whites, but I felt that I would somehow slip up and betray myself. I doffed my hat, stood a respectful distance from the desk, looked as unbookish as possible, and waited for the white patrons to be taken care of. When the desk was clear of people, I still waited. The white librarian looked at me.

"What do you want, boy?"

As though I did not possess the power of speech, I stepped forward and simply handed her the forged note, not parting my lips.

"What books by Mencken does he want?" she asked.

"I don't know, ma'am," I said, avoiding her eyes.

"Who gave you this card?"

"Mr. Falk," I said.

"Where is he?"

"He's at work, at the M—Optical Company," I said. "I've been in here for him before."

"I remember," the woman said. "But he never wrote notes like this."

Oh, God, she's suspicious. Perhaps she would not let me have the books? If she had turned her back at that moment, I would have ducked out the door and never gone back. Then I thought of a bold idea.

"You can call him up, ma'am," I said, my heart pounding.

"You're not using these books, are you?" she asked pointedly.

"Oh, no, ma'am. I can't read."

"I don't know what he wants by Mencken," she said under her breath.

I knew now that I had won; she was thinking of other things and the race question had gone out of her mind. She went to the shelves. Once or twice she looked over her shoulder at me, as though she was still doubtful. Finally she came forward with two books in her hand.

"I'm sending him two books," she said. "But tell Mr. Falk to come in next time, or send me the names of the books he wants. I don't know what he wants to read."

I said nothing. She stamped the card and handed me the books. Not daring to glance at them, I went out of the library, fearing that the woman would call me back for further questioning. A block away from the library I opened one of the books and read a title: *A Book of Prefaces*. I was nearing my nineteenth birthday and I did not know how to pronounce the word "preface." I thumbed the pages and saw strange words and strange names. I shook my head, disappointed. I looked at the other book; it was called *Prejudices*. I knew what that word meant; I had heard it all my life. And right off I was on guard against Mencken's books. Why would a man want to call a book *Prejudices*? The word was so stained with all my memories of racial hate that I could not conceive of anybody using it for a title. Perhaps I had made a mistake about Mencken? A man who had prejudices must be wrong.

When I showed the books to Mr. Falk, he looked at me and frowned.

"That librarian might telephone you," I warned him.

"That's all right," he said. "But when you're through reading those books, I want you to tell me what you get out of them."

That night in my rented room, while letting the hot water run over my can of pork and beans in the sink, I opened *A Book of Prefaces* and began to read. I was jarred and shocked by the style, the clear, clean, sweeping sentences. Why did he write like that? And how did one write like that? I pictured the man as a raging demon, slashing with his pen, consumed with hate, denouncing everything American, extolling everything European or German, laughing at the weaknesses of people, mocking God, authority. What was this? I stood up, trying to realize what reality lay behind the meaning of the words . . . Yes, this man was fighting, fighting with words. He was using words as a weapon, using them as one would use a club. Could words be weapons? Well, yes, for here they were. Then, maybe, perhaps, I could use them as a weapon? No. It frightened me. I read on and what amazed me was not what he said, but how on earth anybody had the courage to say it.

Occasionally I glanced up to reassure myself that I was alone in the room. Who were these men about whom Mencken was talking so passionately? Who was Anatole France? Joseph Conrad? Sinclair Lewis, Sherwood Anderson, Dostoevski, George Moore, Gustave Flaubert, Maupassant, Tolstoy, Frank Harris, Mark Twain, Thomas Hardy, Arnold Bennett, Stephen Crane, Zola, Norris, Gorky, Bergson, Ibsen, Balzac, Bernard Shaw, Dumas, Poe, Thomas Mann, O. Henry, Dreiser, H. G. Wells, Gogol, T. S. Eliot, Gide, Baudelaire, Edgar Lee Masters, Stendhal, Turgenev, Huneker, Nietzche, and scores of others? Were these men real? Did they exist or had they existed? And how did one pronounce their names?

I ran across many words whose meanings I did not know, and I either looked them up in a dictionary or, before I had a chance to do that, encountered the word in a context that made its meaning clear. But what strange world was this? I concluded the book with the conviction that I had somehow overlooked something terribly important in life. I had once tried to write, had once reveled in feeling, had let my crude imagination roam, but the impulse to dream had been slowly beaten out of me by experience. Now

it surged up again and I hungered for books, new ways of looking and seeing. It was not a matter of believing or disbelieving what I read, but of feeling something new, of being affected by something that made the look of the
world different.

As dawn broke I ate my pork and beans, feeling dopey, sleepy. I went to
work, but the mood of the book would not die; it lingered, coloring everything I saw, heard, did. I now felt that I knew what the white men were feeling. Merely because I had read a book that had spoken of how they lived and
thought, I identified myself with that book. I felt vaguely guilty. Would I,
filled with bookish notions, act in a manner that would make the whites dislike me?

I forged more notes and my trips to the library became frequent. Reading grew into a passion. My first serious novel was Sinclair Lewis's *Main
Street*. It made me see my boss, Mr. Gerald, and identify him as an American type. I would smile when I saw him lugging his golf bags into the office.
I had always felt a vast distance separating me from the boss, and now I felt
closer to him, though still distant. I felt now that I knew him, that I could
feel the very limits of his narrow life. And this had happened because I had
read a novel about a mythical man called George F. Babbitt.

The plots and stories in the novels did not interest me so much as the
point of view revealed. I gave myself over to each novel without reserve,
without trying to criticize it; it was enough for me to see and feel something
different. And for me, everything was something different. Reading was like
a drug, a dope. The novels created moods in which I lived for days. But I
could not conquer my sense of guilt, my feeling that the white men around
me knew that I was changing, that I had begun to regard them differently.

Whenever I brought a book to the job, I wrapped it in newspaper—a
habit that was to persist for years in other cities and under other circumstances. But some of the white men pried into my packages when I was
absent and they questioned me.

"Boy, what are you reading those books for?"

"Oh, I don't know, sir."

"That's deep stuff you're reading, boy."

"I'm just killing time, sir."

"You'll addle your brains if you don't watch out."

I read Dreiser's *Jennie Gerhardt* and *Sister Carrie* and they revived in
me a vivid sense of my mother's suffering; I was overwhelmed. I grew
silent, wondering about the life around me. It would have been impossible
for me to have told anyone what I derived from these novels, for it was
nothing less than a sense of life itself. All my life had shaped me for the
realism, the naturalism of the modern novel, and I could not read enough of
them.

Steeped in new moods and ideas, I bought a ream of paper and tried to
write; but nothing would come, or what did come was flat beyond telling. I
discovered that more than desire and feeling were necessary to write and I
dropped the idea. Yet I still wondered how it was possible to know people
sufficiently to write about them? Could I ever learn about life and people?

To me, with my vast ignorance, my Jim Crow station in life, it seemed a task impossible of achievement. I now knew what being a Negro meant. I could endure the hunger. I had learned to live with hate. But to feel that there were feelings denied me, that the very breath of life itself was beyond my reach, that more than anything else hurt, wounded me. I had a new hunger.

In buoying me up, reading also cast me down, made me see what was possible, what I had missed. My tension returned, new, terrible, bitter, surging, almost too great to be contained. I no longer *felt* that the world about me was hostile, killing; I *knew* it. A million times I asked myself what I could do to save myself, and there were no answers. I seemed forever condemned, ringed by walls.

I did not discuss my reading with Mr. Falk, who had lent me his library card; it would have meant talking about myself and that would have been too painful. I smiled each day, fighting desperately to maintain my old behavior, to keep my disposition seemingly sunny. But some of the white men discerned that I had begun to brood.

"Wake up there, boy!" Mr. Olin said one day.

"Sir!" I answered for the lack of a better word.

"You act like you've stolen something," he said.

I laughed in the way I knew he expected me to laugh, but I resolved to be more conscious of myself, to watch my every act, to guard and hide the new knowledge that was dawning within me.

If I went north, would it be possible for me to build a new life then? But how could a man build a life upon vague, unformed yearnings? I wanted to write and I did not even know the English language. I bought English grammars and found them dull. I felt that I was getting a better sense of the language from novels than from grammars. I read hard, discarding a writer as soon as I felt that I had grasped his point of view. At night the printed page stood before my eyes in sleep.

Mrs. Moss, my landlady, asked me one Sunday morning:

"Son, what is this you keep on reading?"

"Oh, nothing. Just novels."

"What you get out of 'em?"

"I'm just killing time," I said.

"I hope you know your own mind," she said in a tone which implied that she doubted if I had a mind.

I knew of no Negroes who read the books I liked and I wondered if any Negroes ever thought of them. I knew that there were Negro doctors, lawyers, newspapermen, but I never saw any of them. When I read a Negro newspaper I never caught the faintest echo of my preoccupation in its pages. I felt trapped and occasionally, for a few days, I would stop reading. But a vague hunger would come over me for books, books that opened up new avenues of feeling and seeing, and again I would forge another note to the white librarian. Again I would read and wonder as only the naive and unlettered can read and wonder, feeling that I carried a secret, criminal burden about with me each day.

That winter my mother and brother came and we set up housekeeping, buying furniture on the installment plan, being cheated and yet knowing no way to avoid it. I began to eat warm food and to my surprise found that regular meals enabled me to read faster. I may have lived through many illnesses and survived them, never suspecting that I was ill. My brother obtained a job and we began to save toward the trip north, plotting our time, setting tentative dates for departure. I told none of the white men on the job that I was planning to go north; I knew that the moment they felt I was thinking of the North they would change toward me. It would have made them feel that I did not like the life I was living, and because my life was completely conditioned by what they said or did, it would have been tantamount to challenging them.

I could calculate my chances for life in the South as a Negro fairly clearly now.

I could fight the southern whites by organizing with other Negroes, as my grandfather had done. But I knew that I could never win that way; there were many whites and there were but few blacks. They were strong and we were weak. Outright black rebellion could never win. If I fought openly I would die and I did not want to die. News of lynchings were frequent.

I could submit and live the life of a genial slave, but that was impossible. All of my life had shaped me to live by my own feelings and thoughts. I could make up to Bess and marry her and inherit the house. But that, too, would be the life of a slave; if I did that, I would crush to death something within me, and I would hate myself as much as I knew the whites already hated those who had submitted. Neither could I ever willingly present myself to be kicked, as Shorty had done. I would rather have died than do that.

I could drain off my restlessness by fighting with Shorty and Harrison. I had seen many Negroes solve the problem of being black by transferring their hatred of themselves to others with a black skin and fighting them. I would have to be cold to do that, and I was not cold and I could never be.

I could, of course, forget what I had read, thrust the whites out of my mind, forget them; and find release from anxiety and longing in sex and alcohol. But the memory of how my father had conducted himself made that course repugnant. If I did not want others to violate my life, how could I voluntarily violate it myself?

I had no hope whatever of being a professional man. Not only had I been so conditioned that I did not desire it, but the fulfillment of such an ambition was beyond my capabilities. Well-to-do Negroes lived in a world that was almost as alien to me as the world inhabited by whites.

What, then, was there? I held my life in my mind, in my consciousness each day, feeling at times that I would stumble and drop it, spill it forever. My reading had created a vast sense of distance between me and the world in which I lived and tried to make a living, and that sense of distance was increasing each day. My days and nights were one long, quiet, continuously contained dream of terror, tension, and anxiety. I wondered how long I could bear it.

Jerre Mangione
(1909–)

Born and raised in Rochester, New York, Jerre Mangione was the child of Sicilian immigrants supported by the father's work as a pastry cook and paperhanger. Forbidden to speak English at home, he left the Sicilian neighborhood of his youth for the education at Syracuse University that enabled him to pursue his ambitions as a writer. Graduating in 1931, he worked during the Depression years in various writing and editorial positions, including a stint with the Federal Writers Project. Mount Allegro *(1943) established his reputation and led to Guggenheim and other fellowships, while he continued to work in government, advertising, and public relations. From 1961 until his retirement in 1977 he taught at the University of Pennsylvania.*

Written as nonfiction, Mount Allegro *was published as a novel when the publishers decided it would sell more copies that way, but although Mangione changed the names, the book remains primarily a memoir of his relationship to his Sicilian-American heritage. It tells of his childhood in Rochester, his breaking away to go to college, his first visit to the country of his ancestors. For the 1981 edition, the fifth, he wrote a "Finale," about the disappearance of his old neighborhood.*

Mangione's concern for things Sicilian is continued in two other books that focus on his relatives: Reunion in Sicily *(1950) and* A Passion for Sicilians: The World Around Danilo Dolci *(1968). Other books of nonfiction include* America Is Also Italian *(1969),* The Dream and the Deal: Federal Writers Project, 1936–43 *(1972), and* An Ethnic at Large: A Memoir of the Thirties and Forties *(1978). Novels are* The Ship and the Flame *(1948) and* Night Search *(1965).*

[From] Mount Allegro

Welcome to Girgenti

THE TALK OF MY ROCHESTER RELATIVES kept flashing through my mind and made nearly everything in Sicily seem familiar. Only two things took me by complete surprise: the poverty and the scenery. I had heard and read a great deal about Sicily's poor living conditions but, without actually coming face to face with them, I should never have known how shocking they were; I might never have realized that human beings could live in such poverty and still preserve their dignity.

The scenery was a revelation because I had come to Sicily expecting to see green meadows, softly undulating hills, and long stretches of vegetation. What I saw made me understand what time and nostalgia must have done to my relatives' memories. Within an hour after I took the train from Palermo to Girgenti I was plunged into a Wagnerian maze of naked solid-rock mountains. Precipices and cliffs arched overhead dangerously, like monsters of mythology frozen, solid, and shaved. Pluto and the Gates of Hades, indeed. It was a wonder that Sicilians were not a cringing people; a wonder that their eyes and hearts had any softness.

It was better toward the sea, near Girgenti. The blue of the Mediterranean was like daylight after the dark terror of the mountains. There was less nakedness. You often spotted patches of green where lemon, almond, and olive trees bloomed, wonderfully indifferent to the ravages of Nature around them. You could see the sky more easily. It made everything seem more gentle.

My entrance into Girgenti was as casual as though I had lived in the city all my life and were coming back from a weekened jaunt in Palermo. The conductor actually asked me if I had enjoyed my excursion in Palermo and when I told him I was from New York, he looked me over suspiciously and remarked that I 'didn't look like an American.' A few phrases of my personal concoction of Sicilian convinced him that I must be a foreigner; but I was depressed instead of flattered by his first impression. I had the terrifying feeling that I was going to be swallowed into this island of rock and never see America again. It was a worry that stayed with me all the way through Sicily and even on the mainland of Italy, where there were plenty of American consuls around.

The fear that the Fascists might get me was not entirely a product of my imagination. In the few days I had been in Italy I had already been severely cross-examined by Fascist officials in both Naples and Palermo. My American passport had made no noticeable impression on them. It was only after I produced the letter to the Minister of Propaganda that they stopped treating me as though I might be a spy or a deserter and believed that I was what I claimed to be.

When we reached the top of the mountain overlooking Girgenti, the train paused and exchanged whistles with another train. Sicilian trains seemed incapable of meeting each other without stopping and exchanging such endearments. The conductor stuck his head out of the door and called over to the engineer of the other train.

'One of my passengers says he is the son of Peppino Amoroso, the pastrymaker,' he yelled.

The engineer stretched his neck to get a good look at me and I obligingly made myself as conspicuous as possible. '*Ah si, lu figliu di Peppino,*'[1] he remarked nonchalantly, as though my father had left Sicily the day before. 'How is your father?' he asked politely. Then, when his engine was puffing away, he said: 'Give him my regards when you see him. Tell him his old friend Cicco Spina was asking about him.'

The train began to descend into Girgenti.

Pindar[2] called the city 'the most beautiful among mortal cities,' and a historian of its Greek period said that its people built as if they would never have to die and ate as though they would die tomorrow. Nature and man must have been more lavish then. All that is left of the Greeks' city is what was formerly the acropolis. Yet it still has beauty. It starts from the top of a long hill and unrolls itself down to a plain of olive trees and Greek temples, continuing down to the edge of the island to Porto Empedocle on the Mediterranean, the port town where my father and Luigi Pirandello[3] were born.

From the hilltop I could see the Mediterranean, with the golden-colored temples in between contrasting their brilliance with the dazzling blue of the sea. Immediately below me, nearly halfway down the slope, were the streets and houses of Girgenti, huddled together as closely as my relatives at a party. This was the city the Greeks called Akragas, the Romans and the Fascists called Agrigento, and my relatives called Girgenti. In deference to the latter, I preferred to think of it as Girgenti.

The Fascists also changed the names of the principal streets. The main street, which was known to my relatives as the Via Atenea, in honor of their Greek forbears, was now the Via Roma. But the street still overlooked the Greek temples and the sea; apparently, there was nothing the Fascists could do about that.

Most of the city's streets were little more than alleys cutting their way through the sloping huddle of stone houses like so many narrow gulleys. There was no pattern to them and, like people who try to avoid each other but do not succeed, they met at the most unexpected places. A local patriot explained to me that the narrowness of the streets and their lack of pattern were part of a grand strategy to resist the numerous armies who tried to take Girgenti. Civilian defense in those days was highly effective. From the second-story windows of their homes, the townspeople would empty buckets of scalding water and hot oil onto the swarms of invaders clogged in the

---

1. "Ah yes, the son of Peppino."

2. Pindar (518?–c. 438 B.C.), Greek lyric poet, lived for a time in Girgenti.

3. (1867–1936), Italian playwright.

streets below. Many a Carthaginian, I was told, was burned to death that way.

A large committee of uncles and cousins, some of them looking amazingly like me, were waiting for me at the station. At first they were solemn and polite and, as they took turns kissing and embracing me, they asked the usual questions about my journey and the health of my parents. I could not make out one relative from another. I kissed and let myself be kissed and knew that each one was closely related in some way, but I was too bewildered by their numbers to identify them.

One of my relatives, a man six feet tall who resembled an Irishman I knew in New York, sensed that I did not know who he was. With tears in his eyes, he caught me in his arms again and asked: 'Don't you know me? I am your father's brother, your Uncle Pitrinu.' He seemed hurt because I had not known it instinctively. I had once seen a photograph of him but it had been so retouched and prettified that it bore little resemblance to him.

I was at once struck by the fact that there were no women present. Later, when I learned to what extent the women of Girgenti were excluded from the lives of their menfolk, it did not seem so strange. I asked them where Rosario Alfano was. They told me he had gone to visit a sick relative in Messina but would be back to see me before I left.

They led me off to the car Uncle Pitrinu had rented especially for the occasion. On the way they stopped everyone they met and said: 'Meet the son of Peppino Amoroso. His name is Gerlando and he is from North America.' They were proud that I had come so far to see them, though a little disturbed by the fact that I had traveled from Palermo third class along with the peasants. As soon as they heard me laugh with them, they dropped their solemnity and treated me as though they had always known me. What did I do for a living? How much did I earn? What did the Americans think of Italy's victory over Ethiopia?[4]

They were disappointed in all my answer to these questions, but cheered up considerably when I showed them the letter to the Minister of Propaganda. After that, I was an important personage and was henceforth introduced to people as 'the son of Peppino Amoroso who has a letter of introduction to the Minister of Propaganda.' Inevitably, of course, I had to produce the letter to prove that the relative who was introducing me was not a liar.

They were amused by my brand of Sicilian. What in the world did I mean by such words as *conduttore, boto, signa*? They had never, of course, heard them. The true origin of *baccauso* first dawned on me then. Fortunately, there were enough authentic Sicilian words in my sentences to carry their meaning. Sometimes I managed to use a Sicilian idiom and then there would be a howl of laughter and congratulations, almost amounting to relief, for I was thereby establishing my identity with them.

They quarreled as to where I should stay. Each relative wanted me to be

---

4. Italy invaded Ethiopia in 1935, defeating it in 1936 and making it a part of Italian East Africa.

his guest and threatened to become offended if I did not accept his hospitality. I refused to decide and said I would leave it up to them. After much wrangling, they agreed I should first stay with my father's uncle, Stefano, because he was the oldest and because he had treated my father like a son after his parents died. After that, I was to stay with my Uncle Pitrinu because he was the closest of kin.

There was some dispute about this point. It developed that Uncle Pitrinu had not been on good terms with my father for the past twenty years. My father had loaned him three hundred dollars to come to America, which my uncle used instead to marry and set up a funeral establishment in Porto Empedocle. He had never returned the money nor answered my father's letters asking for it. But my relatives decided that inasmuch as Uncle Pitrinu had demonstrated his brotherly love by coming all the way from Porto Empedocle—five miles away—and paying for the rent of the car hired in my honor, he had a right to extend his hospitality to his American nephew for a few weeks. After that I could stay with . . .

I interrupted, pointing out that I could only be in Sicily a short time; and that I planned to visit several Italian cities to gather material for articles. They had known me less than a half-hour and already they were appalled to think that I could bear to leave them. 'You can come back to Italy some other time and see those cities. They will still be there. We may not,' they argued.

And my cousin Nardo said: 'I'll get you all the material you want for articles. I will introduce you to men in Girgenti who have read many books. They will tell you anything you want to know.' They talked of my departure with such eloquence and pain that I wondered whether they had forgotten I was staying a few weeks and not leaving that afternoon.

My Uncle Stefano skillfully put an end to the discussion. 'We must remember,' he said solemnly, 'that Gerlando has a letter to the Minister of Propaganda. He must take it to Rome and deliver it in person.' They were grateful for the explanation; it proved that I was not heartless. 'You just can't afford to keep a Minister waiting too long,' they explained to each other.

In their eagerness to show how much they loved me, they deluged me with hospitality. They poured it on me unmercifully, particularly at meal times. Breakfast and the midday meal were simple enough, but the evening repast was usually interspersed with noisy debates. I would insist I had eaten and drunk more than enough; they would tell me I had barely begun and pile my dish high with food again. '*Mangia, mangia,*[5] they urged. 'Eat it without bread, but eat it,' they would finally say in desperation. And, in desperation, I would try to eat more, though my appetite had long since been satisfied, for it was hopeless fighting their obsession to stuff me with food.

They took turns at dining me and each one tried to feed me more than the others. Some of the older relatives who remembered my father's fondness for sea-food and assumed I shared it went out of their way to cook the most exotic species they could buy. It was obvious that none of them could

5. "Eat, eat."

afford the quantities of food they served me, yet each family swore that their meal was but a snack and that I was starving myself before their very eyes. Two or three times I tried to buy some of the provisions, but they became offended at these attempts and forgave me only on the ground that I was an American and must have been brought up among a lot of Indians.

Their poverty made their hospitality seem all the more painful. The most prosperous of my relatives were the few who were civil-service employees and earned about seventy-five dollars a month. Their food and clothing expenses were easily as high as those in an average American city. In addition, they paid many fees and taxes unknown to my Rochester relatives, among them an artisan tax, and taxes on their furniture and even on outdoor stairways (so many lire for each step). I could not understand how most of my relatives could keep up with their taxes and living expenses; they were masons, carpenters, and laborers who worked only occasionally and did not earn nearly as much as the civil-service employees.

Like bureaucrats the world over, the civil-service workers were the most loquacious and faithful supporters of the Government. Their boasting was only equaled by that of the college boys who had had Fascism drilled into them from childhood. Those were days of drunken hope for such patriots, probably the only exultant ones the Fascists had enjoyed since they had come into power. Ethiopia had just been won and every loyal Fascist felt like a Caesar holding the world by the tail. 'Soon,' a young law student declaimed to me, 'we're going to show the world that the French are an effeminate race who can't fight and the English a weak and treacherous nation always trying to betray Italy.'

One of the most ardent Fascists I talked with was my cousin Nardo, who had a clerical job in the postoffice. He was fond of bragging that his two sons, eleven and twelve, could handle guns and bayonets like adult soldiers. The boys were just as proud of themselves and would come to see me in their smart black uniforms, demanding to be photographed. Their sister Ciccina, a handsome girl of fourteen, kept singing the latest Fascist songs to me and quoting resonant excerpts from Mussolini's speeches.

The children and the parents were disturbed by my lack of enthusiasm. They dragged out a book that must easily have weighed fifty pounds. It had been published in celebration of the Fascist Party's tenth anniversary and showed scores of roads, bridges, postoffices, and railway stations built since Mussolini took over. Nearly all of them were constructed in the more northern Italian cities around regions popular with tourists.

I asked why their government was doing nothing to improve some of the small towns I had visited around Girgenti where the housing conditions were disgusting and there was no water supply. I pointed out that even in Girgenti there were one-room homes occupied by an entire family and its livestock.

'That all takes time,' Nardo assured me. 'You must have fish blood in you if you can't respond to the wonderful things Mussolini has done for Italy. Take, for example, the train schedules. . . .'

I begged him to spare me that. He showed me another book containing memoirs and souvenirs of the Fascist revolution. On one page was pictured a group of Black Shirts holding up clubs and castor oil bottles as proudly as though they were trophies won at an athletic match.

Nardo's daughter pointed to them and gloated: 'That's how our Duce[6] got rid of the horrible Communists. If they try anything funny again, he'll give them some more whacks and lots of castor oil.' I shuddered, and she laughed. She did not realize I was shuddering for her and the rest of the patriots who would some day have to face the truth about their black-shirted heroes.

The patriots were noisy but relatively few. Most of my relatives showed no inclination to ballyhoo Fascism and were plainly skeptical of the daily newspaper accounts that described Ethiopia as the land of milk and honey. 'If Ethiopia is such a wonderful country, why haven't the English taken it over before?' one of them whispered to me.

The peasants, desperately poor and eager to grasp any straw of hope, were the most gullible. On a bus I heard one say to another, 'It must be wonderful to earn money every day.'

'Lucky dogs,' the other said, referring to some relatives who had been sent to Ethiopia to work. 'Some day they will be riding around in automobiles as they do in Brooklyn and we'll be writing them letters begging for money.'

'*Chi lu sa?*'[7] the first replied. 'Perhaps we too can be sent to Ethiopia. Then our relatives will be writing *us* for money.'

The proverty of the city was nothing compared to that of the little towns around it. You had only to take one look at them to know why their people had flocked in groves to foreign countries where they might eat and live as men should. My mother's home town was typical of such towns. The natives called it Munderialli but its official name was Realmonte. To reach it I climbed a steep hill from the railroad station.

Once I got to the top, the only heartening sight was the Mediterranean coming into a wide inlet about a mile away, with small vine-covered hills popping up gaily in between. The town was arranged on a plateau and completely exposed to the sun. There wasn't a tree or a bit of grass anywhere.

The nearest water supply was seven miles away. Every morning a man with a mule and a cart brought a barrel of water to Realmonte and sold it to the natives in bottles. An inferior quality of water was sold in barrels for washing purposes—so inferior that it had given many of the natives an eye disease which prevented them from migrating to America when our doors were still wide open.

Except for the rather elegant stone houses built for the priest, the mayor, and a few of the natives who had returned from America with dollars, the buildings had dismally regular features and were built close together. They were mostly of dark yellow stucco and arranged in rows along perfectly straight alleys. Realmonte had produced many clever masons, among them some of my Rochester relatives, but apparently they

---

6. Leader—popular term for Benito Mussolini (1883–1945).

7. "Who knows?"

had been able to do little for the beauty of the town except to make certain that everything was built in straight lines.

My aunt's house, no better or worse than the dozens of other homes I visited, had two rooms and a small hole in the wall just large enough to hold a stove. The floors and walls were of rough cement; the beams of the ceiling stuck out like the bones of a skinny man. There was no toilet in the house and no privy outside. On the walls were pasted long bulletins distributed by the Government telling Italians what to think of Mussolini and the Versailles Treaty.[8]

My aunt lived there with her two daughters and a thirty-year-old son. Andrea was eager to marry and was attracted to a girl in town who had the proper amount of linen for her dowry, but the marriage seemed to be out of the question because there was no one else to support his mother and sisters. One of the sisters was named Annunziata. On the first day we met she half-playfully suggested that we get married so that I could take her away to America. During the past year she had received as many as four proposals from young men of highly respectable families, but she said she was obliged to turn them down because she did not have the necessary dowry.

'I wish I could go to America,' she said. 'I hear that if a man and woman want to be married there, they simply go to church and then have a feast and that's all there is to it. What a wonderful country! Here she has to have linens and money if she wants to marry a man with a respectable background. And do you know that in Porto Empedocle a girl has to provide all the furniture besides the money and the linen. Do you wonder that there are so many spinsters there?'

My aunt had my mother's combination of strength and gentleness. She was one of the few relatives I met who was bitterly opposed to the 'Government' and did not hesitate to say so. 'The taxes are driving us crazy,' she would say again and again. 'If your mother did not send us clothes now and then, God knows what we should wear. Andrea earns eight lire (sixty cents then) a day when he works. How can a family of four possibly live on that?'

The 'Government' was one thing, but Il Duce was obviously something else in her mind. 'The only people we can be proud of in Italy are our King and our Duce. They are both men of genius and will keep us out of war. Andrea says that only the other day Mussolini in person took an airplane trip around this coast to make certain we were well protected. He must have flown right over our town.'

My aunt and cousins, like my relatives in Girgenti, were proud of me because I was an American. They put on their Sunday clothes and told everyone that 'Margarita's son' was visiting them. If anyone dared say that I spoke their language 'almost like a native,' they loudly resented it because they thought it detracted from my prestige as an American.

Andrea wore a suit I recognized as one I had discarded several years ago, and every day I was there my aunt wore the black silk dress I had brought

---

8. Treaty of 1919 that ended World War I, but left many, including Italians, dissatisfied with its provisions.

for her from New York. I asked her why she did not wear colors and pointed out that, after all, her husband had died all of five years ago.

'In Munderialli we are cursed with stupid ideas,' she said. 'I'm afraid I shall have to wear black till I die. Then they can dress me in anything they please. One thing I shall always hold against your uncle, *bonarma*, is that he would never consent to moving to another town. Most of the people here are common peasants who don't know any better and I have to put up with their ideas.'

On a Friday they bought a chicken for me and insisted I eat it while they fed on spaghetti. I objected so much that the chicken became cold, but in the end I had to eat every bit of it so that they would not be offended. The youngest daughter, Zina, who was the most devout, was the only one who said she would not eat meat on Fridays. The rest of them agreed that 'If we can afford to buy meat, the good Lord doesn't mind when we eat it.' Apparently God was as understanding in Sicily as he was in Rochester.

Every afternoon we visited persons who had known my mother when she lived there. Most of them were related to me. They all said I looked like my mother and showed me pictures of her as a young girl to prove they were right. One of them exclaimed: 'How strange Destiny is! A young girl leaves Munderialli for a land across the ocean, and thirty-five years later a young man arrives and tells us he is her son.'

Many of them anxiously asked me if their relatives in America had given me 'a little something' for them. They invariably meant dollar bills. In most instances I had to say no. I tried to explain that times were hard in America; that their relatives there were barely managing to earn a living and could only send their greetings. I could tell from their eyes that they didn't believe me. One particularly disappointed mother, who had received neither money nor greetings, asked me if there was something 'peculiar' about the American air that made people forget easily. Her son had not written her a line for ten years. 'I can't understand it,' she said. 'He used to love me so much. I had all I could do to persuade him to join his brothers in America.'

The townspeople would stare at us from their balconies and dark doorways as we walked along the streets through the chickens and the garbage. There were hardly any men around, and many of the women were gray-haired and dressed in black. My aunt would often stop to introduce me to some 'special friend of the family.' Related or not, they asked the same questions about the health of my mother, my age and my salary, the ages of my brother and sisters and whether or not they were married.

Some of them, when they learned I lived in New York, asked me questions that went something like this: 'Do you know so-and-so? He lives on such-and-such a street. Surely, you must have come across him. He is short and dark and has a funny scar on his forehead. They took particular pains to round up the three or four natives who had been to America and could speak some English. As soon as I was introduced to one of them, a crowd would form around us and beg us to speak *Americano*. As we tried to say a few sentences, the crowd would laugh uproariously and have a great deal of fun mimicking us.

One of the ex-Americans I met worked in the local post-office. In New

York, he had helped dig the Brooklyn subway. 'When there was no more
work, I came home and bought myself a job with the money I saved digging
the subway. The United States is a nice place but only when you are working.' He was a Fascist and spent considerable time explaining how Mussolini
was bringing glory to Italy. He justified Mussolini's imperialism on the
ground that Italy was overpopulated.

Why, then, I asked, was he asking for larger families? He laughed mis-
chievously and, pointing his forefinger to the center of his forehead, said,
'Ah, Mussolini is a very smart man.'

The other two ex-Americans were not nearly so patriotic. One of them
said he had made a 'big mistake' in leaving the United States and begged me
to do what I could to help him get back. 'I returned after I had saved a few
dollars because I thought living expenses here were less. Now they have
become higher than they were in America. We'll be paying taxes next for
the privilege of breathing.' For more than a year he had been trying to get
permission from the American consul in Palermo to return to America. He
had even written Mussolini a long letter explaining how impossible it was
for him to live in Italy and support his family on the salary he made as a
mason, but so far had received no reply. Like my aunt, he blamed his troubles on the 'Government,' not on Mussolini.

The third ex-American had no illusions about Fascism and took great
delight in expressing himself on the subject in four-letter Anglo-Saxon
words. 'Believe me, fellow, it is better to be dying in America than to be alive
and kicking in this country,' he assured me. He had lived in Brooklyn for
eight years, until the authorities learned that he had entered the country ille-
gally, and deported him. Now he was scheming to get back. As soon as he had
saved some money, he would pretend he wanted to work in Ethiopia. Once he
got there he would escape to Egypt. He was confident he would find a ship
there on its way to New York with a captain who could be bribed to take him
along. 'I'm going to get back to America if it is the last thing I do,' he said.

On my last evening in town, I sat on the piazza with a group of men,
exchanging thoughts while we watched the lighthouse in the distance
sweeping the Mediterranean with a large round ray. The younger men
avoided talking politics and asked questions about Hollywood movie stars
and the height of American skyscrapers. In the group was a young policeman named Vincenzo, who was home on leave from his station in Rome. He
quizzed me about the New York police, asking where they got their graft
now that Prohibition was over; if it was true that most of them had flat feet,
and whether or not they were popular with women.

It developed that his last question had a direct bearing on one of Vincenzo's recent and sad experiences as a policeman. The average Italian, he
pointed out, dislikes the *sbirro* (cop) on general principles. Dressed in civilian
clothes on a night off, he was strolling about looking for some girl who
would respond to his flirtations. In this way he made the acquaintance of a
young brunette, who was the daughter of a tobacconist. For the sake of expediency, Vincenzo told her he was a government clerk. Everything progressed

nicely until one evening when Vincenzo absent-mindedly walked into her father's store to buy some cigarettes. Behind the counter was the girl. The moment she realized I was a policeman,' he said mournfully, 'it was the end of everything. She has refused to have anything to do with me since.'

The older men preferred to talk of politics, but everything they said was a repetition of what had appeared in the Fascist press. I could almost finish the sentences they began.

'Some day,' one of them said, 'we shall be able to go to Ethiopia and live like kings.'

'That will mean the end of Munderialli,' one of the young men replied. He turned to me. 'Did you know that there are more people of Munderialli in America than there are here? The only reason everyone didn't leave was because they were either too old or had something wrong with their eyes.'

An elderly man resented this attitude. 'Wait until they finish painting the railroad station, then you will see that Munderialli will have a place on the map. And in a couple of years, when Mussolini lays in the water pipes, Munderialli will be quite a nice place to live in.'

'Yes,' answered the young man, 'if the taxes don't get us by that time.'

We talked until the lights went out. The old men told me that Italy and Germany could lick anybody but did not want war, that the Soviet Union was no good, and that the United States was their great friend and ally.

The next day I left town on a train that was a half-hour late.

Pietro diDonato
(1911–1992)

The son of an Italian immigrant bricklayer, Pietro diDonato was born in West Hoboken, New Jersey. After losing his father in a construction accident, he went to work when he was not much more than a child, helping to support his mother and numerous younger siblings. Trained as a bricklayer, he found himself out of work during the Depression, picked up an education from reading in public libraries, and began to write. From "Christ in Concrete," a story in Esquire, *sprang the autobiographical novel* Christ in Concrete *(1939), a harrowing account of tragedies brought on by haste and greed in the construction of America's monumental cities.*

A huge critical and popular success, Christ in Concrete *begins with the death of the father, Geremio, and traces the immediate effects on the family, including the son's beginnings as a bricklayer and the subsequent death of an uncle. For two decades after the publication of the novel, diDonato remained mostly silent, but in* Three Circles of Light *(1960) he took up the story again, enlarging the account to include the years before the father's death. In both books, diDonato's prose is staccato, laced with colloquialisms, and his plotting is episodic. Although* Christ in Concrete *remains the stronger book, taken together the two present a memorable picture of one family's experiences from the period around World War II into the nineteen twenties.*

DiDonato's other works include two religious biographies, *Immigrant Saint: The Life of Mother Cabrini* (1960) and *The Penitent* (1962), and a miscellany, *Naked Author* (1970).

———

[From] *Christ in Concrete*

Geremio

1

MARCH WHISTLED STINGING SNOW against the brick walls and up the gaunt girders. Geremio, the foreman, swung his arms about, and gaffed the men on.

Old Nick, the "Lean," stood up from over a dust-flying brick pile, tapped the side of his nose and sent an oyster directly to the ground. "Master Geremio, the Devil himself could not break his tail any harder than we here."

Burly Julio of the walrus mustache and known as the "Snoutnose" let fall the chute door of the concrete hopper and sang over in the Lean's direction: "Mari-Annina's belly and the burning night will make of me once more a milk-mouthed stripling lad . . ."

The Lean loaded his wheelbarrow and spat furiously. "Sons of two-legged dogs . . . despised of even the Devil himself! Work! Sure! For America beautiful will eat you and spit your bones into the earth's hole! Work!"

And with that his wiry frame pitched the barrow violently over the rough floor.

Snoutnose waved his head to and fro and with mock pathos wailed, "Sing on, O guitar of mine . . ."

Short, cheery-faced Tomas, the scaffoldman, paused with hatchet in hand and tenpenny spike sticking out from small dicelike teeth to tell the Lean as he went by, in a voice that all could hear, "Ah, father of countless chicks, the old age is a carrion!"

Geremio chuckled and called to him. "Hey, little Tomas, who are you to talk? You and big-titted Cola can't even hatch an egg, whereas the Lean has just to turn the door-knob of his bedroom and old Philomena becomes a balloon!"

Coarse throats tickled and mouths opened wide in laughter.

The Lean pushed his barrow on, his face cruelly furrowed with time and struggle. Sirupy sweat seeped from beneath his cap, down his bony nose and turned icy at its end. He muttered to himself. "Saints up, down, sideways and inside out! How many more stones must I carry before I'm overstuffed with the light of day! I don't understand . . . blood of the Virgin, I don't understand!"

Mike the "Barrel-mouth" pretended he was talking to himself and yelled out in his best English . . . he was always speaking English while the rest carried on in their native Italian. "I don't know myself, but somebodys whose gotta bigga buncha keeds and he alla times talka from somebodys elsa!"

Geremio knew it was meant for him and he laughed. "On the tomb of Saint Pimple-legs, this little boy my wife is giving me next week shall be the last! Eight hungry little Christians to feed is enough for any man."

Tomas nodded to the rest. "Sure, Master Geremio had a telephone call from the next bambino. Yes, it told him it had a little bell between instead of a rose bush. . . . It even told him its name!"

"Laugh, laugh all of you," returned Geremio, "but I tell you that all my kids must be boys so that they someday will be big American builders. And then I'll help them to put the gold away in the basements!"

A great din of riveting shattered the talk among the fast-moving men. Geremio added a handful of Honest tobacco to his corncob, puffed strongly, and cupped his hands around the bowl for a bit of warmth. The chill day caused him to shiver, and he thought to himself: Yes, the day is cold, cold . . . but who am I to complain when the good Christ Himself was crucified?

Pushing the job is all right (when has it been otherwise in my life?), but this job frightens me. I feel the building wants to tell me something; just as one Christian to another. Or perhaps the Easter week is making of me a spirit-seeing pregnant woman. I don't like this. Mr. Murdin tells me, Push it up! That's all he knows. I keep telling him that the underpinning should be doubled and the old material removed from the floors, but he keeps the inspector drunk and . . . "Hey, Ashes-ass! Get away from under that pilaster! Don't pull the old work. Push it away from you or you'll have a nice present for Easter if the wall falls on you!" . . . Well, with the help of God I'll see this job through. It's not my first, nor the . . . "Hey, Patsy number two! Put more cement in that concrete; we're putting up a building, not an Easter cake!"

Patsy hurled his shovel to the floor and gesticulated madly. "The padrone Murdin-sa tells me, 'Too much, too much! Lil' bit is plenty!' And you tell me I'm stingy! The rotten building can fall after I leave!"

Six floors below, the contractor called. "Hey, Geremio! Is your gang of dagos dead?"

Geremio cautioned the men. "On your toes, boys. If he writes out slips, someone won't have big eels on the Easter table."

The Lean cursed that the padrone could take the job and all the Saints for that matter and shove it . . .!

Curly-headed Lazarene, the roguish, pigeon-toed scaffoldman, spat a cloud of tobacco juice and hummed to his own music . . . "Yes, certainly yes to your face, master padrone . . . and behind, This to you and all your kind!"

The day, like all days, came to an end. Calloused and bruised bodies sighed, and numb legs shuffled toward shabby railroad flats . . .

"Ah, bella casa mio. Where my little freshets of blood and my good woman await me. Home where my broken back will not ache so. Home where midst the monkey chatter of my piccolinos I will float off to blessed slumber with my feet on the chair and the head on the wife's soft full breast."

These great child-hearted ones leave one another without words or ceremony, and as they ride and walk home, a great pride swells the breast . . .

"Blessings to Thee, O Jesus. I have fought winds and cold. Hand to hand I have locked dumb stones in place and the great building rises. I have earned a bit of bread for me and mine."

The mad day's brutal conflict is forgiven, and strained limbs prostrate themselves so that swollen veins can send the yearning blood coursing and pulsating deliciously as though the body mountained leaping streams.

The job alone remained behind . . . and yet, they also, having left the bigger part of their lives with it. The cold ghastly beast, the Job, stood stark, the eerie March wind wrapping it in sharp shadows of falling dusk.

That night was a crowning point in the life of Geremio. He bought a house! Twenty years he had helped to mold the New World. And now he was to have a house of his own! What mattered that it was no more than a wooden shack? It was his own!

He had proudly signed his name and helped Annunziata to make her X on the wonderful contract that proved them owners. And she was happy to think that her next child, soon to come, would be born under their own rooftree. She heard the church chimes, and cried to the children, "Children, to bed! It is near midnight. And remember, shut-mouth to the paesanos! Or they will send the evil eye to our new home even before we put foot."

The children scampered off to the icy yellow bedroom where three slept in one bed and three in the other. Coltishly and friskily they kicked about under the covers; their black iron-cotton stockings not removed . . . what! and freeze the peanut-little toes?

Said Annunziata, "The children are so happy, Geremio; let them be, for even I would dance a Tarantella." And with that she turned blushing. He wanted to take her on her word. She patted his hands, kissed them, and whispered. "Our children will dance for us . . . in the American style someday."

Geremio cleared his throat and wanted to sing. "Yes, with joy I could sing in a richer feeling than the great Caruso." He babbled little old-country couplets and circled the room until the tenant below tapped the ceiling.

Annunziata whispered, "Geremio, to bed and rest. Tomorrow is a day for great things . . . and the day on which our Lord died for us."

The children were now hard asleep. Heads under the cover, over . . . snotty noses whistling, and little damp legs entwined.

In bed Geremio and Annunziata clung closely to each other. They mumbled figures and dates until fatigue stilled their thoughts. And with chubby Johnny clutching fast his bottle and warmed between them . . . life breathed heavily, and dreams entertained in far, far worlds, the nation-builder's brood.

But Geremio and Annunziata remained for a long while staring into the darkness . . . silently.

At last Annunziata spoke. "Geremio?"

"Yes?"

"This job you are now working . . ."

"So?"

"You used always to tell me about what happened on the jobs . . . who was jealous, and who praised . . ."

"You should know by now that all work is the same . . ."

"Geremio. The month you have been on this job, you have not spoken a word about the work . . . And I have felt that I am walking into a dream. Is the work dangerous? Why don't you answer . . .?"

2

Job loomed up damp, shivery gray. Its giant members waiting.

Builders donned their coarse robes, and waited.

Geremio's whistle rolled back into his pocket and the symphony of struggle began.

Trowel rang through brick and slashed mortar rivets were machine-gunned fast with angry grind Patsy number one check Patsy number two check the Lean three check Julio four steel bellowed back at hammer donkey engines coughed purple Ashes-ass Pietro fifteen chisel point intoned stone thin steel whirred and wailed through wood liquid stone flowed with dull rasp through iron veins and hoist screamed through space Rosario the Fat twenty-four and Giacomo Sangini check . . . The multitudinous voices of a civilization rose from the surroundings and melted with the efforts of the Job.

The Lean as he fought his burden on looked forward to only one goal, the end. The barrow he pushed, he did not love. The stones that brutalized his palms, he did not love. The great God Job, he did not love. He felt a searing bitterness and a fathomless consternation at the queer consciousness that inflicted the ever mounting weight of structures that he *had to! had to!* raise above his shoulders! When, when and where would the last stone be? Never . . . did he bear his toil with the rhythm of song! Never . . . did his gasping heart knead the heavy mortar with lilting melody! A voice within him spoke in wordless language.

The language of worn oppression and the despair of realizing that his life had been left on brick piles. And always, there had been hunger and her bastard, the fear of hunger.

Murdin bore down upon Geremio from behind and shouted:

"Goddammit, Geremio, if you're givin' the men two hours off today with pay, why the hell are they draggin' their tails? And why don't you turn that skinny old Nick loose, and put a young wop in his place?"

"Now listen-a to me, Mister Murdin—"

"Don't give me that! And bear in mind that there are plenty of good barefoot men in the streets who'll jump for a day's pay!"

"Padrone—padrone, the underpinning gotta be make safe and . . ."

"Lissenyawopbastard! if you don't like it, you know what you can do!" And with that he swung swaggering away.

The men had heard, and those who hadn't knew instinctively.

The new home, the coming baby, and his whole background, kept the fire from Geremio's mouth and bowed his head. "Annunziata speaks of scouring the ashcans for the children's bread in case I didn't want to work on a job where. . . . But am I not a man, to feed my own with these hands? Ah, but day will end and no boss in the world can then rob me the joy of my home!"

Murdin paused for a moment before descending the ladder.

Geremio caught his meaning and jumped to, nervously directing the rush of work. . . . No longer Geremio, but a machinelike entity.

The men were transformed into single, silent beasts. Snoutnose steamed through ragged mustache whip-lashing sand into mixer Ashes-ass dragged under four-by-twelve beam Lean clawed wall knots jumping in jaws masonry crumbled dust billowed thundered choked . . .

At noon, dripping noses were blown, old coats thrown over shoulders, and foot-long sandwiches were toasted at the end of wire over the flames. Shadows were once again personalities. Laughter added warmth.

Geremio drank his wine from an old-fashioned magnesia bottle and munched a great pepper sandwich . . . no meat on Good Friday.

Said one, "Are some of us to be laid off? Easter is upon us and communion dresses are needed and . . ."

That, while Geremio was dreaming of the new house and the joys he could almost taste. Said he, "Worry not. You should know Geremio." It then all came out. He regaled them with his wonderful joy of the new house. He praised his wife and children one by one. They listened respectfully and returned him well wishes and blessings. He went on and on. . . . "Paul made a radio—all by himself, mind you! One can hear *Barney Google* and many American songs!"

"A radio!"

"An electric machine like magic—yes."

"With music and Christian voices?"

"That is nothing to what he shall someday accomplish!"

"Who knows," suggested Giacomo amazed, "but that Dio has deigned to gift you with a Marconi[1] . . ."

"I tell you, son of Geremio shall never never lay bricks! Paulie mine will study from books—he will be the great builder! This very moment I can see him . . . How proud he!"

Said they in turn: "Master Geremio, in my province it is told that for good luck in a new home, one is to sprinkle well with salt . . . especially the corners, and on moving day sweep with a new broom to the center and pick all up—but do not sweep it out over the threshold!"

"That may be, Pietro. But, Master Geremio, it would be better in my mind that holy water should bless. And also a holy picture of Saint Joseph guarding the door."

"The Americans use the shoe of a horse . . . there must be something in that. One may try . . ."

Snoutnose knew a better way. "You know, you know." He ogled his eyes and smacked his lips. Then, reaching out his hands over the hot embers . . . "To embrace a goose-fat breast and bless the house with the fresh milk. And one that does not belong to the wife . . . that is the way!"

Acid-smelling di Nobilis were lit. Geremio preferred his corncob. And Lazarene "tobacco-eater" proudly chawed his quid . . . in the American style.

The ascent to labor was made, and as they trod the ladder, heads turned and eyes communed with the mute flames of the brazier whose warmth they were leaving, not with willing heart, and in that fleeting moment the breast wanted much to speak of hungers that never reached the tongue.

About an hour later, Geremio called over to Pietro, "Pietro, see if Mister Murdin is in the shanty and tell him I must see him! I will convince him that the work must not go on like this . . . just for the sake of a little more profit!"

Pietro came up soon. "The padrone is not coming up. He was drinking from a large bottle of whisky and cursed in American words that if you did not carry out his orders—"

---

1. Guglielmo Marchese Marconi (1874–1937), Italian physicist and pioneer in wireless telegraphy.

Geremio turned away disconcerted, stared dumbly at the structure and mechanically listed in his mind's eye the various violations of construction safety. An uneasy sensation hollowed him. The Lean brought down an old piece of wall and the structure palsied. Geremio's heart broke loose and out-thumped the floor's vibrations, a rapid wave of heat swept him and left a chill touch in its wake. He looked about to the men, a bit frightened. They seemed usual, life-size, and moved about with the methodical deftness that made the moment then appear no different than the task of toil had ever been.

Snoutnose's voice boomed into him. "Master Geremio, the concrete is re-ady!"

"Oh yes, yes, Julio." And he walked gingerly toward the chute, but not without leaving behind some part of his strength, sending out his soul to wrestle with the limbs of Job, who threatened in stiff silence. He talked and joked with Snoutnose. Nothing said anything, nor seemed wrong. Yet a vague uneasiness was to him as certain as the foggy murk that floated about Job's stone and steel.

"Shall I let the concrete down now, Master Geremio?"

"Well, let me see—no, hold it a minute. Hey, Lazarene! Tighten the chute cables!"

Snoutnose straightened, looked about, and instinctively rubbed the sore small of his spine. "Ah," sighed he, "all the men feel as I—yes, I can tell. They are tired but happy that today is Good Friday and we quit at three o'clock—"And he swelled in human ecstasy at the anticipation of food, drink and the hairy flesh-tingling warmth of wife, and then, extravagant rest.

Geremio gazed about and was conscious of seeming to understand many things. He marveled at the strange feeling which permitted him to sense the familiarity of life. And yet—all appeared unreal, a dream pungent and nostalgic.

Life, dream, reality, unreality, spiraling ever about each other. "Ha," he chuckled, "how and from where do these thoughts come?"

Snoutnose had his hand on the hopper latch and was awaiting the word from Geremio. "Did you say something, Master Geremio?"

"Why yes, Julio, I was thinking—funny! A—yes, what is the time—yes, that is what I was thinking."

"My American can of tomatoes says ten minutes from two o'clock. It won't be long now, Master Geremio."

Geremio smiled. "No, about an hour . . . and then, home."

"Oh, but first we stop at Mulberry Street, to buy their biggest eels, and the other finger-licking stuffs."

Geremio was looking far off, and for a moment happiness came to his heart without words, a warm hand stealing over. Snoutnose's words sang to him pleasantly, and he nodded.

"And Master Geremio, we ought really to buy the sea-fruits with the shells—you know, for the much needed steam they put into the—"

He flushed despite himself and continued, "It is true, I know it—especially the juicy clams . . . uhmn, my mouth waters like a pump."

Geremio drew on his unlit pipe and smiled acquiescence. The men around him were moving to their tasks silently, feeling of their fatigue, but absorbed in contemplations the very same as Snoutnose's. The noise of labor seemed not to be noise, and as Geremio looked about, life settled over him a gray concert—gray forms, atmosphere and gray notes . . . Yet his off-tone world felt so near, and familiar.

"Five minutes from two," swished through Snoutnose's mustache.

Geremio automatically took out his watch, rewound and set it. Lazarene had done with the cables. The tone and movement of the scene seemed to Geremio strange, differently strange, and yet, a dream familiar from a timeless date. His hand went up in motion to Julio. The molten stone gurgled low, and then with heightening rasp. His eyes followed the stone-cementy pudding, and to his ears there was no other sound than its flow. From over the roofs somewhere, the tinny voice of *Barney Google* whined its way, hooked into his consciousness and kept itself a revolving record beneath his skullplate.

"Ah, yes, *Barney Google*, my son's wonderful radio machine . . . wonderful Paul." His train of thought quickly took in his family, home and hopes. And with hope came fear. Something within asked, "Is it not possible to breathe God's air without fear dominating with the pall of unemployment? And the terror of production for Boss, Boss and Job? To rebel is to lose all of the very little. To be obedient is to choke. O dear Lord, guide my path."

Just then, the floor lurched and swayed under his feet. The slipping of the underpinning below rumbled up through the undetermined floors.

Was he faint or dizzy? Was it part of the dreamy afternoon? He put his hands in front of him and stepped back, and looked up wildly. "No! No!"

The men poised stricken. Their throats wanted to cry out and scream but didn't dare. For a moment they were a petrified and straining pageant. Then the bottom of their world gave way. The building shuddered violently, her supports burst with the crackling slap of wooden gunfire. The floor vomited upward. Geremio clutched at the air and shrieked agonizingly. "Brothers, what have we done? Ahhh-h, children of ours!" With the speed of light, balance went sickeningly awry and frozen men went flying explosively. Job tore down upon them madly. Walls, floors, beams became whirling, solid, splintering waves crashing with detonations that ground man and material in bonds of death.

The strongly shaped body that slept with Annunziata nights and was perfect in all the limitless physical quantities thudded as a worthless sack amongst the giant débris that crushed fragile flesh and bone with centrifugal intensity.

Darkness blotted out his terror and the resistless form twisted, catapulted insanely in its directionless flight, and shot down neatly and deliberately between the empty wooden forms of a foundation wall pilaster in upright position, his blue swollen face pressed against the form and his arms outstretched, caught securely through the meat by the thin round bars of reinforcing steel.

The huge concrete hopper that was sustained by an independent structure of thick timber wavered a breath or so, its heavy concrete rolling uneasily until a great sixteen-inch wall caught it squarely with all the terrific verdict of its dead weight and impelled it downward through joists, beams and masonry until it stopped short, arrested by two girders, an arm's length above Geremio's head; the gray concrete gushing from the hopper mouth, and sealing up the mute figure.

Giacomo had been thrown clear of the building and dropped six floors to the street gutter, where he lay writhing.

The Lean had evinced no emotion. When the walls descended, he did not move. He lowered his head. One minute later he was hanging in mid-air, his chin on his chest, his eyes tearing loose from their sockets, a green foam bubbling from his mouth and his body spasming, suspended by the shreds left of his mashed arms, pinned between a wall and a girder.

A two-by-four hooked little Tomas up under the back of his jumper and swung him around in a circle to meet a careening I-beam. In the flash that he lifted his frozen cherubic face, its shearing edge sliced through the top of his skull.

When Snoutnose cried beseechingly, "Saint Michael!" blackness enveloped him. He came to in a world of horror. A steady stream, warm, thick, and sickening as hot wine, bathed his face and clogged his nose, mouth, and eyes. The nauseous sirup that pumped over his face clotted his mustache red and drained into his mouth. He gulped for air, and swallowed blood. As he breathed, the pain shocked him to oppressive semiconsciousness. The air was wormingly alive with cries, screams, moans, and dust, and his crushed chest seared him with a thousand fires. He couldn't see, nor breathe enough to cry. His right hand moved to his face and wiped at the gelatinizing substance, but it kept coming on, and a heartbreaking moan wavered about him, not far. He wiped his eyes in subconscious despair. Where was he? What kind of a dream was he having? Perhaps he wouldn't wake up in time for work, and then what? But how queer; his stomach beating him, his chest on fire, he sees nothing but dull red, only one hand moving about, and a moaning in his face!

The sound and clamor of the rescue squads called to him from far off.

Ah, yes, he's dreaming in bed, and, far out in the streets, engines are going to a fire. Oh, poor devils! Suppose his house were on fire? With the children scattered about in the rooms he could not remember! He must do his utmost to break out of this dream! He's swimming under water, not able to raise his head and get to the air. He must get back to consciousness to save his children!

He swam frantically with his one right hand, and then felt a face beneath its touch. A face! It's Angelina alongside of him! Thank God, he's awake! He tapped her face. It moved. It felt cold, bristly, and wet. "It moves so. What is this?" His fingers slithered about grisly sharp bones and in a gluey, stringy, hollow mass, yielding as wet macaroni. Gray light brought sight, and hysteria punctured his heart. A girder lay across his chest, his right hand clutched a grotesque human mask, and suspended almost on top of him was the twitching, faceless body of Tomas. Julio fainted with an inarticulate sigh. His fingers loosed and the bodiless headless face dropped and fitted to the side of his face while the drippings above came slower and slower.

The rescue men cleaved grimly with pick and ax.

Geremio came to with a start . . . far from their efforts. His brain told him instantly what had happened and where he was. He shouted wildly. "Save me! Save me! I'm being buried alive!"

He paused exhausted. His genitals convulsed. The cold steel rod upon which they were impaled froze his spine. He shouted louder and louder. "Save me! I am hurt badly! I can be saved I can—save me before it's too late!" But the cries went no farther than his own ears. The icy wet concrete reached his chin. His heart appalled. "In a few seconds I will be entombed. If I can only breathe, they will reach me. Surely, they will!" His face was quickly covered, its flesh yielding to the solid sharp-cut stones. "Air! Air!" screamed his lungs as he was completely sealed. Savagely he bit into the wooden form pressed upon his mouth. An eighth of an inch of its surface splintered off. Oh, if he could only hold out long enough to bite even the smallest hole through to air! He must! There can be no other way! He must! There can be no other way! He is responsible for his family! He cannot leave them like this! He didn't want to die! This could not be the answer to life! He had bitten halfway through when his teeth snapped off to the gums in the uneven conflict. The pressure of the concrete was such, and its effectiveness so thorough, that the wooden splinters, stumps of teeth, and blood never left the choking mouth.

Why couldn't he go any farther?

Air! Quick! He dug his lower jaw into the little hollowed space and gnashed in choking agonized fury. Why doesn't it go through! Mother of Christ, why doesn't it give? Can there be a notch, or two-by-four stud behind it? Sweet Jesu! No! No! Make it give . . . Air! Air!

He pushed the bone-bare jaw maniacally; it splintered, cracked, and a jagged fleshless edge cut through the form, opening a small hole to air. With a desperate burst the lung-prisoned air blew an opening through the shredded mouth and whistled back greedily a gasp of fresh air. He tried to breathe, but it was impossible. The heavy concrete was settling immutably and its rich cement-laden grout ran into his pierced face. His lungs would not expand and were crushing in tighter and tighter under the settling concrete.

"Mother mine—mother of Jesu—Annunziata—children of mine—dear, dear, for mercy, Jesu-Giuseppe e' Mari," his blue foamed tongue called. It then distorted in a shuddering coil and mad blood vomited forth. Chills and fire played through him and his tortured tongue stuttered, "Mercy, blessed Father—salvation, most kind Father—Saviour—Saviour of His children, help me—adored Saviour—I kiss your feet eternally—you are my Lord—there is but one God—you are my God of infinite mercy—Hail Mary divine Virgin—our Father who art in heaven hallowed be thy—name—our Father—my Father," and the agony excruciated with never-ending mount, "our Father—Jesu, Jesu, soon Jesu, hurry dear Jesu Jesu! Je-sssu . . .!" His mangled voice trebled hideously, and hung in jerky whimperings. Blood vessels burst like mashed flower stems. He screamed. "Show yourself now, Jesu! Now is the time! Save me! Why don't you come! Are you there! I cannot stand it—ohhh, why do you let it happen—where are you? Hurry hurry hurry!"

His bones cracked mutely and his sanity went sailing distorted in the limbo of the subconscious. With the throbbing tones of an organ in the hollow background, the fighting brain disintegrated and the memories of a baffled lifetime sought outlet.

He moaned the simple songs of barefoot childhood, scenes flashed desperately on and off, and words and parts of words came pitifully high and low from his inaudible lips.

Paul's crystal-set earphones pressed the sides of his head tighter and tighter, the organ boomed the mad dance of the Tarentella, and the hysterical mind sang cringingly and breathlessly, "Jesu my Lord my God my all Jesu my Lord my God my all Jesu my Lord my God my all Jesu my Lord my God my all."

Carlos Bulosan
(1913–1956)

The Bulosan family's small farm on the island of Luzon in the Philippines afforded a very meager existence to a large number of children; Carlos was the youngest boy. At the age of seventeen, he sailed for Seattle, Washington, using most of his scant savings for a steerage ticket. He had completed only three years of school and spoke almost no English.

Shortly after his arrival at the beginning of the Great Depression (1930), he was caught up in the effort to unionize cannery and agricultural workers. He was active in union activities all his life; one of his last jobs was editing a cannery workers' yearbook in Seattle. He held other jobs in Alaska and the Northwest, but spent most of his time in California.

Bulosan's health was always poor. In addition to serious injuries, he suffered from tuberculosis and spent two years (1936–1938) in the Los Angeles County Hospital where doctors removed one lung and all the ribs on his right side. During his hospitalization, he read a book a day and after his discharge, especially when he was out of work, he spent long hours in the Los Angeles Public Library.

His first publication, a story called "The End of the War" appeared in the New Yorker in 1944; five years later he wrote, "I am trying to write every day in the midst of utter misery and starvation." Bulosan depicted prejudice against Filipinos and the ways in which they were exploited by employers and labor contractors. In America Is in the Heart (1946), he depicted the lives of a largely male, uneducated, and unskilled group on the fringes of society from the perspective of "one who longed to become a part of America." America Is in the Heart *is a three-part memoir dealing with life in his native* barrio, *his immigration, experiences as a wanderer and migrant worker, and apprenticeship as a writer. The following passages are taken from the middle section and depict his wandering in the early thirties on the West Coast.*

———

[From] *America Is in the Heart*

[*West Coast Wanderings*]

CHAPTER XV

LIKE A THUNDERING RIVER the train rushed toward Pasco, crossing wide, level lands, and passing through badlands, plateaus, and rill-marked hills. At Grandview, a prairie town whose sharp winds cut through the valleys and swept the plains, a dozen men jumped on and several of them came to my car. Two looked like professional hoboes, but the others were young men in search of work. I did not notice that there was a girl among them until we reached Kennewick,[1] when the railroad detectives came to the boxes and

---

1. All the towns mentioned are along the southern border of central Washington.

scattered us among the trees. When they were gone and we had run back to the car, I learned that she was with her brother, who was younger than she. They were on their way to California where an uncle was waiting for them.

The sun went down slowly and sudden darkness came over the land. I sat back in my corner and tried to sleep, brushing off the obscene conversations of the men around me. Then in the middle of the night, isolated in a corner of the box, I was awakened by the young girl's whimpering. She was desperately struggling with someone in the dark, breathing as though she were being choked to death. Then I heard her fall heavily on the floor, and she began to sob hopelessly. Her assailant dragged her to my corner. I could hear the man fumbling at her. He was tearing hungrily at her clothes. I strained my eyes in the dark to see what was happening. After a while the girl did not struggle any more. She turned lifelessly toward me, and in the dark I could hear her agony.

With a sudden revulsion, I got up and felt for the man. But someone struck me on the head, and I rolled on the floor. There was silence for a long time; then as I returned to consciousness, I heard the stifled sobbing of the girl again. Another man approached her. . . .

When the train stopped many of the men in our car jumped out. The girl crawled about in the dark searching for her brother.

"Bill—Bill, honey, where are you?" she whispered.

But the boy had disappeared in the night. Afraid and alone, she leaned against the wall and cried brokenly. I got up from my corner and looked out. We were in Hood, on the Columbia River. It was still dark, but I could hear the rushing water and, somewhere on the other side of the town, the sharp whistle of another train. The girl spread some newspapers on the floor and lay down to sleep. I struck a match and watched her face affectionately. She looked a little like my older sister, Francisca. There was a sudden rush of warm feeling in me, yearning to comfort her with the words I knew. This ravished girl and this lonely night, in a freight train bound for an unknown city. . . . I could not hold back the tears that came to my eyes.

When we reached Portland it was already after midnight. The girl walked with me in the streets.

"Where are you going?" she asked me.

"I am looking for an address," I said, trying to make her understand my broken English. "But the houses are too dark."

"Do you have a friend here?" But she did not wait for an answer. "Let's go back to the station," she suggested.

We found a train about ready to leave for California. A few men came into the car where the girl and I were sitting. Then a woman came in with her husband, who was carrying a baby. There was a Negro boy with a harmonica; he kept playing for hours, stopping only to say "Salem!" "Eugene!" "Klamath Falls!"[2] when we passed through those places.

The girl leaned on me and went to sleep, her breath warming my face. I

---

2. Traveling from north to south in Oregon.

dozed off and did not waken until the following morning. The girl was gone, but the newspapers on which she had lain were still warm. Everybody was gone except the Negro boy with the harmonica. He was still playing. I kept staring at him because it was the first time I had ever seen a black person.

"Where are you going, boy?" he asked.

"California, sir," I said.

He laughed, "*Sir?*"

"Yes, sir," I said again.

"Boy, you are far from California!" He laughed aloud, taking up the harmonica again.

I opened the door and looked out. The train was still moving. When the train stopped at the station, the Negro began to laugh again.

"Boy, boy, boy!" he screamed. "This is Reno, Nevada!"

I went to the door again and looked out. Then I saw the startling sign:

RENO, THE BIGGEST SMALL CITY IN THE WORLD!

The girl had left three strands of her brown hair on my shoulder. I picked them up and wrapped them in a piece of newspaper. I do not know why I did it, but felt somehow that I would meet her again. Innocent-looking she was, and forlorn, and I felt that there was a bond between us, a bond of fear and a common loneliness.

When the Negro told me what train to take to California, I thanked him and left, hoping I would encounter him again. The cars were full of hoboes and drifting men, who sat on the floor eating stale bread and drinking cold coffee. The wide desert land was shimmering with heat, and except for a bit of brush here and there, it reminded me of my escape with Julio across the Rattlesnake Mountains.

At last we came to some mountains, tall frowning mountains, and deep, narrow rivers rushing down the canyons. I counted thirteen short tunnels before we came out to the border of California, rolling across a wide land of luxuriant vegetation and busy towns. Then there was a river, and not far off the town of Marysville loomed above a valley of grapes and sugar beets, all green and ready for the summer harvest.

I wanted to stop and walk around town, but some of the hoboes told me that there were thousands of Filipinos in Stockton. I remained on the same train until it got to Sacramento, where I boarded another that took me to Stockton. It was twilight when the train pulled into the yards. I asked some of the hoboes where I could find Chinatown, for there I would be sure to find my countrymen.

"El Dorado Street," they said.

It was like a song, for the words actually mean "the land of gold." I did not know that I wanted gold in the new land, but the name was like a song. I walked slowly in the streets, avoiding the business district and the lights. Then familiar signs glowed in the coming night, and I began to walk faster. I saw many Filipinos in magnificent suits standing in front of poolrooms and gambling houses. There must have been hundreds in the street somewhere, waiting for the night.

I walked eagerly among them, looking into every face and hoping to see a familiar one. The asparagus season was over and most of the Filipino farmhands were in town, bent on spending their earnings because they had no other place to go. They were sitting in the bars and poolrooms, in the dance halls and gambling dens; and when they had lost or spent all their money, they went to the whorehouses and pawed at the prostitutes.

I entered a big gambling house on El Dorado and Lafayette Streets, where ten prostitutes circulated, obscenely clutching at some of the gamblers. I went to a stove in the middle of the room where a pot of tea was boiling. I filled a cup and then another, and the liquid warmed my empty stomach. This was to save me in harsher times, in the hungry years of my life in America. Dirnking tea in Chinese gambling houses was something tangible, and gratifying, and perhaps it was because of this that most of the Filipino unemployed frequented these places.

I was still drinking when a Chinese came out of a back room with a gun and shot a Filipino who was standing by a table. When the bullet hit the Filipino, he turned toward the Chinese with a stupid look of surprise. I saw his eyes and I knew that the philosophers lied when they said death was easy and beautiful. I knew that there was nothing better than life, even a hard life, even a frustrated life. Yes, even a broken-down gambler's life. And I wanted to live.

I ran to the door without looking back. I ran furiously down the street. A block away, I stopped in a doorway and stood, shivering, afraid, and wanting to spit out the tea that I had drunk in the gambling house. When my heart ceased pounding, I walked blindly up a side street. I had not gone far when I saw a building ablaze.

"What is it?" I asked a Filipino near me.

"It is the Filipino Federation Building," he said. "I don't agree with this organization, but I know why the building is burning. I know the Chinese gambling lords control this town."

I did not know what he meant. I looked at him with eager eyes.

"I don't know what you mean," I said. "I've just arrived in the United States."

"My name is Claro," he said, extending a long, thin hand, and coughing behind the other. "I came from Luna, in the province of La Union. Let us go to my restaurant and I will explain everything to you. Are you hungry, boy?"

He was not much older than I, and he spoke my dialect.

"I have not eaten for two days," I said. "You see, I took the freight train in Sunnyside, Washington."

Claro hugged me. When he entered the restaurant, he locked the door and put down the shades.

"I don't want the swine in the street to see us," he said, going to the stove. "They disgust me with their filthy interest in money. That is why I am always behind in my bills. I like good people, so I am keeping this restaurant for them."

I watched him prepare vegetable soup and fry a piece of chicken. When the pot started to boil, Claro put a record on a portable phonograph at the other end of the counter; then there was a sudden softness in his face, and his eyes shone. He had put on a Strauss waltz. Going back to the stove, Claro raised his hands expertly above his head in the manner of boleros and started to dance, swaying gracefully in the narrow space between the stove and the counter. He was smiling blissfully, and when someone knocked on the door he stopped suddenly and shouted:

"Go away! The place is closed for tonight!"

When he had placed everything on the counter, Claro took a chair and sat near me.

"Listen, my friend," he said. "The Chinese syndicates, the gambling lords, are sucking the blood of our people. The Pinoys work every day in the fields but when the season is over their money is in the Chinese vaults! And what do the Chinese do? Nothing! I see them only at night in their filthy gambling dens waiting for the Filipinos to throw their hard-earned money on the tables. Why, the Chinese control this town! The local banks can't do business without them, and the farmers, who badly need the health and interest of their Filipino workers, don't want to do anything because they borrow money from the banks. See!"

I was too hungry to listen. But I was also beginning to understand what he was trying to say.

"Perhaps in another year I will be able to understand what you are saying, Claro," I said.

"Stay away from Stockton," he warned me. "Stay away from the Chinese gambling houses, and the dance halls and the whorehouses operated by Americans. Don't come back to this corrupt town until you are ready to fight for our people!"

I thanked him and walked hastily to the door. I hurried to the freight yards. I was fortunate enough to find an empty boxcar. I sat in a corner and tried to sleep, but Claro's words kept coming back to me. He wanted me to go back to fight for our people when I was ready. I knew I would go back, but how soon I did not know. I would go back to Claro and his town. His food had warmed me and I felt good.

Chapter XVI

I began to be afraid, riding alone in the freight train. I wanted suddenly to go back to Stockton and look for a job in the tomato fields, but the train was already traveling fast. I was in flight again, away from an unknown terror that seemed to follow me everywhere. Dark flight into another place, toward other enemies. But there was a clear sky and the night was ablaze with stars. I could still see the faint haze of Stockton's lights in the distance, a halo arching above it and fading into a backdrop of darkness.

In the early morning the train stopped a few miles from Niles, in the midst of a wide grape field. The grapes had been harvested and the bare vines were falling to the ground. The apricot trees were leafless. Three railroad detectives jumped out of a car and ran toward the boxcars. I ran to the vineyard and hid behind a smudge pot, waiting for the next train from Stockton. A few bunches of grapes still hung on the vines, so I filled my pockets and ran for the tracks when the train came. It was a freight and it stopped to pick up carloads of grapes; when it started moving again the empties were full of men.

I crawled to a corner of a car and fell asleep. When I awakened the train was already in San Jose. I jumped outside and found another freight going south. I swung aboard and found several hoboes drinking cans of beer. I sat and watched them sitting solemnly, as though there were no more life left in the world. They talked as though there were no more happiness left, as though life had died and would not live again. I could not converse with them, and this barrier made me a stranger. I wanted to know them and to be a part of their life. I wondered what I had in common with them beside the fact that we were all on the road rolling to unknown destinations.

When I reached Salinas, I walked to town and went to a Mexican restaurant on Soledad Street. I was drinking coffee when I saw the same young girl who had disappeared in the night. She was passing by with an old man. I ran to the door and called to her, but she did not hear me. I went back to my coffee wondering what would become of her.

I avoided the Chinese gambling houses, remembering the tragedy in Stockton. Walking on the dark side of the street as though I were hunted, I returned eagerly to the freight yards. I found the hoboes sitting gloomily in the dark. I tried a few times to jump into the boxcars, but the detectives chased me away. When the freights had gone the detectives left.

Then an express from San Francisco came and stopped to pick up a few passengers. The hoboes darted out from the dark and ran to the rods. When I realized that I was the only one left, I grabbed the rod between the coal car and the car behind it. Then the express started, gathering speed as it nosed its way through the night.

I almost fell several times. The strong, cold wind lashed sharply at my face. I put the crook of my arm securely about the rod, pinching myself when I feared that I was going to sleep. It was not yet autumn and the sky was clear, but the wind was bitter and sharp and cut across my face like a knife. When my arm went to sleep, I beat it to life with my fist. It was the only way I could save myself from falling to my death.

I was so exhausted and stiff with the cold when I reached San Luis Obispo that I could scarcely climb down. I stumbled when I reached the ground, rolling over on my stomach as though I were headless. Then I walked to town, where I found a Filipino who took me in his car to Pismo Beach. The Filipino community was a small block near the sea—a block of poolrooms, gambling houses, and little green cottages where prostitutes were doing business. At first I did not know what the cottages were, but I saw many Filipinos going into them from the gambling houses near by. Then I guessed what they were, because cottages such as these were found in every Filipino community.

I went into one of the cottages and sat in the warm little parlor where the Filipinos were waiting their turn to go upstairs. Some of the prostitutes were sitting awkwardly in the men's laps, wheedling them. Others were dancing cheek to cheek, swaying their hips suggestively. The Filipinos stood around whispering lustily in their dialects. The girls were scantily dressed, and one of them was nude. The nude girl put her arms around me and started cooing lasciviously.

I was extricated from her by the same Filipino who had taken me into his car in San Luis Obispo. He came into the house and immediately took the girl upstairs. In ten minutes he was down again and asked me if I would like to ride with him to Lompoc. I had heard of the place when I was in Seattle, so naturally I was interested. We started immediately and in about two hours had passed through Santa Maria.

Beyond the town, at a railroad crossing, highway patrolmen stopped our car. Speaking to me in our dialect, Doro, my companion, said:

"These bastards probably want to see if we have a white woman in the car."

"Why?" I asked him, becoming frightened.

"They think every Filipino is a pimp," he said. "But there are more pimps among them than among all the Filipinos in the world put together. I will kill one of these bastards someday!"

They questioned Doro curtly, peered into the car, and told us to go on.

I came to know afterward that in many ways it was a crime to be a Filipino in California. I came to know that the public streets were not free to my people: we were stopped each time these vigilant patrolmen saw us driving a car. We were suspect each time we were seen with a white woman. And perhaps it was this narrowing of our life into an island, into a filthy segment of American society, that had driven Filipinos like Doro inward, hating everyone and despising all positive urgencies toward freedom.

When we reached the mountains to the right of the highway, we turned toward them and started climbing slowly, following the road that winds around them like a taut ribbon. We had been driving for an hour when we reached the summit, and suddenly the town of Lompoc shone like a constellation of stars in the deep valley below. We started downward, hearing the strong wind from the sea beating against the car. Then we came to the edge of the town, and church bells began ringing somewhere near a forest.

It was the end of the flower season, so the Filipino workers were all in town. They stood on the sidewalks and in front of Japanese stores showing their fat rolls of money to the girls. Gambling was going on in one of the old buildings, in the Mexican district, and in a café across the street Mexican girls and Filipinos were dancing. I went inside the café and sat near the counter, watching the plump girls dancing drunkenly.

I noticed a small Filipino sitting forlornly at one of the tables. He was smoking a cigar and spitting like a big man into an empty cigar box on the floor. When the juke box stopped playing he jumped to the counterman for some change. He put the nickels in the slot, waving graciously to the dancers although he never danced himself. Now and then a Filipino would go into the back room where the gamblers were playing cards and cursing loudly.

The forlorn Filipino went to the counter again and asked for change. He put all the nickels in the slot and bought several packages of cigarettes. He threw the cigarettes on the table near the juke box and then called to the old Mexican men who were sitting around the place. The Mexicans rushed for the table, grabbing the cigarettes. The Filipino went out lighting another big cigar.

I followed him immediately. He walked slowly and stopped now and then to see if I was following him. There was some mysterious force in him that attracted me. When he came to a large neon sign which said Landstrom Café, he stopped and peered through the wide front window. Then he entered a side door and climbed the long stairs.

I opened the door quietly and entered. I heard him talking to a man in one of the rooms upstairs. When I reached the landing a hard blow fell on my head. I rolled on the floor. Then I saw him with a gun in his hand, poised to strike at my head again. Standing behind him was my brother Amado, holding a long-bladed knife.

I scrambled to my feet screaming: "Brother, it is me! It is Allos! Remember?"

My brother told his friend to stop. He came near me, walking around me suspiciously. He stepped back and folded the blade of the knife. There was some doubt in his face.

"I am your brother," I said again, holding back the tears in my eyes. "I am Allos! Remember the village of Mangusmana? Remember when you beat our *carabao* in the rain? When you touched my head and then ran to Binalonan? Remember, Amado?" I was not only fighting for my life, but also for a childhood bond that was breaking. Frantically I searched in my mind for other remembrances of the past which might remind him of me, and re-establish a bridge between him and my childhood.

"Remember when I fell from the coconut tree and you were a janitor in the *presidencia*?" I said. "And you brought some magazines for me to read? Then you went away to work in the sugar plantations of Bulacan?"

"If you are really my brother tell me the name of our mother," he said casually.

"Our mother's name is Meteria," I said. "That is what the people call her. But her real name is Autilia Sampayan. We used to sell salted fish and salt in the villages. Remember?"

My brother grabbed me affectionately and for a long time he could not say a word. I knew, then, that he had loved my mother although he had had no chance to show it to her. Yes, to him, and to me afterward, to know my mother's name was to know the password into the secrets of the past, into childhood and pleasant memories; but it was also a guiding star, a talisman, a charm that lights us to manhood and decency.

"It has been so long, Allos," Amado said at last. "I had almost forgotten you. Please forgive me, brother. . . ."

"My name is Alfredo," said his friend. "I nearly killed you!" He laughed guiltily, putting the gun in his pocket. "Yes, I almost killed you, Allos!"

My brother opened the door of their room. It was a small room, with one broken chair and a small window facing the street. Their clothes were hanging on a short rope that was strung between the door and a cracked mirror. I sat on the edge of the bed, waiting for my brother to speak. Alfredo started playing solitaire on the table, laughing whenever he cheated himself.

"Go out in the hall and wash your hands," said my brother. "Then we will go downstairs for something to eat. Where is your suitcase?"

"I don't have any—now," I said. "I lost it when I was in Seattle."

"Have you been in Seattle?" he asked.

"I have been in Alaska, too," I said. "And other places."

"You should have written to me," he said. "You shouldn't have come to America. But you can't go back now. You can never go back, Allos."

I could hear men shouting in a bar two blocks down the street. Then church bells started ringing again, and the wind from the sea carried their message to the farmhouses in the canyon near the river. I knew that as long as there was a hope for the future somewhere I would not stop trying to reach it. I looked at my brother and Alfredo and knew that I would never stay with them, to rot and perish in their world of brutality and despair. I knew that I wanted something which would ease my fear and stop my flight from dawn to dawn.

"Life is tough, Carlos," said my brother. "I had a good job for some time, but the depression came. I had to do something. I had to live, Carlos!"

I did not know what he was trying to tell me. But I noticed that he had started using my Christian name. I noticed, too, that he spoke to me in English. His English was perfect. Alfredo's English was perfect also, but his accent was still strong. Alfredo tried to speak the way my brother spoke, but his uncultured tongue twisted ridiculously about in his mouth and the words did not come out right.

"We are in the bootleg racket," said my brother. "Alfredo and I will make plenty of money. But it is dangerous."

"I like money," Alfredo said. "It is everything."

They spoke with cynicism, but there was a grain of wisdom in their words. We were driving a borrowed car toward a farmhouse, away from the flower fields that made Lompoc famous. We drove across a dry river and into a wide orchard, then Alfredo knocked on the door. An Italian came to the door and told us to follow him into the back yard.

"How many bottles do you want?" he asked my brother, starting to dig under a eucalyptus tree.

"I think I can sell two dozen," said Amado.

"The big size?" asked the Italian.

"The big size," Alfredo said.

The Italian looked at me suspiciously. When he had all the bottles ready, Amado paid him, and the Italian opened a small bottle and passed it around to us. I refused to drink, and Alfredo laughed. Then we went to the car and drove carefully to town.

They disappeared with the bottles, peddling their bootleg whisky in gambling houses and places of questionable reputation. They were boisterous when they entered the room, throwing their money on the bed and talking excitedly. They were disappointed when I told them that I wanted to go to Los Angeles.

"Don't you want to go into business with us?" Alfredo asked me.

"Maybe I will come back someday," I said.

"Well, I was hoping you would want to begin early," he said. There was a note of genuine disappointment in his voice. He put some money in my pocket. "Here is something for you to remember me by."

"If you would like to go to school," said my brother in parting, "just let me know. But whatever you do, Carlos, don't lose your head. Good-bye!"

I sat in the bus and watched them walking toward the Mexican district. I wanted to cry because my brother was no longer the person I had known in Binalonan. He was no longer the gentle, hard-working janitor in the *presidencia*. I remembered the time when he had gone to Lingayen to cook for my brother Macario! Now he had changed, and I could not understand him any more.

"Please, God, don't change me in America!" I said to myself, looking the other way so that I would not cry.

Ralph Ellison
(1914–)

Ralph Waldo Ellison was born in Oklahoma City only seven years after the territory became a state. Growing up in the fluid social structure of the frontier, he glimpsed the creative potential inherent in a racially and ethnically diverse population.

His earliest creative interest was in music, especially the improvisational methods of jazz musicians. He enrolled in Tuskegee Institute in 1933, intending to study classical composition. During his second year, he took a literature course and experienced for the first time the emotional power of writing. Driven by financial worries, he left school and went to New York City where he hoped to be able to support himself while studying. In

Harlem he met Langston Hughes, who introduced him to the work of André Malraux. Richard Wright helped him get work writing essays and fiction for such leftist publications as New Challenge *and* New Masses. *Two of his best-known short stories, "Flying Home" and "King of the Bingo Game," were published in magazines during this period; there is no collection of his short fiction.*

Invisible Man (1952), Ellison's National Book Award-winning novel, was selected in a 1965 Book Week *poll of critics as the most significant work of fiction of the post-war period. It has continued to be viewed as a major work. Excerpts from a second novel, set in the South and spanning a long period of history, have been published in literary journals. Ellison is the author of two collections of essays:* Shadow and Act *(1964) and* Going to the Territory *(1986).*

Studies include Robert G. O'Meally, *The Craft of Ralph Ellison* (1980), and Alan Nadel, *Invisible Criticism: Ralph Ellison and the American Canon* (1988)

Flying Home

WHEN TODD CAME TO, he saw two faces suspended above him in a sun so hot and blinding that he could not tell if they were black or white. He stirred, feeling pain that burned as though his whole body had been laid open to the sun which glared into his eyes. For a moment an old fear of being touched by white hands seized him. Then the very sharpness of the pain began slowly to clear his head. Sounds came to him dimly. He done come to. Who are they? he thought. Naw he aint, I coulda sworn he was white. Then he heard clearly:

"You hurt bad?"

Something within him uncoiled. It was a Negro sound.

"He's still out," he heard.

"Give 'im time. . . . Say, son, you hurt bad?"

Was he? There was that awful pain. He lay rigid, hearing their breathing and trying to weave a meaning between them and his being stretched painfully upon the ground. He watched them warily, his mind traveling back over a painful distance. Jagged scenes, swiftly unfolding as in a movie trailer, reeled through his mind, and he saw himself piloting a tailspinning plane and landing and landing and falling from the cockpit and trying to stand. Then, as in a great silence, he remembered the sound of crunching bone, and now, looking up into the anxious faces of an old Negro man and a boy from where he lay in the same field, the memory sickened him and he wanted to remember no more.

"How you feel, son?"

Todd hesitated, as though to answer would be to admit an inacceptable weakness Then, "It's my ankle," he said.

"Which one?"

"The left."

With a sense of remoteness he watched the old man bend and remove his boot, feeling the pressure ease.

"That any better?"

"A lot. Thank you."

He had the sensation of discussing someone else, that his concern was with some far more important thing, which for some reason escaped him.

"You done broke it bad," the old man said. "We have to get you to a doctor."

He felt that he had been thrown into a tailspin. He looked at his watch; how long had he been here? He knew there was but one important thing in the world, to get the plane back to the field before his officers were displeased.

"Help me up," he said. "Into the ship."

"But it's broke too bad. . . ."

"Give me you arm!"

"But, son . . .

Clutching the old man's arm he pulled himself up, keeping his left leg clear, thinking, "I'd never make him understand," as the leather-smooth face came parallel with his own.

"Now, let's see."

He pushed the old man back, hearing a bird's insistent shrill. He swayed oddily. Blackness washed over him, like infinity.

"You best sit down."

"No, I'm O.K."

"But, son, You jus' gonna make it worse. . . ."

It was a fact that everything in him cried out to deny, even against the flaming pain in his ankle. He would have to try again.

"You mess with that ankle they have to cut your foot off," he heard.

Holding his breath, he started up again. It pained so badly that he had to bite his lips to keep from crying out and he allowed them to help him down with a pang of despair.

"It's best you take it easy. We gon' git you a doctor."

Of all the luck, he thought. Of all the rotten luck, now I have done it. The fumes of high-octane gasoline clung in the heat taunting him.

We kin ride him into town on old Ned," the boy said.

Ned? He turned, seeing the boy point toward an ox team browsing where the burned blade of a plow marked the end of a furrow. Thoughts of himself riding an ox through the town, past streets full of white faces, down the concrete runways of the airfield made swift images of humiliation in his mind. With a pang he remembered his girl's last letter. "Todd," she had written, "I don't need the papers to tell me you had the intelligence to fly. And I have always known you to be as brave as anyone else. The papers annoy me. Don't you be contented to prove over and over again that you're brave or skillful just because you're black. Todd. I think they keep beating that dead horse because they don't want to say why you boys are not yet fighting. I'm really disappointed, Todd. Anyone with brains can learn to fly, but then what? What about using it, and who will you use it for? I wish, dear, you'd write about this. I sometimes think they're playing a trick on us. It's very humiliating. . . ." He wiped cold sweat from his face, thinking, What does she know of humiliation? She's never been down South. Now the humiliation would come. When you must have them judge you, knowing that they never accept your mistakes as your own, but hold it against your whole race—that was humiliation. Yes and humiliation was when you could never be simply yourself, when you were always a part of this old black ignorant man. Sure, he's all right. Nice and kind and helpful. But he's not you. Well, there's one humiliation I can spare myself.

"No," he said, "I have orders not to leave the ship. . . ."

"Aw," the old man said. Then turning to the boy, "Teddy, then you better hustle down to Mister Graves and get him to come. . . ."

"No, wait!" he protested before he was fully aware. Graves might be white. "Just have him get word to the field, please. They'll take care of the rest."

He saw the boy leave, running.

"How far does he have to go?"

"Might' nigh a mile."

He rested back, looking at the dusty face of his watch. But now they know something has happened, he thought. In the ship there was a perfectly good radio, but it was useless. The old fellow would never operate it. That buzzard knocked me back a hundred years, he thought. Irony danced within him like the gnats circling the old man's head. With all I've learned I'm dependent upon this "peasant's" sense of time and space. His leg throbbed. In the plane, instead of time being measured by the rhythms of pain and a kid's legs, the instruments would have told him at a glance. Twisting upon his elbows he saw where dust had powdered the plane's fuselage, feeling the lump form in his throat that was always there when he thought of flight. It's crouched there, he thought, like the abandoned shell of a locust. I'm naked without it. Not a machine, a suit of clothes you wear. And with a sudden embarrassment and wonder he whispered, "It's the only dignity I have. . . ."

He saw the old man watching, his torn overalls clinging limply to him in the heat. He felt a sharp need to tell the old man what he felt. But that would be meaningless. If I tried to explain why I need to fly back, he'd think I was simply afraid of white officers. But it's more than fear . . . a sense of anguish clung to him like the veil of sweat that hugged his face. He watched the old man, hearing him humming snatches of a tune as he admired the plane. He felt a furtive sense of resentment. Such old men often came to the field to watch the pilots with childish eyes. At first it had made him proud; they had been a meaningful part of a new experience. But soon he realized they did not understand his accomplishments and they came to shame and embarrass him, like the distasteful praise of an idiot. A part of the meaning of flying had gone then, and he had not been able to regain it. If I were a prizefighter I would be more human, he thought. Not a monkey doing tricks, but a man. They were pleased simply that he was a Negro who could fly, and that was not enough. He felt cut off from them by age, by understanding, by sensibility, by technology and by his need to measure himself against the mirror of other men's appreciation. Somehow he felt betrayed, as he had when as a child he grew to discover that his father was dead. Now for him any real appreciation lay with his white officers; and with them he could never be sure. Between ignorant black men and condescending whites, his course of flight seemed mapped by the nature of things away from all needed and natural landmarks, under some sealed orders, couched in ever more technical and mysterious terms, his path curved swiftly away from both the shame the old man symbolized and the cloudy terrain of white men's regard. Flying blind, he knew but one point of landing and there he would receive his wings. After that the enemy would appreciate his skill and he would assume his deepest meaning, he thought sadly, neither from those who condescended nor from those who praised without understanding, but from the enemy who would recognize his manhood and skill in terms of hate. . . .

He sighed, seeing the oxen making queer, prehistoric shadows against the dry brown earth.

"You just take it easy, some," the old man soothes. "That boy won't take long. Crazy as he is about airplanes."

"I can wait," he said.

"What kinda airplane you call this here'n?"

"An Advanced Trainer," he said, seeing the old man smile. His fingers were like gnarled dark wood against the metal as he touched the low-slung wing.

"'Bout how fast can she fly?"

"Over two hundred an hour."

"Lawd! That's so fast I bet it don't seem like you moving!"

Holding himself rigid, Todd opened his flying suit. The shade had gone and he lay in a ball of fire.

"You mind if I take a look inside? I was always curious to see. . . ."

"Help yourself. Just don't touch anything."

He heard him climb upon the metal wing, grunting. Now the questions would start. Well, so you don't have to think to answer. . . .

He saw the old man looking over into the cockpit, his eyes bright as a child's.

"You must have to know a lot to work all these here things."

He was silent, seeing him step down and kneel beside him.

"Son, how come you want to fly way up there in the air?"

Because it's the most meaningful act in the world . . . because it makes me less like you, he thought.

But he said: "Because I like it, I guess. It's as good a way to fight and die as I know."

"Yeah? I guess you right," the old man said. "But how long you think before they gonna let you all fight?"

He tensed. This was the question all Negroes asked, put with the same timid hopefulness and longing that always opened a greater void within him than that he had felt beneath the plane the first time he had flown. He felt light-headed. It came to him suddenly that there was something sinister about the conversation, that he was flying unwillingly into unsafe and uncharted regions. If he could only be insulting and tell this old man who was trying to help him to shut up!

"I bet you one thing . . ."

"Yes?"

"That you was plenty scared coming down."

He did not answer. Like a dog on a trail the old man seemed to smell out his fears and he felt anger bubble within him.

"You sho' scared me. When I seen you coming down in that thing with it a-rollin' and a-jumpin' like a pitchin' hoss, I thought sho' you was a goner. I almost had me a stroke!"

He saw the old man grinning, "Ever'thin's been happening round here this morning, come to think of it."

"Like what?" he asked.

"Well, first thing I know, here come two white fellers looking for Mister Rudolph, that's Mister Graves's cousin. That got me worked up right away. . . ."

"Why?"

"Why? 'Cause he done broke outta the crazy house, that's why. He liable to kill somebody," he said. "They oughta have him by now though. Then here you come. First I think it's one of them white boys. Then dog-gone if you don't fall outta there. Lawd, I'd done heard about you boys but I haven't never seen one o' you-all. Cain't tell you how it felt to see somebody what look like me in a airplane!"

The old man talked on, the sound steaming around Todd's thoughts like air flowing over the fuselage of a flying plane. You were a fool, he thought, remembering how before the spin the sun had blazed bright against the bill-board signs beyond the town, and how a boy's blue kite had bloomed beneath him, tugging gently in the wind like a strange, odd-shaped flower. He had once flown such kites himself and tried to find the boy at the end of the invisible cord. But he had been flying too high and too fast. He had climbed steeply away in exultation. Too steeply, he thought. And one of the first rules you learn is that if the angle of thrust is too steep the plane goes into a spin. And then, instead of pulling out of it and going into a dive you let a buzzard panic you. A lousy buzzard!

"Son, what made all that blood on the glass?"

"A buzzard," he said, remembering how the blood and feathers had sprayed back against the hatch. It had been as though he had flown into a storm of blood and blackness.

"Well, I declare! They's lots of 'em around here. They after dead things. Don't eat nothing what's alive."

"A little bit more and he would have made a meal out of me," Todd said grimly.

"They bad luck all right. Teddy's got a name for 'em, calls 'em jim-crows," the old man laughed.

"It's a damned good name."

"They the damnedest birds. Once I seen a hoss all stretched out like he was sick, you know. So I hollers, 'Gid up from there, suh!' Just to make sho! An' doggone, son, if I don't see two ole jimcrows come flying right up outa that hoss's insides! Yessuh! The sun was shinin' on 'em and they couldn't a been no greasier if they'd been eating barbecue."

Todd thought he would vomit, his stomach quivered.

"You made that up," he said.

"Nawsuh! Saw him just like I see you."

"Well, I'm glad it was you."

"You see lots a funny things down here, son."

"No, I'll let you see them," he said.

"By the way, the white folks round here don't like to see you boys up there in the sky. They ever bother you?"

"No."

"Well, they'd like to."

"Someone always wants to bother someone else," Todd said. "How do you know?"

"I just know."

"Well," he said defensively, "no one has bothered us."

Blood pounded in his ears as he looked away into space. He turned, seeing a black spot in the sky, and strained to confirm what he could not clearly see.

"What does that look like to you?" he asked excitedly.

"Just another bad luck, son."

Then he saw the movement of wings with disappointment. It was gliding smoothly down, wings outspread, tail feathers gripping the air, down swiftly—gone behind the green screen of trees. It was like a bird he had imagined there, only the sloping branches of the pines remained, sharp against the pale stretch of sky. He lay barely breathing and stared at the point where it had disappeared, caught in a spell of loathing and admiration. Why did they make them so disgusting and yet teach them to fly so well? It's like when I was up in heaven, he heard, starting.

The old man was chuckling, rubbing his stubbled chin.

"What did you say?"

"Sho', I died and went to heaven . . . maybe by time I tell you about it they be done come after you."

"I hope so," he said wearily.

"You boys ever sit around and swap lies?"

"Not often. Is this going to be one?"

"Well, I ain't so sho', on account of it took place when I was dead."

The old man paused, "That wasn't no lie 'bout the buzzards, though."

"All right," he said.

"Sho' you want to hear 'bout heaven?"

"Please," he answered, resting his head upon his arm.

"Well, I went to heaven and right away started to sproutin' me some wings. Six good ones, they was. Just like them the white angels had. I couldn't hardly believe it. I was so glad that I went off on some clouds by myself and tried 'em out. You know, 'cause I didn't want to make a fool outta myself the first thing. . . ."

It's an old tale, Todd thought. Told me years ago. Had forgotten. But at least it will keep him from talking about buzzards.

He closed his eyes, listening.

". . . First thing I done was to git up on a low cloud and jump off. And doggone, boy, if them wings didn't work! First I tried the right; then I tried the left; then I tried 'em both together. Then Lawd, I started to move on out among the folks. I let 'em see me. . . ."

He saw the old man gesturing flight with his arms, his face full of mock pride as he indicated an imaginary crowd, thinking, It'll be in the newspapers, as he heard, ". . . so I went and found me some colored angels—somehow I didn't believe I was an angel till I seen a real black one, ha, yes! Then I was sho'—but they tole me I better come down 'cause us colored folks had to wear a special kin' a harness when we flew. That was how come they wasn't flyin'. Oh yes, an' you had to be extra strong for a black man even, to fly with one of them harnesses. . . ."

This is a new turn, Todd thought, what's he driving at?

"So I said to myself, I ain't gonna be bothered with no harness! Oh naw! 'Cause if God let you sprout wings you oughta have sense enough not to let nobody make you wear something what gits in the way of flyin'. So I starts to flyin'. Heck, son," he chuckled, his eyes twinkling, "you know I had to let ev'ybody know that old Jefferson could fly good as anybody else. And I could too, fly smooth as a bird! I could even loop-the-loop—only I had to make sho' to keep my long white robe down roun' my ankles. . . ."

Todd felt uneasy. He wanted to laugh at the joke, but his body refused, as of an independent will. He felt as he had as a child when after he had chewed a sugar-coated pill which his mother had given him, she had laughed at his efforts to remove the terrible taste.

". . . Well," he heard, "I was doing all right 'til I got to speeding. Found out I could fan up a right strong breeze, I could fly so fast. I could do all kin'sa stunts too. I started flying up to the stars and divin' down and zooming roun' the moon. Man, I like to scare the devil outa some ole white angels. I was raisin' hell. Not that I meant any harm, son. But I was just feeling good. It was so good to know I was free at last. I accidently knocked the tops offa some stars and they tell me I caused a storm and a coupla lynchings down here in Macon County—though I swear I believe them boys what said that was making up lies on me. . . ."

He's mocking me, Todd thought angrily. He thinks it's a joke. Grinning down at me . . . His throat was dry. He looked at his watch; why the hell didn't they come? Since they had to, why? One day I was flying down one of them heavenly streets. You got yourself into it, Todd thought. Like Jonah in the whale.

"Justa throwin' feathers in everybody's face. An' ole Saint Peter called me in. Said, 'Jefferson, tell me two things, what you doin' flyin' without a harness; an' how come you flyin' so fast?' So I tole him I was flyin' without a harness 'cause it got in my way, but I couldn'ta been flyin' so fast, 'cause I wasn't usin' but one wing. Saint Peter said, 'You wasn't flyin' with but one wing?' 'Yessuh,' I says, scared-like. So he says, 'Well, since you got sucha extra fine pair of wings you can leave off yo' harness awhile. But from now on none of that there one-wing flyin', 'cause you gittin' up too damn much speed!'"

And with one mouth full of bad teeth you're making too damned much talk, thought Todd. Why don't I send him after the boy? His body ached from the hard ground and seeking to shift his position he twisted his ankle and hated himself for crying out.

"It gittin' worse?"

"I . . . I twisted it," he groaned.

"Try not to think about it, son. That's what I do."

He bit his lip, fighting pain with counter-pain as the voice resumed its rhythmical droning. Jefferson seemed caught in his own creation.

". . . After all that trouble I just floated roun' heaven in slow motion. But I forgot, like colored folks will do, and got to flyin' with one wing again. This time I was restin' my old broken arm and got to flyin' fast enough to shame the devil. I was comin' so fast, Lawd, I got myself called befo' ole Saint Peter again. He said, 'Jeff, didn't I warn you 'bout that speedin'?' 'Yessuh,' I says, 'but it was an accident.' He looked at me sad-like and shook his head and I knowed I was gone. He said, 'Jeff, you and that speedin' is a danger to the heavenly community. If I was to let you keep on flyin', heaven wouldn't be nothin' but uproar. Jeff, you got to go!' Son, I argued and pleaded with that old white man, but it didn't do a bit of good. They rushed me straight to them pearly gates and gimme a parachute and a map of the state of Alabama . . ."

Todd heard him laughing so that he could hardly speak, making a screen between them upon which his humiliation glowed like fire.

"Maybe you'd better stop awhile," he said, his voice unreal.

"Ain't much more," Jefferson laughed. "When they gimme the parachute ole Saint Peter ask me if I wanted to say a few words before I went. I felt so bad I couldn't hardly look at him, specially with all them white angels standin' around. Then somebody laughed and made me mad. So I tole him, 'Well, you done took my wings. And you puttin' me out. You got charge of things so's I can't do nothing' about it. But you got to admit just this: While I was up here I was the flyinest sonofabitch what ever hit heaven!'"

At the burst of laughter Todd felt such an intense humiliation that only great violence would wash it away. The laughter which shook the old man like a boiling purge set up vibrations of guilt within him which not even the intricate machinery of the plane would have been adequate to transform and he heard himself screaming, "Why do you laugh at me this way?"

He hated himself at that moment, but he had lost control. He saw Jefferson's mouth fall open, "What—?"

"Answer me!"

His blood pounded as though it would surely burst his temples and he tried to reach the old man and fell, screaming, "Can I help it because they won't let us actually fly? Maybe we are a bunch of buzzards feeding on a dead horse, but we can hope to be eagles, can't we? Can't we?"

He fell back, exhausted, his ankle pounding. The saliva was like straw in his mouth. If he had the strength he would strangle this old man. This grinning, gray-headed clown who made him feel as he felt when watched by the white officers at the field. And yet this old man had neither power, prestige, rank nor technique. Nothing that could rid him of this terrible feeling. He watched him, seeing his face struggle to express a turmoil of feeling.

"What you mean, son? What you talking 'bout . . .?"

"Go away. Go tell your tales to the white folks."

"But I didn't mean nothing like that. . . . I . . . I wasn't tryin' to hurt your feelings. . . ."

"Please. Get the hell away from me!"

"But I didn't, son. I didn't mean all them things a-tall."

Todd shook as with a chill, searching Jefferson's face for a trace of the mockery he had seen there. But now the face was somber and tired and old. He was confused. He could not be sure that there had ever been laughter there, that Jefferson had ever really laughed in his whole life. He saw Jefferson reach out to touch him and shrank away, wondering if anything except the pain, now causing his vision to waver, was real. Perhaps he had imagined it all.

"Don't let it get you down, son," the voice said pensively.

He heard Jefferson sigh wearily, as though he felt more than he could say. His anger ebbed, leaving only the pain.

"I'm sorry," he mumbled.

"You just wore out with pain, was all. . . ."

He saw him through a blur, smiling. And for a second he felt the embarrassed silence of understanding flutter between them.

"What you was doin' flyin' over this section, son? Wasn't you scared they might shoot you for a crow?"

Todd tensed. Was he being laughed at again. But before he could decide, the pain shook him and a part of him was lying calmly behind the screen of pain that had fallen between them, recalling the first time he had ever seen a plane. It was as though an endless series of hangars had been shaken ajar in the air base of his memory and from each, like a young wasp emerging from its cell, arose the memory of a plane.

The first time I ever saw a plane I was very small and planes were new in the world. I was four-and-a-half and the only plane that I had ever seen

was a model suspended from the ceiling of the automobile exhibit at the
State Fair. But I did not know that it was only a model. I did not know how
large a real plane was, nor how expensive. To me it was a fascinating toy,
complete in itself, which my mother said could only be owned by rich little
white boys. I stood rigid with admiration, my head straining backwards as I
watched the gray little plane describing arcs above the gleaming tops of the
automobiles. And I vowed that, rich or poor, someday I would own such a
toy. My mother had to drag me out of the exhibit and not even the merry-
go-round, the Ferris wheel, or the racing horses could hold my attention for
the rest of the Fair. I was too busy imitating the tiny drone of the plane with
my lips, and imitating with my hands the motion, swift and circling, that it
made in flight.

After that I no longer used the pieces of lumber that lay about our back
yard to construct wagons and autos . . . now it was used for airplanes. I built
biplanes, using pieces of board for wings, a small box for the fuselage,
another piece of wood for the rudder. The trip to the Fair had brought something new into my small world. I asked my mother repeatedly when the Fair
would come back again. I'd lie in the grass and watch the sky, and each fighting bird became a soaring plane. I would have been good a year just to have
seen a plane again. I became a nuisance to everyone with my questions
about airplanes. But planes were new to the old folks, too, and there was little that they could tell me. Only my uncle knew some of the answers. And
better still, he could carve propellers from pieces of wood that would whirl
rapidly in the wind, wobbling noisily upon oiled nails.

I wanted a plane more than I'd wanted anything, more than I wanted
the red wagon with rubber tires, more than the train that ran on a track with
its train of cars. I asked my mother over and over again:

"Mamma?"

"What do you want, boy?" she'd say.

"Mamma, will you get mad if I ask you?" I'd say.

"What do you want now? I ain't got time to be answering a lot of fool
questions. What do you want?"

"Mamma, when you gonna get me one . . .?" I'd ask.

"Get you one what?" she'd say.

"You know, Mamma; what I been asking you. . . ."

"Boy," she'd say, "if you don't want a spanking you better come on an'
tell me what you talking about so I can get on with my work."

"Aw, Mamma, you know. . . ."

"What I just tell you?" she'd say.

"I mean when you gonna buy me a airplane."

"AIRPLANE! Boy, is you crazy? How many times I have to tell you to
stop that foolishness. I done told you them things cost too much. I bet I'm
gon' wham the living daylight out of you if you don't quit worrying me
'bout them things!"

But this did not stop me, and a few days later I'd try all over again.

Then one day a strange thing happened. It was spring and for some reason I had been hot and irritable all morning. It was a beautiful spring. I could feel it as I played barefoot in the backyard. Blossoms hung from the thorny black locust trees like clusters of fragrant white grapes. Butterflies flickered in the sunlight above the short new dew-wet grass. I had gone in the house for bread and butter and coming out I heard a steady unfamiliar drone. It was unlike anything I had ever heard before. I tried to place the sound. It was no use. It was a sensation like that I had when searching for my father's watch, heard ticking unseen in a room. It made me feel as though I had forgotten to perform some task that my mother had ordered . . . then I located it, overhead. In the sky, flying quite low and about a hundred yards off was a plane! It came so slowly that it seemed barely to move. My mouth hung wide; my bread and butter fell into the dirt. I wanted to jump up and down and cheer. And when the idea struck I trembled with excitement: "Some little white boy's plane's done flew away and all I got to do is stretch out my hands and it'll be mine!" It was a little plane like that at the Fair, flying no higher than the eaves of our roof. Seeing it come steadily forward I felt the world grow warm with promise. I opened the screen and climbed over it and clung there, waiting. I would catch the plane as it came over and swing down fast and run into the house before anyone could see me. Then no one could come to claim the plane. It droned nearer. Then when it hung like a silver cross in the blue directly above me I stretched out my hand and grabbed. It was like sticking my finger through a soap bubble. The plane flew on, as though I had simply blown my breath after it. I grabbed again, frantically, trying to catch the tail. My fingers clutched the air and disappointment surged tight and hard in my throat. Giving one last desperate grasp, I strained forward. My fingers ripped from the screen, I was falling. The ground burst hard against me. I drummed the earth with my heels and when my breath returned, I lay there bawling.

My mother rushed through the door.

"What's the matter, chile! What on earth is wrong with you?"

"It's gone! It's gone!"

"What gone?"

"The airplane . . ."

"Airplane?"

"Yessum, jus' like the one at the Fair. . . . I . . . I tried to stop it an' it kep' right on going . . ."

"When, boy?"

"Just now," I cried, through my tears.

"Where it go, boy, what way?"

"Yonder, there . . ."

She scanned the sky, her arms akimbo and her checkered apron flapping in the wind as I pointed to the fading plane. Finally she looked down at me, slowly shaking her head.

"It's gone! It's gone!" I cried.

"Boy, is you a fool?" she said. "Don't you see that there's a real airplane 'stead of one of them toy ones?"

"Real . . .?" I forgot to cry. "Real?"

"Yass, real. Don't you know that thing you reaching for is bigger'n a auto? You here trying to reach for it and I bet it's flying 'bout two hundred miles higher'n this roof." She was disgusted with me. "You come on in this house before somebody else sees what a fool you done turned out to be. You must think these here lil ole arms of you'n is mighty long. . . ."

I was carried into the house and undressed for bed and the doctor was called. I cried bitterly, as much from the disappointment of finding the plane so far beyond my reach as from the pain.

When the doctor came I heard my mother telling him about the plane and asking if anything was wrong with my mind. He explained that I had had a fever for several hours. But I was kept in bed for a week and I constantly saw the plane in my sleep, lying just beyond my fingertips, sailing so slowly that it seemed barely to move. And each time I'd reach out to grab it I'd miss and through each dream I'd hear my grandma warning:

> Young man, young man,
> Yo' arms too short
> To box with God. . . .

"Hey, son!"

At first he did not know where he was and looked at the old man pointing, with blurred eyes.

"Ain't that one of you-all's airplanes coming after you?"

As his vision cleared he saw a small black shape above a distant field, soaring through waves of heat. But he could not be sure and with the pain he feared that somehow a horrible recurring fantasy of being split in twain by the whirling blades of a propeller had come true.

"You think he sees us?" he heard.

"See? I hope so."

"He's coming like a bat outa hell!"

Straining, he heard the faint sound of a motor and hoped it would soon be over.

"How you feeling?"

"Like a nightmare," he said.

"Hey, he's done curved back the other way!"

"Maybe he saw us," he said. "Maybe he's gone to send out the ambulance and ground crew." And, he thought with despair, maybe he didn't even see us.

"Where did you send the boy?"

"Down to Mister Graves," Jefferson said. "Man what owns this land."

"Do you think he phoned?"

Jefferson looked at him quickly.

"Aw sho'. Dabney Graves is got a bad name on accounta them killings but he'll call though. . . ."

"What killings?"

"Them five fellers . . . ain't you heard?" he asked with surprise.

"No."

"Everybody knows 'bout Dabney Graves, especially the colored. He done killed enough of us."

Todd had the sensation of being caught in a white neighborhood after dark.

"What did they do?" he asked.

"Thought they was men," Jefferson said. "An' some he owed money, like he do me. . . ."

"But why do you stay here?"

"You black, son."

"I know, but . . ."

"You have to come by the white folks, too."

He turned away from Jefferson's eyes, at once consoled and accused. And I'll have to come by them soon, he thought with despair. Closing his eyes, he heard Jefferson's voice as the sun burned blood-red upon his lips.

"I got nowhere to go," Jefferson said, "an' they'd come after me if I did. But Dabney Graves is a funny fellow. He's all the time making jokes. He can be mean as hell, then he's liable to turn right around and back the colored against the white folks. I seen him do it. But me, I hates him for that more'n anything else. 'Cause just as soon as he gits tired helping a man he don't care what happens to him. He just leaves him stone cold. And then the other white folks is double hard on anybody he done helped. For him it's just a joke. He don't give a hilla beans for nobody—but hisself. . . ."

Todd listened to the thread of detachment in the old man's voice. It was as though he held his words arm's length before him to avoid their destructive meaning.

"He'd just as soon do you a favor and then turn right around and have you strung up. Me, I stays outa his way 'cause down here that's what you gotta do."

If my ankle would only ease for a while, he thought. The closer I spin toward the earth the blacker I become, flashed through his mind. Sweat ran into his eyes and he was sure that he would never see the plane if his head continued whirling. He tried to see Jefferson, what it was that Jefferson held in his hand? It was a little black man, another Jefferson! A little black Jefferson that shook with fits of belly-laughter while the other Jefferson looked on with detachment. Then Jefferson looked up from the thing in his hand and turned to speak, but Todd was far away, searching the sky for a plane in a hot dry land on a day and age he had long forgotten. He was going mysteriously with his mother through empty streets where black faces peered from behind drawn shades and someone was rapping at a window and he was looking back to see a hand and a frightened face frantically beckoning from a cracked door and his mother was looking down the empty perspective of the street and shaking her head and hurrying him along and at first it was only a flash he saw and a motor was droning as through the sun-glare he saw it gleaming silver as it circled and he was seeing a burst like a puff of white smoke and hearing his mother yell, Come along, boy, I got no time for

them fool airplanes, I got no time, and he saw it a second time, the plane flying high, and the burst appeared suddenly and fell slowly, billowing out
sparkling like fireworks and he was watching and being hurried along as the
air filled with a flurry of white pinwheeling cards that caught in the wind
and scattered over the rooftops and into the gutters and a woman was running and snatching a card and reading it and screaming and he darted into
the shower, grabbing as in winter he grabbed for snowflakes and bounding
away at his mother's, Come in here, boy! Come on, I say! and he was watching as she took the card away, seeing her face grow puzzled and turning taut
as her voice quavered, "Niggers Stay From The Polls," and died to a moan of
terror as he saw the eyeless sockets of a white hood staring at him from the
card and above he saw the plane spiraling gracefully, agleam in the sun like a
fiery sword. And seeing it soar he was caught, transfixed between a terrible
horror and a horrible fascination.

The sun was not so high now, and Jefferson was calling and gradually he
saw three figures moving across the curving roll of the field.

"Look like some doctors, all dressed in white," said Jefferson.

They're coming at last, Todd thought. And he felt such a release of tension within him that he thought he would faint. But no sooner did he close
his eyes than he was seized and he was struggling with three white men
who were forcing his arms into some kind of coat. It was too much for him,
his arms were/pinned to his sides as the pain blazed in his eyes, he realized
that it was a straitjacket. What filthy joke was this?

"That oughta hold him, Mister Graves," he heard.

His total energies seemed focused in his eyes as he searched their faces.
That was Graves; the other two wore hospital uniforms. He was poised
between two poles of fear and hate as he heard the one called Graves saying,
"He looks kinda purty in that there suit, boys. I'm glad you dropped by."

"This boy ain't crazy, Mister Graves," one of the others said. "He needs
a doctor, not us. Don't see how you led us way out here anyway. It might be
a joke to you, but your cousin Rudolph liable to kill somebody. White folks
or niggers, don't make no difference. . . ."

Todd saw the man turn red with anger. Graves looked down upon him,
chuckling.

"This nigguh belongs in a straitjacket, too, boys. I knowed that the minit
Jeff's kid said something 'bout a nigguh flyer. You all know you cain't let the
nigguh git up that high without his going crazy. The nigguh brain ain't built
right for high altitudes. . . ."

Todd watched the drawling red face, feeling that all the unnamed horror
and obscenities that he had ever imagined stood materialized before him.

"Let's git outta here," one of the attendants said.

Todd saw the other reach toward him, realizing for the first time that he
lay upon a stretcher as he yelled.

"Don't put your hands on me!"

They drew back, surprised.

"What's that you say, nigguh?" asked Graves.

He did not answer and thought that Graves's foot was aimed at his head. It landed on his chest and he could hardly breathe. He coughed helplessly, seeing Graves's lips stretch taut over his yellow teeth, and tried to shift his head. It was as though a half-dead fly was dragging slowly across his face and a bomb seemed to burst within him. Blasts of hot, hysterical laughter tore from his chest, causing his eyes to pop and he felt that the veins in his neck would surely burst. And then a part of him stood behind it all, watching the surprise in Graves's red face and his own hysteria. He thought he would never stop, he would laugh himself to death. It rang in his ears like Jefferson's laughter and he looked for him, centering his eyes desperately upon his face, as though somehow he had become his sole salvation in an insane world of outrage and humiliation. It brought a certain relief. He was suddenly aware that although his body was still contorted it was an echo that no longer rang in his ears. He heard Jefferson's voice with gratitude.

"Mister Graves, the Army done tole him not to leave his airplane."

"Nigguh, Army or no, you gittin' off my land! That airplane can stay 'cause it was paid for by taxpayers' money. But you gittin' off. An' dead or alive, it don't make no difference to me."

Todd was beyond it now, lost in a world of anguish.

"Jeff," Graves said, "you and Teddy come and grab holt. I want you to take this here black eagle over to that nigguh airfield and leave him."

Jefferson and the boy approached him silently. He looked away, realizing and doubting at once that only they could release him from his overpowering sense of isolation.

They bent for the stretcher. One of the attendants moved toward Teddy.

"Think you can manage it, boy?"

"I think I can, suh," Teddy said.

"Well, you better go behind then, and let yo' pa go ahead so's to keep that leg elevated."

He saw the white men walking ahead as Jefferson and the boy carried him along in silence. Then they were pausing and he felt a hand wiping his face; then he was moving again. And it was as though he had been lifted out of his isolation, back into the world of men. A new current of communication flowed between the man and boy and himself. They moved him gently. Far away he heard a mockingbird liquidly calling. He raised his eyes, seeing a buzzard poised unmoving in space. For a moment the whole afternoon seemed suspended and he waited for the horror to seize him again. Then like a song within his head he heard the boy's soft humming and saw the dark bird glide into the sun and glow like a bird of flaming gold.

Saul Bellow
(1915–)

Born in Montreal to Russian-Jewish parents newly arrived from St. Peters-
burg, Saul Bellow was raised in Chicago and attended The University of
Chicago and Northwestern University. After several years of supporting
his writing career with teaching and odd jobs, a 1948 Guggenheim Fellow-
ship stipend enabled him to live and write for two years in Paris. He
returned to New York, living and teaching in the East for a dozen years
before settling in Chicago.

Often his subject matter is the immigrant or second-generation experi-
ence, but his protagonists are not confined to a single category. In settings
ranging from urban ethnic ghettos to Iron Curtain countries or remote
African villages, they are searchers for the moral truths beneath varied
everyday experiences.

The recipient of many honors, including three National Book Awards,
the French Croix de Chevalier des Arts et Lettres, and the Pulitzer Prize,
Bellow was awarded the Nobel Prize for Literature in 1976.

Among his best-known works are The Adventures of Augie March
(1953), a picaresque novel of search for personal meaning; Henderson the
Rain King *(1959), in which a Gentile millionaire travels to Africa in search*
of his soul; and two studies of the artistic mind, Herzog *(1964) and* Humboldt's Gift *(1975). In* The Dean's December *(1982) an academic observer,*
wrenched from his scholarly isolation, compares life in American inner-city
slums with life under totalitarian regimes; the protagonist of More Die of
Heartbreak *(1987) observes his uncle, a famous botanist, struggle with the*
unscrupulous family he marries into.

"A Silver Dish" is from a collection of five stories, Him with His Foot in
His Mouth *(1984). Among Bellow's other novels, novellas, and story collec-*
tions are Dangling Man *(1944),* The Victim *(1947),* Seize the Day *(1956),*
Mosby's Memoirs and Other Stories *(1968),* Mr. Sammler's Planet *(1970),*
and A Theft *(1989).*

Scholarly studies include Mark Harris, *Saul Bellow: Drumlin Woodchuck* (1980);
Jonathan Wilson, *On Bellow's Planet: Readings from the Dark Side* (1985); and
Ellen Pifer, *Saul Bellow against the Grain* (1990).

A *Silver* Dish

WHAT DO YOU DO ABOUT DEATH—in this case, the death of an old father? If you're a modern person, sixty years of age, and a man who's been around, like Woody Selbst, what do you do? Take this matter of mourning, and take it against a contemporary background. How, against a contemporary background, do you mourn an octogenarian father, nearly blind, his heart enlarged, his lungs filling with fluid, who creeps, stumbles, gives off the odors, the moldiness or gassiness, of old men. I *mean!* As Woody put it, be realistic. Think what times these are. The papers daily give it to you—the Lufthansa pilot in Aden is described by the hostages on his knees, begging the Palestinian terrorists not to execute him, but they shoot him through the head. Later they themselves are killed. And still others shoot others, or shoot themselves. That's what you read in the press, see on the tube, mention at dinner. We know now what goes on daily through the whole of the human community, like a global death-peristalsis.

Woody, a businessman in South Chicago, was not an ignorant person. He knew more such phrases than you expect a tile contractor (offices, lobbies, lavatories) to know. The kind of knowledge he had was not the kind for which you get academic degrees. Although Woody had studied for two years in a seminary, preparing to be a minister. Two years of college during the Depression was more than most high-school graduates could afford. After that, in his own vital, picturesque, original way (Morris, his old man, was also, in his days of nature, vital and picturesque), Woody had read up on many subjects, subscribed to *Science* and other magazines that gave real information, and had taken night courses at De Paul and Northwestern in ecology, criminology, existentialism. Also he had traveled extensively in Japan, Mexico, and Africa, and there was an African experience that was especially relevant to mourning. It was this: on a launch near the Murchison Falls in Uganda, he had seen a buffalo calf seized by a crocodile from the bank of the White Nile. There were giraffes along the tropical river, and hippopotamuses, and baboons, and flamingos and other brilliant birds crossing the bright air in the heat of the morning, when the calf, stepping into the river to drink, was grabbed by the hoof and dragged down. The parent buffaloes couldn't figure it out. Under the water the calf still threshed, fought, churned the mud. Woody, the robust traveler, took this in as he sailed by, and to him it looked as if the parent cattle were asking each other dumbly what had happened. He chose to assume that there was pain in this, he read brute grief into it. On the White Nile, Woody had the impression that he had gone back to the pre-Adamite past, and he brought reflections on this impression home to South Chicago. He brought also a bundle of hashish from Kampala. In this he took a chance with the customs inspectors, banking perhaps on his broad build, frank face, high color. He didn't look like a wrongdoer, a bad guy; he looked like a good guy. But he liked taking chances. Risk was a wonderful stimulus. He threw down his trenchcoat on the customs counter. If the inspectors searched the pockets, he was prepared to say that the coat wasn't his. But he got away with it, and the Thanksgiving turkey was stuffed with hashish. This was much enjoyed. That was practically the last feast at which Pop, who also relished risk or defiance, was present. The hashish Woody had tried to raise in his backyard from the Africa seeds didn't take. But behind his warehouse, where the Lincoln Continental was parked, he kept a patch of marijuana. There was no harm at all in Woody, but he didn't like being entirely within the law. It was simply a question of self-respect.

After that Thanksgiving, Pop gradually sank as if he had a slow leak. This went on for some years. in and out of the hospital, he dwindled, his mind wandered, he couldn't even concentrate enough to complain, except in exceptional moments on the Sundays Woody regularly devoted to him. Morris, an amateur who once was taken seriously by Willie Hoppe, the great pro himself, couldn't execute the simplest billiard shots anymore. He could only conceive shots; he began to theorize about impossible three-cushion combinations. Halina, the Polish women with whom Morris had lived for over forty years as man and wife, was too old herself now to run to the hospital. So Woody had to do it. There was Woody's mother, too—a Christian convert—needing care; she was over eighty and frequently hospitalized. Everybody had diabetes and pleurisy and arthritis and cataracts and cardiac pacemakers. And everybody had lived by the body, but the body was giving out.

There were Woody's two sisters as well, unmarried, in their fifties, very Christian, very straight, still living with Mama in an entirely Christian bungalow. Woody, who took full responsibility for them all, occasionally had to put one of the girls (they had become sick girls) in a mental institution. Nothing severe. The sisters were wonderful women, both of them gorgeous once, but neither of the poor things was playing with a full deck. And all the factions had to be kept separate—Mama, the Christian convert; the fundamentalist sisters; Pop, who read the Yiddish paper as long as he could still see print; Halina, a good Catholic. Woody, the seminary forty years behind him, described himself as an agnostic. Pop had no more religion than you could find in the Yiddish paper, but he made Woody promise to bury him among Jews, and that was where he lay now, in the Hawaiian shirt Woody had bought for him at the tilers' convention in Honolulu. Woody would allow no undertaker's assistant to dress him, but came to the parlor and buttoned the stiff into the shirt himself, and the old man went down looking like Ben-Gurion[1] in a simple wooden coffin, sure to rot fast. That was how Woody wanted it all. At the graveside, he had taken off and folded his jacket, rolled up his sleeves on thick freckled biceps, waved back the little tractor standing by, and shoveled the dirt himself. His big face, broad at the bottom,

---

1. David Ben-Gurion (1886–1973), the first prime minister of Israel.

narrowed upward like a Dutch house. And, his small good lower teeth taking hold of the upper lip in his exertion, he performed the final duty of a son. He was very fit, so it must have been emotion, not the shoveling, that made him redden so. After the funeral, he went home with Halina and her son, a decent Polack like his mother, and talented, too—Mitosh played the organ at hockey and basketball games in the Stadium, which took a smart man because it was a rabble-rousing kind of occupation—and they had some drinks and comforted the old girl. Halina was true blue, always one hundred percent for Morris.

Then for the rest of the week Woody was busy, had jobs to run, office responsibilities, family responsibilities. He lived alone; as did his wife; as did his mistress: everybody in a separate establishment. Since his wife, after fifteen years of separation, had not learned to take care of herself, Woody did her shopping on Fridays, filled her freezer. He had to take her this week to buy shoes. Also, Friday night he always spent with Helen—Helen was his wife de facto. Saturday he did his big weekly shopping. Saturday night he devoted to Mom and his sisters. So he was too busy to attend to his own feelings except, intermittently, to note to himself, "First Thursday in the grave." "First Friday, and fine weather." "First Saturday; he's got to be getting used to it." Under his breath he occasionally said, "Oh, Pop."

But it was Sunday that hit him, when the bells rang all over South Chicago—the Ukrainian, Roman Catholic, Greek, Russian, African Methodist churches, sounding off one after another. Woody had his offices in his warehouse, and there had built an apartment for himself, very spacious and convenient, in the top story. Because he left every Sunday morning at seven to spend the day with Pop, he had forgotten by how many churches Selbst Tile Company was surrounded. He was still in bed when he heard the bells, and all at once he knew how heartbroken he was. This sudden big heartache in a man of sixty, a practical, physical, healthy-minded, and experienced man, was deeply unpleasant. When he had an unpleasant condition, he believed in taking something for it. So he thought: What shall I take? There were plenty of remedies available. His cellar was stocked with cases of Scotch whisky, Polish vodka, Armagnac, Moselle, Burgundy. There were also freezers with steaks and with game and with Alaskan king crab. He bought with a broad hand—by the crate and by the dozen. But in the end, when he got out of bed, he took nothing but a cup of coffee. While the kettle was heating, he put on his Japanese judo-style suit and sat down to reflect.

Woody was moved when things were *honest*. Bearing beams were honest, undisguised concrete pillars inside highrise apartments were honest. It was bad to cover up everything. He hated faking. Stone was honest. Metal was honest. These Sunday bells were very straight. They broke loose, they wagged and rocked, and the vibrations and the banging did something for him—cleansed his insides, purified his blood. A bell was a one-way throat, had only one thing to tell you and simply told it. He listened.

He had had some connections with bells and churches. He was after all something of a Christian. Born a Jew, he was a Jew facially, with a hint of Iroquois or Cherokee, but his mother had been converted more than fifty years ago by her brother-in-law, the Reverend Doctor Kovner. Kovner, a rabbinical student who had left the Hebrew Union College in Cincinnati to become a minister and establish a mission, had given Woody a partly Christian upbringing. Now, Pop was on the outs with these fundamentalists. He said that the Jews came to the mission to get coffee, bacon, canned pineapple, day-old bread, and dairy products. And if they had to listen to sermons, that was okay—this was the Depression and you couldn't be too particular—but he knew they sold the bacon.

The Gospels said it plainly: "Salvation is from the Jews."

Backing the Reverend Doctor were wealthy fundamentalists, mainly Swedes, eager to speed up the Second Coming by converting all Jews. The foremost of Kovner's backers was Mrs. Skoglund, who had inherited a large dairy business from her late husband. Woody was under her special protection.

Woody was fourteen years of age when Pop took off with Halina, who worked in his shop, leaving his difficult Christian wife and his converted son and his small daughters. He came to Woody in the backyard one spring day and said, "From now on you're the man of the house." Woody was practicing with a golf club, knocking off the heads of dandelions. Pop came into the yard in his good suit, which was too hot for the weather, and when he took off his fedora the skin of his head was marked with a deep ring and the sweat was sprinkled over his scalp—more drops than hairs. He said, "I'm going to move out." Pop was anxious, but he was set to go—determined. "It's no use. I can't live a life like this." Envisioning the life Pop simply *had* to live, his free life, Woody was able to picture him in a billiard parlor, under the El tracks in a crap game, or playing poker at Brown and Koppel's upstairs. "You're going to be the man of the house," said Pop. "It's okay. I put you all on welfare. I just got back from Wabansia Avenue, from the relief station." Hence the suit and the hat. "They're sending out a caseworker." Then he said, "You got to lend me money to buy gasoline—the caddie money you saved."

Understanding that Pop couldn't get away without his help, Woody turned over to him all he had earned at the Sunset Ridge Country Club in Winnetka. Pop felt that the valuable life lesson he was transmitting was worth far more than these dollars, and whenever he was conning his boy a sort of high-priest expression came down over his bent nose, his ruddy face. The children, who got their finest ideas at the movies, called him Richard Dix.[2] Later, when the comic strip came out, they said he was Dick Tracy.[3]

As Woody now saw it, under the tumbling bells, he had bankrolled his own desertion. Ha ha! He found this delightful; and especially Pop's attitude of "That'll teach you to trust your father." For this was a demonstration on

---

2. Silent movie actor with a square jaw, popular in the twenties.

3. Square-jawed comic strip hero.

behalf of real life and free instincts, against religion and hypocrisy. But mainly it was aimed against being a fool, the disgrace of foolishness. Pop had it in for the Reverend Doctor Kovner, not because he was an apostate (Pop couldn't have cared less), not because the mission was a racket (he admitted that the Reverend Doctor was personally honest), but because Doctor Kovner behaved foolishly, spoke like a fool, and acted like a fiddler. He tossed his hair like a Paganini[4] (this was Woody's addition; Pop had never even heard of Paganini). Proof that he was not a spiritual leader was that he converted Jewish women by stealing their hearts. "He works up all those broads," said Pop. "He doesn't even know it himself, I swear he doesn't know how he gets them."

From the other side, Kovner often warned Woody, "Your father is a dangerous person. Of course, you love him; you should love him and forgive him, Voodrow, but you are old enough to understand he is leading a life of wice."

It was all petty stuff: Pop's sinning was on a boy level and therefore made a big impression on a boy. And on Mother. Are wives children, or what? Mother often said, "I hope you put that brute in your prayers. Look what he has done to us. But only pray for him, don't see him." But he saw him all the time. Woodrow was leading a double life, sacred and profane. He accepted Jesus Christ as his personal redeemer. Aunt Rebecca took advantage of this. She made him work. He had to work under Aunt Rebecca. He filled in for the janitor at the mission and settlement house. In winter, he had to feed the coal furnace, and on some nights he slept near the furnace room, on the pool table. He also picked the lock of the storeroom. He took canned pineapple and cut bacon from the flitch with his pocketknife. He crammed himself with uncooked bacon. He had a big frame to fill out.

Only now, sipping Melitta coffee, he asked himself: Had he been so hungry? No, he loved being reckless. He was fighting Aunt Rebecca Kovner when he took out his knife and got on a box to reach the bacon. She didn't know, she couldn't prove that Woody, such a frank, strong, positive boy, who looked you in the eye, so direct, was a thief also. But he was also a thief. Whenever she looked at him, he knew that she was seeing his father. In the curve of his nose, the movement of his eyes, the thickness of his body, in his healthy face, she saw that wicked savage Morris.

Morris, you see, had been a street boy in Liverpool—Woody's mother and her sister were British by birth. Morris's Polish family, on their way to America, abandoned him in Liverpool because he had an eye infection and they would all have been sent back from Ellis Island. They stopped awhile in England, but his eyes kept running and they ditched him. They slipped away, and he had to make out alone in Liverpool at the age of twelve. Mother came of better people. Pop, who slept in the cellar of her house, fell in love with her. At sixteen, scabbing[5] during a seamen's strike, he shoveled

---

4. Niccolo Paganini (1782–1840), Italian violinist.

5. Taking the job of a striking worker.

his way across the Atlantic and jumped ship in Brooklyn. He became an American, and America never knew it. He voted without papers, he drove without a license, he paid no taxes, he cut every corner. Horses, cards, billiards, and women were his lifelong interests, in ascending order. Did he love anyone (he was so busy)? Yes, he loved Halina. He loved his son. To this day, Mother believed that he had loved her most and always wanted to come back. This gave her a chance to act the queen, with her plump wrists and faded Queen Victoria face. "The girls are instructed never to admit him," she said. The Empress of India speaking.

Bell-battered Woodrow's soul was whirling this Sunday morning, indoors and out, to the past, back to his upper corner of the warehouse, laid out with such originality—the bells coming and going, metal on naked metal, until the bell circle expanded over the whole of steel-making, oil-refining, power-producing mid-autumn South Chicago, and all its Croatians, Ukrainians, Greeks, Poles and respectable blacks heading for their churches to hear Mass or to sing hymns.

Woody himself had been a good hymn singer. He still knew the hymns. He had testified,[6] too. He was often sent by Aunt Rebecca to get up and tell a churchful of Scandihoovians that he, a Jewish lad, accepted Jesus Christ. For this she paid him fifty cents. She made the disbursement. She was the bookkeeper, fiscal chief, general manager of the mission. The Reverend Doctor didn't know a thing about the operation. What the Doctor supplied was the fervor. He was genuine, a wonderful preacher. And what about Woody himself? He also had fervor. He was drawn to the Reverend Doctor. The Reverend Doctor taught him to lift up his eyes, gave him his higher life. Apart from this higher life, the rest was Chicago—the ways of Chicago, which came so natural that nobody thought to question them. So, for instance, in 1933 (what ancient, ancient times!), at the Century of Progress World's Fair, when Woody was a coolie and pulled a rickshaw, wearing a peaked straw hat and trotting with powerful, thick legs, while the brawny red farmers—his boozing passengers—were laughing their heads off and pestered him for whores, he, although a freshman at the seminary, saw nothing wrong, when girls asked him to steer a little business their way, in making dates and accepting tips from both sides. He necked in Grant Park with a powerful girl who had to go home quickly to nurse her baby. Smelling of milk, she rode beside him on the streetcar to the West Side, squeezing his rickshaw puller's thigh and wetting her blouse. This was the Roosevelt Road car. Then, in the apartment where she lived with her mother, he couldn't remember that there were any husbands around. What he did remember was the strong milk odor. Without inconsistency, next morning he did New Testament Greek: The light shineth in darkness—*to fos en te skotia fainei*—and the darkness comprehended it not.

And all the while he trotted between the shafts on the fairgrounds he had one idea, nothing to do with these horny giants having a big time in the

---

6. Made a statement of personal religious experience at a church service.

city: that the goal, the project, the purpose was (and he couldn't explain why he thought so; all evidence was against it)—God's idea was that this world should be a love world, that it should eventually recover and be entirely a world of love. He wouldn't have said this to a soul, for he could see himself how stupid it was—personal and stupid. Nevertheless, there it was at the center of his feelings. And at the same time, Aunt Rebecca was right when she said to him, strictly private, close to his ear even, "You're a little crook, like your father."

There was some evidence for this, or what stood for evidence to an impatient person like Rebecca. Woody matured quickly—he had to—but how could you expect a boy of seventeen, he wondered, to interpret the viewpoint, the feelings, of a middle-aged woman, and one whose breast had been removed? Morris told him that this happened only to neglected women, and was a sign. Morris said that if titties were not fondled and kissed, they got cancer in protest. It was a cry of the flesh. And this had seemed true to Woody. When his imagination tried the theory on the Reverend Doctor, it worked out—he couldn't see the Reverend Doctor behaving in that way to Aunt Rebecca's breasts! Morris's theory kept Woody looking from bosoms to husbands and from husbands to bosoms. He still did that. It's an exceptionally smart man who isn't marked forever by the sexual theories he hears from his father, and Woody wasn't all that smart. He knew this himself. Personally, he had gone far out of his way to do right by women in this regard. What nature demanded. He and Pop were common, thick men, but there's nobody too gross to have ideas of delicacy.

The Reverend Doctor preached, Rebecca preached, rich Mrs. Skoglund preached from Evanston, Mother preached. Pop also was on a soapbox. Everyone was doing it. Up and down Division Street, under every lamp, almost, speakers were giving out: anarchists, Socialists, Stalinists, single-taxers, Zionists, Tolstoyans, vegetarians, and fundamentalist Christian preachers—you name it. A beef, a hope, a way of life or salvation, a protest. How was it that the accumulated gripes of all the ages took off so when transplanted to America?

And that fine Swedish immigrant Aase (Osie, they pronounced it), who had been the Skoglunds' cook and married the eldest son, to become his rich, religious widow—she supported the Reverend Doctor. In her time she must have been built like a chorus girl. And women seem to have lost the secret of putting up their hair in the high basketry fence of braid she wore. Aase took Woody under her special protection and paid his tuition at the seminary. And Pop said . . . But on this Sunday, at peace as soon as the bells stopped banging, this velvet autumn day when the grass was finest and thickest, silky green: before the first frost, and the blood in your lungs is redder than summer air can make it and smarts with oxygen, as if the iron in your system was hungry for it, and the chill was sticking it to you in every breath . . . Pop, six feet under, would never feel this blissful sting again. The last of the bells still had the bright air streaming with vibrations.

On weekends, the institutional vacancy of decades came back to the warehouse and crept under the door of Woody's apartment. It felt as empty on Sundays as churches were during the week. Before each business day, before the trucks and the crews got started, Woody jogged five miles in his Adidas suit. Not on this day still reserved for Pop, however. Although it was tempting to go out and run off the grief. Being alone hit Woody hard this morning. He thought: Me and the world; the world and me. Meaning that there always was some activity to interpose, an errand or a visit, a picture to paint (he was a creative amateur), a massage, a meal—a shield between himself and that troublesome solitude which used the world as its reservoir. But Pop! Last Tuesday, Woody had gotten into the hospital bed with Pop because he kept pulling out the intravenous needles. Nurses stuck them back, and then Woody astonished them all by climbing into bed to hold the struggling old guy in his arms. "Easy, Morris, Morris, go easy." But Pop still groped feebly for the pipes.

When the tolling stopped, Woody didn't notice that a great lake of quiet had come over his kingdom, the Selbst Tile warehouse. What he heard and saw was an old red Chicago streetcar, one of those trams the color of a stockyard steer. Cars of this type went out before Pearl Harbor—clumsy, big-bellied, with tough rattan seats and brass grips for the standing passengers. Those cars used to make four stops to the mile, and ran with a wallowing motion. They stank of carbolic or ozone and throbbed when the air compressors were being charged. The conductor had his knotted signal cord to pull, and the motorman beat the foot gong with his mad heel.

Woody recognized himself on the Western Avenue line and riding through a blizzard with his father, both in sheepskins and with hands and faces raw, the snow blowing in from the rear platform when the doors opened and getting into the longitudinal cleats of the floor. There wasn't warmth enough inside to melt it. And Western Avenue was the longest car line in the world, the boosters said, as if it was a thing to brag about. Twenty-three miles long, made by a draftsman with a T square, lined with factories, storage buildings, machine shops, used-car lots, trolley barns, gas stations, funeral parlors, six-flats, utility buildings, and junkyards, on and on from the prairies on the south to Evanston on the north. Woodrow and his father were going north to Evanston, to Howard Street, and then some, to see Mrs. Skoglund. At the end of the line they would still have about five blocks to hike. The purpose of the trip? To raise money for Pop. Pop had talked him into this. When they found out, Mother and Aunt Rebecca would be furious, and Woody was afraid, but he couldn't help it.

Morris had come and said, "Son, I'm in trouble. It's bad."

"What's bad, Pop?"

"Halina took money from her husband for me and has to put it back before old Bujak misses it. He could kill her."

"What did she do it for?"

"Son, you know how the bookies collect? They send a goon. They'll break my head open."

"Pop! You know I can't take you to Mrs. Skoglund."

"Why not? You're my kid, aren't you? The old broad wants to adopt you, doesn't she? Shouldn't I get something out of it for my trouble? What am I—outside? And what about Halina? She puts her life on the line, but my own kid says no."

"Oh, Bujak wouldn't hurt her."

"Woody, he'd beat her to death."

Bujak? Uniform in color with his dark-gray work clothes, short in the legs, his whole strength in his tool-and-die-maker's forearms and black fingers; and beat-looking—there was Bujak for you. But, according to Pop, there was big, big violence in Bujak, a regular boiling Bessemer inside his narrow chest. Woody could never see the violence in him. Bujak wanted no trouble. If anything, maybe he was afraid that Morris and Halina would gang up on him and kill him, screaming. But Pop was no desperado murderer. And Halina was a calm, serious woman. Bujak kept his savings in the cellar (banks were going out of business). The worst they did was to take some of his money, intending to put it back. As Woody saw him, Bujak was trying to be sensible. He accepted his sorrow. He set minimum requirements for Halina: cook the meals, clean the house, show respect. But at stealing Bujak might have drawn the line, for money was different, money was vital substance. If they stole his savings he might have had to take action, out of respect for the substance, for himself—self-respect. But you couldn't be sure that Pop hadn't invented the bookie, the goon, the theft—the whole thing. He was capable of it, and you'd be a fool not to suspect him. Morris knew that Mother and Aunt Rebecca had told Mrs. Skoglund how wicked he was. They had painted him for her in poster colors—purple for vice, black for his soul, red for Hell flames: a gambler, smoker, drinker, deserter, screwer of women, and atheist. So Pop was determined to reach her. It was risky for everybody. The Reverend Doctor's operating costs were met by Skoglund Dairies. The widow paid Woody's seminary tuition; she bought dresses for the little sisters.

Woody, now sixty, fleshy and big, like a figure for the victory of American materialism, sunk in his lounge chair, the leather of its armrests softer to his fingertips than a woman's skin, was puzzled and, in his depths, disturbed by certain blots within him, blots of light in his brain, a blot combining pain and amusement in his breast (how did *that* get there?). Intense thought puckered the skin between his eyes with a strain bordering on headache. Why had he let Pop have his way? Why did he agree to meet him that day, in the dim rear of the poolroom?

"But what will you tell Mrs. Skoglund?"

"The old broad? Don't worry, there's plenty to tell her, and it's all true. Ain't I trying to save my little laundry-and-cleaning shop? Isn't the bailiff coming for the fixtures next week?" And Pop rehearsed his pitch on the Western Avenue car. He counted on Woody's health and his freshness. Such a straightforward-looking body was perfect for a con.

Did they still have such winter storms in Chicago as they used to have?

Now they somehow seemed less fierce. Blizzards used to come straight down from Ontario, from the Arctic, and drop five feet of snow in an afternoon. Then the rusty green platform cars, with revolving brushes at both ends, came out of the barns to sweep the tracks. Ten or twelve streetcars followed in slow processions, or waited, block after block.

There was a long delay at the gates of Riverview Park, all the amusements covered for the winter, boarded up—the dragon's-back high-rides, the Bobs, the Chute, the Tilt-a-Whirl, all the fun machinery put together by mechanics and electricians, men like Bujak the tool-and-die-maker, good with engines. The blizzard was having it all its own way behind the gates, and you couldn't see far inside; only a few bulbs burned behind the palings. When Woody wiped the vapor from the glass, the wire mesh of the window guards was stuffed solid at eye level with snow. Looking higher, you saw mostly the streaked wind horizontally driving from the north. In the seat ahead, two black coal heavers, both in leather Lindbergh flying helmets, sat with shovels between their legs, returning from a job. They smelled of sweat, burlap sacking, and coal. Mostly dull with black dust, they also sparkled here and there.

There weren't many riders. People weren't leaving the house. This was a day to sit legs stuck out beside the stove, mummified by both the outdoor and the indoor forces. Only a fellow with an angle, like Pop, would go and buck such weather. A storm like this was out of the compass, and you kept the human scale by having a scheme to raise fifty bucks. Fifty soldiers! Real money in 1933.

"That woman is crazy for you," said Pop.

"She's just a good woman, sweet to all of us."

"Who knows what she's got in mind. You're a husky kid. Not such a kid, either."

"She's a religious woman. She really has religion."

"Well, your mother isn't your only parent. She and Rebecca and Kovner aren't going to fill you up with their ideas. I know your mother wants to wipe me out of your life. Unless I take a hand, you won't even understand what life is. Because they don't know—those silly Christers."

"Yes, Pop."

"The girls I can't help. They're too young. I'm sorry about them, but I can't do anything. With you it's different."

He wanted me like himself, an American.

They were stalled in the storm, while the cattle-colored car waited to have the trolley reset in the crazy wind, which boomed, tingled, blasted. At Howard Street they would have to walk straight into it, due north.

"You'll do the talking at first," said Pop.

Woody had the makings of a salesman, a pitchman. He was aware of this when he got to his feet in church to testify before fifty or sixty people. Even though Aunt Rebecca made it worth his while, he moved his own heart when he spoke up about his faith. But occasionally, without notice, his heart went away as he spoke religion and he couldn't find it anywhere. In its absence, sincere behavior got him through. He had to rely for delivery on his face, his voice—on behavior. Then his eyes came closer and closer together. And in this approach of eye to eye he felt the strain of hypocrisy. The twisting of his face threatened to betray him. It took everything he had to keep looking honest. So, since he couldn't bear the cynicism of it, he fell back on mischievousness. Mischief was where Pop came in. Pop passed straight through all those divided fields, gap after gap, and arrived at his side, bent-nosed and broad-faced. In regard to Pop, you thought of neither sincerity nor insincerity. Pop was like the man in the song: he wanted what he wanted when he wanted it. Pop was physical; Pop was digestive, circulatory, sexual. If Pop got serious, he talked to you about washing under the arms or in the crotch or of drying between your toes or of cooking supper, of baked beans and fried onions, of draw poker or of a certain horse in the fifth race at Arlington. Pop was elemental. That was why he gave such relief from religion and paradoxes, and things like that. Now Mother *thought* she was spiritual, but Woody knew that she was kidding herself. Oh, yes, in the British accent she never gave up she was always talking to God or about Him—please God, God willing, praise God. But she was a big substantial bread-and-butter down-to-earth woman, with down-to-earth duties like feeding the girls, protecting, refining, keeping pure the girls. And those two protected doves grew up so overweight, heavy in the hips and thighs, that their poor heads looked long and slim. And mad. Sweet but cuckoo—Paula cheerfully cuckoo, Joanna depressed and having episodes.

"I'll do my best by you, but you have to promise, Pop, not to get me in Dutch with Mrs. Skoglund."

"You worried because I speak bad English? Embarrassed? I have a mockie accent?"

"It's not that. Kovner has a heavy accent, and she doesn't mind."

"Who the hell are those freaks to look down on me? You're practically a man and your dad has a right to expect help from you. He's in a fix. And you bring him to her house because she's bighearted, and you haven't got anybody else to go to."

"I got you, Pop."

The two coal trimmers stood up at Devon Avenue. One of them wore a woman's coat. Men wore women's clothing in those years, and women men's, when there was no choice. The fur collar was spiky with the wet, and sprinkled with soot. Heavy, they dragged their shovels and got off at the front. The slow car ground on, very slow. It was after four when they reached the end of the line, and somewhere between gray and black, with snow spouting and whirling under the street lamps. In Howard Street, autos were stalled at all angles and abandoned. The sidewalks were blocked. Woody led the way into Evanston, and Pop followed him up the middle of the street in the furrows made earlier by trucks. For four blocks they bucked the wind and then Woody broke through the drifts to the snowbound mansion, where they both had to push the wrought-iron gate because of the drift behind it. Twenty rooms or more in this dignified house and nobody in them but Mrs. Skoglund and her servant Hjordis, also religious.

As Woody and Pop waited, brushing the slush from their sheepskin collars and Pop wiping his big eyebrows with the ends of his scarf, sweating and freezing, the chains began to rattle and Hjordis uncovered the air holes of the glass storm door by turning a wooden bar. Woody called her "monk-faced." You no longer see women like that, who put no female touch on the face. She came plain, as God made her. She said, "Who is it and what do you want?"

"It's Woodrow Selbst. Hjordis? It's Woody."

"You're not expected."

"No, but we're here."

"What do you want?"

"We came to see Mrs. Skoglund."

"What for do you want to see her?"

"Just tell her we're here."

"I have to tell her what you came for, without calling up first."

"Why don't you say it's Woody with his father, and we wouldn't come in a snowstorm like this if it wasn't important."

The understandable caution of women who live alone. Respectable old-time women, too. There was no such respectability now in those Evanston houses, with their big verandas and deep yards and with a servant like Hjordis, who carried at her belt keys to the pantry and to every closet and every dresser drawer and every padlocked bin in the cellar. And in High Episcopal Christian Science Women's Temperance Evanston, no tradespeople rang at the front door. Only invited guests. And here, after a ten-mile grind through the blizzard, came two tramps from the West Side. To this mansion where a Swedish immigrant lady, herself once a cook and now a philanthropic widow, dreamed, snowbound, while frozen lilac twigs clapped at her storm windows, of a new Jerusalem and a Second Coming and a Resurrection and a Last Judgment. To hasten the Second Coming, and all the rest, you had to reach the hearts of these scheming bums arriving in a snowstorm.

Sure, they let us in.

Then in the heat that swam suddenly up to their muffled chins Pop and Woody felt the blizzard for what it was; their cheeks were frozen slabs. They stood beat, itching, trickling in the front hall that *was* a hall, with a carved newel post staircase and a big stained-glass window at the top. Picturing Jesus with the Samaritan woman. There was a kind of Gentile closeness to the air. Perhaps when he was with Pop, Woody made more Jewish observations than he would otherwise. Although Pop's most Jewish characteristic was that Yiddish was the only language he could read a paper in. Pop was with Polish Halina, and Mother was with Jesus Christ, and Woody ate uncooked bacon from the flitch. Still, now and then he had a Jewish impression.

Mrs. Skoglund was the cleanest of women—her fingernails, her white neck, her ears—and Pop's sexual hints to Woody all went wrong because she was so intensely clean, and made Woody think of a waterfall, large as she was, and grandly built. Her bust was big. Woody's imagination had investigated this. He thought she kept things tied down tight, very tight. But she lifted both arms once to raise a window and there it was, her bust, beside him, the whole unbindable thing. Her hair was like the raffia you had to soak before you could weave with it in a basket class—pale, pale. Pop, as he took his sheepskin off, was in sweaters, no jacket. His darting looks made him seem crooked. Hardest of all for these Selbsts with their bent noses and big, apparently straightforward faces was to look honest. All the signs of dishonesty played over them. Woody had often puzzled about it. Did it go back to the muscles, was it fundamentally a jaw problem—the projecting angles of the jaws? Or was it the angling that went on in the heart? The girls called Pop Dick Tracy, but Dick Tracy was a good guy. Whom could Pop convince? Here Woody caught a possibility as it flitted by. Precisely because of the way Pop looked, a sensitive person might feel remorse for condemning unfairly or judging unkindly. Just because of a face? Some must have bent over backward. Then he had them. Not Hjordis. She would have put Pop into the street then and there, storm or no storm. Hjordis was religious, but she was wised up, too. She hadn't come over in steerage and worked forty years in Chicago for nothing.

Mrs. Skoglund, Aase (Osie), led the visitors into the front room. This, the biggest room in the house, needed supplementary heating. Because of fifteen-foot ceilings and high windows, Hjordis had kept the parlor stove burning. It was one of those elegant parlor stoves that wore a nickel crown, or miter, and this miter, when you moved it aside, automatically raised the hinge of an iron stove lid. That stove lid underneath the crown was all soot and rust, the same as any other stove lid. Into this hole you tipped the scuttle and the anthracite chestnut[7] rattled down. It made a cake or dome of fire visible through the small isinglass[8] frames. It was a pretty room, three-quarters paneled in wood. The stove was plugged into the flue of the marble fireplace, and there were parquet floors and Axminster carpets and cranberry-colored tufted Victorian upholstery, and a kind of Chinese étagère, inside a cabinet, lined with mirrors and containing silver pitchers, trophies won by Skoglund cows, fancy sugar tongs and cut-glass pitchers and goblets. There were Bibles and pictures of Jesus and the Holy Land and that faint Gentile odor, as if things had been rinsed in a weak vinegar solution.

"Mrs. Skoglund, I brought my dad to you. I don't think you ever met him," said Woody.

"Yes, Missus, that's me, Selbst."

Pop stood short but masterful in the sweaters, and his belly sticking out, not soft but hard. He was a man of the hard-bellied type. Nobody intimidated Pop. He never presented himself as a beggar. There wasn't a cringe in

---

7. Hard coal, high in carbon content.
8. Semitransparent sheets of mica.

him anywhere. He let her see at once by the way he said "Missus" that he was independent and that he knew his way around. He communicated that he was able to handle himself with women. Handsome Mrs. Skoglund, carrying a basket woven out of her own hair, was in her fifties—eight, maybe ten years his senior.

"I asked my son to bring me because I know you do the kid a lot of good. It's natural you should know both of his parents."

"Mrs. Skoglund, my dad is in a tight corner and I don't know anybody else to ask for help."

This was all the preliminary Pop wanted. He took over and told the widow his story about the laundry-and-cleaning business and payments overdue, and explained about the fixtures and the attachment notice, and the bailiff's office and what they were going to do to him; and he said, "I'm a small man trying to make a living."

"You don't support your children," said Mrs. Skoglund.

"That's right," said Hjordis.

"I haven't got it. If I had it, wouldn't I give it? There's bread lines and soup lines all over town. Is it just me? What I have I divvy with. I give the kids. A bad father? You think my son would bring me if I was a bad father into your house? He loves his dad, he trusts his dad, he knows his dad is a good dad. Every time I start a little business going I get wiped out. This one is a good little business, if I could hold on to that little business. Three people work for me, I meet a payroll, and three people will be on the street, too, if I close down. Missus, I can sign a note and pay you in two months. I'm a common man, but I'm a hard worker and a fellow you can trust."

Woody was startled when Pop used the word "trust." It was as if from all four corners a Sousa[9] band blew a blast to warn the entire world: "Crook! This is a crook!" But Mrs. Skoglund, on account of her religious preoccupations, was remote. She heard nothing. Although everybody in this part of the world, unless he was crazy, led a practical life, and you'd have nothing to say to anyone, your neighbors would have nothing to say to you, if communications were not of a practical sort, Mrs. Skoglund, with all her money, was unworldly—two-thirds out of this world.

"Give me a chance to show what's in me," said Pop, "and you'll see what I do for my kids."

So Mrs. Skoglund hesitated, and then she said she'd have to go upstairs, she'd have to go to her room and pray on it and ask for guidance—would they sit down and wait. There were two rocking chairs by the stove. Hjordis gave Pop a grim look (a dangerous person) and Woody a blaming one (he brought a dangerous stranger and disrupter to injure two kind Christian ladies). Then she went out with Mrs. Skoglund.

As soon as they left, Pop jumped up from the rocker and said in anger, "What's this with the praying? She has to ask God to lend me fifty bucks?"

Woody said, "It's not you, Pop, it's the way these religious people do."

---

9. John Philip Sousa (1854–1932), American bandmaster and composer of marches.

"No," said Pop. "She'll come back and say that God wouldn't let her."

Woody didn't like that; he thought Pop was being gross and he said, "No, she's sincere. Pop, try to understand: she's emotional, nervous, and sincere, and tries to do right by everybody."

And Pop said, "That servant will talk her out of it. She's a toughie. It's all over her face that we're a couple of chiselers."

"What's the use of us arguing," said Woody. He drew the rocker closer to the stove. His shoes were wet through and would never dry. The blue flames fluttered like a school of fishes in the coal fire. But Pop went over to the Chinese-style cabinet or étagère and tried the handle, and then opened the blade of his penknife and in a second had forced the lock of the curved glass door. He took out a silver dish.

"Pop, what is this?" said Woody.

Pop, cool and level, knew exactly what this was. He relocked the étagère, crossed the carpet, listened. He stuffed the dish under his belt and pushed it down into his trousers. He put the side of his short thick fingers to his mouth.

So Woody kept his voice down, but he was all shook up. He went to Pop and took him by the edge of his hand. As he looked into Pop's face, he felt his eyes growing smaller and smaller, as if something were contracting all the skin on his head. They call it hyperventilation when everything feels tight and light and close and dizzy. Hardly breathing, he said, "Put it back, Pop."

Pop said, "It's solid silver, it's worth dough."

"Pop, you said you wouldn't get me in Dutch."

"It's only insurance in case she comes back from praying and tells me no. If she says yes, I'll put it back."

"How?"

"It'll get back. If I don't put it back, you will."

"You picked the lock. I couldn't. I don't know how."

"There's nothing to it."

"We're going to put it back now. Give it here."

"Woody, it's under my fly, inside my underpants. Don't make such a noise about nothing."

"Pop, I can't believe this."

"For cry-ninety-nine, shut your mouth. If I didn't trust you I wouldn't have let you watch me do it. You don't understand a thing. What's with you?"

"Before they come down, Pop, will you dig that dish out of your long johns."

Pop turned stiff on him. He became absolutely military. He said, "Look, I order you!"

Before he knew it, Woody had jumped his father and begun to wrestle with him. It was outrageous to clutch your own father, to put a heel behind him, to force him to the wall. Pop was taken by surprise and said loudly, "You want Halina killed? Kill her! Go on, you be responsible." He began to resist, angry, and they turned about several times, when Woody, with a trick he had learned in a Western movie and used once on the playground, tripped him and they fell to the ground. Woody, who already outweighed the old man by twenty pounds, was on top. They landed on the floor beside the stove, which stood on a tray of decorated tin to protect the carpet. In this position, pressing Pop's hard belly, Woody recognized that to have wrestled him to the floor counted for nothing. It was impossible to thrust his hand under Pop's belt to recover the dish. And now Pop had turned furious, as a father has every right to be when his son is violent with him, and he freed his hand and hit Woody in the face. He hit him three or four times in mid-face. Then Woody dug his head into Pop's shoulder and held tight only to keep from being struck and began to say in his ear, "Jesus, Pop, for Christ sake remember where you are. Those women will be back!" But Pop brought up his short knee and fought and butted him with his chin and rattled Woody's teeth. Woody thought the old man was about to bite him. And because he was a seminarian, he thought: Like an unclean spirit. And held tight. Gradually Pop stopped thrashing and struggling. His eyes stuck out and his mouth was open, sullen. Like a stout fish. Woody released him and gave him a hand up. He was then overcome with many bad feelings of a sort he knew the old man never suffered. Never, never. Pop never had these groveling emotions. There was his whole superiority. Pop had no such feelings. He was like a horseman from Central Asia, a bandit from China. It was Mother, from Liverpool, who had the refinement, the English manners. It was the preaching Reverend Doctor in his black suit. You have refinements, and all they do is oppress you? The hell with that.

The long door opened and Mrs. Skoglund stepped in, saying, "Did I imagine, or did something shake the house?"

"I was lifting the scuttle to put coal on the fire and it fell out of my hand. I'm sorry I was so clumsy," said Woody.

Pop was too huffy to speak. With his eyes big and sore and the thin hair down over his forehead, you could see by the tightness of his belly how angrily he was fetching his breath, though his mouth was shut.

"I prayed," said Mrs. Skoglund.

"I hope it came out well," said Woody.

"Well, I don't do anything without guidance, but the answer was yes, and I feel right about it now. So if you'll wait, I'll go to my office and write a check. I asked Hjordis to bring you a cup of coffee. Coming in such a storm."

And Pop, consistently a terrible little man, as soon as she shut the door, said, "A check? Hell with a check. Get me the greenbacks."

"They don't keep money in the house. You can cash it in her bank tomorrow. But if they miss that dish, Pop, they'll stop the check, and then where are you?"

As Pop was reaching below the belt, Hjordis brought in the tray. She was very sharp with him. She said, "Is this a place to adjust clothing, Mister? A men's washroom?"

"Well, which way is the toilet, then?" said Pop.

She had served the coffee in the seamiest mugs in the pantry, and she bumped down the tray and led Pop down the corridor, standing guard at the bathroom door so he shouldn't wander about the house.

Mrs. Skoglund called Woody to her office and after she had given him the folded check said that they should pray together for Morris. So once more he was on his knees, under rows and rows of musty marbled-cardboard files, by the glass lamp by the edge of the desk, the shade with flounced edges, like the candy dish. Mrs. Skoglund, in her Scandinavian accent—an emotional contralto—raising her voice to Jesus-uh Christ-uh, as the wind lashed the trees, kicked the side of the house, and drove the snow seething on the windowpanes, to send light-uh, give guidance-uh, put a new heart-uh in Pop's bosom. Woody asked God only to make Pop put the dish back. He kept Mrs. Skoglund on her knees as long as possible. Then he thanked her, shining with candor (as much as he knew how), for her Christian generosity and he said, "I know that Hjordis has a cousin who works at the Evanston YMCA. Could she please phone him and try to get us a room tonight so that we don't have to fight the blizzard all the way back? We're almost as close to the Y as to the car line. Maybe the cars have even stopped running."

Suspicious Hjordis, coming when Mrs. Skoglund called to her, was burning now. First they barged in, made themselves at home, asked for money, had to have coffee, probably left gonorrhea on the toilet seat. Hjordis, Woody remembered, was a woman who wiped the doorknobs with rubbing alcohol after guests had left. Nevertheless, she telephoned the Y and got them a room with two cots for six bits.

Pop had plenty of time, therefore, to reopen the étagère, lined with reflecting glass or German silver (something exquisitely delicate and tricky), and as soon as the two Selbsts had said thank you and goodbye and were in midstreet up to the knees in snow, Woody said, "Well, I covered for you. Is that thing back?"

"Of course it is," said Pop.

They fought their way to the small Y building, shut in wire grille and resembling a police station—about the same dimensions. It was locked, but they made a racket on the grille, and a small black man let them in and shuffled them upstairs to a cement corridor with low doors. It was like the small-mammal house in Lincoln Park. He said there was nothing to eat, so they took off their wet pants, wrapped themselves tightly in the khaki army blankets, and passed out on their cots.

First thing in the morning, they went to the Evanston National Bank and got the fifty dollars. Not without difficulties. The teller went to call Mrs Skoglund and was absent a long time from the wicket. "Where the hell has he gone?" said Pop.

But when the fellow came back, he said, "How do you want it?"

Pop, said, "Singles." He told Woody, "Bujak stashes it in one-dollar bills."

But by now Woody no longer believed Halina had stolen the old man's money.

Then they went into the street, where the snow-removal crews were at work. The sun shone broad, broad, out of the morning blue, and all Chicago would be releasing itself from the temporary beauty of those vast drifts.

"You shouldn't have jumped me last night, Sonny."

"I know, Pop, but you promised you wouldn't get me in Dutch."

"Well, it's okay. We can forget it, seeing you stood by me."

Only, Pop had taken the silver dish. Of course he had, and in a few days Mrs. Skoglund and Hjordis knew it, and later in the week they were all waiting for Woody in Kovner's office at the settlement house. The group included the Reverend Doctor Crabbie, head of the seminary, and Woody, who had been flying along, level and smooth, was shot down in flames. He told them he was innocent. Even as he was falling, he warned that they were wronging him. He denied that he or Pop had touched Mrs. Skoglund's property. The missing object—he didn't even know what it was—had probably been misplaced, and they would be very sorry on the day it turned up. After the others were done with him, Dr. Crabbie said that until he was able to tell the truth he would be suspended from the seminary, where his work had been unsatisfactory anyway. Aunt Rebecca took him aside and said to him, "You are a little crook, like your father. The door is closed to you here."

To this Pop's comment was "So what, kid?"

"Pop, you shouldn't have done it."

"No? Well, I don't give a care, if you want to know. You can have the dish if you want to go back and square yourself with all those hypocrites."

"I didn't like doing Mrs. Skoglund in the eye, she was so kind to us."

"Kind?"

"Kind."

"Kind has a price tag."

Well, there was no winning such arguments with Pop. But they debated it in various moods and from various elevations and perspectives for forty years and more, as their intimacy changed, developed, matured.

"Why did you do it, Pop? For the money? What did you do with the fifty bucks?" Woody, decades later, asked him that.

"I settled with the bookie, and the rest I put in the business."

"You tried a few more horses."

"I maybe did. But it was a double, Woody. I didn't hurt myself, and at the same time did you a favor."

"It was for me?"

"It was too strange of a life. That life wasn't *you*, Woody. All those women . . . Kovner was no man, he was an in-between. Suppose they made you a minister? Some Christian minister! First of all, you wouldn't have been able to stand it, and second, they would throw you out sooner or later."

"Maybe so."

"And you wouldn't have converted the Jews, which was the main thing they wanted."

"And what a time to bother the Jews," Woody said. "At least *I* didn't bug them."

Pop had carried him back to his side of the line, blood of his blood, the same thick body walls, the same coarse grain. Not cut out for a spiritual life. Simply not up to it.

Pop was no worse than Woody, and Woody was no better than Pop. Pop wanted no relation to theory, and yet he was always pointing Woody toward a position—a jolly, hearty, natural, likable, unprincipled position. If Woody had a weakness, it was to be unselfish. This worked to Pop's advantage, but he criticized Woody for it, nevertheless. "You take too much on yourself," Pop was always saying. And it's true that Woody gave Pop his heart because Pop was so selfish. It's usually the selfish people who are loved the most. They do what you deny yourself, and you love them for it. You give them your heart.

Remembering the pawn ticket for the silver dish, Woody startled himself with a laugh so sudden that it made him cough. Pop said to him after his expulsion from the seminary and banishment from the settlement house, "You want in again? Here's the ticket. I hocked that thing. It wasn't so valuable as I thought."

"What did they give?"

"Twelve-fifty was all I could get. But if you want it you'll have to raise the dough yourself, because I haven't got it anymore."

"You must have been sweating in the bank when the teller went to call Mrs. Skoglund about the check."

"I was a little nervous," said Pop. "But I didn't think they could miss the thing so soon."

That theft was part of Pop's war with Mother. With Mother, and Aunt Rebecca, and the Reverend Doctor. Pop took his stand on realism. Mother represented the forces of religion and hypochondria. In four decades, the fighting never stopped. In the course of time, Mother and the girls turned into welfare personalities and lost their individual outlines. Ah, the poor things, they became dependents and cranks. In the meantime, Woody, the sinful man, was their dutiful and loving son and brother. He maintained the bungalow—this took in roofing, pointing, wiring, insulation, air-conditioning—and he paid for heat and light and food, and dressed them all out of Sears, Roebuck and Wieboldt's, and bought them a TV, which they watched as devoutly as they prayed. Paula took courses to learn skills like macramé-making and needlepoint, and sometimes got a little job as recreational worker in a nursing home. But she wasn't steady enough to keep it. Wicked Pop spent most of his life removing stains from people's clothing. He and Halina in the last years ran a Cleanomat in West Rogers Park—a so-so business resembling a laundromat—which gave him leisure for billiards, the horses, rummy and pinochle. Every morning he went behind the partition to check out the filters of the cleaning equipment. He found amusing things that had been thrown into the vats with the clothing—sometimes, when he got lucky, a locket chain or a brooch. And when he had fortified the cleaning fluid, pouring all that blue and pink stuff in from plastic jugs, he read the

Forward over a second cup of coffee, and went out, leaving Halina in charge. When they needed help with the rent, Woody gave it.

After the new Disney World was opened in Florida, Woody treated all his dependents to a holiday. He sent them down in separate batches, of course. Halina enjoyed this more than anybody else. She couldn't stop talking about the address given by an Abraham Lincoln automaton. "Wonderful, how he stood up and moved his hands, and his mouth. So real! And how beautiful he talked." Of them all, Halina was the soundest, the most human, the most honest. Now that Pop was gone, Woody and Halina's son, Mitosh, the organist at the Stadium, took care of her needs over and above Social Security, splitting expenses. In Pop's opinion, insurance was a racket. He left Halina nothing but some out-of-date equipment.

Woody treated himself, too. Once a year , and sometimes oftener, he left his business to run itself, arranged with the trust department at the bank to take care of his gang, and went off. He did that in style, imaginatively, expensively. In Japan, he wasted little time in Tokyo. He spent three weeks in Kyoto and stayed at the Tawaraya Inn, dating from the seventeenth century or so. There he slept on the floor, the Japanese way, and bathed in scalding water. He saw the dirtiest strip show on earth, as well as the holy places and the temple gardens. He visited also Istanbul, Jerusalem, Delphi, and went to Burma and Uganda and Kenya on safari, on democratic terms with drivers, Bedouins, bazaar merchants. Open, lavish, familiar, fleshier and fleshier but (he jogged, he lifted weights) still muscular—in his naked person beginning to resemble a Renaissance courtier in full costume—becoming ruddier every year, an outdoor type with freckles on his back and spots across the flaming forehead and the honest nose. In Addis Ababa he took an Ethiopian beauty to his room from the street and washed her, getting into the shower with her to soap her with his broad, kindly hands. In Kenya he taught certain American obscenities to a black woman so that she could shout them out during the act. On the Nile, below Murchison Falls, those fever trees rose huge from the mud, and hippos on the sandbars belched at the passing launch, hostile. One of them danced on his spit of sand, springing from the ground and coming down heavy, on all fours. There, Woody saw the buffalo calf disappear, snatched by the crocodile.

Mother, soon to follow Pop, was being lightheaded these days. In company, she spoke of Woody as her boy—"What do you think of my Sonny?"—as though he was ten years old. She was silly with him, her behavior was frivolous, almost flirtatious. She just didn't seem to know the facts. And behind her all the others, like kids at the playground, were waiting their turn to go down the slide: one on each step, and moving toward the top.

Over Woody's residence and place of business there had gathered a pool of silence of the same perimeter as the church bells while they were ringing, and he mourned under it, this melancholy morning of sun and autumn. Doing a life survey, taking a deliberate look at the gross side of his case—of the other side as well, what there was of it. But if this heartache continued, he'd go out and run it off. A three-mile jog—five, if necessary. And you'd think that this jogging was an entirely physical activity, wouldn't you? But there was something else in it. Because, when he was a seminarian, between the shafts of his World's Fair rickshaw, he used to receive, pulling along (capable and stable), his religious experiences while he trotted. Maybe it was all a single experience repeated. He felt truth coming to him from the sun. He received a communication that was also light and warmth. It made him very remote from his horny Wisconsin passengers, those farmers whose whoops and whore cries he could hardly hear when he was in one of his states. And again out of the flaming of the sun would come to him a secret certainty that the goal set for this earth was that it should be filled with good, saturated with it. After everything preposterous, after dog had eaten dog, after the crocodile death had pulled everyone into his mud. It wouldn't conclude as Mrs. Skoglund, bribing him to round up the Jews and hasten the Second Coming, imagined it, but in another way. This was his clumsy intuition. It went no further. Subsequently, he proceeded through life as life seemed to want him to do it.

There remained one thing more this morning, which was explicitly physical, occurring first as a sensation in his arms and against his breast and, from the pressure, passing into him and going into his breast.

It was like this: When he came into the hospital room and saw Pop with the sides of his bed raised, like a crib, and Pop, so very feeble, and writhing, and toothless, like a baby, and the dirt already cast into his face, into the wrinkles—Pop wanted to pluck out the intravenous needles and he was piping his weak death noise. The gauze patches taped over the needles were soiled with dark blood. Then Woody took off his shoes, lowered the side of the bed, and climbed in and held him in his arms to soothe and still him. As if he were Pop's father, he said to him, "Now, Pop. Pop." Then it was like the wrestle in Mrs. Skoglund's parlor, when Pop turned angry like an unclean spirit and Woody tried to appease him, and warn him, saying, "Those women will be back!" Beside the coal stove, when Pop hit Woody in the teeth with his head and then became sullen, like a stout fish. But this struggle in the hospital was weak—so weak! In his great pity, Woody held Pop, who was fluttering and shivering. From those people, Pop had told him, you'll never find out what life is, because they don't know what it is. Yes, Pop—well, what is it, Pop? Hard to comprehend that Pop, who was dug in for eighty-three years and had done all he could to stay, should now want nothing but to free himself. How could Woody allow the old man to pull the intravenous needles out? Willful Pop, he wanted what he wanted when he wanted it. But what he wanted at the very last Woody failed to follow, it was such a switch.

After a time, Pop's resistance ended. He subsided and subsided. He rested against his son, his small body curled there. Nurses came and looked. They disapproved, but Woody, who couldn't spare a hand to wave them out, motioned with his head toward the door. Pop, whom Woody thought he had stilled, only had found a better way to get around him. Loss of heat was the way he did it. His heat was leaving him. As can happen with small animals while you hold them in your hand, Woody presently felt him cooling. Then, as Woody did his best to restrain him, and thought he was succeeding, Pop divided himself. And when he was separated from his warmth, he slipped into death. And there was his elderly, large, muscular son, still holding and pressing him when there was nothing anymore to press. You could never pin down that self-willed man. When he was ready to make his move, he made it—always on his own terms. And always, always, something up his sleeve. That was how he was.

Louis Chu
(1915–1970)

The Chu family emigrated from Toishan, a village near Canton, China, when Louis was a boy of nine. He was educated in the public schools of Newark, New Jersey, and at Upsala College, New York University, and the New School for Social Research. As an American soldier in World War II, he served in China. After the war he returned to his native land to marry, bringing his new wife out of the country just prior to the Communist takeover of 1949.

Back in New York, he was employed by the New York City Welfare Department and became director of a social service center. He was also a Chinatown celebrity as an officer of the Soo Yuen Benevolent Association and host of a popular radio program called "Chinese Festival."

Chu's Eat a Bowl of Tea *(1961) is unique in its realistic portrait of the "bachelor society" ambiance of Chinese-American enclaves prior to the end of World War II. In the nineteenth and early twentieth centuries, most settlers from China were men: Some had left wives and children behind, others made arranged marriages and fathered children in China, but only the male children were apt to follow their fathers. After the Chinese Exclusion Act was repealed in 1943 and increased immigration of refugees from Communism was allowed, more women and whole families began to arrive, and the male-dominated society was transformed.*

Chu's satiric novel is set in the transitionary period. Wah Gay and Lee Gong, two old friends in New York's Chinatown, arrange a marriage between their offspring, Ben Loy—a waiter in a Connecticut restaurant— and Mei Oi—left behind with her mother in a village near Canton. The young people meet and marry in China and settle in New York. The marriage is troubled by his impotence and her infidelity, but the newlyweds are ultimately able to settle their differences and settle down to a contented life in San Francisco, separate from both fathers.

The dialogue accurately recreates the speakers' Sze Yup dialect, com-

plete with curses referring to incest, sodomy, and death. Settings include the family association meeting rooms, barbershops, and mah jong clubs where the men gather to drink, gossip, and gamble.

The following sections describing the marriage arrangements, Mei Oi's arrival in America, and the American family association wedding banquet are excerpted from the 1961 edition.

[From] *Eat a Bowl of Tea*

[A Chinese Wedding]

IV

THE FOLLOWING AFTERNOON, when Wah Gay[1] got up at one o'clock, Lee Gong was already there rattling the door knob trying to get in.

The proprietor unlocked the door. "So early today?"

"Yes. I couldn't get any sleep last night."

The two had been friends for many years. Up till ten years ago, they had been friends who rarely saw each other. Wang Wah Gay, after a short stay in New York, had gone out to Chicago, where he became co-owner of the New Canton Restaurant on North Clark Street with his elder brother Wang Wah Lim.[2] Elder brother Lim was in charge of the kitchen; while little brother Gay, because of his greater knowledge of the English language, was a combination manager-cashier-waiter.

On the other hand, Lee Gong's only contact with the restaurant business had been a short three months spent as a dishwasher in a Chinese restaurant on 59th Street. This was when he first had arrived in New York from China and the restaurant since then had changed hands many times.

"I didn't get much sleep either," said Wah Gay. "What was the matter with you? Why didn't you get any sleep?"

"That . . . that young man who was here yesterday," Lee Gong sat down

---

1. The groom's father operates a gambling club called Money Come.
2. Wang is the family name, listed first by Chinese tradition.

on the sofa and lit a cigarette, "I forgot to ask you his name." He tried to make it sound casual.

"You mean the one who brought me the letter?"

"Yes, that's right," Lee Gong said impatiently.

"That was my little boy." Wah Gay tried hard to keep from laughing out loud. "Come to think of it, it was the first time he has been here."

Lee Gong knew that his friend Wah Gay's son had arrived in this country a few years ago. Other than that he knew nothing. And he had had no reason to want to know more. In spite of the many letters he had been getting from his wife, Jung Shee, in China, urging him to find a suitable husband for their daughter Mei Oi, who was of a very marriageable age—just eighteen—Lee Gong had been of the opinion that his daughter was still young and there was plenty of time to find her a husband.

His many years in America had made him frown on the customary early marriages in China. During idle discussions at the Money Come, Lee Gong had often spoken out against early marriages and dependence upon the support of the parents. While he had expected Jung Shee to keep harping at him to search for a husband for Mei Oi from the Golden Mountain,[3] he had paid little attention to these letters until yesterday, when he saw the young man whom he suspected was Wah Gay's son.

"How many years has he got?" he pursued in earnest.

"This year he is twenty-four."

"A very commendable boy."

Wah Gay was not born yesterday. The moment Lee Gong mentioned Ben Loy he knew what his old friend had in mind. But he didn't want Lee Gong to know that he knew. He was rather proud of his son Ben Loy. He had kept him on the straight path. Any girl would be lucky to have his son for a husband.

"Where does your boy work?" pursued Lee Gong.

"Ben Loy is working in Stanton, Connecticut, at the China Pagoda."

It was almost two o'clock now and Money Come soon had enough players to start a game of mah-jong.[4]

* * *

XII

Mei Oi had met her father for the first time at Idlewild Airport[5] when she and her husband arrived from San Francisco. She had not known which one

---

3. The term used by Chinese immigrants to refer to America, especially San Francisco.

4. Played with 144 domino-like tiles, usually by four players.

5. Former name of John F. Kennedy Airport on Long Island, New York.

was her father until the white-haired, slightly-built man wearing a brown, double-breasted suit that needed pressing edged forward and called out, "Mei Oi!"

"Papa!" Mei Oi was trying to find some resemblance between this man and the pictures that she had seen of him back home, pictures that had been taken a long time ago. Her father placed an arm around her shoulder, "Daughter, daughter!"

"She's air-sick," volunteered Ben Loy. A gust of wind raised and lowered everybody's hair.

The larger man with a cigar in his mouth next stepped forward. His hand went up to his mouth and the cigar dropped out of sight. "*Ah Sow,*" he bowed slightly.

Mei Oi blushed. "*Lao Yair,*" she bowed, assuming this man was her father-in-law.

Ben Loy's father, Wah Gay, extended his hand to his new daughter-in-law; but Mei Oi failed to take it, whereupon he quickly switched it to his son. "Loy, how are you?"

"Ah Loy!" Lee Gong shook hands with his son-in-law.

They hailed a taxi and headed for Manhattan. Mei Oi was sick from the plane ride. To her the trip downtown was an endless stream of turns and stops. Turns and stops. She only half-heartedly answered her father's question about her mother and the village. Her father-in-law thoughtfully put out his cigar.

"We must give a banquet to celebrate the wedding," said Wah Gay as the taxi rolled down Second Avenue toward Chinatown. "After all, you, Ah Loy, are my only son." He turned to the bride's father, "You, my good friend . . . you have only this little girl . . . heh heh. It's only right we should give a banquet in honor of the marriage."

Later that day Wah Gay and Lee Gong brought noodles and won ton, telling the young ones that these were good for Mei Oi's upset stomach.

* * *

XIV

Wah Gay went ahead with plans for a marriage banquet. He had considered not having the party at all, but he dismissed the idea quickly. After all, Ben Loy was his only son. During the father's many-times-ten-years in New York, he had been invited to all kinds of celebrations: Weddings, hair-cut parties, departures for China, new arrivals from China. During the days when two Chinese opera companies played to standing room only, he was frequently invited to sit down and dine with the stage celebrities after the show. Now, with the return of Ben Loy and his bride, it was only fitting that the brand-new father-in-law invite his friends and cousins to celebrate the auspicious occasion. The banquet at the village did not count, according to Wah Gay. This was New York, where another set of friends and cousins waited expectantly.

This probably would be only the beginning, for what would be more proper and natural than to celebrate the birth of a grandchild in another year or so? Wah Gay beamed when he thought of a yet-to-be-born grandchild. He would become a grandpa. Just thinking about it made him happy.

With two hundred and fifty invitation cards in raised gold letters already sent out, Wah Gay once more settled down to relax at his favorite pastime and occupation. Normally in-laws among the Chinese would shy away from the gaming tables when the other was present, in order to avoid any possible embarrassment. But as far as Wah Gay and Lee Gong were concerned, the marriage of their offspring placed no such restriction on their social activities. The two continued to play mah-jong just like old times.

There was, however, one added chore for Wah Gay. A steady stream of invited guests would come in to congratulate him, each bearing a red envelope containing money. To the bearer of each envelope, Wah Gay would say, "Heh heh, there's no need for this, old friend." He would hand each a red printed thank-you card and a cigar. He kept the thank-you cards handy, right next to the mah-jongs. When he had received fifteen to twenty of these money-bearing envelopes, he would tie them with a rubber band to keep them more orderly. Soon his desk in the back room began to bulge with these envelopes and their contents. Wah Gay himself would not open them. He would turn them over to his son and daughter-in-law after the banquet.

The day of the banquet broke clear and sunny but, toward the latter part of the afternoon, the sun began to fade and patches of clouds floated eastward. An hour before banquet time, a slight drizzle began to descend upon Chinatown. The neon lights on Mott Street came on earlier than usual. The streets and sidewalks soon were wet. A semi-darkness commenced creeping upon this city within a city.

Automobiles and taxis stopped and crawled. Started and stopped. People darted in and out of traffic. Umbrellas bobbed up and down. Neon lights flickered in the distance. The wetness of the asphalt pavement reflected the lit-up pagoda roof of the Grand China Restaurant.

There had been no mah-jong playing for Wah Gay this afternoon. He and Lee Gong had been sitting idly in the basement club house until 5:30, when they trotted over to a cigar store on Chatham Square to pick up cigarettes and cigars for the banquet. Wah Gay found out, when he called to check, that the liquor had been delivered to the restaurant by Wing Lee Wei Company.

When the two fathers arrived at the restaurant, Ah Song, the club house hanger-on, and Chong Loo, the rent collector, were already there. Wah Gay had asked them to help out at the banquet. Chong Loo tore a small opening in each package of cigarettes and placed one to a table. Ah Song instructed the waiters to open a bottle of Haig and Haig and a bottle of Johnnie Walker for each table. Outside in the vestibule, the flowers which the florist had delivered a few minutes earlier awaited attention. Ah Song asked one of the waiters for a flower vase with which to decorate the head table.

Dinner at six, show up at seven. That's a prevailing Chinese custom. Although the invitation card said six o'clock, in all probability the dinner would not start until sometime after seven. Ben Loy and his bride did not arrive until a few minutes after six. Mei Oi's face was flushed slightly from the brisk walk to the restaurant. Her red satin Chinese gown fitted her snugly.

The moment the couple entered the restaurant, Ah Song appeared at the doorway with roses for Mei Oi. He proceeded to pin the flowers on Mei Oi's gown, while the bridegroom stood by awkwardly. From where they sat watching, the respective fathers-in-law were open-mouthed at the scene. The bride's face reddened noticeably.

Wah Gay, his face flushed, and mindful of Ah Song's reputation with women, was angry at himself for having asked Ah Song to help out. Ordinarily the incident itself would have been nothing scandalous; but Ah Song was famous for this sort of thing.

Wah Gay leaned over to Lee Gong and whispered, "That sonovabitch Ah Song is no damned good." They hoped that not too many of the guests had seen the episode. It had occurred in the vestibule, screened off from the rest of the dining room by a partition.

Ben Loy quickly steered his bride toward the head table, where no guests had been seated yet. Wah Gay now stood by the entrance, welcoming the arriving guests, while Lee Gong was sitting nearby, content to let his old friend play the host. Wang Chuck Ting, also sitting nearby, had been asked by Wah Gay to be master of ceremonies. Now, as Ben Loy and Mei Oi approached the head table, the president of the Wang Association got up and nodded to them. He shook hands with Ben Loy and bowed slightly to the bride. The seating of the bridal couple created a babble among the guests as they whispered comments on the bride's beauty.

After having seated Mei Oi at the head table, Ben Loy joined his father at the reception line. Children were running helter-skelter in all directions. Waiters were bringing ice cubes and ginger ale for the tables. The manager came out of his cashier's cage and walked over to the microphone, which was at the left of the head table, and tested it by counting into it.

The guests continued to stream in, reaching a crescendo at about six-thirty, and then began to taper off. Smoke filled the dining room rapidly.

The drizzle, light as it was, had brought out an assortment of umbrellas and these were evident everywhere throughout the large dining room. As the room became more fully filled, the waiters had to twist and turn to make their way through the zig-zagged pattern of round tables, which were much too close together. Shortly after six-forty-five, the stream of arriving guests had dwindled to a trickle. Those who had arrived early were getting restless. There was much turning of heads and frequent consultation with their watches. The late arrivals were expecting the commencement of speeches momentarily. Wah Gay, now seated at the head table, looked in the direction of the doorway to see if anyone else was coming in. Then he consulted his watch. Five minutes past seven. He leaned over and whispered into Wang Chuck Ting's ear.

The President of the Wang Association, a man in his seventies, who would look quite at home with a vest pocket watch and a gold chain dangling across his slightly bulging stomach, slowly got up and walked over to the microphone. "Uncles, brothers, aunts, sisters, and honored guests, little brother appreciates the privilege tonight to welcome you all on behalf of our host, Mr. Cousin Wah Gay. He has set these inadequate tables for you as a token of thanks and appreciation for your generous gifts. Although his beloved son, Mr. Cousin Ben Loy, and Mr. Lee Gong's daughter, Miss Lee Mei Oi, have been married in the old country, Mr. Cousin Wah Gay is not one to forget his friends and cousins and relatives in New York. On the occasion of the marriage of his son Ben Loy to Miss Lee, he wants to share this happiness with you all. . . . Now I would like to introduce to you the President of the Wang Association, Mr. Cousin Fook Ming, to say a few words . . ."

The guests stirred in their seats and applauded politely. Some craned their necks to see who was going to talk. Many were indifferent. A man almost directly opposite the banquet chairman got up and walked over to the microphone. He was a pale, thin, bespectacled man in his late fifties. Actually he was a Vice-President of the Wang Association, but, in keeping with custom, he was introduced as President. "First of all," he began, "I want to introduce to you our host, Mr. Cousin Wah Gay."

Wang Wah Gay got up and beamingly acknowledged the applause.

"Mr. Lee Gong, father of the lovely bride."

Lee Gong got up and bowed to the upturned, smiling faces.

"The bride and bridegroom, Mr. and Mrs. Ben Loy."

The newlyweds rose and waved to the guests. The applause was by far the loudest.

"And now I would like to introduce some officers of the Wang Association . . . Mr. Cousin Ping Wah, Treasurer of the Association . . . Mr. Cousin Won Duck, Chinese Language Secretary . . . Mr. Cousin Kuen Jay, English Language Secretary . . . Mr. Eng Ho Soon, President of Ping On Tong . . ."

The obliging audience applauded everybody who rated an introduction. Many consulted their watches for the second and third time. Children drained dry their glasses of water. Here and there a mother cautioned her restless youngster to keep quiet.

Wang Chuck Ting next introduced Wang Doo Ott, Second Vice-President of the Wang Association, but he, too, was introduced as *the* president of the Association. "On behalf of Mr. Cousin Wah Gay," began Vice-President Doo Ott, "the bride and bridegroom, I want to thank you all for the many gifts, for the monies, thank you for your time. By your presence here tonight, you have given our host a big face. . . . Please drink heartily."

Wang Chuck Ting again got up. "I invite you to drink many drinks and to use your chop sticks generously. We all hope that by this time next year, we will once again lift up our glasses and drink many drinks."

Another round of applause broke out among the guests. At the head table, Ben Loy gazed at the carnation in his lapel, while Mei Oi opened her pocketbook and took a quick glance at the tiny mirror. Ben Loy eyed her longingly. He was very proud of her tonight. He thought she looked very lovely in her red gown.

Someone at the table said, "Next year we will drink to the first baby."

Embarrassed, Mei Oi lowered her eyes and focused them on the chop sticks in front of her.

Wang Chuck Ting continued, "Today is an excellent day for a holiday. The rain and wind will bring good fortune and good luck to the newlyweds."

When the toastmaster finally sat down he turned to Ben Loy. "Little brother, how did you come to pick such a lovely bride?"

Ben Loy mumbled that the bride had been already picked out for him by his father. To this Wang Chuck Ting chuckled, "I wish *my* father had been so good at picking himself a daughter-in-law!" Laughter broke out at the table. Hardly had the laughter died down, when Chuck Ting opened his mouth again. "Heh heh, next year around this time, we'll drink again. We'll drink to their first-born."

A shy smile appeared on Mei Oi's face, now fully flushed. Ben Loy tried to suppress a grin.

A few late comers straggled in and, after looking around, found seats without too much inconvenience to the rest of the guests. The pandemonium of the crowd blended with the clinking of ice cubes being gingerly dropped into glasses. Wah Gay cheerfully picked up one of the bottles and started pouring for his distinguished guests. He even poured one for his new daughter-in-law, who feebly protested that she did not drink. Right away a chorus of protests arose from the other guests.

"If you never drank before in your life," said Wang Chuck Ting, "tonight you must drink, for tonight is a big holiday."

The crimson of Mei Oi's face deepened. From a nearby table, unnoticed by Mei Oi, Ah Song stole repeated glances in her direction.

By the time the waiters brought out the *little dishes*, the guests were famished. They attacked the food with enthusiasm. Soon the sweet and pungent spareribs, the one-thousand-year eggs, the spiced gizzards, and shrimp chips were gone. Next the waiters brought out a large bowl of soup for each table. Ben Loy gazed at the thick shark-fin soup sprinkled with powdery Virginia ham. After a moment's hesitation, he picked up the small ladle in front of him and began serving the guests.

"Let's not stand on ceremony," Chuck Ting protested. He reached over and picked up Wah Gay's bowl. "Here, fill up your father's first."

"Don't forget the bride," someone said. Ben Loy sheepishly picked up Mei Oi's bowl.

"I just want a little," she said.

Chuck Ting raised his glass. "Let's drink to the bride and bridegroom."

The soup was followed by *Wor Shew Up, Bird's Nest Chicken, Lobster Egg Roll, Mushrooms, Squabs* . . . all in rapid succession amidst clinking glasses. The guests toasted many drinks. And gradually stomachs were moving closer toward the edge of the table. Wah Gay cupped his hand to his mouth and whispered to Lee Gong, "Let's go."

Each took with him a cup and a bottle. They stopped at their own table. "A drink of many thanks to you," said Wah Gay and Lee Gong, raising their cups. "Good fortune all year round!"

"Good fortune all year round!" the guests rose with their glasses in response. The two hosts moved on quickly to the next table, then the next, until they had gone around to every table, thanking the guests, pouring drinks for them. Many of the guests jovially predicted that they would drink again next year at the haircut party of the first grandchild. Wah Gay and Lee Gong laughed happily at these predictions.

As soon as they returned to their own table, Wah Gay signaled to Ben Loy and his cousin, Wing Sim, who had come from Connecticut for the festivity and was sitting at the next table with his wife, Eng Shee. It was time for Ben Loy and Wing Sim to make the rounds. After a hasty huddle to decide what brand of whiskey to take along, they started off with a first stop at the head table, with Wing Sim pouring the drinks and Ben Loy doing the toasting. Earlier Wing Sim had suggested that he carry two bottles, one to be filled with tea for Ben Loy. But the bridegroom shrugged this precautionary measure off, saying that he would not get drunk.

Ah Song got up and glanced in the direction of Ben Loy. He walked over and was about to join the two cousins when Chuck Ting intervened. "Ah Song, there's no need for you to accompany them. They'll manage by themselves."

Ah Song retreated to his own table, but not without another furtive glance at Mei Oi.

Chong Loo joined the bridegroom and Wing Sim with a tray full of chopped betel nuts and now offered these to the guests. The married adults at each table took a piece of the chopped nuts wrapped in red paper and left a tiny envelope of money on the tray. Before moving on to the next table, Chong Loo scooped up the red envelopes and stuffed them into the brown paper bag carried for this purpose, and replenished the tray with the chopped nuts.

While all this was going on the waiters continued to bring out additional dishes: *Abalone, Chicken Guy Que,* and many others.

Mrs. Wing Sim, who was not many years older than the bride, now accompanied Mei Oi for the tea ceremony. On a little round service tray, the older woman carried ten cups filled with tea, first to the head table. Mei Oi stood next to her, holding her folded fan up to her chin.

"Drink tea, sirs," announced Mrs. Wing Sim, extending the tray to the center of the table. The guests rose, each picking up a cup of tea and sipping it. The cups were then put back on the tray. Most of them were still nearly full. Little red envelopes began dropping onto the tray beside the cups. Ben Loy's aunt, Mrs. Wang Wah Lim, was ready with a brown paper bag to receive the red envelopes. She had flown in from Chicago especially for the party.

As soon as the cups were refilled, the hostesses moved on to the next table. At each stop, the same refrain greeted them: "Heh heh, next year we will drink again." And Mei Oi would raise her fan a little higher.

When the tea ceremony was over, Ah Song walked briskly to a waiter's stand in the back and brought back several boxes of cigars. He proceeded to pass out the cigars to the men at each table.

By the time the guests were ready to leave, it was close to nine o'clock. Ah Song was holding the door open. Wah Gay, Lee Gong, and Ben Loy stood by and smilingly nodded to the departing guests.

"Thank you many times, great uncle."

"Thank you."

"Thank you, Mr. Wang."

"Thank you, Mr. Lee."

"Today you have given me a big face."

"You have a kind heart."

"Thank you for the big face."

Yoshiko Uchida
(1921–1992)

A nisei, or second-generation Japanese American, Uchida was born in Alameda, California. She was a senior at the University of California, Berkeley when, after the bombing of Pearl Harbor, Americans of Japanese descent were ordered into "relocation camps." With her family, she spent five months in the horse barns at Tanforan Racetrack before they were assigned to Topaz, a camp in the Utah desert. Uchida taught in the camp elementary school until the spring of 1943 when she was allowed to accept a fellowship for graduate study at Smith College, where she earned her master's degree.

After the war, Uchida took secretarial work so that she could reserve time in the evenings for her writing. Her first book, The Dancing Kettle and Other Japanese Folk Tales *(1949), was well received, and a Ford Foundation grant allowed her to visit Japan for the first time, where she collected more traditional lore, published in* The Magic Listening Cap *(1955), illustrated*

*with her own drawings. She has published more than twenty-five books for
adults and young readers.*

*The children of immigrants were a special concern to her. She wrote,
"Through my books I hope to give young Asian Americans a sense of their
past and to reinforce their self-esteem and self-knowledge. At the same
time, I want to dispel the stereotypic image held by many non-Asians about
the Japanese and write about them as real people. *** I write to celebrate
our common humanity, for the basic elements of humanity are present in
all our strivings."*

Autobiographical accounts include *Journey to Topaz: A Story of the Japanese-
American Evacuation* (1971), *Journey Home* (1978), and *Desert Exile: The Uproot-
ing of a Japanese-American Family* (1982). *Picture Bride* (1987) is a novel. *"Tears of
Autumn"* is from *The Forbidden Stitch* (1989).

Tears of Autumn

HANA OMIYA STOOD AT THE RAILING of the small ship that shuddered toward
America in a turbulent November sea. She shivered as she pulled the folds
of her silk kimono close to her throat and tightened the wool shawl about
her shoulders.

She was thin and small, her dark eyes shadowed in her pale face, her
black hair piled high in a pompadour that seemed too heavy for so slight a
woman. She clung to the moist rail and breathed the damp salt air deep into
her lungs. Her body seemed leaden and lifeless, as though it were simply the
vehicle transporting her soul to a strange new life, and she longed with
childlike intensity to be home again in Oka Village.

She longed to see the bright persimmon dotting the barren trees beside
the thatched roofs, to see the fields of golden rice stretching to the mountains where only last fall she had gathered plum white mushrooms, and to
see once more the maple trees lacing their flaming colors through the green
pine. If only she could see a familiar face, eat a meal without retching, walk
on solid ground, and stretch out at night on a *tatami* mat instead of in a hard
narrow bunk. She thought now of seeking the warm shelter of her bunk but
could not bear to face the relentless smell of fish that penetrated the lower
decks.

Why did I ever leave Japan? she wondered bitterly. Why did I ever listen to my uncle? And yet she knew it was she herself who had begun the chain of events that placed her on this heaving ship. It was she who had first planted in her uncle's mind the thought that she would make a good wife for Taro Takeda, the lonely man who had gone to America to make his fortune in Oakland, California.

It all began one day when her uncle had come to visit her mother.

"I must find a nice young bride," he had said, startling Hana with this blunt talk of marriage in her presence. She blushed and was ready to leave the room when her uncle quickly added, "My good friend Takeda has a son in America. I must find someone willing to travel to that far land."

This last remark was intended to indicate to Hana and her mother that he didn't consider this a suitable prospect for Hana, who was the youngest daughter of what once had been a fine family. Her father, until his death fifteen years ago, had been the largest landholder of the village and one of its last samurai.[1] They had once had many servants and field hands, but now all that was changed. Their money was gone. Hana's three older sisters had made good marriages, and the eldest remained in their home with her husband to carry on the Omiya name and perpetuate the homestead. Her other sisters had married merchants in Osaka and Nagoya and were living comfortably.

Now that Hana was twenty-one, finding a proper husband for her had taken on an urgency that produced an embarrassing secretive air over the entire matter. Usually, her mother didn't speak of it until they were lying side by side on their quilts at night. Then, under the protective cover of darkness, she would suggest one name and then another, hoping that Hana would indicate an interest in one of them.

Her uncle spoke freely of Taro Takeda only because he was so sure Hana would never consider him. "He is a conscientious, hardworking man who has been in the United States for almost ten years. He is thirty-one, operates a small shop, and rents some rooms above the shop where he lives." Her uncle rubbed his chin thoughtfully. "He could provide well for a wife," he added.

"Ah," Hana's mother said softly.

"You say he is successful in this business?" Hana's sister inquired.

"His father tells me he sells many things in his shop—clothing, stockings, needles, thread, and buttons—such things as that. He also sells bean paste, pickled radish, bean cake, and soy sauce. A wife of his would not go cold or hungry."

They all nodded, each of them picturing this merchant in varying degrees of success and affluence. There were many Japanese emigrating to America these days, and Hana had heard of the picture brides who went with nothing more than an exchange of photographs to bind them to a strange man.

---

1. Member of the feudal military class.

"Taro San is lonely," her uncle continued. "I want to find for him a fine young woman who is strong and brave enough to cross the ocean alone."

"It would certainly be a different kind of life," Hana's sister ventured, and for a moment, Hana thought she glimpsed a longing ordinarily concealed behind her quiet, obedient face. In that same instant, Hana knew she wanted more for herself than her sisters had in their proper, arranged, and loveless marriages. She wanted to escape the smothering strictures of life in her village. She certainly was not going to marry a farmer and spend her life working beside him planting, weeding, and harvesting in the rice paddies until her back became bent from too many years of stooping and her skin was turned to brown leather by the sun and wind. Neither did she particularly relish the idea of marrying a merchant in a big city as her two sisters had done. Since her mother objected to her going to Tokyo to seek employment as a teacher, perhaps she would consent to a flight to America for what seemed a proper and respectable marriage.

Almost before she realized what she was doing, she spoke to her uncle. "Oji San, perhaps I should go to America to make this lonely man a good wife."

"You, Hana Chan?" Her uncle observed her with startled curiosity. "You would go all alone to a foreign land so far away from your mother and family?"

"I would not allow it." Her mother spoke fiercely. Hana was her youngest and she had lavished upon her the attention and latitude that often befall the last child. How could she permit her to travel so far, even to marry the son of Takeda who was known to her brother?

But now, a notion that had seemed quite impossible a moment before was lodged in his receptive mind, and Hana's uncle grasped it with the pleasure that comes from an unexpected discovery.

"You know," he said looking at Hana, "it might be a very good life in America."

Hana felt a faint fluttering in her heart. Perhaps this lonely man in America was her means of escaping both the village and the encirclement of her family.

Her uncle spoke with increasing enthusiasm of sending Hana to become Taro's wife. And the husband of Hana's sister, who was head of their household, spoke with equal eagerness. Although he never said so, Hana guessed he would be pleased to be rid of her, the spirited younger sister who stirred up his placid life with what he considered radical ideas about life and the role of women. He often claimed that Hana had too much schooling for a girl. She had graduated from Women's High School in Kyoto, which gave her five more years of schooling that her older sister.

"It has addled her brain—all that learning from those books," he said when he tired of arguing with Hana.

A man's word carried much weight for Hana's mother. Pressed by the two men, she consulted her other daughters and their husbands. She discussed the matter carefully with her brother and asked the village priest.

Finally, she agreed to an exchange of family histories and an investigation was begun into Taro Takeda's family, his education, and his health, so they would be assured there was no insanity or tuberculosis or police records concealed in his family's past. Soon Hana's uncle was devoting his energies entirely to serving as go-between for Hana's mother and Taro Takeda's father.

When at last an agreement to the marriage was almost reached, Taro wrote his first letter to Hana. It was brief and proper and gave no more clue to his character than the stiff formal portrait taken at his graduation from middle school. Hana's uncle had given her the picture with apologies from his parents, because it was the only photo they had of him and it was not a flattering likeness.

Hana hid the letter and photograph in the sleeve of her kimono and took them to the outhouse to study in private. Squinting in the dim light and trying to ignore the foul odor, she read and reread Taro's letter, trying to find the real man somewhere in the sparse unbending prose.

By the time he sent her money for her steamship tickets, she had received ten more letters, but none revealed much more of the man than the first. In none did he disclose his loneliness or his need, but Hana understood this. In fact, she would have recoiled from a man who bared his intimate thoughts to her so soon. After all, they would have a lifetime together to get to know one another.

So it was that Hana had left her family and sailed alone to America with a small hope trembling inside of her. Tomorrow, at last, the ship would dock in San Francisco and she would meet face to face the man she was soon to marry. Hana was overcome with excitement at the thought of being in America, and terrified of the meeting about to take place. What would she say to Taro Takeda when they first met, and for all the days and years after?

Hana wondered about the flat above the shop. Perhaps it would be luxuriously furnished with the finest of brocades and lacquers, and perhaps there would be a servant, although he had not mentioned it. She worried whether she would be able to manage on the meager English she had learned at Women's High School. The overwhelming anxiety for the day to come and the violent rolling of the ship were more than Hana could bear. Shuddering in the face of the wind, she leaned over the railing and became violently and wretchedly ill.

By five the next morning, Hana was up and dressed in her finest purple silk kimono and coat. She could not eat the bean soup and rice that appeared for breakfast and took only a few bites of the yellow pickled radish. Her bags, which had scarcely been touched since she boarded the ship, were easily packed, for all they contained were her kimonos and some of her favorite books. The large willow basket, tightly secured by a rope, remained under the bunk, untouched since her uncle had placed it there.

She had not befriended the other women in her cabin, for they had lain in their bunks for most of the voyage, too sick to be company to anyone. Each morning Hana had fled the closeness of the sleeping quarters and spent most of the day huddled in a corner of the deck, listening to the lonely songs of some Russians also travelling to an alien land.

As the ship approached land, Hana hurried up to the deck to look out at the gray expanse of ocean and sky, eager for a first glimpse of her new homeland.

"We won't be docking until almost noon," one of the deckhands told her.

Hana nodded, "I can wait," she answered, but the last hours seemed the longest.

When she set foot on American soil at last, it was not in the city of San Francisco as she had expected, but on Angel Island, where all third-class passengers were taken. She spent two miserable days and nights waiting, as the immigrants were questioned by officials, examined for trachoma and tuberculosis, and tested for hookworm by a woman who collected their stools on tin pie plates. Hana was relieved she could produce her own, not having to borrow a little from someone else, as some of the women had to do. It was a bewildering, degrading beginning, and Hana was sick with anxiety, wondering if she would ever be released.

On the third day, a Japanese messenger from San Francisco appeared with a letter for her from Taro. He had written it the day of her arrival, but it had not reached her for two days.

Taro welcomed her to America, and told her that the bearer of the letter would inform Taro when she was to be released so he could be at the pier to meet her.

The letter eased her anxiety for a while, but as soon as she was released and boarded the launch for San Francisco, new fears rose up to smother her with a feeling almost of dread.

The early morning mist had become a light chilling rain, and on the pier black umbrellas bobbed here and there, making the task of recognition even harder. Hana searched desperately for a face that resembled the photo she had studied so long and hard. Suppose he hadn't come. What would she do then?

Hana took a deep breath, lifted her head and walked slowly from the launch. The moment she was on the pier, a man in a black coat, wearing a derby and carrying an umbrella, came quickly to her side. He was of slight build, not much taller than she, and his face was sallow and pale. He bowed stiffly and murmured, "You have had a long trip, Miss Omiya. I hope you are well."

Hana caught her breath. "You are Takeda San?" she asked.

He removed his hat and Hana was further startled to see that he was already turning bald.

"You are Takeda San?" she asked again. He looked older than thirty-one.

"I am afraid I no longer resemble the early photo my parents gave you. I am sorry."

Hana had not meant to begin like this. It was not going well.

"No, no," she said quickly. "It is just that I . . . that is, I am terribly nervous. . . ." Hana stopped abruptly, too flustered to go on.

"I understand," Taro said gently. "You will feel better when you meet my friends and have some tea. Mr. and Mrs. Toda are expecting you in Oakland. You will be staying with them until . . ." He couldn't bring himself to mention the marriage just yet and Hana was grateful he hadn't.

He quickly made arrangements to have her baggage sent to Oakland then led her carefully along the rain-slick pier toward the streetcar that would take them to the ferry.

Hana shuddered at the sight of another boat, and as they climbed to its upper deck she felt a queasy tightening of her stomach.

"I hope it will not rock too much," she said anxiously. "Is it many hours to your city?"

Taro laughed for the first time since their meeting, revealing the gold fillings of his teeth. "Oakland is just across the bay," he explained. "We will be there in twenty minutes."

Raising a hand to cover her mouth, Hana laughed with him and suddenly felt better. I am in America now, she thought, and this is the man I came to marry. Then she sat down carefully beside Taro, so no part of their clothing touched.

John Okada
(1923–1971)

Born and raised in Seattle, Washington, John Okada received two bachelor's degrees—in English and library science—from the University of Washington and a master's degree in English from Columbia University. He served as a sergeant in the U.S. Air Force in World War II.

Okada had a difficult time placing his first novel, No-No Boy, with a publisher. In a 1956 letter to the Charles Tuttle Company (who did publish the book the following year), Okada explained that the Japanese immigrant experience "has never been told in fiction and only in fiction can the hopes and fears and joys and sorrows of people be adequately recorded. I feel an urgency to write of the Japanese in the United States for the Issei [immigrant generation] are rapidly vanishing and I should regret it if their chapter in American history should die with them."

Okada told his publisher that he was at work on a second novel with an

Issei protagonist, but he never succeeded in having it published before he died of a heart attack. His widow, Dorothy, offered his manuscripts and papers to the University of California at Los Angeles, but they were not familiar with his work and not interested in the collection. Discouraged, she burned all the papers, and the rest of his writing was lost. No-No Boy was also ignored when first published; it was rescued from obscurity by students of Asian-American heritage in the 1970s.

Ichiro, the novel's American-born protagonist, has been interned with his family in a relocation camp. When he is asked, in a questionnaire circulated by the government, whether he is willing to serve in the U.S. armed services and renounce all loyalty to Japan, he answers both questions in the negative, becomes a no-no boy, and is imprisoned for his refusal to serve. On his return to Seattle, Ichiro finds that most of his contemporaries reject him for what they regard as his treasonous decision; his younger brother joins the army to make up for Ichiro's actions. At the same time, his mother and some of her friends are convinced that Japan has won the war. Kenji, who has returned from the army with a leg wound that will not heal, is the only person who understands the conflicts Ichiro faces and remains loyal to him. The opening chapter of the novel describes the internal and external conflicts Ichiro faces.

[From] No-No Boy

[Ichiro's Return]

1

TWO WEEKS AFTER his twenty-fifth birthday, Ichiro got off a bus at Second and Main in Seattle. He had been gone four years, two in camp and two in prison.

Walking down the street that autumn morning with a small, black suitcase, he felt like an intruder in a world to which he had no claim. It was just enough that he should feel this way, for, of his own free will, he had stood before the judge and said that he would not go in the army. At the time there was no other choice for him. That was when he was twenty-three, a man of twenty-three. Now, two years older, he was even more of a man.

Christ, he thought to himself, just a goddamn kid is all I was. Didn't know enough to wipe my own nose. What the hell have I done? What am I doing back here? Best thing I can do would be to kill some son of a bitch and head back to prison.

He walked toward the railroad depot where the tower with the clocks on all four sides was. It was a dirty looking tower of ancient brick. It was a dirty city. Dirtier, certainly, than it had a right to be after only four years.

Waiting for the light to change to green, he looked around at the people standing at the bus stop. A couple of men in suits, half a dozen women who failed to arouse him even after prolonged good behavior, and a young Japanese with a lunch bucket. Ichiro studied him, searching in his mind for the name that went with the round, pimply face and the short-cropped hair. The pimples were gone and the face had hardened, but the hair was still cropped. The fellow wore green, army-fatigue trousers and an Eisenhower jacket—Eto Minato. The name came to him at the same time as did the horrible significance of the army clothes. In panic, he started to step off the curb. It was too late. He had been seen.

"Itchy!" That was his nickname.

Trying to escape, Ichiro urged his legs frenziedly across the street.

"Hey, Itchy!" The caller's footsteps ran toward him.

An arm was placed across his back. Ichiro stopped and faced the other Japanese. He tried to smile, but could not. There was no way out now.

"I'm Eto. Remember?" Eto smiled and extended his palm. Reluctantly, Ichiro lifted his own hand and let the other shake it.

The round face with the round eyes peered at him through silver-rimmed spectacles. "What the hell! It's been a long time, but not that long. How've you been? What's doing?"

"Well . . . that is, I'm . . ."

"Last time must have been before Pearl Harbor. God, it's been quite a while, hasn't it? Three, no, closer to four years, I guess. Lotsa Japs coming back to the Coast. Lotsa Japs in Seattle. You'll see 'em around. Japs are funny that way. Gotta have their rice and saké and other Japs. Stupid, I say. The smart ones went to Chicago and New York and lotsa places back east, but there's still plenty coming back out this way." Eto drew cigarettes from his breast pocket and held out the package. "No? Well, I'll have one. Got the habit in the army. Just got out a short while back. Rough time, but I made it. Didn't get out in time to make the quarter, but I'm planning to go to school. How long you been around?"

Ichiro touched his toe to the suitcase. "Just got in. Haven't been home yet."

"When'd you get discharged?"

A car grinding its gears started down the street. He wished he were in it. "I . . . that is . . . I never was in."

Eto slapped him good-naturedly on the arm. "No need to look so sour. So you weren't in. So what? Been in camp all this time?"

"No." He made an effort to be free of Eto with his questions. He felt as if he were in a small room whose walls were slowly closing in on him. "It's been a long time, I know, but I'm really anxious to see the folks."

"What the hell. Let's have a drink. On me. I don't give a damn if I'm late to work. As for your folks, you'll see them soon enough. You drink, don't you?"

"Yeah, but not now."

"Ahh," Eto was disappointed. He shifted his lunch box from under one arm to the other.

"I've really got to be going."

The round face wasn't smiling any more. It was thoughtful. The eyes confronted Ichiro with indecision which changed slowly to enlightenment and then to suspicion. He remembered. He knew.

The friendliness was gone as he said: "No-no boy, huh?"

Ichiro wanted to say yes. He wanted to return the look of despising hatred and say simply yes, but it was too much to say. The walls had closed in and were crushing all the unspoken words back down into his stomach. He shook his head once, not wanting to evade the eyes but finding it impossible to meet them. Out of his big weakness the little ones were branching, and the eyes he didn't have the courage to face were ever present. If it would have helped to gouge out his own eyes, he would have done so long ago. The hate-churned eyes with the stamp of unrelenting condemnation were his cross and he had driven the nails with his own hands.

"Rotten bastard. Shit on you." Eto coughed up a mouthful of sputum and rolled his words around it: "Rotten, no-good bastard."

Surprisingly, Ichiro felt relieved. Eto's anger seemed to serve as a release to his own naked tensions. As he stooped to lift the suitcase a wet wad splattered over his hand and dripped onto the black leather. The legs of his accuser were in front of him. God in a pair of green fatigues, U.S. Army style. They were the legs of the jury that had passed sentence upon him. Beseech me, they seemed to say, throw your arms about me and bury your head between my knees and seek pardon for your great sin.

"I'll piss on you next time," said Eto vehemently.

He turned as he lifted the suitcase off the ground and hurried away from the legs and the eyes from which no escape was possible.

Jackson Street started at the waterfront and stretched past the two train depots and up the hill all the way to the lake, where the houses were bigger and cleaner and had garages with late-model cars in them. For Ichiro, Jackson Street signified that section of the city immediately beyond the railroad tracks between Fifth and Twelfth Avenues. That was the section which used to be pretty much Japanese town. It was adjacent to Chinatown and most of the gambling and prostitution and drinking seemed to favor the area.

Like the dirty clock tower of the depot, the filth of Jackson Street had increased. Ichiro paused momentarily at an alley and peered down the passage formed by the walls of two sagging buildings. There had been a door there at one time, a back door to a movie house which only charged a nickel. A nickel was a lot of money when he had been seven or nine or eleven. He wanted to go into the alley to see if the door was still there.

Being on Jackson Street with its familiar store fronts and taverns and restaurants, which were somehow different because the war had left its mark on them, was like trying to find one's way out of a dream that seemed real most of the time but wasn't really real because it was still only a dream. The war had wrought violent changes upon the people, and the people, in turn, working hard and living hard and earning a lot of money and spending it on whatever was available, had distorted the profile of Jackson Street. The street had about it the air of a carnival without quite succeeding at becoming one. A shooting gallery stood where once had been a clothing store; fish and chips had replaced a jewelry shop; and a bunch of Negroes were horsing around raucously in front of a pool parlor. Everything looked older and dirtier and shabbier.

He walked past the pool parlor, picking his way gingerly among the Negroes, of whom there had been only a few at one time and of whom there seemed to be nothing but now. They were smoking and shouting and cussing and carousing and the sidewalk was slimy with their spittle.

"Jap!"

His pace quickened automatically, but curiosity or fear or indignation or whatever it was made him glance back at the white teeth framed in a leering dark brown which was almost black.

"Go back to Tokyo, boy." Persecution in the drawl of the persecuted.

The white teeth and brown-black leers picked up the cue and jigged to the rhythmical chanting of "Jap-boy, To-ki-yo; Jap-boy, To-ki-yo . . ."

Friggin' niggers, he uttered savagely to himself and, from the same place deep down inside where tolerance for the Negroes and the Jews and the Mexicans and the Chinese and the too short and too fat and too ugly abided because he was Japanese and knew what it was like better than did those who were white and average and middle class and good Democrats or liberal Republicans, the hate which was unrelenting and terrifying seethed up.

Then he was home. It was a hole in the wall with groceries crammed in orderly confusion on not enough shelving, into not enough space. He knew what it would be like even before he stepped in. His father had described the place to him in a letter, composed in simple Japanese characters because otherwise Ichiro could not have read it. The letter had been purposely repetitive and painstakingly detailed so that Ichiro should not have any difficulty finding the place. The grocery store was the same one the Ozakis had operated for many years. That's all his father had had to say. Come to the grocery store which was once the store of the Ozakis. The Japanese characters, written simply so that he could read them, covered pages of directions as if he were a foreigner coming to the city for the first time.

Thinking about the letter made him so mad that he forgot about the Negroes. He opened the door just as he had a thousand times when they had lived farther down the block and he used to go to the Ozakis' for a loaf of bread or a jar of pickled scallions, and the bell tinkled just as he knew it would. All the grocery stores he ever knew had bells which tinkled when one opened the door and the familiar sound softened his inner turmoil.

"Ichiro?" The short, round man who came through the curtains at the back of the store uttered the name preciously as might an old woman. "Ya, Ichiro, you have come home. How good that you have come home!" The gently spoken Japanese which he had not heard for so long sounded strange. He would hear a great deal of it now that he was home, for his parents, like most of the old Japanese, spoke virtually no English. On the other hand, the children, like Ichiro, spoke almost no Japanese. Thus they communicated, the old speaking Japanese with an occasional badly mispronounced word or two of English; and the young, with the exception of a simple word or phrase of Japanese which came fairly effortlessly to the lips, resorting almost constantly to the tongue the parents avoided.

The father bounced silently over the wood flooring in slippered feet toward his son. Fondly, delicately, he placed a pudgy hand on Ichiro's elbow and looked up at his son who was Japanese but who had been big enough for football and tall enough for basketball in high school. He pushed the elbow and Ichiro led the way into the back, where there was a kitchen, a bathroom and one bedroom. He looked around the bedroom and felt like puking. It was neat and clean and scrubbed. His mother would have seen to that. It was just the idea of everybody sleeping in the one room. He wondered if his folks still pounded flesh.

He backed out of the bedroom and slumped down on a stool. "Where's Ma?"

"Mama is gone to the bakery." The father kept his beaming eyes on his son who was big and tall. He shut off the flow of water and shifted the metal teapot to the stove.

"What for?"

"Bread," his father said in reply, "bread for the store."

"Don't they deliver?"

"Ya, they deliver." He ran a damp rag over the table, which was spotlessly clean.

"What the hell is she doing at the bakery then?"

"It is good business, Ichiro." He was at the cupboard, fussing with the tea cups and saucers and cookies. "The truck comes in the morning. We take enough for the morning business. For the afternoon, we get soft, fresh bread. Mama goes to the bakery."

Ichiro tried to think of a bakery nearby and couldn't. There was a big Wonder Bread bakery way up on Nineteenth, where a nickel used to buy a bagful of day-old stuff. That was thirteen and a half blocks, all uphill. He knew the distance by heart because he'd walked it twice every day to go to grade school, which was a half-block beyond the bakery or fourteen blocks from home.

"What bakery?"

The water on the stove began to boil and the old man flipped the lid on the pot and tossed in a pinch of leaves. "Wonder Bread."

"Is that the one up on Nineteenth?"

"Ya."

"How much do you make on bread?"

"Let's see," he said pouring the tea, "Oh, three, four cents. Depends."

"How many loaves does Ma get?"

"Ten or twelve. Depends."

Ten loaves at three or four cents' profit added up to thirty or forty cents. He compromised at thirty-five cents and asked the next question: "The bus, how much is it?"

"Oh, let's see." He sipped the tea noisily, sucking it through his teeth in well regulated gulps. "Let's see. Fifteen cents for one time. Tokens are two for twenty-five cents. That is twelve and one-half cents."

Twenty-five cents for bus fare to get ten loaves of bread which turned a profit of thirty-five cents. It would take easily an hour to make the trip up and back. He didn't mean to shout, but he shouted: "Christ, Pa, what else do you give away?"

His father peered over the teacup with a look of innocent surprise.

It made him madder. "Figure it out. Just figure it out. Say you make thirty-five cents on ten loaves. You take a bus up and back and there's twenty-five cents shot. That leaves ten cents. On top of that, there's an hour wasted. What are you running a business for? Your health?"

Slup went the tea through his teeth, slup, slup, slup. "Mama walks." He sat there looking at his son like a benevolent Buddha.

Ichiro lifted the cup to his lips and let the liquid burn down his throat. His father had said "Mama walks" and that made things right with the world. The overwhelming simplicity of the explanation threatened to evoke silly giggles which, if permitted to escape, might lead to hysterics. He clenched his fists and subdued them.

At the opposite end of the table the father had slupped the last of his tea and was already taking the few steps to the sink to rinse out the cup.

"Goddammit, Pa, sit down!" He'd never realized how nervous a man his father was. The old man had constantly been doing something every minute since he had come. It didn't figure. Here he was, round and fat and cheerful-looking and, yet, he was going incessantly as though his trousers were crawling with ants.

"Ya, Ichiro, I forget you have just come home. We should talk." He resumed his seat at the table and busied his fingers with a box of matches.

Ichiro stepped out of the kitchen, spotted the cigarettes behind the cash register, and returned with a pack of Camels. Lighting a match, the old man held it between his fingers and waited until the son opened the package and

put a cigarette in his mouth. By then the match was threatening to sear his
fingers. He dropped it hastily and stole a sheepish glance at Ichiro, who
reached for the box and struck his own match.

"Ichiro." There was a timorousness in the father's voice. Or was it
apology?

"Yeah."

"Was it very hard?"

"No. It was fun." The sarcasm didn't take.

"You are sorry?" He was waddling over rocky ground on a pitch-black
night and he didn't like it one bit.

"I'm okay, Pa. It's finished. Done and finished. No use talking about it."

"True," said the old man too heartily. "it is done and there is no use to
talk." The bell tinkled and he leaped from the chair and fled out of the
kitchen.

Using the butt of the first cigarette, Ichiro lit another. He heard his
father's voice in the store.

"Mama. Ichiro. Ichiro is here."

The sharp, lifeless tone of his mother's words flipped through the
silence and he knew that she hadn't changed.

"The bread must be put out."

In other homes mothers and fathers and sons and daughters rushed into
hungry arms after week-end separations to find assurance in crushing
embraces and loving kisses. The last time he saw his mother was over two
years ago. He waited, seeing in the sounds of the rustling waxed paper the
stiff, angular figure of the woman stacking the bread on the rack in neat,
precise piles.

His father came back into the kitchen with a little less bounce and began
to wash the cups. She came through the curtains a few minutes after, a
small, flat-chested, shapeless woman who wore her hair pulled back into a
tight bun. Hers was the awkward, skinny body of a thirteen-year-old which
had dried and toughened through the many years following but which had
developed no further. He wondered how the two of them had ever gotten
together long enough to have two sons.

"I am proud that you are back," she said. "I am proud to call you my
son."

It was her way of saying that she had made him what he was and that
the thing in him which made him say no to the judge and go to prison for
two years was the growth of a seed planted by the mother tree and that she
was the mother who had put this thing in her son and that everything that
had been done and said was exactly as it should have been and that that was
what made him her son because no other would have made her feel the pride
that was in her breast.

He looked at his mother and swallowed with difficulty the bitterness
that threatened to destroy the last fragment of understanding for the
women who was his mother and still a stranger because, in truth, he could

not know what it was to be a Japanese who breathed the air of America and yet had never lifted a foot from the land that was Japan.

"I've been talking with Pa," he said, not knowing or caring why except that he had to say something.

"After a while, you and I, we will talk also." She walked through the kitchen into the bedroom and hung her coat and hat in a wardrobe of cardboard which had come from Sears Roebuck. Then she came back through the kitchen and out into the store.

The father gave him what was meant to be a knowing look and uttered softly: "Doesn't like my not being in the store when she is out. I tell her the bell tinkles, but she does not understand."

"Hell's bells," he said in disgust. Pushing himself out of the chair violently, he strode into the bedroom and flung himself out on one of the double beds.

Lying there, he wished the roof would fall in and bury forever the anguish which permeated his every pore. He lay there fighting with his burden, lighting one cigarette after another and dropping ashes and butts purposely on the floor. It was the way he felt, stripped of dignity, respect, purpose, honor, all the things which added up to schooling and marriage and family and work and happiness.

It was to please her, he said to himself with teeth clamped together to imprison the wild, meaningless, despairing cry which was forever straining inside of him. Pa's okay, but he's a nobody. He's a goddamned, fat, grinning, spineless nobody. Ma is the rock that's always hammering, pounding, pounding, pounding in her unobtrusive, determined, fanatical way until there's nothing left to call one's self. She's cursed me with her meanness and the hatred that you cannot see but which is always hating. It was she who opened my mouth and made my lips move to sound the words which got me two years in prison and an emptiness that is more empty and frightening than the caverns of hell. She's killed me with her meanness and hatred and I hope she's happy because I'll never know the meaning of it again.

"Ichiro."

He propped himself up on an elbow and looked at her. She had hardly changed. Surely, there must have been a time when she could smile and, yet, he could not remember.

"Yeah?"

"Lunch is on the table."

As he pushed himself off the bed and walked past her to the kitchen, she took broom and dustpan and swept up the mess he had made.

There were eggs, fried with soy sauce, sliced cold meat, boiled cabbage, and tea and rice. They all ate in silence, not even disturbed once by the tinkling of the bell. The father cleared the table after they had finished and dutifully retired to watch the store. Ichiro had smoked three cigarettes before his mother ended the silence.

"You must go back to school."

He had almost forgotten that there had been a time before the war when he had actually gone to college for two years and studiously applied himself to courses in the engineering school. The statement staggered him. Was that all there was to it? Did she mean to sit there and imply that the four intervening years were to be casually forgotten and life resumed as if there had been no four years and no war and no Eto who had spit on him because of the thing he had done?

"I don't feel much like going to school."

"What will you do?"

"I don't know."

"With an education, your opportunities in Japan will be unlimited. You must go and complete your studies."

"Ma," he said slowly, "Ma, I'm not going to Japan. Nobody's going to Japan. The war is over. Japan lost. Do you hear? Japan lost."

"You believe that?" It was said in the tone of an adult asking a child who is no longer a child if he really believed that Santa Claus was real.

"Yes, I believe it. I know it. America is still here. Do you see the great Japanese army walking down the streets? No. There is no Japanese army any more."

"The boat is coming and we must be ready."

"The boat?"

"Yes." She reached into her pocket and drew out a worn envelope.

The letter had been mailed from Sao Paulo, Brazil, and was addressed to a name that he did not recognize. Inside the envelope was a single sheet of flimsy, rice paper covered with intricate flourishes of Japanese characters.

"What does it say?"

She did not bother to pick up the letter. "To you who are a loyal and honorable Japanese, it is with humble and heartfelt joy that I relay this momentous message. Word has been brought to us that the victorious Japanese government is presently making preparations to send ships which will return to Japan those residents in foreign countries who have steadfastly maintained their faith and loyalty to our Emperor. The Japanese government regrets that the responsibilities arising from the victory compels them to delay in the sending of the vessels. To be among the few who remain to receive this honor is a gratifying tribute. Heed not the propaganda of the radio and newspapers which endeavor to convince the people with lies about the allied victory. Especially, heed not the lies of your traitorous countrymen who have turned their backs on the country of their birth and who will suffer for their treasonous acts. The day of glory is close at hand. The rewards will be beyond our greatest expectations. What we have done, we have done only as Japanese, but the government is grateful. Hold your heads high and make ready for the journey, for the ships are coming."

"Who wrote that?" he asked incredulously. It was like a weird nightmare. It was like finding out that an incurable strain of insanity pervaded the family, an intangible horror that swayed and taunted beyond the grasp of reaching fingers.

"A friend in South America. We are not alone."

"We *are* alone," he said vehemently. "This whole thing is crazy. You're crazy. I'm crazy. All right, so we made a mistake. Let's admit it."

"There has been no mistake. The letter confirms."

"Sure it does. It proves there's crazy people in the world besides us. If Japan won the war, what the hell are we doing here? What are you doing running a grocery store? It doesn't figure. It doesn't figure because we're all wrong. The minute we admit that, everything is fine. I've had a lot of time to think about all this. I've thought about it, and every time the answer comes out the same. You can't tell me different any more."

She sighed ever so slightly. "We will talk later when you are feeling better." Carefully folding the letter and placing it back in the envelope, she returned it to her pocket. "It is not I who tell you that the ship is coming. It is in the letter. If you have come to doubt your mother—and I'm sure you do not mean it even if you speak in weakness—it is to be regretted. Rest a few days. Think more deeply and your doubts will disappear. You are my son, Ichiro."

No, he said to himself as he watched her part the curtains and start into the store. There was a time when I was your son. There was a time that I no longer remember when you used to smile a mother's smile and tell me stories about gallant and fierce warriors who protected their lords with blades of shining steel and about the old woman who found a peach in the stream and took it home and, when her husband split it in half, a husky little boy tumbled out to fill their hearts with boundless joy. I was that boy in the peach and you were the old woman and we were Japanese with Japanese feelings and Japanese pride and Japanese thoughts because it was all right then to be Japanese and feel and think all the things that Japanese do even if we lived in America. Then there came a time when I was only half Japanese because one is not born in America and raised in America and taught in America and one does not speak and swear and drink and smoke and play and fight and see and hear in America among Americans in American streets and houses without becoming American and loving it. But I did not love enough, for you were still half my mother and I was thereby still half Japanese and when the war came and they told me to fight for America, I was not strong enough to fight you and I was not strong enough to fight the bitterness which made the half of me which was you bigger than the half of me which was America and really the whole of me that I could not see or feel. Now that I know the truth when it is too late and the half of me which was you is no longer there, I am only half of me and the half that remains is American by law because the government was wise and strong enough to know why it was that I could not fight for America and did not strip me of my birthright. But it is not enough to be American only in the eyes of the law and it is not enough to be only half an American and know that it is an empty half. I am not your son and I am not Japanese and I am not American. I can go someplace and tell people that I've got an inverted stomach and that I am an American, true and blue and Hail Columbia, but the army wouldn't have me because of the stomach. That's easy and I would do it, only I've got to convince myself first and that I cannot do. I wish with all my heart that I were Japanese or that I were American. I am neither and I blame you and I blame myself and I blame the world which is made up of many countries which fight with each other and kill and hate and destroy but not enough, so that they must kill and hate and destroy again and again and again. It is so easy and simple that I cannot understand it at all. And the reason I do not understand it is because I do not understand you who were the half of me that is no more and because I do not understand what it was about that half that made me destroy the half of me which was American and the half which might have become the whole of me if I had said yes I will go and fight in your army because that is what I believe and want and cherish and love . . .

Defeatedly, he crushed the stub of a cigarette into an ash tray filled with many other stubs and reached for the package to get another. It was empty and he did not want to go into the store for more because he did not feel much like seeing either his father or mother. He went into the bedroom and tossed and groaned and half slept.

Maya Angelou
(1928–)

Born Marguerite Johnson in St. Louis, Missouri, Maya Angelou lived with her brother Bailey in the home of their paternal grandmother in Stamps, Arkansas, after the breakup of their parents' marriage. She was educated in segregated public schools in Arkansas and in California and New York, where she studied dance and drama.

Her theatrical credits include a twenty-two-nation tour of Porgy and Bess *sponsored by the U.S. State Department and roles in Jean Genet's* The Blacks *and* Cabaret for Freedom, *which she co-authored with Godfrey Cambridge. She has appeared in films and television productions, written music for films and composed screenplays, and written and acted in plays for both stage and television. A strong voice for civil rights and sexual equality, she served as an officer of the Southern Christian Leadership Conference aud was a newspaper editor in Egypt and a university official in Ghana.*

Angelou, the author of several poetry collections, is best known for her autobiographical writing. The first book in the series, I Know Why the Caged Bird Sings, *was warmly received by the critics and nominated for the National Book Award. It covers the author's childhood and adolescence, up to the age of sixteen. In it, Angelou graphically describes instances of bigotry and child abuse without sentiment or self-pity and illuminates the lives of rural blacks trapped in economic servitude and schoolchildren cheated by attendance at separate and unequal schools. Other autobiographical volumes are* Gather Together in My Name *(1974),* Singin' and Swingin' and Gettin' Merry Like Christmas *(1976),* The Heart of a Woman *(1981), and* All God's Children Need Traveling Shoes *(1987). Her four-volume* Collected Poems *appeared in 1986.*

[From] I Know Why the Caged Bird Sings

23 [Graduation Day]

THE CHILDREN IN STAMPS trembled visibly with anticipation. Some adults were excited too, but to be certain the whole young population had come down with graduation epidemic. Large classes were graduating from both the grammar school and the high school. Even those who were years removed from their own day of glorious release were anxious to help with preparations as a kind of dry run. The junior students who were moving into the vacating classes' chairs were tradition-bound to show their talents for leadership and management. They strutted through the school and around the campus exerting pressure on the lower grades. Their authority was so new that occasionally if they pressed a little too hard it had to be overlooked. After all, next term was coming, and it never hurt a sixth grader to have a play sister in the eighth grade, or a tenth-year student to be able to call a twelfth grader Bubba. So all was endured in a spirit of shared understanding. But the graduating classes themselves were the nobility. Like travelers with exotic destinations on their minds, the graduates were remarkably forgetful. They came to school without their books, or tablets or even pencils. Volunteers fell over themselves to secure replacements for the missing equipment. When accepted, the willing workers might or might not be thanked, and it was of no importance to the pregraduation rites. Even teachers were respectful of the now quiet and aging seniors, and tended to speak to them, if not as equals, as beings only slightly lower than themselves. After tests were returned and grades given, the student body, which acted like an extended family, knew who did well, who excelled, and what piteous ones had failed.

Unlike the white high school, Lafayette County Training School distinguished itself by having neither lawn, nor hedges, nor tennis court, nor climbing ivy. Its two buildings (main classrooms, the grade school and home economics) were set on a dirt hill with no fence to limit either its boundaries or those of bordering farms. There was a large expanse to the left of the school which was used alternately as a baseball diamond or a basketball court. Rusty hoops on the swaying poles represented the permanent recreational equipment, although bats and balls could be borrowed from the P. E. teacher if the borrower was qualified and if the diamond wasn't occupied.

Over this rocky area relieved by a few shady tall persimmon trees the graduating class walked. The girls often held hands and no longer bothered to speak to the lower students. There was a sadness about them, as if this old world was not their home and they were bound for higher ground. The boys, on the other hand, had become more friendly, more outgoing. A decided change from the closed attitude they projected while studying for finals. Now they seemed not ready to give up the old school, the familiar paths and classrooms. Only a small percentage would be continuing on to college—one of the South's A & M (agricultural and mechanical) schools, which trained Negro youths to be carpenters, farmers, handymen, masons, maids, cooks and baby nurses. Their future rode heavily on their shoulders, and blinded them to the collective joy that had pervaded the lives of the boys and girls in the grammar school graduating class.

Parents who could afford it had ordered new shoes and ready-made clothes for themselves from Sears and Roebuck or Montgomery Ward. They also engaged the best seamstresses to make the floating graduating dresses and to cut down secondhand pants which would be pressed to a military slickness for the important event.

Oh, it was important, all right. Whitefolks would attend the ceremony, and two or three would speak of God and home, and the Southern way of life, and Mrs. Parsons, the principal's wife, would play the graduation march while the lower-grade graduates paraded down the aisles and took their seats below the platform. The high school seniors would wait in empty classrooms to make their dramatic entrance.

In the Store I was the person of the moment. The birthday girl. The center. Bailey had graduated the year before, although to do so he had had to forfeit all pleasures to make up for his time lost in Baton Rouge.

My class was wearing butter-yellow piqué dresses, and Momma[1] launched out on mine. She smocked the yoke into tiny crisscrossing puckers, then shirred the rest of the bodice. Her dark fingers ducked in and out of the lemony cloth as she embroidered raised daisies around the hem. Before she considered herself finished she had added a crocheted cuff on the puff sleeves, and a pointy crocheted collar.

I was going to be lovely. A walking model of all the various styles of fine hand sewing and it didn't worry me that I was only twelve years old and merely graduating from the eighth grade. Besides, many teachers in Arkansas Negro schools had only that diploma and were licensed to impart wisdom.

The days had become longer and more noticeable. The faded beige of former times had been replaced with strong and sure colors. I began to see my classmates' clothes, their skin tones, and the dust that waved off pussy willows. Clouds that lazed across the sky were objects of great concern to me. Their shiftier shapes might have held a message that in my new happiness and with a little bit of time I'd soon decipher. During that period I looked at the arch of heaven so religiously my neck kept a steady ache. I had taken to smiling more often, and my jaws hurt from the unaccustomed activity. Between the two physical sore spots, I suppose I could have been uncomfortable, but that was not the case. As a member of the winning team (the graduating class of 1940) I had outdistanced unpleasant sensations by miles. I was headed for the freedom of open fields.

Youth and social approval allied themselves with me and we trammeled memories of slights and insults. The wind of our swift passage remodeled my features. Lost tears were pounded to mud and then to dust. Years of withdrawal were brushed aside and left behind, as hanging ropes of parasitic moss.

My work alone had awarded me a top place and I was going to be one of the first called in the graduating ceremonies. On the classroom blackboard, as well as on the bulletin board in the auditorium, there were blue stars and white stars and red stars. No absences, no tardinesses, and my academic work was among the best of the year. I could say the preamble to the Constitution even faster than Bailey. We timed ourselves often: "Wethepeopleof-theUnitedStatesinordertoformamoreperfectunion . . ." I had memorized the Presidents of the United States from Washington to Roosevelt in chronological as well as alphabetical order.

My hair pleased me too. Gradually the black mass had lengthened and thickened, so that it kept at last to its braided pattern, and I didn't have to yank my scalp off when I tried to comb it.

Louise and I had rehearsed the exercises until we tired out ourselves.

---

1. Angelou's name for her grandmother, Mrs. Annie Henderson, owner of the Wm. Johnson General Merchandise Store.

Henry Reed was class valedictorian. He was a small, very black boy with hooded eyes, a long, broad nose and an oddly shaped head. I had admired him for years because each term he and I vied for the best grades in our class. Most often he bested me, but instead of being disappointed I was pleased that we shared top places between us. Like many Southern Black children, he lived with his grandmother, who was as strict as Momma and as kind as she knew how to be. He was courteous, respectful and soft-spoken to elders, but on the playground he chose to play the roughest games. I admired him. Anyone, I reckoned, sufficiently afraid or sufficiently dull could be polite. But to be able to operate at a top level with both adults and children was admirable.

His valedictory speech was entitled "To Be or Not to Be." The rigid tenth-grade teacher had helped him write it. He'd been working on the dramatic stresses for months.

The weeks until graduation were filled with heady activities. A group of small children were to be presented in a play about buttercups and daisies and bunny rabbits. They could be heard throughout the building practicing their hops and their little songs that sounded like silver bells. The older girls (nongraduates, of course) were assigned the task of making refreshments for the night's festivities. A tangy scent of ginger, cinnamon, nutmeg and chocolate wafted around the home economics building as the budding cooks made samples for themselves and their teachers.

In every corner of the workshop, axes and saws split fresh timber as the woodshop boys made sets and stage scenery. Only the graduates were left out of the general bustle. We were free to sit in the library at the back of the building or look in quite detachedly, naturally, on the measures being taken for our event.

Even the minister preached on graduation the Sunday before. His subject was, "Let your light so shine that men will see your good works and praise your Father, Who is in Heaven." Although the sermon was purported to be addressed to us, he used the occasion to speak to backsliders, gamblers and general ne'er-do-wells. But since he had called our names at the beginning of the service we were mollified.

Among Negroes the tradition was to give presents to children going only from one grade to another. How much more important this was when the person was graduating at the top of the class. Uncle Willie and Momma had sent away for a Mickey Mouse watch like Bailey's. Louise gave me four embroidered handkerchiefs. (I gave her three crocheted doilies.) Mrs. Sneed, the minister's wife, made me an underskirt to wear for graduation, and nearly every customer gave me a nickel or maybe even a dime with the instruction "Keep on moving to higher ground," or some such encouragement.

Amazingly the great day finally dawned and I was out of bed before I knew it. I threw open the back door to see it more clearly, but Momma said, "Sister, come away from that door and put your robe on."

I hoped the memory of that morning would never leave me. Sunlight was itself still young, and the day had none of the insistence maturity would bring it in a few hours. In my robe and barefoot in the backyard, under cover of going to see about my new beans, I gave myself up to the gentle warmth and thanked God that no matter what evil I had done in my life He had allowed me to live to see this day. Somewhere in my fatalism I had expected to die, accidentally, and never have the chance to walk up the stairs in the auditorium and gracefully receive my hard-earned diploma. Out of God's merciful bosom I had won reprieve.

Bailey came out in his robe and gave me a box wrapped in Christmas paper. He said he had saved his money for months to pay for it. It felt like a box of chocolates, but I knew Bailey wouldn't save money to buy candy when we had all we could want under our noses.

He was as proud of the gift as I. It was a soft-leather-bound copy of a collection of poems by Edgar Allan Poe, or, as Bailey and I called him, "Eap." I turned to "Annabel Lee" and we walked up and down the garden rows, the cool dirt between our toes, reciting the beautifully sad lines.

Momma made a Sunday breakfast although it was only Friday. After we finished the blessing, I opened my eyes to find the watch on my plate. It was a dream of a day. Everything went smoothly and to my credit. I didn't have to be reminded or scolded for anything. Near evening I was too jittery to attend to chores, so Bailey volunteered to do all before his bath.

Days before, we had made a sign for the Store, and as we turned out the lights Momma hung the cardboard over the doorknob. It read clearly: CLOSED. GRADUATION.

My dress fitted perfectly and everyone said that I looked like a sunbeam in it. On the hill, going toward the school, Bailey walked behind with Uncle Willie, who muttered, "Go on, Ju." He wanted him to walk ahead with us because it embarrassed him to have to walk so slowly. Bailey said he'd let the ladies walk together, and the men would bring up the rear. We all laughed, nicely.

Little children dashed by out of the dark like fireflies. Their crepe-paper dresses and butterfly wings were not made for running and we heard more than one rip, dryly, and the regretful "uh uh" that followed.

The school blazed without gaiety. The windows seemed cold and unfriendly from the lower hill. A sense of ill-fated timing crept over me, and if Momma hadn't reached for my hand I would have drifted back to Bailey and Uncle Willie, and possibly beyond. She made a few slow jokes about my feet getting cold, and tugged me along to the now-strange building.

Around the front steps, assurance came back. There were my fellow "greats," the graduating class. Hair brushed back, legs oiled, new dresses and pressed pleats, fresh pocket handkerchiefs and little handbags, all homesewn. Oh, we were up to snuff, all right. I joined my comrades and didn't even see my family go in to find seats in the crowded auditorium.

The school band struck up a march and all classes filed in as had been rehearsed. We stood in front of our seats, as assigned, and on a signal from the choir director, we sat. No sooner had this been accomplished than the band started to play the national anthem. We rose again and sang the song, after which we recited the pledge of allegiance. We remained standing for a brief minute before the choir director and the principal signaled to us, rather desperately I thought, to take our seats. The command was so unusual that our carefully rehearsed and smooth-running machine was thrown off. For a full minute we fumbled for our chairs and bumped into each other awkwardly. Habits change or solidify under pressure, so in our state of nervous tension we had been ready to follow our usual assembly pattern: the American national anthem, then the pledge of allegiance, then the song every Black person I knew called the Negro National Anthem. All done in the same key, with the same passion and most often standing on the same foot.

Finding my seat at last, I was overcome with a presentiment of worse things to come. Something unrehearsed, unplanned, was going to happen, and we were going to be made to look bad. I distinctly remember being explicit in the choice of pronoun. It was "we," the graduating class, the unit, that concerned me then.

The principal welcomed "parents and friends" and asked the Baptist minister to lead us in prayer. His invocation was brief and punchy, and for a second I thought we were getting back on the high road to right action. When the principal came back to the dais, however, his voice had changed. Sounds always affected me profoundly and the principal's voice was one of my favorites. During assembly it melted and lowed weakly into the audience. It had not been in my plan to listen to him, but my curiosity was piqued and I straightened up to give him my attention.

He was talking about Booker T. Washington,[2] our "late great leader," who said we can be as close as the fingers on the hand, etc. . . . Then he said a few vague things about friendship and the friendship of kindly people to those less fortunate than themselves. With that his voice nearly faded, thin, away. Like a river diminishing to a stream and then to a trickle. But he cleared his throat and said, "Our speaker tonight, who is also our friend, came from Texarkana to deliver the commencement address, but due to the irregularity of the train schedule, he's going to, as they say, 'speak and run.'" He said that we understood and wanted the man to know that we were most grateful for the time he was able to give us and then something about how we were willing always to adjust to another's program, and without more ado—"I give you Mr. Edward Donleavy."

Not one but two white men came through the door offstage. The shorter one walked to the speaker's platform, and the tall one moved over to the center seat and sat down. But that was our principal's seat, and already occupied. The dislodged gentleman bounced around for a long breath or two before the Baptist minister gave him his chair, then with more dignity than the situation deserved, the minister walked off the stage.

---

2. Booker T. Washington (1856–1915), founder of Tuskegee Institute.

Donleavy looked at the audience once (on reflection, I'm sure that he wanted only to reassure himself that we were really there), adjusted his glasses and began to read from a sheaf of papers.

He was glad "to be here and to see the work going on just as it was in the other schools."

At the first "Amen" from the audience I willed the offender to immediate death by choking on the word. But Amens and Yes, sir's began to fall around the room like rain through a ragged umbrella.

He told us of the wonderful changes we children in Stamps had in store. The Central School (naturally, the white school was Central) had already been granted improvements that would be in use in the fall. A well-known artist was coming from Little Rock to teach art to them. They were going to have the newest microscopes and chemistry equipment for their laboratory. Mr. Donleavy didn't leave us long in the dark over who made these improvements available to Central High. Nor were we to be ignored in the general betterment scheme he had in mind.

He said that he had pointed out to people at a very high level that one of the first-line football tacklers at Arkansas Agricultural and Mechanical College had graduated from good old Lafayette County Training School. Here fewer Amen's were heard. Those few that did break through lay dully in the air with the heaviness of habit.

He went on to praise us. He went on to say how he had bragged that "one of the best basketball players at Fisk sank his first ball right here at Lafayette County Training School."

The white kids were going to have a chance to become Galileos and Madame Curies and Edisons and Gauguins, and our boys (the girls weren't even in on it) would try to be Jesse Owenses and Joe Louises.

Owens and the Brown Bomber were great heroes in our world, but what school official in the white-goddom of Little Rock had the right to decide that those two men must be our only heroes? Who decided that for Henry Reed to become a scientist he had to work like George Washington Carver,[3] as a bootblack, to buy a lousy microscope? Bailey was obviously always going to be too small to be an athlete, so which concrete angel glued to what country seat had decided that if my brother wanted to become a lawyer he had to first pay penance for his skin by picking cotton and hoeing corn and studying correspondence books at night for twenty years?

The man's dead words fell like bricks around the auditorium and too many settled in my belly. Constrained by hard-learned manners I couldn't look behind me, but to my left and right the proud graduating class of 1940 had dropped their heads. Every girl in my row had found something new to do with her handkerchief. Some folded the tiny squares into love knots, some into triangles, but most were wadding them, then pressing them flat on their yellow laps.

---

3. George Washington Carver (1864?–1943). A member of the Tuskegee faculty, he dedicated himself to finding uses for southern agricultural crops and thereby improving the region's economy.

On the dais, the ancient tragedy was being replayed. Professor Parsons sat, a sculptor's reject, rigid. His large, heavy body seemed devoid of will or willingness, and his eyes said he was no longer with us. The other teachers examined the flag (which was draped stage right) or their notes, or the windows which opened on our now-famous playing diamond.

Graduation, the hush-hush magic time of frills and gifts and congratulations and diplomas, was finished for me before my name was called. The accomplishment was nothing. The meticulous maps, drawn in three colors of ink, learning and spelling decasyllabic words, memorizing the whole of *The Rape of Lucrece*—it was for nothing. Donleavy had exposed us.

We were maids and farmers, handymen and washerwomen, and anything higher that we aspired to was farcical and presumptuous.

Then I wished that Gabriel Prosser and Nat Turner had killed all whitefolks in their beds and that Abraham Lincoln had been assassinated before the signing of the Emancipation Proclamation, and that Harriet Tubman had been killed by that blow on her head and Christopher Columbus had drowned in the *Santa Maria*.

It was awful to be Negro and have no control over my life. It was brutal to be young and already trained to sit quietly and listen to charges brought against my color with no chance of defense. We should all be dead. I thought I should like to see us all dead, one on top of the other. A pyramid of flesh with the whitefolks on the bottom, as the broad base, then the Indians with their silly tomahawks and teepees and wigwams and treaties, the Negroes with their mops and recipes and cotton sacks and spirituals sticking out of their mouths. The Dutch children should all stumble in their wooden shoes and break their necks. The French should choke to death on the Louisiana Purchase (1803) while silk-worms ate all the Chinese with their stupid pigtails. As a species, we were an abomination. All of us.

Donleavy was running for election, and assured our parents that if he won we could count on having the only colored paved playing field in that part of Arkansas. Also—he never looked up to acknowledge the grunts of acceptance—also, we were bound to get some new equipment for the home economics building and the workshop.

He finished, and since there was no need to give any more than the most perfunctory thank-you's, he nodded to the men on the stage, and the tall white man who was never introduced joined him at the door. They left with the attitude that now they were off to something really important. (The graduation ceremonies at Lafayette County Training School had been a mere preliminary.)

The ugliness they left was palpable. An uninvited guest who wouldn't leave. The choir was summoned and sang a modern arrangement of "Onward, Christian Soldiers," with new words pertaining to graduates seeking their place in the world. But it didn't work. Elouise, the daughter of the Baptist minister, recited "Invictus," and I could have cried at the impertinence of "I am the master of my fate, I am the captain of my soul."

My name had lost its ring of familiarity and I had to be nudged to go

and receive my diploma. All my preparations had fled. I neither marched up
to the stage like a conquering Amazon, nor did I look in the audience for
Bailey's nod of approval. Marguerite Johnson, I heard the name again, my
honors were read, there were noises in the audience of appreciation, and I
took my place on the stage as rehearsed.

I thought about colors I hated: ecru, puce, lavender, beige and black.

There was shuffling and rustling around me, then Henry Reed was giving his valedictory address, "To Be or Not to Be." Hadn't he heard the
whitefolks? We couldn't *be*, so the question was a waste of time. Henry's
voice came out clear and strong. I feared to look at him. Hadn't he got the
message? There was no "nobler in the mind" for Negroes because the world
didn't think we had minds, and they let us know it. "Outrageous fortune"?
Now, that was a joke. When the ceremony was over I had to tell Henry Reed
some things. That is, if I still cared. Not "rub," Henry, "erase." "Ah, there's
the erase." Us.

Henry had been a good student in elocution. His voice rose on tides of
promise and fell on waves of warnings. The English teacher had helped him
to create a sermon winging through Hamlet's soliloquy. To be a man, a doer,
a builder, a leader, or to be a tool, an unfunny joke, a crusher of funky toadstools. I marveled that Henry could go through with the speech as if we had
a choice.

I had been listening and silently rebutting each sentence with my eyes
closed; then there was a hush, which in an audience warns that something
unplanned is happening. I looked up and saw Henry Reed, the conservative,
the proper, the A student, turn his back to the audience and turn to us (the
proud graduating class of 1940) and sing, nearly speaking,

> Lift ev'ry voice and sing
> Till earth and heaven ring
> Ring with the harmonies of Liberty . . .

It was the poem written by James Weldon Johnson. It was the music composed by J. Rosamond Johnson. It was the Negro national anthem. Out of
habit we were singing it.

Our mothers and fathers stood in the dark hall and joined the hymn of
encouragement. A kindergarten teacher led the small children onto the stage
and the buttercups and daisies and bunny rabbits marked time and tried to
follow:

> Stony the road we trod
> Bitter the chastening rod
> Felt in the days when hope, unborn, had died.
> Yet with a steady beat
> Have not our weary feet
> Come to the place for which our fathers sighed?

Every child I knew had learned that song with his ABC's and along with "Jesus Loves Me This I Know." But I personally had never heard it before. Never heard the words, despite the thousands of times I had sung them. Never thought they had anything to do with me.

On the other hand, the words of Patrick Henry had made such an impression on me that I had been able to stretch myself tall and trembling and say, "I know not what course others may take, but as for me, give me liberty or give me death."

And now I heard, really for the first time:

> We have come over a way that with tears has been watered,
> We have come, treading our path through the blood of the slaughtered.

While echoes of the song shivered in the air, Henry Reed bowed his head, said "Thank you," and returned to his place in the line. The tears that slipped down many faces were not wiped away in shame.

We were on top again. As always, again. We survived. The depths had been icy and dark, but now a bright sun spoke to our souls. I was no longer simply a member of the proud graduating class of 1940; I was a proud member of the wonderful, beautiful Negro race.

Oh, Black known and unknown poets, how often have your auctioned pains sustained us? Who will compute the lonely nights made less lonely by your songs, or by the empty pots made less tragic by your tales?

If we were a people much given to revealing secrets, we might raise monuments and sacrifice to the memories of our poets, but slavery cured us of that weakness. It may be enough, however, to have it said that we survive in exact relationship to the dedication of our poets (include preachers, musicians and blues singers).

Nash Candelaria
(1928–)

Although he was born in Los Angeles, Nash Candelaria considers himself "a New Mexican by heritage and sympathy," because his forebears were among the founders of Albuquerque, and his interest as a writer is in the history and culture of that region. One of his ancestors, Juan, wrote a history of New Mexico in 1776, and Candelaria has explored the region's later history, including its involvement in the Mexican War and the problems of cultural conflict with white settlers.

He received a bachelor of science degree from the University of California at Los Angeles and served as a second lieutenant in the U.S. Air Force. Although he was able to write full time for a short period in the eighties, he has been employed by computer and scientific instrument firms most of his life, writing fiction in his leisure time.

Candelaria's trilogy of novels, Memories of the Alhambra *(1977),* Not by the Sword *(1982), and* Inheritance of Strangers *(1984), consists of historical narratives dealing with New Mexicans who are proud of their descent from Spanish conquistadors but ignore their Native American heritage.* The Day the Cisco Kid Shot John Wayne *(1988) is a collection of twelve short stories concerned with relations between Hispanic Americans and their Anglo neighbors. "El Patron" is taken from* Cuentos Chicanos *(1984), edited by Rudolfo A. Anaya and Antonio Marquez.*

El Patrón

MY FATHER-IN-LAW'S HIERARCHY is, in descending order: Dios, El Papa, y el patrón. It is to these that mere mortals bow, as in turn el patrón bows to El Papa, and El Papa bows to Dios.

God and the Pope are understandable enough. It's this el patrón, the boss, who causes most of our trouble. Whether it's the one who gives you work and for it pay, the lifeblood of hardworking little people—or others: Our parents (fathers affectionately known as jefe, mothers known merely as mama, military commanders el capitán), or any of the big shots in the government el alcalde, el gobernador, el presidente and never forget la policía[1]).

It was about some such el patrón trouble that Señor Martínez boarded the bus in San Diego and headed north toward L.A.—and us.

Since I was lecturing to a midafternoon summer school class at Southwestern U., my wife, Lola, picked up her father at the station. When I arrived home, they were sitting politely in the living room talking banalities: "Yes, it does look like rain. But if it doesn't rain, it might be sunny. If only the clouds would blow away."

Lola had that dangerous look on her face that usually made me start

---

1. The mayor, governor, president, and police.

talking too fast and too long in hope of shifting her focus. It never worked. She'd sit there with a face like a brown-skinned kewpie doll whose expression was slowly turning into that of an angry maniac. When she could no longer stand it, she'd give her father a blast: "You never talk to me about anything important, you macho, chauvinist jumping bean!" Then it would escalate to nastiness from there.

But tonight it didn't get that far. As I entered Señor Martínez rose, dressed neatly in his one suit as for a wedding or a funeral, and politely shook my hand. Without so much as a glance at Lola, he said, "Why don't you go to the kitchen with the other women."

"There are no other women," Lola said coldly. She stood and belligerently received my kiss on the cheek before leaving.

Señor Martínez was oblivious to her reaction, sensing only the absence of "woman," at which he visibly relaxed and sat down.

"Rosca," he said, referring to me as he always did by my last name. "Tito is in trouble with the law."

His face struggled between anger and sadness, tinged with a crosscurrent of confusion. Tito was his pride and joy. His only son after four daughters. A twilight gift born to his wife at a time when he despaired of ever having a son, when their youngest daughter, Lola, was already ten years old and their oldest daughter twenty.

"He just finished his examinations at the state university. He was working this summer to save money for his second year when this terrible thing happened."

I could not in my wildest fantasies imagine young Vicente getting into any kind of trouble. He had always impressed me as a bright, polite young man who would inspire pride in any father. Even when he and old Vicente had quarreled about Tito going to college instead of working full-time, the old man had grudgingly come around to seeing the wisdom of it. But now. The law! I was stunned.

"Where is he?" I asked, imagining the nineteen-year-old in some filthy cell in the San Diego jail.

"I don't know." Then he looked over his shoulder toward the kitchen, as if to be certain no one was eavesdropping. "I think he went underground."

Underground! I had visions of drug-crazed revolutionary zealots. Bombs exploding in federal buildings. God knows what kind of madness.

"They're probably after him," he went on. Then he paused and stared at me as if trying to understand. "Tito always looked up to you and Lola. Of all the family it would be you he would try to contact. I want you to help me." Not help *Tito*, I thought, but help *me*.

I went to the cabinet for the bottle that I keep there for emergencies. I took a swallow to give me enough courage to ask the question. "What . . . did . . . he do?"

Señor Martínez stared limply at the glass in his hand. "You know," he said, "my father fought with Pancho Villa."

Jesus! I thought. If everyone who told me his father had fought with Pancho Villa was telling the truth, that army would have been big enough to conquer the world. Besides—what did this have to do with Tito?

"When my turn came," he continued, "I enlisted in the Marines at Camp Pendleton. Fought los Japonés in the Pacific." Finally he took a swallow of his drink and sat up stiffly as if at attention. "The men in our family have never shirked their duty!" He barked like the Marine corporal he had once been.

It slowly dawned on me what this was all about. It had been *the* topic all during summer school at Southwestern U. Registration for the draft. "No blood for Mideast oil!" the picket signs around the campus post office had shouted. "Boycott the Exxon army!"

"I should never have let him go to college," Señor Martínez said. "That's where he gets such crazy radical ideas. From those rich college boys whose parents can buy them out of all kinds of trouble."

"So he didn't register," I said.

"The FBI is probably after him right now. It's a federal crime you know. And the Canadians don't want draft dodgers either."

He took a deep swallow and polished off the rest of his drink in one gulp, putting the empty glass on the coffee table. There, his gesture seemed to say, now you know the worst.

Calmer now, he went on to tell me more. About the American Civil War; a greater percentage of Spanish-speaking men of New Mexico had joined the Union Army than the men from any other group in any other state in the Union. About the Rough Riders, including young Mexican-Americans, born on horseback, riding roughest of all over the Spanish in Cuba. About the War-to-End-All-Wars, where tough, skinny, brown-faced doughboys from farms in Texas, New Mexico, Arizona, Colorado, and California gave their all "Over There." About World War II, from the New Mexico National Guard captured at Bataan to the tough little Marines whom he was proud to fight alongside; man for man there were more decorations for bravery among Mexican-Americans than among any other group in this war. Then Korea, where his younger brother toughed it out in the infantry. Finally Vietnam, where kids like his nephew, Pablo, got it in some silent, dark jungle trying to save a small country from the Communists.

By now he had lost his calm. There were tears in his eyes, partly from the pride he felt in this tradition of valor in war. But partly for something else, I thought. I could almost hear his son's reply to his impassioned call to duty: "Yes, Papá. So we could come back, if we survived, to our jobs as busboys and ditch diggers; *that's* why I have to go to college. I don't want to go to the Middle East and fight and die for some oil company when you can't even afford to own a car. If the Russians invaded our country, I would defend it. If a robber broke into our house, I would fight him. If someone attacked you, I would save you. But this? No, papá."

But now Tito was gone. God knows where. None of his three sisters in San Diego had seen him. Nor any of his friends in the neighborhood or school or work.

I could hear preparations for dinner from the kitchen. Señor Martínez and I had another tragito[2] while Lolita and Junior ate their dinner early, the sounds of their childish voices piercing through the banging of pots and pans.

When Lola called me Emiliano instead of by my nickname, Pata, I knew we were in for a lousy meal. Everything her father disliked must have been served. It had taken some kind of perverse gourmet expending a tremendous amount of energy to fix such rotten food. There was that nothing white bread that presses together into a doughy flat mass instead of the tortillas papá thrived on. There was a funny little salad with chopped garbage in it covered by a blob of imitation goo. There was no meat. No meat! Just all those sliced vegetables in a big bowl. Not ordinary vegetables like beans and potatoes and carrots, but funny, wiggly long things like wild grass . . . or worms. And quivering cubes of what must have been whale blubber.

Halfway through the meal, as Señor Martínez shuffled the food around on his plate like one of our kids resisting what was good for them, the doorbell rang.

"You'd better get that, Emiliano," Lola said, daring me to refuse by her tone of voice and dagger-throwing glance.

Who needs a fight? In a sense I was the lucky one because I could leave the table and that pot of mess-age. When I opened the door, a scraggly young man beamed a weak smile at me. "I hitchhiked from San Diego," Tito said.

Before I could move onto the steps and close the door behind me, he stumbled past me into the house. Tired as he was, he reacted instantly to seeing his father at the table. "You!" he shouted, then turned and bolted out the door.

Even tired he could run faster than I, so I hopped into the car and drove after him while Lola and Señor Martínez stood on the steps shouting words at me that I couldn't hear.

Two blocks later Tito finally climbed into the car after I bribed him with a promise of dinner at McDonald's. While his mouth was full I tried to talk some sense into him, but to no avail. He was just as stubborn as his father and sister. Finally, I drove him to the International House on campus where the housing manager, who owed me a favor, found him an empty bed.

"You should have *made* him come back with you," Lola nagged at me that night.

"He doesn't want to be under the same roof with his father." From her thoughtful silence I knew that she understood and probably felt the same way herself. When I explained to her what it was all about—her father had said nothing to her—it looked for a moment as if she would get out of bed, stomp to the guest room, and heave Señor Martínez out into the street.

The next day seemed like an endless two-way shuttle between our

---

2. Little drink.

house and the I House. First me. Then Lola. If Señor Martínez had had a car and could drive, he would have followed each of us.

Our shuttle diplomacy finally wore them down. I could at last discern cracks in father's and son's immovable positions.

"Yes. Yes. I love my son."

"I love my father."

"I know. I know. Adults should be able to sit down and air their differences, no matter how wrong he is."

"Maybe tomorrow. Give me a break. But definitely not at mealtime. I can't eat while my stomach is churning."

The difficulty for me, as always, was in keeping my opinions to myself. Lola didn't have that problem. After all, they were her brother and father, so she felt free to say whatever she pleased.

"The plan is to get them to talk," I said to her. "If they can talk they can reach some kind of understanding."

"Papá has to be set straight," she said. "As usual, he's wrong, but he always insists it's someone else who messed things up."

"He doesn't want Tito to go to jail."

"That's Tito's choice!" Of course she was right; they were both right.

The summit meeting was set for the next afternoon. Since I had only one late morning lecture, I would pick up Tito, feed him a Big Mac or two, then bring him to the house. Lola would fix Señor Martínez some nice tortillas and chili, making up for that abominable dinner of the night before last. Well fed, with two chaperones mediating, we thought they could work something out.

When Tito and I walked into the house, my hope started to tremble and develop goose bumps. It was deathly silent and formal. Lola had that dangerous look on her face again. The macho, chauvinist jumping bean sat stiffly in his suit that looked like it had just been pressed—all shiny and sharply creased, unapproachable and potentially cutting, an inanimate warning of what lay behind Señor Martínez's stone face.

Tito and I sat across from the sofa and faced them. Or rather I faced them. Both Tito and Señor Martínez were looking off at an angle from each other, not daring to touch glances. I smiled, but no one acknowledged it so I gave it up. Then Lola broke the silence.

"What this needs is a woman's point-of-view," she began.

That's all Señor Martínez needed. The blast his eyes shot at her left her open-mouthed and silent as he interrupted. "I don't want you to go to jail!" He was looking at Lola, but he meant Tito.

Tito's response was barely audible, and I detected a trembling in his voice. "You'd rather I got killed on some Arabian desert," he said.

The stone face cracked. For a moment it looked as if Señor Martínez would burst into tears. He turned his puzzled face from Lola toward his son. "No," he said. "Is that what you think?" Then, when Tito did not answer, he said, "You're my only son, and damn it! Sons are supposed to obey their fathers!"

"El patrón, El Papa, and Dios," Tito said with a trace of bitterness.

But Lola could be denied no longer. "Papá, how old were you when you left Mexico for the U.S.?" She didn't expect an answer, so didn't give him time to reply. "Sixteen, wasn't it? And what did your father say?"

Thank God that smart-ass smile of hers was turned away from her father. She knew she had him, and he knew it too, but she didn't need her smirk to remind him of it.

He sighed. The look on his face showed that sometimes memories were best forgotten. When he shook his head but did not speak, Lola went on. She too had seen her father's reaction, and her voice lost its hard edge and became more sympathetic.

"He disowned you, didn't he? Grandpa disowned you. Called you a traitor to your own country. A deserter when things got tough."

"I did not intend to stay in Mexico and starve," he said. He looked around at us one by one as if he had to justify himself. "He eventually came to Los Estados Unidos himself. He and Mamá died in that house in San Diego."

"What did you think when Grandpa did that to you?"

No answer was necessary. "Can't you see, Papá?" Lola pleaded, meaning him and Tito. He could see.

Meanwhile Tito had been watching his father as if he had never seen him before. I guess only the older children had heard Papá's story of how he left Mexico.

"I don't intend to go to jail, Papá," Tito said, "I just have to take a stand along with thousands of others. In the past old men started wars in which young men died in order to preserve old men's comforts. It just has to stop. There's never been a war without a draft. Never a draft without registration. And this one is nothing but craziness by el patrón in Washington, D.C. If enough of us protest, maybe he'll get the message."

"They almost declared it unconstitutional," I said. "They may yet."

"Because they aren't signing women," Papá said in disgust. But from the look on Lola's face, I'd pick her over him in any war.

"If they come after me, I'll register," Tito said. "But in the meantime I have to take this stand."

There. It was out. They had had their talk in spite of their disagreements.

"He's nineteen," Lola said. "Old enough to run his own life."

Señor Martínez was all talked out. He slumped against the back of the sofa. Even the creases in his trousers seemed to have sagged. Tito looked at his sister, and his face brightened.

"Papá," Tito said. "I . . . I'd like to go home, if you want me to."

On Papá's puzzled face I imagined I could read the words: "My father fought with Pancho Villa." But it was no longer an accusation, only a simple statement of fact. Who knows what takes more courage—to fight or not to fight?

"There's a bus at four o'clock," Señor Martínez said.

Later I drove them in silence to the station. Though it felt awkward, it wasn't a bad silence. There are more important ways to speak than with words, and I could feel that sitting shoulder to shoulder beside me, father and son had reached some accord.

Papá still believed in el patrón, El Papa, and Dios. What I hoped they now saw was that Tito did too. Only in his case, conscience overrode el patrón, maybe even El Papa. In times past, popes too declared holy wars that violated conscience. For Tito, conscience was the same as Dios. And I saw in their uneasy truce that love overrode their differences.

I shook their hands as they boarded the bus, and watched the two similar faces, one old, one young, smile sadly at me through the window as the Greyhound pulled away.

When I got back home, Junior and Lolita were squabbling over what channel to watch on TV. I rolled my eyes in exasperation, ready to holler at them, but Lola spoke up first.

"I'm glad Papá got straightened out. The hardest thing for parents with their children is to let go."

Yeah, I started to say, but she stuck her head into the other room and told Junior and Lolita to stop quarreling or they were going to get it.

Toni Morrison
(1931–)

Born Chloe Anthony Wofford in Loraine, Ohio, Toni Morrison was edu-cated at Howard University and at Cornell, where she wrote her master's degree thesis on suicide in the novels of Virginia Woolf and William Faulkner. She taught English at Texas Southern University from 1955 through 1957, then at Howard from 1957 to 1964. While at Howard, she married Harold Morrison, but the marriage did not last, and she left Wash-ington, D.C., to support herself and her sons by editorial work at Random House in New York City and by teaching in surrounding universities. At Random House, her editorial work included books by black authors such as Toni Cade Bambera, Angela Davis, and Gayle Jones. Meanwhile, she had begun her own writing, and by the late 1970s she had established herself as a major author. In 1984 she accepted an endowed chair as Professor of the Humanities at the State University of New York at Albany and in 1989 moved from there to another endowed chair at Princeton University.

A short story formed the germ of Morrison's first novel, The Bluest Eye

(1969), set in her home town, Loraine, Ohio. Much of her later work builds on the matter introduced here, as the world of her novels is frequently rural, northern, and black, with her characters cruelly twisted and their aspirations thwarted by pressures of poverty and ignorance born of their exclusion from mainstream America. In Sula *(1973), she explores the lives of two women, childhood friends in a town much like Lorain. In* Song of Solomon *(1977) she extends her range and depth in a longer work involving many more characters that focuses on the search of a northern black for the southern clues to his inherited identity. In* Tar Baby *(1981) she introduces more sophisticated characters, with whites playing prominent parts, as she tells of love in Paris, on a Caribbean island, and in New York and the rural South.* Beloved *(1987) has received special praise. A harrowing story set in the north not long after the Civil War, it presents the pain engendered by slavery as a continuous presence that is most memorably embodied in the ghost of a girl murdered by her mother to save her from slave catchers.* Jazz *(1992) is a story of love and violence set in New York City in 1926. Constructed as a series of riffs, it moves to the nineteenth-century South to play off the rural past of the main characters against their city present.*

Morrison's *Playing in the Dark: Whiteness and the Literary Imagination* (1992) is an essay in criticism. A study is Gary D. Schmidt, *Toni Morrison* (1990).

———

[From] *Sula*

1922

IT WAS TOO COOL for ice cream. A hill wind was blowing dust and empty Camels wrappers about their ankles. It pushed their dresses into the creases of their behinds, then lifted the hems to peek at their cotton underwear. They were on their way to Edna Finch's Mellow House, an ice-cream parlor catering to nice folks—where even children would feel comfortable, you know, even though it was right next to Reba's Grill and just one block down from the Time and a Half Pool Hall. It sat in the curve of Carpenter's Road, which, in four blocks, made up all the sporting life available in the Bottom. Old men and young ones draped themselves in front of the Elmira Theater, Irene's Palace of Cosmetology, the pool hall, the grill and the other sagging business enterprises that lined the street. On sills, on stoops, on crates and broken chairs they sat tasting their teeth and waiting for something to distract them. Every passerby, every motorcar, every alteration in stance caught their attention and was commented on. Particularly they watched women. When a woman approached, the older men tipped their hats; the young ones opened and closed their thighs. But all of them, whatever their age, watched her retreating view with interest.

Nel and Sula walked through this valley of eyes chilled by the wind and heated by the embarrassment of appraising stares. The old men looked at their stalklike legs, dwelled on the cords in the backs of their knees and remembered old dance steps they had not done in twenty years. In their lust, which age had turned to kindness, they moved their lips as though to stir up the taste of young sweat on tight skin.

Pig meat. The words were in all their minds. And one of them, one of the young ones, said it aloud. Softly but definitively and there was no mistaking the compliment. His name was Ajax, a twenty-one-year-old pool haunt of sinister beauty. Graceful and economical in every movement, he held a place of envy with men of all ages for his magnificently foul mouth. In fact he seldom cursed, and the epithets he chose were dull, even harmless. His reputation was derived from the way he handled the words. When he said "hell" he hit the *h* with his lungs and the impact was greater than the achievement of the most imaginative foul mouth in the town. He could say "shit" with a nastiness impossible to imitate. So, when he said "pig meat" as Nel and Sula passed, they guarded their eyes lest someone see their delight.

It was not really Edna Finch's ice cream that made them brave the stretch of those panther eyes. Years later their own eyes would glaze as they cupped their chins in remembrance of the inchworm smiles, the squatting haunches, the track-rail legs straddling broken chairs. The cream-colored trousers marking with a mere seam the place where the mystery curled. Those smooth vanilla crotches invited them; those lemon-yellow gabardines beckoned to them.

They moved toward the ice-cream parlor like tightrope walkers, as thrilled by the possibility of a slip as by the maintenance of tension and balance. The least sideways glance, the merest toe stub, could pitch them into those creamy haunches spread wide with welcome. Somewhere beneath all of that daintiness, chambered in all that neatness, lay the thing that clotted their dreams.

Which was only fitting, for it was in dreams that the two girls had first met. Long before Edna Finch's Mellow House opened, even before they marched through the chocolate halls of Garfield Primary School out onto the playground and stood facing each other through the ropes of the one vacant swing ("Go on." "No. You go."), they had already made each other's acquaintance in the delirium of their noon dreams. They were solitary little girls whose loneliness was so profound it intoxicated them and sent them stumbling into Technicolored visions that always included a presence, a someone, who, quite like the dreamer, shared the delight of the dream. When Nel, an only child, sat on the steps of her back porch surrounded by the high silence of her mother's incredibly orderly house, feeling the neatness pointing at her back, she studied the poplars and fell easily into a picture of herself lying on a flowered bed, tangled in her own hair, waiting for some fiery prince. He approached but never quite arrived. But always, watching the dream along with her, were some smiling sympathetic eyes. Someone as interested as she herself in the flow of her imagined hair, the thickness of the mattress of flowers, the voile sleeves that closed below her elbows in gold-threaded cuffs.

Similarly, Sula, also an only child, but wedged into a household of throbbing disorder constantly awry with things, people, voices and the slamming of doors, spent hours in the attic behind a roll of linoleum galloping through her own mind on a gray-and-white horse tasting sugar and smelling roses in full view of a someone who shared both the taste and the speed.

So when they met, first in those chocolate halls and next through the ropes of the swing, they felt the ease and comfort of old friends. Because each had discovered years before that they were neither white nor male, and that all freedom and triumph was forbidden to them, they had set about creating something else to be. Their meeting was fortunate, for it let them use each other to grow on. Daughters of distant mothers and incomprehensible fathers (Sula's because he was dead; Nel's because he wasn't), they found in each other's eyes the intimacy they were looking for.

Nel Wright and Sula Peace were both twelve in 1922, wishbone thin and easy-assed. Nel was the color of wet sandpaper—just dark enough to escape the blows of the pitch-black truebloods and the contempt of old women who worried about such things as bad blood mixtures and knew that the origin of a mule and a mulatto were one and the same. Had she been any lighter-skinned she would have needed either her mother's protection on the way to school or a streak of mean to defend herself. Sula was a heavy brown with large quiet eyes, one of which featured a birthmark that spread from the middle of the lid toward the eyebrow, shaped something like a stemmed rose. It gave her otherwise plain face a broken excitement and blue-blade threat like the keloid[1] scar of the razored man who sometimes played checkers with her grandmother. The birthmark was to grow darker as the years passed, but now it was the same shade as her gold-flecked eyes, which, to the end, were as steady and clean as rain.

Their friendship was as intense as it was sudden. They found relief in each other's personality. Although both were unshaped, formless things, Nel seemed stronger and more consistent than Sula, who could hardly be counted on to sustain any emotion for more than three minutes. Yet there was one time when that was not true, when she held on to a mood for weeks, but even that was in defense of Nel.

Four white boys in their early teens, sons of some newly arrived Irish people, occasionally entertained themselves in the afternoon by harassing black schoolchildren. With shoes that pinched and woolen knickers that made red rings on their calves, they had come to this valley with their par-

---

1. A hard excrescence on the skin.

ents believing as they did that it was a promised land—green and shimmering with welcome. What they found was a strange accent, a pervasive fear of their religion and firm resistance to their attempts to find work. With one exception the older residents of Medallion scorned them. The one exception was the black community. Although some of the Negroes had been in Medallion before the Civil War (the town didn't even have a name then), if they had any hatred for these newcomers it didn't matter because it didn't show. As a matter of fact, baiting them was the one activity that the white Protestant residents concurred in. In part their place in this world was secured only when they echoed the old residents' attitude toward blacks.

These particular boys caught Nel once, and pushed her from hand to hand until they grew tired of the frightened helpless face. Because of that incident, Nel's route home from school became elaborate. She, and then Sula, managed to duck them for weeks until a chilly day in November when Sula said, "Let's us go on home the shortest way."

Nel blinked, but acquiesced. They walked up the street until they got to the bend of Carpenter's Road where the boys lounged on a disused well. Spotting their prey, the boys sauntered forward as though there were nothing in the world on their minds but the gray sky. Hardly able to control their grins, they stood like a gate blocking the path. When the girls were three feet in front of the boys, Sula reached into her coat pocket and pulled out Eva's paring knife. The boys stopped short, exchanged looks and dropped all pretense of innocence. This was going to be better than they thought. They were going to try and fight back, and with a knife. Maybe they could get an arm around one of their waists, or tear. . .

Sula squatted down in the dirt road and put everything on the ground: her lunchpail, he reader, her mittens, her slate. Holding the knife in her right hand, she pulled the slate toward her and pressed her left forefinger down hard on its edge. Her aim was determined but inaccurate. She slashed off only the tip of her finger. The four boys stared open-mouthed at the wound and the scrap of flesh, like a button mushroom, curling in the cherry blood that ran into the corners of the slate.

Sula raised her eyes to them. Her voice was quiet. "If I can do that to myself, what you suppose I'll do to you?"

The shifting dirt was the only way Nel knew that they were moving away; she was looking at Sula's face, which seemed miles and miles away.

But toughness was not their quality—adventuresomeness was—and a mean determination to explore everything that interested them, from one-eyed chickens high-stepping in their penned yards to Mr. Buckland Reed's gold teeth, from the sound of sheets flapping in the wind to the labels on Tar Baby's wine bottles. And they had no priorities. They could be distracted from watching a fight with mean razors by the glorious smell of hot tar being poured by roadmen two hundred yards away.

In the safe harbor of each other's company they could afford to abandon the ways of other people and concentrate on their own perceptions of things. When Mrs. Wright reminded Nel to pull her nose, she would do it enthusiastically but without the least hope in the world.

"While you sittin' there, honey, go 'head and pull your nose."

"It hurts, Mamma."

"Don't you want a nice nose when you grow up?"

After she met Sula, Nel slid the clothespin under the blanket as soon as she got in the bed. And although there was still the hateful hot comb to suffer through each Saturday evening, its consequences—smooth hair—no longer interested her.

Joined in mutual admiration they watched each day as though it were a movie arranged for their amusement. The new theme they were now discovering was men. So they met regularly, without even planning it, to walk down the road to Edna Finch's Mellow House, even though it was too cool for ice cream.

Then summer came. A summer limp with the weight of blossomed things. Heavy sunflows were weeping over fences; iris curling and browning at the edges far away from their purple hearts; ears of corn letting their auburn hair wind down to their stalks. And the boys. The beautiful, beautiful boys who dotted the landscape like jewels, split the air with their shouts in the field, and thickened the river with their shining wet backs. Even their footsteps left a smell of smoke behind.

It was in that summer, the summer of their twelfth year, the summer of the beautiful black boys, that they became skittish, frightened and bold—all at the same time.

In that mercury mood in July, Sula and Nel wandered about the Bottom barefoot looking for mischief. They decided to go down by the river where the boys sometimes swam. Nel waited on the porch of 7 Carpenter's Road while Sula ran into the house to go to the toilet. On the way up the stairs, she passed the kitchen where Hannah sat with two friends, Patsy and Valentine. The two women were fanning themselves and watching Hannah put down some dough, all talking casually about one thing and another, and had gotten around, when Sula passed by, to the problems of child rearing.

"They a pain."

"Yeh. Wish I'd listened to mamma. She told me not to have 'em too soon."

"Anytime atall is too soon for me."

"Oh, I don't know. My Rudy minds his daddy. He just wild with me. Be glad when he growed and gone."

Hannah smiled and said, "Shut your mouth. You love the ground he pee on."

"Sure I do. But he still a pain. Can't help loving your own child. No matter what they do."

"Well, Hester grown now and I can't say love is exactly what I feel."

"Sure you do. You love her, like I love Sula. I just don't like her. That's the difference."

"Guess so. Likin' them is another thing."

"Sure. They different people, you know . . ."

She only heard Hannah's words, and the pronouncement sent her flying up the stairs. In bewilderment, she stood at the window fingering the curtain edge, aware of a sting in her eye. Nel's call floated up and into the window, pulling her away from dark thoughts back into the bright, hot daylight.

They ran most of the way.

Heading toward the wide part of the river where trees grouped themselves in families darkening the earth below. They passed some boys swimming and clowning in the water, shrouding their words in laughter.

They ran in the sunlight, creating their own breeze, which pressed their dresses into their damp skin. Reaching a kind of square of four leaf-locked trees which promised cooling, they flung themselves into the four-cornered shade to taste their lip sweat and contemplate the wildness that had come upon them so suddenly. They lay in the grass, their foreheads almost touching, their bodies stretched away from each other at a 180-degree angle. Sula's head rested on her arm, an undone braid coiled around her wrist. Nel leaned on her elbows and worried long blades of grass with her fingers. Underneath their dresses flesh tightened and shivered in the high coolness, their small breasts just now beginning to create some pleasant discomfort when they were lying on their stomachs.

Sula lifted her head and joined Nel in the grass play. In concert, without ever meeting each other's eyes, they stroked the blades up and down, up and down. Nel found a thick twig and, with her thumbnail, pulled away its bark until it was stripped to a smooth, creamy innocence. Sula looked about and found one too. When both twigs were undressed Nel moved easily to the next stage and began tearing up rooted grass to make a bare spot of earth. When a generous clearing was made, Sula traced intricate patterns in it with her twig. At first Nel was content to do the same. But soon she grew impatient and poked her twig rhythmically and intensely into the earth, making a small neat hole that grew deeper and wider with the least manipulation of her twig. Sula copied her, and soon each had a hole the size of a cup. Nel began a more strenuous digging and, rising to her knee, was careful to scoop out the dirt as she made her hole deeper. Together they worked until the two holes were one and the same. When the depression was the size of a small dishpan, Nel's twig broke. With a gesture of disgust she threw the pieces into the hole they had made. Sula threw hers in too. Nel saw a bottle cap and tossed it in as well. Each then looked around for more debris to throw into the hole: paper, bits of glass, butts of cigarettes, until all of the small defiling things they could find were collected there. Carefully they replaced the soil and covered the entire grave with uprooted grass.

Neither one had spoken a word.

They stood up, stretched, then gazed out over the swift dull water as an unspeakable restlessness and agitation held them. At the same instant each girl heard footsteps in the grass. A little boy in too big knickers was coming up from the lower bank of the river. He stopped when he saw them and picked his nose.

"Your mamma tole you to stop eatin' snot, Chicken," Nel hollered at him through cupped hands.

"Shut up," he said, still picking.

"Come up here and say that."

"Leave him 'lone, Nel. Come here, Chicken. Lemme show you something."

"Naw."

"You scared we gone take your bugger away?"

"Leave him 'lone, I said. Come on, Chicken. Look. I'll help you climb a tree."

Chicken looked at the tree Sula was pointing to—a big double beech with low branches and lots of bends for sitting.

He moved slowly toward her.

"Come on, Chicken, I'll help you up."

Still picking his nose, his eyes wide, he came to where they were standing. Sula took him by the hand and coaxed him along. When they reached the base of the beech, she lifted him to the first branch, saying, "Go on. Go on. I got you." She followed the boy, steadying him, when he needed it, with her hand and her reassuring voice. When they were as high as they could go, Sula pointed to the far side of the river.

"See? Bet you never saw that far before, did you?"

"Uh uh."

"Now look down there." They both leaned a little and peered through the leaves at Nel standing below, squinting up at them. From their height she looked small and foreshortened.

Chicken Little laughed.

"Y'all better come on down before you break your neck," Nel hollered.

"I ain't never coming down," the boy hollered back.

"Yeah. We better. Come on, Chicken."

"Naw. Lemme go."

"Yeah, Chicken. Come on, now."

Sula pulled his leg gently.

"Lemme go."

"OK, I'm leavin' you." She started on.

"Wait!" he screamed.

Sula stopped and together they slowly worked their way down.

Chicken was still elated. "I was way up there, wasn't I? Wasn't I? I'm a tell my brovver."

Sula and Nel began to mimic him: "I'm a tell my brovver; I'm a tell my brovver."

Sula picked him up by his hands and swung him outward then around and around. His knickers ballooned and his shrieks of frightened joy startled the birds and the fat grasshoppers. When he slipped from her hands and sailed away out over the water they could still hear his bubbly laughter.

The water darkened and closed quickly over the place where Chicken Little sank. The pressure of his hard and tight little fingers was still in Sula's palms as she stood looking at the closed place in the water. They expected him to come back up, laughing. Both girls stared at the water.

Nel spoke first. "Somebody saw." A figure appeared briefly on the opposite shore.

The only house over there was Shadrack's. Sula glanced at Nel. Terror widened her nostrils. Had he seen?

The water was so peaceful now. There was nothing but the baking sun and something newly missing. Sula cupped her face for an instant, then turned and ran up to the little plank bridge that crossed the river to Shadrack's house. There was no path. It was as though neither Shadrack nor anyone else ever came this way.

Her running was swift and determined, but when she was close to the three little steps that led to his porch, fear crawled into her stomach and only the something newly missing back there in the river made it possible for her to walk up the three steps and knock at the door.

No one answered. She stared back, but thought again of the peace of the river. Shadrack would be inside, just behind the door ready to pounce on her. Still she could not go back. Ever so gently she pushed the door with the tips of her fingers and heard only the hinges weep. More. And then she was inside. Alone. The neatness, the order startled her, but more surprising was the restfulness. Everything was so tiny, so common, so unthreatening. Perhaps this was not the house of the Shad. The terrible Shad who walked about with his penis out, who peed in front of ladies and girl-children, the only black who could curse white people and get away with it, who drank in the road from the mouth of the bottle, who shouted and shook in the streets. This cottage? This sweet old cottage? With its made-up bed? With its rag rug and wooden table? Sula stood in the middle of the little room and in her wonder forgot what she had come for until a sound at the door made her jump. He was there in the doorway looking at her. She had not heard his coming and now he was looking at her.

More in embarrassment than terror she averted her glance. When she called up enough courage to look back at him, she saw his hand resting upon the door frame. His fingers, barely touching the wood, were arranged in a graceful arc. Relieved and encouraged (no one with hands like that, no one with fingers that curved around wood so tenderly could kill her), she walked past him out of the door, feeling his gaze turning, turning with her.

At the edge of the porch, gathering the wisps of courage that were fast leaving her, she turned once more to look at him, to ask him . . . had he . . . ?

He was smiling, a great smile, heavy with lust and time to come. He nodded his head as though answering a question, and said, in a pleasant conversational tone, a tone of cooled butter, "Always."

Sula fled down the steps, and shot through the greenness and the baking sun back to Nel and the dark closed place in the water. There she collapsed in tears.

Nel quieted her. "Sh, sh. Don't, don't. You didn't mean it. It ain't your fault. Sh. Sh. Come on, le's go, Sula. Come on, now. Was he there? Did he see? Where's the belt to your dress?"

Sula shook her head while she searched her waist for the belt.

Finally she stood up and allowed Nel to lead her away. "He said, 'Always. Always.'"

"What?"

Sula covered her mouth as they walked down the hill. Always. He had answered a question she had not asked, and its promise licked at her feet.

A bargeman, poling away from the shore, found Chicken late that afternoon stuck in some rocks and weeds, his knickers ballooning about his legs. He would have left him there but noticed that it was a child, not an old black man, as it first appeared, and he prodded the body loose, netted it and hauled it aboard. He shook his head in disgust at the kind of parents who would drown their own children. When, he wondered, will those people ever be anything but animals, fit for nothing but substitutes for mules, only mules didn't kill each other the way niggers did. He dumped Chicken Little into a burlap sack and tossed him next to some egg crates and boxes of wool cloth. Later, sitting down to smoke on an empty lard tin, still bemused by God's curse and the terrible burden his own kind had of elevating Ham's sons,[2] he suddenly became alarmed by the thought that the corpse in this heat would have a terrible odor, which might get into the fabric of his woolen cloth. He dragged the sack away and hooked it over the side, so that the Chicken's body was half in and half out of the water.

Wiping the sweat from his neck, he reported his find to the sheriff at Porter's Landing, who said they didn't have no niggers in their county, but that some lived in those hills 'cross the river, up above Medallion. The bargeman said he couldn't go all the way back there, it was every bit of two miles. The sheriff said whyn't he throw it on back into the water. The bargeman said he never shoulda taken it out in the first place. Finally they got the man who ran the ferry twice a day to agree to take it over in the morning.

That was why Chicken Little was missing for three days and didn't get to the embalmer's until the fourth day, by which time he was unrecognizable to almost everybody who once knew him, and even his mother wasn't deep down sure, except that it just had to be him since nobody could find him. When she saw his clothes lying on the table in the basement of the mortuary, her mouth snapped shut, and when she saw his body her mouth flew wide open again and it was seven hours before she was able to close it and make the first sound.

So the coffin was closed.

The Junior Choir, dressed in white, sang "Nearer My God to Thee" and "Precious Memories," their eyes fastened on the songbooks they did not need, for this was the first time their voices presided at a real-life event.

Nel and Sula did not touch hands or look at each other during the funeral. There was a space, a separateness, between them. Nel's legs had turned to granite and she expected the sheriff or Reverend Deal's pointing finger at any moment. Although she knew she had "done nothing," she felt convicted and hanged right there in the pew—two rows down from her parents in the children's section.

---

2. Ham, son of Noah, was traditionally the ancestor of the black race (*cf.* Genesis ix: 25–26).

Sula simply cried. Soundlessly and with no heaving and gasping for breath, she let the tears roll into her mouth and slide down her chin to dot the front of her dress.

As Reverend Deal moved into his sermon, the hands of the women unfolded like pairs of raven's wings and flew high above their hats in the air. They did not hear all of what he said; they heard the one word, or phrase, or inflection that was for them the connection between the event and themselves. For some it was the term "Sweet Jesus." And they saw the Lamb's eye and the truly innocent victim: themselves. They acknowledged the innocent child hiding in the corner of their hearts, holding a sugar-and-butter sandwich. That one. The one who lodged deep in their fat, thin, old, young skin, and was the one the world had hurt. Or they thought of their son newly killed and remembered his legs in short pants and wondered where the bullet went in. Or they remembered how dirty the room looked when their father left home and wondered if that is the way the slim, young Jew felt, he who for them was both son and lover and in whose downy face they could see the sugar-and-butter sandwiches and feel the oldest and most devastating pain there is: not the pain of childhood, but the remembrance of it.

Then they left their pews. For with some emotions one has to stand. They spoke, for they were full and needed to say. They swayed, for the rivulets of grief or of ecstasy must be rocked. And when they thought of all that life and death locked into that little closed coffin they danced and screamed, not to protest God's will but to acknowledge it and confirm once more their conviction that the only way to avoid the Hand of God is to get in it.

In the colored part of the cemetery, they sank Chicken Little in between his grandfather and an aunt. Butterflies flew in and out of the bunches of field flowers now loosened from the top of the bier and lying in a small heap at the edge of the grave. The heat had gone, but there was no breeze to lift the hair of the willows.

Nel and Sula stood some distance away from the grave, the space that had sat between them in the pews had dissolved. They held hands and knew that only the coffin would lie in the earth; the bubbly laughter and the press of fingers in the palm would stay above ground forever. At first, as they stood there, their hands were clenched together. They relaxed slowly until during the walk back home their fingers were laced in as gentle a clasp as that of any two young girlfriends trotting up the road on a summer day wondering what happened to butterflies in the winter.

Ved Mehta
(1934–)

Born in Lahore (in India then, Pakistan after the 1947 partition), Ved Parkash Mehta was blinded as a result of childhood meningitis; one of his earliest memories is tearfully saying goodbye to his father at age five as he left home to begin his education at an orphanage for the blind in Bombay. Later, aware of his bleak prospects in India, he sought admission to thirty schools for the blind in Europe and the United States. Accepted by the Arkansas School for the Blind in Little Rock, he left India at fifteen. From Arkansas, he went to Pomona College in California, where he began his first book, Face to Face: An Autobiography *(1957), published the year after his graduation. Interested in history, he secured fellowships that took him to Balliol College, Oxford, for a second B.A. (1959) and then to Harvard for an M.A. (1961). Meanwhile, his writing had caught the attention of the editor of* The New Yorker, *and in 1961 he joined the staff of that magazine, where most of his work has since appeared before its publication in books. "I don't belong to any single tradition," he has said. "I am an amalgam of five cultures—Indian, British, American, blind and* The New Yorker." *Living in New York City, in 1975 he became an American citizen.*

Mehta's autobiographical books are masterpieces of the genre, monuments to the industry, memory, and sweeping perceptions of an extraordinary human being. By 1989 he had completed a series of six mature volumes, to which he gave the general name "Continents of Exile." It includes Daddyji *(1972), a portrait of his father;* Mamaji *(1979), with its focus on his mother;* Vedi *(1982), on his schooling in Bombay;* The Ledge between the Streams *(1984), covering his family life in the tumultuous years for India of 1940 to 1949;* Sound-Shadows of the New World *(1985), about his years as a foreign-born blind student in Arkansas; and* The Stolen Light *(1989), on life as a Pomona undergraduate.*

Among Mehta's many other books are a number of nonfiction works on India, including Walking the Indian Streets *(1960),* Portrait of India *(1970),* Mahatma Gandhi and His Apostles *(1977),* The New India *(1978), and* A Family Affair: India under Three Prime Ministers *(1982). In* The

Photographs of Chachaji: The Making of a Documentary Film *(1980) he describes the filming of his "Chachaji: My Poor Relation." Works of fiction include* Delinquent Chacha *(1976), a novel, and* Three Stories of the Raj *(1986).*

———

The Cloud Has Spread Its Dark Hair[1]

Indian Youth Asks Admittance to ASB

A 14-year-old blind youth from Simla, India, who has completed all of the training available to him in his native country, is seeking admittance to the Arkansas School for the Blind to further his education. [I was actually fifteen.]

Members of the blind school board at a recent meeting authorized James M. Woolly, school superintendent, to investigate the youth's situation. . . .

In his letter to Mr. Woolly, a letter he typed himself in English, the youth said:

"And there is no more scope in India for my studies as I have gained from St. Dunstan's what they could teach me. Now I have great wish to come over to your school, and hope that you will be kind enough to admit me."

He indicated a desire to complete the full course offered at the Arkansas School and was also interested in university examinations offered at the completion of the course.

—*Little Rock (Ark.) Democrat,*
February 20, 1949

Finally, I was in America. Ever since I could remember, I had been hearing about it from my father, Daddyji, as "God's own country." He had come here from India to continue his medical studies, and now I was here as a student. I'd been trying to come for at least eight years—since I was seven years old. The morning after I arrived, I sat down at a typewriter and wrote a letter home:

---

1. The first chapter of *Sound-Shadows of the New World* (1985).

544 West 113 Street, Apt. 4A
New York 25, N.Y., U.S.A.
16th August, 1949

My Dearest Daddyjee,

I reached New York yesterday. It was a very long Journey than we expected it to be. It took me 47 hours to get here. Mrs. John di Francesco came to receive me at the aerodrome.

Now I think I better tell you something about my journey. The Journey was quite boring and tiring. I reached London, by London timings, at 9:15 A.M. Cousin Nitya Nand was there to meet me. But the Plane did not stop there for long.

The people who met us at Aerodrome in Delhi and said they would look after me did not even come to me in the plane once, and I never even knew where they were. As a matter of fact. I—whatever I did was by myself.

I just now have had a word on telephone with Mr. Woolly. He wants me at Arkansas School for the Blind as soon as possible. He says the school will open in three weeks time from today. I rang Mr. Woolly because I came to know by Mr. and Mrs. di Francesco that there is lots of Infantile Paralysis going on in Arkansas. But Mr. Woolly has assuredly said that they are better off there than in New York. He left it to me when I wish to come I can come, but he said the sooner the better it is from his point of view. I think I shall leave for Arkansas on the 26th of this month. Mr. and Mrs. di Francesco will be going on six days holidays to Maine from the 27th. They say I am welcome to go with them if I wish to. But I am still thinking. Mr. and Mrs. di Francesco are very nice people.

I shall write you a very long letter as soon as I can get a good typewriter for long time. That I do not hope to get here in New York. Daddyjee I do not like to say anymore what I feel. I am very homesick.

The bag which you bought me with a zip on it which you said will be very useful as a second bag was open on the way by breaking the zip, and all the Ivory things which you presented me were removed except one piece. Some of my clothes were also stolen. It was discovered there and then, at the New York aerodrome that the bag has been broken. It was also examined by the people over there. All the shirts which we kept in that were taken away. And instead of my things there was one hair brush and one shaving creams bottle which was not mine. I gave same back to them. The bag is absolutely spoilt. We have put down a claim for my things. But I do not know whether they will give it or not. The one piece which was left was the salt cellar. Mrs. di Francesco tells me that the price of it here in New York is 12 Dollars. She also seems to seen other ivory pieces in shops over here and she says that they are very very expensive. Only if I have had those to sell I would have made at least one and a half months living expenses in School. I have put down a claim for over One hundred Dollars because they are even more expensive over here.

With love to all and respects.

Your affectionate Son,
Ved

At the airport in New Delhi, there had been dozens of relatives all around, laughing and clapping. Suddenly, they were embracing me, and there was such a rush and confusion that people embracing me were themselves being embraced. Then Daddyji and I were walking to the Pan American airplane, dirt crunching under our feet. Daddyji fell into conversation with a couple of Sikh passengers walking just ahead of us and found out that they were going to New York on the same airplane. "This is my fifteen-year-old blind son, Ved," he said, introducing me to them. (I have been totally blind since I was four years old, as a result of meningitis.) "He's travelling alone for the first time—you see, he's going to America for his studies. I'd be grateful if you could give him assistance along the way if he needs it." I wanted to hide, out of embarrassment, but I had never travelled anywhere alone or gone so far away, and I said nothing.

"Most certainly, most certainly," the two Sikhs said, and clicked their tongues.

We dropped behind. "Son, you must build up your health," Daddyji said. "Ninety-one pounds for a boy five feet five is a very low weight. Even the officer who gave me permission to accompany you to the plane remarked on how thin you look for your age."

I had never been on an airplane before. There were steps going up and up and up. They were so narrow that Daddyji and I had to go single file, and they were tinny and flimsy and shook under us, creating a little storm. Inside, the floor sloped upward, and the ceiling was so low that I had to walk with my head bowed.

"Another thing—you'll have to learn not to be so shy," Daddyji was saying. His voice sounded painfully loud to me through the haze of voices in the plane.

"I'm not shy," I snapped irritably.

At my seat, we embraced quickly, like two Punjabi adults, and he hurried away, leaving me sad at my outburst. I had no idea when we might meet again.

There was a pair of seats on each side of the aisle. My seat was next to a window. I sat strapped in it, wondering how high off the ground I was and whether anyone in my family could see through the window. I tried to smile, as I always did for photographs—which, of course, I couldn't see, but which I would overhear others commenting on.

It was very hot: it was the middle of August, and we had not had any monsoon rains for days.

Daddyji had been gone no more than a few minutes when I heard the hasty rustle of a sari. It was Mamaji. She planted a kiss on my forehead, her face wet with tears. "Let God keep you," she said.

I struggled to unstrap myself, but before I could she was gone. My forehead burned. I had not been kissed since I was a small boy—since I was eight or nine, perhaps.

Almost immediately, the airplane under me roared and trembled. An air hostess who sounded very American came up and said, over my head, "Above you there are two buttons—the red one is for calling me, and the green one is a reading light."

I nodded knowingly. It is just as well she doesn't realize I can't see, I thought. This way, she won't be oversolicitous.

Several times, I thought that we had left the ground, but then the tires bumped along the runway or the plane lurched to a stop. I began to feel that we would never get off. I'd often had the same feeling during the months of preparation for going to America, when I was waiting to complete the required medical tests, to get inoculations, to have my picture and finger-prints taken, and to hear from the various authorities concerned with pass-port, visa, foreign exchange, and police clearance.

Finally, the airplane paused, then raced along the runway. I held my breath. Then I felt the airplane shaking in the air as it rose like a speeded-up lift cage. The airplane levelled off, but there was no letup in the roar. It all but blocked out my hearing, and I wondered how I would survive it for such a long journey.

In my flight bag I had a Braille copy of "Murder on the Orient Express," by Agatha Christie. At first, I felt awkward about reading Braille in public, but I got bored just sitting, so I took the book out and started it.

"Is that Braille you're reading?" the air hostess asked, bending over me.

I nodded sheepishly.

She sighed and went away.

The rest of the journey is a jumble of disconnected memories. I remem-ber that I felt frightened when we landed in Karachi; all of us in my family were refugees from Pakistan, and I was wary of being in a Muslim country. I fell asleep reading. I had to go hungry for a long time, because I didn't want to confess that I didn't know how to use a knife and fork. We landed in some place, but I didn't catch its name. Everybody got off, and I waited for some-one to help me, but no one came—neither the air hostess nor the two Sikhs. We went high up in the air and it got very cold, and I had to breathe very fast. My ears popped repeatedly. They hurt so badly that I thought I would go deaf. We were in Damascus. The man who was cleaning and restocking the plane helped me off and showed me to a restaurant in the airport. The waiter there did not speak English; I had to order food through an inter-preter. Luckily, they had Indian food, and I ate my fill with my fingers. In one place, it was sleeting, and the airline people gave us raincoats to walk to a small waiting room, where we had to wait for two hours. We stopped in London. Cousin Nitya Nand had come from Cambridge specially to meet me, but it took so long for me to find someone to take me to a bus, for the bus to take me to Customs, and for the Customs people to clear me to go to the visitors' lounge, where Cousin Nitya Nand was waiting, that we had time only to exchange a few pieces of news before I had to get back on the bus.

After forty-seven hours, we reached New York. It was two o'clock on the afternoon of the fifteenth of August.

At the airport, I was questioned by an immigration official. "You're blind—totally blind—and they gave you a visa? You say it's for your studies, but studies where?"

"At the Arkansas School for the Blind. It is in Little Rock, in Arkansas."

He shuffled through the pages of a book. Sleep was in my eyes. Drops of sweat were running down my back. My shirt and trousers felt dirty.

"Arkansas School is not on our list of approved schools for foreign students."

"I know," I said. "That is why the immigration officials in Delhi gave me only a visitor's visa. They said that when I got to the school I should tell the authorities to apply to be on your list of approved schools, so that I could get a student visa." I showed him a big manila envelope I was carrying; it contained my chest X-rays, medical reports, and fingerprint charts, which were necessary for a student visa, and which I'd had prepared in advance.

"Why didn't you apply to an approved school in the first place and come here on a proper student visa?" he asked, looking through the material.

My knowledge of English was limited. With difficulty, I explained to him that I had applied to some thirty schools but that, because I had been able to get little formal education in India, the Arkansas School was the only one that would accept me; that I had needed a letter of acceptance from an American school to get dollars sanctioned by the Reserve Bank of India; and that now that I was in America I was sure I could change schools if the Arkansas School was not suitable or did not get the necessary approval.

Muttering to himself, the immigration official looked up at me, down at his book, and up at me again. He finally announced, "I think you'll have to go to Washington and apply to get your visa changed to a student visa before you can go to any school."

I recalled things that Daddyji used to say as we were growing up: "In life, there is only fight or flight. You must always fight," and "America is God's own country. People there are the most hospitable and generous people in the world." I told myself I had nothing to worry about. Then I remembered that Daddyji had mentioned a Mr. and Mrs. Dickens in Washington—they were friends of friends of his—and told me that I could get in touch with them in case of emergency.

"I will do whatever is necessary," I now said to the immigration official. "I will go to Washington."

He hesitated, as if he were thinking something, and then stamped my passport and returned it to me. "We Mehtas carry our luck with us," Daddyji used to say. He is right, I thought.

The immigration official suddenly became helpful, as if he were a friend. "You shouldn't have any trouble with the immigration people in Washington," he said, and asked, "Is anybody meeting you here?"

"Mr. and Mrs. di Francesco," I said.

Mrs. di Francesco was a niece of Manmath Nath Chatterjee, whom Daddyji had known when he himself was a student, in London, in 1920. Daddyji had asked Mr. Chatterjee, who had a Scottish-American wife and was now settled in Yellow Springs, Ohio, if he could suggest anyone with whom I might stay in New York, so that I could get acclimatized to American before proceeding to the Arkansas School, which was not due to open until the eleventh of September. Mr. Chatterjee had written back that, as it happened, his wife's niece was married to John di Francesco, a singer who was totally blind, and that Mr. and Mrs. di Francesco lived in New York, and would be delighted to meet me at the airport and keep me as a paying guest at fifteen dollars a week.

"How greedy of them to ask for money!" I had cried when I learned of the arrangement. "People come and stay with us for months and we never ask for an anna.[2]

Daddyji had said, "In the West, people do not, as a rule, stay with relatives and friends but put up in hotels, or in houses as paying guests. That is the custom there. Mr. and Mrs. di Francesco are probably a young, struggling couple who could do with a little extra money."

The immigration official now came from behind the counter, led me to an open area, and shouted, with increasing volume, "Fransisco! . . . Franchesca! . . . De Franco!" I wasn't sure what the correct pronunciation was, but his shouting sounded really disrespectful. I asked him to call for Mr. and Mrs. di Francesco softly. He bellowed, "Di Fransesco!"

No one came. My mouth went dry. Mr. and Mrs. di Francesco had sent me such a warm invitation. I couldn't imagine why they would have let me down or what I should do next.

Then I heard the footsteps of someone running toward us. "Here I am. You must be Ved. I'm Muriel di Francesco. I'm sorry John couldn't come." I noted that the name was pronounced the way it was spelled, and that hers was a Yankee voice—the kind I had heard when I first encountered Americans at home, during the war—but it had the sweetness of the voices of my sisters.

We shook hands; she had a nice firm grip. I had an impulse to call her Auntie Muriel—at home, an older person was always called by an honorific, like "Auntie" or "Uncle"—but I greeted her as Daddyji had told me that Westerners liked to be greeted: "Mrs. di Francesco, I'm delighted to make your acquaintance."

"You had a terrible trip, you poor boy. What a terrible way to arrive!" Mrs. di Francesco said in the taxi. "Imagine, everything stolen from a bag!"

One bag had contained clothes. The other, a holdall, had contained (in addition to some extra shirts) a number of ivory curios—statues of Lord Krishna, "no evil" monkeys, brooches with a little pattern on them—which Daddyji had bought with the idea that I could sell them at great profit. "You can take the ivory curios to a shop in Little Rock and ask the shop to sell them for you—on commission, of course," he had said. "In America, a lot of people earn and learn. Who knows? Maybe we could start an ivory-export-import business in a year or so, when I retire from government service." He was deputy director general of health services in the Indian government. "I expect there is a great deal of demand over there for hand-carved things."

---

2. A small coin, 1/16th of a rupee.

The fact that neither of us had ever sold even a second-hand gramophone didn't stop us from dreaming.

I didn't want Mrs. di Francesco to feel bad, so I made light of the theft. "The other bag is still full," I said.

"The ivory things must have been really valuable," she said. She had helped me fill out the insurance-claim forms. "What a bad introduction to America!"

"But it could have happened in Delhi."

She regaled the taxi-driver with the story, as if she and I were long-standing friends. "And we had to wait at the airport for two whole hours, filling out insurance forms. And he only knew the prices in rubles."

"Rupees," I said.

"Is that right?" the taxi-driver said, from the front seat. "Well, it shouldn't have happened to you, son."

I leaned toward the half-open window and listened for the roar of street crowds, the cries of hawkers, the clatter of tonga[3] wheels, the trot of tonga horses, the crackle of whips, the blasts of Klaxons, the trills of police whistles, the tinkling of bicycle bells—but all I heard was the steady hiss and rush of cars. "In America, you can really travel fast and get places," I said.

Mrs. di Francesco took both my hands in hers and broke into open, unrestrained laughter. I have never heard a woman laugh quite like that, I thought.

"What are you laughing at?" I asked.

"I'd just noticed that all this time you had your hand in your breast pocket. Are you afraid of having your wallet stolen, too?"

I was embarrassed. I hadn't realized what I had been doing.

The taxi-driver took a sharp turn.

"Where are we?" I asked.

"On Broadway," Mrs. di Francesco said.

"Is Broadway a wide road?" I asked.

She laughed. "A very wide avenue—it's the center of the universe."

At home, the center was a circle, but here the center, it seemed, was a straight line. At home, I often felt I was on a merry-go-round, circling activities that I couldn't join in. Here I would travel in taxis amid new friends and have adventures. I tried to voice my thoughts.

"Poor boy, you have difficulty with the language," Mrs. di Francesco said, gently pressing my hand.

"English is difficult," I said, and I tried to make a joke. "When I was small and first learning English, I was always confusing 'chicken' and 'kitchen.'"

"'Chicken' and 'kitchen,'" Mrs. di Francesco repeated, and laughed.

"I have enough trouble speaking English," the taxi-driver said. "I could never learn to speak Hindu."

---

3. A two-wheeled, horse-drawn vehicle.

"Hindi," I said, correcting him.

"You see?" the taxi-driver said.

Mrs. di Francesco laughed, and the taxi-driver joined in.

After a while, the taxi came to a stop. "Here we are at home, on a Hundred and Thirteenth Street between Broadway and Amsterdam," Mrs. di Francesco said.

Though I was carrying a bank draft for eighty dollars, I had only two dollars in cash, which a family friend had given me for good luck. I handed it to Mrs. di Francesco for the taxi.

"That won't be enough," she said.

"But it is *seven rupees!*" I cried. "At home, one could hire a tonga for a whole day for that."

"This is New York," she said. She clicked open her purse and gave some money to the taxi-driver.

The taxi-driver put my bags on the curb, shook my hand, and said, "If I go to India, I will remember not to become a tonga driver." He drove away.

We picked up the luggage. Mrs. di Francesco tucked my free hand under her bare arm with a quick motion and started walking. A woman at home would probably have cringed at the touch of a stranger's hand under her arm, I thought, but thinking this did not stop me from making a mental note that the muscle of her arm was well developed.

We went into a house, and walked up to Mr. and Mrs. di Francesco's apartment, on the fourth floor. Mr. di Francesco opened the door and kissed Mrs. di Francesco loudly. Had a bomb exploded, I could not have been more surprised. They'll catch something, I thought. I had never heard any grownups kissing at home—not even in films.

Mr. di Francesco shook my hand. He had a powerful grip and a powerful voice. He took me by the shoulder and almost propelled me to a couch. "This is going to be your bed," he said. "I'm sorry I couldn't come to the airport. Anyway, I knew you wouldn't mind being greeted by a charming lady." He doesn't have a trace of the timid, servile manner of music masters and blind people at home, I thought.

"We had a delightful ride from the airport," I said.

Mr. di Francesco wanted to know why we were so late, and Mrs. di Francesco told him about the theft.

"What bad luck!" he said.

"But I got here," I said.

"That's the spirit," he said, laughing.

"John, thank you for starting dinner," Mrs. di Francesco said from what I took to be the kitchen.

"Oh, you cook!" I exclaimed. I had never heard of a blind person who could cook.

"Yes, I help Muriel," he said. "We don't have servants here, as they do in your country. We have labor-saving devices." He then showed me around the apartment, casually tapping and explaining—or putting my hand on—

various unfamiliar things: a stove that did not burn coal or give out smoke; an ice chest that stood on end and ran on electricity; a machine that toasted bread; a bed for two people; and a tub in which one could lie down. I was full of questions, and asked how natural gas from the ground was piped into individual apartments, and how people could have so much hot water that they could lie down in it. At home, a husband and wife never slept in one bed, but I didn't say anything about that, because I felt shy.

"Do you eat meat?" Mrs. di Francesco asked me from the kitchen. "Aunt Rita—Mrs. Chatterjee—didn't know."

"Yes, I do eat meat," I called back to her. I started worrying about how I would cut it.

Mrs. di Francesco sighed with relief. "John and I hoped that you weren't a vegetarian. We're having spaghetti and meatballs, which are made of beef. Is that all right?"

I shuddered. As a Hindu, I had never eaten beef, and the mere thought of it was revolting. But I recalled another of Daddyji's sayings, "When in Rome, do as the Romans do," and said, "I promised my father that I would eat anything and everything in America and gain some weight."

Mrs. di Francesco brought out the dinner and served it to us at a small table. "The peas are at twelve and the spaghetti and meatballs at six," she said. I must have looked puzzled, because she added, "John locates his food on a plate by the clock dial. I thought all blind people knew—"

"You forget that India has many primitive conditions," Mr. di Francesco interrupted. "Without a doubt, work for the blind there is very backward."

I bridled. "There is nothing primitive or backward in India."

There was a silence, in which I could hear Mr. di Francesco swallowing water. I felt very much alone. I wished I were back home.

"I didn't mean it that way," Mr. di Francesco said.

"I'm sorry," I said, and then, rallying a little, confessed that Braille watches were unheard of in India—that I had first read about them a year or so earlier in a British Braille magazine, and then it had taken me several months to get the foreign exchange and get a Braille pocket watch from Switzerland.

"Then how do blind people there know what time it is—whether it is day or night?" Mr. di Francesco asked.

"They have to ask someone, or learn to tell from the morning and night sounds. I suppose that things *are* a little backward there. That is why I had to leave my family and come here for education."

"The food is getting cold," Mrs. di Francesco said.

I picked up my fork and knife with trembling fingers and aimed for six. I suddenly wanted to cry.

"You look homesick," Mrs. di Francesco said.

I nodded, and tried to eat. A sense of relief engulfed me: we had mutton meatballs at home all the time, and they didn't require a knife. But the relief was short-lived: I had never had spaghetti, and the strands were long and tended to bunch together. They stretched from my mouth to my plate—a sign of my Indian backwardness, I thought. I longed for the kedgeree[4] at home, easily managed with a spoon.

Mrs. di Francesco reached over and showed me how to wrap the spaghetti around my fork, shake it, and pick it up. Even so, I took big bites when I thought that Mrs. di Francesco was not looking—when she was talking to Mr. di Francesco. Later in the meal, it occurred to me that I was eating the food Daddyji had eaten when he was a student abroad. I resolutely bent my face over the plate and started eating in earnest.

Mrs. di Francesco took away our plates and served us something else, and I reached for my spoon.

"That's eaten with a fork," she said.

I attacked it with a fork, "It is a pudding with a crust!" I cried. "I have never eaten anything like it."

"It's not a pudding—it's apple pie," Mrs. di Francesco said. "By the way, we're having scrambled eggs for breakfast. Is that all right?"

I confessed that I didn't know what they were, and she described them to me.

"Oh, I know—rumble-tumble eggs!" I exclaimed. "I like them very much."

They both laughed. "British—Indian English is really much nicer than American English," Mr. di Francesco said. "You should keep it. In fact, I'll adopt 'rumble-tumble.'"

I felt sad that I had come to America for my studies instead of going to England first, as Daddyji had done. But no school in England had accepted me.

"We've heard so much about India from Uncle Manmath," Mrs. di Francesco said. "It must be a very exciting place."

"Yes, tell us about India," Mr. di Francesco said.

I felt confused. I couldn't think of what to say or how to say it.

"You look tired," Mrs. di Francesco said, patting me on the arm.

"I cannot think of the right English words sometimes," I said.

Mrs. di Francesco cleared some things off the table and said, "Don't worry. Now that you're here, your English will improve quickly."

She went to the kitchen and started washing the plates while Mr. di Francesco and I lingered at the table—much as we might at home.

I asked Mr. di Francesco how he had become self-supporting and independent, with a place of his own.

"You make it sound so romantic, but it's really very simple," he said. He spoke in a matter-of-fact way. "I spent twelve years at the Perkins Institution for the Blind, in Massachusetts. I entered when I was seven, and left when I was nineteen."

"Perkins!" I cried. "I have been trying to go there since I was seven.

---

4. A cooked dish of rice and other ingredients.

First, they would not have me because of the war. But after the war they would not have me, either—they said that I would end up a 'cultural misfit.'"

"What does that mean?"

"They said that bringing Eastern people to the West at a young age leads to 'cultural maladjustment'—and they said, 'Blindness is a maladjustment in itself.'"

"But now you're here. I'll call Perkins tomorrow and tell them that the damage is already done, and that your cultural maladjustment would be much worse if your were to end up in Arkansas." He laughed.

"Do you really think they will take me? Dr. Farrell, the director at Perkins, is a very stubborn man."

"They certainly should. Unlike Massachusetts, Arkansas is a very poor state. Arkansas School for the Blind is a state school. They are required to accept all the blind children in the state free of charge. In fact, you'll probably be the only one there paying for board and tuition. The school is bound to have a lot of riffraff. It's no place to improve your English. In Arkansas, you'll lose all your nice Britishisms and acquire a terrible Southern drawl. You have to go to Perkins. I know Dr. Farrell."

I was excited. "Perkins is said to be the best school for the blind anywhere. How did you like it? How was your life there?"

"Life at Perkins? It was probably no different from that of millions of other kids. We played and studied." He added obligingly, "It was a lot of fun."

Fun—so that's what it was, I thought. That is the difference between all the things he did at school and all the things I missed out on by not going to a good school.

"And after Perkins?"

"After Perkins, I studied voice at the New England Conservatory, where Muriel and I met. Then I came to New York, started giving voice lessons, married Muriel, and here I am."

"There must be more to tell."

"There really isn't."

"Did Mrs. di Francesco's parents not object? She is sighted."

"I wasn't asking to marry Muriel's parents. She could do what she pleased. This is America."

* * *

N. Scott Momaday
(1934–)

N. Scott Momaday was born in Lawton, Oklahoma, and raised in various places, including the Jemez Pueblo, New Mexico. His parents were both teachers, his father also a painter and his mother a writer. Kiowa by ancestry, he was given the Indian name Tsoai-talee, or "Rock-tree-Boy," in honor of a Kiowa legend associated with Devil's Tower in Wyoming; later, both the tower and the legend became important to his writing. Momaday graduated from the University of New Mexico in 1958 and then attended Stanford University, earning an M.A. in 1960 and a Ph.D. in English in 1963. He has since taught at the University of California at Berkeley, Stanford, and the University of Arizona.

After editing The Complete Poems of Frederick Goddard Tuckerman *(1965), presenting works of a reclusive New Englander of the nineteeth century, Momaday turned more exclusively to his own writing. In much of his work he has attempted to reclaim his Kiowa heritage, which he has said became vitally important to him only in adulthood when "I suddenly realized that my father had grown up speaking a language that I didn't grow up speaking," that among his father's ancestors, who had migrated from Canada, were "peoples I knew nothing about." In* House Made of Dawn *(1968), a Pulitzer Prize-winning novel, he wove into a contemporary story insistent threads of history and myth, establishing the pattern for later prose works.* The Way to Rainy Mountain *(1969) brings similar and sometimes identical material closer to home by presenting it as a memoir, with illustrations by the author's father.* The Names: A Memoir *(1976) continues the project, combining personal memories with ancestral stories.* The Ancient Child *(1989), a novel, portrays an artist of mixed blood torn between his Anglo ambitions and Kiowa heritage.*

Momaday's poetry is collected in *Angle of Geese* (1973) and *The Gourd Dancer* (1976). Studies include Martha Scott Trimble, *N. Scott Momaday* (1973), and Matthias Schubnell, *N. Scott Momaday: The Cultural and Literary Background* (1985).

[From] The Way to Rainy Mountain[1]

Headwaters

Noon in the intermountain plain:
There is scant telling of the marsh—
A log, hollow and weather-stained,
An insect at the mouth, and moss—
Yet waters against the roots,
Stand brimming to the stalks. What moves?
What moves on this archaic force
Was wild and welling at the source.

Prologue

THE JOURNEY BEGAN one day long ago on the edge of the northern Plains. It was carried on over a course of many generations and many hundreds of miles. In the end there were many things to remember, to dwell upon and talk about.

"You know, everything had to begin. . . ." For the Kiowas the beginning was a struggle for existence in the bleak northern mountains. It was there, they say, that they entered the world through a hollow log. The end, too, was a struggle, and it was lost. The young Plains culture of the Kiowas withered and died like grass that is burned in the prairie wind. There came a day like destiny; in every direction, as far as the eye could see, carrion lay out in the land. The buffalo was the animal representation of the sun, the essential and sacrificial victim of the Sun Dance. When the wild herds were destroyed, so too was the will of the Kiowa people; there was nothing to sustain them in spirit. But these are idle recollections, the mean and ordinary agonies of human history. The interim was a time of great adventure and nobility and fulfillment.

Tai-me[2] came to the Kiowas in a vision born of suffering and despair. "Take me with you," Tai-me said, "and I will give you whatever you want."

---

1. Earlier versions of the Introduction appeared in *The Reporter*, January 26, 1967, and *House Made of Dawn* (1968). Rainy Mountain is in southwest Oklahoma.

2. In the words of the Priest of the Sun in Momaday's *House Made of Dawn*, "Tai-me was their sun dance doll, their most sacred fetish. * * * The story of the coming of Tai-me has existed for hundreds of years by word of mouth. It represents the oldest and best idea that man has of himself."

And it was so. The great adventure of the Kiowas was a going forth into the heart of the continent. They began a long migration from the headwaters of the Yellowstone River eastward to the Black Hills and south to the Wichita Mountains. Along the way they acquired horses, the religion of the Plains, a love and possession of the open land. Their nomadic soul was set free. In alliance with the Comanches they held dominion in the southern Plains for a hundred years. In the course of that long migration they had come of age as a people. They had conceived a good idea of themselves; they had dared to imagine and determine who they were.

In one sense, then, the way to Rainy Mountain is preeminently the history of an idea, man's idea of himself, and it has old and essential being in language. The verbal tradition by which it has been preserved has suffered a deterioration in time. What remains is fragmentary: mythology, legend, lore, and hearsay—and of course the idea itself, as crucial and completed as it ever was. That is the miracle.

The journey herein recalled continues to be made anew each time the miracle comes to mind, for that is peculiarly the right and responsibility of the imagination. It is a whole journey, intricate with motion and meaning; and it is made with the whole memory, that experience of the mind which is legendary as well as historical, personal as well as cultural. And the journey is an evocation of three things in particular: a landscape that is incomparable, a time that is gone forever, and the human spirit, which endures. The imaginative experiece and the historical express equally the traditions of man's reality. Finally, then, the journey recalled is among other things the revelation of one way in which these traditions are conceived, developed, and interfused in the human mind. There are on the way to Rainy Mountain many landmarks, many journeys in the one. From the beginning the migration of the Kiowas was an expression of the human spirit, and that expression is most truly made in terms of wonder and delight: "There were many people, and oh, it was beautiful. That was the beginning of the Sun Dance. It was all for Tai-me, you know, and it was a long time ago."

INTRODUCTION

A single knoll rises out of the plain in Oklahoma, north and west of the Wichita Range. For my people, the Kiowas, it is an old landmark, and they gave it the name Rainy Mountain. The hardest weather in the world is there. Winter brings blizzards, hot tornadic winds arise in the spring, and in summer the prairie is an anvil's edge. The grass turns brittle and brown, and it cracks beneath your feet. There are green belts along the rivers and creeks, linear groves of hickory and pecan, willow and witch hazel. At a distance in July or August the steaming foliage seems almost to writhe in fire. Great green and yellow grasshoppers are everywhere in the tall grass, popping up like corn to sting the flesh, and tortoises crawl about on the red earth, going nowhere in the plenty of time. Loneliness is an aspect of the land. All things in the plain are isolate; there is no confusion of objects in the eye, but *one* hill or *one* tree or *one* man. To look upon that landscape in the early morning, with the sun at your back, is to lose the sense of proportion. Your imagination comes to life, and this, you think, is where Creation was begun.

I returned to Rainy Mountain in July. My grandmother had died in the spring, and I wanted to be at her grave. She had lived to be very old and at last infirm. Her only living daughter was with her when she died, and I was told that in death her face was that of a child.

I like to think of her as a child. When she was born, the Kiowas were living that last great moment of their history. For more than a hundred years they had controlled the open range from the Smoky Hill River to the Red, from the head-waters of the Canadian to the fork of the Arkansas and Cimarron. In alliance with the Comanches, they had ruled the whole of the southern Plains. War was their sacred business, and they were among the finest horsemen the world has ever known. But warfare for the Kiowas was preeminently a matter of disposition rather than of survival, and they never understood the grim, unrelenting advance of the U.S. Cavalry. When at last, divided and ill-provisioned, they were driven onto the Staked Plains in the cold rains of autumn, they fell into panic. In Palo Duro Canyon[3] they abandoned their crucial stores to pillage and had nothing then but their lives. In order to save themselves, they surrendered to the soldiers at Fort Sill[4] and were imprisoned in the old stone corral that now stands as a military museum. My grandmother was spared the humiliation of those high gray walls by eight or ten years, but she must have known from birth the affliction of defeat, the dark brooding of old warriors.

Her name was Aho, and she belonged to the last culture to evolve in North America. Her forebears came down from the high country in western Montana nearly three centuries ago. They were a mountain people, a mysterious tribe of hunters whose language has never been positively classified in any major group. In the late seventeenth century they began a long migration to the south and east. It was a journey toward the dawn, and it led to a golden age. Along the way the Kiowas were befriended by the Crows, who gave them the culture and religion of the Plains. They acquired horses, and their ancient nomadic spirit was suddenly free of the ground. They acquired Tai-me, the sacred Sun Dance doll, from that moment the object and symbol of their worship, and so shared in the divinity of the sun. Not least, they acquired the sense of destiny, therefore courage and pride. When they entered upon the southern Plains they had been transformed. No longer were they slaves to the simple necessity of survival; they were a lordly and dangerous society of fighters and thieves, hunters and priests of the sun.

---

3. In Texas.
4. Near Lawton, Oklahoma.

According to their origin myth, they entered the world through a hollow log. From one point of view, their migration was the fruit of an old prophecy, for indeed they emerged from a sunless world.

Although my grandmother lived out her long life in the shadow of Rainy Mountain, the immense landscape of the continental interior lay like memory in her blood. She could tell of the Crows, whom she had never seen, and of the Black Hills, where she had never been. I wanted to see in reality what she had seen more perfectly in the mind's eye, and traveled fifteen hundred miles to begin my pilgrimage.

Yellowstone, it seemed to me, was the top of the world, a region of deep lakes and dark timber, canyons and waterfalls. But, beautiful as it is, one might have the sense of confinement there. The skyline in all directions is close at hand, the high wall of the woods and deep cleavages of shade. There is a perfect freedom in the mountains, but it belongs to the eagle and the elk, the badger and the bear. The Kiowas reckoned their stature by the distance they could see, and they were bent and blind in the wilderness.

Descending eastward, the highland meadows are a stairway to the plain. In July the inland slope of the Rockies is luxuriant with flax and buckwheat, stonecrop and larkspur. The earth unfolds and the limit of the land recedes. Clusters of trees, and animals grazing far in the distance, cause the vision to reach away and wonder to build upon the mind. The sun follows a longer course in the day, and the sky is immense beyond all comparison. The great billowing clouds that sail upon it are shadows that move upon the grain like water, dividing light. Farther down, in the land of the Crows and Blackfeet, the plain is yellow. Sweet clover takes hold of the hills and bends upon itself to cover and seal the soil. There the Kiowas paused on their way; they had come to the place where they must change their lives. The sun is at home on the plains. Precisely there does it have the certain character of a god. When the Kiowas came to the land of the Crows, they could see the dark lees of the hills at dawn across the Bighorn River, the profusion of light on the grain shelves, the oldest deity ranging after the solstices. Not yet would they veer southward to the caldron of the land that lay below; they must wean their blood from the northern winter and hold the mountains a while longer in their view. They bore Tai-me in procession to the east.

A dark mist lay over the Black Hills, and the land was like iron. At the top of a ridge I caught sight of Devil's Tower upthrust against the gray sky as if in the birth of time the core of the earth had broken through its crust and the motion of the world was begun. There are things in nature that engender an awful quiet in the heart of man; Devil's Tower is one of them. Two centuries ago, because they could not do otherwise, the Kiowas made a legend at the base of the rock. My grandmother said:

> Eight children were there at play, seven sisters and their brother. Suddenly the boy was struck dumb; he trembled and began to run upon his hands and feet. His fingers became claws, and his body was covered with fur. Directly there was a bear where the boy had been. The sisters were terrified; they ran, and the bear after them. They came to the stump of a great tree, and the tree spoke to

them. It bade them climb upon it, and as they did so it began to rise into the air. The bear came to kill them, but they were just beyond its reach. It reared against the tree and scored the bark all around with its claws. The seven sisters were borne into the sky, and they became the stars of the Big Dipper.

From that moment, and so long as the legend lives, the Kiowas have kinsmen in the night sky. Whatever they were in the mountains, they could be no more. However tenuous their well-being, however much they had suffered and would suffer again, they had found a way out of the wilderness.

My grandmother had a reverence for the sun, a holy regard that now is all but gone out of mankind. There was a wariness in her, and an ancient awe. She was a Christian in her later years, but she had come a long way about, and she never forgot her birthright. As a child she had been to the Sun Dances; she had taken part in those annual rites, and by them she had learned the restoration of her people in the presence of Tai-me. She was about seven when the last Kiowa Sun Dance was held in 1887 on the Washita River above Rainy Mountain Creek. The buffalo were gone. In order to consummate the ancient sacrifice—to impale the head of a buffalo bull upon the medicine tree—a delegation of old men journeyed into Texas, there to beg and barter for an animal from the Goodnight herd. She was ten when the Kiowas came together for the last time as a living Sun Dance culture. They could find no buffalo; they had to hand an old hide from the sacred tree. Before the dance could begin, a company of soldiers rode out from Fort Sill under orders to disperse the tribe. Forbidden without cause the essential act of their faith, having seen the wild herds slaughtered and left to rot upon the ground, the Kiowas backed away forever from the medicine tree. That was July 20, 1890, at the great bend of the Washita. My grandmother was there. Without bitterness, and for as long as she lived, she bore a vision of deicide.

Now that I can have her only in memory, I see my grandmother in the several postures that were peculiar to her: standing at the wood stove on a winter morning and turning meat in a great iron skillet; sitting at the south window, bent above her beadwork, and afterwards, when her vision failed, looking down for a long time into the folds of her hands; going out upon a cane, very slowly as she did when the weight of age came upon her; praying. I remember her most often at prayer. She made long, rambling prayers out of suffering and hope, having seen many things. I was never sure that I had the right to hear, so exclusive were they of all mere custom and company. The last time I saw her she prayed standing by the side of her bed at night, naked to the waist, the light of a kerosene lamp moving upon her dark skin. Her long, black hair, always drawn and braided in the day, lay upon her shoulders and against her breasts like a shawl. I do not speak Kiowa, and I never understood her prayers, but there was something inherently sad in the sound, some merest hesitation upon the syllables of sorrow. She began in a high and descending pitch, exhausting her breath to silence; then again and again—and always the same intensity of effort, of something that is, and is not, like urgency in the human voice. Transported so in the dancing light among the shadows of her room, she seemed beyond the reach of time. But that was illusion; I think I knew then that I should not see her again.

Houses are like sentinels in the plain, old keepers of the weather watch. There, in a very little while, wood takes on the appearance of great age. All colors wear soon away in the wind and rain, and then the wood is burned gray and the grain appears and the nails turn red with rust. The window-panes are black and opaque; you imagine there is nothing within, and indeed there are many ghosts, bones given up to the land. They stand here and there against the sky, and you approach them for a longer time than you expect. They belong in the distance; it is their domain.

Once there was a lot of sound in my grandmother's house, a lot of coming and going, feasting and talk. The summers there were full of excitement and reunion. The Kiowas are a summer people; they abide the cold and keep to themselves, but when the season turns and the land becomes warm and vital they cannot hold still; an old love of going returns upon them. The aged visitors who came to my grandmother's house when I was a child were made of lean and leather, and they bore themselves upright. They wore great black hats and bright ample shirts that shook in the wind. They rubbed fat upon their hair and wound their braids with strips of colored cloth. Some of them painted their faces and carried the scars of old and cherished enmities. They were an old council of warlords, come to remind and be reminded of who they were. Their wives and daughters served them well. The women might indulge themselves; gossip was at once the mark and compensation of their servitude. They made loud and elaborate talk among themselves, full of jest and gesture, fright and false alarm. They went abroad in fringed and flowered shawls, bright beadwork and German silver. They were at home in the kitchen, and they prepared meals that were banquets.

There were frequent prayer meetings, and great nocturnal feasts. When I was a child I played with my cousins outside, where the lamplight fell upon the ground and the singing of the old people rose up around us and carried away into the darkness. There were a lot of good things to eat, a lot of laughter and surprise. And afterwards, when the quiet returned. I lay down with my grandmother and could hear the frogs away by the river and feel the motion of the air.

Now there is a funeral silence in the rooms, the endless wake of some final word. The walls have closed in upon my grandmother's house. When I returned to it in mourning, I saw for the first time in my life how small it was. It was late at night, and there was a white moon, nearly full. I sat for a long time on the stone steps by the kitchen door. From there I could see out across the land; I could see the long row of trees by the creek, the low light upon the rolling plains, and the stars of the Big Dipper. Once I looked at the moon and caught sight of a strange thing. A cricket had perched upon the handrail, only a few inches away from me. My line of vision was such that the creature filled the moon like a fossil. It had gone there, I thought, to live and die, for there, of all places, was its small definition made whole and eternal. A warm wind rose up and purled like the longing within me.

The next morning I awoke at dawn and went out on the dirt road to Rainy Mountain. It was already hot, and the grasshoppers began to fill the air. Still, it was early in the morning, and the birds sang out of the shadows. The long yellow grass on the mountain shone in the bright light, and a scissortail hied above the land. There, where it ought to be, at the end of a long and legendary way, was my grandmother's grave. Here and there on the dark stones were ancestral names. Looking back once, I saw the mountain and came away.

Maxine Hong Kingston
(1940–)

The daughter of immigrants from the Pearl River area of south China, Maxine Hong Kingston was born in Stockton, California. She was educated in the Stockton public schools and the University of California at Berkeley.

Her father, Tom, who named himself after Thomas Edison, lived alone in the United States for nearly two decades before he was able to bring his wife over. Left behind in China, Mrs. Hong trained to become an obstetrician and practiced medicine. When the couple was finally reunited in 1939, she joined her husband in the family laundry business.

Kingston's first publication, Woman Warrior: Memories of a Girlhood Among Ghosts *(1976), is a mixture of fiction and autobiography. In it Kingston blends family stories and the traditional lore her mother taught her with her own existence in the English-speaking world to recreate the experience of growing up straddling two cultures.*

China Men *(1980) recounts the historical experience of male immigrants like her grandfathers, uncles, and father. Living bachelor existences, they worked at railroad building and mining and in laundries or restaurants to earn enough money to retire to their homeland or bring the families they had left behind in China to the United States.*

In Tripmaster Monkey *(1989), Kingston invents a fictional protagonist, Wittman Ah Sing, a Berkeley student who considers himself a reincarnation of the mythical Monkey King, said to have brought the Buddhist scriptures from India to China. It is Wittman's ambition to write a play that will draw together the divergent cultures he finds around him and articulate a message of human unity.*

Kingston has taught at several universities, including her alma mater,

*the University of California, Berkeley. The following narrative of the build-
ing of the transcontinental railroad is taken from* China Men.

———

The Grandfather of the Sierra Nevada Mountains

THE TRAINS USED TO CROSS THE SKY. The house jumped and dust shook down
from the attic. Sometimes two trains ran parallel going in opposite directions; the railroad men walked on top of the leaning cars, stepped off one
train onto the back of the other, and traveled the opposite way. They headed
for the caboose while the train moved against their walk, or they walked
toward the engine while the train moved out from under their feet. Hoboes
ran alongside, caught the ladders, and swung aboard. I would have to learn
to ride like that, choose my boxcar, grab a ladder at a run, and fling myself
up and sideways into an open door. Elsewhere I would step smoothly off.
Bad runaway boys lost their legs trying for such rides. The train craunched
past—pistons stroking like elbows and knees, the coal cars dropping coal,
cows looking out between the slats of the cattle-cars, the boxcars almost
stringing together sentences—Hydro-Cushion, Georgia Flyer, Route of the
Eagle—and suddenly sunlight filled the windows again, the slough wide
again and waving with tules, for which the city was once named; red-winged
blackbirds and squirrels settled. We children ran to the tracks and found the
nails we'd placed on them; the wheels had flattened them into knives that
sparked.

Once in a while an adult said, "Your grandfather built the railroad." (Or
"Your grandfathers built the railroad." Plural and singular are by context.)
We children believed that it was that very railroad, those trains, those tracks
running past our house; our own giant grandfather had set those very logs
into the ground, poured the iron for those very spikes with the big heads
and pounded them until the heads spread like that, mere nails to him. He
had built the railroad so that trains would thunder over us, on a street that
inclined toward us. We lived on a special spot of the earth, Stockton, the
only city on the Pacific coast with three railroads—the Santa Fe, Southern
Pacific, and Western Pacific. The three railroads intersecting accounted for

the flocks of hoboes. The few times that the train stopped, the cows moaned all night, their hooves stumbling crowdedly and banging against the wood.

Grandfather left a railroad for his message: We had to go somewhere difficult. Ride a train. Go somewhere important. In case of danger, the train was to be ready for us.

The railroad men disconnected the rails and took the steel away. They did not come back. Our family dug up the square logs and rolled them downhill home. We collected the spikes too. We used the logs for benches, edged the yard with them, made bases for fences, embedded them in the ground for walkways. The spikes came in handy too, good for paperweights, levers, wedges, chisels. I am glad to know exactly the weight of ties and the size of nails.

Grandfather's picture hangs in the dining room next to an equally large one of Grandmother, and another one of Guan Goong, God of War and Literature. My grandparents' similarity is in the set of their mouths; they seem to have hauled with their mouths. My mouth also feels the tug and strain of weights in its corners. In the family album, Grandfather wears a greatcoat and Western shoes, but his ankles show. He hasn't shaved either. Maybe he became sloppy after the Japanese soldier bayoneted his head for not giving directions. Or he was born slow and without a sense of direction.

The photographer came to the village regularly and set up a spinet, potted trees, an ornate table stacked with hardbound books of matching size, and a backdrop with a picture of paths curving through gardens into panoramas; he lent his subjects dressy ancient mandarin clothes, Western suits, and hats. An aunt tied the fingers of the lame cousin to a book, the string leading down his sleeve; he looks like he's carrying it. The family hurried from clothes chests to mirrors without explaining to Grandfather, hiding Grandfather. In the family album are group pictures with Grandmother in the middle, the family arranged on either side of her and behind her, second wives at the ends, no Grandfather. Grandmother's earrings, bracelets, and rings are tinted jade green, everything and everybody else black and white, her little feet together neatly, two knobs at the bottom of her gown. My mother, indignant that nobody had readied Grandfather, threw his greatcoat over his nightclothes, shouted, "Wait! Wait!" and encouraged him into the sunlight. "Hurry," she said, and he ran, coat flapping, to be in the picture. She would have slipped him into the group and had the camera catch him like a peeping ghost, but Grandmother chased him away. "What a waste of film," she said. Grandfather always appears alone with white stubble on his chin. He was a thin man with big eyes that looked straight ahead. When we children talked about overcoat men, exhibitionists, we meant Grandfather, Ah Goong, who must have yanked open that greatcoat—no pants.

MaMa was the only person to listen to him, and so he followed her everywhere, and talked and talked. What he liked telling was his journeys to the Gold Mountain. He wasn't smart, yet he traveled there three times. Left to himself, he would have stayed in China to play with babies or stayed in the United States once he got there, but Grandmother forced him to leave both places. "Make money," she said. "Don't stay here eating." "Come home," she said.

Ah Goong sat outside her open door when MaMa worked. (In those days a man did not visit a good woman alone unless married to her.) He saw her at her loom and came running with his chair. He told her that he had found a wondrous country, really gold, and he himself had gotten two bags of it, one of which he had had made into a ring. His wife had given that ring to their son for his wedding ring. "That ring on your finger," he told Mother, "proves that the Gold Mountain exists and that I went there."

Another of his peculiarities was that he heard the crackles, bangs, gun-shots that go off when the world lurches; the gears on its axis snap. Listening to a faraway New Year, he had followed the noise and come upon the blasting in the Sierras. (There is a Buddhist instruction that that which is most elusive must, of course, be the very thing to be pursued; listen to the farthest sound.) The Central Pacific hired him on sight; chinamen had a natural talent for explosions. Also there were not enough workingmen to do all the labor of building a new country. Some of the banging came from the war to decide whether or not black people would continue to work for nothing.

Slow as usual, Ah Goong arrived in the spring; the work had begun in January 1863. The demon that hired him pointed up and up, east above the hills of poppies. His first job was to fell a redwood, which was thick enough to divide into three or four beams. His tree's many branches spread out, each limb like a little tree. He circled the tree. How to attack it? No side looked like the side made to be cut, nor did any ground seem the place for it to fall. He axed for almost a day the side he'd decided would hit the ground. Halfway through, imitating the other lumberjacks, he struck the other side of the tree, above the cut, until he had to run away. The tree swayed and slowly dived to earth, creaking and screeching like a green animal. He was so awed, he forgot what he was supposed to yell. Hardly any branches broke; the tree sprang, bounced, pushed at the ground with its arms. The limbs did not wilt and fold; they were a small forest, which he chopped. The trunk lay like a long red torso; sap ran from its cuts like crying blind eyes. At last it stopped fighting. He set the log across sawhorses to be cured over smoke and in the sun.

He joined a team of men who did not ax one another as they took alternate hits. They blew up the stumps with gunpowder. "It was like uprooting a tooth," Ah Goong said. They also packed gunpowder at the roots of a whole tree. Not at the same time as the bang but before that, the tree rose from the ground. It stood, then plunged with a tearing of veins and muscles. It was big enough to carve a house into. The men measured themselves against the upturned white roots, which looked like claws, a sun with claws. A hundred men stood or sat on the trunk. They lifted a wagon on it and took a photograph. The demons[1] also had their photograph taken.

---

1. The white people, non-Chinese.

Because these mountains were made out of gold, Ah Goong rushed over to the root hole to look for gold veins and ore. He selected the shiniest rocks to be assayed later in San Francisco. When he drank from the streams and saw a flash, he dived in like a duck; only sometimes did it turn out to be the sun or the water. The very dirt winked with specks.

He made a dollar a day salary. The lucky men gambled, but he was not good at remembering game rules. The work so far was endurable. "I could take it," he said.

The days were sunny and blue, the wind exhilarating, the heights god-like. At night the stars were diamonds, crystals, silver, snow, ice. He had never seen diamonds. He had never seen snow and ice. As spring turned into summer, and he lay under that sky, he saw the order in the stars. He recognized constellations from China. There—not a cloud but the Silver River, and there, on either side of it—Altair and Vega, the Spinning Girl and the Cowboy, far, far apart. He felt his heart breaking of loneliness at so much blue-black space between star and star. The railroad he was building would not lead him to his family. He jumped out of his bedroll. "Look! Look!" Other China Men jumped awake. An accident? An avalanche? Injun demons? "The stars," he said. "The stars are here." "Another China Man gone out of his mind," men grumbled. "A sleepwalker." "Go to sleep, sleep-walker." "There. And there," said Ah Goong, two hands pointing. "The Spinning Girl and the Cowboy. Don't you see them?" "Homesick China Man," said the China Men and pulled their blankets over their heads. "Didn't you know they were here? I could have told you they were here. Same as in China. Same moon. Why not same stars?" "Nah. Those are American stars."

Pretending that a little girl was listening, he told himself the story about the Spinning Girl and the Cowboy: A long time ago they had visited earth, where they met, fell in love, and married. Instead of growing used to each other, they remained enchanted their entire lifetimes and beyond. They were too happy. They wanted to be doves or two branches of the same tree. When they returned to live in the sky, they were so engrossed in each other that they neglected their work. The Queen of the Sky scratched a river between them with one stroke of her silver hairpin—the river a galaxy in width. The lovers suffered, but she did devote her time to spinning now, and he herded his cow. The King of the Sky took pity on them and ordered that once each year, they be allowed to meet. On the seventh day of the seventh month (which is not the same as July 7), magpies form a bridge for them to cross to each other. The lovers are together for one night of the year. On their parting, the Spinner cries the heavy summer rains.

Ah Goong's discovery of the two stars gave him something to look forward to besides meals and tea breaks. Every night he located Altair and Vega and gauged how much closer they had come since the night before. During the day he watched the magpies, big black and white birds with round bodies like balls with wings; they were a welcome sight, a promise of meetings. He had found two familiars in the wilderness: magpies and stars. On the meeting day, he did not see any magpies nor hear their chattering jaybird cries. Some black and white birds flew overhead, but they may have been American crows or late magpies on their way. Some men laughed at him, but he was not the only China Man to collect water in pots, bottles, and canteens that day. The water would stay fresh forever and cure anything. In ancient days the tutelary gods of the mountains sprinkled corpses with this water and brought them to life. That night, no women to light candles, burn incense, cook special food, Grandfather watched for the convergence and bowed. He saw the two little stars next to Vega—the couple's children. And bridging the Silver River, surely those were black flapping wings of magpies and translucent-winged angels and faeries. Toward morning, he was awakened by rain, and pulled his blankets into his tent.

The next day, the fantailed orange-beaked magpies returned. Altair and Vega were beginning their journeys apart, another year of spinning and herding. Ah Goong had to find something else to look forward to. The Spinning Girl and the Cowboy met and parted six times before the railroad was finished.

When cliffs, sheer drops under impossible overhangs, ended the road, the workers filled the ravines or built bridges over them. They climbed above the site for tunnel or bridge and lowered one another down in wicker baskets made stronger by the lucky words they had painted on four sides. Ah Goong got to be a basketman because he was thin and light. Some basketmen were fifteen-year-old boys. He rode the basket barefoot, so his boots, the kind to stomp snakes with, would not break through the bottom. The basket swung and twirled, and he saw the world sweep underneath him; it was fun in a way, a cold new feeling of doing what had never been done before. Suspended in the quiet sky, he thought all kinds of crazy thoughts, that if a man didn't want to live any more, he could just cut the ropes or, easier, tilt the basket, dip, and never have to worry again. He could spread his arms, and the air would momentarily hold him before he fell past the buzzards, hawks, and eagles, and landed impaled on the tip of a sequoia. This high and he didn't see any gods, no Cowboy, no Spinner. He knelt in the basket though he was not bumping his head against the sky. Through the wickerwork, slivers of depths darted like needles, nothing between him and air but thin rattan. Gusts of wind spun the light basket. "Aiya," said Ah Goong. Winds came up under the basket, bouncing it. Neighboring baskets swung together and parted. He and the man next to him looked at each other's faces. They laughed. They might as well have gone to Malaysia to collect bird nests. Those who had done high work there said it had been worse; the birds screamed and scratched at them. Swinging near the cliff, Ah Goong stood up and grabbed it by a twig. He dug holes, then inserted gunpowder and fuses. He worked neither too fast nor too slow, keeping even with the others. The basketmen signaled one another to light the fuses. He struck match after match and dropped the burnt matches over the sides. At last his fuse caught; he waved, and the men above pulled hand over hand hauling him up, pulleys creaking. The scaffolds stood like a row of gibbets. Gallows trees along a ridge. "Hurry, hurry," he said. Some impatient men clambered up their ropes. Ah Goong ran up the ledge road they'd cleared and watched the explosions, which banged almost synchronously, echoes booming like war. He moved his scaffold to the next section of cliff and went down in the basket again, with bags of dirt, and set the next charge.

This time two men were blown up. One knocked out or killed by the explosion fell silently, the other screaming, his arms and legs struggling. A desire shot out of Ah Goong for an arm long enough to reach down and catch them. Much time passed as they fell like plummets. The shreds of baskets and a cowboy hat skimmed and tacked. The winds that pushed birds off course and against mountains did not carry men. Ah Goong also wished that the conscious man would fall faster and get it over with. His hands gripped the ropes, and it was difficult to let go and get on with the work. "It can't happen twice in a row," the basketmen said the next trip down. "Our chances are very good. The trip after an accident is probably the safest one." They raced to their favorite basket, checked and double-checked the four ropes, yanked the strands, tested the pulleys, oiled them, reminded the pulleymen about the signals, and entered the sky again.

Another time, Ah Goong had been lowered to the bottom of a ravine, which had to be cleared for the base of a trestle, when a man fell, and he saw his face. He had not died of shock before hitting bottom. His hands were grabbing at air. His stomach and groin must have felt the fall all the way down. At night Ah Goong woke up falling, though he slept on the ground, and heard other men call out in their sleep. No warm women tweaked their ears and hugged them. "It was only a falling dream," he reassured himself.

Across a valley, a chain of men working on the next mountain, men like ants changing the face of the world, fell, but it was very far away. Godlike, he watched men whose faces he could not see and whose screams he did not hear roll and bounce and slide like a handful of sprinkled gravel.

After a fall, the buzzards circled the spot and reminded the workers for days that a man was dead down there. The men threw piles of rocks and branches to cover bodies from sight.

The mountainface reshaped, they drove supports for a bridge. Since hammering was less dangerous than the blowing up, the men played a little; they rode the baskets swooping in wide arcs; they twisted the ropes and let them unwind like tops. "Look at me," said Ah Goong, pulled open his pants, and pissed overboard, the wind scattering the drops. "I'm a waterfall," he said. He had sent a part of himself hurtling. On rare windless days he watched his piss fall in a continuous stream from himself almost to the bottom of the valley.

One beautiful day, dangling in the sun above a new valley, not the desire to urinate but sexual desire clutched him so hard he bent over in the basket. He curled up, overcome by beauty and fear, which shot to his penis. He tried to rub himself calm. Suddenly he stood up tall and squirted out into space. "I *am* fucking the world," he said. The world's vagina was big, big as the sky, big as a valley. He grew a habit: whenever he was lowered in the basket, his blood rushed to his penis, and he fucked the world.

Then it was autumn, and the wind blew so fiercely, the men had to postpone the basketwork. Clouds moved in several directions at once. Men pointed at dust devils, which turned their mouths crooked. There was ceaseless motion; clothes kept moving; hair moved; sleeves puffed out. Nothing stayed still long enough for Ah Goong to figure it out. The wind sucked the breath out of his mouth and blew thoughts from his brains. The food convoys from San Francisco brought tents to replace the ones that whipped away. The baskets from China, which the men saved for high work, carried cowboy jackets, long underwear, Levi pants, boots, earmuffs, leather gloves, flannel shirts, coats. They sewed rabbit fur and deerskin into the linings. They tied the wide brims of their cowboy hats over their ears with mufflers. And still the wind made confusing howls into ears, and it was hard to think.

The days became nights when the crews tunneled inside the mountain, which sheltered them from the wind, but also hid the light and sky. Ah Goong pickaxed the mountain, the dirt filling his nostrils through a cowboy bandanna. He shoveled the dirt into a cart and pushed it to a place that was tall enough for the mule, which hauled it the rest of the way out. He looked forward to cart duty to edge closer to the entrance. Eyes darkened, nose plugged, his windy cough worse, he was to mole a thousand feet and meet others digging from the other side. How much he'd pay now to go swinging in a basket. He might as well have gone to work in a tin mine. Coming out of the tunnel at the end of a shift, he forgot whether it was supposed to be day or night. He blew his nose fifteen times before the mucus cleared again.

The dirt was the easiest part of tunneling. Beneath the soil, they hit granite. Ah Goong struck it with his pickax, and it jarred his bones, chattered his teeth. He swung his sledgehammer against it, and the impact rang in the dome of his skull. The mountain that was millions of years old was locked against them and was not to be broken into. The men teased him, "Let's see you fuck the world now." "Let's see you fuck the Gold Mountain now." But he no longer felt like it. "A man ought to be made of tougher material than flesh," he said. "Skin is too soft. Our bones ought to be filled with iron." He lifted the hammer high, careful that it not pull him backward, and let it fall forward of its own weight against the rock. Nothing happened to that gray wall; he had to slam with strength and will. He hit at the same spot over and over again, the same rock. Some chips and flakes broke off. The granite looked everywhere the same. It had no softer or weaker spots anywhere, the same hard gray. He learned to slide his hand up the handle, lift, slide and swing, a circular motion, hammering, hammering, hammering. He would bite like a rat through that mountain. His eyes couldn't see; his nose couldn't smell; and now his ears were filled with the noise of hammering. This rock is what is real, he thought. This rock is what real is, not clouds or mist, which make mysterious promises, and when you go through them are nothing. When the foreman measured at the end of twenty-four hours of pounding, the rock had given a foot. The hammering went on day and night. The men worked eight hours on and eight hours off. They worked on all eighteen tunnels at once. While Ah Goong slept, he could hear the sledgehammers of other men working in the earth. The steady banging reminded him of holidays and harvests; falling asleep, he heard the women chopping mincemeat and the millstones striking.

The demons in boss suits came into the tunnel occasionally, measured with a yardstick, and shook their heads. "Faster," they said. "Faster. China-men too slow. Too slow." "Tell us we're slow," the China Men grumbled. The ones in top tiers of scaffolding let rocks drop, a hammer drop. Ropes tangled around the demons' heads and feet. The cave China Men muttered and flexed, glared out of the corners of their eyes. But usually there was no diversion—one day the same as the next, one hour no different from another—the beating against the same granite.

After tunneling into granite for about three years, Ah Goong understood the immovability of the earth. Men change, men die, weather changes, but a mountain is the same as permanence and time. This mountain would have taken no new shape for centuries, ten thousand centuries, the world a still, still place, time unmoving. He worked in the tunnel so long, he learned to see many colors in black. When he stumbled out, he tried to talk about time. "I felt time," he said. "I saw time. I saw world." He tried again, "I saw what's real. I saw time, and it doesn't move. If we break through the mountain, hollow it, time won't have moved anyway. You translators ought to tell the foreigners that."

Summer came again, but after the first summer, he felt less nostalgia at the meeting of the Spinning Girl and the Cowboy. He now knew men who had been in this country for twenty years and thirty years, and the Cowboy's one year away from his lady was no time at all. His own patience was longer. The stars were meeting and would meet again next year, but he would not have seen his family. He joined the others celebrating Souls' Day, the holiday a week later, the fourteenth day of the seventh month. The supply wagons from San Francisco and Sacramento brought watermelon, meat, fish, crab, pressed duck. "There, ghosts, there you are. Come and get it." They displayed the feast complete for a moment before falling to, eating on the dead's behalf.

In the third year of pounding granite by hand, a demon invented dynamite.[2] The railroad workers were to test it. They had stopped using gunpowder in the tunnels after avalanches, but the demons said that dynamite was more precise. They watched a scientist demon mix nitrate, sulphate, and glycerine, then flick the yellow oil, which exploded off his fingertips. Sitting in a meadow to watch the dynamite detonated in the open, Ah Goong saw

2. Alfred Nobel (1833–1896) perfected a combination of nitroglycerine and kieselguhr, a diatomaceous earth, in 1866. It was more stable than pure nitroglycerine. Concerned about possible misuse of dynamite and other explosives developed by his family business, he left money for the prizes named after him for contributions in various fields that promote international peace.

the men in front of him leap impossibly high into the air; then he felt a
shove as if from a giant's unseen hand—and he fell backward. The boom
broke the mountain silence like fear breaking inside stomach and chest and
groin. No one had gotten hurt; they stood up laughing and amazed, looking
around at how they had fallen, the pattern of the explosion. Dynamite was
much more powerful than gunpowder. Ah Goong had felt a nudge, as if
something kind were moving him out of harm's way. "All of a sudden I was
sitting next to you." "Aiya. If we had been nearer, it would have killed us."
"If we were stiff, it would have gone through us." "A fist." "A hand." "We
leapt like acrobats." Next time Ah Goong flattened himself on the ground,
and the explosion rolled over him.

He never got used to the blasting; a blast always surprised him. Even
when he himself set the fuse and watched it burn, anticipated the explosion,
the bang—*bahng* in Chinese—when it came, always startled. It cleaned the
crazy words, the crackling, and bingbangs out of his brain. It was like New
Year's, when every problem and thought was knocked clean out of him by
firecrackers, and he could begin fresh. He couldn't worry during an explosion, which jerked every head to attention. Hills flew up in rocks and dirt.
Boulders turned over and over. Sparks, fires, debris, rocks, smoke burst up,
not at the same time as the boom (*bum*) but before that—the sound a separate occurrence, not useful as a signal.

The terrain changed immediately. Streams were diverted, rockscapes
exposed. Ah Goong found it difficult to remember what land had looked like
before an explosion. It was a good thing the dynamite was invented after the
Civil War to the east was over.

The dynamite added more accidents and ways of dying, but if it were
not used, the railroad would take fifty more years to finish. Nitroglycerine
exploded when it was jounced on a horse or dropped. A man who fell with it
in his pocket blew himself up into red pieces. Sometimes it combusted
merely standing. Human bodies skipped through the air like puppets and
made Ah Goong laugh crazily as if the arms and legs would come together
again. The smell of burned flesh remained in rocks.

In the tunnels, the men bored holes fifteen to eighteen inches deep with
a power drill, stuffed them with hay and dynamite, and imbedded the fuse in
sand. Once, for extra pay, Ah Goong ran back in to see why some dynamite
had not gone off and hurried back out again; it was just a slow fuse. When
the explosion settled, he helped carry two-hundred-, three-hundred-, five-
hundred-pound boulders out of the tunnel.

As a boy he had visited a Taoist monastery where there were nine
rooms, each a replica of one of the nine hells. Lifesize sculptures of men and
women were spitted on turning wheels. Eerie candles under the suffering
faces emphasized eyes poked out, tongues pulled, red mouths and eyes, and
real hair, eyelashes, and eyebrows. Women were split apart and men dismembered. He could have reached out and touched the sufferers and the
implements. He had dug and dynamited his way into one of these hells.

"Only here there are eighteen tunnels, not nine, plus all the tracks between them," he said.

One day he came out of the tunnel to find the mountains white, the evergreens and bare trees decorated, white tree sculptures and lace bushes everywhere. The men from snow country called the icicles "ice chopsticks." He sat in his basket and slid down the slopes. The snow covered the gouged land, the broken trees, the tracks, the mud, the campfire ashes, the unburied dead. Streams were stilled in mid-run, the water petrified. That winter he thought it was the task of the human race to quicken the world, blast the freeze, fire it, redden it with blood. He had to change the stupid slowness of one sunrise and one sunset per day. He had to enliven the silent world with sound. "The rock," he tried to tell the others. "The ice." "Time."

The dynamiting loosed blizzards on the men. Ears and toes fell off. Fingers stuck to the cold silver rails. Snowblind men stumbled about with bandannas over their eyes. Ah Goong helped build wood tunnels roofing the track route. Falling ice scrabbled on the roofs. The men stayed under the snow for weeks at a time. Snowslides covered the entrances to the tunnels, which they had to dig out to enter and exit, white tunnels and black tunnels. Ah Goong looked at his gang and thought, If there is an avalanche, these are the people I'll be trapped with, and wondered which ones would share food. A party of snowbound barbarians had eaten the dead.[3] Cannibals, thought Ah Goong, and looked around. Food was not scarce; the tea man brought whiskey barrels of hot tea, and he warmed his hands and feet, held the teacup to his nose and ears. Someday, he planned, he would buy a chair with metal doors for putting hot coal inside it. The magpies did not abandon him but stayed all winter and searched the snow for food.

The men who died slowly enough to say last words said, "Don't leave me frozen under the snow. Send my body home. Burn it and put the ashes in a tin can. Take the bone jar when you come down the mountain." "When you ride the fire car back to China, tell my descendants to come for me." "Shut up," scolded the hearty men. "We don't want to hear about bone jars and dying." "You're lucky to have a body to bury, not blown to smithereens." "Stupid man to hurt yourself," they bawled out the sick and wounded. How their wives would scold if they brought back deadmen's bones. "Aiya. To be buried here, nowhere." "But this is somewhere," Ah Goong promised. "This is the Gold Mountain. We're marking the land now. The track sections are numbered, and your family will know where we leave you." But he was a crazy man, and they didn't listen to him.

Spring did come, and when the snow melted, it revealed the past year, what had happened, what they had done, where they had worked, the lost

---

3. The Donner party, a group of emigrants to California during the winter of 1846–1847, were stranded in the Sierra Nevada Mountains for several months. Only about half of the original 87 members of the group survived. The survivors disagreed about what had happened during their isolation, but the view that cannibalism had occurred was widely held.

tools, the thawing bodies, some standing with tools in hand, the bright rails. "Remember Uncle Long Winded Leong?" "Remember Strong Back Wong?" "Remember Lee Brother?" "And Fong Uncle?" They lost count of the number dead; there is no record of how many died building the railroad. Or maybe it was demons doing the counting and chinamen not worth counting. Whether it was good luck or bad luck, the dead were buried or cairned next to the last section of track they had worked on. "May his ghost not have to toil," they said over graves. (In China a woodcutter ghost chops eternally; people have heard chopping in the snow and in the heat.) "Maybe his ghost will ride the train home." The scientific demons said the transcontinental railroad would connect the West to Cathay. "What if he rides back and forth from Sacramento to New York forever?" "That wouldn't be so bad. I hear the cars will be like houses on wheels." The funerals were short. "No time. No time," said both China Men and demons. The railroad was as straight as they could build it, but no ghosts sat on the tracks; no strange presences haunted the tunnels. The blasts scared ghosts away.

When the Big Dipper pointed east and the China Men detonated nitroglycerine and shot off guns for the New Year, which comes with the spring, these special bangs were not as loud as the daily bangs, not as numerous as the bangs all year. Shouldn't the New Year be the loudest day of all to obliterate the noises of the old year? But to make a bang of that magnitude, they would have to blow up at least a year's supply of dynamite in one blast. They arranged strings of chain reactions in circles and long lines, banging faster and louder to culminate in a big bang. And most importantly, there were random explosions—surprise. Surprise. SURPRISE. They had no dragon, the railroad their dragon.

The demons invented games for working faster, gold coins for miles of track laid, for the heaviest rock, a grand prize for the first team to break through a tunnel. Day shifts raced against night shifts, China Men against Welshmen, China Men against Irishmen, China Men against Injuns and black demons. The fastest races were China Men against China Men, who bet on their own teams. China Men always won because of good teamwork, smart thinking, and the need for the money. Also, they had the most workers to choose teams from. Whenever his team won anything, Ah Goong added to his gold stash. The Central Pacific or Union Pacific won the land on either side of the tracks it built.

One summer day, demon officials and China Man translators went from group to group and announced, "We're raising the pay—thirty-five dollars a month. Because of your excellent work, the Central Pacific Railroad is giving you a four-dollar raise per month." The workers who didn't know better cheered. "What's the catch?" said the smarter men. "You'll have the opportunity to put in more time," said the railroad demons. "Two more hours per shift." Ten-hour shifts inside the tunnels. "It's not ten hours straight," said the demons. "You have time off for tea and meals. Now that you have dynamite, the work isn't so hard." They had been working for three and a half years already, and the track through the Donner Summit was still not done.

The workers discussed the ten-hour shift, swearing their China Man obscenities. "Two extra hours a day—sixty hours a month for four dollars." "Pig catcher demons." "Snakes." "Turtles." "Dead demons." "A human body can't work like that." "The demons don't believe this is a human body. This is a chinaman's body." To bargain, they sent a delegation of English speakers, who were summarily noted as troublemakers, turned away, docked.

The China Men, then, decided to go on strike and demand forty-five dollars a month and the eight-hour shift. They risked going to jail and the Central Pacific keeping the pay it was banking for them. Ah Goong memorized the English, "Forty-five dollars a month—eight-hour shift." He practiced the strike slogan: "Eight hours a day good for white man, all the same good for China Man."

The men wrapped barley and beans in ti leaves, which came from Hawaii via San Francisco, for celebrating the fifth day of the fifth month (not May but mid-June, the summer solstice). Usually the way the red string is wound and knotted tells what flavors are inside—the salty barley with pickled egg, or beans and pork, or the gelatin pudding. Ah Goong folded ti leaves into a cup and packed it with food. One of the literate men slipped in a piece of paper with the strike plan, and Ah Goong tied the bundle with a special pattern of red string. The time and place for the revolution against Kublai Khan[4] had been hidden inside autumn mooncakes. Ah Goong looked from one face to another in admiration. Of course, of course. No China Men, no railroad. They were indispensable labor. Throughout these mountains were brothers and uncles with a common idea, free men, not coolies, calling for fair working conditions. The demons were not suspicious as the China Men went gandying up and down the tracks delivering the bundles tied together like lines of fish. They had exchanged these gifts every year. When the summer solstice cakes came from other camps, the recipients cut them into neat slices by drawing the string through them. The orange jellies, which had a red dye stick inside soaked in lye, fell into a series of sunrises and sunsets. The aged yolks and the barley also looked like suns. The notes gave a Yes strike vote. The yellow flags to ward off the five evils—centipedes, scorpions, snakes, poisonous lizards, and toads—now flew as banners.

The strike began on Tuesday morning, June 25, 1867. The men who were working at that hour walked out of the tunnels and away from the tracks. The ones who were sleeping slept on and rose as late as they pleased. They bathed in streams and shaved their moustaches and wild beards. Some went fishing and hunting. The violinists tuned and played their instruments. The drummers beat theirs at the punchlines of jokes. The gamblers shuffled and played their cards and tiles. The smokers passed their pipes, and the drinkers bet for drinks by making figures with their hands. The cooks made party food. The opera singers' falsettos almost perforated the mountains. The men sang new songs about the railroad. They made up verses and

---

4. Kublai Khan (1216–1294), the founder of the Mongol dynasty in China, grandson of Genghis Khan.

shouted Ho at the good ones, and laughed at the rhymes. Oh, they were madly singing in the mountains. The storytellers told about the rise of new kings. The opium smokers when they roused themselves told their florid images. Ah Goong sifted for gold. All the while the English-speaking China Men, who were being advised by the shrewdest bargainers, were at the demons' headquarters repeating the demand: "Eight hours a day good for white man, all the same good for China Man." They had probably negotiated the demons down to nine-hour shifts by now.

The sounds of hammering continued along the tracks and occasionally there were blasts from the tunnels. The scabby white demons had refused to join the strike. "Eight hours a day good for white man, all the same good for China Man," the China Men explained to them. "Cheap John Chinaman," said the demons, many of whom had red hair. The China Men scowled out of the corners of their eyes.

On the second day, artist demons climbed the mountains to draw the China Men for the newspapers. The men posed bare-chested, their fists clenched, showing off their arms and backs. The artists sketched them as perfect young gods reclining against rocks, wise expressions on their handsome noble-nosed faces, long torsos with lean stomachs, a strong arm extended over a bent knee, long fingers holding a pipe, a rope of hair over a wide shoulder. Other artists drew faeries with antennae for eyebrows and brownies with elvish tails; they danced in white socks and black slippers among mushroom rings by moonlight.

Ah Goong acquired another idea that added to his reputation for craziness: The pale, thin Chinese scholars and the rich men fat like Buddhas were less beautiful, less manly than these brown muscular railroad men, of whom he was one. One of ten thousand heroes.

On the third day, in a woods—he would be looking at a deer or a rabbit or an Injun watching him before he knew what he was seeing—a demon dressed in a white suit and tall hat beckoned him. They talked privately in the wilderness. The demon said, "I Citizenship Judge invite you to be U.S. citizen. Only one bag gold." Ah Goong was thrilled. What an honor. He would accept this invitation. Also what advantages, he calculated shrewdly; if he were going to be jailed for this strike, an American would have a trial. The Citizenship Judge unfurled a parchment sealed with gold and ribbon. Ah Goong bought it with one bag of gold. "You vote," said the Citizenship Judge. "You talk in court, buy land, no more chinaman tax." Ah Goong hid the paper on his person so that it would protect him from arrest and lynching. He was already a part of this new country, but now he had it in writing.

The fourth day, the strikers heard that the U.S. Cavalry was riding single file up the tracks to shoot them. They argued whether to engage the Army with dynamite. But the troops did not come. Instead the cowardly demons blockaded the food wagons. No food. Ah Goong listened to the optimistic China Men, who said, "Don't panic. We'll hold out forever. We can hunt. We can last fifty days on water." The complainers said, "Aiya. Only saints can do that. Only magic men and monks who've practiced." The China Men refused to declare a last day for the strike.

The foresighted China Men had cured jerky, fermented wine, dried and strung orange and grapefruit peels, pickled and preserved leftovers. Ah Goong, one of the best hoarders, had set aside extra helpings from each meal. This same quandary, whether to give away food or to appear selfish, had occurred during each of the six famines he had lived through. The food-less men identified themselves. Sure enough, they were the shiftless, piggy, arrogant type who didn't worry enough. The donors scolded them and shamed them the whole while they were handing them food: "So you lived like a grasshopper at our expense." "Fleaman." "You'll be the cause of our not holding out long enough." "Rich man's kid. Too good to hoard." Ah Goong contributed some rice crusts from the bottoms of pans. He kept how much more food he owned a secret, as he kept the secret of his gold. In apology for not contributing richer food, he repeated a Mohist[5] saying that had guided him in China: "The superior man does not push humaneness to the point of stupidity.'" He could hear his wife scolding him for feeding strangers. The opium men offered shit and said that it calmed the appetite.

On the fifth and sixth days, Ah Goong organized his possessions and patched his clothes and tent. He forebore repairing carts, picks, ropes, baskets. His work-habituated hands arranged rocks and twigs in designs. He asked a reader to read again his family's letters. His wife sounded like herself except for the polite phrases added professionally at the beginnings and the ends. "Idiot," she said, "why are you taking so long? Are you wasting the money? Are you spending it on girls and gambling and whiskey? Here's my advice to you: Be a little more frugal. Remember how it felt to go hungry. Work hard." He had been an idle man for almost a week. "I need a new dress to wear to weddings. I refuse to go to another banquet in the same old dress. If you weren't such a spendthrift, we could be building the new courtyard where we'll drink wine among the flowers and sit about in silk gowns all day. We'll hire peasants to till the fields. Or lease them to tenants, and buy all our food at market. We'll have clean fingernails and toenails." Other relatives said, "I need a gold watch. Send me the money. Your wife gambles it away and throws parties and doesn't disburse it fairly among us. You might as well come home." It was after one of these letters that he had made a bonus investigating some dud dynamite.

Ah Goong did not spend his money on women. The strikers passed the word that a woman was traveling up the railroad and would be at his camp on the seventh and eighth day of the strike. Some said she was a demoness and some that she was a Chinese and her master a China Man. He pictured a nurse coming to bandage wounds and touch foreheads or a princess surveying her subjects; or perhaps she was a merciful Jesus demoness. But she was a pitiful woman, led on a leash around her waist, not entirely alive. Her owner sold lottery tickets for the use of her. Ah Goong did not buy one. He took out his penis under his blanket or bared it in the woods and thought

---

5. Mohism, the doctrines of Motze, which advocate universal love of mankind and government by monarchy.

about nurses and princesses. He also just looked at it, wondering what it was that it was for, what a man was for, what he had to have a penis for.

There was rumor also of an Injun woman called Woman Chief, who led a nomadic fighting tribe from the eastern plains as far as these mountains. She was so powerful that she had four wives and many horses. He never saw her though.

The strike ended on the ninth day. The Central Pacific announced that in its benevolence it was giving the workers a four-dollar raise, not the fourteen dollars they had asked for. And that the shifts in the tunnels would remain eight hours long. "We were planning to give you the four-dollar raise all along," the demons said to diminish the victory. So they got thirty-five dollars a month and the eight-hour shift. They would have won forty-five dollars if the thousand demon workers had joined the strike. Demons would have listened to demons. The China Men went back to work quietly. No use singing and shouting over a compromise and losing nine days' work.

There were two days that Ah Goong did cheer and throw his hat in the air, jumping up and down and screaming Yippee like a cowboy. One: the day his team broke through the tunnel at last. Toward the end they did not dynamite but again used picks and sledge-hammers. Through the granite, they heard answering poundings, and answers to their shouts. It was not a mountain before them any more but only a wall with people breaking through from the other side. They worked faster. Forward. Into day. They stuck their arms through the holes and shook hands with men on the other side. Ah Goong saw dirty faces as wonderous as if he were seeing Nu Wo, the creator goddess who repairs cracks in the sky with stone slabs; sometimes she peeks through and human beings see her face. The wall broke. Each team gave the other a gift of half a tunnel, dug. They stepped back and forth where the wall had been. Ah Goong ran and ran, his boots thudding to the very end of the tunnel, looked at the other side of the mountain, and ran back, clear through the entire tunnel. All the way through.

He spent the rest of his time on the railroad laying and bending and hammering the ties and rails. The second day the China Men cheered was when the engine from the West and the one from the East rolled toward one another and touched. The transcontinental railroad was finished. They Yippee'd like madmen. The white demon officials gave speeches. "The Greatest Feat of the Nineteenth Century," they said. "The Greatest Feat in the History of Mankind," they said. "Only Americans could have done it," they said, which is true. Even if Ah Goong had not spent half his gold on Citizenship Papers, he was an American for having built the railroad. A white demon in top hat tap-tapped on the gold spike, and pulled it back out. Then one China Man held the real spike, the steel one, and another hammered it in.[6]

While the demons posed for photographs, the China Men dispersed. It

---

6. The Union Pacific (built westward from Nebraska) and the Central Pacific (built eastward from California) met at Promontory Point, Utah, on May 10, 1869.

was dangerous to stay. The Driving Out had begun. Ah Goong does not appear in railroad photographs. Scattering, some China Men followed the north star in the constellation Tortoise the Black Warrior to Canada, or they kept the constellation Phoenix ahead of them to South America or the White Tiger west or the Wolf east. Seventy lucky men rode the Union Pacific to Massachusetts for jobs at a shoe factory. Fifteen hundred went to Fou Loy Company in New Orleans and San Francisco, several hundred to plantations in Mississippi, Georgia, and Arkansas, and sugarcane plantations in Louisiana and Cuba. (From the South, they sent word that it was a custom to step off the sidewalk along with the black demons when a white demon walked by.) Seventy went to New Orleans to grade a route for a railroad, then to Pennsylvania to work in a knife factory. The Colorado State Legislature passed a resolution welcoming the railroad China Men to come build the new state. They built railroads in every part of the country—the Alabama and Chattanooga Railroad, the Houston and Texas Railroad, the Southern Pacific, the railroads in Louisiana and Boston, the Pacific Northwest, and Alaska. After the Civil War, China Men banded the nation North and South, East and West, with crisscrossing steel. They were the binding and building ancestors of this place.

Ah Goong would have liked a leisurely walk along the tracks to review his finished handiwork, or to walk east to see the rest of his new country. But instead, Driven Out, he slid down mountains, leapt across valleys and streams, crossed plains, hid sometimes with companions and often alone, and eluded bandits who would hold him up for his railroad pay and shoot him for practice as they shot Injuns and jackrabbits. Detouring and backtracking, his path wound back and forth to his railroad, a familiar silver road in the wilderness. When a train came, he hid against the shaking ground in case a demon with a shotgun was hunting from it. He picked over camps where he had once lived. He was careful to find hidden places to sleep. In China bandits did not normally kill people, the booty the main thing, but here the demons killed for fun and hate. They tied pigtails to horses and dragged chinamen. He decided that he had better head for San Francisco, where he would catch a ship to China.

Perched on hillsides, he watched many sunsets, the place it was setting, the direction he was going. There were fields of grass that he tunneled through, hid in, rolled in, dived and swam in, suddenly jumped up laughing, suddenly stopped. He needed to find a town and human company. The spooky tumbleweeds caught in barbed wire were peering at him, waiting for him; he had to find a town. Towns grew along the tracks as they did along rivers. He sat looking at a town all day, then ducked into it by night.

At the familiar sight of a garden laid out in a Chinese scheme—vegetables in beds, white cabbages, red plants, chives, and coriander for immortality, herbs boxed with boards—he knocked on the back door. The China Man who answered gave him food, the appropriate food for the nearest holiday, talked story, exclaimed at how close their ancestral villages were to each other. They exchanged information on how many others lived how near, which towns had Chinatowns, what size, two or three stores or a block, which towns to avoid. "Do you have a wife?" they asked one another. "Yes. She lives in China. I have been sending money for twenty years now." They exchanged vegetable seeds, slips, and cuttings, and Ah Goong carried letters to another town or China.

Some demons who had never seen the likes of him gave him things and touched him. He also came across lone China Men who were alarmed to have him appear, and, unwelcome, he left quickly; they must have wanted to be the only China Man of that area, the special China Man.

He met miraculous China Men who had produced families out of nowhere—a wife and children, both boys and girls. "Uncle," the children called him, and he wanted to stay to be the uncle of the family. The wife washed his clothes, and he went on his way when they were dry.

On a farm road, he came across an imp child playing in the dirt. It looked at him, and he looked at it. He held out a piece of sugar; he cupped a grassblade between his thumbs and whistled. He sat on the ground with his legs crossed, and the child climbed into the hollow of his arms and legs. "I wish you were my baby," he told it. "My baby." He was very satisfied sitting there under the humming sun with the baby, who was satisfied too, no squirming. "My daughter," he said. "My son." He couldn't tell whether it was a boy or a girl. He touched the baby's fat arm and cheeks, its gold hair, and looked into its blue eyes. He made a wish that it not have to carry a sledgehammer and crawl into the dark. But he would not feel sorry for it; other people must not suffer any more than he did, and he could endure anything. Its mother came walking out into the road. She had her hands above her like a salute. She walked tentatively toward them, held out her hand, smiled, spoke. He did not understand what she said except "Bye-bye." The child waved and said, "Bye-bye," crawled over his legs, and toddled to her. Ah Goong continued on his way in a direction she could not point out to a posse looking for a kidnapper chinaman.

Explosions followed him. He heard screams and went on, saw flames outlining black windows and doors, and went on. He ran in the opposite direction from gunshots and the yell—*eeha awha*—the cowboys made when they herded cattle and sang their savage songs.

Good at hiding, disappearing—decades unaccounted for—he was not working in a mine when forty thousand chinamen were Driven Out of mining. He was not killed or kidnapped in the Los Angeles Massacre, though he gave money toward ransoming those whose toes and fingers, a digit per week, and ears grotesquely rotting or pickled, and scalped queues, were displayed in Chinatowns. Demons believed that the poorer a chinaman looked, the more gold he had buried somewhere, that chinamen stuck together and would always ransom one another. If he got kidnapped, Ah Goong planned, he would whip out his Citizenship Paper and show that he was an American. He was lucky not to be in Colorado when the Denver demons burned all chinamen homes and businesses, nor in Rock Springs, Wyoming, when the miner demons killed twenty-eight or fifty chinamen. The Rock Springs Massacre began in a large coal mine owned by the Union Pacific; the outnumbered chinamen were shot in the back as they ran to Chinatown, which the demons burned. They forced chinamen out into the open and shot them; demon women and children threw the wounded back in the flames. (There was a rumor of a good white lady in Green Springs who hid China Men in the Pacific Hotel and shamed the demons away.) The hunt went on for a month before federal troops came. The count of the dead was inexact because bodies were mutilated and pieces scattered all over the Wyoming Territory. No white miners were indicted, but the government paid $ 150,000 in reparations to victims' families. There were many family men, then. There were settlers—abiding China Men. And China Women. Ah Goong was running elsewhere during the Drivings Out of Tacoma, Seattle, Oregon City, Albania, and Marysville. The demons of Tacoma packed all its chinamen into boxcars and sent them to Portland, where they were run out of town. China Men returned to Seattle, though, and refused to sell their land and stores but fought until the army came; the demon rioters were tried and acquitted. And when the Boston police imprisoned and beat 234 chinamen, it was 1902, and Ah Goong had already reached San Francisco or China, and perhaps San Francisco again.

In Second City (Sacramento), he spent some of his railroad money at the theater. The main actor's face was painted red with thick black eyebrows and long black beard, and when he strode onto the stage, Ah Goong recognized the hero, Guan Goong; his puppet horse had red nostrils and rolling eyes. Ah Goong's heart leapt to recognize hero and horse in the wilds of America. Guan Goong murdered his enemy—crash! bang! of cymbals and drum—and left his home village—sad, sad flute music. But to the glad clamor of cymbals entered his friends—Liu Pei (pronounced the same as Running Nose) and Chang Fei. In a joyful burst of pink flowers, the three men swore the Peach Garden Oath. Each friend sang an aria to friendship; together they would fight side by side and live and die one for all and all for one. Ah Goong felt as warm as if he were with friends at a party. Then Guan Goong's archenemy, the sly Ts'ao Ts'ao, captured him and two of Liu Pei's wives, the Lady Kan and the Lady Mi. Though Ah Goong knew they were boy actors, he basked in the presence of Chinese ladies. The prisoners traveled to the capital, the soldiers waving horsehair whisks, signifying horses, the ladies walking between horizontal banners, signifying palanquins. All the prisoners were put in one bedroom, but Guan Goong stood all night outside the door with a lighted candle in his hand, singing an aria about faithfulness. When the capital was attacked by a common enemy, Guan Goong fought the biggest man in one-to-one combat, a twirling, jumping sword dance that strengthened the China Men who watched it. From afar Guan Goong's two partners heard about the feats of the man with the red face and intelligent horse. The three friends were reunited and fought until they secured their rightful kingdom.

Ah Goong felt refreshed and inspired. He called out Bravo like the demons in the audience, who had not seen theater before. Guan Goong, the God of War, also God of War and Literature, had come to America—Guan Goong, Grandfather Guan, our own ancestor of writers and fighters, of actors and gamblers, and avenging executioners who mete out justice. Our own kin. Not a distant ancestor but Grandfather.

In the Big City (San Francisco), a goldsmith convinced Ah Goong to have his gold made into jewelry, which would organize it into one piece and also delight his wife. So he handed over a second bag of gold. He got it back as a small ring in a design he thought up himself, two hands clasping in a handshake. "So small?" he said, but the goldsmith said that only some of the ore had been true gold.

He got a ship out of San Francisco without being captured near the docks, where there was a stockade full of jailed chinamen; the demonesses came down from Nob Hill and took them home to be servants, cooks, and baby-sitters.

Grandmother liked the gold ring very much. The gold was so pure, it squished to fit her finger. She never washed dishes, so the gold did not wear away. She quickly spent the railroad money, and Ah Goong said he would go to America again. He had a Certificate of Return and his Citizenship Paper.

But this time, there was no railroad to sell his strength to. He lived in a basement that was rumored to connect with tunnels beneath Chinatown. In an underground arsenal, he held a pistol and said, "I feel the death in it." "The holes for the bullets were like chambers in a beehive or wasp nest," he said. He was inside the earth when the San Francisco Earthquake and Fire began. Thunder rumbled from the ground. Some say he died falling into the cracking earth. It was a miraculous earthquake and fire. The Hall of Records burned completely. Citizenship Papers burned, Certificates of Return, Birth Certificates, Residency Certificates, passenger lists, Marriage Certificates— every paper a China Man wanted for citizenship and legality burned in that fire. An authentic citizen, then, had no more papers than an alien. Any paper a China Man could not produce had been "burned up in the Fire of 1906." Every China Man was reborn out of that fire a citizen.

Some say the family went into debt to send for Ah Goong, who was not making money; he was a homeless wanderer, a shiftless, dirty, jobless man with matted hair, ragged clothes, and fleas all over his body. He ate out of garbage cans. He was a louse eaten by lice. A fleaman. It cost two thousand dollars to bring him back to China, his oldest sons signing promissory notes for one thousand, his youngest to repay four hundred to one neighbor and six hundred to another. Maybe he hadn't died in San Francisco, it was just his papers that burned; it was just that his existence was outlawed by Chinese Exclusion Acts. The family called him Fleaman. They did not understand his accomplishments as an American ancestor, a holding, homing ancestor of this place. He'd gotten the legal or illegal papers burned in the San Francisco Earthquake and Fire; he appeared in America in time to be a citizen and to father citizens. He had also been seen carrying a child out of the fire, a child of his own in spite of the laws against marrying. He had built a railroad out of sweat, why not have an American child out of longing?

Daniela Gioseffi
(1941–)

Born in Orange, New Jersey, Daniela Gioseffi attended Montclair State College and received a master of fine arts degree from the Catholic University. She has worked as a professional actress, given poetry readings on college campuses, written plays—including an adaptation of Turgenev's Fathers and Sons—*and performed on radio and television. A novel,* The Great American Belly Dance, *appeared in 1977.* Eggs in the Lake *(1979) is a poetry collection.* Women on War: Global Voices for Survival, *her sixth book, won the American Book Award. The following story, "Rosa in Television Land," is taken from* From the Margin: Writings in Italian Americana *(1991), edited by Anthony Julian Tamburri, Paolo A. Giordano, and Fred L. Gardaphé.*

Rosa in Television Land

ROSA, A PEAR-SHAPED WOMAN who faintly resembles an aging Sophia Loren, limps peacefully through Brooklyn's Red Hook section past the groceries or fruit stands of her usual route along Smith Street. She has no idea of the peculiar events that await her. Trucks are unloaded by denim-clad workers as wooden crates filled with fruits and boxes of canned goods roll noisily down unloading ramps, aluminum wheels purring in the morning bustle. Groggy-faced children gambol toward a red brick public school which Rosa Della Rosa passes precisely at eight o'clock every weekday morning of her life. Rosa holds her head a little higher as she walks past the school, knowing that she was never able to attend it.

A schoolboy, just ahead of Rosa, stops to pick up a delinquent grapefruit which has rolled from a broken crate onto the sidewalk. He aims it at the seat of his schoolmate's pants. As the boys scurry into the schoolyard, Rosa bends down into the gutter to rescue the fruit and deposit it in her string shopping bag. "Only trees should throw fruit to the ground!" she exclaims softly, repeating an adage her mother learned long ago in southern Italy, where the wasting of food was considered a sin against the earth. Rosa, by her act of salvage, hopes to redeem the schoolboy's soul from his naive prank, as well as have a nice piece of citrus for her breakfast.

As she stands, Rosa pats the bun at the back of her neck, which is held with a large Florentine hairpin her mother brought long ago from the Old Country. She winds her long grey hair in the same way every morning and secures it exactly as her mother did her own. Not a strand is out of place. Her sturdy black oxford heels serve her well as she boards the bus at the corner of Atlantic Avenue. She smooths her black dress and coat into place as she slides her seventy-eight-year-old body into the seat behind the driver— just as she has for over twenty-five years. Retirement has never once occurred to her. Her birth certificate was lost long ago in Italy. She simply pretends with the help of a worn baptismal certificate, that she's under retirement age. Since she works efficiently enough, the factory manager has never bothered to check into it. To the few faint hairs that grow on her chin, she pays no mind. Girlish vanities and dreams of romance have long ago faded with her fading irises.

"Rosa, you look beautiful and happy today! What's the spark in your eyes?." asks the bus driver who's seen Rosa board his bus every work day for the past ten years, from 1966, when he began working his morning route, to 1976.

"*Niente*. Nothing at all. I looka da same as yesterday. Dis dress is just like de other one. I wash one; wear one. Wash one; wear the other! Why do you joke? I found a good grapefruit for breakfast, so I smile more. But, it's a nice day, *sì*?

"*Sì*. Sunny as Italy!" The driver, an African-American, agrees.

"No, nowhere is sunny as Italia!" Rosa smiles and laughs, "except Africa. *Sì*? But almosta!"

Rosa disembarks from the crowded bus full of screaming high school students and enters a small factory where she takes the elevator to the third floor, removes her coat, and sits as she always does, every weekday morning of her life, at the end of a long conveyor belt which carries tiny boxes, row upon row, past her inspection. It's Rosa's job to make sure that each box contains exactly eight pieces of candy-coated laxative gum. Then, she takes lid after lid in her right hand, clamps it down with her left, and transfers the closed box to another conveyor beside her where it passes along to be automatically sealed in cellophane.

Rosa Della Rosa has worked in the chocolate laxative factory on Atlantic

Avenue since her husband died thirty years ago. She never considers staying home and collecting social security, as it would be shameful to take government funds. Financial help can only be accepted from *la famiglia*, and the only family Rosa has left is her ailing older sister, Helena, for whom she cares. She was unable to have children with her husband, and now, all her family is dead except for Helena, feeble and bedridden, with whom she lives in an old Red Hook tenement apartment. Rosa's father declared long ago that any man who would have so little pride as to accept welfare is "a lazy bum." Rosa never managed to make the distinctions between hard-earned social security and welfare or charity.

She lives in a world of simple infinitives where the answer to the mystery of life is: to wake to work to sleep to see to say to drink to eat to walk to go and to come, to be born and to die. She speaks only the minimum of English needed to get her through her evenly patterned days. As a girl, she remembers nearly starving to death when crops failed after World War I, creating a severe famine throughout southern Italy. Her father, after the First World War, sick of watching his family's agony, worked and bartered his way to the New World. A few months later, he sent steerage passage tickets from New York so that Rosa, her mother, and her older sister, Helena, could follow. Later, her brothers were brought, too, and finally the whole family was reunited on Mulberry Street in New York. From that tearful reunion, they lived in a small, crowded apartment, huddling around a coal stove in freezing winter and fanning themselves for relief on the fire escape in sweltering summer.

The mid-morning factory whistle sounds, and Rosa gladly goes down to the basement for her coffeebreak. She meets with her fellow women workers there, around an aluminum percolator, to rest and talk of husbands, children, family crises, and the price of food. Rosa, considered indomitably cheerful, always sits in a corner of the room, nibbling her daily piece of anisette toast, now and then offering a bit of wisdom to the conversation. "Children, dey gotta have da rules, butta da rules musta be putta widda love from *la famiglia*." When the other women complain of their husbands' behavior, she always states, as if for the first time, "A man, he no can cry too mucha; is a woman's work to cry, to worry, to make a nice housa, cooka da food and lova da bambinos. Da man, he pusha here and he pusha dere, but he no can afford to cry!"

Since Rosa seldom says anything that can be debated, the younger women nod their head in affirmation and continue with their chatter. This morning, the conversation goes differently than ever before. Domenica, a petite curly-haired brunette of forty-three, sits beside Rosa and speaks animatedly:

"Listen, Rosa, I figured out how you can earn the money for Helena's hospital bed—the one I showed you in the catalog—so you don't have to hurt your back no more helping her to sit up! My nephew, Don, is casting director for a commercial television studio—ya know? Where they make commercials to sell things on TV? Well, he was over for dinner last night and he's looking for a nice elderly lady to do a false denture adhesive commercial, and I told him about you. He wants her to have a cheerful smile and a foreign accent and look like everybody's sweet old grandmother. 'I wish you'd give Rosa, where I work, the job,' I says to him! Because of your sister's hospital bed. He says, okay, he would use you if he could. I showed him your picture that I took with the other women—at Christmas—when my kids gave me that new polaroid camera. Don says you look just like his grandmother—my mother, Lisa, who passed away not long ago. I hadn't really thought about it until he said it, but it's true, you do. And Rosa, guess what? He's coming by this afternoon to meet you and maybe take you for a screen test. He says he'll make sure they pay you good, if he can use you!"

Domenica's dark eyes sparkle with cheerful enthusiasm. "Just think, Rosa, you'll be on *television*!" Domenica is proud to have something so exciting to tell everybody, but Rosa feels embarrassed by the public admission of her need for money.

"Holy Mary, Domenica! Um no needa money. Uma save lidda by lidda. But, uma be so glad to meet you nephew!" Rosa feels that to introduce one to a member of one's family is to bestow a great honor of friendship.

When the workday ends, she rushes to the lavatory to wash her hands and recomb her hair into a fresh knot. As she carefully smooths down her black skirt and picks a few pieces of lint from it, Domenica enters excitedly. "He's here. Don's here! I saw him from the window!" She quickly hurries Rosa to the elevator and out onto busy Atlantic Avenue. A bright yellow taxi stands at the curb and a young, dark-haired, fair-skinned man alights from it. Domenica, short and olive-skinned, gives her tall blue-eyed nephew a warm hug and proudly introduces him to Rosa.

"*Mi piace! Piacere!*" Rosa beams.

"My pleasure, too, Mrs. Della Rosa. I think you might do fine for our spot, but I want to take you to the studio with me now for a quick test, to see how you come out on camera. I can take you right there in this cab and get you back home in a couple of hours."

Rosa instantly fills Don with nostalgic memories of his grandmother who died several weeks earlier. Don's grandmother was his staunch defender from the wrath of his parents all through his youth. When things were difficult during his teen years at home, he went to live with his grandmother, who indulged him greatly with food, affection, and approval. The smell of Rosa, a mixture of garlic and rose water, fills Don with a pleasant sensation of remembered solace. He immediately treats Rosa with gentle respect, despite her limited command of English. He decides to personally escort her through the entire job to make things easier for her.

"Me, get in a taxi?" Rosa shys away hardly capable of being persuaded to break the regular pattern of her day. "*Mama mid!* It's very nice, but uma go home to my sister and cooka da minestrone for her supper!"

"Oh, for heaven's sakes, Rosa, I'll stop by and look in on Helena and explain. I have the extra keys you gave me to keep safe for you. I'll get her anything she needs until you get home. You'll be home soon, anyway! You can use the money you make from the commercial for the bed to make Helena more comfortable. She'll understand. Don came all this way just to meet you!"

She lowers her eyes. She doesn't mean to insult Domenica or her nephew's efforts. She's seen just enough television to know what a commercial is, but she can't believe what's happening. The idea of a taxi ride fills her with trepidation. At last, she consents to embark with Don. The cab speeds quickly up the avenue toward the Brooklyn Bridge. As it buzzes over the metal groundwork of the big bridge, Rosa sits stiffly upright hanging onto the backrest in front of her. Accustomed to subways and buses, she's never driven over the Brooklyn Bridge in all her years in the city. Her dark pupils dart about as the huge cables of the bridge and its lofty granite arches loom over her. The sudden change in her routine puts her in a state of shock as Don escorts her into the television studio with its bright lights, chrome, cameras, wires, and bustling personnel. She can do nothing but stare, listen, smell, sense what's happening. Her heart throbs, but she smiles and murmurs, *"Piacere!"* assuring everyone that meeting them is her pleasure. She holds her worn black leather purse to her bosom to keep her hands from trembling. Still, they shake a little as they caress the familiar leather.

Rosa is placed before the camera at different angles and asked to smile and say her name. She complies humbly with Don's every wish.

"Well, Mrs. Della Rosa, the producer agrees. You'll do just fine. You'll be on camera for about half a minute and you'll only need to say one sentence.

". . . Which we'll teach you. Don't worry about a thing!" Don adds reassuringly. "We're taping on Monday at an old Victorian farmhouse in Morristown, New Jersey. I'll bring you there in a studio limousine."

Rosa's not at all sure about what the producer or Don is describing, but she understands she'll go in a car with Don next Monday to a place somewhere outside the city. What concerns her most is having to take a day off from work at the factory—something she's done so rarely that the thought fills her with dread.

"Rosa, you'll make more on Monday than you make in a month at the factory!" Domenica is proud to exclaim aloud at Friday morning's coffee break. "Don says so!" Domenica stretches her small frame to its full four-foot eleven-inch height and smooths her curly brown hair as she stands beside the perking percolator.

"Madre di Dio!"[1] Rosa crosses herself, though she rarely goes to church. She believes what her father told her: "Most priests are thieves who want to take from a hardworking man and his family, so they can have nice dinners with plenty of wine!" Her father, like his father before him, had wearied of paying indulgences to the local churchmen who ran his village in southern Italy—while the North and the Vatican seemed to grow richer on the back of the starving South. "Faith in God is infinite, but the Church is

---

1. "Mother of God!"

infinitely corrupt!" Her father often declared with passionate conviction. "Hail Mary!"

Monday morning dawns and Rosa in wonder sits nervously by her kitchen window, peering diligently out into the street for Don's arrival. She sips coffee and nibbles a piece of anisette toast. She has never ventured from the Red Hook ghetto of immigrant Italians, with its rapidly arriving and integrating Hispanic community, since her husband died thirty years ago. She asks little from life. Ordinary daily bread is good enough and anisette toast to her is a great luxury. When she can't, out of agitation, finish the piece she's begun, she carefully wraps it in wax paper and puts it back in the bread box.

Around her, Rosa has watched soul after soul writhe in the agonies of ambition. Though she's full of empathy for their miseries and longings, she's content to care for Helena and feed an occasional neglected child of the neighborhood or a stray animal. She knows every family on her block, and all the local storekeepers. Sometimes she tries to comfort a widow with soup or herb teas, home remedies learned long ago from her mother. Rosa wrings an old lace and linen handkerchief and clutches her purse to her bosom as she peers nervously out the window through the fire escape to the street, watching for Don's car to appear.

The bun at the back of her neck has been more painstakingly arranged than usual. Rosa remembers the last time she left Brooklyn was to go to her parents' funeral in Manhattan's Little Italy. In their late eighties, they had died twenty years ago, within two days of each other, half frozen in the bad winter weather when their apartment house furnace failed. Rosa is ashamed that she wasn't able to relieve their poverty beyond taking the burden of Helena from them. Her three brothers were better able to make money for the family, but they'd all been killed—one in World War II, another in the Korean War, and her eldest in a construction accident when he was sixty-three, a few years before their elderly parents died. As she sits vigilantly awaiting Don, she recalls that her food-bearing visits to her parents meant much in their old age, when they retired from factory work but neglected to collect social security.

Rosa's husband was a mason, a bricklayer like her brothers. One of her brothers introduced him to her, and when they were married, her husband brought her to live near his family in Brooklyn. Rosa's father was able to offer no dowry, as in the Old Country, so she felt fortunate to find a husband at all. Though Rosa earned money for the family table from her factory work, her father was always worried about her virginity and honor, and sorrowful over Helena's aging maidenhood, in a city whose customs he never really understood. He was greatly relieved when Rosa married, but Rosa's mother was heartbroken to have her daughter move away from their neighborhood village.

As the studio limousine speeds through the Lincoln Tunnel, Don remarks to Rosa how they are riding through a tube under the water. Frightened, Rosa holds her breath from the carbon monoxide fumes and fears she will drown under the Hudson River. To all Don offers, Rosa nods her head in constant awe, exclaiming. "*Madre di Dio!*"

With Don's help, Rosa finally alights from the studio car which brings them to a plush green lawn in the back of a huge white Victorian mansion in Morristown. Rosa sighs in wide-eyed wonder. Voluptuous sunlit shrubs, trees, flowers of every bright springtime color, sweet smells of pine and fresh mown grass surround her. This, she decides, at last must be the America my family was promised by the ticket salesman who came to our village—who sold us steerage passage aboard a steamship to the New World. This is the America bathed in golden light that lit our dreams as we rocked across the sea on our sickening voyage. This is the America my family never saw! Here the trees are as green as *Apulia's* olive groves! "Blue sky, sunlight like *patria mia!*"[2] Rosa sighs.

"*Che belleza! Madre mia!*"[3] She gasps breathlessly to Don: "Um no can believa dis! Brooklyn *è brutto*,[4] butta dis? *Simulare la Provincia d'Apulia! Bellisima!*[5] Dis isa America uma dream when um holda my Mamma's skirt ona da cold oceana! Uma wisha Helena coulda see disa! Uma wisha Mamma and Papa coulda see dis bella America! *Madre mia!*" Rosa crosses herself at the thought of her parents sharing the sight with her.

Don leads Rosa to the edge of a giant picnic table where she is greeted by a makeup artist who begins staring at her face, but not her eyes still wide with amazement. She's made to sit in a folding chair while she's powdered and rouged and lined with mascara. "Ina my ola village, only a *putana*[6] putsa paint ona *la faccia!*[7] she jokes with the makeup artist who pays her no mind as he doesn't understand what she's saying. "Don't talk, it ruins the lips!" he commands. Rosa humbly stilled, thinks to herself how in Puglese villages along the Adriatic coast across from the Greek Islands, the women wear black dresses after their husbands die and go to church every day to say the rosary. They keep their hair in a bun and work in the fields until they are too old to. Her mother never wore any powder or rouge, saying it was only for bad women.

As the makeup man continues to fuss over Rosa's face, she takes in more of the scene around them. A long redwood picnic table is spread on the sprawling, manicured lawn around which tremendous pine trees loom in dark green splendor, accented against a clear blue sky. No factory stacks or noises rise in the distance. On the seemingly infinite table, Rosa stares in

---

2.. My country.

3. "What beauty! My mother!"

4. Ugly.

5. "Like the province of Apulia! Beautiful."

6. Whore.

7. Face.

wonder at the plentiful food. Great roasted hams with glistening pineapple slices shining in silver trays and glowing with glazed red cherries. Platters of roasted turkeys, crisp and brown, stand beside bowls of cooked yellow corn dripping with butter. Great mounds of shiny fruit spill forth from gleaming porcelain bowls beside sparkling crystal goblets from which electric blue linen napkins are puffed. Sumptuous loaves of bread, rolls, pies, cakes, cookies of every description and bright ripe vegetables in abundant variety, radiant with the cool sunshine of early spring. The air fresh and crisp, the tranquil countryside mesmerizes Rosa. "At lasta, uma see America ina my family's dreams," She remarks as the makeup man, who pays no attention to her words, finishes.

A cicada, singing in a nearby tree makes the sound man curse aloud to break her spell. "If that goddamned bug doesn't quit singing loud enough to be taken for a frigging buzz saw or a jet stream," he shouts to the director, "we'll have to end up doing a voice-over back at the studio!"

Shocked out of her reveries by the coarse language, her visage prepared for the camera, Rosa is abruptly greeted by the director who immediately begins drumming a sentence into her head while the costume mistress wraps and ties a crisply starched, magnificently flowered blue and red apron over Rosa's plain black dress. The director makes her smile broadly and repeat the sentence over and over again, until she thinks her head will burst from the strain of stress and gesture. Don stands by and helps her drill until, finally, after several minutes, the crew breaks for a rest before the rolling of the camera. When at last they pause, the powdered, smiling Rosa in her brightly colored apron can grin perfectly into the big red light on the camera, hold a lacquered cob of yellow corn beside her face, and say "Uma always use *Ultragrip* ona my dentures to enjoy my family pic-a-niks!"

During the break, while the prop girls scurry about putting finishing touches on the set and the director gives commands to the several extras who will be used to represent Rosa's family, Don explains to her: "There's a child psychiatrist and pediatrician on the set to supervise the children. They get paid $150 per hour!" Don points to a man and a woman beside several children and toddlers dressed in gingham country frocks and suits. There are two babies sitting in highchairs and several pseudo-relatives of every age now gathering around the huge picnic table. Don explains that they will pretend to be picnicking merrily behind her as she stands before the table to recite her line, smiling into the camera. "Considering the prop girls, director, sound and camera men, studio personnel, commercial script writer, our salaries at the ad agency, yours and the other actors' fees, remote control rig, trucks and transportation, this commercial will probably cost close to three-quarters of a million dollars to produce!"

"Holy Mother of God!" Rosa sighs in disbelief. "Um betcha da food alone costa alot a money! Did you ever see such a bigga table, such a bigga turkey ina you life?"

"Yeah, and not one 'spicy meatball' anywhere!" Don teases, smiling.

"This is an All-American feast!" He enjoys Rosa's wide-eyed wonder at the incredible world of television into which he has benevolently brought her.

"Okay, Mrs. Della Rosa. Ready on the set!" calls the director.

"*Si signore*. Uma ready!" Rosa answers, practicing her smile at him. "Uma ready." She remarks to Don as he leads her to her spot on the set, "Uma lika to smile. You can take da smile from you face and put ina you heart, widda a feast likka dis in you eyes!"

All becomes hushed; then, at the director's cue, the pseudo-relatives behind Rosa, on camera, begin to gesture and laugh as if at a picnic. Rosa, as she was bid, holds up her lacquered cob of corn, smiles broadly into the red light on the camera, and repeats her line: "Uma *always* use *Ultragrip* ona my dentures to *enjoy* my family pic-a-nicks!"

"Cut!" shouts the director, "Mrs. Della Rosa, the corn was hiding your face too much. Hold it away to the side of your face, with your pinky out more!"

Don explains from the sidelines in Italian. He murmurs reassuringly.

Si signore!" Rosa nods obediently and moves the corn away from her face. She sticks out her pinky in a delicate gesture.

"Ready, cut two, take two!" the stage manager claps his board. "Roll um!" and so the process is repeated through several takes until the director is satisfied with the results.

"Okay! Cut and print!" He finally shouts and perfunctorily adds, "Thanks everybody. You can go home. Dismissed!"

Rosa can hardly take the smile from her face. It seems frozen there from repetition. The muscles of her cheeks ache.

"Well, Rosa," exclaims Don. "You're a star! You'll be watching yourself on television before you know it!"

"Helena will no believe when she sees me! Holy Mother of God!"

While Don tends to business, Rosa sits exhausted on a bench at the edge of the picnic table. She watches the prop girls begin to dismantle the set. Too excited to eat breakfast or lunch, her ordeal now over, Rosa's mouth waters at the glorious repast. Before she can think of tasting a morsel, the prop and set workers begin shoveling the platters of food into the huge, black plastic garbage bags. Rosa's eyes gape in silent horror as bread, rolls, pies, cakes, corn, vegetables, fruits, and amazingly glazed hams are swept from sight, bagged as garbage. In utter disbelief, Rosa sees the feast of her dreams unceremoniously destroyed, shoveled into garbage bags, thrown to the ground.

Finally, unable to contain herself, she asks quietly, "Whadda you gonna do with dat bigga turkey? Uma know a nice orphanage ina Brooklyn. . ."

The prop mistress is used to being asked such scavaging questions by perpetually starving actors dismissed from sets. Without giving Rosa even a sidelong glance, she answers contemptuously, "Throw it away with the rest of the perishable props, of course! Salvaging perishables from sets complicates tax matters. Excuse me." She reaches over Rosa, grabs the turkey platter, and slides the sumptuous roasted bird into a black plastic sack full of cracked and crumbling pies, cookies, and squashed fruit. It lands with a sloppy thud, spraying soggy crumbs over Rosa's flowered apron.

Don reappears as a costume girl bids Rosa to stand while she removes the apron. As Don escorts her home through the Lincoln Tunnel again, she does not speak or exclaim anything in Holy-Mother-of-God phrases. In her mind she sees the food of her dreams behind the house of her dreams shoveled into a huge black plastic mouth of hell as her starving parents, Helena, her brothers, and herself, as a child, look on with saddened faces, somber with shadows of death.

"Well, Rosa, what do you think of Television Land?" Don questions cheerfully.

"*Non capisco nulla di niente. Non capisco, Signore. Non capisco,*"[8] Rosa utters softly. Don decides she is weary from her exciting day, as she rests back against the cushions of the limousine, her eyes half-closed. When they arrive in front of her tenement home in Red Hook, Don helps Rosa out of the car and to the door, thinking that she is tired just as his grandmother would be after such a long and eventful day. "Will you be all right, Mrs. Della Rosa?"

"*Si, molte grazie, Signore. Grazie mille.*"[9] Rosa puts her hands on Don's arm as if in sympathy and nods weakly. She enters her hallway without turning back. "*Buona notte!*"[1]

"Good night, to you, too." Don watches her grey hair disappear into the darkness.

She slowly climbs the stairs to her apartment and, in the dim light of the landing, opens the door, depositing the keys in her worn black purse which she leaves, as always, on the old hall table. She peers into the dusky bedroom, where Helena wheezes quietly in her sleep. Without turning on any lights to brighten the twilight kitchen, she goes to the sink and washes her hands with soap and cold water—because the hot water tap hasn't worked for years like the one in the bathroom does, but it's too close to the bedroom and sound of hissing pipes might wake Helena out of her pain-filled respite from slow dying.

Rosa goes to the bread box and extracts from its near empty depths the waxed-paper-wrapped, half-eaten pieces of anisette toast left over from her vigilant breakfast at the window. She sits again by the window and peers into the coming night, as slowly she chews the dry bread with her quite good, very old, real teeth, crushing it crumb by crumb, morsel by precious morsel.

---

8. "I don't understand anything about it. I don't understand, mister. I don't understand."

9. "Yes, many thanks, mister. A thousand thanks."

1. "Goodnight!"

Joseph Geha
(1944–)

Joseph Geha was born in 1944 in Zahleh, Lebanon, where his family name has been known since before the Middle Ages. His mother was from Damascus, Syria; the parents' marriage had been arranged in the traditional way.

Sailing on the first steamship to leave Beirut harbor after World War II, the Geha family emigrated to the United States in 1946. They settled in Toledo, Ohio, where they operated a grocery store and lived in the upstairs apartment. Like most of their Lebanese Christian neighbors, Geha's parents spoke primarily Arabic, so Joseph and his sister did not learn English until they went to school.

Geha went from the Toledo public schools to the University of Toledo, earning both a bachelor's and a master's degree. He has written poetry, fiction, and plays about the conflicts within the immigrant culture of Middle Eastern families in northern Ohio and southeast Michigan. In 1988 he was awarded a fellowship grant from the National Endowment for the Arts. He has taught at Southwest Missouri State College and Bowling Green State University and is currently on the faculty of Iowa State University.

"News from Phoenix" is taken from Through and Through: Toledo Stories *(1990).*

News from Phoenix

AFTER THREE YEARS IN AMERICA, Isaac's mother was still afraid of Jews. Damascus remained fresh in her, the dark evenings huddled with her sisters, fearful and giggling around the brazier while her uncle told stories. He was an archimandrite[1] in the Maronite Church, and even now Sofia trembled at the thought of him. His cassock reeked sweat and incense, and she remembered, too, the thick bitter smell of the Turkish anise drink he favored, how his beard glistened oil as he sipped—and such stories! No! She put both hands to her ears and shouted at her husband: "Amos!"

Who paid no attention. It was closing time, and Isaac's father stood at the cash register counting money. His lips made the quick, breathy sounds of numbers.

"Amos, they are Jews!" she shouted. "Jews!" as if that word said it all, and anyone who had an ounce of sense would understand.

Isaac was almost six years old and he had heard her stories, her uncle the archimandrite's stories, of what Jews did to little Christian children, of throats slit and blood taken for secret ceremonies, the children found white and limp in the morning, thrown into some alley behind the weavers' market or the gold *souq*.[2] Even so, he did not understand. (What had Charlotte and Erwin Klein to do with all that?) But he became frightened anyway. Somehow there had been danger in the ride downtown for ice cream and the little gifts Charlotte had bought. He and his brother had just had a narrow escape, that much he understood, and he began to cry. Then Demitri, younger than Isaac by three years, took his thumb from his mouth and gave out that slow, toneless wail of his that understood nothing except that Isaac was crying.

"Hoost!" The sound came from their father, and immediately the boys fell silent. "*Izraiyeen* take you!" Amos cursed his wife with the angel of death. He slapped the money into the cash drawer. "Look how you're scaring them—why?" His voice was big, although he was not yet shouting. That would come. "Give them back the toys." He wiped his hands across the belly of his apron and waited.

Sofia lowered her eyes. Then, whispering a prayer against the Evil Eye, she handed the package of crayons to Isaac and the balsa wood airplane to Demitri.

"Hoost!" Amos said again. She turned away, but her lips continued to move, silently, as little as the syllables of the prayer would allow.

Demitri tossed the airplane, and the four of them watched it float up in a gentle arc. It banked just shy of the flypaper that hung in coils above the butcher block, hesitated, then dropped abruptly into a banana crate.

"G'wan now," Amos said in English. "G'wan, take da ara-blane downstairs."

They obeyed, Demitri following Isaac into the cellar. Beneath the stairs was the toilet stool. Isaac nudged the lid down with his toe, then sat listening to the voices above while his brother threw and chased the airplane among the racks of empty soda pop bottles. His father's shouting, when it came,

---

1. Head of a monastery or group of monasteries.
2. Bazaar.

would be full of curses, but it would be brief. Afterward a silence would fall between them, stiff with exaggerated politeness; and in the silence his curses—of blood, of lineage and the womb that gives issue—would hover above the tiny store and the flat upstairs until finally, through small familiar signals of regret, Amos took them back one by one.

And the two of them would have something warm to drink then, they always did. Sofia lit the gas burner and stirred the base of the Turkish samovar around and around in the flame, adding anise seed in pinched doses until its strong licorice smell filled the kitchen, and still Amos would say "More . . . more," and she would add another pinch, and yet another. The yellow brew, called *yensoun*, remained syrupy even after it settled. Amos drank it that way. Into her own cup Sofia first spooned plenty of sugar, and when she poured for herself she poured *yensoun* and cream at the same time, two-handed, lest the cream curdle in the strong brew.

Sometimes Isaac asked for a taste, but always they told him no, that it was too strong for children, and they would send him out of the kitchen. So he would sit in the front room and listen to the silence dissolve between them, Sofia gazing into the dregs of Amos's cup and finding journeys there, money, business for the store, news from a friend. Her voice would grow high, child-like with foretelling, and soon Amos would be laughing.

Because, after all, his wife wasn't a mean woman. He told people that. More like a child, he told them, she believed everything. Blood and secret ceremonies—an uncle's bogeyman stories! And would an archimandrite, in the Latin rite equal to a monsignor, tell such horrors to a child? Probably not. Probably she simply remembered the stories that way, adding his authority to them later, as children sometimes do; and who would curse a child? Especially one so often ignored, left to herself here in a tiny flat above a tiny store, surrounded by taverns and pawnshops and the blue-eyed bums asking for wine. America was hardly what a child must have expected it to be. A child, he told people, given to petulance when things were boring, when the weather was hot and there was nothing to do.

Isaac pressed his nose to the doorscreen and stared at the way the air wiggled between buses and trucks and automobiles when there was a red light. Too hot for business, his father had said. Amos was sitting behind the counter with his cousin Milad, playing a hand of *baserah*. There had been no customers for hours. Sofia stood at the display window with a piece of newspaper, fanning herself and Demitri, who stood close by her despite the heat. It was quiet in the store, only flies and the rustle of paper. Now and then Uncle Milad would mutter something at his cards—Arabic or English, it was hard to tell with the cigar in his mouth.

"But there is nothing to do in this country!" Sofia shouted as if in the middle of an argument. Isaac started at the suddenness of her voice. The men looked up. Amos kinked an eyebrow but said nothing, and after a moment Milad gathered the cards and began shuffling them.

"The children! Poor things, look how they have nothing to do."

"Take them to the park," Amos said. He nodded for Milad to deal.

"I do not know the buses."

Milad dealt, and the men studied their cards.

"I do not know the buses," she said again. "You must come with us."

Amos glared up at her. Even Isaac understood: customers or no, business is still business.

Have they been to the *arta muzeem?*" Milad asked.

"Truly," Amos said, "take them to the *ara muzeema.*"

"What is that?"

"It is free. They have pictures on the walls. You can go look at the pictures."

"And sometimes music, too," Milad said. "Violins, pianos."

Sofia thought a moment.

"And in the summer," Milad added, *aira condition.*"

"Still, I do not know the buses."

"You do not have to change buses," Amos said. "It is right here on Monroe Street. That way, not even four kilometers."

"The driver will not understand me."

Milad put down the cards. "I will take them in my *machina.*"

"Sit down," Amos said. "It is your play."

Sofia knew only the Adams bus that went downtown and the Jefferson bus that brought her back. Her English was still terribly broken, even after three years; some said she wasn't trying to learn. Charlotte Klein had offered to drive her to a high school where English was taught at night, but Sofia refused to go. She wouldn't leave the children alone, she said. Also, Charlotte Klein was a Jew.

"Take the bus on the corner and say to the driver: *De ara muzeema,*" Amos said. "Sit behind him, and he will tell you when he reaches it."

"*D'Aram muzeema,*" Sofia sighed, then she put down the newspaper. "*D'arama amuzeema.*"

Amos gave her money from the cash drawer. "And dress up the boys," he said.

She washed Isaac and Demitri and had them put on the blue trousers with suspenders and the white shirts they wore for church. Then she packed a shopping bag with lunch.

When the bus arrived, Sofia told the driver several times but he still couldn't understand her. Finally, Isaac tried, speaking slowly and carefully, and the man appeared to understand. They sat behind the driver, Demitri moaning a little because he was still afraid of buses and the noise of traffic. While Isaac wasn't afraid, he could never seem to get used to the diesel smell that buses had, nor the whine of gears building, but not enough, not quite enough, before the releasing lurch and hiss of the air brakes. It went on that way for blocks until at last the driver turned to them. "This is it," he said.

Sofia looked at him.

"Your stop, ma'am."

Sofia smiled.

"The art museum," the driver said. "Ar-rt mew-see-uhm."

Isaac understood first and took his mother's hand. But after the bus had moved away, leaving them on the sidewalk, they saw no art museum, no pictures on walls; only a hot summer confusion of streets and buildings and changing traffic lights. Although there were signs set low in the power-trimmed lawns, the words were meaningless to them. After a moment Sofia took a few steps in one direction, turned—the boys wheeling beside her in wide arcs—and started in another; then she stopped. She began to curse the art museum and the bus driver and Amos, too, using not the exact pronunciation of the profanity but changing a letter or a syllable, therefore cursing but not the words of cursing, not the words of anything, and so not a sin.

They crossed the street and waited for the homeward bus. But no sooner had they sat on the bench than they began to hear music from, it seemed, just around the corner. They listened to it a while. Finally, the return bus nowhere in sight, they picked up the shopping bag and turned the corner.

The music was coming from loudspeakers atop the roof of a small, white building. There were pictures painted on the walls and windows, bright cartoon shapes of blue and yellow and orange. Little plastic pennants flapped from wires. Above it all, high on a white post, was a painting of a red horse with wings.

Sofia and Isaac and Demitri sat down on the tiny lawn in front of the place, took out their lunch—lamb meat patties, turnips pickled in beet juice, rolled grape leaves, olives, and cheese and fruit—and began to eat.

"*Aira condition,*" Sofia snorted. She fanned herself with a piece of waxed paper.

Automobiles drove onto the lot, and the attendants in spotless new uniforms immediately began polishing the windshields. Children pointed and laughed from back-seat windows. Someone in a green car, a woman or a young man, yelled "Hey, Gypsies!" as the car pulled into traffic. Sofia understood that word. She stood and cast a sign after the car—thumb and two fingers clenched, the fig—and shouted as she did so, forgetting to change the letters or the syllables. Sitting down again, she said a blessing to erase the curse.

A horn honked from the street behind them. The boys turned together; it was Charlotte and Erwin Klein. "Mama, mama!" Demitri shouted in the only English he knew. Sofia would not turn to look. "Hoost," she said. When Demitri began to move, she grasped him by the suspenders and pulled him down. Charlotte got out of her car, smiling as she always smiled whenever she saw Demitri. She bent over and spoke to Sofia in careful, distinct English. Isaac understood. She was offering them a ride home. Sofia also understood (that much Isaac could tell) but she opened her hands and shook her head no. "*Yahood,*" she said to Isaac and Demitri, *Jews,* so they would understand.

Charlotte was a small, very thin woman. She had straight hair, and Isaac thought it pretty just now how outdoor light changed it from blonde to almost red. Her eyes, however, weren't pretty at all. Magnified by glasses, they seemed too large for her face, and the harlequin slant of the frames made them look squinty. But Isaac never paid much attention to eyes; he would always remember hers as blue, maybe. It was mouths that he looked to. Tears or laughter or anger, for him it was the turn of the mouth that each time signaled first, and not the eyes. (Once, when Amos had removed his belt and stamped after the boys as they cowered together in a corner, Isaac pulled loose of Demitri and said, "Papa, your pants are gonna fall down!" and he remembered how his father had stopped short, and, although his eyes never blinked even, one side of his mouth began working against the laughter. Twisting and clenching against it, before he dropped the belt and shuffled into the kitchen where Mama was already laughing.) Charlotte had a wide, full-lipped mouth, with that little bleb of flesh in the center of the upper lip that Isaac would forever like in a woman, associating it somehow with generosity and kindness.

Charlotte looked back at the car. She exaggerated a shrug, and Erwin waved her the come-on sign with his arm. Sofia continued to smile at all this as if she understood none of it. Charlotte talked a moment with Erwin at the car, then Erwin went inside the white building and stood at the pay phone in the window. When they drove away, Sofia was still smiling, looking straight ahead.

Only minutes passed before Milad pulled up his ancient creaking automobile and told them to get in quickly, quickly. When they got home, Amos was furious.

The building where the Kleins lived and where Erwin Klein had his law office was within walking distance of the store, but toward downtown and away from the bums; an area where the streets began to be lined with trees and shrubs set in white half-barrels. Doormen wearing gold braid stood beneath scalloped marquees fringed with gold. The buildings they served housed expensive shops on the lower floors, as well as the offices of doctors, brokers, attorneys like Erwin Klein. From the paneled lobbies elevators carried residents to their apartments. One rainy afternoon Charlotte took the boys up there with her, to the elegant quiet of her living room where Demitri was fascinated by his blue image in the blue-tinted mirror top of the coffee table.

She had no children. Married in her mid-thirties and resigned, it seemed, to never having them, she made Demitri her favorite. It was only natural; Demitri had the deep brown eyes that women liked, and his mile-a-minute Arabic must have sounded cute to an American. Demitri took to her as well, and soon she was driving him to the dimestore or the Saturday movies. Of course, Isaac went, too, so there would be no jealousy.

Sofia raised her voice against all this, "In their temple they learn the Evil Eye!" and Amos would blow up at her, "Think of it, a woman childless at her age, just think of it!" Then he would add, "You are no neighbor."

Two years ago when Milad Yakoub first sold the butcher shop to Amos, it was Erwin Klein who had taken care of the legal matters—the loan, the transfer of deed, licenses for beer and wine to carry out. "He understands business," Milad had told Amos in Arabic. "Trust him and keep your mouth shut." And so when Erwin advised that the name, "Yakoub Market," was worth something to the business, Amos kept his mouth shut and did not change the name of the store to his own. Later, when Erwin suggested a line of party products—soft drinks and packaged snack foods—Amos trusted the advice. He ordered from the wholesaler according to a list Erwin drew up for him, and he realized a profit and an increase in business.

"This one," Amos told the boys in English, "he is schooled," and he would raise one hand toward Erwin, indicating a respectful silence.

Erwin did look like a smart man; he had a high wide forehead, glasses, and a straight, even line of a mouth that could answer squarely to anything, or so it seemed to Isaac. He was very tall, too, and very, very skinny. "He was sick probably all his life," was how Sofia saw it. "Probably his mother had thin milk." And indeed there was a kind of sickliness about him, even his laugh; you expected it to be bigger than it was. Nevertheless, he did laugh, breaking the respectful silence as he lifted Demitri up almost to the ceiling of the store. Then he would pick up Isaac, too, so there would be no jealousy.

In June of their third year in America, Amos received a letter from Saint Patrick School informing him that Isaac would not be admitted into the first grade. That same morning he took both boys and walked them hand in hand to the school. Two nuns who were standing in the foyer with their black bookbags made a fuss over Demitri, and Amos let them. Then he asked to see the nun whose signature appeared at the bottom of the letter.

She was an old woman with a quick, friendly smile, and yes, she remembered Isaac well. Several weeks before, she had observed him during a series of tests, how he'd fretted in tight-lipped defeat over nursery rhymes and geometric puzzles and even her own simple directions. So, when Amos began to explain that his son was bright and his only problem was that he didn't know English well enough yet since they almost never spoke it at home, her smile vanished. She interrupted him with a stiff shake of her head, no. Amos tried again—"Maybe, Mum, wit' the extra help," and "Maybe wit' special books,"—but the more he tried the more she seemed to grow impatient. Isaac could see it all in the set of her mouth. Finally, when his father asked to speak with the principal, her lips formed a rigid curve: *These people,* she was thinking. But she didn't want trouble, Isaac could see that too, and after a moment she signaled them to follow her down the polished halls to the office.

The principal must have been expecting them; she was adamant from the start. "This boy," she said, busily moving a sheaf of papers from one corner of her desk to the other, "is simply not ready for first grade, at least not at Saint Patrick's." And that was all. An uneasy silence followed, then the principal stood up as if to dismiss them. But Amos remained seated, smiling; he was trying everything.

"Listen, Mum," he said, "I have a joke. . . ."

He usually tried this with customers when they complained about prices or the freshness of the meat. The joke was one of his funny ones, about the rabbi and the priest. Even so, the principal kept a stone face all through it; when it was ended, she was actually frowning.

Outside, Amos cursed both nuns by name, a short vicious curse concerning, as Isaac would always remember, nipples and squirting blood.

Then he brightened. He hitched his trousers and told the boys to wait for him here on the school steps while he went across the street.

Beyond the traffic Isaac saw a row of small shops. "What for, Papa?"

"What for? Telephone. Never mind what for!"

Isaac watched him go. He looked silly, hurrying off toward a phone booth in those large gray trousers, the butt-fold wagging left right left like a tail. But Isaac could not turn away from it; his eyes fixed themselves on that rear as it worked anxiously through the indifferent roar of Monroe Street for his sake alone. Poor butt; his father was trying everything.

When Amos returned, he gathered the boys to him and sat down on the steps beneath the principal's window. He began to sob loudly, all the time muttering curses and wiping his eyes with a red handkerchief, although Isaac could see that there was nothing to wipe. Now and then Amos would look up at the window, pause, then bury his face in Isaac's neck or Demitri's curls. At last the door opened, and soon Isaac was again sitting with his brother in a corner of the principal's office.

She was still firm, but this time she spoke slowly, in little words, the way some people talk to bums. But this time it was Amos who interrupted. "I called up a friend onna telephone," he said. "Him he's gonna talk for me."

The principal sighed. "All right," she said, "all right."

Finally, Erwin Klein arrived. He had on sneakers and tennis shorts and a white v-neck sweater, but when he began talking everything changed. He spoke such perfect English—so rapidly Isaac could barely make it out—and with such confidence that he looked the principal directly in the eye. He didn't look sick at all that day. He was handsome without his glasses, sunburned on the cheeks and forehead, and skinny, yes, but so much taller than Amos. When he was finished, the principal's stone face had relaxed into a smile. "Well, yes," she agreed, "I suppose it's worth a try."

At that, Amos made an exaggerated, grateful bow. "*Kes umeek,*" he said in Arabic, *Your mother's vulva.* She smiled. Demitri began to giggle, and she reached out and touched his curls the way a mother would. Isaac could see then that she wasn't a mean person, not really. She just didn't want trouble.

And so Isaac was admitted into the first grade. With the help of a novice nun who tutored him after school, his English improved greatly, and by the following June he would become one of the five gold-star readers in his class.

Amos showed his gratitude to the Kleins: the groceries he had delivered to their door were always wholesale. And even Sofia's protests began to diminish; eventually, she said nothing at all. It was in October of Isaac's first year of school that she told her husband about the slowness she'd been noticing in Charlotte, a slight change in her walk, and the way her mind seemed to be on other things. Then, one night Sofia dreamed of a death, and she awoke laughing.

"Good news!" she said at breakfast. "Soon they will have their own."

"How?" Amos was still in his nightshirt.

"In dreams, death always means a birth."

"Who died?"

"Missus Charlotte—so it will be a boy. Think of it, they will have their own now."

"*Inshallah*," Amos said, *God willing.*

But even in the happiness of that moment, while his mother stirred the samovar of *yensoun*, clucking on like a nested pigeon, Isaac saw his father's eyebrow go up in doubt.

The doubt vanished one Saturday afternoon, only a week or so later, when Erwin stopped by the store. It seemed one of his usual after-lunch visits except that when he spoke his voice had a forced casualness to it. Finally, unable to mask his feelings any longer, he told Amos that Charlotte had seen the doctor and that, yes, it was certain.

Amos laughed. "Good news!" he said in Arabic, echoing Sofia's words. Then he leaned over the butcher block and muttered something that Isaac didn't catch, and both men began to laugh. Leaving Sofia to watch the store, Amos led Erwin into the back room and opened a bottle of Jewish wine with the star on it.

Less than a month later, the baby was born dead. When the phone rang with the news, Isaac was doing his after-school chores, carrying empty soda pop bottles down the basement stairs to sort them.

"Missus Charlotte!" Amos smiled. And forever in Isaac's memory of that day his father would be standing at the pay phone, smiling and listening, and his smile fading. "No, Mum, he is not here. He was here after the lunch, but not now. Downtown, he tell me."

Sofia, too, had sensed something wrong. She put Demitri down from her lap and stood up.

"He don' say no more"—his voice was shaking now—"only downtown. No, Mum, I don't know where." He listened a moment more, then nodded his head quickly and hung up. Rushing, searching his pockets, talking to himself and to Sofia, he scooped some dimes from the cash drawer and ran back to the phone.

"Where?" Sofia asked.

"He's downtown! Where? Shut up! Downtown!"

Amos inserted a dime and dialed. "Quickly!" he said over his shoulder, but Sofia was already out the door. Isaac saw her pass the display window pulling on her coat as she hurried down the sidewalk in the direction of Charlotte's street.

A woman's voice came on the line. Amos was polite to her, but he could not keep his voice from shouting. Then there was Doctor Binatti's voice, big even over the phone.

Amos began in Arabic, caught himself, and started again in English. Then he noticed the boys, Isaac with pop bottles hanging from both hands, and he turned a little away and said the rest quietly into the receiver.

Hanging up, he said "Close your mouth," and Isaac closed his mouth.

A customer came into the store, then another. Demitri began to fuss, and Isaac took his hand and led him upstairs for a nap. When he returned, his father was slicing liver for the first customer's order. After a while, Isaac went down into the basement and used the toilet, remembering later to jiggle the handle. Then he continued sorting—Coke, Hires, Whistle, and Crush. He came up again at the sound of the back door, but it was not his mother, only one of the bums looking to earn wine money. His father sent the man away; there wasn't any work. Later, Amos made liverwurst sandwiches. Demitri awoke from his nap, and they ate. Amos drank a beer after his sandwich. Sofia still was not back.

"G'wan, get out-a-side," Amos told the boys in English, but Isaac lingered in the back of the store. Demitri, eyes liquid and calm and understanding nothing, stayed by his brother.

When Sofia came in, her face was white. She sat on a stool behind the counter while Amos finished with a customer. She had been crying, and when she spoke she used Arabic so the customer would not understand. "Little, little," she began, so quietly that Isaac could barely make out the rest. "Small as my hand," she said, "but perfect." The customer left. Isaac crept toward the front so he could hear. "Perfect," Sofia said again. "Everything. It even had a little pee-pee."

Amos looked down and made a noise with his tongue, tch.

"And Mister Erwin?" he asked.

"He was downtown."

"Woman, I know that. Has he been told?"

She nodded. "He is there now. He is going with her to the hospital."

Amos made the sound again, tch.

"Even so, it is all as God would have it," Sofia said, and Amos looked at her. She smiled. "It did not die a Jew. While Doctor Binatti he was busy, I took water from the kitchen," she was not looking at his face, "and gave it baptism."

Amos turned away from her. "Watch the store," he said. He came to the back of the store and stood there a moment, looking down at the spattered sawdust beneath the butcher block. Then he noticed Isaac. Nudging the boy aside, he lifted a soda pop crate and carried it down into the cellar.

Isaac listened at the doorway. He could hear the roar and suck of the toilet, its float frozen with rust. He heard his father lift the tank lid and adjust the valve. Then Isaac, too, picked up a soda pop crate.

Amos was standing before a row of bottle racks, head down, his arms loaded with bottles. He was sorting them. "Tch," he said when he heard Isaac behind him, but he did not send the boy away. After a minute, Sofia followed, carrying Demitri.

"What is it, Amos?" she asked, but he kept his back to her. "I shouldn't have?"

Amos turned around. Isaac could see that he was ready to blow up. Then it went out of his face. He sat down on a soda pop crate and put the bottles at his feet. "Is this how you watch the store? No matter." He spoke quietly. "No difference." Then he looked up, blinking into the lightbulb behind Sofia's head. "Go upstairs. Make *yensoun*," he said, his fingers dangling helpless among the bottles. "I want something warm to drink."

In December Amos phoned to invite the Kleins for Christmas Eve dinner. Although it was practically a last-minute idea ("So what if they are Jews," he told Sofia as he dialed, perhaps forgetting that the idea had been hers in the first place, "how can Christmas offend them?") the Kleins not only accepted, they arrived, like a bachelor uncle, two hours early. "Before the stores close," they explained, and they took the boys to a shopping center— Isaac unsure about seeing Santa, Demitri breathless with excitement—and brought them back loaded with gifts. They brought red wine with them, too, with the star on it, and after dinner sat drinking and talking, asking Sofia about the customs of Christmas in the old country. Then they told of a vacation they were planning to begin in January, an extended tour of the southwest and Mexico.

"To get away from Ohio's winter," Charlotte said. Isaac glanced briefly at Erwin. His face was pale, the corners of his mouth pinched in. There was a brief silence, then Amos turned the talk to houses; he was seriously considering a place across town from the store. As he began to describe its two storeys, its yard, and its real neighborhood, far from the bums and broken glass, Sofia's face glowed.

Then Charlotte confessed that they, too, were looking to move, and that this was another reason for their trip. Phoenix had wonderful sunshine, she said, year round, and the—she paused—the facilities there had been highly recommended.

And it was then that Isaac began to sense that things were changing. Soon everything would be different, and somehow he would have to accustom himself.

Later, when the others were busy—Erwin putting together a toy ferris wheel for Demitri, Sofia busy with dessert—Charlotte and Amos sat down together on the couch and began to talk very quietly. Isaac didn't think it was right to listen on purpose.

"And if anything happens to him," Charlotte removed her glasses and put them back on again, "well, I don't know what I'll do." But she said it as if she did know what.

After dessert there was, of course, *yensoun*. Charlotte and Erwin exchanged glances, then laughed in disbelief at the third or fourth time Amos called out "More!" and Sofia added yet another pinch.

They laughed again, afterward, when Sofia began reading the cups—

journeys and money and love. The drink must have heartened her; she told how her uncle the archimandrite had taught her to read cups, and when she began to describe the man himself ("Hees beard, it come down to here, an' my father he said you can comb a pounda grease outta it!") there was another peal of laughter.

But what if anything did happen? The thought came to Isaac amid the laughter, himself laughing. Erwin looked so thin, sitting back from the table now, balancing the tiny cup and saucer on the bone of his knee. And if anything did happen, then the news, when it came, would come from Phoenix.

Turning to the stove, Isaac took the samovar in one hand, the creamer in the other, and poured himself a cup as he'd seen his mother do it, two-handed. If she noticed, she said nothing; and his father, looking his way now, also said nothing. So Isaac took a sip. It was bitter despite the sugar and milk, and terribly strong, as he'd always imagined it would be. But somehow the adults had liked it. They were laughing harder than ever now, probably at the face he was making. Charlotte and Erwin had drunk theirs without even wincing. Maybe they were used to it, maybe he wasn't. He took another sip to accustom himself.

That night Erwin showed Isaac how to load his Christmas camera with color film, but when it was done and Isaac put his eye to the viewfinder, Erwin turned his face away. Isaac understood; there was no need for his father's warning, the raised eyebrow. Charlotte wore a blue dress that night.

Charles Johnson
(1948–)

A graphic artist as well as a writer, Charles Johnson published two collections of cartoons and contributed drawings to such national publications as Ebony *and the* Chicago Tribune *before he began winning critical attention for his writing with his first published novel,* Faith and the Good Thing *(1974). Since then he has published four more books, written scripts for television, and been selected in a survey conducted by the University of Southern California as one of the ten best short story writers in America.*

Johnson was born in Evanston, Illinois, received a bachelor's and a master's degree from Southern Illinois University and studied with the novelist John Gardner. His writing for television includes the award-winning "Booker" (1983) for the Public Broadcasting System. He has taught creative writing at the University of Washington, been fiction editor for the Seattle

Review, *lectured abroad for the U.S. Information Agency, and published numerous critical articles.*

His third novel, Middle Passage, *won the National Book Award for fiction in 1990. It is a rich mixture of historical details about the slave trade, with philosophy, mystery, humor, and satiric observations about contemporary life and race relations.*

Johnson is a practicing Buddhist; his writing reveals his fascination with both European and Asian branches of philosophy. He comments, "one might say that in fiction I attempt to interface Eastern and Western philosophical traditions, always with the hope that some new perception of experience—especially 'black experience'—will emerge from these meditations."

Other publications include Black Humor *(1970);* Half-Past Nation Time *(1972);* Oxherding Tale *(1982);* The Sorcerer's Apprentice *(1986), a short story collection; and* Being and Race: Black Writing Since 1970. *The following story is from* The Sorcerer's Apprentice.

Exchange Value

ME AND MY BROTHER, Loftis, came in by the old lady's window. There was some kinda boobytrap—boxes of broken glass—that shoulda warned us Miss Bailey wasn't the easy mark we made her to be. She been living alone for twenty years in 4-B down the hall from Loftis and me, long before our folks died—a hincty, halfbald West Indian woman with a craglike face, who kept her door barricaded, shutters closed, and wore the same sorry-looking outfit—black wingtip shoes, cropfingered gloves in winter, and a man's floppy hat—like maybe she dressed half-asleep or in a dark attic. Loftis, he figured Miss Bailey had some grandtheft dough stashed inside, jim, or leastways a shoebox full of money, 'cause she never spent a nickel on herself, not even for food, and only left her place at night.

Anyway, we figured Miss Bailey was gone. Her mailbox be full, and Pookie White, who run the Thirty-ninth Street Creole restaurant, he say she ain't dropped by in days to collect the handouts he give her so she can get by. So here's me and Loftis, tipping around Miss Bailey's blackdark kitchen. The floor be littered with fruitrinds, roaches, old food furred with blue mold. Her dirty dishes be stacked in a sink feathered with cracks, and it looks like the old lady been living, lately, on Ritz crackers and Department of

Agriculture (Welfare Office) peanut butter. Her toilet be stopped up, too, and, on the bathroom floor, there's five Maxwell House coffee cans full of shit. Me, I was closing her bathroom door when I whiffed this evil smell so bad, so thick, I could hardly breathe, and what air I breathed was stifling, like solid fluid in my throatpipes, like broth or soup. "Cooter," Loftis whisper, low, across the room, "you smell that?" He went right on sniffing it, like people do for some reason when something be smelling stanky, then took out his headrag and held it over his mouth. "Smells like something crawled up in here and died!" Then, head low, he slipped his long self into the living room. Me, I stayed by the window, gulping for air, and do you know why?

You oughta know, up front, that I ain't too good at this gangster stuff, and I had a real bad feeling about Miss Bailey from the get-go. Mama used to say it was Loftis, not me, who'd go places—I see her standing at the sideboard by the sink now, big as a Frigidaire, white flour to her elbows, a washtowel over her shoulder, while we ate a breakfast of cornbread and syrup. Loftis, he graduated fifth at DuSable High School, had two gigs and, like Papa, he be always wanting the things white people had out in Hyde Park, where Mama did daywork sometimes. Loftis, he be the kind of brother who buys *Esquire*, sews Hart, Schaffner & Marx labels in Robert Hall suits, talks properlike, packs his hair with Murray's; and he took classes in politics and stuff at the Black People's Topographical Library in the late 1960s. At thirty, he make his bed military-style, reads *Black Scholar* on the bus he takes to the plant, and, come hell or high water, plans to make a Big Score. Loftis, he say I'm 'bout as useful on a hustle—or when it comes to getting ahead—as a headcold, and he says he has to count my legs sometimes to make sure I ain't a mule, seeing how, for all my eighteen years, I can't keep no job and sorta stay close to home, watching TV, or reading *World's Finest* comic books, or maybe just laying dead, listening to music, imagining I see faces or foreign places in water stains on the wallpaper, 'cause some days, when I remember Papa, then Mama, killing theyselves for chump change—a pitiful li'l bowl of porridge—I get to thinking that even if I ain't had all I wanted, maybe I've had, you know, all I'm ever gonna get.

"Cooter," Loftis say from the living room. "You best get in here quick."

Loftis, he'd switched on Miss Bailey's bright, overhead living room lights, so for a second I couldn't see and started coughing—the smell be so powerful it hit my nostrils like coke—and when my eyes cleared, shapes come forward in the light, and I thought for an instant like I'd slipped in space. I seen why Loftis called me, and went back two steps. See, 4-B's so small if you ring Miss Bailey's doorbell, the toilet'd flush. But her living room, webbed in dust, be filled to the max with dollars of all denominations, stacks of stock in General Motors, Gulf Oil, and 3M Company in old White Owl cigar boxes, battered purses, or bound in pink rubber bands. It be like the kind of cubby-hole kids play in, but filled with . . . *things*: everything, like a world inside the world, you take it from me, so like picturebook scenes of plentifulness you could seal yourself off in here and settle forever. Loftis and me both drew breath suddenly. There be unopened cases of Jack Daniel's, three safes cemented to the floor, hundreds of matchbooks, unworn clothes, a fuel-burning stove, dozens of wedding rings, rubbish, World War II magazines, a carton of a hundred canned sardines, mink stoles, old rags, a birdcage, a bucket of silver dollars, thousands of books, paintings, quarters in tobacco cans, two pianos, glass jars of pennies, a set of bagpipes, an almost complete Model A Ford dappled with rust, and, I swear, three sections of a dead tree.

"Damn!" My head be light; I sat on an upended peach crate and picked up a bottle of Jack Daniel's.

"Don't you touch *any*thing!" Loftis, he panting a little; he slap both hands on a table. "Not until we inventory this stuff."

"Inventory? Aw, Lord, Loftis," I say, "something ain't *right* about this stash. There could be a curse on it. . . ."

"Boy, sometime you act weak-minded."

"For real, Loftis, I got a feeling. . . ."

Loftis, he shucked off his shoes, and sat down heavily on the lumpy arm of a stuffed chair. "Don't say *any*thing." He chewed his knuckles, and for the first time Loftis looked like he didn't know his next move. "Let me think, okay?" He squeezed his nose in a way he has when thinking hard, sighed, then stood up and say, "There's something you better see in that bedroom yonder. Cover up your mouth."

"Loftis, I ain't going in there."

He look at me right funny then. "She's a miser, that's all. She saves things."

"But a tree?" I say. "Loftis, a *tree* ain't normal!"

"Cooter, I ain't gonna tell you twice."

Like always, I followed Loftis, who swung his flashlight from the plant—he a night watchman—into Miss Bailey's bedroom, but me, I'm thinking how trippy this thing is getting, remembering how, last year, when I had a paper route, the old lady, with her queer, crablike walk, pulled my coat for some change in the hallway, and when I give her a handful of dimes, she say, like one of them spooks on old-time radio, "Thank you, Co-o-oter," then gulped the coins down like aspirin, no lie, and scurried off like a hunchback. Me, I wanted no parts of this squirrely old broad, but Loftis, he holding my wrist now, beaming his light onto a low bed. The room had a funny, museumlike smell. Real sour. It was full of dirty laundry. And I be sure the old lady's stuff had a terrible string attached when Loftis, looking away, lifted her bedsheets and a knot of black flies rose. I stepped back and held my breath. Miss Bailey be in her long-sleeved flannel nightgown, bloated, like she'd been blown up by a bicycle pump, her old face caved in with rot, fly-blown, her fingers big and colored like spoiled bananas. Her wristwatch be ticking softly beside a half-eaten hamburger. Above the bed, her wall had roaches squashed in little swirls of bloodstain. Maggots clustered in her eyes, her ears, and one fist-sized rat hissed inside her flesh. My eyes snapped shut. My knees failed; then I did a Hollywood faint. When I surfaced, Loftis, he be sitting beside me in the living room, where he'd drug me, reading a wrinkled, yellow article from the *Chicago Daily Defender*.

"Listen to this," Loftis say. "Elnora Bailey, forty-five, a Negro house-maid in the Highland Park home of Henry Conners, is the beneficiary of her employer's will. An old American family, the Conners arrived in this country on the *Providence* shortly after the voyage of the *Mayflower*. The family flourished in the early days of the 1900s.' . . ." He went on, getting breath: "'A distinguished and wealthy industrialist, without heirs or a wife, Conners willed his entire estate to Miss Bailey of 3347 North Clark Street for her twenty years of service to his family.' . . ." Loftis, he give that Geoffrey Holder laugh of his, low and deep; then it eased up his throat until it hit a high note and tipped his head back onto his shoulders. "Cooter, that was before we was born! Miss Bailey kept this in the Bible next to her bed."

Standing, I braced myself with one hand against the wall. "She didn't earn it?"

"Naw." Loftis, he folded the paper—"Not one penny"—and stuffed it in his shirt pocket. His jaw looked tight as a horseshoe. "Way I see it," he say, "this was her one shot in a lifetime to be rich, but being country, she had backward ways and blew it." Rubbing his hands, he stood up to survey the living room. "Somebody's gonna find Miss Bailey soon, but if we stay on the case—Cooter, don't square up on me now—we can tote everything to our place before daybreak. Best we start with the big stuff."

"But why didn't she *use* it, huh? Tell me that?"

Loftis, he don't pay me no mind. When he gets an idea in his head, you can't dig it out with a chisel. How long it took me and Loftis to inventory, then haul Miss Bailey's queer old stuff to our crib, I can't say, but that cranky old ninnyhammer's hoard come to $879,543 in cash money, thirty-two bank books (some deposits be only $5), and me, I wasn't sure I was dreaming or what, but I suddenly flashed on this feeling, once we left her flat, that all the fears Loftis and me had about the future be gone, 'cause Miss Bailey's property was the past—the power of that fellah Henry Conners trapped like a bottle spirit—which we could live off, so it was the future, too, pure potential: can *do*. Loftis got to talking on about how that piano we pushed home be equal to a thousand bills, jim, which equals, say, a bad TEAC A-3340 tape deck, or a down payment on a deuce-and-a-quarter. Its value be (Loftis say) that of a universal standard of measure, relational, unreal as number, so that tape deck could turn, magically, into two gold lamé suits, a trip to Tijuana, or twenty-five blow jobs from a ho—we had $879,543 worth of wishes, if you can deal with that. Be like Miss Bailey's stuff is raw energy, and Loftis and me, like wizards, could transform her stuff into anything else at will. All we had to do, it seemed to me, was decide exactly what to exchange it for.

While Loftis studied this over (he looked funny, like a potato trying to say something, after the inventory, and sat, real quiet, in the kitchen), I filled my pockets with fifties, grabbed me a cab downtown to grease, yum, at one of them high-hat restaurants in the Loop. . . . But then I thought better of it, you know, like I'd be out of place—just another jig putting on airs—and scarfed instead at a ribjoint till both my eyes bubbled. This fat lady making fishburgers in the back favored an old hardleg baby-sitter I once had, a Mrs. Paine who made me eat ocher,[1] and I wanted so bad to say, "Loftis and me Got Ovuh," but I couldn't put that in the wind, could I, so I hatted up. Then I copped a boss silk necktie, cashmere socks, and a whistle-slick maxi leather jacket on State Street, took cabs *every*where, but when I got home that evening, a funny, Pandora-like feeling hit me. I took off the jacket, boxed it—it looked trifling in the hallway's weak light—and, tired, turned my key in the door. I couldn't get in. Loftis, he'd changed the lock and, when he finally let me in, looking vaguer, crabby, like something out of the Book of Revelations, I seen this elaborate, booby-trapped tunnel of cardboard and razor blades behind him, with a two-foot space just big enough for him or me to crawl through. That wasn't all. Two bags of trash from the furnace room downstairs be sitting inside the door. Loftis, he give my leather jacket this evil look, hauled me inside, and hit me upside my head.

"How much this thing set us back?"

"Two fifty." My jaws got tight; I toss him my receipt. "You want me to take it back? Maybe I can get something else. . . ."

Loftis, he say, not to me, but to the receipt, "Remember the time Mama give me that ring we had in the family for fifty years? And I took it to Merchandise Mart and sold it for a few pieces of candy?" He hitched his chair forward and sat with his elbows on his knees. "That's what you did, Cooter. You crawled into a Clark bar." He commence to rip up my receipt, then picked up his flashlight and keys. "As soon as you buy something you *lose* the power to buy something." He button up his coat with holes in the elbows, showing his blue shirt, then turned 'round at the tunnel to say, "Don't touch Miss Bailey's money, or drink her splo, or do *any*thing until I get back."

"Where you going?"

"To work. It's Wednesday, ain't it?"

"You going to work?"

"Yeah."

"You got to go *really*? Loftis," I say, "what you brang them bags of trash in here for?"

"It ain't trash!" He cut his eyes at me. "There's good clothes in there. Mr. Peterson tossed them out, he don't care, but I saw some use in them, that's all."

"Loftis . . ."

"Yeah?"

"What we gonna do with all this money?"

Loftis pressed his fingers to his eyelids, and for a second he looked caged, or like somebody'd kicked him in his stomach. Then he cut me some

---

1. Okra.

slack: "Let me think on it tonight—it don't pay to rush—then we can TCB, okay?"

Five hours after Loftis leave for work, that old blister Mr. Peterson, our landlord, he come collecting rent, find Mrs. Bailey's body in apartment 4-B, and phoned the fire department. Me, I be folding my new jacket in tissue paper to keep it fresh, adding the box to Miss Bailey's unsunned treasures when two paramedics squeezed her on a long stretcher through a crowd in the hallway. See, I had to pin her from the stairhead, looking down one last time at this dizzy old lady, and I seen something in her face, like maybe she'd been poor as Job's turkey for thirty years, suffering that special Negro fear of using up what little we get in this life—Loftis, he call that entropy—believing in her belly, and for all her faith, jim, that there just ain't no more coming tomorrow from grace, or the Lord, or from her own labor, like she can't kill nothing, and won't nothing die . . . so when Conners will her his wealth, it put her through changes, she be spellbound, possessed by the promise of life, panicky about depletion, and locked now in the past 'cause every purchase, you know, has to be a poor buy: a loss of life. Me, I wasn't worried none. Loftis, he got a brain trained by years of talking trash with people in Frog Hudson's barbershop on Thirty-fifth Street. By morning, I knew, he'd have some kinda wheeze worked out.

But Loftis, he don't come home. Me, I got kinda worried. I listen to the hi-fi all day Thursday, only pawing outside to peep down the stairs, like that'd make Loftis come sooner. So Thursday go by; and come Friday the head's out of kilter—first there's an ogrelike belch from the toilet bowl, then water bursts from the bathroom into the kitchen—and me, I can't call the super (How do I explain the tunnel?), so I gave up and quit bailing. But on Saturday, I could smell greens cooking next door. Twice I almost opened Miss Bailey's sardines, even though starving be less an evil than eating up our stash, but I waited till it was dark and, with my stomach talking to me, stepped outside to Pookie White's lay a hard-luck story on him, and Pookie, he give me some jambalaya and gumbo. Back home in the living room, finger-feeding myself, barricaded in by all that hope-made material, the Kid felt like a king in his counting room, and I copped some Zs in an armchair till I heard the door move on its hinges, then bumping in the tunnel, and a heavy-footed walk thumped into the bedroom.

"Loftis?" I rubbed my eyes. "You back?" It be Sunday morning. Six-thirty sharp. Darkness dissolved slowly into the strangeness of twilight, with the rays of sunlight surging at exactly the same angle they fall each evening, as if the hour be an island, a moment outside time. Me, I'm afraid Loftis gonna fuss 'bout my not straightening up, letting things go. I went into the bathroom, poured water in the one-spigot washstand—brown rust come bursting out in flakes—and rinsed my face. "Loftis, you supposed to be home four days ago. Hey," I say, toweling my face, "you okay?" How come he don't answer me? Wiping my hands on the seat on my trousers, I tipped into Loftis's room. He sleeping with his mouth open. His legs be drawn up, both fists clenched between his knees. He'd kicked his blanket on the floor. In his sleep, Loftis laughed, or moaned, it be hard to tell. His eyelids, not quite shut, show slits of white. I decided to wait till Loftis wake up for his decision, but turning, I seen his watch, keys, and what looked in the first stain of sunlight to be a carefully wrapped piece of newspaper on his nightstand. The sunlight swelled to a bright shimmer, focusing the bedroom slowly like solution do a photographic image in the developer. And then something so freakish went down I ain't sure it took place. Fumble-fingered, I unfolded the paper, and inside be a blemished penny. It be like suddenly somebody slapped my head from behind. Taped on the penny be a slip of paper, and on the paper be the note "Found while walking down Devon Avenue." I hear Loftis mumble like he trapped in a nightmare. "Hold tight," I whisper. "It's all right." Me, I wanted to tell Loftis how Miss Bailey looked four days ago, that maybe it didn't have to be like that for us—did it?— because we could change. Couldn't we? Me, I pull his packed sheets over him, wrap up the penny, and, when I locate Miss Bailey's glass jar in the living room, put it away carefully, for now, with the rest of our things.

Leslie Marmon Silko
(1948–)

Leslie Marmon Silko, born in Albuquerque, New Mexico, was brought up on the nearby Laguna Pueblo Reservation where both the whites and the Native Americans of her ancestry had lived for several generations. As a child she learned from her great-aunt and her great-grandmother the traditional stories of their tribe. Her first publication, Laguna Woman; Poems *(1974) acknowledges her debt to them.*

Ceremony (1977), her widely acclaimed first novel, deals with the suffering of Tayo, a mixed-blood veteran of World War II who is haunted by his experiences, especially because he saw a resemblance between the Japanese enemy he was ordered to kill and his own uncle. His mental healing is achieved with the help of the mixed-blood healer, Old Betonie, who uses traditional ritual to bring Tayo into harmony with his culture and with nature.

During a period of living with Inuit tribespeople in Bethel, Alaska, Silko learned the myths of that Native American culture and blended those myths with her own family background and Laguna tradition in a collection of poetry, photographs, and stories called Storyteller, *published in 1981.*

*The same year she was awarded a MacArthur Foundation Fellowship,
enabling her to take a leave from her teaching position at the University of
Arizona and concentrate on her writing.*

Silko's second novel, Almanac of the Dead *(1991), set mostly in present-
day Arizona and Mexico, is an ambitious polemic, woven of history, myth,
and fiction. Opposed in deadly struggle are the ecologically destructive
ways of the European invaders and the earth-centered traditions of the
Native Americans.*

The Delicacy and Strength of Lace (1986), edited by Anne Wright, records Silko's
correspondence with the poet James Wright. The present text is taken from *Storyteller*.

———

The Man to Send Rain Clouds

THEY FOUND HIM under a big cottonwood tree. His Levi jacket and pants
were faded light blue so that he had been easy to find. The big cotton-wood
tree stood apart from a small grove of winterbare cottonwoods which grew
in the wide, sandy arroyo. He had been dead for a day or more, and the
sheep had wandered and scattered up and down the arroyo. Leon and his
brother-in-law, Ken, gathered the sheep and left them in the pen at the sheep
camp before they returned to the cottonwood tree. Leon waited under the
tree while Ken drove the truck through the deep sand to the edge of the
arroyo. He squinted up at the sun and unzipped his jacket—it sure was hot
for this time of year. But high and northwest the blue mountains were still
in snow. Ken came sliding down the low, crumbling bank about fifty yards
down, and he was bringing the red blanket.

Before they wrapped the old man, Leon took a piece of string out of his
pocket and tied a small gray feather in the old man's long white hair. Ken
gave him the paint. Across the brown wrinkled forehead he drew a streak of
white and along the high cheekbones he drew a strip of blue paint. He
paused and watched Ken throw pinches of corn meal and pollen into the
wind that fluttered the small gray feather. Then Leon painted with yellow
under the old man's broad nose, and finally, when he had painted green
across the chin, he smiled.

"Send us rain clouds, Grandfather." They laid the bundle in the back of the pickup and covered it with a heavy tarp before they started back to the pueblo.

They turned off the highway onto the sandy pueblo road. Not long after they passed the store and post office they saw Father Paul's car coming toward them. When he recognized their faces he slowed his car and waved for them to stop. The young priest rolled down the car window.

"Did you find old Teofilo?" he asked loudly.

Leon stopped the truck. "Good morning, Father. We were just out to the sheep camp. Everything is O.K. now."

"Thank God for that. Teofilo is a very old man. You really shouldn't allow him to stay at the sheep camp alone."

"No, he won't do that any more now."

"Well, I'm glad you understand. I hope I'll be seeing you at Mass this week—we missed you last Sunday. See if you can get old Teofilo to come with you." The priest smiled and waved at them as they drove away.

Louise and Teresa were waiting. The table was set for lunch, and the coffee was boiling on the black iron stove. Leon looked at Louise and then at Teresa.

"We found him under a cottonwood tree in the big arroyo near sheep camp. I guess he sat down to rest in the shade and never got up again." Leon walked toward the old man's bed. The red plaid shawl had been shaken and spread carefully over the bed, and a new brown flannel shirt and pair of stiff new Levi's were arranged neatly beside the pillow. Louise held the screen door open while Leon and Ken carried in the red blanket. He looked small and shriveled, and after they dressed him in the new shirt and pants he seemed more shrunken.

It was noontime now because the church bells rang the Angelus. They ate the beans with hot bread, and nobody said anything until after Teresa poured the coffee.

Ken stood up and put on his jacket. "I'll see about the gravediggers. Only the top layer of soil is frozen. I think it can be ready before dark."

Leon nodded his head and finished his coffee. After Ken had been gone for a while, the neighbors and clanspeople came quietly to embrace Teofilo's family and to leave food on the table because the gravediggers would come to eat when they were finished.

The sky in the west was full of pale yellow light. Louise stood outside with her hands in the pockets of Leon's green army jacket that was too big for her. The funeral was over, and the old men had taken their candles and medicine bags and were gone. She waited until the body was laid into the pickup before she said anything to Leon. She touched his arm, and he noticed that her hands were still dusty from the corn meal that she had sprinkled around the old man. When she spoke, Leon could not hear her.

"What did you say? I didn't hear you."

"I said that I had been thinking about something."

"About what?"

"About the priest sprinkling holy water for Grandpa. So he won't be thirsty."

Leon stared at the new moccasins that Teofilo had made for the ceremonial dances in the summer. They were nearly hidden by the red blanket. It was getting colder, and the wind pushed gray dust down the narrow pueblo road. The sun was approaching the long mesa where it disappeared during the winter. Louise stood there shivering and watching his face. Then he zipped up his jacket and opened the truck door. "I'll see if he's there."

Ken stopped the pickup at the church, and Leon got out; and then Ken drove down the hill to the graveyard where people were waiting. Leon knocked at the old carved door with its symbols of the Lamb. While he waited he looked up at the twin bells from the king of Spain with the last sunlight pouring around them in their tower.

The priest opened the door and smiled when he saw who it was. "Come in! What brings you here this evening?"

The priest walked toward the kitchen, and Leon stood with his cap in his hand, playing with the earflaps and examining the living room—the brown sofa, the green armchair, and the brass lamp that hung down from the ceiling by links of chain. The priest dragged a chair out of the kitchen and offered it to Leon.

"No thank you, Father. I only came to ask you if you would bring your holy water to the graveyard."

The priest turned away from Leon and looked out the window at the patio full of shadows and the dining-room windows of the nuns' cloister across the patio. The curtains were heavy, and the light from within faintly penetrated; it was impossible to see the nuns inside eating supper. "Why didn't you tell me he was dead? I could have brought the Last Rites anyway."

Leon smiled. "It wasn't necessary, Father."

The priest stared down at his scuffed brown loafers and the worn hem of his cassock. "For a Christian burial it was necessary."

His voice was distant, and Leon thought that his blue eyes looked tired.

"It's O.K. Father, we just want him to have plenty of water."

The priest sank down into the green chair and picked up a glossy missionary magazine. He turned the colored pages full of lepers and pagans without looking at them.

"You know I can't do that, Leon. There should have been the Last Rites and a funeral Mass at the very least."

Leon put on his green cap and pulled the flaps down over his ears. "It's getting late, Father. I've got to go."

When Leon opened the door Father Paul stood up and said, "Wait." He left the room and came back wearing a long brown overcoat. He followed Leon out the door and across the dim churchyard to the adobe steps in front of the church. They both stooped to fit through the low adobe entrance. And when they started down the hill to the graveyard only half of the sun was visible above the mesa.

The priest approached the grave slowly, wondering how they had managed to dig into the frozen ground; and then he remembered that this was New Mexico, and saw the pile of cold loose sand beside the hole. The people stood close to each other with little clouds of steam puffing from their faces. The priest looked at them and saw a pile of jackets, gloves, and scarves in the yellow, dry tumbleweeds that grew in the graveyard. He looked at the red blanket, not sure that Teofilo was so small, wondering if it wasn't some perverse Indian trick—something they did in March to ensure a good harvest—wondering if maybe old Teofilo was actually at sheep camp corraling the sheep for the night. But there he was, facing into a cold dry wind and squinting at the last sunlight, ready to bury a red wool blanket while the faces of his parishioners were in shadow with the last warmth of the sun on their backs.

His fingers were stiff, and it took him a long time to twist the lid off the holy water. Drops of water fell on the red blanket and soaked into dark icy spots. He sprinkled the grave and the water disappeared almost before it touched the dim, cold sand; it reminded him of something—he tried to remember what it was, because he thought if he could remember he might understand this. He sprinkled more water; he shook the container until it was empty, and the water fell through the light from sundown like August rain that fell while the sun was still shining, almost evaporating before it touched the wilted squash flowers.

The wind pulled at the priest's brown Franciscan robe and swirled away the corn meal and pollen that had been sprinkled on the blanket. They lowered the bundle into the ground, and they didn't bother to untie the stiff pieces of new rope that were tied around the ends of the blanket. The sun was gone, and over on the highway the eastbound lane was full of headlights. The priest walked away slowly. Leon watched him climb the hill, and when he had disappeared within the tall, thick walls, Leon turned to look up at the high blue mountains in the deep snow that reflected a faint red light from the west. He felt good because it was finished, and he was happy about the sprinkling of the holy water; now the old man could send them big thunder-clouds for sure.

Jamaica Kincaid
(1949–)

Born in St. John's, Antigua, West Indies, as Elaine Potter Richardson, Kincaid was raised in poverty and educated in government schools in what was then a British colony. At seventeen, she left home to become a babysitter in Scarsdale, New York. Hoping to attend college, but unprepared by her West Indian schooling, she attended night classes, then left her position in Scarsdale for three years as an au pair *girl on New York's Upper East Side. After earning a high school diploma, she took classes at the New School for Social Research and spent a year on a scholarship at Franconia College in New Hampshire before returning to New York, where she changed her name to Jamaica Kincaid and began to write. Acquaintance with a writer for* The New Yorker *led to pieces in "The Talk of the Town" and eventually to fiction.*

"When I left home," she has said, "I never wanted to know another Antiguan." For nineteen years she didn't see her mother. Yet her life experiences have become the stuff of her fiction. "I'm someone who writes to save her life," she has said. "I mean, I can't imagine what I would do if I didn't write. I would be dead or I would be in jail because—what else could I do?" At the Bottom of the River (1983) is a collection of stories focused on girlhood experience in Antigua. The novel Annie John (1985) ranges over similar material to tell of a girl's growing up. The heroine of Lucy (1990) comes from her island home to be a nursemaid in New York.

Mariah[1]

ONE MORNING IN EARLY MARCH, Mariah said to me, "You have never seen spring, have you?" And she did not have to await an answer, for she already knew. She said the word "spring" as if spring were a close friend, a friend who had dared to go away for a long time and soon would reappear for their passionate reunion. She said, "Have you ever seen daffodils pushing their way up out of the ground? And when they're in bloom and all massed together, a breeze comes along and makes them do a curtsy to the lawn stretching out in front of them. Have you ever seen that? When I see that, I feel so glad to be alive." And I thought, So Mariah is made to feel alive by some flowers bending in the breeze. How does a person get to be that way?

I remembered an old poem I had been made to memorize when I was ten years old and a pupil at Queen Victoria Girls' School. I had been made to memorize it, verse after verse, and then had recited the whole poem to an auditorium full of parents, teachers, and my fellow pupils. After I was done, everybody stood up and applauded with an enthusiasm that surprised me, and later they told me how nicely I had pronounced every word, how I had placed just the right amount of special emphasis in places where that was needed, and how proud the poet, now long dead, would have been to hear his words ringing out of my mouth. I was then at the height of my two-faced-ness: that is, outside I seemed one way, inside I was another; outside false, inside true. And so I made pleasant little noises that showed both modesty and appreciation, but inside I was making a vow to erase from my mind, line by line, every word of that poem. The night after I had recited the poem, I dreamt, continously it seemed, that I was being chased down a narrow cobbled street by bunches and bunches of those same daffodils that I had vowed to forget, and when finally I fell down from exhaustion they all piled on top of me, until I was buried deep underneath them and was never seen again. I had forgotten all of this until Mariah mentioned daffodils, and now I told it to her with such an amount of anger I surprised both of us. We were standing quite close to each other, but as soon as I had finished speaking, without a second of deliberation we both stepped back. It was only one step that was made, but to me it felt as if something that I had not been aware of had been checked.

Mariah reached out to me and, rubbing her hand against my cheek, said, "What a history you have." I thought there was a little bit of envy in her voice, and so I said, "You are welcome to it if you like."

After that, each day, Mariah began by saying, "As soon as spring

---

1. First published in *The New Yorker*, "Mariah" forms a part of the novel *Lucy* (1990), the source of the present text.

comes," and so many plans would follow that I could not see how one little spring could contain them. She said we would leave the city and go to the house on one of the Great Lakes, the house where she spent her summers when she was a girl. We would visit some great gardens. We would visit the zoo—a nice thing to do in springtime; the children would love that. We would have a picnic in the park as soon as the first unexpected and unusually warm day arrived. An early-evening walk in the spring air—that was something she really wanted to do with me, to show me the magic of a spring sky.

On the very day it turned spring, a big snowstorm came, and more snow fell on that day than had fallen all winter. Mariah looked at me and shrugged her shoulders. "How typical," she said, giving the impression that she had just experienced a personal betrayal. I laughed at her, but I was really wondering, How do you get to be a person who is made miserable because the weather changed its mind, because the weather doesn't live up to your expectations? How do you get to be that way?

While the weather sorted itself out in various degrees of coldness, I walked around with letters from my family and friends scorching my breasts. I had placed these letters inside my brassiere, and carried them around with me wherever I went. It was not from feelings of love and longing that I did this; quite the contrary. It was from a feeling of hatred. There was nothing so strange about this, for isn't it so that love and hate exist side by side? Each letter was a letter from someone I had loved at one time without reservation. Not too long before, out of politeness, I had written my mother a very nice letter, I thought, telling her about the first ride I had taken in an underground train. She wrote back to me, and after I read her letter, I was afraid to even put my face outside the door. The letter was filled with detail after detail of horrible and vicious things she had read or heard about that had taken place on those very same underground trains on which I traveled. Only the other day, she wrote, she had read of an immigrant girl, someone my age exactly, who had had her throat cut while she was a passenger on perhaps the very same train I was riding.

But, of course, I had already known real fear. I had known a girl, a schoolmate of mine, whose father had dealings with the Devil. Once, out of curiosity, she had gone into a room where her father did his business, and she had looked into things that she should not have, and she became possessed. She took sick, and we, my other schoolmates and I, used to stand in the street outside her house on our way home from school and hear her being beaten by what possessed her, and hear her as she cried out from the beatings. Eventually she had to cross the sea, where the Devil couldn't follow her, because the Devil cannot walk over water. I thought of this as I felt the sharp corners of the letters cutting into the skin over my heart. I thought, On the one hand there was a girl being beaten by a man she could not see; on the other there was a girl getting her throat cut by a man she could see. In this great big world, why should my life be reduced to these two possibilities?

When the snow fell, it came down in thick, heavy glops, and hung on the trees like decorations ordered for a special occasion—a celebration no one had heard of, for everybody complained. In all the months that I had lived in this place, snowstorms had come and gone and I had never paid any attention, except to feel that snow was an annoyance when I had to make my way through the mounds of it that lay on the sidewalk. My parents used to go every Christmas Eve to a film that had Bing Crosby standing waist-deep in snow and singing a song at the top of his voice. My mother once told me that seeing this film was among the first things they did when they were getting to know each other, and at the time she told me this I felt strongly how much I no longer liked even the way she spoke; and so I said, barely concealing my scorn, "What a religious experience that must have been." I walked away quickly, for my thirteen-year-old heart couldn't bear to see her face when I had caused her pain, but I couldn't stop myself.

In any case, this time when the snow fell, even I could see that there was something to it—it had a certain kind of beauty; not a beauty you would wish for every day of your life, but a beauty you could appreciate if you had an excess of beauty to begin with. The days were longer now, the sun set later, the evening sky seemed lower than usual, and the snow was the color and texture of a half-cooked egg white, making the world seem soft and lovely and—unexpectedly, to me—nourishing. That the world I was in could be soft, lovely, and nourishing was more than I could bear, and so I stood there and wept, for I didn't want to love one more thing in my life, didn't want one more thing that could make my heart break into a million little pieces at my feet. But all the same, there it was, and I could not do much about it; for even I could see that I was too young for real bitterness, real regret, real hard-heartedness.

The snow came and went more quickly than usual. Mariah said that the way the snow vanished, as if some hungry being were invisibly swallowing it up, was quite normal for that time of year. Everything that had seemed so brittle in the cold of winter—sidewalks, buildings, trees, the people themselves—seemed to slacken and sag a bit at the seams. I could now look back at the winter. It was my past, so to speak, my first real past—a past that was my own and over which I had the final word. I had just lived through a bleak and cold time, and it is not to the weather outside that I refer. I had lived through this time, and as the weather changed from cold to warm it did not bring me along with it. Something settled inside me, something heavy and hard. It stayed there, and I could not think of one thing to make it go away. I thought, So this must be living, this must be the beginning of the time people later refer to as "years ago, when I was young."

My mother had a friendship with a woman—a friendship she did not advertise, for this woman had spent time in jail. Her name was Sylvie; she had a scar on her right cheek, a human-teeth bite. It was as if her cheek were a half-ripe fruit and someone had bitten into it, meaning to eat it, but then realized it wasn't ripe enough. She had gotten into a big quarrel with another woman over this: which of the two of them a man they both loved should live with. Apparently Sylvie said something that was unforgivable, and the other woman flew into an even deeper rage and grabbed Sylvie in an embrace, only it was not an embrace of love but an embrace of hatred, and she left Sylvie with the marked cheek. Both women were sent to jail for public misconduct, and going to jail was something that for the rest of their lives no one would let them forget. It was because of this that I was not allowed to speak to Sylvie, that she was not allowed to visit us when my father was at home, and that my mother's friendship with her was supposed to be a secret. I used to observe Sylvie, and I noticed that whenever she stopped to speak, even in the briefest conversation, immediately her hand would go up to her face and caress her little rosette (before I knew what it was, I was sure that the mark on her face was a rose she had put there on purpose because she loved the beauty of roses so much she wanted to wear one on her face), and it was as if the mark on her face bound her to something much deeper than its reality, something that she could not put into words. One day, outside my mother's presence, she admired the way my corkscrew plaits fell around my neck, and then she said something that I did not hear, for she began by saying, "Years ago when I was young," and she pinched up her scarred cheek with her fingers and twisted it until I thought it would fall off like a dark, purple plum in the middle of her pink palm, and her voice became heavy and hard, even though she was laughing all the time she spoke. That is how I came to think that heavy and hard was the beginning of living, real living; and though I might not end up with a mark on my cheek, I had no doubt that I would end up with a mark somewhere.

I was standing in front of the kitchen sink one day, my thoughts centered, naturally, on myself, when Mariah came in—danced in, actually—singing an old song, a song that was popular when her mother was a young woman, a song she herself most certainly would have disliked when she was a young woman and so she now sang it with an exaggerated tremor in her voice to show how ridiculous she still found it. She twirled herself wildly around the room and came to a sharp stop without knocking over anything, even though many things were in her path.

She said, "I have always wanted four children, four girl children. I love my children." She said this clearly and sincerely. She said this without doubt on the one hand or confidence on the other. Mariah was beyond doubt or confidence. I thought, Things must have always gone her way, and not just for her but for everybody she has ever known from eternity; she has never had to doubt, and so she has never had to grow confident; the right thing always happens to her; the thing she wants to happen happens. Again I thought, How does a person get to be that way?

Mariah said to me, "I love you." And again she said it clearly and sincerely, without confidence or doubt. I believed her, for if anyone could love a young woman who had come from halfway around the world to help her take care of her children, it was Mariah. She looked so beautiful standing there in the middle of the kitchen. The yellow light from the sun came in through a window and fell on the pale-yellow linoleum tiles of the floor, and on the walls of the kitchen, which were painted yet another shade of pale yellow, and Mariah, with her pale-yellow skin and yellow hair, stood still in this almost celestial light, and she looked blessed, no blemish or mark of any kind on her cheek or anywhere else, as if she had never quarreled with anyone over a man or over anything, would never have to quarrel at all, had never done anything wrong and had never been to jail, had never had to leave anywhere for any reason other than a feeling that had come over her. She had washed her hair that morning and from where I stood I could smell the residue of the perfume from the shampoo in her hair. Then underneath that I could smell Mariah herself. The smell of Mariah was pleasant. Just that—pleasant. And I thought, But that's the trouble with Mariah—she smells pleasant. By then I already knew that I wanted to have a powerful odor and would not care if it gave offense.

On a day on which it was clear that there was no turning back as far as the weather was concerned, that the winter season was over and its return would be a noteworthy event, Mariah said that we should prepare to go and spend some time at the house on the shore of one of the Great Lakes. Lewis would not accompany us. Lewis would stay in town and take advantage of our absence, doing things that she and the children would not enjoy doing with him. What these things were I could not imagine. Mariah said we would take a train, for she wanted me to experience spending the night on a train and waking up to breakfast on the train as it moved through freshly plowed fields. She made so many arrangements—I had not known that just leaving your house for a short time could be so complicated.

Early that afternoon, because the children, my charges, would not return home from school until three, Mariah took me to a garden, a place she described as among her favorites in the world. She covered my eyes with a handkerchief, and then, holding me by the hand, she walked me to a spot in a clearing. Then she removed the handkerchief and said, "Now, look at this." I looked. It was a big area with lots of thick-trunked, tall trees along winding paths. Along the paths and underneath the trees were many, many yellow flowers the size and shape of play teacups, or fairy skirts. They looked like something to eat and something to wear at the same time; they looked beautiful; they looked simple, as if made to erase a complicated and unnecessary idea. I did not know what these flowers were, and so it was a mystery to me why I wanted to kill them. Just like that. I wanted to kill them. I wished that I had an enormous scythe; I would just walk down the path, dragging it alongside me, and I would cut these flowers down at the place where they emerged from the ground.

Mariah said, "These are daffodils. I'm sorry about the poem, but I'm hoping you'll find them lovely all the same."

There was such joy in her voice as she said this, such a music, how could I explain to her the feeling I had about daffodils—that it wasn't exactly daffodils, but that they would do as well as anything else? Where should I start? Over here or over there? Anywhere would be good enough, but my heart and my thoughts were racing so that every time I tried to talk I stammered and by accident bit my own tongue.

Mariah, mistaking what was happening to me for joy at seeing daffodils for the first time, reached out to hug me, but I moved away, and in doing that I seemed to get my voice back. I said, "Mariah, do you realize that at ten years of age I had to learn by heart a long poem about some flowers I would not see in real life until I was nineteen?"

As soon as I said this, I felt sorry that I had cast her beloved daffodils in a scene she had never considered, a scene of conquered and conquests; a scene of brutes masquerading as angels and angels portrayed as brutes. This woman who hardly knew me loved me, and she wanted me to love this thing—a grove brimming over with daffodils in bloom—that she loved also. Her eyes sank back in her head as if they were protecting themselves, as if they were taking a rest after some unexpected hard work. It wasn't her fault. It wasn't my fault. But nothing could change the fact that where she saw beautiful flowers I saw sorrow and bitterness. The same thing could cause us to shed tears, but those tears would not taste the same. We walked home in silence. I was glad to have at last seen what a wretched daffodil looked like.

When the day came for us to depart to the house on the Great Lake, I was sure that I did not want to go, but at midmorning I received a letter from my mother bringing me up to date on things she thought I would have missed since I left home and would certainly like to know about. "It still has not rained since you left," she wrote. "How fascinating," I said to myself with bitterness. It had not rained once for over a year before I left. I did not care about that any longer. The object of my life now was to put as much distance between myself and the events mentioned in her letter as I could manage. For I felt that if I could put enough miles between me and the place from which that letter came, and if I could put enough events between me and the events mentioned in the letter, would I not be free to take everything just as it came and not see hundreds of years in every gesture, every word spoken, every face?

On the train, we settled ourselves and the children into our compartments—two children with Mariah, two children with me. In one of the few films I had seen in my life so far, some people on a train did this—settled into their compartments. And so I suppose I should have felt excitement at doing something I had never done before and had only seen done in a film. But almost everything I did now was something I had never done before, and so the new was no longer thrilling to me unless it reminded me of the past. We went to the dining car to eat our dinner. We sat at tables—the children by themselves. They had demanded that, and had said to Mariah that they would behave, even though it was well known that they always did. The other people sitting down to eat dinner all looked like Mariah's relatives; the people waiting on them all looked like mine. The people who looked like my relatives were all older men and very dignified, as if they were just emerging from a church after Sunday service. On closer observation, they were not at all like my relatives; they only looked like them. My relatives always gave backchat. Mariah did not seem to notice what she had in common with the other diners, or what I had in common with the waiters. She acted in her usual way, which was that the world was round and we all agreed on that, when I knew that the world was flat and if I went to the edge I would fall off.

That night on the train was frightening. Every time I tried to sleep, just as it seemed that I had finally done so, I would wake up sure that thousands of people on horseback were following me, chasing me, each of them carrying a cutlass to cut me up into small pieces. Of course, I could tell it was the sound of the wheels on the tracks that inspired this nightmare, but a real explanation made no difference to me. Early that morning, Mariah left her own compartment to come and tell me that we were passing through some of those freshly plowed fields she loved so much. She drew up my blind, and when I saw mile after mile of turned-up earth, I said, a cruel tone to my voice, "Well, thank God I didn't have to do that." I don't know if she understood what I meant, for in that one statement I meant many different things.

When we got to our destination, a man Mariah had known all her life, a man who had always done things for her family, a man who came from Sweden, was waiting for us. His name was Gus, and the way Mariah spoke his name it was as if he belonged to her deeply, like a memory. And, of course, he was a part of her past, her childhood: he was there, apparently, when she took her first steps; she had caught her first fish in a boat with him; they had been in a storm on the lake and their survival was a miracle, and so on. Still, he was a real person, and I thought Mariah should have long separated the person Gus standing in front of her in the present from all the things he had meant to her in the past. I wanted to say to him, "Do you not hate the way she says your name, as if she owns you?" But then I though about it and could see that a person coming from Sweden was a person altogether different from a person like me.

We drove through miles and miles of country-side, miles and miles of nothing. I was glad not to live in a place like this. The land did not say, "Welcome. So glad you could come." It was more, "I dare you to stay here." At last we came to a small town. As we drove through it, Mariah became excited; her voice grew low, as if what she was saying only she needed to hear. She would exclaim with happiness or sadness, depending, as things passed before her. In the half a year or so since she had last been there, some things had changed, some things had newly arrived, and some things had vanished completely. As she passed through this town, she seemed to forget she was the wife of Lewis and the mother of four girl children. We left the small town and a silence fell on everybody, and in my own case I felt a kind of despair. I felt sorry for Mariah; I knew what she must have gone through, seeing her past go swiftly by in front of her. What an awful thing that is, as if the ground on which you are standing is being slowly pulled out from under your feet and beneath is nothing, a hole through which you fall forever.

The house in which Mariah had grown up was beautiful, I could immediately see that. It was large, sprawled out, as if rooms had been added onto it when needed, but added on all in the same style. It was modeled on the farmhouse that Mariah's grandfather grew up in, somewhere in Scandinavia. It had a nice veranda in front, a perfect place from which to watch rain fall. The whole house was painted a soothing yellow with white trim, which from afar looked warm and inviting. From my room I could see the lake. I had read of this lake in geography books, had read of its origins and its history, and now to see it up close was odd, for it looked so ordinary, gray, dirty, unfriendly, not a body of water to make up a song about. Mariah came in, and seeing me studying the water she flung her arms around me and said, "Isn't it great?" But I wasn't thinking that at all. I slept peacefully, without any troubling dreams to haunt me; it must have been that knowing there was a body of water outside my window, even though it was not the big blue sea I was used to, brought me some comfort.

Mariah wanted all of us, the children and me, to see things the way she did. She wanted us to enjoy the house, all its nooks and crannies, all its sweet smells, all its charms, just the way she had done as a child. The children were happy to see things her way. They would have had to be four small versions of myself not to fall at her feet in adoration. But I already had a mother who loved me, and I had come to see her love as a burden and had come to view with horror the sense of self-satisfaction it gave my mother to hear other people comment on her great love for me. I had come to feel that my mother's love for me was designed solely to make me into an echo of her; and I didn't know why, but I felt that I would rather be dead than become just an echo of someone. That was not a figure of speech. Those thoughts would have come as a complete surprise to my mother, for in her life she had found that her ways were the best ways to have, and she would have been mystified as to how someone who came from inside her would want to be anyone different from her. I did not have an answer to this myself. But there it was. Thoughts like these had brought me to be sitting on the edge of a Great Lake with a woman who wanted to show me her world and hoped that I would like it, too. Sometimes there is no escape, but often the effort of trying will do quite nicely for a while.

I was sitting on the veranda one day with these thoughts when I saw Mariah come up the path, holding in her hands six grayish-blackish fish. She said, "Taa-daah! Trout!" and made a big sweep with her hands, holding the fish up in the light, so that rainbowlike colors shone on their scales. She sang out, "I will make you fishers of men," and danced around me. After she stopped, she said, "Aren't they beautiful? Gus and I went out in my old boat—my very, very old boat—and we caught them. My fish. This is supper. Let's go feed the minions."

It's possible that what she really said was "millions," not "minions."

Certainly she said it in jest. But as we were cooking the fish, I was thinking about it. "Minions." A word like that would haunt someone like me; the place where I came from was a dominion of someplace else. I became so taken with the word "dominion" that I told Mariah this story: When I was about five years old or so, I had read to me for the first time the story of Jesus Christ feeding the multitudes with seven loaves and a few fishes. After my mother had finished reading this to me, I said to her, "But how did Jesus serve the fish? boiled or fried?" This made my mother look at me in amazement and shake her head. She then told everybody she met what I had said, and they would shake their heads and say, "What a child!" It wasn't really such an unusual question. In the place where I grew up, many people earned their living by being fishermen. Often, after a fisherman came in from sea and had distributed most of his fish to people with whom he had such an arrangement, he might save some of them, clean and season them, and build a fire, and he and his wife would fry them at the seashore and put them up for sale. It was quite a nice thing to sit on the sand under a tree, seeking refuge from the hot sun, and eat a perfectly fried fish as you took in the view of the beautiful blue sea, former home of the thing you were eating. When I had inquired about the way the fish were served with the loaves, to myself I had thought, Not only would the multitudes be pleased to have something to eat, not only would they marvel at the miracle of turning so little into so much, but they might go on to pass a judgment on the way the food tasted. I know it would have mattered to me. In our house, we all preferred boiled fish. It was a pity that the people who recorded their life with Christ never mentioned this small detail, a detail that would have meant a lot to me.

When I finished telling Mariah this, she looked at me, and her blue eyes (which I would have found beautiful even if I hadn't read millions of books in which blue eyes were always accompanied by the word "beautiful") grew dim as she slowly closed the lids over them, then bright again as she opened them wide and then wider.

A silence fell between us; it was a deep silence, but not too thick and not too black. Through it we could hear the clink of the cooking utensils as we cooked the fish Mariah's way, under flames in the oven, a way I did not like. And we could hear the children in the distance screaming—in pain or pleasure, I could not tell.

Mariah and I were saying good night to each other the way we always did, with a hug and a kiss, but this time we did it as if we both wished we hadn't gotten such a custom started. She was almost out of the room when she turned and said, "I was looking forward to telling you that I have Indian blood, that the reason I'm so good at catching fish and hunting birds and roasting corn and doing all sorts of things is that I have Indian blood. But now, I don't know why, I feel I shouldn't tell you that. I feel you will take it the wrong way."

This really surprised me. What way should I take this? Wrong way?

Right way? What could she mean? To look at her, there was nothing remotely like an Indian about her. Why claim a thing like that? I myself had Indian blood in me. My grandmother is a Carib Indian. That makes me one-quarter Carib Indian. But I don't go around saying that I have some Indian blood in me. The Carib Indians were good sailors, but I don't like to be on the sea; I only like to look at it. To me my grandmother is my grandmother, not an Indian. My grandmother is alive; the Indians she came from are all dead. If someone could get away with it, I am sure they would put my grandmother in a museum, as an example of something now extinct in nature, one of a handful still alive. In fact, one of the museums to which Mariah had taken me devoted a whole section to people, all dead, who were more or less related to my grandmother.

Mariah says, "I have Indian blood in me," and underneath everything I could swear she says it as if she were announcing her possession of a trophy. How do you get to be the sort of victor who can claim to be the vanquished also?

I now heard Mariah say, "Well," and she let out a long breath, full of sadness, resignation, even dread. I looked at her; her face was miserable, tormented, ill-looking. She looked at me in a pleading way, as if asking for relief, and I looked back, my face and my eyes hard; no matter what, I would not give it.

I said, "All along I have been wondering how you got to be the way you are. Just how it was that you got to be the way you are."

Even now she couldn't let go, and she reached out, her arms open wide, to give me one of her great hugs. But I stepped out of its path quickly, and she was left holding nothing. I said it again. I said, "How do you get to be that way?" The anguish on her face almost broke my heart, but I would not bend. It was hollow, my triumph, I could feel that, but I held on to it just the same.

Amy Tan
(1952–)

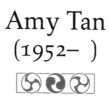

Amy Tan is one of three children born to a Chinese immigrant family settled in Oakland, California. Her parents stressed educational achievement and hoped that she would become a neurosurgeon and an accomplished pianist. She chose instead to study English and linguistics, earning her bachelor and master's degrees from San Jose State University and studying toward a Ph.D. at the University of California, Berkeley.

After several years as an educational administrator and free lance business writer, she turned to writing fiction. Drawing on the narratives of her childhood—family memories, Chinese fairy stories, and the parables told by her mother and father, a Baptist minister—Tan fashioned compelling short stories. Her success in placing them in national magazines foreshadowed the public reaction to her first novel.

The Joy Luck Club (1989) was an instant success, making the best seller list almost immediately after its publication. Interweaving sixteen stories about four mother and daughter pairs, Tan explores the relations between Chinese- and American-born women. The four immigrant characters— Suyuan Woo, An-mei Hsu, Lindo Jong, and Ying-Ying St. Clair—having fled the horrors of World War II, find themselves in San Francisco, where they form a club to share customs and food, support and criticize each other, and play mah jong.

Forty years later, when Suyuan Woo dies, the remaining trio invite her daughter Jing-mei to fill the vacant place at the game table and in their circle. Jing-mei comes to understand that she is a surrogate not only for her own mother but also for the three surviving women's American daughters who, like her, discount their Chinese heritage.

Traveling to China to reunite her mother's shattered past, Jing-mei recognizes the strong pull of her ancestry, a force the other three daughters also come to appreciate in other ways.

Tan's second novel, The Kitchen God's Wife (1991), chronicles the experiences of two immigrant women from different classes and regions whose strong bond is forged in the tragedy of war.

The following story, "Half and Half," from The Joy Luck Club, is narrated by Rose Hsu Jordan, the American-born daughter of An-mei Hsu.

Half and Half

AS PROOF OF HER FAITH, my mother used to carry a small leatherette Bible when she went to the First Chinese Baptist Church every Sunday. But later, after my mother lost her faith in God, that leatherette Bible wound up wedged under a too-short table leg, a way for her to correct the imbalances of life. It's been there for over twenty years.

My mother pretends that Bible isn't there. Whenever anyone asks her what it's doing there, she says, a little too loudly, "Oh, this? I forgot." But I know she sees it. My mother is not the best housekeeper in the world, and after all these years that Bible is still clean white.

Tonight I'm watching my mother sweep under the same kitchen table, something she does every night after dinner. She gently pokes her broom around the table leg propped up by the Bible. I watch her, sweep after sweep, waiting for the right moment to tell her about Ted and me, that we're getting divorced. When I tell her, I know she's going to say, "This cannot be."

And when I say that it is certainly true, that our marriage is over, I know what else she will say: "Then you must save it."

And even though I know it's hopeless—there's absolutely nothing left to save—I'm afraid if I tell her that, she'll still persuade me to try.

I think it's ironic that my mother wants me to fight the divorce. Seventeen years ago she was chagrined when I started dating Ted. My older sisters had dated only Chinese boys from church before getting married.

Ted and I met in a politics of ecology class when he leaned over and offered to pay me two dollars for the last week's notes. I refused the money and accepted a cup of coffee instead. This was during my second semester at UC Berkeley, where I had enrolled as a liberal arts major and later changed to fine arts. Ted was in his third year in pre-med, his choice, he told me, ever since he dissected a fetal pig in the sixth grade.

I have to admit that what I initially found attractive in Ted were precisely the things that made him different from my brother and the Chinese boys I had dated: his brashness; the assuredness in which he asked for things and expected to get them; his opinionated manner; his angular face and lanky body; the thickness of his arms; the fact that his parents immigrated from Tarrytown, New York, not Tientsin, China.

My mother must have noticed these same differences after Ted picked me up one evening at my parents' house. When I returned home, my mother was still up, watching television.

"He is American," warned my mother, as if I had been too blind to notice. "A *waigoren*."

"I'm American too," I said. "And it's not as if I'm going to marry him or something."

Mrs. Jordan also had a few words to say. Ted had casually invited me to a family picnic, the annual clan reunion held by the polo fields in Golden Gate Park. Although we had dated only a few times in the last month—and certainly had never slept together, since both of us lived at home—Ted introduced me to all his relatives as his girlfriend, which, until then, I didn't know I was.

Later, when Ted and his father went off to play volleyball with the others, his mother took my hand, and we started walking along the grass, away from the crowd. She squeezed my palm warmly but never seemed to look at me.

"I'm so glad to meet you *finally*," Mrs. Jordan said. I wanted to tell her I wasn't really Ted's girlfriend, but she went on. "I think it's nice that you and Ted are having such a lot of fun together. So I hope you won't misunderstand what I have to say."

And then she spoke quietly about Ted's future, his need to concentrate on his medical studies, why it would be years before he could even think about marriage. She assured me she had nothing whatsoever against minorities; she and her husband, who owned a chain of office-supply stores, personally knew many fine people who were Oriental, Spanish, and even black. But Ted was going to be in one of those professions where he would be judged by a different standard, by patients and other doctors who might not be as understanding as the Jordans were. She said it was so unfortunate the way the rest of the world was, how unpopular the Vietnam War was.

"Mrs. Jordan, I am not Vietnamese," I said softly, even though I was on the verge of shouting. "And I have no intention of marrying your son."

When Ted drove me home that day, I told him I couldn't see him anymore. When he asked me why, I shrugged. When he pressed me, I told him what his mother had said, verbatim, without comment.

"And you're just going to sit there! Let my mother decide what's right?" he shouted, as if I were a co-conspirator who had turned traitor. I was touched that Ted was so upset.

"What should we do?" I asked, and I had a pained feeling I thought was the beginning of love.

In those early months, we clung to each other with a rather silly desperation, because, in spite of anything my mother or Mrs. Jordan could say, there was nothing that really prevented us from seeing one another. With imagined tragedy hovering over us, we become inseparable, two halves creating the whole: yin and yang. I was victim to his hero. I was always in danger and he was always rescuing me. I would fall and he would lift me up. It was exhilarating and draining. The emotional effect of saving and being saved was addicting to both of us. And that, as much as anything we ever did in bed, was how we made love to each other: conjoined where my weakness needed protection.

"What should we do?" I continued to ask him. And within a year of our first meeting we were living together. The month before Ted started medical school at UCSF we were married in the Episcopal church, and Mrs. Jordan sat in the front pew, crying as was expected of the groom's mother. When Ted finished his residency in dermatology, we bought a run-down three-story Victorian with a large garden in Ashbury Heights. Ted helped me set up a studio downstairs so I could take in work as a free-lance production assistant for graphic artists.

Over the years, Ted decided where we went on vacation. He decided what new furniture we should buy. He decided we should wait until we moved into a better neighborhood before having children. We used to discuss some of these matters, but we both knew the question would boil down to my saying, "Ted, you decide." After a while, there were no more discussions. Ted simply decided. And I never thought of objecting. I preferred to ignore the world around me, obsessing only over what was in front of me: my T-square, my X-acto knife, my blue pencil.

But last year Ted's feelings about what he called "decision and responsibility" changed. A new patient had come to him asking what she could do about the spidery veins on her cheeks. And when he told her he could suck the red veins out and make her beautiful again, she believed him. But instead, he accidentally sucked a nerve out, and the left side of her smile fell down and she sued him.

After he lost the malpractice lawsuit—his first, and a big shock to him I now realize—he started pushing me to make decisions. Did I think we should buy an American car or a Japanese car? Should we change from whole-life to term insurance? What did I think about that candidate who supported the contras? What about a family?

I thought about things, the pros and the cons. But in the end I would be so confused, because I never believed there was ever any one right answer, yet there were many wrong ones. So whenever I said, "You decide," or "I don't care," or "Either way is fine with me," Ted would say in his impatient voice, "No, *you* decide. You can't have it both ways, none of the responsibility, none of the blame."

I could feel things changing between us. A protective veil had been lifted and Ted now started pushing me about everything. He asked me to decide on the most trivial matters, as if he were baiting me. Italian food or Thai. One appetizer or two. Which appetizer. Credit card or cash. Visa or Master-Card.

Last month, when he was leaving for a two-day dermatology course in Los Angeles, he asked if I wanted to come along and then quickly, before I could say anything, he added, "Never mind, I'd rather go alone."

"More time to study," I agreed.

"No, because you can never make up your mind about anything," he said.

And I protested, "But it's only with things that aren't important."

"Nothing is important to you, then," he said in a tone of disgust.

"Ted, if you want me to go, I'll go."

And it was as if something snapped in him. "How the hell did we ever get married? Did you just say 'I do' because the minister said 'repeat after me'? What would you have done with your life if I had never married you? Did it ever occur to you?"

This was such a big leap in logic, between what I said and what he said, that I though we were like two people standing apart on separate mountain peaks, recklessly leaning forward to throw stones at one another, unaware of the dangerous chasm that separated us.

But now I realize Ted knew what he was saying all along. He wanted to show me the rift. Because that evening he called from Los Angeles and said he wanted a divorce.

Ever since Ted's been gone, I've been thinking. Even if I had expected it, even if I had known what I was going to do with my life, it still would have knocked the wind out of me.

When something that violent hits you, you can't help but lose your balance and fall. And after you pick yourself up, you realize you can't trust anybody to save you—not your husband, not your mother, not God. So what can you do to stop yourself from tilting and falling all over again.

My mother believed in God's will for many years. It was as if she had turned on a celestial faucet and goodness kept pouring out. She said it was faith that kept all these good things coming our way, only I thought she said "fate," because she couldn't pronounce that "th" sound in "faith."

And later, I discovered that maybe it was fate all along, that faith was just an illusion that somehow you're in control. I found out the most *I* could have was hope, and with that I was not denying any possibility, good or bad. I was just saying, if there is a choice, dear God or whatever you are, here's where the odds should be placed.

I remember the day I started thinking this. It was such a revelation to me. It was the day my mother lost her faith in God. She found that things of unquestioned certainty could never be trusted again.

We had gone to the beach, to a secluded spot south of the city near Devil's Slide. My father had read in *Sunset* magazine that this was a good place to catch ocean perch. And although my father was not a fisherman but a pharmacist's assistant who had once been a doctor in China, he believed in his *nengkan*, his ability to do anything he put his mind to. My mother believed she had *nengkan* to cook anything my father had a mind to catch. It was this belief in their *nengkan* that had brought my parents to America. It had enabled them to have seven children and buy a house in the Sunset district with very little money. It had given them the confidence to believe their luck would never run out, that God was on their side, that the house gods had only benevolent things to report and our ancestors were pleased, that lifetime warranties meant our lucky streak would never break, that all the elements were in balance, the right amount of wind and water.

So there we were, the nine of us: my father, my mother, my two sisters, four brothers, and myself, so confident as we walked along our first beach. We marched in single file across the cool gray sand, from oldest to youngest. I was in the middle, fourteen years old. We would have made quite a sight, if anyone else had been watching, nine pairs of bare feet trudging, nine pairs of shoes in hand, nine black-haired heads turned toward the water to watch the waves tumbling in.

The wind was whipping the cotton trousers around my legs and I looked for some place where the sand wouldn't kick into my eyes. I saw we were standing in the hollow of a cove. It was like a giant bowl, cracked in half, the other half washed out to sea. My mother walked toward the right, where the beach was clean, and we all followed. On this side, the wall of the cove curved around and protected the beach from both the rough surf and the wind. And along this wall, in its shadow, was a reef ledge that started at the edge of the beach and continued out past the cove where the water became rough. it seemed as though a person could walk out to sea on this reef, although it looked very rocky and slippery. On the other side of the cove, the wall was more jagged, eaten away by the water. It was pitted with crevices, so when the waves crashed against the wall, the water spewed out of these holes like white gulleys.

Thinking back, I remember that this beach cove was a terrible place, full of wet shadows that chilled us and invisible specks that flew into our eyes and made it hard for us to see the dangers. We were all blind with the newness of this experience, a Chinese family trying to act like a typical American family at the beach.

My mother spread out an old striped bedspread, which flapped in the wind until nine pairs of shoes weighed it down. My father assembled his long bamboo fishing pole, a pole he had made with his own two hands, remembering its design from his childhood in China. And we children sat huddled shoulder to shoulder on the blanket, reaching into the grocery sack full of bologna sandwiches, which we hungrily ate salted with sand from our fingers.

Then my father stood up and admired his fishing pole, its grace, its strength. Satisfied, he picked up his shoes and walked to the edge of the beach and then onto the reef to the point just before it was wet. My two older sisters. Janice and Ruth, jumped up from the blanket and slapped their thighs to get the sand off. Then they slapped each other's back and raced off down the beach shrieking. I was about to get up and chase them, but my mother nodded toward my four brothers and reminded me: *"Dangsying tamende shenti."* which means "Take care of them," or literally, "Watch out for their bodies." These bodies were the anchors of my life. Matthew, Mark, Luke, and Bing. I fell back onto the sand, groaning as my throat grew tight, as I made the same lament. "Why?" why did *I* have to care for them?

And she gave me the same answer. *"Yiding."*

I must. Because they were my brothers. My sisters had once taken care of me. how else could I learn responsibility? How else could I appreciate what my parents had done for me?

Matthew, Mark, and Luke were twelve, ten, and nine, old enough to keep themselves loudly amused. They had already buried Luke in a shallow grave of sand so that only his head stuck out. Now they were starting to pat together the outline of a sand-castle wall on top of him.

But Bing was only four, easily excitable and easily bored and irritable. He didn't want to play with the other brothers because they had pushed him off to the side, admonishing him, "No, Bing, you'll just wreck it."

So Bing wandered down the beach, walking stiffly like an ousted emperor, picking up shards of rock and chunks of driftwood and flinging them with all his might into the surf. I trailed behind, imagining tidal waves and wondering what I would do if one appeared. I called to Bing every now and then. "Don't go too close to the water. You'll get your feet wet." And I thought how much I seemed like my mother, always worried beyond reason inside, but at the same time talking about the danger as if it were less than it really was. The worry surrounded me, like the wall of the cove, and it made me feel everything had been considered and was now safe.

My mother had a superstition, in fact, that children were predisposed to certain dangers on certain days, all depending on their Chinese birthdate. It was explained in a little Chinese book called *The Twenty-Six Malignant Gates*. There, on each page, was an illustration of some terrible danger that awaited young innocent children. In the corners was a description written in Chinese, and since I couldn't read the characters, I could only see what the picture meant.

The same little boy appeared in each picture: climbing a broken tree limb, standing by a falling gate, slipping in a wooden tub, being carried away by a snapping dog, fleeing from a bolt of lighting. And in each of these pictures stood a man who looked as if he were wearing a lizard costume. He had a big crease in his forehead, or maybe it was actually that he had two round horns. In one picture, the lizard man was standing on a curved bridge, laughing as he watched the little boy falling forward over the bridge rail, his slippered feet already in the air.

It would have been enough to think that even one of these dangers could befall a child. And even though the birthdates corresponded to only one danger, my mother worried about them all. This was because she couldn't figure out how the Chinese dates, based on the lunar calendar, translated into American dates. So by taking them all into account, she had absolute faith she could prevent every one of them.

The sun had shifted and moved over the other side of the cove wall. Everything had settled into place. My mother was busy keeping sand from blowing onto the blanket, then shaking sand out of shoes, and tacking corners of blankets back down again with the now clean shoes. My father was still standing at the end of the reef, patiently casting out, waiting for *nengkan* to manifest itself as a fish. I could see small figures farther down on the beach, and I could tell they were my sisters by their two dark heads and yellow pants. My brothers' shrieks were mixed with those of seagulls. Bing had found an empty soda bottle and was using this to dig sand next to the dark cove wall. And I sat on the sand, just where the shadows ended and the sunny part began.

Bing was pounding the soda bottle against the rock, so I called to him. "Don't dig so hard. You'll bust a hole in the wall and fall all the way to China." And I laughed when he looked at me as though he thought what I said was true. He stood up and started walking toward the water. He put one foot tentatively on the reef, and I warned him, "Bing."

"I'm gonna see Daddy," he protested.

"Stay close to the wall, then, away from the water," I said "Stay away from the mean fish."

And I watched as he inched his way along the reef, his back hugging the bumpy cove wall. I still see him, so clearly that I almost feel I can make him stay there forever.

I see him standing by the wall, safe, calling to my father, who looks over his shoulder toward Bing. How glad I am that my father is going to watch him for a while! Bing starts to walk over and then something tugs on my father's line and he's reeling as fast as he can.

Shouts erupt. Someone had thrown sand in Luke's face and he's jumped out of his sand grave and thrown himself on top of Mark, thrashing and kicking. My mother shouts for me to stop them. And right after I pull Luke off Mark, I look up and see Bing walking alone to the edge of the reef. In the confusion of the fight, nobody notices. I am the only one who sees what Bing is doing.

Bing walks one, two, three steps. His little body is moving so quickly, as if he spotted something wonderful by the water's edge. And I think, *He's going to fall in.* I'm expecting it. And just as I think this, his feet are already in the air, in a moment of balance, before he splashes into the sea and disappears without leaving so much as a ripple in the water.

*		*		*

I sank to my knees watching that spot where he disappeared, not moving, not saying anything. I couldn't make sense of it. I was thinking. Should I run to the water and try to pull him out? Should I shout to my father? Can I rise on my legs fast enough? Can I take it all back and forbid Bing from joining my father on the ledge?

And then my sisters were back, and one of them said, "Where's Bing?" There was silence for a few seconds and then shouts and sands flying as everybody rushed past me toward the water's edge. I stood there unable to move as my sisters looked by the cove wall, as my brothers scrambled to see what lay behind pieces of driftwood. My mother and father were trying to part the waves with their hands.

We were there for many hours. I remembered the search boats and the sunset when dusk came. I had never seen a sunset like that a bright orange flame touching the water's edge and then fanning out, warming the sea. When it became dark, the boats turned their yellow orbs on and bounced up and down on the dark shiny water.

As I look back, it seems unnatural to think about the colors of the sunset and boats at a time like that. But we all had strange thoughts. My father was calculating minutes, estimating the temperature of the water, readjusting his estimate of when Bing fell. My sisters were calling, "Bing! Bing!" as if he were hiding in some bushes high above the beach cliffs. My brothers sat in the car, quietly reading comic books. And when the boats turned off their yellow orbs, my mother went for a swim. She had never swum a stroke in her life, but her faith in her own *nengkan* convinced her that what these Americans couldn't do, she could. She could find Bing.

And when the rescue people finally pulled her out of the water, she still had her *nengkan* intact. Her hair, her clothes, they were all heavy with the cold water, but she stood quietly, calm and regal as a mermaid queen who had just arrived out of the sea. The police called off the search, put us all in our car, and sent us home to grieve.

I had expected to be beaten to death, by my father, by my mother, by my sisters and brothers. I knew it was my fault. I hadn't watched him closely enough, and yet I saw him. But as we sat in the dark living room, I heard them, one by one whispering their regrets.

"I was selfish to want to go fishing," said my father.

"We shouldn't have gone for a walk," said Janice, while Ruth blew her nose yet another time.

"Why'd you have to throw sand in my face?" moaned Luke. "Why'd you have to make me start a fight?"

And my mother quietly admitted to me, "I told you to stop their fight. I told you to take your eyes off him."

If I had had any time at all to feel a sense of relief, it would have quickly evaporated, because my mother also said, "So now I am telling you, we must go and find him, quickly, tomorrow morning." And everybody's eyes looked down. But I saw it as my punishment: to go out with my mother, back to the beach, to help her find Bing's body.

Nothing prepared me for what my mother did the next day. When I woke up, it was still dark and she was already dressed. On the kitchen table was a thermos, a teacup, the white leatherette Bible, and the car keys.

"Is Daddy ready?" I asked.

"Daddy's not coming," she said.

"Then how will we get there? Who will drive us?"

She picked up the keys and I followed her out the door to the car. I wondered the whole time as we drove to the beach how she had learned to drive overnight. She used no map. She drove smoothly ahead, turning down Geary, then the Great Highway, signaling at all the right times, getting on the Coast Highway and easily winding the car around the sharp curves that often led inexperienced drivers off and over the cliffs.

When we arrived at the beach, she walked immediately down the dirt path and over to the end of the reef ledge, where I had seen Bing disappear. She held in her hand the white Bible. And looking out over the water, she called to God, her small voice carried up by the gulls to heaven. It began with "Dear God" and ended with "Amen," and in between she spoke in Chinese.

"I have always believed in your blessings." she praised God in that same tone she used for exaggerated Chinese compliments. "We knew they would come. We did not question them. You decisions were our decisions. You rewarded us for our faith.

"In return we have always tried to show our deepest respect. We went to your house. We brought you money. We sang your songs. You gave us more blessings. And now we have misplaced one of them. We were careless.

This is true. We had so many good things, we couldn't keep them in our mind all the time.

"So maybe you hid him from us to teach us a lesson, to be more careful with your gifts in the future. I have learned this. I have put it in my memory. And now I have come to take Bing back."

I listened quietly as my mother said these words, horrified. And I began to cry when she added, "Forgive us for his bad manners. My daughter, this one standing here, will be sure to teach him better lessons of obedience before he visits you again."

After her prayer, her faith was so great that she saw him, three times, waving to her from just beyond the first wave. *"Nale"*—There! And she would stand straight as a sentinel, until three times her eyesight failed her and Bing turned into a dark spot of churning seaweed.

My mother did not let her chin fall down. She walked back to the beach and put the Bible down. She picked up the thermos and teacup and walked to the water's edge. Then she told me that the night before she had reached back into her life, back when she was a girl in China, and this is what she had found.

"I remember a boy who lost his hand in a firecracker accident," she said. "I saw the shreds of this boy's arm, his tears, and then I heard his mother's claim that he would grow back another hand, better than the last. This mother said she would pay back an ancestral debt ten times over. She would use a water treatment to soothe the wrath of Chu Jung, the three-eyed god of fire. And true enough, the next week this boy was riding a bicycle, both hands steering a straight course past my astonished eyes!"

And then my mother became very quiet. She spoke again in a thoughtful, respectful manner.

"An ancestor of ours once stole water from a sacred well. Now the water is trying to steal back. We must sweeten the temper of the Coiling Dragon who lives in the sea. And then we must make him loosen his coils from Bing by giving him another treasure he can hide."

My mother poured out tea sweetened with sugar into the teacup, and threw this into the sea. And then she opened her fist. In her palm was a ring of watery blue sapphire, a gift from her mother, who had died many years before. This ring, she told me, drew coveting stares from women and made them inattentive to the children they guarded so jealously. This would make the Coiling Dragon forgetful of Bing. She threw the ring into the water.

But even with this, Bing did not appear right away. For an hour or so, all we saw was seaweed drifting by. And then I saw her clasp her hands to her chest, and she said in a wondrous voice. "See, it's because we were watching the wrong direction." And I saw Bing trudging wearily at the far end of the beach, his shoes hanging in his hand, his dark head over in exhaustion. I could feel what my mother felt. The hunger in our hearts was instantly filled. And then the two of us, before we could even get to our feet, saw him light a cigarette, grow tall, and become a stranger.

"Ma, let's go," I said as softly as possible.

"He's there," she said firmly. She pointed to the jagged wall across the water. "I see him. He is in a cave, sitting on a little step above the water. He is hungry and a little cold, but he has learned now not to complain too much."

And then she stood up and started walking across the sandy beach as though it were a solid paved path, and I was trying to follow behind, struggling and stumbling in the soft mounds. She marched up the steep path to where the car was parked, and she wasn't even breathing hard as she pulled a large inner tube from the trunk. To this lifesaver, she tied the fishing line from my father's bamboo pole. She walked back and threw the tube into the sea, holding on to the pole.

"This will go where Bing is. I will bring him back," she said fiercely. I had never heard so much *nengkan* in my mother's voice.

The tube followed her mind. It drifted out, toward the other side of the cove where it was caught by stronger waves. The line became taut and she strained to hold on tight. But the line snapped and then spiraled into the water.

We both climbed toward the end of the reef to watch. The tube had now reached the other side of the cove. A big wave smashed it into the wall. The bloated tube leapt up and then it was sucked in, under the wall and into a cave. It popped out. Over and over again, it disappeared, emerged, glistening black, faithfully reporting it had seen Bing and was going back to try to pluck him from the cave. Over and over again, it dove and popped back up again, empty but still hopeful. And then, after a dozen or so times, it was sucked into the dark recess, and when it came out, it was torn and lifeless.

At that moment, and not until that moment, did she give up. My mother had a look on her face that I'll never forget. It was one of complete despair and horror, for losing Bing, for being so foolish as to think she could use faith to change fate. And it made me angry—so blindingly angry—that everything had failed us.

I know now that I had never expected to find Bing, just as I know now I will never find a way to save my marriage. My mother tells me, though, that I should still try.

"What's the point?" I say. "There' no hope. There's no reason to keep trying."

"Because you must," she says. "This is not hope. Not reason. This is your fate. This is your life, what you must do."

"So what can I do?"

And my mother says, "You must think for yourself, what you must do. If someone tells you, then you are not trying." And then she walks out of the kitchen to let me think about this.

I think about Bing, how I knew he was in danger, how I let it happen. I think about my marriage, how I had seen the signs, really I had. But I just let it happen. And I think now that fate is shaped half by expectation, half by inattention. But somehow, when you lose something you love, faith takes over. You have to pay attention to what you lost. You have to undo the expectation.

My mother, she still pays attention to it. That Bible under the table, I know she sees it. I remember seeing her write in it before she wedged it under.

I lift the table and slide the Bible out. I put the Bible on the table, flipping quickly through the pages, because I know it's there. On the page before the New Testament begins, there's a section called "Deaths," and that's where she wrote "Bing Hsu" lightly, in erasable pencil.

Louise Erdrich
(1954–)

A member of the Turtle Mountain Band of Chippewa, Louise Erdrich was born in Little Falls, Minnesota, and was brought up in Wahpeton, North Dakota, near the reservation. Her parents were teachers in the Bureau of Indian Affairs School serving the reservation.

She received her undergraduate training in anthropology at Dartmouth College, where she met her future husband, the novelist Michael Dorris, a faculty member in Native American studies. Erdrich completed a master's degree at Johns Hopkins University the following year and returned to Dartmouth as a writer in residence.

Encouraged by her parents with nickel "royalties" for each story she wrote and "publication" in home-made construction paper books, Erdrich thought of herself as a writer when she was very young. Her short fiction began appearing in magazines and anthologies in 1981. In 1984 she published two books: Jacklight, *a collection of poetry, and* Love Medicine, *a National Book Critics Circle Award-winning novel.*

The Beet Queen *(1986) and* Tracks *(1988), like the earlier novel, deal with Native American and mixed-blood families in North Dakota. The writing has been compared to Faulkner or the "magical realist" writers of South America with its blending of divergent voices and interrelated stories. The same characters or members of the same families appear in the three novels, a loosely tied trilogy.*

Erdrich and Dorris published a collaborative novel, The Crown of Columbus, *in 1991. "The Red Convertible" is from* Love Medicine.

The Red Convertible

(1974)

LYMAN LAMARTINE

I WAS THE FIRST ONE to drive a convertible on my reservation. And of course it was red, a red Olds. I owned that car along with my brother Henry Junior. We owned it together until his boots filled with water on a windy night and he bought out my share. Now Henry owns the whole car, and his younger brother Lyman (that's myself), Lyman walks everywhere he goes.

How did I earn enough money to buy my share in the first place? My one talent was I could always make money. I had a touch for it, unusual in a Chippewa. From the first I was different that way, and everyone recognized it. I was the only kid they let in the American Legion Hall to shine shoes, for example, and one Christmas I sold spiritual bouquets for the mission door to door. The nuns let me keep a percentage. Once I started, it seemed the more money I made the easier the money came. Everyone encouraged it. When I was fifteen I got a job washing dishes at the Joliet Café, and that was where my first big break happened.

It wasn't long before I was promoted to bussing tables, and then the short order cook quit and I was hired to take her place. No sooner than you know it I was managing the Joliet. The rest is history. I went on managing. I soon become part owner, and of course there was no stopping me then. It wasn't long before the whole thing was mine.

After I'd owned the Joliet for one year, it blew over in the worst tornado ever seen around here. The whole operation was smashed to bits. A total loss. The fryalator was up in a tree, the grill torn in half like it was paper. I was only sixteen. I had it all in my mother's name, and I lost it quick, but before I lost it I had every one of my relatives, and their relatives, to dinner, and I also bought that red Olds I mentioned, along with Henry.

The first time we saw it! I'll tell you when we first saw it. We had gotten a ride up to Winnipeg, and both of us had money. Don't ask me why, because we never mentioned a car or anything, we just had all our money. Mine was cash, a big bankroll from the Joliet's insurance. Henry had two checks—a week's extra pay for being laid off, and his regular check from the Jewel Bearing Plant.

We were walking down Portage anyway, seeing the sights, when we saw it. There it was, parked, large as life. Really as *if* it was alive. I though of the word *repose*, because the car wasn't simply stopped, parked, or whatever. That car reposed, calm and gleaming, a FOR SALE sign in its left front window. Then, before we had thought it over at all, the car belonged to us and our pockets were empty. We had just enough money for gas back home.

We went places in that car, me and Henry. We took off driving all one whole summer. We started off toward the Little Knife River and Mandaree in Fort Berthold and then we found ourselves down in Wakpala somehow, and then suddenly we were over in Montana on the Rocky Boys, and yet the summer was not even half over. Some people hang on to details when they travel, but we didn't let them bother us and just lived our everyday lives here to there.

I do remember this one place with willows. I remember I laid under those trees and it was comfortable. So comfortable. The branches bent down all around me like a tent or a stable. And quiet, it was quiet, even though there was a powwow close enough so I could see it going on. The air was not too still, not too windy either. When the dust rises up and hangs in the air around the dancers like that, I feel good. Henry was asleep with his arms thrown wide. Later on, he woke up and we started driving again. We were somewhere in Montana, or maybe on the Blood Reserve—it could have been anywhere. Anyway it was where we met the girl.

All her hair was in buns around her ears, that's the first thing I noticed about her. She was posed alongside the road with her arm out, so we stopped. That girl was short, so short her lumber shirt looked comical on her, like a nightgown. She had jeans on and fancy moccasins and she carried a little suitcase.

"Hop on in," says Henry. So she climbs in between us.

"We'll take you home," I says. "Where do you live?"

"Chicken," she says.

"Where the hell's that?" I ask her.

"Alaska."

"Okay," says Henry, and we drive.

We got up there and never wanted to leave. The sun doesn't truly set there in summer, and the night is more a soft dusk. You might doze off, sometimes, but before you know it you're up again, like an animal in nature. You never feel like you have to sleep hard or put away the world. And things would grow up there. One day just dirt or moss, the next day flowers and long grass. The girl's name was Susy. Her family really took to us. They fed us and put us up. We had our own tent to live in by their house, and the kids would be in and out of there all day and night. They couldn't get over me and Henry being brothers, we looked so different. We told them we knew we had the same mother, anyway.

One night Susy came in to visit us. We sat around in the tent talking of this thing and that. The season was changing. It was getting darker by that time, and the cold was even getting just a little mean. I told her it was time for us to go. She stood up on a chair.

"You never seen my hair," Susy said.

That was true. She was standing on a chair, but still, when she unclipped her buns the hair reached all the way to the ground. Our eyes opened. You couldn't tell how much hair she had when it was rolled up so neatly. Then my brother Henry did something funny. He went up to the chair and said, "Jump on my shoulders." So she did that, and her hair reached down past his waist, and he started twirling, this way and that, so her hair was flung out from side to side.

"I always wondered what it was like to have long pretty hair," Henry says. Well we laughed. It was a funny sight, the way he did it. The next morning we got up and took leave of those people.

On to greener pastures, as they say. It was down through Spokane and across Idaho then Montana and very soon we were racing the weather right along under the Canadian border through Columbus, Des Lacs, and then we were in Bottineau County and soon home. We'd made most of the trip, that summer, without putting up the car hood at all. We got home just in time, it turned out, for the army to remember Henry had signed up to join it.

I don't wonder that the army was so glad to get my brother that they turned him into a Marine. He was built like a brick out-house anyway. We liked to tease him that they really wanted him for his Indian nose. He had a nose big and sharp as a hatchet, like the nose on Red Tomahawk, the Indian who killed Sitting Bull, whose profile is on signs all along the North Dakota highways. Henry went off to training camp, came home once during Christmas, then the next thing you know we got an overseas letter from him. It was 1970, and he said he was stationed up in the northern hill country. Whereabouts I did not know. He wasn't such a hot letter writer, and only got off two before the enemy caught him. I could never keep it straight, which direction those good Vietnam soldiers were from.

I wrote him back several times, even though I didn't know if those letters would get through. I kept him informed all about the car. Most of the time I had it up on blocks in the yard or half taken apart, because that long trip did a hard job on it under the hood.

I always had good luck with numbers, and never worried about the draft myself. I never even had to think about what my number was. But Henry was never lucky in the same way as me. It was at least three years before Henry came home. By then I guess the whole war was solved in the government's mind, but for him it would keep on going. In those years I'd put his car into almost perfect shape. I always thought of it as his car while he was gone, even though when he left he said, "Now it's yours," and threw me his key.

"Thanks for the extra key," I'd said. "I'll put it up in your drawer just in case I need it." He laughed.

When he came home, though, Henry was very different, and I'll say this: the change was no good. You could hardly expect him to change for the better, I know. But he was quiet, so quiet, and never comfortable sitting still anywhere but always up and moving around. I thought back to times we'd sat still for whole afternoons, never moving a muscle, just shifting our weight along the ground, talking to whoever sat with us, watching things. He'd always had a joke, then, too, and now you couldn't get him to laugh, or when he did it was more the sound of a man choking, a sound that stopped up the throats of other people around him. They got to leaving him alone most of the time, and I didn't blame them. It was a fact: Henry was jumpy and mean.

I'd bought a color TV set for my mom and the rest of us while Henry was away. Money still came very easy. I was sorry I'd ever bought it though, because of Henry. I was also sorry I'd bought color, because with black-and-white the pictures seem older and farther away. But what are you going to do? He sat in front of it, watching it, and that was the only time he was completely still. But it was the kind of stillness that you see in a rabbit when it freezes and before it will bolt. He was not easy. He sat in his chair gripping the armrests with all his might, as if the chair itself was moving at a high speed and if he let go at all he would rocket forward and maybe crash right through the set.

Once I was in the room watching TV with Henry and I heard his teeth click at something. I looked over, and he'd bitten through his lip. Blood was going down his chin. I tell you right then I wanted to smash that tube to pieces. I went over to it but Henry must have known what I was up to. He rushed from his chair and shoved me out of the way, against the wall. I told myself he didn't know what he was doing.

My mom came in, turned the set off real quiet, and told us she had made something for supper. So we went and sat down. There was still blood going down Henry's chin, but he didn't notice it and no one said anything, even though every time he took a bite of his bread his blood fell onto it until he was eating his own blood mixed in with the food.

While Henry was not around we talked about what was going to happen to him. There were no Indian doctors on the reservation, and my mom was afraid of trusting Old Man Pillager because he courted her long ago and was jealous of her husbands. He might take revenge through her son. We were afraid that if we brought Henry to a regular hospital they would keep him.

"They don't fix them in those places," Mom said; "they just give them drugs."

"We wouldn't get him there in the first place," I agreed, "so let's just forget about it."

Then I thought about the car.

Henry had not even looked at the car since he'd gotten home, though like I said, it was in tip-top condition and ready to drive. I thought the car might bring the old Henry back somehow. So I bided my time and waited for my chance to interest him in the vehicle.

One night Henry was off somewhere. I took myself a hammer. I went out to that car and I did a number on its underside. Whacked it up. Bent the tail pipe double. Ripped the muffler loose. By the time I was done with the car it looked worse than any typical Indian car that has been driven all its life on reservation roads, which they always say are like government promises—full of holes. It just about hurt me, I'll tell you that! I threw dirt in the carburetor and I ripped all the electric tape off the seats. I made it look just as beat up as I could. Then I sat back and waited for Henry to find it.

Still, it took him over a month. That was all right, because it was just getting warm enough, not melting, but warm enough to work outside.

"Lyman," he says, walking in one day, "that red car looks like shit."

"Well it's old," I says. "You got to expect that."

"No way!" says Henry. "That car's a classic! But you went and ran the piss right out of it, Lyman, and you know it don't deserve that. I kept that car in A-one shape. You don't remember. You're too young. But when I left, that car was running like a watch. Now I don't even know if I can get it to start again, let alone get it anywhere near its old condition."

"Well you try," I said, like I was getting mad, "but I say it's a piece of junk."

Then I walked out before he could realize I knew he'd strung together more than six words at once.

After that I thought he'd freeze himself to death working on that car. He was out there all day, and at night he rigged up a little lamp, ran a cord out the window, and had himself some light to see by while he worked. He was better than he had been before, but that's still not saying much. It was easier for him to do the things the rest of us did. He ate more slowly and didn't jump up and down during the meal to get this or that or look out the window. I put my hand in the back of the TV set, I admit, and fiddled around with it good, so that it was almost impossible now to get a clear picture. He didn't look at it very often anyway. He was always out with that car or going off to get parts for it. By the time it was really melting outside, he had it fixed.

I had been feeling down in the dumps about Henry around this time. We had always been together before. Henry and Lyman. But he was such a loner now that I didn't know how to take it. So I jumped at the chance one day when Henry seemed friendly. It's not that he smiled or anything. He just said, "Let's take that old shitbox for a spin." Just the way he said it made me think he could be coming around.

We went out to the car. It was spring. The sun was shining very bright. My only sister, Bonita, who was just eleven years old, came out and made us stand together for a picture. Henry leaned his elbow on the red car's windshield, and he took his other arm and put it over my shoulder, very carefully, as though it was heavy for him to lift and he didn't want to bring the weight down all at once.

"Smile," Bonita said, and he did.

That picture. I never look at it anymore. A few months ago, I don't know why, I got his picture out and tacked it on the wall. I felt good about Henry at the time, close to him. I felt good having his picture on the wall, until one night when I was looking at television. I was a little drunk and stoned. I looked up at the wall and Henry was staring at me. I don't know what it was, but his smile had changed, or maybe it was gone. All I know is I couldn't stay in the same room with that picture. I was shaking. I got up, closed the door, and went into the kitchen. A little later my friend Ray came over and we both went back into that room. We put the picture in a brown bag, folded the bag over and over tightly, then put it way back in a closet.

I still see that picture now, as if it tugs at me, whenever I pass that closet door. The picture is very clear in my mind. It was so sunny that day Henry had to squint against the glare. Or maybe the camera Bonita held flashed like a mirror, blinding him, before she snapped the picture. My face is right out in the sun, big and round. But he might have drawn back, because the shadows on his face are deep as holes. There are two shadows curved like little hooks around the ends of his smile, as if to frame it and try to keep it there—that one, first smile that looked like it might have hurt his face. He has his field jacket on and the worn-in clothes he'd come back in and kept wearing ever since. After Bonita took the picture, she went into the house and we got into the car. There was a full cooler in the trunk. We started off, east, toward Pembina and the Red River because Henry said he wanted to see the high water.

The trip over there was beautiful. When everything starts changing, drying up, clearing off, you feel like your whole life is starting. Henry felt it, too. The top was down and the car hummed like a top. He'd really put it back in shape, even the tape on the seats was very carefully put down and glued back in layers. It's not that he smiled again or even joked, but his face looked to me as if it was clear, more peaceful. It looked as though he wasn't thinking of anything in particular except the bare fields and windbreaks and houses we were passing.

The river was high and full of winter trash when we got there. The sun was still out, but it was colder by the river. There were still little clumps of dirty snow here and there on the banks. The water hadn't gone over the banks yet, but it would, you could tell. It was just at its limit, hard swollen, glossy like an old gray scar. We made ourselves a fire, and we sat down and watched the current go. As I watched it I felt something squeezing inside me and tightening and trying to let go all at the same time. I knew I was not not just feeling it myself; I knew I was feeling what Henry was going through at that moment. Except that I couldn't stand it, the closing and opening. I jumped to my feet. I took Henry by the shoulders and I started shaking him. "Wake up," I says, "wake up, wake up, wake up!" I didn't know what had come over me. I sat down beside him again.

His face was totally white and hard. Then it broke, like stones break all of a sudden when water boils up inside them.

"I know it," he says. "I know it. I can't help it. It's no use."

We start talking. He said he knew what I'd done with the car. It was obvious it had been whacked out of shape and not just neglected. He said he wanted to give the car to me for good now, it was no use. He said he'd fixed it just to give it back and I should take it.

"No way," I says, "I don't want it."

"That's okay," he says, "you take it."

"I don't want it, though," I says back to him, and then to emphasize, just to emphasize, you understand, I touch his shoulder. He slaps my hand off.

"Take that car," he says.

"No," I say, "make me," I say, and then he grabs my jacket and rips the arm loose. That jacket is a class act, suede with tags and zippers. I push Henry backwards, off the log. He jumps up and bowls me over. We go down in a clinch and come up swinging hard, for all we're worth, with our fists. He socks my jaw so hard I feel like it swings loose. Then I'm at his ribcage and land a good one under his chin so his head snaps back. He's dazzled. He looks at me and I look at him and then his eyes are full of tears and blood and at first I think he's crying. But no, he's laughing. "Ha! Ha!" he says. "Ha! Ha! Take good care of it."

"Okay," I says, "okay, no problem. Ha! Ha!"

I can't help it, and I start laughing, too. My face feels fat and strange, and after a while I get a beer from the cooler in the trunk, and when I hand it to Henry he takes his shirt and wipes my germs off. "Hoof-and-mouth disease," he says. For some reason this cracks me up, and so we're really laughing for a while, and then we drink all the rest of the beers one by one and throw them in the river and see how far, how fast, the current takes them before they fill up and sink.

"You want to go on back?" I ask after a while. "Maybe we could snag a couple nice Kashpaw girls."

He says nothing. But I can tell his mood is turning again.

"They're all crazy, the girls up here, every damn one of them."

"You're crazy too," I say, to jolly him up. "Crazy Lamartine boys!"

He looks as though he will take this wrong at first. His face twists, then clears, and he jumps up on his feet. "That's right!" he says. "Crazier 'n hell. Crazy Indians!"

I think it's the old Henry again. He throws off his jacket and starts swinging his legs out from the knees like a fancy dancer. He's down doing something between a grouse dance and a bunny hop, no kind of dance I ever saw before, but neither has anyone else on all this green growing earth. He's wild. He wants to pitch whoopee! He's up and at me and all over. All this time I'm laughing so hard, so hard my belly is getting tied up in a knot.

"Got to cool me off!" he shouts all of a sudden. Then he runs over to the river and jumps in.

There's boards and other things in the current. It's so high. No sound comes from the river after the splash he makes, so I run right over. I look around. It's getting dark. I see he's halfway across the water already, and I know he didn't swim there but the current took him. It's far. I hear his voice, though, very clearly across it.

"My boots are filling," he says.

He says this in a normal voice, like he just noticed and he doesn't know what to think of it. Then he's gone. A branch comes by. Another branch. And I go in.

By the time I get out of the river, off the snag I pulled myself onto, the sun is down. I walk back to the car, turn on the high beams, and drive it up the bank. I put it in first gear and then I take my foot off the clutch. I get out, close the door, and watch it plow softly into the water. The headlights reach in as they go down, searching, still lighted even after the water swirls over the back end. I wait. The wires short out. It is all finally dark. And then there is only the water, the sound of it going and running and going and running and running.